D1544875

Oswald Mosley

Oswald Mosley

Robert Skidelsky

HOLT, RINEHART AND WINSTON
New York

It is a universal law: everyone who *acts* breeds both good and evil. With some it's more good, with others more evil.

Alexander Solzhenitsyn, *Cancer Ward*

Library of Congress Cataloging in Publication Data

Skidelsky, Robert Jacob Alexander, 1939–
Oswald Mosley.

1. Mosley, Sir Oswald, bart., 1896–
DA574.M6S55   942.084′092′4   [B]   74–6941
ISBN 0–03–086580–8

Printed in Great Britain by
Redwood Burn Limited
Trowbridge & Esher

TO ALEX

Contents

List of Illustrations

Between pages 256 and 257

Acknowledgments are due for the following photographs: The Royal Aero Club, 1*a*; *Illustrated London News*, 1*b*, 3*b*; Central Press, 2; *London Express*, 3*a*; PLA Photos, 4*a*; *Evening Standard*, 4*b*; Radio Times Hulton Picture Library, 5*a*, 5*b*, 6*a*, 6*b*; PA-Reuter, 7*a*; John Warburton, 7*b*.

Figure 2 is reproduced by permission of the Estate of David Low.

Acknowledgments

IT IS always a pleasure to acknowledge help, though in this case a number of people who contributed valuable impressions prefer not to be mentioned. It is a particular pleasure to thank my wife. She typed the book in draft many more times than she would care to remember. Her encouragement and cheerfulness sustained me through many discouraging moments.

I must also thank Sir Oswald and Lady Mosley, as well as other members of the family – especially his sons, Nicholas, Michael, Alexander and Max, and his daughter Mrs Vivien Forbes-Adam – who helped me generously with their time and in other ways.

Sir Oswald and Lady Mosley and Alexander Mosley, my Oxford friend Philip Williams, David Calleo, my colleague at the School of Advanced International Studies, Washington, and Sir John Riddell have all read the manuscript wholly or in part, and have all contributed very helpful suggestions in writing and in conversation. Simon Newman and Sandra Brazaitis greatly assisted with the research for the earlier sections of the book; Andrew Goodman in the final, frantic rush. It is even more important than usual in such cases to claim entire personal responsibility for the result.

In the course of working on this book, I have had the benefit of many conversations with my subject, and have therefore been in a position to form an estimate of his character independently of other people's testimony or written records. It may be argued that any such personal relationship is bound to make the biographer unduly sympathetic and thus warp his critical faculty. There is no inherent reason why this should be so. The better one comes to know someone the more one can grow to dislike him, as apparently happened in the case of G. M. Young and Stanley Baldwin. The role of ' participant-observer ' is, of course, delicate; but, provided the observer has all his wits about him, it can be extremely rewarding. This is particularly true in biography, whose aim is to ' get inside ' the subject and explain to the reader what moves him, what gives meaning to his life. In any case, the role of biographer, as I conceive it, is not that of prosecutor; it comes somewhere between that of counsel for the defence and judge. This has special relevance to Mosley. Mosley has always been, and will always continue to be, an extremely controversial figure. The trouble is that practically everything written or said about him that has come before the public in recent years has been from the prosecution point of view. It is time that the case for Mosley was made by the historian; and in my judgment sufficient time has now elapsed for one to be able to view his life and the causes he espoused with both detachment and sympathy. If, therefore, this book presents him in a more favourable light than that to which many readers are accustomed, I can only hope that they will see this as his due, and not the result of excessive personal influence exerted by a living subject on his biographer.

I should like to thank the Warden and Fellows of Nuffield College, Oxford, for electing me to a research fellowship in order to embark on this book, and the Trustees of the Thank-offering to Britain Fund for giving me a research fellowship at the British Academy to enable me to do the work on Mosley and British fascism which forms the middle section of the book.

I would also like to thank Mr J. Gwyn Morgan, the Assistant General Secretary of the Labour Party, for permission to use the Minutes of the National Executive Committee of the Labour Party for the years 1924–31; Mr Nigel Nicolson, for permission to see Harold Nicolson's unpublished papers in Balliol College Library; and the Home Office, for guiding me to the files of the Metropolitan Police at the Public Record Office. To the librarians of Transport House, Balliol College, the Public Record Office and the Franklin D. Roosevelt Library, together with the Librarian at Kedleston Castle (Curzon Papers) and Mr Tom Harrisson of the Mass Observation Archive at Sussex University my warmest thanks are due for their help and co-operation. Mr P. L. Rees of York University also kindly supplied me with a very full bibliography on Mosley and British fascism. For that remarkable institution, the London Library, I have nothing but praise – for the range of its books, and the kindness and helpfulness of its staff. Finally, no author can have been so fortunate in having such a patient and encouraging publisher as I have had in Mr James Wright of Macmillan.

So many people have helped me in so many small ways with this book that I cannot mention all. But I should like to thank especially the following: the late Mr W. E. D. Allen, Earl Baldwin of Bewdley, Mr R. Reynell Bellamy, the late Mr A. K. Chesterton, Mr E. J. Hamm, Sir Roy Harrod, Mr R. E. Lewis, Mr E. Rolph, Mr Beverley Nichols, Professor G. W. Paish, Mr Richard Payne, the late Mr Sidney Potter, Mrs Ursula Potter, Mr R. W. Ratcliffe, Lord Rothermere, Mr R. Row, Mr Hugh Thomas, Mr A. W. Tuke, Mr Charles Wegg Prosser, Mr Hugh Ross Williamson and the late Mr Allan Young.

ROBERT SKIDELSKY

Introduction

IT MAY be of some interest to the reader to explain how this biography came to be written. I first encountered Sir Oswald Mosley early in 1961, when I was an undergraduate at Oxford. Mosley had been invited to the Oxford Union (debating society) to speak against a motion proposing that South Africa be expelled from the Commonwealth. He was sixty-four years old, a big man, over six feet, running somewhat to fat at the time, with a trim moustache set in a chubby face. His main opponent was Mr Jeremy Thorpe, now the Liberal leader, whose wit and passion had long made him a favourite with university audiences, and who launched into a sweeping denunciation of enormities which unfitted South Africa for membership of any civilised community of nations. This is what the Union wanted to hear and it cheered him loudly. Mosley evidently had a hopeless task. His main point was that if we insisted on condemning every country which failed to live up to our particular moral requirements we would soon have no friends left in the world. But the highlight of his speech came when he trapped Mr Thorpe in a series of brilliantly timed and calculated exchanges which the Liberal M.P. seemed to have won completely till Mosley demolished him with a final crushing rejoinder. It was a superb example of the art of public debating, which failed to win the vote, but won for Mosley an ovation. My interest in him was born at this point. I greatly admire courage and intelligence, and it had taken the one for a man as unpopular as Mosley to come to the Union at all, and the other for him to gain a triumph in that stronghold of liberalism. How was it that someone with Mosley's outstanding gifts had come to occupy such a low and generally despised position in the national life? Here was the start of an investigation which, on and off, was to occupy me for the next twelve years.

I should at this point say something about my own political ideas and how they related to my growing interest in Mosley. From 1961 onwards I was actively involved in the Labour Party, both at the university level and in the Campaign for Democratic Socialism. It was Hugh Gaitskell's courage, in face of the bitterest denunciations from his own party, in fighting for what he believed to be right, that really attracted me to Labour politics at the time. To be drawn into politics by the personality of a leader may seem immature. Yet there is a sound reason for it. On the quality of the leadership depends the possibility of action. This truth has never, it seems to me, been adequately grasped by social democratic

parties. They spend their lives talking about the world to come;
yet saddle themselves for the most part with leaders who are all too
obviously content with the world as it is: hence the literature of
' betrayal ' which pours out in unceasing flood from social democratic pens.   Early on in my reading about Mosley I was struck by
the dedication of John Strachey's book *Revolution by Reason* (1925):
' To O.M. who may some day do the things of which we dream.'
This exactly paralleled my own feelings about Gaitskell, though not
about his successor.   The Mosley of the 1920s seemed to have all
the attributes that I wanted from a Labour leader – bold policies,
unflinching courage, eloquent language, compassion, popular
appeal.   As the Labour Government of 1964 staggered from disaster to disaster under an obviously inadequate prime minister,
Mosley took shape in my mind as Labour's ' lost leader '.

This view comes out strongly in my book *Politicians and the Slump*,
published a few days after the forced devaluation of the pound in
November 1967, and based on my postgraduate research into a
previous Labour government – that of Ramsay MacDonald in 1929–
31 – and its handling of the unemployment problem.   Mosley was
Chancellor of the Duchy of Lancaster in that government, resigning
from office when the Cabinet rejected his proposal for a British
' New Deal '.   He is the hero of that book, as he deserves to be,
A. J. P. Taylor rightly remarking that he alone ' rose to the height
of the challenge '.   The failure of the Labour Party, and indeed
the whole political Establishment, to do so is the other theme of the
book.   The rejection of the Mosley Memorandum was a decisive
moment in twentieth century British history: ' the moment when
the British people resolved unwittingly to stand on the ancient
ways '.*   It was the sense of the inadequacy of a whole political
class, reinforced by the equally discreditable performance of the
class of the 1960s into which Mr Cecil King has provided such an
illuminating insight, that determined me to reopen the Mosley case.
This book is the result.

Where did the case then stand?† Until fairly recently the usual
interpretation of Mosley was that he was a political adventurer
who, having failed to make it in the Conservative Party, then joined
the Labour Party where the prospects of promotion seemed brighter.
Having failed to sweep the Labour Party with his demagogic economic proposals, he then set himself up as a fascist, that being the
thing for an adventurer to do just then, hoping to win power
through a mixture of violence and anti-semitism.   This finally
revealed him to the British people for the rotter he was, and he was

*A. J. P. Taylor, *English History 1914–1945* (1965), p. 286.
†Mosley's own autobiography, *My Life*, appeared in 1968, after I had started
on my own book. This has made possible a much more informed appraisal,
but of course he emphasises what is important for him.

interned during the Second World War for supporting Hitler. Afterwards he tried a brief comeback by stirring up racial hatred, and since then has languished in well-deserved oblivion and obloquy.   It is important to mention this interpretation, however grotesque it may seem, because this is the way Mosley has been presented to the British people by the bulk of the national press for the major part of his political life.

By the time I started work on the biography, this view had been substantially modified, at least for the period of his life up to 1931. Mosley's character and motives were still suspect, but the striking originality of his economic proposals of 1930 was increasingly recognised; also that they foreshadowed in a remarkable way much of what has since come to pass.   *Politicians and the Slump* provided the first detailed (and, I should add, accurate) account of the Mosley Memorandum.   However, Mosley before 1930 remained largely unknown.   Mr Taylor wrote (1965): ' It is impossible to say where Mosley got his ideas from.   Perhaps he devised them himself.' One can now say a good deal more about this and I have tried to do so in Chapter 7.   I may have failed to do full justice to the creative ferment in the Birmingham Labour Party of the mid-1920s, partly owing to the lack of first-hand accounts.   But it must have been a highly stimulating atmosphere, with Mosley, Strachey, Brailsford, Wise, Lloyd and others chewing over ideas derived from J. A. Hobson, from the latest books and articles by Keynes, from the experience of war-time planning.   Mosley was the first to break through to a modern economic policy with his so-called Birmingham Proposals of 1925, but the Independent Labour Party was not far behind with its Living Wage policy.   It is still astonishing to see how a whole set of ideas can vanish without trace, only to reappear years later as entirely new.   This was indeed the fate of Mosley's scheme.   He wanted to reflate the economy by expanding the money supply, to plan incomes to avoid inflation, to channel the new money into the declining areas, to plan foreign trade, to float the pound – all astonishingly modern but, as Professor Pollard says, an ' isolated *tour de force* '.   The New Party programme, *A National Policy*, drafted by Mosley's collaborators Strachey, Bevan, W. J. Brown and Allan Young in 1931 is another example of an impressive, though forgotten, document.   Both might have saved the Labour Party much trouble, and the British people much anguish, had their message been digested sooner.

The problem of Mosley's originality is not of course resolved just by reference to the Birmingham Labour Party of the mid-1920s. I have laid particular stress on the values derived from his landed background – a genuine, not a spurious, one, going back hundreds of years – and particularly on that aspect of it which emphasised the responsibility of rulers for the welfare and happiness of the people. Mosley was well placed to challenge liberal economics, because he had grown up in, as he calls it, a ' feudal world '.   One of the striking facts about the modern world is the way in which pre-liberal ideas have come back into fashion as the liberal econo-mic order developed in the nineteenth century crumbled under the impact of depression.   This movement was already well under way before Mosley was born.   The fact that he brought to politics attitudes derived from earlier traditions was one of the reasons why he was able to participate creatively in the modern political pro-cess.   Another was the impact of the First World War.   This was a highly problematic experience for Mosley and crucial, in my view, to an understanding of why he went ' wrong '.   I will come to this in a moment.   Here it is only necessary to mention three ' creative ' consequences: first, it gave him a sense of mission, a genuine com-mitment to a politician's phrase, the Land Fit for Heroes; secondly, it provided him with an alternative model of social and economic organisation – ' war socialism '; thirdly, it gave him a new outlook on foreign policy.   Britain should never fight again except in its own self-defence.   This resolution, expressed repeatedly in his ' isolationist ' foreign-policy stands of the 1920s, is of immense importance in any fair assessment of Mosley's opposition to the Second World War.

That Mosley made original and important contributions to the economic and political debate before 1931 will not, I think, be generally disputed.   The case for reassessment of Mosley after 1931 is bound to seem much weaker.   Questions are likely to be of two kinds.   Is there any reason for bothering with what Mosley said or thought after 1931, considering that it has had no discernible influence?   Is there any case for a reassessment of the things he did after 1931 – his political methods, his decision to go fascist?

The case for continuing to take Mosley's ideas seriously is more substantial than the practical consideration that for much of his life after 1945 there is little else to write about.   In the first place, the creativity with which he is now generally credited before 1931 did not suddenly disappear when he put on a black shirt.   Rather, a highly unusual and penetrating mind went on developing and refining certain basic positions present only in embryo in the 1920s. Secondly, Mosley's political stands provide a mordant and ironic commentary on the history of his own lifetime.   To study Mosley's thought is to be presented with an alternative history of Great Britain in the twentieth century, a history of ' what might have been' which has a fascination of its own.   But it would be mistake to treat it merely as fantasy.   Mosley had a remarkable gift for being in tune with the main historical tendencies of his age.   When his responses to twentieth century challenges are set side by side with those of Britain's rulers, it is *their* lack of attunement to the new age that appears so striking. Mosley may have been out of tune with the British political culture; but Britain itself was notably failing to adapt its nineteenth century ideas to twentieth century reality. Mosley may best be seen as an ' authoritarian modernizer ' in a society which had ' resolved unwittingly to stand on the ancient ways '.* It was the inherent difficulty of this position, as much as Mosley's ' character defects ', which wrecked his political career. But the very quality of futurism which helped bring his political ambitions to dust keeps his ideas fresh for present and succeeding generations.

These ideas – economic, political, philosophical – are explored at some length in this book. Here I just want to say a word about his most distinctive contribution, namely his vision of a world divided up into blocs, each supplying its own material needs and expressing its own spiritual possibilities. This was an outgrowth of his economic nationalism of the 1920s. Mosley traced both war and economic disruption to a single source: the ' unlimited geographic option in profits ' in Leo Amery's graphic phrase, which embroiled governments in the defence of the economic interests of their nationals in faraway places, and which placed social life at the mercy of the disruptive forces of international trade and finance. In reaction to this he developed his programme of ' national socialism ' in which ' insulation ' of the domestic economy was to go hand in hand with ' isolation ' in foreign affairs. But this programme of political control over economic life came up squarely against the equally modern fact of interdependence. The isolated, self-sufficient state was an anachronism in a world in which no nation, except possibly the largest, could hope to provide unaided its own means of sustenance and defence, and in which ideas, knowledge, business organisation and travel were increasingly international. The problem – far from being resolved today – was how to reconcile political control over economic life with the transnational character of modern business activity. One answer was to build a superstructure of international institutions to regulate what has in effect become an international community: a world state in embryo. Mosley has always rejected this as unworkable and unnatural. The gap between the national community which held the allegiance of the masses and the international community which already existed in the minds of the business and intellectual élites was too great to be bridged in a single leap. Mosley's alternative was an ' extension of patriotism ' to an area sufficiently large to provide most of its foodstuffs and raw materials and sufficiently

*This is the view of Henry Ashby Turner (' Fascism and Modernization ', *World Politics*, June 1972) which has the great merit of bypassing the futile attempt of trying to classify Mosley according to the conventional political categories of ' Right ' and ' Left '.

homogeneous culturally to form a political community. Like many
Europeans at different times he saw America as the pioneer of
the enlarged nation of the future.

Mosley's earliest version of the bloc was the British Empire. It
was because he wanted to weld the Empire into a political and economic unit in the 1930s that he insisted that Germany must be
allowed a bloc of its own as well. After the Second World War
he wanted Britain to lead the defeated and demoralised European
nations into a new European community. He was always haunted
by the nightmare of Britain's manhood being poured away to
defend the crumbling nineteenth century international system
which it had pioneered, rather than being harnessed to building,
with like-minded countries, the higher civilisation which science
made possible. It is at least a tenable proposition that Britain's
economic and political decline has resulted from the attempt, culminating in Pyrrhic victories in two world wars, to do the former,
not the latter. Britain today is the economic ' sick man of Europe '
and its current debility threatens with collapse the Common Market
which it finally joined in 1971, twenty-four years after Mosley first
campaigned for European union. It was against the background
of what he saw as a continually inadequate political response to the
problems of change that Mosley developed his argument for a
higher type of statesman.

This background of a failing political class is highly relevant to
any assessment of Mosley's political style. The conventional view
today is that he was a man with a first-class brain but a second-class
character. He has been accused of appalling judgment, colossal vanity,
suicidal impatience. He was a man who revelled in violence and, by
stirring up hatred, earned the undying hatred of others. He had
an insatiable lust for power. According to Baldwin he was a ' cad '.

Sound judgment – in the choice of men, in the choice of the
moment to act – is obviously important in politics, though there is
something suspect about the phrase itself, which suggests a cautious
mediocrity. In one sense, Mosley's judgment of people was good:
he recognised genius, respected professional expertise. His advocacy of the cause of Keynes in the 1920s is an example: a man hopelessly ' unsound ' by the debilitated standards of the time. Where
genius was clearly absent, Mosley was less reliable. He under-
rated good men, and could be taken in by scoundrels. In particular his intense mistrust of the ' sound ' men led him to idealise
political outlaws who gave him a bad name with the serious public.

Mosley was undoubtedly vain. He took great pains over his
own appearance and gestures. He believed that he alone had the
answer to Britain's problems. Psychoanalysts might have a field
day speculating about the sources of his extraordinary sense of
personal destiny, his dreams of glory. The picture that might

emerge is that of a man who continually needed to compensate for a lack of self-esteem, the product perhaps of a loveless childhood. But such evidence as we have, admittedly fragmentary, suggests that Mosley's ambition was grounded in an exceptionally affectionate and supportive home background. He was adored by his mother and paternal grandfather; and his adult ambitions were sustained not only by the constant support of his mother, but by the admiration and loyalty of the two remarkable women who were his wives. Perhaps his personal milieu at all stages of his career may have been *too* supportive for his own political good. It is tempting to relate his notorious impatience – ' he must have what he wants immediately,' wrote Harold Laski – to the absence of frustration in his own childhood. But perhaps a more fundamental reason for it was the impact of war. The First World War was for the eighteen-year-old Mosley such a forced growth that he found it difficult thereafter to adjust to any sense of ' peace-time '. His whole historical view was foreshortened. He always underestimated the time it would take, or need, for things to happen.

In the conventional interpretation there is a straight line between Mosley's ' character defects ' and what are regarded as his unsavoury political methods. To the charge of demagogy first levelled in the Smethwick by-election of 1926 were added the charges of stirring up hatred against the Jews and provoking and using political violence in the 1930s. These matters are discussed at some length in the book. It is far from my intention to defend or excuse everything Mosley did in his political life. Sometimes his political judgment was at fault; sometimes he acted sincerely but with an insensitivity to the feelings of others; sometimes he rationalised bad means by reference to the good ends to which they were directed.

However, it is important to distinguish between those aspects of his political behaviour which are genuinely reprehensible, and those which are so only from the cosy perspective of Whitehall – a perspective too often adopted by historians trying to make themselves even more respectable than civil servants. Many of the charges against Mosley, in my view, are ' administrative ' charges disguised as moral charges. Mosley was a challenger in a political society which had settled down to a middle-aged consensus. His approach in his ' populist ' periods was to rouse people against the ' corrupt interests ' in the old Radical style. The result was an inevitable heightening of tension which could lead to violence. In fact the level of political violence in England in the 1930s was very low and the evidence, I believe, shows that Mosley in this respect was as much, if not more, sinned against than sinning. But it was still unacceptable to the ' mature ' democracy that England had suddenly become. It is strange how quickly the idea of con-

sensus politics had taken hold. It was in striking contrast to the
reality of the fifteen years or so before the First World War which
were marked by domestic violence far greater than anything seen in
the 1930s. The nearest parallel to Mosley then was the young
Lloyd George, in full cry against the Boer War. There was the
same populism, the same attack on the ' corrupt interests ' (including Jewish financiers) and an even greater violence: for example, a
man was killed at Lloyd George's Birmingham meeting of 1901.
Lloyd George saw the parallel clearly enough; hence his interestingly tolerant attitude toward the events of Olympia.

Political style has to be judged in relation to needs. One might
argue that Britain had to compensate in the inter-war years for
political and economic decline, and also guard itself against the
threat of political revolution, by an enhanced civility in politics;
and that it was the genius of the British political system to have
realised this. On the other hand it might be claimed that the
more urgent task was to find some way to reversing that decline,
with its tragic symbol of continuous mass unemployment, and that
consensus politics was the least appropriate way of discovering it.
The vacuous goodwill of MacDonald and Baldwin did not provide
any answer to the problems facing Britain: it merely papered over
the cracks of a failing society. The politics of accommodation
reached, in this period, such a peak of perfection that it became
almost impossible to inject any new ideas into the political process
through ordinary political means. As Taylor has rightly remarked,
' the very forces which made Great Britain peaceful and stable prevented her from becoming the country of the New Deal '. Yet
the very virtues of a system can become vices if they preclude adaptation to new realities. The peace and stability of which Taylor
writes was – and perhaps is – too close to *rigor mortis* to permit any
facile dismissal of Mosley as a mere unscrupulous troublemaker.
Lord Boothby has written of him: ' I have not seen his equal in
political courage.' More political courage and less political smooth-
ness would have served Britain well.

The golden rule in English politics is to stick to your party.
If you do that anything will be forgiven you in time. Mosley broke
this rule. It was his ambition, many argue, that finally betrayed
him. Not content with ordinary political prizes he grasped for
supreme power by aping the methods which had brought success
to Mussolini and Hitler. Mosley himself naturally gives a different
explanation. He justified his break from conventional politics, and
continues to justify it, by reference to the decadence of the existing
élites and the need to replace them by ' new men ' born out of
' struggle '. The real explanation, I believe, is more complex.
Mosley was not satisfied with ordinary political prizes, but this was
not because he lusted for power. Neither do I see the decision he

took in 1931–2 as the rational decision he makes it out to be, though
rational calculation entered into it.

To understand the decision for fascism I believe we must go back
to the less creative consequences on Mosley of his First World War
experience. We find in him the same duality of attitude that
marked so many of the articulate survivors of that holocaust – a
hatred of war and the people who run it and cause it, but at the
same time a nostalgic yearning for, and idealisation of, the ' spirit
of the trenches '. Mosley's real problem was that his sense of
political mission awakened by the war co-existed with an inability
to settle down again to normal civilian life, with its conventional
standards of success and achievements, its conventional pace and
morality. (One must remember, too, that he had been uprooted
from the land, the ultimate source of his values and spiritual health.)
What held him to politics in the 1920s, despite the strong pull of
hedonism, was his view of himself in the Labour Party as part of an
army on the march towards the realisation of his dreams. This
belief was totally shattered by Labour's political betrayal of 1930–1.
The army was revealed as a rabble which had ' taken to its heels
on the Day of Judgment '. Under the traumatic impact of this
collapse, the emotional syndrome of the war survivor reasserted itself: the emptiness of civilian existence, the fraudulence of politics.
Mosley fled back to the trenches. Rationally, he persuaded himself that he was building an improved instrument for action, but
in fact he was removing himself from the plane of effective action.
Perhaps he realised this. There is some evidence to suggest that
he never expected his fascist enterprise to succeed or, more precisely,
that success was not its main object, which was to enable Mosley
and many of the men who joined him to live the only life which had
meaning for them. The Spenglerian concepts of ' exhaustion '
and ' renewal ' had for Mosley a deeply personal significance.
His movement was his way back to health.

What I have tried to do in this book is to set the personal life of
Mosley in the context of the decline of Britain. Britain had two
great war-leaders. It failed to find a great peace-leader; and its
recent history shows that winning the peace is even more important
than winning the war. Mosley might have been that leader. He
destroyed himself; and was destroyed by the very spirit of negation
against which he fought so valiantly. The past cannot be undone.
But a better appreciation of it may lessen the inhibition of the present against allowing Mosley's voice to be heard on any issue affecting the future. The exclusion of Mosley from the contemporary
dialogue as a punishment without end is both mean and unwise.
For the following pages show that the ideas and values in whose
name Mosley has been pilloried do not offer the only, or even the
most secure, guide to the unknown.

Chapter 1

Feudal Livery

A BIOGRAPHY is more than just a description and evaluation of someone's life. It is an attempt to understand how it was that a person came to act and behave in the way he did, hold the opinions he did – in short, how he came to be the man he was. This raises a particular problem with Oswald Mosley, who seems to stand, in so many ways, apart not only from his time but from his country. He calls to mind the contemporary jingle about Charles James Fox: 'Though he's British by birth, he's foreign in his heart.' As we shall show, this view represents a serious oversimplification. Nevertheless, it helps to define the problem of Mosley. His fiery political energy seems to spring from sources other than those of a parliamentary tradition worn smooth by time; his fertile mind is stocked with ideas that seem to have no roots in the British political soil. Even his ferocious, dark, good looks seem to come from Mediterranean rather than from northern shores.

No man can be completely explained by his background; and not all backgrounds have equal explanatory value. In Mosley's case, to start with background is not just the biographer's conventional piety. It serves the immediate purpose of placing Mosley firmly in a British tradition at a particular point in time. Mosley comes from the country gentry of England. He is heir to its values and its way of life. However, he was born into it at a highly complex moment of transition for English society as a whole. On the one hand, the values of the land from which Mosley came had been defeated and crushed by the triumph of urban, middle-class England and the forces of economic liberalism which accompanied its rise; on the other hand, those forces themselves were starting to be challenged by the rise of the working class and the decay of Britain's world position. These facts offer an important preliminary insight into Mosley's career. They place him in British society and help explain his alienation from that society at a point in time when the possibilities of an attack on the whole liberal position were opening up. From a biographical point of view, Mosley's life can be seen as an attempt to reintegrate his background into the mainstream of twentieth century English life at a time when English society itself was starting to be threatened by the forces which had earlier destroyed his family position.

For the modern Mosley story, 1846 was a date of double significance. In the world of national politics it marked the repeal of the Corn Laws which had protected the position of the land – a revolution, in the words of Halévy, ' more momentous than that of 1832, as momentous, indeed, as that of 1688 '. In the little world of the Mosley family, 1846 was also momentous: it marked the formal end of the Mosley manorial régime at Manchester. The two events, in fact, were part of the same happening: the expulsion of the Mosleys from Manchester was merely a minor engagement in the Waterloo of the social system that had governed England since the Middle Ages. In 1846 capitalism celebrated its final victory over feudalism; the new class of businessmen won its blood-less triumph over the country gentlemen of England. It is not without significance in our story that the *coup de grâce* both to the Mosleys at Manchester and to the landed interest of England should have been delivered by the same man: Richard Cobden. Oswald Mosley set out to avenge a family, as well as a class, defeat.

The Mosley connection with Manchester goes back at least to the middle of the fifteenth century when a Jenkyn Moseley appears as a burgess of Hough, a hamlet in the manor of Manchester. Family tradition, as family traditions are apt to, traces the descent back much earlier – to the Mosleys of Moseley in Staffordshire. According to the local historian who has made the most extensive study of the family lineage, ' this descent has never been proved, and is probably unprovable. The surname of Mosley, variously spelled, was by no means uncommon in several counties, and it occurs in Lancashire early in the fourteenth century.'[1] The earliest Mosley ancestors were probably yeomen farmers: by the fifteenth and sixteenth centuries they had moved into the cloth trade. Edward Mosley (born *c*.1500) is described as a ' merchant ', owner of ' one tenement in Moston '. His four sons – Oswald, Nicholas, Anthony and Francis – are all variously described as ' merchants ', ' clothiers ' or ' clothworkers '. It was they who laid the foundations of the family fortune. Manchester had already become an important centre of an English cloth trade stimulated by the influx of French, Walloon and Dutch artisans, and by the growing demand of the opulent princes of the Renaissance. Oswald, Anthony and Francis handled the Manchester side of the family business; Nicholas went to London to arrange for the sale of the fabrics there, and their shipment abroad. Of Nicholas, a contemporary poet wrote:

To Russia, to Tartasie, France and Italy,
Your homme-spunne clothe he yearly made to see.

Family legend has built up Nicholas Mosley into a kind of com-mercial Francis Drake who earned his knighthood through privateer-ing: a worthy ancestor for a twentieth century political buccaneer. In fact, there was little of the freebooter about Nicholas. As a wealthy merchant he became prominent in the City and in the civic administration of London, and by this route he became Lord Mayor of London in 1599. He earned his knighthood in 1600 not by organising raids on the Spanish Main, but through his exceptional skill in extorting taxation from the reluctant City business community.[2] In addition, a grateful Queen Elizabeth gave him a carved oak bedstead, and a family motto, *Mos Legem Regit* (' Custom Rules the Law '), a royal pun. (It was about this time that the spelling of the name took its present form of Mosley.) According to his contemporaries, Sir Nicholas cared not ' who was loser so he thereby did gayne ' and died in bed at the age of eighty-five clutching a bag containing £400 in gold sovereigns and railing at his sons for not taking after him in money-making.[3]

As a result of their business successes, the Mosleys found themselves in possession of substantial amounts of liquid cash at the moment when great landed estates came flooding onto the market, bankrupted by the extravagance of their feudal owners. Then, as later, purchase of an estate was the quickest way up the social ladder. Sometime in the 1570s, Earl de la Warr mortgaged the manor of Manchester to Nicholas Mosley as security for a loan. When he failed to pay it back, Nicholas Mosley purchased de la Warr's estates, and became lord of the manor of Manchester in 1596, building an appropriate seat, Hough End Hall, to a design by Inigo Jones, on the site of his father's tenement. He is also recorded as purchasing other properties in Lancashire, Cheshire and Shropshire. His son Edward, M.P. for Preston and attorney-general for Lancashire, added to his father's holdings by buying the estate of Rolleston-on-Dove, Staffordshire, in 1614: this was to become the main family seat. Two more properties, in Derbyshire and Leicestershire, were bought in the 1630s. The other branches of the family also converted their profits into land. In 1608, Anthony Mosley's son Oswald bought the manor of Ancoats from Lord Byron's ancestor, Sir John Byron, for £250. With the failure of Sir Nicholas's male heirs, the Manchester, Rolleston and Ancoats estates were united in the person of Sir Oswald Mosley of Ancoats, after a long litigation, early in the eighteenth century. However, the present Sir Oswald is a direct descendant of another branch of Anthony's family, which gained the family estates in the person of Sir John Parker Mosley in 1780. The rise of the Mosleys by a combination of business acumen and royal favour is by no means untypical of the social changes taking place in England at the end of the sixteenth and early seventeenth centuries.

Having prospered through royal patronage, the Mosleys not unnaturally took the King's side in the Civil War. Sir Edward Mosley loaned his needy sovereign £20,000 in 1642: for this he was rewarded with a baronetcy. (The present Sir Oswald Mosley is the sixth baronet of the third creation dating from 1781.) Later

that year, Charles I ordered his ' trustye and well-beloved ' Sir
Edward Mosley, High Sheriff of Staffordshire, to raise ' sufficient
forces of horse and foote, to be paid by the county, and to put the
same into the castle of Tutbury [adjoining the Rolleston estate] for
the defence and securetie of the same against all levies of the rebels,
and other ill-affected persons in that or the neighbouring counties '.
This Sir Edward did.   However, the family legend of his last stand
at Tutbury against Cromwell has no foundation.   In fact, Sir
Edward Mosley was taken prisoner at the battle of Middlewich in
1643; the royal castle of Tutbury was surrendered by Lord Lough-
borough to Sir William Brereton three years later and was demolished on the orders of Parliament.   Mosley grew up in the shadow
of its imposing ruins.[4]   For Sir Edward, backing the wrong side
proved an expensive business.   The Mosley estates were seques-
tered, pending payment of a heavy fine.   Sir Edward did not help
matters by getting hopelessly into debt and abandoning himself to
a life of wild debauch in London.[5]   On his death, the family,
gathering together their last resources, recovered their lands by
paying the fine of £4874, reckoned to be about one-tenth of their
value.   With Manchester's conduit, or water pipe, ' flowing with
pure claret ', Nicholas Mosley of Ancoats celebrated the Restoration in fine style, by marching 200 of the original troop he had
raised for the King through its streets – a performance which his
descendant was to emulate almost 300 years later.   It was a fitting
climax to the expansionist phase of family history.

Having made their pile, the Mosleys abandoned their connection
with commerce and settled down to the life of wealthy country
gentry, made more spacious by the rising rents of their landed and
urban properties as Georgian England slowly prepared itself for
industrial take-off.   Family legend tells of a brief flirtation with
Bonnie Prince Charlie in 1745, but in general there was little hanker-
ing after adventure.[6]   The Mosleys raised large families and had
their fair share of success in marrying off their eligible daughters.
The Tudor hall at Rolleston acquired a Georgian façade; it was
surrounded by parks and formal gardens for the delight of the ladies;
the young gentlemen would amuse themselves rather more boister-
ously at Eton and Brasenose College, Oxford.   There were stately
processions round the main family homes.   There was even an
eccentric, the Reverend Sir John Mosley (d.1779) who, perhaps
inspired by Mandeville's *Fable of the Bees*, constructed elaborate
follies on his estate to provide employment for the poor.   The Mosleys remained a county, not a national, family, content, in the
words of a local historian, ' with the by-paths rather than the main
road of history '.

This failure to break through to national importance has some
bearing on our story.   The accepted *cursus honorum* in the modern

rise of great English families has been ' trade, a fortune, the acquisition of an estate, a baronetcy, membership of Parliament, and finally a peerage '.[7] The transition from baronetcy to peerage generally, though not invariably, was the transition from country gentry to landed aristocracy, with its corollary shift of interest from local to national politics, county to metropolitan life. The Mosleys never became one of the great families of England, though at times they almost did. This was not through lack of money. By the early nineteenth century, if not before, the family certainly had an annual income in excess of the £10,000 considered the minimum financial qualification for aristocratic status – enough to support both a country house and a town house in London.[8] But they did not choose to accept the aristocratic responsibility of national leadership. Between 1661 and 1807 no Mosley sat in Parliament. Sir Oswald Mosley, the present baronet's great-great-grandfather, then became Whig M.P. for North Staffordshire. But apart from his unorthodox support for Samuel Whitbread's 1808 resolution calling for peace with Napoleon[9]– an interesting anticipation of his descendant's attitude to the Hitler war – he made no mark; and on his retirement in 1837 recorded ruefully in his *Memoir* that ' with the exception of having been introduced to many *talented*, and to a few *pious*, men, he found that . . . his expectations ended in nothing but vanity and vexations of the spirit '.

Perhaps the Mosleys remained too attached to the soil of their native Staffordshire, too absorbed in the affairs of Manchester, fully to take the plunge into national, London-based, politics. But their position as greater gentry on the fringe of national politics left an ambiguous legacy. As country gentry they remained more parochial and anti-cosmopolitan than the aristocracy, more attached to traditional values, more cut off from industrial, middle-class England, suspicious of the politics of accommodation practised by their aristocratic leaders at Westminster (it was the country gentlemen, not the aristocracy, who revolted against the repeal of the Corn Laws in 1846).[10] On the other hand, his Whig parliamentary ancestor gave Mosley a sense of identification with the tradition of a reforming landed aristocracy, willing to accommodate, and even lead, the forces of change to stave off revolution. Perhaps Mosley's own particular combination of conservatism and radicalism can be traced back to his family's divided loyalties.

The brightest jewel in the Mosley crown was the manor of Manchester; it was here, too, that history displayed one of its richest ironies. Grown by 1800 from a collection of family estates, hamlets and villages into the first great centre of the new industrial civilisation – ' from this foul drain ', wrote de Tocqueville, ' the greatest stream of human industry flows out to fertilise the world ' – Manchester had not yet escaped from its legal status as a manorial village, governed by a medieval court-leet over which Mosley's bailiff presided and which was still theoretically responsible for the 'upkeep' of the 'estate'. The clash between a decaying feudalism and a rising capitalism here developed at its most dramatic. It centred on that touchstone of the modern world, the freedom of the market.

Chief among the Mosleys' manorial rights was the exclusive ownership of all fairs and markets; and with it the right to specify at what times and under what conditions goods might be sold. (In return, they had to provide and maintain sites – a Mosley built the first Manchester Exchange in 1739.)   As business expanded, the lords of the manor received an increasingly lucrative income from tollage and stallage – taxes on goods entering the market and on the rental of stalls.   To the rising Manchester 'shopocracy' these manorial rights were intolerable insults.   The tax was simply 'un-earned increment' – a classic case of aristocratic privilege.   The regulations were bureaucratic interferences with business, based on obsolete economic doctrines.   Here was the crux of the matter. The privilege of holding markets was justified by its protective function in shielding the local population from economic fluctua-tions; the income derived from it a kind of endowment to enable the lord of the manor to fulfil that protective role.   In a society de-pendent upon local resources and therefore vulnerable to natural catastrophes such as plague or harvest failure, the regulation of the food supply so as to prevent the population from rioting and starv-ing was the chief object of the local authorities.   The whole system of regulations was essentially designed to prevent 'hucksters' (generally strangers) from disrupting the food supply by under-cutting the declared price in private transactions thereby ruining farmers; or cornering stocks to force a price rise thereby making it impossible for the poor to buy bread.   The lord's tollage and stallage were basically protective duties levied on 'foreign' traders.[11]   The Industrial Revolution completely transformed this defensive outlook.   With vast profits to be made nationally and internationally, merchants and manufacturers alike demanded the emancipation of the market from the web of feudal restrictions; and were becoming wealthy and self-confident enough to make their will prevail.

The merchants' first offensive was launched in 1782 when Messrs Chadwick & Archer set up 114 unauthorised meatstalls in Poolford. Sir John Parker Mosley brought and won an action for trespass but, as the family *Memoir* sadly noted, the merchants were able 'to combine together for . . . defraying the expenses of a trial . . . while the unprotected Lord of the Manor was at his own cost subjected to vexatious and expensive lawsuits for the maintenance and pre-servation of his rights'.[12]   No doubt partly because of the expense of this and other litigations, Sir Oswald Mosley tried in 1808 to sell his rights for £80,000 to the police commissioners (a kind of supplementary local authority set up by statute in 1792 to take over some of the functions of the failing court-leet). But the price was considered too high, and the manorial régime shuffled on for another thirty-seven years.

The final phase of the struggle in the 1830s and 1840s revealed a new alignment of local forces, significant for the future: the landed oligarchs who ruled through the manorial system joined together with the ' common people ' in resisting the demands of the middle-class reformers. The Municipal Corporations Act of 1835, following hard on the first Reform Act, provided that the inhabitant householders of any town or borough could obtain incorporation (that is, an elected local government) by petition to the Privy Council. The reformers were galvanised by Richard Cobden, who on 19 October 1837 attended a meeting of the court-leet for the first time as one of the jurors. It was a revealing experience. The meeting was held in the manor court-room, ' large and altogether destitute of furniture, whose row of tall old-fashioned windows would, but for the crust of smoke and dirt that covered them, have afforded a cheerful light. The atmosphere of the room was heavy and stale. . . . To the left of the door lay a heap of sawdust. . . . A filthy white dog, with black spots, had curled himself upon this tempting bed; and he lifted up his ears with excusable surprise at the shrill tones of the crier, who now opened the court with the usual " O yes ", followed by an unintelligible jargon of Saxon, old English, and Norman epithets. . . . '13 Cobden's anger boiled over when at the end of the meeting Mosley's steward presented him and the other jurors with tickets entitling them to a court-leet dinner provided by Sir Oswald. ' Well, what in the world does this mean?' asked Cobden. ' Is it that in this great town of Manchester we are still living under the feudal system? Does Sir Oswald Mosley, living up in Derbyshire, send his mandate down here for us to come into this dingy hole to elect a government for Manchester, and then go and get a ticket for soup at his expense? Why, now I will put an end to this thing.'

The Tories and Radicals launched a vigorous counter-offensive. ' Working Men Beware,' they cried.

We must have no Middle-Class Government. No Whig Corporation – No New Police – No Turtle-Fed Aldermen – no cotton-lord Mayors – No Civic Banquets – No Golden-Mace, Collars and Orders – No Wine Cellars stored out of a new borough rate. . . . The Whigs are not our Friends, their Reform tends to establish a Shopocracy to rule over and grind down the Poor.

The ' Tory Radical ' Chartists argued that the ' reported tyranny of the Lord of the Manor was all a fudge' to mask the reality of New Poor Law oppression. The Municipal Reformers collected 11,830 signatures for a petition; Sir Oswald Mosley retaliated with 31,947 ' anti-incorporators '. An enquiry reduced the number of ' genuine ' Cobdenite petitioners to 7984, while the anti-incorporation figure was whittled down hugely to 8694, a reduction in the adverse balance achieved only by the ' heroic exertion ' of Cobden and his friends. Nevertheless, despite the narrow majority for the continuance of the manorial régime, incorporation was conceded by the Privy Council in 1838. The decision was contested in the courts for a number of years afterwards, but the battle had been lost.

In 1846, Sir Oswald Mosley agreed to sell his manorial rights, which he said represented an annual income of £9114 16s 8d, for a capital sum of £200,000. The major part of the Mosleys' private property in Manchester was leased out, injudiciously, on 999-year leases, from which Mosley still draws ground-rents. The last meeting of the court-leet was held in May 1846. In the words of Manchester's historian Arthur Redford,

> Cobden denounced the ' feudal monopoly ' of the Mosleys as vehemently as he denounced the agricultural monopoly of the rural landowners; and many of his Manchester disciples must have derived a peculiar gratification from the fact that the downfall of the Corn Laws, in 1846, accompanied the abolition of the manorial control over the local cornmarket and the extinction of the Manchester Court Leet.[14]

But in the ebb and flow of events there are few final victories or defeats; and the issues apparently so conclusively settled in 1846 were to be fought all over again as the Cobdenite dream turned into the nightmare of the Great Depression of the inter-war years.

Thereafter the Mosleys did not fight the nineteenth century: they simply ignored it. What was left after the Manchester débâcle was 4000 acres of farmland, chiefly in Staffordshire. Here a tiny feudal enclave survived into the twentieth century. The Black Country might be getting blacker, but the Mosleys had no connection with either the potteries or the metal works of Staffordshire: younger sons flocked into the Army or the Church in even greater profusion than before. Halfway between Manchester and Birmingham, Rolleston lost touch with both. After the family's expulsion from Manchester, the old Tudor–Georgian hall had symbolically burnt to the ground, to be replaced by an ugly, sprawling, Victorian pile. Here the gargantuan Sir Tonman Mosley reigned till 1879. He was succeeded by Sir Oswald Mosley, the present Mosley's grandfather, whose wife had already given birth to yet another Oswald, Mosley's father, in 1873.

Mosley's mother's family was also Staffordshire gentry, though on a much less grand scale than the Mosleys: oddly enough, it was the female line which furnished the family name Heathcote, with Mosley's maternal grandfather Justinian Edwards taking the additional name Heathcote by royal licence in 1870. The Heathcotes first appear in *Burke's Landed Gentry* in the eighteenth century at Apedale near Stoke-on-Trent. Sir Richard Edensor Heathcote had been Tory M.P. for Stoke-on-Trent in 1835–6 and Justinian Edwards Heathcote represented the same division from 1886–92: he regaled the young Mosley with stories of Parnell. The discovery of coal on their Staffordshire land had brought their farming activities, but not their wealth, to an end; and about the middle of the nineteenth century they migrated to the more salubrious surroundings of Market Drayton, Shropshire, where Mosley's mother, Katherine Maud, was born in 1874, the second in a family of three sisters and two brothers. She married the heir of Rolleston, Oswald Mosley, in 1895; and their eldest child, Oswald Ernald, the subject of this biography, was born on 16 November 1896.

Katherine Maud was 5 feet 10 inches tall, with hooded eyes and a large mouth as the chief features of a strong face. She was noted for her firm Christian principles, shading off into spiritualism later on in life. Her son did not take after her in this respect: like many others brought up as believers in an age of scepticism, Mosley adapted his family's religion to the demands of secular salvation. She was passionately devoted to animals and to the sports of the field. Without intellectual or artistic interests, she had considerable practical common sense. This was to come in very useful in the upbringing of her children, since her marriage to Mosley's father did not last. He was a hard-riding, hard-drinking, hard-living, Tory squire, much given to expletives, whose early escapades had led to a hurried removal from Eton at the age of sixteen. He died of cirrhosis of the liver, at fifty-four, his dissipations, according to the family doctor, Lord Horder, being enough to have killed several men. His wasted energy is not untypical of that of a class which has lost its function, but retains its values, and of an eldest son in an aristocratic world who has nothing to do except await the succession. He went on sowing his wild oats well into his marriage, and this prompted Katherine Maud, a determined woman, to secure a judicial separation. Taking her three children with her (John and Edward had followed in quick succession to Oswald) she left him never to return. From the age of five, Mosley was brought up by his mother at Belton Hall, near Market Drayton, Shropshire. He saw his father only occasionally.

The two main people in Mosley's childhood were his mother and his paternal grandfather, Sir Oswald Mosley, at Rolleston. Both idolised him: to his mother 'Tom was God'* noted a contemporary of the 1920s, a substitute for a husband; to his grandfather he was substitute for a son, since Mosley's father was as great a disappointment to his father as he was to his wife. In these two relationships may be found a clue to Mosley's own supreme self-esteem, which was to be such a marked feature of his subsequent career. Freud wrote, 'A man who has been the indisputable favourite of his mother keeps for life the feeling of a conqueror.' To his mother, Mosley was the man of the house from an early age, 'my man-child' as she called him.[15] This support was never withdrawn. A lady of strong Tory convictions, she followed her son through all his political vicissitudes, even going so far as to put on a black shirt in the 1930s: her faith in his star remained undimmed till the day of her death. By his grandfather, Mosley was treated ostentatiously as a son and heir, but with the fond indulgence given to a grandson. The old Sir Oswald burst into tears when Mosley told him he had volunteered for the Royal Flying Corps in 1914 – 'astonishing in such a man; he explained that . . . I was all he had'.[16]

Mosley, who made some study of psychology in his war-time imprisonment, has discounted psychoanalytic explanations as applied to him – understandably enough, for their tendency is to 'explain' his actions in terms of unconscious drives rather than as rational responses to real problems. As his career developed along eccentric lines he was wont to attack the modern 'witchdoctors' who attempted to label worthy rebels like himself 'maladjusted'. He did not hesitate, however, to apply Freudian ideas to others: 'Behind the conscious mind operates every atavistic impulse,' he later wrote about his opponents. His lament that psychologists study disease rather than health may strike one as special pleading but there was nothing obviously diseased about Mosley's childhood.[17] Unlike Goebbels, he did not grow up with any physical deformities; his home life was secure and affectionate. Mosley was someone who bears out to an extraordinary extent Karl Jaspers' dictum that 'Man . . . is not what he is simply once and for all, but a process' – and one moreover directed by conscious effort or will.[18]

If the problem of motivation cannot be settled by an appeal to Mosley's childhood experiences, especially in view of what little we know about them, the source of his social and personal values can be much more clearly related to the influence of a whole way of life which survived the loss of Manchester. Mosley himself talks of growing up in a feudal world:

> Like medieval life, the economy was practically self-contained.
> Farms, the garden, shooting and the large well-stocked cellars

*Mosley was known as Tom to his friends in the 1920s.

satisfied most needs; the same wagon which took our produce a few miles to be sold in Burton-on-Trent would return well loaded with a fine variety of the best beers. There was little need to go outside the closed and charmed circle, and we children never did. Our time was divided between farms, gardens and carpenter's shop, where the bearded Pritchard presided over a corps of experts who kept all things going as their forbears had done for generations. . . .

Again in feudal fashion, the warmest and most intimate friendships developed between us and these people, so characteristic of traditional England, not only in their daily occupations, but in the strong bonds of mutual sympathy in life's events, birth, marriage, death, occasions sad and festive: this was really a classless society.[19]

Mosley's adored and adoring grandfather was clearly a paternalist of the old school, who took his obligations and his rights very seriously. He was not without enterprise: the diversification from arable to livestock farming to counter the North American grain invasions of the 1880s saved the Rolleston economy for another generation. As a young man, he worked with his labourers in the field from dawn to dusk. He raised a prize-winning shorthorn herd, placed his pedigree bulls at the disposal of his tenants for a nominal fee, and remitted a portion of their rents in hard times. He built cottages and a recreation hall for his workpeople, maintained a school for their children, an almshouse for the aged, a church for their spiritual health, and threw open his grounds to fêtes and fairs for their entertainment. His solicitude on one occasion took a positively Tolstoyan turn when he started baking a special wholemeal bread at the stone mill of Rolleston: ' Standard Bread ' provided Northcliffe's *Daily Mail* with one of its earliest journalistic stunts, and Rolleston was deluged for samples of the health-giving loaves.

All this activity, however, took place within a carefully structured social hierarchy in which each person had his place and function. The Hall stood at its apex with its own internal economy of butlers, manservants, housemaids and cooks: two still-maids would be engaged exclusively in making cakes. There were thirty gardeners. People for miles around were tenants or employees, or in some way dependent on the Rolleston economy. Mosley's grandfather was as conscious of his dignities as of his responsibilities. A Rolleston countrywoman has provided a vivid sketch of a vanished world:

Sir Oswald Mosley, 4th baronet, reigned supreme in those days – and when the Mosley yellow coach and four prancing horses passed through the lodge gates, through the village and into the town of Burton, the postillions on the near horse blow-

ing a horn, footmen in superb livery standing at the back, it was indeed an event that the people delighted to see: women curtsied, men doffed their caps and the curate made obeisance.
. . .

Just as his grandfather had fought to maintain the manorial rights in Manchester, so Mosley's grandfather (in vain) fought a lawsuit costing thousands of pounds to maintain the family's ancestral right to the exclusive use of a number of pews in the east aisle of St Mary's parish church, Rolleston. At the request of King Edward VII (a personal friend) Sir Oswald gave a canon of Windsor, Leonard Tyrwhitt, the living which was in his gift:

> No sooner had the squire installed Canon Tyrwhitt in the snug family rectory than the feud broke into flame, with the parson trying to turn the squire out of a pew of which his family had had undisputed possession for 300 years.
>
>   This let loose one of the most remarkable and stubborn controversies ever waged 'twixt priest and patron. But it was robbed of its uglier features at one or two points by Canon Tyrwhitt's quick sense of humour. For instance, the Sunday after Sir Oswald's expropriation the rector announced his text: ' For if there come into your assembly a man with a gold ring in goodly apparel, and there comes in also a poor man in vile raiment, and ye have respect of him that weareth the gay clothing and say unto him "Sit here in a good place", and say to the poor man "Stand thou here or sit here under my footstool", are ye not then partial in yourselves and become of evil thoughts?' The press added ' Sturgeon himself, master of apt quotation as he was, never made a happier hit '.[20]

By this curious route, the class struggle came at last to Rolleston. Yet this was not the class struggle of Victorian England. As de Tocqueville wrote:

> Thus, although in aristocratic society the master and servant have no natural resemblance, although, on the contrary, they are placed at an immense distance on the scale of human beings by their fortune, education and opinions, yet time ultimately binds them together. They are connected by a long series of common reminiscences, and however different they may be, they grow alike; while in democracies, where they are naturally almost alike, they always remain strangers to one another.[21]

The influence of this setting in forming Mosley's own social values emerges in his belief in a ' self-contained ' economy with its corollary of a revived agriculture, the paternal solicitude for his ' own people ', his functional view of society with its rejection of the ' crude class divisions of the city '[22] and, more trivially, his frequent recourse to litigation to protect his rights and his good name.

Another aspect of background is what Mosley himself describes as ' the long continuing influence of the pagan world ', inseparable from a society not just with roots in the soil but with roots in a value system which long antedated the civilisation of towns and universities.   Violence was ever present in nature, and it found its reflection in the life-style of those who lived close to it: in the love of cockfighting and bull-baiting which survived in Staffordshire and Lancashire well into the nineteenth century;* in the ' sports of the field ', the religion of the country gentry; in the tradition of prize-fighting and ' gentleman ' boxers: Mosley's grandfather and father as well as Mosley himself were all notable boxers, and boxing matches between squire and prize-fighter, or between father and son, were staged in Rolleston's ballroom.   These activities were pastimes; but they had been, and to some extent still were, functional to the education of a warrior class which in England, as all over Europe, was still largely recruited from land-based aristocracies and peasants.   Mosley carried from his background an ' attitude to manhood ', to the giving and receiving of punishment, which was as much at variance with the norms of contemporary political life as is the ethic of an army with those of contemporary civilian life.

In most social histories of Victorian England, the aristocracy merges insensibly into the bourgeois world of sobriety and industry so that it might seem almost eccentric to talk of the survival of a specifically aristocratic life-style.[23]   The new mood of serious high-mindedness certainly affects the Mosleys. It can be seen in the career of Sir John Parker Mosley, the first baronet of the third creation (1781), who starts out life as a debauched dandy, but then

*Bull-baiting certainly went on in the vicinity of Tutbury and Rolleston Hall till early in the nineteenth century.   In its original form the annual Bull-feast was instituted by Tutbury Castle's owner, John of Gaunt, in the fourteenth century, as an amusement for his Spanish bride, Constance of Castile.   To the accompaniment of much revelry and eating, the bull, provided for the occasion by the Prior of Tutbury, had his horns sawn off, his ears cropped, his tail cut off at the stump, and his nostrils filled with pepper.   He was then set loose, no one being allowed to approach within forty feet of him except the minstrels.   If the bull escaped capture during the day he remained the property of the Prior; if any of the minstrels could take hold of him and cut off a tuft of hair as proof of capture, the bull would be brought to the bailiff's house, tied with collar and rope and baited with dogs, after which the minstrels might sell, kill or divide him among themselves as they liked.   In degenerate form this festival lasted officially until 1778 and unofficially for much longer.   (Sir Oswald Mosley, *History of the Castle, Priory and Town of Tutbury, in the County of Stafford* (1832) pp. 86 ff.)

takes to praying to God alone in his study, banishes all theatrical entertainment from his household and is known as Methodist in the county. Piety, too, marks his grandson, Sir Oswald Mosley, author of the *Memoir*, who urges his children to 'devoutly read the Sacred Book' so as better to resist the promptings of the Devil.

What distinguishes the aristocracy and gentry from the bourgeoisie in this new world of Evangelical piety and middle-class utilitarianism is nothing more than a nuance, a subterranean tradition hard to pin down. It is perhaps best expressed in the phrase 'high spirits': the lingering tradition of the dandy, of 'sowing one's wild oats', of practical joking, of conspicuous display, of eccentricity, of idiosyncratic speech; all perhaps products of the self-confidence alone possessed by those born at the apex of an unchallenged social pyramid, who instinctively feel that anything they do must be justified. In religion the difference was between the old worldly Church of England and the new Evangelicalism: when Lord Melbourne exclaimed, 'Things are coming to a pretty pass when religion is allowed to invade private life', he was voicing the eighteenth century protest against the nineteenth. In education, the difference is between Eton and Rugby: the 'graceful insolence of an aristocracy victorious over religion and learning alike' had no place in the world of Dr Arnold and the high-minded Victorian educational reformers. Mosley was heir to the tradition of the dandy, of the aristocratic playboy. Confidence in hereditary rank is an important element in his story: however far he strayed from the path of orthodoxy, he always had a fall-back position which could not be snatched from him.

For Mosley, unlike his brothers and, one suspects, thousands of young men brought up in similar circumstances, these values achieved the status of a personal and social philosophy because they became conscious, articulated: ideas in the mind, to be carried through life long after the setting in which they took root had disappeared. Such glimpses as we have of his childhood suggest a solitary, imaginative boy, prone to day-dreaming and introspection. He was far from fitting automatically into the life-style of the country gentry, unlike his brother Edward who became a regular army officer. Horse riding, an indispensable accomplishment in that world, held secret terrors for him as a child, conquered only by immense effort.[24] Similarly, Mosley himself admits that he was never any good with his hands. But it is precisely those experiences which cannot be mastered easily or naturally which acquire special significance in one's emotional or imaginative life. At the same time, we must insist that class background can no more explain what Mosley did with his life than can upbringing. The family tradition and its predicament leads us to the point of departure in Mosley's life: it cannot see us through to his ultimate destination. Eric Bentley's comment on Nietzsche's *Zarathustra* is apposite: 'The old aristocratic modes of feeling are to be grafted onto the thought of a new evolutionary futurism.'

At the age of nine Mosley was sent away to West Down, a small preparatory school for Winchester. (The decision apparently had already been made to send him to Winchester rather than Eton; to the Heathcote, rather than to the Mosley, school.) The headmaster, Lionel Helbert, was a fresh-air fanatic: Mosley's most vivid memory of West Down was the intense cold. Otherwise he got into the school Cricket XI and took up boxing. But before he could achieve any real distinction at West Down he was pressing to move on to Winchester. He entered in September 1909 at the age of twelve, almost a year earlier than normal. As he notes in his autobiography, he lacked a 'calm, male influence' to say to him, 'What's the hurry?'[25]

There is a marked coolness in Mosley's references to the public school system. 'It seemed to me', he writes, 'a trivial existence, "cribbed, cabined and confined" by many of the silliest shibboleths of the bourgeois world. Apart from games, the dreary waste of public school existence was only relieved by learning and homosexuality; at that time I had no capacity for the former and I never had any taste for the latter.'[26]

Winchester, like all the public schools except Eton, had been adapted in the nineteenth century to serve the needs and aspirations of the upper middle classes who formed its clientèle. Strongly influenced by Jowett of Balliol, Dr Ridding, who became headmaster in 1866, deliberately set out to produce administrators for Victorian and Imperial England. He built new classrooms, introduced a modern curriculum, emphasised examinations, developed organised games and out-of-school activities. The house system, designed to produce a standardised product of high average ability, favouring the 'good mixer' at the expense of the bright individual, was an ideal forcing-ground for the civil service to which the school increasingly sent its best products. The tone of pre-war Winchester was Asquithian liberalism; its most eminent and, in a way, characteristic product, Lord Grey, Asquith's foreign secretary. The complacency, the intellectual distinction, the absolute sense of rectitude, the wealth of Byzantine 'Notions' or customs regulating the minutest details of schoolboy life, all reflected the self-esteem and security of upper middle-class England, the glow of a sun about to set.[27]

Mosley was a fish out of water in his three years at Winchester. By sixteen he was already eager to get out into the world, and once more persuaded his mother to take him away. His housemaster, Mr Bell of Branston's House, agreed. 'He always seemed too old for us,' he said. Not for Mosley was the public-school *cursus honorum*, culminating at eighteen or nineteen in glittering honours, and painful recollections of vanished glory and romantic friendships.

What impression did he make on his contemporaries? There is general agreement that he was an aloof boy who kept very much to himself and showed little interest in house 'activities' whether virtuous or vicious (a contemporary notes that a common activity at the time was ' balls ragging ' but Mosley ' would have no part of that '). He seems to have had no particular friends or enemies; he was neither ' socialised ' nor was he a rebel, but went his own way, sustained, so it is said, by almost daily letters from his mother. He was known to be a skilful boxer and this no doubt protected him from any bullying to which his strangeness might have given rise. One boy, a couple of terms his junior, recalls a painful incident:

> On one occasion he knocked me down to my great surprise! It was entirely my fault – sometime in 1911, I expect. There had been something in the *Daily Mail* about his grandfather's advocating the eating of Standard Bread; and several of us were baiting him with cries of ' Standard Bread ' ' Standard Bread ' as he went to put something away in his cupboard. He suddenly turned round, and I found myself on the floor.

At a time when most fourteen-year-olds are merely pretty, Mosley was already handsome. A contemporary recalls him as ' very tall, with striking, dark, good looks: he could easily have been made up into a stage villain'. His thick black hair was parted in the middle as was the custom, and one Wykehamist remembers him spending a lot of time combing it in front of the mirror: already he was very conscious of his appearance. His rapid growth must have left him rather unco-ordinated, for contemporaries recall him as a man with a shuffling walk, which for a time earned him the nickname of Cloppy Claude.

He never took kindly to authority. As a junior he used to enliven his housemaster's evenings by standing outside his study singing the music-hall ditty: ' Up to one of your tricks again, naughty, naughty boy'. Nor did he welcome fagging, or 'sweating' as it was known at Winchester. A contemporary recalls him as ' making a bitterly sarcastic remark on one occasion about the food at dinner, which I thought of as typical of him '.

To most boys in his house he appeared stupid, or at least totally uninterested in work, and when he left early he was assumed to have been ' superjanned' (superannuated). Certainly he was no academic high flier; but his quality was not entirely unappreciated. A contemporary (one of Mosley's friends at Winchester) writes:

> I had a great friend among the Winchester dons of that period called Malcolm Robertson, who went by the name of ' the Bobber '. . . . One day I was talking to the Bobber about

men who had been in the school with me and made the remark
that I could never understand how Mosley could ever have
been talked of as a future Conservative Prime Minister.
Robertson said: 'Oh, can't you? I always put his intelligence on a very high plane. He had wonderful imagination
and could write a first-class essay.'

At Sandhurst, his essays were apparently cited as models of precision
and clarity. Mosley himself writes of his intellectual development:
'Roughly my rhythm was, clever from nine to eleven, half-witted
from eleven to around sixteen, from sixteen to nineteen a gradual
recovery of my faculties. . . .'[28] He attributes the decay of his
faculties in the public-school period, not implausibly, to his
exceptionally rapid growth.

Perhaps the most intimate glimpse of Mosley at Winchester is
provided in the following comment:

> He had been in the school for 2 years when I got there, but I
> got a remove from the form I'd been put in . . . . and so in my
> second term there I found myself in the same form as him.
> It was the custom there for boys in the same form to 'go over'
> the work of the following day together in what was known as
> Toye-time, in ordinary parlance 'prep'. And that I used to
> do with him, so in spite of the gap in ages between us and the
> difference – great difference – in home background I did see
> quite a bit of him. Indeed I used to say almost till fairly re-
> cently that he couldn't be very brainy as I did his work for
> him for a year, and alas no one can accuse me of being an
> intellectual. Now, I feel sure that this lack of progress on his
> part was due either to idleness or lack of interest, not to lack
> of ability. . . .
>
> I think that he was perhaps rather amused at dazzling one
> with such a different upbringing and completely different
> standard of wealth with accounts of his visits to Truefitts, of
> his tailor in Savile Row and the life of his home.
>
> The same sort of thing was true of his other contacts. I
> remember it being said that when Miss Bell, who kept house
> for our house-master, G. W. Bell, had offered him coffee or
> cocoa or something of the sort . . . he replied – pretty crushingly –
> that he was more accustomed to a whisky and soda. I sup-
> pose he was not then more than 16. I remember, too, he was
> apt to treat the house-butler, a most worthy soul, in a pretty
> *de haut en bas* way, which probably reflected the gulf between
> master and man which would have still been more noticeable
> in his father's household than that of more ordinary folk.
>
> As to his attitude to other ' men ' in the House I don't think
> he had any close friends. . . . I'd say he kept himself to himself

in a community in which there was no privacy – no individual studies, or anything like that.*

Mosley found a refuge from this world of boys, governed by 'Notions', in the gymnasium. There he spent practically the whole of his spare time, becoming an accomplished boxer and fencer. Sergeant Ryan and Sergeant-Major Adam, both products of the Regular Army, and respectively in charge of boxing and fencing, were, he recalls 'by far the most potent influences on my young life'.[29] His respect for them, as for the 'bearded Pritchard' on his family estate, was the respect for the expert which was to remain with him always. Boxing came first in his life, and under the enthusiastic supervision of Ryan, a runner-up in the army feather-weight championships, he developed a formidable straight left which was to serve him in good stead many years later. Boxing, he still maintains, provided 'some food for the mind and character. These fights were clean and fair, were soon forgotten and left no malice. Until human nature becomes pure spirit, is not this among the better disciplines for the animal within us?'[30] Starting the New Party, twenty years later, he announced that he would defend his meetings with 'the good clean English fist'.

Boxing gave way to fencing, once the Headmaster, who disliked competitive boxing, had refused to allow him to box at the public school competition. He showed such natural aptitude that at the age of fifteen he won the public schools championship at both sabre and foil, recovering in the final of the foils from three-one down to take the next four hits and the championship. To such an extent was his life kept separate from that of the house that even at this distance of time several contemporaries remember their 'extreme surprise' when the news of Mosley's victory was announced one day by the housemaster: they hadn't even known that he had taken up fencing.

Riding, hunting, then boxing and fencing: these were the sports at which Mosley excelled. It is, of course, nonsense to suggest that they reveal the character of a solitary incapable of 'team effort', or a love of fighting. What they do reveal is the strong pull of ancestral voices: for these sports are *par excellence* the highly stylised survivals of the aristocratic *function* in feudal society and the aristocratic *style* of war.

* Mosley questions this account. 'Toye Time could not possibly have permitted the co-operation described. The toyes were like small stalls for ponies with open ends. During preparation we could not speak to each other or even throw notes to each other, as we were under continual very strict surveillance.... Equally I do not believe for a moment that I could have made the silly observation about whisky and soda and I certainly would not have treated the house butler in that fashion as people in my world were always trained to show the utmost courtesy in such conditions.'

The Public Schools Fencing Championship was the climax of Mosley's school career. He wanted to try for the British, and subsequently the world, fencing championship. These plans never materialised, but despite his injured leg he fenced for Britain at épée a number of times in the 1930s, making up for lack of mobility with striking aggressiveness.

At seventeen, in January 1914, Mosley entered Sandhurst as a gentleman cadet after a spell of cramming for the examination, interrupted by six weeks in France. He remembers spending at Sandhurst some of ' the most vividly happy days of my life '. He was also involved in an incident which aroused considerable antagonism at the time, and which has evidently lost nothing in the frequent telling.

Sandhurst's history had long been punctuated by rowdiness and violence. The authorities were surprisingly tolerant of these disturbances. Perhaps, as Hugh Thomas, Sandhurst's historian, says, they regarded them as an excellent preparation for war. Some of the rowdiest cadets were to fight and die heroically.

When Mosley came to Sandhurst the rowdiness took the form of a running fight between the cavalry and infantry cadets. Aristocrats, mainly from Eton and Harrow, went overwhelmingly into the élite cavalry regiments; infantry and more-specialised regiments recruited more from middle-class seminaries like Wellington, Bedford Grammar, Charterhouse, Clifton, Haileybury, Marlborough, and U.S.C., Westward Ho!, though a high proportion of middle-class recruits themselves came from military backgrounds.[31] Because of the continuing connection between aristocracy and army, the social struggle between aristocracy and middle class continued in the closed world of Sandhurst long after it had been settled in the wider world outside.

Mosley describes in his memoirs looking round the mess room on his first night at Sandhurst and picking out some fifty or so boys who seemed particularly objectionable. ' Within a month ', he goes on, ' they were my best friends.' The Mosley group, in his own words, was characterised ' by a certain flamboyance of demeanour '. They were the Sandhurst buccaneers, vastly conscious of their own superiority, and no doubt intensely offensive to those who felt no inclination to acknowledge it. Money was freely available to Mosley for the first time in his life. He acquired a sports car and took up polo. Clandestine nocturnal trips to London, brawls with the chuckers-out at the Empire, illegal rides at point-to-points, drunken dinners at Maidenhead and at least one fight in which he knocked out another cadet followed in quick succession. But it was polo that landed him in serious trouble at the end of the summer term, 1914.

Polo had been banned from Sandhurst in 1894, on the ground

that it got too many cadets into debt.   For it required the possession and upkeep of at least two ponies, an expensive business.   It seems, though, that the habit of polo-playing revived among the aristo-cratic cadets.   Mosley took it up with enthusiasm as soon as he arrived and was a member of a Sandhurst team which had won a couple of matches against neighbouring subaltern teams at Alder-shot, although he had apparently not yet acquired his own ponies. One Saturday in June 1914 he had arranged to ride a pony owned by another cadet, intending to buy it if it proved suitable.   He arrived at Aldershot for the match to find that the pony he was ex-pecting to use had been ordered to Wellington instead.   Ponies of other members of the team had been 'misplaced' in a similar fashion, and it is possible that there was a plot to bring Mosley and his friends down a peg or two; or, at any rate, that is how it seemed to them.   In the upshot, the team lost.   What then happened has been the subject of many garbled stories, but the salient point is that Mosley took the lead in the retaliatory action which followed, and was at the centre of the last riot in pre-war Sandhurst.

Later that day, he and two or three friends awaited the offending pony-owner, a third-term cadet, in the billiard room of C Company. As Mosley describes it in *My Life*,[32] ' I was no doubt not very conciliatory, and he appeared to me in no way contrite; I thought, perhaps mistakenly, he was rude.   An argument followed, and ended in a fight, which I won.'   As the other party tells it (after a similar lapse of years): ' There cannot have been much of a fight as it was two or three to one but they had a riding whip (crop, not a cutting whip).'[33]   As Sandhurst cadets of that time remember it, Mosley had ' horsewhipped ' the other man.   This is clearly un-true, since Mosley carried a crop, not a whip.   Also Mosley later became a close friend of the beaten cadet's brother, which hardly seems plausible if he had done something really disgraceful.   (Even if Mosley's account is on the reticent side, what he did can hardly have been as alarming as the activities a few years earlier of Bernard Montgomery and his friends who fought with pokers and even set fire to another cadet.)[34]   At any rate, later that evening, the beaten cadet's friends, fortified by old ale, battered down the door of Mos-ley's room.   In making his escape by the window, Mosley missed his footing and fell to the gravel thirty-five feet below, fracturing his right ankle.   Friends who had assembled rushed him off to the sanatorium.   Later, they counter-attacked.   Skirmishing continu-ed all weekend, as a result of which fifteen cadets, including Mosley, were rusticated.

It is doubtful whether Mosley would have remained in the Army, even had the war not occurred.   He was always in too much of a hurry: also he was one of those for whom the attractions of a disci-plined society fade remarkably if one is not at the top of it.   Besides, in the normal course of events he would have succeeded to the un-changed life of the Rolleston estates.   The Great War, which started less than two months after the Sandhurst incident, put an end to all that.   It gave Mosley a sense of mission which could not be satis-fied by army life; it also made the continuance of Rolleston and its feudal livery unviable.   At the end of the war, 306 years after it had first passed into the hands of the Mosley family, Rolleston was put up for auction.   The great house was pulled down, the estate divided up into separate farms and modern villas.   An established institution of old England had come to an end; the values and ideas associated with it had to be transplanted to a much wider sphere.   Like his famous ancestor, Sir Nicholas, young ' Tom ' Mosley came to London to seek his fortune.

Chapter 2

The Challenge to Liberalism

I

FOR OSWALD MOSLEY the First World War created a radically new situation. He always thought of himself as the spokesman of the war-generation. He had little or no interest in the pre-war world, which to him was simply the liberal era which had perished on the battlefield. In fact liberalism had started on its long decline years before. The war was a catalyst, not a cause. It produced a new man rather than a new idea; a new political savagery rather than a new political force. 'The arsenal was fully assembled by 1918. It was merely a question of waiting for the order to fire,' writes Peter Pulzer. The post-war 'movements of challenge' consisted of the ideas and forces of the late nineteenth century made strident by war and economic collapse.

Historians speak of a 'change of consciousness' in the last decades of the nineteenth century, a 'sense of the demise of an old society'.[1] The society felt to be expiring was liberal society. Starting in the 1870s, liberal forces started to lose ground to their challengers. There are a number of reasons for this. Economic and social change was shifting life from an individual to a collective basis. Business became concentrated in combines and cartels, labour organised in trade unions, electors mobilised in parties, populations crowded into cities. These developments eroded the individualist philosophy which had dominated the nineteenth century. They were also proving incompatible with the doctrine of the minimal state. The forces unleashed by the French and Industrial revolutions – the forces of Mob and Money as Mosley was to call them – had to be controlled if they were not to tear society to pieces. This need was pinpointed by growing economic instability of which the Great Depression of 1873–96 was the first major manifestation. Beyond this was a growing disenchantment with the liberal vision of progress which to many seemed to point to decadence. The attack on liberalism came from many different sides and was inspired by many different motives. Here we are concerned mainly with the challenge to *laissez-faire*, for this was Mosley's own point of departure.

Under the impact of the Great Depression the general belief in the harmonising properties of the market came under organised assault from two sides: socialism and imperialism. In economic thought, socialism's distinct contribution was the theory of underconsumption. According to the early socialist Robert Owen, slumps arise from the ' want of a market . . . coextensive with the means of production', the result of a grossly unequal distribution of the national income. This was the chief economic plank of the more radical marxist theory of capitalist crisis.* Unless wealth were transferred from the accumulating to the consuming classes, periodic and (in the marxist version) deepening breakdowns were inevitable. At the end of the nineteenth century, the underconsumptionist theory was adapted to explain growing international tensions. An inadequate home market transferred capitalist competition from the domestic to the international plane and thus involved governments in the defence of exposed economic interests. Capitalist interdependence, far from abolishing the causes of war as Cobden had claimed, made it more likely. The socialist attack on the market, first developed early in the nineteenth century, had little influence in the golden years of mid-century peace and prosperity. It returned with redoubled force with Depression, as socialist orators drove home the simple and highly acceptable point that crises and wars arise because the rich are too rich and the poor are too poor.

The Great Depression also produced an imperialist challenge to the primacy of the market. (Here we are dealing with the economic aspect of a very complex phenomenon.) What it did was to revive the much earlier mercantilist doctrine that foreign imports destroy domestic employment. The object of mercantilist statecraft was the attainment of the highest possible degree of self-sufficiency (for both economic and strategic reasons) on the basis of a ' closed ' imperial system. Its intellectual underpinning was apparently destroyed by Adam Smith, who claimed that free trade was beneficial to all since it would lead each country to specialise in what it could do best. The coincidence of Depression with the emergence of the United States and Germany as Britain's major industrial competitors shattered this comfortable belief. Free trade, the critics argued, produced not a complementary, but a highly disruptive, system, bringing unemployment and social dislocation to one country after another as national industries were destroyed by cheaper foreign goods.

Socialists and imperialists thus offered different analyses of, and solutions to, the economic problem. Socialists argued that *laissez-faire* failed to allocate production properly between classes.

*In theory, the underconsumptionist point could have been met by state or union action to raise wages. Marx cut off this line of escape for the private-enterprise system by arguing that if wages were raised the rate of profit would fall, thus bringing about collapse by another route. The marxist theory of crises neatly impaled capitalism on the horns of an insoluble dilemma. If it kept down wages it would succumb to a crisis of overproduction. If wages were pushed up it would succumb to a crisis of profitability.

Imperialists charged that it failed to allocate production properly between nations. Both sides believed that the specific imperfections they stressed pushed the system into crisis. For socialists, regular employment and prosperity were to be achieved by redistributing the national income from the rich to the poor; for imperialists, by protecting the home and colonial markets from foreign imports. By the First World War powerful political forces had emerged to champion these views. Marxist parties made their appearance on the left of politics. They were frankly parties of catastrophe, although a significant reformist trend soon appeared arguing that substantial working class gains could be achieved within the capitalist system. On the right, the Depression united the hitherto antagonistic interests of big landlords, big industrialists, and small peasants behind the fight for a tariff. These new alignments were already able to force important policy-changes: after 1873, as Hans Rosenberg writes, continental governments 'began to eliminate the short-lived episode of internal and external free trade'.[2] Bismarck's insurance policy, setting the pattern of European social legislation up to the war, was property's gesture to the working class. Protective tariffs went up in Germany, Italy, Austria, France and the United States; 'half-conscious preparations for autarchy' (Polanyi) led the European powers to stake out colonial claims in Africa and Asia.

But the impact on politics went deeper than this. The possibility of breakdown, always inherent from the 1870s onwards, produced a new political breed – Bonapartists or men of crisis, for whom the 'crisis' and not parliamentary manœuvre or the 'swing of the pendulum' opens up the royal road to power. Such men were less concerned with doctrinal or class distinctions than with the prospect of uniting disparate forces under their leadership in periods of emergency, holding themselves in reserve for that day. The twentieth century is full of examples of this type, war and economic collapse giving them their chance: Joseph Chamberlain may be regarded as their prototype.*

Closely connected with this was the dream of welding the forces of socialism and imperialism into a unified challenge to the dominant liberal order. According to Charles Maurras, founder of Action Française, socialism could be made to fit nationalism 'as a well-made hand fits a beautiful glove'. The underlying assumption was that it was *laissez-faire* which had created the class war.

---

*It is, of course, a mistake to exaggerate the sharpness of the break between one epoch and another. Chamberlain was a transitional figure; his age was a transitional age. But to stress discontinuity is in this case to err on the right side: as Geoffrey Barraclough has pointed out, historians have concentrated too exclusively on the world that was dying, not enough on the new world coming to life (*Introduction to Contemporary History* (1969) p. 31).

Destroy its hold, and a new consensus could be built on the basis of producer interests. Politically, the idea of uniting the ' genuine ' producers against the loafers, parasites and cosmopolitans had obvious attractions. The difficulties, however, were formidable. If the 'challenge' was to society as a whole, the 'response', as Karl Polanyi has pointed out in his brilliant survey, *The Great Transformation*, came from different groups differently affected by change.

A century of capitalist industrialisation, dividing society into competing classes of employers and workers, had alienated large sections of the population from the values of the governing class. The economic philosophy of socialism drew its inspiration from an acute sense of injustice; that of protectionism and imperialism from the quest for security in an uncertain world. The protectionist concern for the welfare of the national community was perfectly genuine; however, it was bound up with the defence of existing inequalities which bypassed the moral issue. Initially, imperialism undoubtedly attracted some working class and socialist support. The turning-point came with the Boer War and Hobson's famous critique. The First World War completed socialism's disenchantment with imperialism, which thereafter became synonymous with war. Socialists, in the main, wanted to build a rational society on the achievements of liberalism. By contrast, imperialists seemed to be figures of the past, re-emerging to rob mankind of its future. Finally, it proved impossible (before the First World War at least) to reconcile the economic programmes of socialists and imperialists. They saw themselves as offering alternative, not complementary, solutions to the economic and social problem, each trying to win over the other. It was left to Mosley, drawing on Keynes, to attempt a genuine intellectual synthesis.

II

The revolt against the liberal political economy was felt in Britain, but in diluted, almost expurgated form. The reason is not far to seek. As pioneers of the first industrial revolution, most Englishmen axiomatically identified their prosperity and their world position with *laissez-faire* at home and free trade abroad. They were therefore all the more disposed to ' stick to the principles that had made England great ', irrespective of temporary misfortunes. This view was not altogether shared by the ' practical men ', whether employers or workers who had to bear the brunt of these misfortunes. But even the practical men swung back to the economics of joy in the last bout of mindless prosperity which wafted Edwardian Britain towards the First World War.

What were these principles that had made England great—at any rate economically? From the very start of the Industrial

Revolution Britain had locked itself into a system of world economy: its great cotton, capital goods and shipbuilding industries were largely created and sustained by foreign demand; a high proportion of British savings were always invested abroad. Britain exported the Industrial Revolution to Europe and North America, while British capital, railways and steamships developed the great primary producing areas of the world and linked them to the manufacturing areas in an integrated world economy. The City of London became the world's financial centre, while the Bank of England in effect managed the international gold standard, a system of multilateral payments which multiplied the arteries of trade. In short, the quest for profit – the mainspring of capitalist enterprise – had led to the elaboration of an economic system in which the direct employment of one British worker in four had come to depend on the foreign appetite for British goods and in which well over fifty per cent of British savings had come to be invested abroad every year. In the words of one historian, ' the satisfactory operation of the British economic system became more and more fully linked with the satisfactory development of the rest of the world '.[3]

Yet to many it seemed that the British position was crumbling. Britain's mid-century boom did not collapse as suddenly as that of the United States or Germany ' amid the debris of bankrupt financiers and cooling blast furnaces ';[4] nevertheless it proved to be the last period till the 1950s when the British economy was able to provide full employment and rising standards of life on a regular basis for people born in Britain. ' There has not since the free trade period been such a decline in our foreign trade . . .,' wrote Robert Giffen, head of the statistical department of the Board of Trade in 1877. The rate of growth of British exports fell from 4·5 per cent in 1850–70 to 2·8 per cent between 1870 and 1913. More worrying, Britain was growing more slowly than Germany and the United States and losing its share of the world market to them. So not only was there an absolute slow-down or 'retardation' in Britain's economic growth, but also it was losing ground relative to its major competitors. Unemployment grew from less than five per cent in mid-century to over seven per cent between 1874 and 1895, and even higher in such 'bad years' as 1907–10. It would have been greater still but for the ability of unions to spread the workload, and emigration which, as Professor Sayers sedately remarks, acted ' as a kind of safety-valve for pockets of population stranded in comparatively unwanted occupations and places '.[5] Between 1880 and 1910 seven million such stranded Britons left their country, 200,000 a year on average, and almost half between the ages of eighteen and thirty. This greatly increased the proportion of drones to active workers in the population (the First World War aggravated this

by inflicting a catastrophe on the same age-group).*   For those who
remained, real wages rose between 1874 and 1896 (though not
after), but this was highly insecure, depending on the fall of imported food and raw-material prices and the ability of unions to
'squeeze profits between stable wages and market-controlled prices',[6]
not on the improved performance of the British economy.   As
labour and capital both fled the country leaving ageing workers and
ageing industrial equipment, Hobson gloomily envisaged Britain as
a retreat of an aristocracy of millionaires 'who will have made their
money where labour was cheapest, and returned to spend it where
life is pleasantest.   No productive work will be possible in England
but such labour as is required for personal service will be procur-
able at a cheap rate, owing to the reluctance of labour to keep pace
with the migration of capital.'[7]

The situation was, of course, open to many conflicting interpretations.   One school of thought maintained that there was
nothing seriously wrong at all.   It seemed vindicated by the sudden
burst of activity just before the First World War which carried
British–and world–trade soaring to new heights.   This period of
1910–13 became the 'normalcy' to which post-war British statesmen were always trying to return.   But what was normal–the
spectacular performance of Britain's traditional exports in this period,
or the tendency to stagnation and even decline that had been visible
between 1875 and 1895?   From a later perspective, 'it was the
extreme prosperity of the last years before the war that . . . looked
paradoxical'.[8]

A more representative view, especially among economists and
political commentators, was that Britain indeed faced a problem,
but it was largely of its own making.   It had rested on its laurels
while other nations had captured its markets.   The British entre-
preneur was no longer the man he was: instead of attending to his
business he spent his time shooting grouse and yachting in the
Mediterranean.   A 'second generation' had lost the business
aptitude of their fathers, possibly because they had been moulded
into conformist muscular Christians at expensive boarding schools
set up specially to turn them into gentlemen.   More generally,
the anti-technical bias of British education meant that only Americans and Germans understood new processes, even when they were
invented by Britons who had somehow triumphed over their native
environment.   Even when the British manufacturer had the wit
to introduce new machinery he was impeded by the British worker,
defensive, suspicious and wedded to the primitive view that more

*The seven million is the total of United Kingdom citizens who left Britain in
these years.   Net emigration (that is, the total of those coming in subtracted
from the total of those going out) comes to 5,700,000 (Peter Mathias, The First
Industrial Nation (1969) p. 452).

machinery meant less employment. 'It was not surprising that the United States and Germany were outstripping England in the race for industrial supremacy,' wrote the French historian Élie Halévy. 'Neither Carnegie nor Krupp had to deal with trade unions.' And so the contemporary catalogue of British failing continued, as it has done in much the same terms ever since.[9]

The economist Alfred Marshall castigated employers for their failure to keep abreast of new ideas: yet his own ideas, those of his profession and those of the governing classes remained firmly rooted in the age of Cobden and Bright. The ' principles that had made England great ' had over the years acquired a special moral sanction that made them almost unchallengeable. Classical economics had arisen as the intellectual by-product of the middle-class struggle against aristocratic privilege and corruption. It never lost the characteristic moral fervour of its political roots. The arguments for free trade were fused by Cobden and Bright into a powerful intellectual, practical and moral synthesis. Free trade was like Christianity: it kept society virtuous. Protection, like paganism, was something one could excuse in the immature, but not in the civilised. To bring the State back into economic life was to bring back the corruption which liberal crusaders had so successfully expelled. Nor were these doctrines for internal consumption only. Mr Corelli Barnett is surely right to emphasise the extent to which the British from the nineteenth century onwards believed firmly in Britain's special mission to bring the true doctrine to the rest of the world.[10] The world was Britain's pasture, free trade its gospel! What was at heart a deeply chauvinistic belief in Britain's inherent superiority was transmuted into a kind of internationalism – a vision of a world set in Britain's mould. In Berlin, British pretensions were viewed with a jaundiced eye. 'In the halls of Parliament', wrote Treitschke, ' one heard only shameless British commercial morality, which, with the Bible in the right hand and the opium pipe in the left, spreads the benefits of civilisation around the world.'[11] The ' British ideology' would never have survived as long as it did in the world at large had it not had a universal appeal, or at home had it not served the interests of powerful economic and political groups. On the other hand, those groups whose interests were not served by it would hardly have made such a poor show in challenging it had not the moral consensus been so firm.

For by the early twentieth century the materials existed for putting forward a completely different interpretation of Britain's prospects in an increasingly unreliable system of world economy. It could be argued that Britain's fundamental problem arose not from the idleness of its businessmen or the stupidity of its workers but from the fact that its export business was partially and perhaps largely self-liquidating. In an earlier period mercantilist writers had warned that 'that trade is the worst . . . that furnishes materials for manufactures in other countries, which afterwards might interfere with some of its own . . .'.[12] Yet this was precisely the trade in which Britain specialised. The economic historian W. J. Ashley claimed accurately enough in 1903 that the 'profit-seeking tendency' of British capital which 'pursues its own immediate gain without any regard to the ultimate effect on national prosperity' had promoted the 'diffusion of manufacturing industry all over the world'.[13] The first consequence was to assist customers to dispense with British manufactures; the second to turn them into competitors in third markets and even in Britain's unprotected home markets. Already by the 1880s British exports had been expelled from industrialised Europe and America, and were starting to be harassed by American and German competition in Latin America and Asia. However, even here the 'profit-seeking tendency' of British capital, which as Feis notes 'remained the quickest and freest to move',[14] threatened the profitable export of British goods. By 1913 most of Britain's textiles went to India and Asia; yet British capital was equipping Japan and China with the latest cotton mills whose products were clearly destined to give Lancashire its *coup de grâce*. For the old argument that inherited skill would triumph over cheap, primitive labour was disposed of by Marshall in language very similar to that used by Mosley in the 1930s: 'the very perfection of the textile and other machinery by which England won her leadership has enabled it to be worked fairly well by backward races'.[15] Provided it could lay its hands on necessary raw materials and on modern machinery 'which did most of the thinking itself' any nation could in time produce for itself most of the things which Britain had previously sent it; and the nineteenth century proliferation of 'infant' industries behind tariff barriers indicated at least a widespread disposition to try.

This sword of Damocles would not have been so threatening had Britain not become so dependent on foreign imports. For inflated imports were a product of inflated exports. The single-minded message of Cobden's Anti-Corn Law League had been: in order to export, you must import. In other words, the need for imports came from the expansion of exports, not the other way round. British capital had developed the agriculture of North America, Australia and Argentina in competition with higher-priced British foodstuffs in order that farmers of those countries could acquire the sterling necessary to buy British manufactures.[16] The result was that British agriculture was ruined by the grain and meat invasions of the 1870s and 1880s and the British worker got cheap food. But his employment – and food – had become that much more dependent on foreign demand for British goods. When the demand ran out, the food ran out. Nor was foreign investment simply a money transaction.   The loan of capital created a sterling debt which could only be repaid by earning sterling.   The easiest place to do so was in a British market open to ' free imports '; naturally the maintenance of such a market became the vested interest of financiers.   Britain became the ' dumping ground for cheap food and subsidised sugar from all over the world ',[17] Lenin noting perceptively that ' the creditor is more permanently attached to the debtor than the seller is to the buyer '.[18]   Thus the initial quest for export markets had expanded imports, which in turn required more exports.   Britain had enmeshed itself in a highly integrated structure of world economy that seemed to be slowly falling to pieces.

The argument was about the dynamics of economic, political and social development.   Was the world being harmonised or torn apart by trade and finance?   The answer to Britain's ' special problem ' depended on the answer to this wider question.   If the former were true, then the British should make themselves more efficient in order to take advantage of expanding world-markets. If, on the other hand, the trend was towards self-sufficiency, then Britain should clearly try to make itself less dependent on world markets.

The question was: how? on what basis?   Here the critics of liberalism divided into two camps, socialist and imperialist.   Both agreed that the problem was to ' create a market '.   But socialists wanted to create a market by raising internal purchasing power; imperialists by clearing foreign markets of competition: redistribution entered the lists against protection, justice against security. The one programme involved seizing political control of the domestic economy in order to create an *internal* market; the other involved seizing political control of foreign economies in order to secure an *external* market.   To imperialists the socialist programme meant the end of profits; to socialists the imperialist programme meant the end of peace.   For all involved in politics these issues between liberalism, socialism and imperialism were important till at least the end of the Second World War; for some they were the crucial issues of debate, the intellectual substance of politics in the age of economic man.   We must now glance at the way the two movements of challenge developed in Britain.

III

The main constituent in the soil of the socialist revival of the 1880s was, as Margaret Cole has pointed out, ' economic surprise – surprise at the failure of Progress '.[19]   As a socialist orator told a working class audience in the early 1880s, ' Not the most skilled, thrifty, and sober worker and wage-earner present but by a turn of bad trade or a bout of ill-health might be reduced to almost helpless

misery.'[20]   No working class demand of this period was more
poignant, or from the perspective of the nineteenth century economist more backward-looking, than the demand for the Right to
Work.   Trade depression 'activated the latent sentiments of
Chartism ',[21] and the Labour Party was formed in 1900 from a
combination of the new socialist societies and the trade unions, radicalised by insecurity and the bitter struggles with employers and
their legal arm, the judiciary, in the 1890s.   The entry of the working class into politics was inevitable following the third Reform Act
of 1884–5; its mobilisation under the banner of socialism was a
direct result of the Depression, and the gaping holes it revealed in
the theory of *laissez-faire*.

From our point of view, what is interesting is the answer English
socialists gave to the question of what was wrong with capitalism,
for on this hinged Labour's response to the inter-war crisis.   There
were two possible approaches: the problem could be tackled from
the moral side or the economic side.   Marx combined both: the
unjust distribution of income (the result of extracting surplus value)
left the workers too poor to buy the goods which capitalists placed
on the market.   This produced periodic capitalist crises.   As
more and more wealth became concentrated in fewer and fewer
hands, the crisis would deepen till the impoverished and desperate
masses would rise up in revolt.   English socialists rejected this view.
As McBriar has explained, ' All the things which Marx's unifying
philosophy bound closely together fell to bits and pieces at the
Fabian touch.'[22]   The Fabians, the main theorists of the English
socialist movement, concentrated on the injustices of the system
without linking them to the demand problem.   They produced a
theory of exploitation similar to Marx's: monopoly ownership of
land and capital, producing ' rent ' for their owners, maintained
' poverty in the midst of plenty '.   The remedy was to tax landlord
and capitalist out of existence, filling their place with state and
municipal enterprise, thus achieving a more equal income distribution and more socially useful production.   This theory was not
linked to any notion of capitalist crisis.   Accepting as they did
Say's Law of Markets, which said that supply always creates its
own demand, most socialists assumed that capitalist fluctuations
were accidents which would disappear in the course of evolution.
They had no better explanation for them than harvest failures, or
Jevons' sunspots.   Even when they proposed measures to tide the
workers over difficult times – as in Beatrice Webb's ' counter-cycle '
programme of public works[23] – they did not question the view that
capitalism was self-adjusting, and that the system's norm was full
employment.

This led to an important political conclusion.   Socialism would
be built on the success of capitalism, not on its failure.   This be-

came the official doctrine of the Labour Party. It was perfectly attuned to its strategy of parliamentary gradualism, a product of its liberal heritage, as well as the bourgeois character of its leadership. Thus, the mainstream of the Labour Party, for all its moral fervour, emerged from the pre-war years with an economic theory and a political strategy which had no connection with the capitalist crisis of the inter-war years.

I emphasise 'mainstream'. J. A. Hobson, whose 'heresy' dates from 1889, provided a link between exploitation, capitalist crisis, and war with his underconsumption theory. Hobson is by far the most significant economic thinker thrown up by the modern left of British politics – a man who rapidly acquired an international reputation with his *Imperialism* (1902). Slumps, he argued, arose from the lack of working-class purchasing power. This in turn led to the export of capital which created imperial rivalries leading to war. If national income were more evenly – and justly – distributed, slumps and, equally important, foreign involvements would disappear.* This 'isolationist' or 'Little England' programme foreshadows in a remarkable way Mosley's 'national socialism' of his Labour Party days.

In its respect for orthodox economic assumptions and orthodox political strategy, the Labour position was very close to that of reformist liberalism. Liberal politicians like Lloyd George realised that a generous dose of social welfare was the only way to keep the working class quiet and save the Liberal Party from extinction. On its intellectual side, the new liberalism associated with T. H. Green mounted a considerable criticism of *laissez-faire*.[24] The practical importance of the development of the 'welfare state' started under Lloyd George and Churchill in the 1900s and reaching its culmination between 1945 and 1951 cannot be overestimated, since it largely enabled British liberal society to survive the blows of depression in the inter-war years. At the same time the new liberalism failed to come to grips with the causes of renewed economic instability, for which its welfare measures were at best a palliative, not a cure. Its rationale for a programme of moderate redistribution was moral, not economic: property must pay a ransom for its privileges in the form of social benefits to be financed out of progressive taxation. The new liberals differed from the socialists only in their estimate of how large the ransom would have to be. But on the central issue of faith in the ability of capitalist

---

*See ch. VI of his *Imperialism*, especially such remarks as 'foreign trade would indeed exist, but there would be no difficulty in exchanging a *small* surplus of our manufactures for the food and raw materials we annually absorbed' and 'There is no necessity to open up new foreign markets; the home markets are capable of indefinite expansion. Whatever is produced in England can be consumed in England.' (My italics)

enterprise to keep the economy moving forward at more or less full employment the two were united. This whole late-Victorian debate on the distribution of wealth ignored the fact that wealth was ceasing to expand.

A more relevant response to the first major breakdown of the nineteenth century trading system was Joseph Chamberlain's campaign for tariff reform (or protection) in 1903. Its background is well conveyed by the following passage from Froude's *Oceana* (1886):

> 'Business' may, probably will, blaze up again, but the growth of it can no longer be regarded as constant, while population increases and hungry stomachs multiply, requiring three meals a day *whatever the condition of the markets*. [My italics]

Froude's 'heresy' is here plain. According to the free traders there should never be a shortage of markets, at any rate not for long. What had most obviously invalidated this assumption was the proliferation of protective tariffs. The Conservative prime minister Arthur Balfour thought Britain was entitled to put on tariffs in order to bargain with other nations to dismantle theirs and thus re-create the free-trade harmonies. But Chamberlain's contention was that these harmonies were themselves an illusion. With capital free to roam the world in search of the highest profit there was practically *nothing* Britain produced today that could not be produced by some other country tomorrow – and in most cases more cheaply.[25] British industries were to be required to undertake prodigies of adaptation to stay competitive – all for nothing. He hammered this theme home at great public meetings up and down the country, which themselves foreshadowed Mosley's crusade in the 1930s. Free traders argued that

> it is your fault if you do not leave the industry which is falling for the industry which is rising. It is an admirable theory, it satisfies everything but an empty stomach. Look how easy it is. Your once great trade of sugar refining is gone. All right, try jam. Your iron trade is gone, never mind. You can make mousetraps. The cotton trade is threatened. Suppose you try doll's eyes. How long is this to go on? Why on earth are you to suppose that the same process which ruined the sugar refining will not in the course of time be applied . . . to something else. . . . You cannot go on forever.[26]

The point was both economic and moral. It would not work; and anyway it was an awful way of life.

Chamberlain's plan to secure Britain's prosperity was simple and bold in conception. Britain must protect its home market against cheap foreign manufactures and create a closed empire market for its own manufactured goods. In return, the dominions would be given an enlarged outlet for their agricultural products in the British market by the exclusion of foreign foodstuffs. The complementary exchange promised by the free traders could thus be secured by an imperial bargain which common sentiment would make possible.

It is easy to pick holes in Chamberlain's plan. He apparently assumed that empire countries would remain content to ' dig, delve and plow ' for Britain. He never considered the possibility that low *British* demand might be an important cause of business difficulties, irrespective of anything that was happening to exports. In other words, he had not moved beyond the conception of a protected system to the idea of an organised or managed one. Once the Government had performed its act of God it was to retire gracefully from the scene leaving ' natural forces ' in command. Why they should prove any more harmonious in the Empire than they had been in the world Chamberlain never made clear. He remained very much a prisoner of the ideology against which he was rebelling.

Nevertheless, Chamberlain is important in our story because he introduces the national community as a value to be defended against free-trade internationalism on one side and working class internationalism on the other. ' I admit I am not cosmopolitan enough to wish to see the happiness, success, or prosperity of American workmen secured by the starvation and misery and suffering of British workmen,' he declared in 1903. It was the economic war generated by free trade that produced the class war preached by Marx. Thus, ending the trade war was the precondition for ending the class war. A country of Britain's size could no longer hope to be self-sufficient. Therefore its protected area had to be larger than itself. The Empire was to hand: it should be developed as an estate for British economic security, and as a fighting force for Britain's military security. ' I am in favour of splendid isolation,' Chamberlain declared, ' but it is not the isolation of an individual whom years may have weakened; it is the isolation of a family standing together through good and evil, for better and for worse.'

Chamberlain's programme attempted explicitly to harmonise the interests of manufacturers and workers on the basis of imperialism, rather than on the failing basis of *laissez-faire* and free trade. As such it was a new departure in politics, threatening to mobilise the forces of discontent into a new political movement drawing support from both the right and the left. ' I feel so much ', remarks Lord Evesham in H. G. Wells' novel *The New Machiavelli* (1911), ' that the best people in every party converge.' The most serious attempt to give this convergence definite political shape was the project for a Social–Imperial Party embracing elements of

socialism, Chamberlain imperialism and Rosebery liberal-imperial-
ism. The Fabian leadership agreed with Chamberlain on the
issues of empire and tariff reform. It accepted 'imperial domination . . . as a modern necessity and only asks that the domination
shall be efficient and sensible ' – a view endorsed by Lord Rosebery.[27] As for tariffs, the Fabian economist Robert Dell argued
that if one believed in conscious control of economic life government
' must consciously control foreign trade '.[28] W. A. S. Hewins, the
first director of that Fabian foundation, the London School of
Economics, ' more than any other single individual, was responsible
for convincing Chamberlain to campaign for Tariff Reform '.[29]
The Fabian rejection of class war in favour of a collectivist–anti-
collectivist alignment also favoured a new grouping.[30] In 1901
Sidney Webb called for a party of National Efficiency displaying
' virility in government ', involving the ' close co-operation of a
group of men of diverse temperaments and varied talents, imbued
with a common faith and a common purpose ', dedicated to removing the slums, destroying the sweated trades and eliminating
inefficiency in government and education. A year later he formed
a dining club, the Coefficients, intended as the ' General Staff '
of a new Social–Imperial Party.[31] Its galaxy of talent included
Viscount Milner, who dreamt of a ' nobler socialism which will
take the place of socialism based on class warfare ', and Carlyon
Bellairs who later supported the British Union of Fascists. Here
we find much of the political ancestry of the inter-war projects with
which Mosley was involved – the Centre Party idea of 1920, the
New Party, the British Union of Fascists.

What were the intellectual foundations of this new political
merger to be? Three leading ideas may be discerned. The first
was the concept of efficiency, with its emphasis on bringing Britain
up to date to meet the challenge of Germany. The second was the
consciousness of living in a new age, to which the *a priori* concepts of
the old political economy no longer applied, and for which a new
political wisdom had to be constructed. Thirdly, the Coefficients
were united in their belief in the inefficiency of parliamentary
democracy. Change was to be brought about by an élite of heroic
technicians: the ' higher types ' of Shaw's plays.[32] Here were the
ideas which Mosley was to take up in the inter-war years.

The pre-war failure of social imperialism as a philosophy and
as a new movement is a matter of history. There were many
reasons – the continued hold of free trade and the strength of the
interests supporting it, the revival of prosperity, the bitterness of
the class cleavage and the hold of party loyalty. Yet one must
not be misled by the convenience of dividing history up into epochs
separated by wars into believing that the projects of this period had
failed simply because they had not yet triumphed by 1914. The

pre-war challengers were surely right in their view that reality no longer corresponded to the beliefs of the Victorians and that a new wisdom was required for a new age. They were overtaken by war which both accelerated the disintegration which provided the setting for their own challenge *and* perpetuated the life of obsolete ideas and institutions; thus imparting a new and savage twist to the struggle when it was resumed in the inter-war years.

Chapter 3

A Special Kind of Experience

THE CALL to arms in 1914 found in Mosley as enthusiastic a response as in most young Englishmen of his generation. There was no doubt in any of their minds that this was an entirely righteous war waged to stop German militarism devouring Europe. ' The foul tornado, centred at Berlin, Is over all the width of Europe whirled, Rending the sails of progress,' wrote the seventeen-year-old Wilfred Owen. The argument alike of old-fashioned liberals, who saw it as a tragic culmination of secret diplomacy cutting across the ' natural harmony of interests ', and of new-fangled socialists, who attributed it to the sinister scramble for world markets, made no impression on the millions of young men who enrolled for their meeting with Destiny. (Two and a half million answered the call to the colours; 950,000 were killed.) Incredible as it may now seem, their fear was that the war would be over before they had a chance to prove themselves. If a deeper, unconscious, impulse can be discerned behind the cheering and flag-waving, the gaiety and enthusiasm, it was surely the longing for purification and comradeship, the desire to escape from a dreary life and a social impasse which was slowly tearing the country to pieces. The same motive, in sombre and cynical form, was present in the minds of leading politicians, both Liberal and Conservative. If for Lord Grey the lamps of Europe were going out, for many parliamentarians the European war was in a very real sense an alternative to civil war. The more timid welcomed it as a relief from the intractable domestic problems of Ireland and industrial unrest; the more imaginative, like Lloyd George, hoped that out of it would emerge a new consensus, a spirit of national unity to heal the gulf between the ' two nations '. No one anticipated the four-year nightmare which was to follow.

With the outbreak of war on 4 August 1914, Sandhurst was re-called several weeks early. The rustications were dropped and Mosley was back in E Company for the final weeks of arduous training. On 6 October 1914 he was commissioned into a crack cavalry regiment, the 16th Queen's Light Dragoons, known as the 16th Lancers, and sent to Curragh, thirty miles from Dublin. Officers of the 16th Lancers were among those who had taken part in the ' Curragh Mutiny ' that spring. Now the men who had refused to coerce Ulster were mostly to die in Flanders.

From Curragh, Mosley applied to join the Royal Flying Corps as an observer, and about Christmas, after the first, terrible, battle of

Ypres, he was posted to 6th Squadron at Bailleul near Poperinghe
on the left flank of the Allied armies.   He remained there for about
four months before returning to England in April 1915 to take his
pilot's certificate at Shoreham.

Why did Mosley volunteer for this virtually unknown infant arm
of the huge military machine?   The R.F.C. had been established
only in 1912.   At the outbreak of the war it had only 150 aircraft
of all types, and Mosley estimates that at the end of 1914 only sixty
men, pilots and observers, were actually flying.   Some Sandhurst
contemporaries allege that his unpopularity at the R.M.C., following him to Curragh, made him eager to seek fresh pastures.   This is
inherently unlikely: the 16th Lancers was an élite regiment, and
Mosley would never have been accepted had he been as unpopular
as some later recollections suggest.   Others claim that the ankle
fracture, sustained in the Sandhurst ' incident ', had not completely
healed and that he joined the R.F.C. so that he wouldn't have to
march.   He himself gives a different explanation: ' How to get to
the front was the burning question of the hour.   One service alone
supplied the answer: the Royal Flying Corps.'[1]   Already a man in a
hurry, Mosley was determined to get to the action even if it meant
a change of party: a recurrent theme in his career.   At a deeper
level there was the attraction of glamour, spectacular danger,
modernity.   Mosley was one of nature's buccaneers, and the R.F.C.
was the home of buccaneers, as air forces have been the world over
ever since.   It was an élite of the brave, the reckless, the versatile.
On the ground massive armies of unknown soldiers were locked in
anonymous slaughter; high above them the knights of the skies
jousted in single combat.   It was as if, for a few brief months, the
spirit of chivalry, killed by the mechanisation and size of armies,
lived again in these aerial tournaments, so often to be followed by
the victor dropping a wreath on the enemy aerodrome to mark the
passing of a valiant opponent.   Europe was being destroyed on the
ground.   Was it being reborn in the air?

One had to be brave, reckless and versatile to fly the flimsy
contraptions of wood, strings and wires which then passed for
aeroplanes.   Their main task was reconnaissance.   The pilot flew
the plane – mostly at this stage BE2Cs and Farman Shorthorns –
while the observer sat in a little wooden seat at the back, marking
enemy concentrations and other landmarks on squared maps.
Parachutes were not allowed, on the ground that they would weaken
the pilot's determination to carry out his mission.   The aeroplane's
maximum ceiling was 6000 feet and its average speed 60–70 miles
per hour though it might drop to 30 miles per hour in an adverse
wind.   Pilots and observers were armed only with rifles and revol-
vers, exchanging small-arms fire through the rigging with any
enemy plane whose path they happened to cross: this was how the

famous duels in the air which were to immortalise such names as 'Johnny' Hawker and on the German side Richthofen started, though later planes were fitted with machine guns firing through the propeller arc.

Gaiety and sudden death: the atmosphere was very much that of 'eat, drink and be merry for tomorrow you die'. The gods having determined one's fate, what was there to do but to live life to the full before the blow fell? 'Their messes', one observer has remarked of the R.F.C., 'were civilised and their billets comfortable. They slept in bed; cheerful fires blazed in mess hearths and some of the best food that Britain and France could produce found its way to their tables. There were welcoming arrays of bottles, and the warm air of their quarters was fragrant with the smoke of Egyptian cigarettes.'[2] To the infantry in their rain-sodden trenches it would have seemed terribly unfair – had they known about it. But theirs was the gaiety of the doomed. Mosley recalls: 'We were like men having dinner together at a country house-party knowing that some must soon leave us for ever; in the end, nearly all.'[3] He wrote to his mother not to grieve if he was killed as he was sure he would find death 'a most interesting experience'.

Modernity: Mosley has always been fascinated by everything modern, by every new breakthrough in technique. He was the greatest of the vicarious technologists with a natural career ahead of him as a social engineer. Air travel – the journey into a new dimension – seemed the natural expression of the new age, and it is a fact that famous aviators were prominent in fascist movements all over Europe.* It was not in the annals of the air, however, that Mosley was to make his mark. He gained his pilot's certificate, but showing off before his mother and admiring relatives at Shoreham in May 1915 he crashed the plane and broke his ankle for a second time, thereby almost certainly saving his life. For before the R.F.C. could reclaim him once again after his convalescence his old regiment, the 16th Lancers, demanded his services. In October 1915 he was in the trenches for the first time, with a leg that had not properly healed up.

From the few to the many; from the fluid to the solid. From all his experiences, however little he enjoyed them at the time, Mosley took away an idea. It is easy to understand his admiration for the R.F.C.: it was an élite of buccaneers, vivacious, daredevil. The Army, though, was solid, mediocre. Yet did not this give it something of the very quality of society itself? And, moreover, was not this very much the kind of society among which he had spent his boyhood – feudal, paternalistic? 'Every man was made to feel that he was a member of a large family and would in all circum-

*And outside Europe: Charles Lindbergh's sympathy with fascism is well known.

stances be looked after. The most intimate confidence was encouraged and freely given with complete trust. The officer must
and would take the utmost trouble to assist any man in his troop or
squadron in any difficulty, either in the regiment or in his private
life.'[4]   The similarity of language with his description of Rolleston
is striking.   Rolleston and the Regiment provided images of social
life at an impressionable age far removed from the normal practice
of peace-time England.   And the aristocratic duality of an uninhi-
bited private world combined with a sense of social responsibility
received reinforcement in the contrasting war-time experiences of
the R.F.C. and the 16th Lancers.

But perhaps the most profound attraction of the military ideal
was its revelation of the power that comes from collective discipline,
so much more formidable than the spectacular, but ephemeral,
exploits of the single knights of the skies.   And it is not surprising
that this revelation was first brought home to him by the performances of the Germans.

Once again let Mosley describe the scene from the second battle of
Ypres (22 April-31 May 1915).   He had been instructed to make
contact with the newly arrived Canadian Expeditionary Force,
with the object of fixing up wireless communication so that they
could easily receive messages from the R.F.C. flyers.   His mission
accomplished he set out back to Poperinghe.

> From a small rise in the ground in the first stage of my return
> journey I looked back to see what was happening.   It was an
> unforgettable spectacle.   As dusk descended there appeared
> to our left the blue-grey masses of the Germans advancing
> steadily behind their lifting curtain of fire, as steadily as if they
> had been on the parade ground of Potsdam.[5]

' They went like Kings in pageant to their imminent death,' wrote
Douglas Jerrold.   ' Troops of that spirit ', Mosley felt, ' can and
will do things which most troops cannot do, and they did.'[6]   What
might a nation in arms not accomplish?   Yet the overpowering
impact of this spectacle did not make him a militarist, though it
gave him an admiration for Germany which he has never lost.   This
– and the constant slaughter in the air and on the ground – made
him conscious only of the tragic waste of human lives and possibilities.   It was the spirit of discipline and sacrifice, rather than the
ends to which it was being directed by the politicians and generals,
that made such a lasting impression on his mind.   The ' noble
inspirations which have been used on all sides for dark purposes of
destruction ' must be harnessed to ' creative achievement '.   Europe
must live, not die.

In the dank trenches the injured leg swelled and rotted, and
Mosley's commanding officer Colonel Eccles finally ordered him

home in March 1916.   He had been invalided out of the war after just under a year of active service.   A couple of operations saved the leg, but left it an inch and a half shorter.   Thereafter he always walked with a pronounced limp.

Brief spells of work at the Ministry of Munitions and the Foreign Office gave Mosley a first-hand impression of a society in arms at home.   By 1917, as R. S. Sayers remarks, Britain had ceased to be a market economy.

> Productive capacity was controlled directly by government departments or indirectly through negotiations with traders and manufacturers.   Raw materials, especially those imported, were purchased by government and doled out to manufacturers for approved production.   Prices were more and more widely fixed, the channels of distribution more and more closely controlled. . . . Employment was controlled . . . by gradual development of a system of reserved occupations, by agreements with trade unions, by direct prohibitions on ' poaching ' of labour, and (without success) by direct prohibitions of strike action.[7]

In war the social ideal drew closer to the military ideal.   Gone, it seemed, were the class animosities and *laissez-faire* principles of the nineteenth century, to be replaced by a mood of solidarity and organisation for survival.   In war, it seemed, the collective triumphed over the individual, the common good over selfishness.   Here was indeed a new-model state – and did it not stand for a truth as profound as the old liberal one?

Suddenly the war was over.   Within a couple of months, the German military machine which in the summer of 1918 hurled the Allies back almost to Paris mysteriously collapsed.   Ludendorff insisted his armies could fight no longer; and the Armistice was signed on 11 November 1918.   With the announcement of an end to the unprecedented slaughter, all restraints in London broke loose in an orgy of rejoicing.

> Work ceased in shops and offices. . . . Crowds surged through the streets, often led by airmen and Dominion troops on leave.   Omnibuses were seized, and people in strange garments caroused on the open upper deck.   A bonfire heaped against the plinth of Nelson's column in Trafalgar Square has left its mark to this day.   Total strangers copulated in doorways and on pavements.   They were asserting the triumph of life over death.[8]

Mosley has given his own memory of that occasion:

> . . . I passed through the festive streets and entered one of London's largest and most fashionable hotels, interested by

the sounds of revelry which echoed from it.   Smooth, smug
people, who had never fought or suffered, seemed to the eyes
of youth – at that moment age-old with sadness, weariness
and bitterness – to be eating, drinking, laughing on the
graves of our companions.   I stood aside from the delirious
throng; silent and alone, ravaged by memory.   Driving purpose had begun; there must be no more war.   I dedicated
myself to politics. . . .[9]

The war, more than any other single experience, shaped Mosley
the man and the politician.   A boy turned overnight into a man –
and in some ways a very old one, as if a lifetime had been compressed into a moment.   The war gave Mosley the ' gift of tongues '
which blazed for over forty years in passionate, eloquent, angry
speeches from platforms up and down the country.   It released in
him the springs of creative energy, whose results were seen in his
successive plans to realise his Land Fit for Heroes.   Cecil Day
Lewis's comment on Wilfred Owen is apposite here: the flowering
of his poetic genius was no gradual development but a ' forced
growth, a revolution in the mind '.   So it was with Mosley.   This
' forced growth ' gave him an immediate problem as a politician.
For a moment it seemed as if the war had induced a ' forced growth '
in society as a whole.   This proved an illusion.   When Reginald
McKenna introduced his famous McKenna Duties in 1915, Lloyd
George scribbled a note across the Cabinet table: ' so the old system
goes destroyed by its own advocates '.   In fact it had only *gone
under* for a few years.   Victorianism survived.   The bankers, merchants and politicians were waiting in the wings for the ' return to
normalcy '.   The divergence – which transcended the simple impatience of the young – between Mosley's time-scale and that of
Britain's rulers had begun.
    This divergence is part of a more general displacement.   The
war, as we have seen, uprooted Mosley from the land.   But in
addition he saw himself from the first as the spokesman of the trench
soldiers – a society of ' new men ' bound together in a special
brotherhood, cut off from those who had remained behind by the
impact of terrible and wonderful truths, contemptuous of the values
of the old world.   In the sensitive survivor hedonism and nihilism
struggled for mastery with idealism.   This double reaction is understandable.   The First World War was a meaningless, atrocious event –
perhaps the most meaningless man-inflicted horror of history.   One
reaction was to say with Nietzsche ' God is dead ', life is meaningless, man a ' useless passion '.   That reaction led forward to the
contemporary doctrine of the absurd.   Side by side with this existed
the feeling that slaughter on this scale *had* to be justified.   Out of
death must come purpose; man must create a new order; and per-

haps in the divine plan evil, too, was an agent of evolution. ' It
is to preserve the future, not the past, that most of those I know are
fighting and have fought,' wrote a young soldier about to die. He
went on: ' It is a glorious comfort to know that the new outlook
on life and humanity . . . will be voiced by those who remain all
the more ardently and passionately because of those that this war
has rendered and will render silent. *Here is death becoming creative. . . .*'[10]   (My italics.)   This was the soldier's memory and the
soldier's resolve that drove Mosley on to ceaseless striving when
pleasure beckoned so invitingly, and which was to drive him into
fascism once a growing sense of betrayal made it impossible for him
to go on ' playing the game '.

If idealism was to give ultimate meaning to Mosley's political
life, it was as a playboy that he first found himself on its fringes.
He plunged into a whirl of pleasure and high society. Through the
War Department of the Foreign Office, he met Aubrey Herbert,
Mark Sykes, Henry Bentinck, Godfrey Locker-Lampson and others
who in turn introduced him to the well known, the well connected
and the brilliant. London hostesses anxious to contribute their bit
to the war effort fêted the dark, handsome Lieutenant Mosley,
invalided out of the front line with a slight but suitably heroic limp.
Eligible young men, too, must have been in scarce supply in the
London of 1916–18.   The death of his grandfather in 1915 had for
the first time given him the money to enjoy life to the full; and war
had not yet become so total, or taxation so prohibitive, as to interfere seriously with the gay social life of the metropolis. Mosley took
a flat in Grosvenor Square; and from there sallied forth to houses of
the famous hostesses of the period – Maud Cunard (mainly political),
Lady Colefax (mainly literary), Maxine Elliott, Nancy Astor and
Mrs Ronnie Greville.   There he met F. E. Smith, Winston Churchill, Asquith, Captain ' Freddie ' Guest and Sir George Younger,
the Liberal and Conservative whips, the Cecil brothers and no
doubt many other more minor political and social luminaries. He
had the looks, presence and manners to succeed – and he did.

This period, too, saw the first flowering of intellectual interests.
In hospital in 1916 he had started reading history and political
biography.   The choice is characteristic.   ' If a man wants to play
tennis well, he should go to Wimbledon and watch the style of the
contemporary champion. If he enters politics, he should read
history and study the form of the great masters of action.'[11]   Certainly by the time he stood for Parliament he had at least a nodding
acquaintance with the lives of the famous English politicians –
Chatham (a particular hero), Pitt, Fox, Gladstone, Disraeli, Lord
Randolph Churchill.   What he particularly noted was the style
of their oratory and the age at which they had embarked on their
political careers.   When he himself entered Parliament at the ripe

age of twenty-two, he comforted himself with the thought that he was doing better than most of them. Had he pursued his historical studies in greater depth he would doubtless have come to the depressing conclusion that wholesome dullness succeeds more frequently in politics than brilliance, which is admired more in retrospect than at the time.

But Mosley studied the history he felt he needed. The history of ' small periods ' and ' small men ' did not interest him. For Mosley history was indispensable aid to fighting the great fight. ' Without history ', writes the Danish critic Georg Brandes, ' the mountain chain of great men and great moments, which runs through millenniums, could not stand clearly and vividly before me.' Years later Mosley wrote: ' I am chiefly concerned with history as a means to action, as the school or staff college which fits us for our task '.[12]

With these awakening interests, Mosley thought of going to university and ' interrogated my Oxford and Cambridge contemporaries in order to discover if they knew much that I didn't. The results were reasonably satisfactory.'[13] The remark is typical. He was a man of 1914–18 and universities taught all the old stuff, which had so little connection with that experience. Mosley was never to go through Keynes' long struggle to escape from established modes of thought, implanted at the universities. He approached the problems of his time with a mind uncluttered by what to him seemed obsolete intellectual luggage. At the same time he imparted to the radical causes with which he came to be associated something of the savagery of the trenches.

Not that life was predominantly serious. At weekend parties, assembled in country houses in the old style, Mosley and companions of the same age indulged to the full the high spirits of young men relaxing after a terrible experience. Staying in Leicestershire (where he first met Harold Nicolson), Mosley arranged a scene in which German officers were supposed to have escaped from a nearby prisoner-of-war camp. After a burst of rifle fire in the grounds, a ' German officer ' was carried into the drawing-room covered with blood, his cap pulled over his head, together with a supposedly dead body of one of the guests he had had shot. Dramatically, the hostess pulled his cap from his head, exclaiming ' You shall be uncovered in the presence of the dead ', only to discover the grinning features of her groom. This love of practical joking remained with Mosley throughout the 1920s, and was to give him a somewhat frivolous image in the staid arena of middle- and working-class politics. Contemporaries would recall a streak of cruelty in his character.

It was F. E. Smith who first suggested to Mosley that he should embark on a political career; and once he expressed interest in the idea both the Coalition whips, Captain ' Freddie ' Guest and Sir George Younger, no doubt appreciative of the electoral value of gallant officers wounded in the service of their country, attempted to enrol him under their respective banners.   Although his background was impeccably Conservative Mosley ' knew little of Conservative sentiment and cared less '.[14]   Party politics was far from his mind.   He thought of himself as a representative of the ' war generation '; whether he entered Parliament as a Coalition Liberal or Unionist made little difference to him.   As it turned out Sir George Younger pressed the matter first, or hardest, and so it was under Conservative auspices that Mosley made his political début. One is reminded of the story of Walter Elliott, who when he received a telegram at the Front from Lanark asking him to stand for Parliament cabled back, ' Certainly, which Party?'   To men of Mosley's age and war experience ' the party ' was of little importance.   What mattered was winning the war and supporting the war leaders; and in the heady atmosphere of war-time national unity Mosley's attitude was that of the majority.

Two opportunities soon arose for adoption as a parliamentary candidate.   The first was for the Stone division of Staffordshire, his home county; the second for the Harrow division of Middlesex. It is to the latter that the controversial honour falls of having launched Mosley on his political career.   In his election speeches Mosley claimed he chose Harrow because he wanted to make his way on his own merits, without advantage of family connection. There was probably something in this.   More important was the fact that Harrow was vastly more convenient – nearer London where his life now centred, and further away from his father at Rolleston, with whom his relations remained less than cordial. It was on 23 July 1918 that Mosley faced the forty-three delegates from the various local Unionist associations – Harrow, Wealdstone, Hanwell, Wembley and Greenford – as one of four candidates on the short list.   His fifteen-minute set speech, learnt by heart, fell flat.   It was, one of the delegates later told him, ' good stuff, but badly chanted '.   What told in his favour, despite his youth, was the lucid and trenchant manner in which he answered questions. His nomination was carried almost unanimously.

Disgruntled local Harrow Conservatives later alleged that Mosley was a Central Office nominee, foisted onto the Harrow Association at the expense of better-qualified local men.[15]   On 20 September 1918, the local newspaper published a letter from a sixty-five-year-old solicitor, A. R. Chamberlayne, attacking the ' party caucus ' which was able to foist men of wealth and connection onto the local associations.   The charge that he was using his wealth to forward his career was to dog Mosley throughout his life.   There is something splendidly old-fashioned in Chamberlayne's complaint about the rejection of worthy nominees (himself, for example!) 'because they will not lower themselves to send in a written application'. It is ironic, too, that the first political charge to be levelled against Mosley was that he was a creature of the party machine.

A fortnight later the *Harrow Observer* printed a vigorous reply from 'Omega'. Dismissing Chamberlayne as a failed politician, 'Omega' declared grandly that 'the electorate will turn with relief from the last throes of these legal intriguers to the original and vigorous reconstruction programmes of the young soldiers who are now appearing in every constituency'. 'Omega' was clearly Mosley himself. He had taken to heart Oscar Wilde's dictum that 'there is only one thing worse than being talked about and that is not being talked about'.

There is little enough mention of reconstruction in Mosley's first speeches. Naturally enough, the emphasis was on winning the war. His argument for doing so is worth reproducing, for it reveals not only his highly rational style of exposition, but also his early realisation of the economic dimension of great power conflicts:

We are all familiar with the ethical reasons for a fight to the finish, but concrete material reasons are not so frequently advanced. A short consideration of a peace under the conditions cited above [i.e., a negotiated peace] will quickly banish all thoughts of such a compromise from the business mind. The conclusion of peace on these terms would mean the triumph of the Middle-European scheme. The Pan-German has long realised that the real power of Germany lies in the East rather than in the West, in the possibility of a vast self-contained Empire stretching from Hamburg to the Persian Gulf. . . .

We now see Russia dismembered with some of her richest though undeveloped lands enslaved body and soul, while the whole country is exposed to the intensive development and commercial exploitation of Germany. There is little doubt that the conquered portions of Russia will in a few years return Germany a rich harvest of developed wealth which will more than wipe out the debt incurred in this war and place her in a position to resume the struggle under conditions which would probably prohibit any other nation ever contesting her right to world domination. She would have at her disposal the vast manpower resources of most of Russia and the Balkans, and would undoubtedly mould this primitive material into a fighting force which would dwarf the aggregate standing armies of the world. Her economic position would be assured by her newly acquired territory, however prolonged the struggle, for she would contain within her own Empire nearly every product essential to the conduct of war together with the food which is necessary to maintain a nation in arms.

Even if we discount the possibility of another war in our time . . . the prospect is not alluring, for ultimate German domination of the world would be assured in an economic if not in a military form. . . . The hypothetical peace I have mentioned would turn Germany into one vast business firm, concentrated on one object, to undersell and crush all competitors in every market of the world. . . . Germany [would hold] three trump cards for a future economic war: (1) Vast tracts of undeveloped land of immeasurable latent wealth . . . (2) the cheapest labour in the world. . . . These primitive Russian and Balkan peoples will work for a wage which over here means starvation and for a length of hours that would kill the more delicately-nurtured Westerner; (3) the Central Empires would possess the shortest, quickest and also the cheapest means of transit from Europe to Asia. . . . In consideration of these three weapons which would remain in the hands of Germany for a *post-bellum* economic war, we may well ask what possibility of successful competition lies in the Free Trade system of England.[16]

Twenty years later he was much less apprehensive about a ' vast self-contained Empire stretching from Hamburg to the Persian Gulf . . . ' but this was because he had in the meantime come to reject the competitive free-trade system in favour of a world of self-sufficient blocs.

By October 1918 it was apparent that the Germans were on the point of collapse. Three days after the armistice was signed on 11 November 1918, Lloyd George went to the country as head of the Coalition. His appeal was basic and overwhelming: trust the man who had produced the shells to produce the houses. As Taylor writes: ' The election was fought around Lloyd George – his past record and his promises for the future.'[17] In a speech in September the prime minister had highlighted the ' plain, homely subjects ' which should receive attention at the forthcoming election – health, education, housing, production and wages. The country which had produced heroes in such numbers should be made a land fit for them to live in. Mosley, of course, received the Coalition 'coupon'. On 25 October, too, Chamberlayne finally entered the ring against him as Independent, backed by a body calling itself the League of Electors. Mosley's first recorded political joke – ' an Independent is a person on whom no one can depend ' – was at Chamberlayne's expense. He could hardly have anticipated that it would be quoted gleefully against him a few years later.

Mosley's first election address is one of the key documents of his life. It expressed the credo of the war-generation, the mood of 1918. The war had given him a vision; and he was to devote the rest of his life to its realisation.

> *Industry:* High wages must be maintained. This can only be achieved by high production based on increased efficiency and organisation. A high standard of life must be ensured by a minimum wage and reduced hours, which are proved to increase rather than curtail production.
>
> *Transport:* Transportation and electrical resources to be controlled and developed by the State.
>
> *Land:* The State must acquire land where necessary at a fair price [for soldiers' smallholdings].
>
> *Housing:* In many cases the State must carry out the work [of slum clearance] itself to ensure speed.
>
> *Education:* Numerous scholarships for higher and university education must be supplied by the State.
>
> *Fiscal Policy:* Preference on duties already existing and hereafter to be imposed must be granted as a long-solicited act of justice for our colonies. Industries essential to the national well-being must be shielded; unfair competition to British industry. . . in the form of ' dumping ' must be stopped.
>
> *Agriculture:* Must be secured by the continuance of the present Corn Production Act.
>
> *Aliens:* Immediate legislation is necessary to prevent undesirable aliens from landing; and for the repatriation of those who are now resident in this country.
>
> *Empire:* Complete unity must be promoted by every means to enable the British Empire to play a leading part in the future League of Nations.

Like most young men who had seen what the state could accomplish in war, Mosley looked to the State to create the 'land fit for heroes'. It was to be a ' controlling and directing ' but not a nationalising state: the State as Leader not as Nanny. It was to be a state which put Britain first – that would guard the British against ' unfair competition', that would preserve Britain for the British. It was to be a state that would create an imperial economic system: ' socialistic imperialism' was how Mosley described his programme in an election speech. It was to be a state that would preserve external peace to make possible the great constructive achievements at home.

How little anything really fundamental changed thereafter. Full production and employment, high wages, decent housing, equal opportunities, a decent environment: these remained the first objects of his passionate endeavours. The means varied, but less than might have been expected. The State always remained in the forefront. The hints of the 'autarchic' economic system disappeared temporarily, only to be revived in the 1930s in fully fledged imperial economics, and in the 1940s in the concept of Europe-Africa. Britain for the British, too, remained a permanent theme. In 1918 the alien was German, in the 1930s Jewish, in the 1950s Black: but the primary loyalty to those with their roots in Britain remained. With the exception of that significant 'extension of patriotism' that propelled Mosley towards Europe in the 1940s, he has fought all his life for the agenda of 1918, returning to it repeatedly with all the enthusiasm of a first love.

The election campaign itself, though mild by the standards of some of his later efforts, did not long remain on this high level of policy. Chamberlayne, as we have seen, introduced the personal note from the start by darkly hinting that Mosley's wealth and connections had 'bought' him the nomination. This charge, Mosley retorted, came ill from a man 'who had travelled from one end of the kingdom to another trying to get returned to Parliament' – an allusion to Chamberlayne's previous unsuccessful electoral efforts (he had stood twice for Glasgow and once for South Shields).[18] 'With the alluring prospect of obtaining £400 a year – a sum they could probably not hope to earn in any other way' it was inevitable that 'freak' candidates should be springing up to oppose him.[19] 'Is it wise', Chamberlayne riposted, 'in times like these to elect a young man of 22, with only a military training, and who seeks to enter Parliament as a step to a " political career "?'[20] The charge of youth gave Mosley no trouble. 'He was quite content to join the ranks of the young men who had entered Parliament in their youth – Fox 19, Pitt 21, Gladstone 22, Palmerston 23, Salisbury 25.'[21] In every crisis 'young men had seized the reins of power' from the 'failed politicians'.[22] 'His opponent had stated that every man of 65 should receive an old age pension and yet at the same time he asked Harrow electors to return him to Parliament (laughter).'[23] 'Would they send their grandfathers into a fresh business?'[24] All this was good knockabout stuff. Yet the charge of youth and inexperience stung Mosley into unkinder reactions. In the next few days, he told an audience early in November, 'they would see the type of the old freak with which they were so familiar in the days of the hustings', 'aborigines of the political world' scrambling up on the 'old time-worn platform of self-interest', thundering 'on the mighty drum of egotism'. He would not follow them into the 'political gutter'.[25]

Angered perhaps by these allusions, Chamberlayne switched to a new line. On 23 November 1918 he claimed that Mosley, despite all the talk of a distinguished military career, had not received his commission till October 1916. This hit a sensitive spot. Mosley immediately instructed his solicitors to inform Chamberlayne that

he had obtained his commission in 1914, not 1916, and to call on
him to withdraw ' the implication . . . that he had failed to qualify
for a commission at the Royal Military College, Sandhurst'.[26]
Chamberlayne then modified his original assertion by stating that
he had understood from the War Office that ' Lieut. Mosley
obtained his appointment as a 2nd Lieutenant in October 1914,
and his full lieutenant's commission in October 1916', but then
went on to expose the heart of his grievance against his opponent:

> If I may be permitted to do so, I would suggest that your
> client should restrain his admirers from making statements
> about his distinguished career in the Army, and so on, and if
> your client would also not make suggestions to the effect
> that his opponent is anxious to get £400 a year income which
> he could not earn in his own occupation, that he is a gutter
> politician and belongs to the stone age, and he is a lost soul
> and so on, it would be more creditable to him.   I know that
> youth is an excuse for many things, but when a gentleman
> aspires to a political career, he should seek advice as to what
> is prudent and likely to reflect credit upon himself in a poli-
> tical contest.[27]

Amidst these acerbities, the election campaign drew to its climax.
In practice little separated the candidates in terms of policy.   As
polling day approached, both Mosley and Chamberlayne, like
Lloyd George himself, abandoned the lofty vision of reconstruction
for a more popular chauvinism.   All undesirable aliens (that is,
Germans) should be deported;* the Kaiser should be tried for war
crimes;   Germany should be squeezed ' until the pips squeaked '.
Both candidates supported Lloyd George.   The point on which
they differed was whether this support should best be provided
by Independents or by the party machines.   Here Mosley undoubtedly had the better of the argument.   A full-page advertise-
ment in the *Harrow Observer* of 13 December 1918 proclaimed in
bold letters:

> Lloyd George Asks You to
> VOTE FOR MOSLEY
> his accredited Coalition Candidate
> Lloyd George is surely the best man to
> settle who are his own loyal supporters
> If you believe in his judgment
> VOTE FOR MOSLEY

*It is remarkable how little the indictment against aliens, of any nationality,
seems to change over time.   Of the Germans Mosley said: ' They had brought
disease amongst them, reduced Englishmen's wages, undersold English goods,
and ruined social life ' (*Harrow Observer*, 29 November 1918).

The Soldier candidate who helped you to Victory,
and now stands for a strong peace.
Let a Soldier finish a Soldier's job
A Vote for an ' Independent ' is a vote against Lloyd George
VOTE FOR MOSLEY

December 14, 1918 was favourable to young soldiers all over the country. 'The astonishing thing', wrote a reporter touring the constituency, 'was the almost unanimous support for Lieut. Mosley. From every other window his face looked out; his carriages careered along the streets; his red favours* met the eye on men, women, and children; his supporters harangued the crowds at street corners; and Mr. Mosley himself was here, there and everywhere.' The oldest elector in the constituency, a Miss Wotton, aged 102, cast the first vote in her life for the youngest successful candidate in the country. The final figures announced a fortnight later (to allow for a postal military vote) gave Mosley 13,950, his opponent 3007. His majority of 10,943 was the fortieth largest in Britain. 'It must be said of the successful candidate that he fought for all he was worth. ... Buoyed up by an ambition for a political career, for which he gives much real promise, he has triumphantly succeeded.'[28] As for Mosley himself, he entered Parliament burning with eagerness to play his part in the 'greatest National Party that the country has ever known . . . a party which was all-embracing, a Party which had in it everything that was worth having.'[29] It was to be a recurring dream.

*Mosley had already chosen Red as his campaign colour, rather than the traditional Tory Blue.

Chapter 4

The Young Crusader

THE 1918 Parliament of 'hard-faced men who looked as if they had done well out of the war' was well named. Over half the 338 Conservative M.P.s who dominated the Coalition were company directors and financiers, grown fat and arrogant on war profits. They supported Lloyd George the war leader, not Lloyd George the social reformer. What would normally have been the radical opposition was fragmented and reduced in strength. A hundred and thirty-six Liberals supported the Coalition. They were Lloyd George's men, practical rather than idealistic. The Asquith Liberals who remained outside the Coalition numbered only twenty-six, Asquith himself losing at East Fife. Into the vacuum created by the dissolution of the historic Liberal Party stepped the Labour Party with $2\frac{1}{2}$ million votes in the country, fifty-nine seats and a brand-new constitution pledging it to the 'common ownership of the means of production, distribution and exchange'. For a long time the significance of this decisive shift of the radical forces to Labour was not registered, least of all by the mediocre Labour leaders returned in 1918 who were content to leave the leadership of the Opposition to the Liberal rump. It was not till MacDonald, Snowden and Henderson managed to get back into Parliament later on that Labour began to look and act more like an alternative government.

The new parliament was conspicuous for the number of new parliamentarians: 260 were entering for the first time. Many of these were the 'hard-faced' men, of whom the brothers Geddes were perhaps the most conspicuous examples. But about a hundred were of the 'war generation', impatient with the old parliamentary 'game' as they called it, determined to create a noble land from the ruins of war. Most of them had entered, like Mosley, as Conservatives or Unionists, but they were not really interested in party labels. Their progressive disillusionment and capitulation was one of the saddest spectacles offered by the life of the new parliament. The novelist Henry Williamson wrote: 'They stammered about a new world, and found that the old world was paramount.' The 'hard-faced' men were in control and, twist and turn as they might, the young men could not escape their clutches. The war which had been fought to make the world safe for democracy turned out in fact to have made it safe for plutocracy. It was against this heartless parliamentary background that the young Mosley had to find his feet and make his way. 'I remember him at that time,' a colleague of 1919 recalled, 'a lonely, detached figure, wandering unhappily about the lobbies of the House, uncertain of his mind. The war, he would say, had planted the seeds of doubt; parties were changing, new political creeds running molten from the crucibles of old faiths, and he did not know which to make his own.'[1]

As was appropriate for an early volunteer to the Royal Flying Corps, Mosley made his maiden speech on 17 February 1919 on the 2nd Reading of the Aerial Navigation Bill. General Seely had just resigned as under-secretary for air, alleging that the control of the Air Council by the War Ministry was stifling the needs of the infant service. After apologising, in the words of his earliest political hero, Chatham, for 'the atrocious crime of being a young man' Mosley spoke briefly, but eloquently, on the dangers of cramping air development by bureaucratic control. 'The peculiar genius of our race', he declared, 'has always manifested itself in strange new enterprises where the individual stood alone, uninspired save by the spirit of adventure in entering new realms and ranges of human activity.'[2] A feature of the speech was the attack on Winston Churchill, secretary of state for war and air, whom Mosley accused of a lack of imagination – a reproof which led *Punch* to comment: 'The idea of anyone regarding our WINSTON as a doddering old fossil!' Every clever, ambitious young politician instinctively knows that he has to prove himself against the ruling, but ageing, champions of the old régime. Just as Lloyd George from the first had taken on the great Joseph Chamberlain, so the twenty-two-year-old Mosley made Churchill – one of the giants of 1918 – his own special target.

Churchill's continued responsibility for military affairs gave Mosley repeated opportunities. Arguing for the independence of the Air Ministry from the War Office, Mosley cast doubts on Churchill's capacity to do both jobs at once. 'We are living', he declared, 'in a period which is seeing what I may call the passing of the superman or the "twilight of the gods".'[3] A few months later he spoke against Churchill's motion to restore scarlet as the dress uniform of the Army. It was a model short speech, combining a lucid statement of the case with some irreverent sallies at the great man's expense. The way Mosley disposes of the argument is a good example of the order and precision of his thinking.

> The right hon. Baronet the Member for the City of London spoke in favour of this proposal. His main argument, as I understood, was that to clothe the Army in red uniform was conducive to *esprit de corps* in the Regular Army. I refuse to believe that the *esprit de corps* of the Regular Army goes no deeper than the tunic. I would remind the right hon. Baronet that, while he and his contemporaries spent practically

the whole of their soldiering in the red tunics, the young men of whom the present Army is composed spent all their time in khaki, and all the glory of their regiments is bound up inseparably with the khaki tradition. His second argument was that this red clothing was conducive to recruiting. It is inconceivable that any young man should join the Army without first consulting some old soldier as to what was to happen in the Army. If he consults one of those old soldiers, he will learn from an expert source that one of the most unpleasant duties of the soldier's life is the cleaning of this red uniform. Hours of his time are wasted in this unproductive duty. The red uniform is extremely unpopular among old soldiers. At any rate, it is open to doubt whether the red uniform will assist recruiting. I do not believe that many men are attracted to the Army by the glamour of a poster or the prospect of amatory success. But, in any case, the right hon. Gentleman has assured us that recruiting for the Regular Army is proceeding satisfactorily, and that the maintenance of His Majesty's Forces will not depend entirely upon the influence of the romantic nursemaid.

The real argument in favour of the red uniform is that on ceremonial occasions it looks nice. That is the beginning and end of the matter. To pursue that argument to its logical conclusion, hon. Members might just as well say that on ceremonial occasions it would look nice to have Whitehall painted pink. The answer in both cases is that in the aesthetic sense the contention may be true, but that from the financial sense we simply cannot afford these luxuries.

Churchill's proposal would cost £3 million. 'This £3,000,000', Mosley went on,

> might be devoted to making this country entirely safe against aerial attack. It might be devoted to the development of our Air Service, to putting it in such a position that it would be unchallenged by any other Air Service in the world. To give an entirely different kind of instance, the League of Nations at the present moment is appealing for a sum of £2,000,000 with which to check the threatened attack of typhus during next winter, which will probably involve the loss of at least a million lives. Two-thirds of this money which is to go to gladdening the eyes of bureaucrats might save a million lives next year.

The speech ended on a lighter note:

> Many of us were inspired with high hopes, when the right hon. Gentleman [Winston Churchill] went to the War Office,

that his realistic outlook and forceful character would be thrown into the scale against the retention of these expensive anachronisms. Those hopes, however, have been dashed to the ground. I fear he is bound too securely to military ambition to realise the necessities of peace. The right hon. Gentleman has developed a reputation for modelling himself upon ambitious precedent. It is scarcely necessary to remind him that the first Napoleon excelled, not merely in the realms of martial display and military achievements, but also in the gentler sphere of peaceful administration. The right hon. Gentleman has already had full opportunity for the display of his genius for war. May I now beg him to turn his attention, flushed as he is with victories won and reverses manfully sustained on far-flung fields – may I beg him to return to the less exciting, but none the less exacting pursuits of peace?[4]

Mosley's early parliamentary efforts read well enough, but no doubt were ' poorly chanted '. He was no natural orator, his voice having a tendency to shrillness and monotony. But he was determined to succeed at this the noblest of all the political arts: the art of public persuasion. Without the traditional political apprenticeship in the Oxford or Cambridge Union, he was obliged to learn on the job. The House of Commons became his School of Rhetoric, and a tedious experience it was for those few Members who sat stoically through Mosley's repeated efforts to get practice, ' of which ', as Churchill put it, ' he stands in much need '. Mosley spared no pains: he sat through endless debates in the hope of catching the Speaker's eye; he studied the form of the great parliamentary orators of the past; he practised replying to points made in debate by attacking the *Times* leader every morning after breakfast; he studied every nuance of gesture and expression in front of a mirror; he even took lessons in voice production. His improvement was rapid.

Mosley, as we have seen, had entered Parliament as a Coalition Unionist. But he was profoundly uninterested in party labels. In so far as the young men of the war generation had a political vision it was to rally together all those of progressive views behind the project of constructing a ' land fit for heroes '. This suggested a new Progressive Party geared to the needs of the post-war world. It may be asked at once why men like Mosley did not turn sooner to the Labour Party as the answer to their problem, and why the bulk of the parliamentary ' war generation ' never in fact embraced the socialist cause. The answer is complex, but understandable. Young men like Mosley were interested in action, not dogma. The whole world of socialist theorising, including the notion of the class struggle, was entirely alien to them. Soldiers who had fought in the war found it difficult to forgive the pacifism of MacDonald, Snowden and many Labour leaders. For people from upper-class backgrounds to associate with Labour was considered far more eccentric and unusual then than it is today: despite the influx of upper-class pacifists opposed to the war, Labour remained a trade-union party, remote from Mosley's whole world and life-experience. Finally, in 1918 Labour was hardly considered a serious challenger for power on its own: an impression reinforced by the performance of the Labour leaders in the House. For all these reasons, while many of the young men of 1918 were anxious to incorporate ' moderate ' or ' patriotic ' Labour in a wider grouping, the option of joining the Labour Party itself simply never occurred to them.

What they tried to do was to organise a new ' Centre ' party under Lloyd George which would stand midway between Reaction on the Right and Revolution on the Left. In the highly charged industrial atmosphere of the immediate post-war years, to avoid the division of politics along class lines seemed to them a task of paramount importance; and they feared with good reason that unless Lloyd George could be reinforced from the Left he would become a prisoner of the hard-faced men of the Right.

On 7 April 1919, therefore, forty M.P.s of both wings of the Coalition decided to form a New Members Parliamentary Committee to hold weekly luncheons to discuss common aims. Oscar Guest, younger brother of the Coalition Liberal Chief Whip, was elected chairman and the Committee included Mosley and Colin Coote (joint secretaries), Walter Elliot, Moore-Brabazon, Cecil L'Estrange Malone (soon to flirt briefly with the Communist Party), Leng-Sturrock and Sir Ernest Wild. The press nicknamed them ' the Babes '.

Mosley, the ' baby ' of the House, was in it from the start. All the members were parliamentary ' new boys '; nearly all of them had fought in the war. Oscar Guest, aged thirty-one, had been a fighter pilot; Moore-Brabazon at the age of twenty-eight had been the first pilot to gain his certificate in the Royal Flying Corps; Colin Coote, twenty-five, had been wounded and decorated. Mosley – ' a tall, dark figure with a limp ', as Colin Coote remembers him – was by and large content to take a back seat. His name hardly ever appears, except in passing, in the press accounts of the ' Centre Party'. Indeed the man who at this stage most interested journalists as a potential national leader was Major Walter Elliot, ' a doctor by profession . . . [and] one of the section of the Eugenists who are for rebuilding the race and correcting the errors with which it has muddled along hitherto '.[5] Such was the quality of post-1918 radicalism!

' We are young in hope and aspiration,' wrote Colin Coote.

' Many of us during the war made a vow that if we " came through " we should devote the rest of our lives to making sure that the war had been worthwhile.'[6]   Mosley was later to remark on a ' certain psychological division ' between those who had fought and those who had stayed behind ' which can perhaps best be expressed in the simple fact that the war generation was more disposed to take the 1918 programmes seriously '.[7]   It was his identification with the returning warriors – with their state of mind, their experiences, their fears, their hopes – that determined Mosley's ultimate political alignment; just as it was the returning warriors themselves, Mussolini's ' aristocracy of the trenches ', who spawned fascist movements all over Europe.

Some inkling of their political aspirations is revealed by a sketch of a new ' Industrial Party ' by Ernest Benn (later an advocate of extreme individualism):

> It would stand for the highest wages and the highest output – two ideals which are absolutely inseparable.   It would tackle in a thorough-going way the problem of unemployment . . . and it would attract to its ranks the better half of the nation by a frank avowal of the necessity for efficiency in all walks of life.   It would declare itself the enemy alike of the reactionary employer and the revolutionary workman.   Within the circle of such a Party trade unions' and employers' federations would both find common aims, in addition to which the great bulk of the people who class themselves neither as capital nor labour would find a practical policy and a definite object . . . which they have utterly failed to secure from the airy ramblings of the old-time politician.[8]

Such thinking, as Mosley justly notes, ' was in the very air of Europe, thrown high by the explosion of the war '.[9]   It made a strong appeal to the hundred-odd war survivors who found themselves in Parliament and who, in Colin Coote's words, ' were not really party men at all ', who believed that the war had shattered the old party shibboleths (' shibboleth ' was a favourite word), and who were anxious to consolidate the *union sacrée* which the war had engendered.[10]   The Coalition, in its own amorphous way, expressed the same thinking.   Even the elderly Austen Chamberlain realised that ' a new world has come into existence with new problems of profound gravity '.   In a speech to the New Members' Group at the Criterion Restaurant on 15 July 1919, Winston Churchill justified the curtailment of traditional party politics not just by reference to the natural desire to preserve the war-time comradeship but because modern problems were technical rather than ideological, calling for managerial skills rather than grand debates on principle.   These twin impulses – the determination to carry over the spirit of war to the tasks of peace and the dawning realisation of the transforming effect of science and technology on political life – were crucial in shaping Mosley's political outlook; and underlay that quest for a new form, a new political framework, in which the spirit of the trenches could find peace-time expression and in which the questions relevant to modern life could be sensibly discussed. The particular solution favoured by the young men of 1918 – a great National Party – may have been naïve, but the quest itself was not eccentric, and in its latter aspect, the search for a political framework adequate to the conditions of contemporary life, still continues.

This first attempt to create a Centre Party of ex-soldiers came to nothing, but the revolt against the old men and their shibboleths found expression in a more light-hearted, but nevertheless significant, escapade of Mosley's early political life. It was as President of the League of Youth and Social Progress that Mosley first achieved a certain notoriety. He later regretted his association with this earnest and rather comic body. ' I exuberantly exploited the youth racket,' he explained. Youth was all the rage in the decade of the 'bright young things'. A Dr Serge Voronoff was peddling his elixir for rejuvenating tired arteries with monkey glands; while the bunglings of the old men, associated with the catastrophes of war, had induced a disposition to pay at any rate lip-service to the youthful qualities of energy and idealism. In Mosley's case, though, there was a more serious motive. He instinctively aligned himself with the young against the old, with the new movement, the new idea, the new form, struggling for expression against the dead weight of the past.

' We can observe quite clearly in the world today', he said in his inaugural address to the League, 8 October 1919,

> two mentalities, two outlooks . . . which we may describe as the mind of 1914 and the mind of today. . . . And so we are driven to a re-division of our political system . . . between the type that merely desires to return as quickly as possible to the year 1914, with its little artificial life, its meanness, its stupendous selfishness, and the type that longs to march forth . . . like Crusaders, to the winning of a better world.

' Beware ', he cried, ' lest old age steal back and rob you of the reward . . . lest the old dead men with their old dead minds embalmed in the tombs of the past creep back to dominate your new age, cleansed of their mistakes in the blood of your generation.'

However, the energies of the young Crusader were soon to be concentrated on a quite different object. In November 1919 he had gone down to support Nancy Astor in the Sutton Division of Plymouth, her husband Colonel Waldorf Astor, who had won the

seat the previous year, having meanwhile been forcibly translated
to the House of Lords.* It was a sparkling campaign, with Lady
Astor characteristically vivacious, if not convincing, in her oratory.
'What have the Conservatives done for the country?' one heckler
wanted to know. 'They have built the British Navy,' replied the
noble lady, who swept into Parliament with an increased majority,
the first woman M.P. ever to be elected. The attraction of Plymouth for Mosley lay less in Lady Astor's vivid personality than
in the presence of a tall, dark girl of twenty-one whom he had met
at Cliveden a little earlier in the year. She was Cynthia, second
daughter of the Foreign Secretary, Earl Curzon of Kedleston,
canvassing energetically on Nancy Astor's behalf. Mosley soon
decided to make her his bride. In love, as elsewhere, he showed
a marked preference for the swift attack. He promptly dispatched
a proposal of marriage by letter. Cynthia refused. She was uncertain of her feelings and wanted more time. But Mosley, a
persistent (and attractive) wooer, pressed his suit energetically, and
finally she gave her consent. Their engagement was announced
on 25 March 1920.

Cynthia – or Cimmie as she was known to her friends – has come
down to us as a somewhat idealised figure. Her undoubted virtues have seemed to shine forth even more strongly by comparison
with her husband's failings. Although Cynthia actively supported
Mosley in all his undertakings, developing great political courage
and considerable platform gifts, she never aroused anything like
the bitter feelings he did. Despite her devotion to the workers'
cause, she remained a figure of the Establishment, in the well-
known tradition of the warm-hearted, emotional person with an
instinctive sympathy for the underdog. Her intellectual understanding of socialism was limited, but she made up for this with an
automatic revolt against any form of injustice. The gossip columns
gushed with conventional phrases about her beauty; but photographs reveal her as handsome rather than beautiful, with prominent teeth, a square chin and a distinct tendency to stoutness.
She played an important part in Mosley's political success, especially
on the human level. Whereas 'Tom' tended to be remote and
deficient in warmth, often giving people the impression of using
them for his own ends, Cynthia was emotional, warm, transparently
sincere. She disarmed suspicion, added the human touch, smoo-
thed personal relations and, especially later in the Labour Party,
came to stand as guarantor for Mosley's own sincerity. Together
they made a very formidable political team. Their marriage was

*The plan was for her to keep the seat temporarily until he could get a Bill passed
enabling him to renounce his peerage. In fact, Nancy Astor remained in Parliament for twenty-six years and her husband was reduced to playing the politician behind the scenes.

not ideally happy, since temperamentally they seem to have been too far apart, but Cynthia adored and admired her husband without understanding him, while he, though often treating her rather cavalierly, loved her after his fashion, and idealised her after her death.

' A popular, beautiful and thoroughly modern girl' is how Cynthia Curzon was described by the popular press at the time of her engagement. Her mother was Mary Leiter, daughter of the Chicago millionaire, Levi Ziegler Leiter, whose fortune in real estate had brought a welcome relief to the heavily mortgaged Curzon properties. In the 1930s it was often suggested that Cimmie was half Jewish, but there is no evidence for this.*

In reaction to the pomp and circumstance of her father's numerous stately homes, Cimmie and her eldest sister Irene (later Baroness Ravensdale) had set up house together in a small maisonette in Mayfair. Even with an aunt nearby to keep a watchful eye, this was considered very daring, and clear proof of her modern outlook. At this period, however, she was living at her father's official residence at No. 1 Carlton House Terrace, and it was to him there that she announced her intention of getting married. Cimmie's relations with Curzon were not always easy; but on this occasion at least he played the part of the solicitous father to perfection, and with his usual addiction to detail.

[Curzon to Grace (his second wife, formerly the Hon. Mrs Alfred Duggan), 21 March 1920]

My darling Girl,
... I was seated at my desk with my boxes at 11.15 p.m. when the door opened and Cim with her eyes alight and an air of intense excitement came into my room and asked if she might speak to me about something. I said at once you have come to tell me that you are engaged – who is the lucky man? Yes she said – she had come to ask my permission to wed young Oswald Mosley M.P. – eldest son of Sir Oswald Mosley BT, a family well known to me in the old days in Derbyshire where they have or had a big place named Rolleston near Burton on Trent now advertised in Country Life as to be sold.

This young Mosley is 23 nearly 2 years older than Cim. He is M.P. for Harrow and one of the youngest members of the House where I believe he has already made something of a mark. She has met [him] in the Salisbury–Astor set since last November. He is reported to be tall, with a dark mous-

---

*According to the *Dictionary of American Biography*, Levi Leiter (1834–1904) was a descendant of James van Leiter, a Dutch Calvinist who came from Amsterdam in 1760. He made his fortune in the dry goods business and in Chicago real estate.

tache and a big nose – nice rather than good-looking.   They
first met in November last when he came down to speak at
Plymouth.   He appears to have spoken to her a little while
ago, when she, though feeling strongly drawn to him, and enjoying his society more than anyone else's did not feel that
she loved him.   Gradually this came and she is now (I am
giving her version throughout) truly in love – I asked if he was
gay or sedate.   She replied that he had started by flirting a
bit with married women but had now (at the age of 23) given
that up and was full of ambition and devoted to a political
career where every sort of prize awaited him.   I said of course
that if she had made her choice and it was a wise one no one
wd welcome it more than myself but that I thought I ought
to see him before finally giving my assent. As I am just off to
Hackwood for the day to see how things are getting on there it
cannot be today, so in the meantime I have written a line
to Lady Salisbury to ask for her report.   I have an idea that
that set looks upon the young man as rather a hero and that
he is really promising.

To tell the truth I was very much relieved that her choice
appeared on the surface to be so good a one, and the child
appeared so genuinely convinced and happy that it warmed
my heart.

I asked if he had any means.   She did not know.   As he
had a motor and a flat she thought yes!

Was he marrying her for love or was he thinking of her
money?   Oh no.   Such an idea had never crossed his mind.

They were going to have a great career together and he
was destined to climb to the very top – with her aid.   I told
her what married life . . . meant – no flying about all over the
world, rushing where she pleased – idle pleasure – in fact her
present existence – but home duties.   The same man day after
day – shaping her pleasures and duties so as to suit his, a good
deal of self-sacrifice and self-restraint. . . . Yes she said she
had weighed all this and there were going to be no flaws in
her idol, no clouds on her horizon.   So there for the moment
I leave it.   It will make life easier for all of us if it is all right,
tho' I suppose that financially it will hit me rather hard. . . .

His first enquiry proved satisfactory.

[Curzon to Grace, 22 March 1920]

. . . Lady Salisbury has given me a good account of young
Mosley who is coming to see me this evening. . . . I don't
want your congrats until you hear from me whether I find
him all right.

Later the bridegroom himself arrived for inspection.

[Curzon to Grace, 23 March 1920]

... The young man Mosley came to see me yesterday evening. ... Very young, tall, slim, dark, rather a big nose, little black moustache, rather a Jewish appearance. ... I put to him the whole case about a young man at 23 taking a young girl of 21 *for life* and all that it meant.   Was he sure of himself, of her, of both of them?   Were they prepared to go in for the big thing for a life time?   She was strong, independent, original.   Could he presume her fidelity and devotion? Could they take the rough as well as the smooth?

It turns out he is quite independent – has practically severed himself from his father who is a spendthrift and a ne'er-do-well.   The estate is in the hands of trustees who will give him £8,000–£10,000 a year straight away and he will ultimately have a clear £20,000 p.a.   He did not even know that Cim was an heiress.

Yesterday I had a satisfactory report about him from Edmund Talbot our Whip in the H of C and today Bob Cecil with whom the young man has worked came to lunch and told me he regarded him as keen, able and promising, not in the first flight, but with a good future before him.   So I have done what I could and have no alternative but to give my consent.

Modern courtship had changed from the old days.   On 25 March Curzon wrote to his wife: 'Where she goes and sleeps I have no idea. ...' Next day, however, she had reappeared, this time with the bridegroom and his mother.

[Curzon to Grace, 26 March 1920]

After I had shut up my letter to you yesterday Lady Mosley, son, and Cim came in to lunch.   The first named a tall, well-dressed rather handsome woman with greying hair and big smiling mouth.   The son also has a rather big smiling – somewhat ugly mouth.   Cim as might be expected is all for rushing everything – expects to get a trousseau, house [ ]* outfit all in a few weeks.   She wanted to dash off tomorrow for Paris without even [ ]* if she could get a room. ... I resisted this and ... suggested it would be much better to proceed more leisurely [sic] here and invite your assistance and get everything in London.   The mother backed me up. ... Cim wants a very quiet wedding of about 50 or 60 people and will not have ... a big society function.

*Word illegible in the original.

> Sometime ago the Dean of Westminster offered to marry
> any of my daughters in the Abbey.   Cim likes the idea if
> only it could be reconciled with the very small party which
> seems a little difficult.   She would greatly prefer to be married
> at Kedleston if it were not so far and the difficulty of putting
> up the . . . guests. . . . I have a new idea for Cim.   Chapel
> Royal St James's which is quite near and only holds about
> 100.   She is enchanted with the prospect.

The limitation of space in the Chapel Royal turned out to be
less of a guarantee of a quiet wedding than Cimmie had hoped
for.   Anonymity was never Lord Curzon's style.   In addition to
the select hundred inside the Chapel Royal on 11 May 1920, several
hundred more were invited to the official reception at the Foreign
Secretary's residence.   The 'very quiet' wedding had escalated
into the highlight of the season: after the gloom cast by war it was
quite like old times.   King George V and Queen Mary attended,
also King Albert and Queen Elizabeth of the Belgians, old friends
of the Curzons who had frequently stayed at Hackwood during
their war-time exile.   The Hon. Bruce Ogilvy, a Sandhurst
friend, was best man; and the ceremony was conducted by the
Reverend Edgar Sheppard, the sub-Dean of the Chapel Royal,
assisted by his son, the Reverend 'Dick' Sheppard, Vicar of
St Martin-in-the-Fields.
   The faded snapshots of 1920 still give a flavour of the Establishment world of high society into which Mosley was making his
official entrance – the portly Lord Curzon leading Cimmie down the
steps of his official residence; Cimmie herself in her dazzling wedding
dress of draped white crêpe with a long train embroidered with
lilies; seven bridesmaids, and a tearful Master Humphrey Falconer
as train-bearer; King George V doffing his top hat in acknowledg-
ment of the cheers of the crowds, twelve deep down Pall Mall;
Queen Mary in her long gown being helped out of her carriage;
society ladies with their knee-length beads, big hats and frilly long
dresses; Bonar Law arriving; Lord Winterton and Lord Robert
Cecil leaving; Lady Curzon curtseying to the King and Queen of
the Belgians; Lady Astor with her head draped with ostrich feathers;
the Duke of Rutland in conversation with the American Ambassador; finally, after it was all over, the select house-party standing
on the steps in front of Hackwood House.   One thinks of the other
photographs – the Blackshirt parades in the 1930s, the squalid
brawls in the Ridley Road in the early 1960s – and it is almost
impossible to put the two together, the two sets of people, the two
sets of circumstances, linked only by the enigmatic personality of
the bridegroom.   Could one imagine any of these stately people
donning a black shirt, being involved in a 'punch-up' with the

' Reds '? Could one imagine the bridegroom himself, elegant to the fingertips in morning coat, top hat, gloves and walking-stick, playing the part of Mussolini? Perhaps the words ' playing a part ' give us a clue. Of all the people present, Mosley alone looks rather unreal, as though he had just stepped onto a stage, turned-up moustaches carefully stuck on, face frozen into a somewhat Mephistophelian grin – Little Red Riding Hood and the Big, Bad Wolf . . . a trick of photography no doubt, yet suggestive of a hitherto barely explored versatility.

The presents were scarcely less imposing than the company. The bride was showered with pearls, diamonds, chinchillas and sables. Oswald gave Cynthia a diamond tiara, a silver wristwatch, a diamond brooch and a sapphire ring. She gave him a set of pearl studs and pin and a golden wristwatch. ' This will surely set the trend for wedding gifts,' foolishly gushed one society columnist. Some volumes of Milton's *Poems* from Lloyd George, Lamb's *Essays* from Godfrey Locker-Lampson, and a bookstand from Lord Robert Cecil hardly seemed to redress the balance in favour of the mind. A brief interlude at Hackwood, and then the couple were off on their honeymoon to Portofino, staying in an old castle perched on a hill in the middle of the bay. London slowly recovered. The beginning of the opera season, the commencement of a run of French plays at the Aldwych, and Lady Cynthia's wedding – what a week it had been!

The years following the war were Dionysian times for that small circle which had the taste and money for it. ' Self-realisation was the aim,' writes Mosley's friend Bob Boothby. Mosley himself recalls: ' We rushed towards life with arms outstretched to embrace the sunshine, and even the darkness, the light and shade which is the essence of existence, every varied enchantment of a glittering, wonderful world; a life rush to be consummated.'[11] The Mosleys were among the Beautiful People of that select circle and they enjoyed themselves in the appropriate style. Ascot, Goodwood, the Eton and Harrow match, Deauville, moonlight bathing in Venice, hunting and polo, great charity balls at Lansdowne House, Chesterfield House and Claridges, West End nightspots till the small hours, and of course the weekend country-house parties – this was the pattern of their social life, faithfully recorded in the issues of *Tatler*, *Lady* and the periodicals devoted to such happenings. Cimmie was described in these early years as ' the personification of the society girl, tall, willowy, with a slightly bored expression, lovely complexion, and expressive blue eyes. She dresses in the most exquisite taste, and is a fine set-off to her handsome husband in whose company she almost invariably appears.' And, as for the night-life of the Member for Harrow, one correspondent noted: ' As he jazzes round the room with his beautiful wife . . . his face is invariably wreathed in smiles.'

A town house of the Queen Anne period was acquired in Smith Square, a few minutes' walk from Parliament and just opposite Transport House; or more accurately two houses which were knocked into one, with a magnificent panelled drawing-room, dominated by a Chirico, running the length of both houses. Cimmie's old Nanny was installed in time for the birth of their first child, Vivien, in 1921 (Queen Elizabeth of Belgium was the god-mother, Lord Robert Cecil the godfather). Nicholas was born two years later. (There is a snap taken about this time showing a rather grim-faced Nanny in broad black hat, Cynthia covered in furs, and Oswald in morning coat, top-hat and rolled umbrella, walking their first baby in the Park.) For country houses they had two at Guildford and Ifield, Sussex, till they bought an old Tudor manor at Denham just outside London in 1926.

' The summits of private happiness were balanced by the heights of public acclaim.' So wrote Mosley many years afterwards. His enormous vitality was able to encompass the two completely sepa-rate lives of the hard-working M.P. and the society *beau*. Many who subscribed to the Puritan doctrine that work is incompatible with pleasure found it difficult to believe that he was serious. ' Is it true that he is a future Prime Minister of England?' asked *Tatler* somewhat dubiously in 1921 after recording yet another appearance on the polo field.

If an image of frivolity was one legacy of the Mosleys' enchanted existence, another which was to be significant when he joined the Labour Party was a deep suspicion of his motives. People are generally very crude about human motivation. Someone like Mosley, they reasoned, had everything he wanted in the way of wealth, social position and political prospects. The ' class betrayal ' with which the Conservatives later credited him must therefore be due to inordinate ambition, to a belief that he could get on faster in a proletarian world which he could dazzle with his wealth and title. On the Labour side, many felt that a rich socialist could not be sincere in his dedication to the workers' cause. Mosley thus developed a reputation of being a mere adventurer. Few consi-dered the possibility that the bright young thing had another side, a desperate earnestness, a recurring nightmare of carnage, a deepen-ing sense of betrayal, that would take more than pleasure to expiate.

With his father-in-law Mosley never got onto close terms. At first both his ' in-laws ' tried to curb his political eccentricities. ' What a fool Tom Mosley is making of himself! If he goes on you should talk to him,' wrote Grace to Curzon on 9 November 1920 soon after he ' crossed the floor ' over the Irish question. But Mosley was determined to make his own career in his own way. Besides there was little to attract him politically to George Nathaniel Curzon, an eighteenth-century autocrat cast in the imperialist mould, disdainful of the League of Nations and profoundly un-interested in Europe. Relations between the two were hardly improved by Mosley's habit of mischievously attacking him in parliamentary debate. Yet the careers of the two men had some obvious parallels.

> How came it that a man who had been given such talents and opportunities, who was inspired by such high ambition, such dogged energy, such burning faith, should have missed the main object of his ambitions, should have been worsted in the struggle by lesser minds, should have failed, ultimately, to make good?

The question Harold Nicolson asks about Curzon might apply equally to his son-in-law.

Differences of temperament and outlook were reinforced by a bitter family quarrel over money. On Curzon's marriage to Mary Leiter in 1895, her father Levi Leiter had settled one million dollars on any children who might result from the marriage. Cynthia's share of all this eventually amounted to about £150,000, or an income of about £9000 a year. In addition, she had been left a little ' nest egg ' of £20,000 by her grandmother. Curzon, who had little money of his own, relied heavily on the incomes which he accepted on behalf of his daughters while they were still in their minority to pay for his regal style of life. ' In a rush of gratitude for his willingness [to agree to their marriage], Cynthia told Curzon that (unlike her eldest sister) she would not insist on taking her allowance away from her father, but would be satisfied with the provision of a substantial marriage settlement.'[12] Why did she change her mind? Curzon himself certainly thought Mosley had something to do with it. On 21 September 1921 he complained to Grace of having received an ' extraordinarily offensive letter from Cim ' claiming more of her inheritance. (In this letter Cimmie had described her father's attitude as ' mean, petty, unwarrantable, unaccountable, and incomprehensible '.) According to Humbert, Curzon's solicitor, Mosley had lost a great deal of money in starting a political newspaper which failed (see below, page 113) and had other bad debts. They had paid £8000 for their house in Guildford.[13] The likeliest explanation for Cynthia's urgent demands to her father is that Mosley was at that time having difficulties with the settlement of his own estate and turned to Cimmie to help him out. Whatever the reason, these money squabbles led to an estrangement between Curzon and his daughter and son-in-law which lasted till Curzon's own death in 1925.

In Cimmie, however, Mosley from the beginning found a wonderful partner. Appearing in the Harrow constituency early in July 1920 to receive a collectively subscribed wedding gift of table silver,

she charmed the crowd with her brief speech of thanks.   A. K. Carlyon, the Constituency President, wrote to Mosley: ' She did it perfectly.   Saying just the right thing in the right way, she *gripped*, as
one of her hearers put it to me afterwards – the heart of her audience
at once.'[14] ' Her victory was greater than her husband's at the polls
18 months ago,' the *Harrow Observer* gallantly remarked.   Thereafter
she was indefatigable in support of Mosley's political career.   The
goodwill she built up in the constituency was presently to be of some
importance as her husband's movement to the Left brought him
into collision with the Harrow Unionist Association.

Chapter 5

'Still the Swine Won't Talk'

MOSLEY HAD arrived at Westminster with a jumble of aspirations, most of them entirely worthy, but with little idea of how to achieve them. He wanted to build a ' land fit for heroes ' – but where was the money to come from? Certainly not from those who were clamouring for a ' return to normalcy '. He was determined to save a fresh generation from being wiped out as his own had been. But how to achieve it? The coalition, for all the brilliance of its leaders, was soon revealed as a cesspit of cynicism and profiteering. Mosley turned away in disgust from the corrupt brilliance of Lloyd George to the purer, if less dazzling, flame of Lord Robert Cecil – one of those genuinely high-minded Tory aristocrats who have done so much through the centuries to preserve England from revolution. If his moralism seemed to verge on holiness (to one journalist he suggested someone ' fed on morning prayers instead of bacon and eggs ') his passionate, non-doctrinaire idealism was perfectly attuned to the mood of an aristocratic ex-officer, radicalised by the war. Moreover, Lord Robert was a man with a cause. His cause was the League of Nations. From the ruins of the old balance-of-power diplomacy would arise a noble edifice to preserve the world from the horrors of a fresh holocaust. To that cause he devoted his life.

Cecil's importance in our story is that he profoundly and permanently influenced Mosley's approach to foreign affairs. He captured him on the rebound from Armageddon and instilled into him a permanent dislike of the alliance system which, in Cecil's view, had produced it. In place of the old balance-of-power diplomacy Lord Robert offered a vision of an international organisation to keep the peace. For some years Mosley made Cecil's cause his own, vigorously championing the League at public meetings up and down the country, and serving on the Executive of the League of Nations Union.* ' There must ', he told his Harrow electors, ' be

*The Minutes of the League of Nations Union (membership 100,000 in 1921) mention Mosley only twice. On 16 June 1921 he ' promised to approach Lord Lonsdale, the Lord Lieutenant of Cumberland in regard to his accepting the Chairmanship of the Cumberland appeal '. On 20 July 1922 he promised to put a question in the House on the composition of the Government's delegation to the League of Nations. Apart from making numerous speeches on behalf of the Union, Mosley's one prominent public intervention in its affairs was at its annual general meeting in 1923 when he clashed with the chairman, Professor

no entangling alliances which inevitably evoke opposition combinations and a return to the balance of power with its division of
Europe into armed camps awaiting their opportunity for attack.'[1]

Nevertheless, there was a vital difference between the Mosley
and Cecil approach to the League. For Mosley the League meant
a concentration of power and the willingness to use power to settle
international problems; it was akin to Shaw's vision of a union of
Higher Powers to keep the unruly lower ones under control.[2] For
Cecil it represented essentially a forum of moral opinion. Cecil's
view was in a sense more realistic as he recognised that no nations
would give up power to the League, but it was part of the dangerous
illusion that speeches at Geneva, unbacked by power, could keep
the peace; an illusion which Mosley, even at his rawest, never
shared. Cecil's position at bottom assumed a harmony of interests
which it needed only ' good sense ' to bring into play; whereas
Mosley held the view that progress and order depend on power,
its availability and constant exercise, and that if the League was
ever to mean anything it must be equipped with power – a difference,
as he would have put it, between the nineteenth century and the
twentieth century mind.

The clash between these two views came to a head when in retalia-
tion for the murder of a couple of Italian officers Mussolini shelled
and occupied the Greek island of Corfu at the end of August 1923.
Mosley wanted to invoke Article 16 of the Covenant which provided
for economic and military sanctions against the aggressor. Cecil, as
the British Government's representative at Geneva, was content to
establish the League's ' competence ' and ' moral authority '. So
the Council duly affirmed its ' competence ' to intervene, while the
Great Powers settled the matter behind its back, giving Mussolini
a diplomatic triumph. Admittedly this latter manœuvre was not
Cecil's fault, but Mosley clearly perceived, what Cecil did not,
that something more than ' competence ' was needed if the League
were to succeed.* What Cecil was later able to look back on as a
modest triumph, Mosley rightly saw as the effective end of the
League. ' We have purchased peace at the price of mortgaging
our future,' he declared. No great nation in the inter-war years
was prepared to hold its power on lease from the Assembly at Geneva,
and once Mosley appreciated this harsh fact he ceased to hitch his

---

Gilbert Murray. Mosley had proposed amendments condemning the Government for not using the League machinery over the Ruhr and for building up a
naval base at Singapore. Gilbert Murray objected to any reference to the
Government on the grounds that the League was a ' non-party ' organisation.
Mosley's first amendment was accepted in modified form, his second was dropped
through lack of time. (*Manchester Guardian*, 20 July 1923.)

*According to Mosley, Cecil wanted to invoke Article 16 as well, but was
dissuaded by Baldwin. (Oswald Mosley, *My Life* (1968) pp. 141–2.)

fervour for peace to that fading star, unlike those whose passion for the League started to wax most ardent when it had been reduced to final impotence. Nevertheless, the Cecilian rejection of traditional Great Power diplomacy proved a permanent legacy, and no one can fully understand Mosley's foreign-policy line in the 1930s without reference to the doctrine preached so earnestly by himself and Lord Robert in 1920.

The other lesson which Cecil taught his willing pupil was the connection between a pacific foreign policy and social reform at home. Once again an old Liberal doctrine hit the raw young M.P. with all the force of a revelation. Foreign adventures drained money from domestic projects; psychologically, their function was to divert people's attention from remediable evils at home. It was in this mood that Mosley started calling for the drastic pruning of inflated government expenditure – ' this parasitical survival of the Great War ', as he put it in a letter to his constituents[3] – and for a time served on Lord Salisbury's People's Economy Union. Mosley was undoubtedly influenced by the post-war revulsion against ' squander-mania ', which under the inefficient Dr Addison's administration at the Ministry of Health meant building remarkably few houses at enormous cost (15,000 in 1920, only 80,000 in 1921). But his prime concern was always with cutting down military spending and overseas commitments in order to release funds for social improvements. ' It went to my heart to think of £100,000,000 being spent in Russia supporting a mere adventure', while the unemployed ' are trying to keep a family on 15s. a week ', he told the House of Commons in 1921. ' It is evident ', he wrote, ' that great economies can be effected by cutting adrift from all extraneous adventures and commitments, and withdrawing to the normal bounds of Empire.'[4] Here again we encounter an attitude that was to prove permanent.

Espousal of such views naturally put Mosley on the left wing of the Coalition, from which position he was exposed to the breezes wafting over from the tiny but still intellectually formidable Liberal Party which at this time occupied little more than the Opposition Front Bench. These breezes grew to gale force when the cause was Free Trade and it is hardly surprising that Mosley was swayed, if not entirely blown over, by them. Under the influence of more enlightened opinions than had been usual in the circles round ' John Bull ' or Johnny Hawker he was beginning to discover the marvellous synchronisation of the liberal system. Peace, Retrenchment and Social Reform all fitted perfectly together as in a beautifully constructed machine. As Lord Robert put it, ' the truth is that the League point of view runs through everything...'. Mosley's mind soon mastered the ' League ' point of view. Its very claim to coherence attracted his orderly mind. Within a year or so he was able to pick his way through the system as unerringly as its most accomplished masters.

Lord Robert Cecil was Mosley's first – and only – living political hero. Of him Mosley later wrote: ' He was nearly a great man, and he was certainly a good man; possibly as great a man as so good a man can be.'[5] Drawn with him into the Cecil orbit were such attractive Tory rebels as Mark Sykes, Billy Ormsby-Gore, Aubrey Herbert and Lord Henry Cavendish Bentinck. Aubrey Herbert, ' half blind and wholly eccentric ' as Robert Boothby dubbed him, had been offered the Crown of Albania and would come to Parliament escorted by two Albanian retainers armed with daggers. Lord Henry Bentinck, descendant of the famous Lord George Bentinck of ' Young England ' fame, came from a tradition of Tory rebels. Was Mosley destined to be his Disraeli? The question suddenly came to be asked when, in a dramatic move, both of them ' crossed the floor ' of the House on 3 November 1920.

For some months previously Mosley's ' Cecilian ' line in foreign policy had been bringing him into collision with the Coalition. He strongly criticised Lloyd George's reliance on the Supreme War Council instead of on the League. In July 1920 he condemned the British–Australian annexation of the former German Pacific colony of Nauru Island as contrary to the Covenant. The British attempt to keep the island's phosphate deposits for their own exclusive use recalled the ' worst days of predatory imperialism '; it was the action of ' sophistical hucksters who still meet in the secret councils of Europe '.[6] A day before he crossed the floor of the House he had been involved in a violent scene at the Cambridge Union when he attacked General Dyer in a debate on Indian constitutional reform. The General's action the previous year in mowing down 379 unarmed civilians at Amritsar (for which he was put on half pay) was described by Mosley as an example of ' Prussian frightfulness ' inspired by racism. The Indian undergraduates applauded lustily, but it was too much for the whites who started a furious opposition which continued for weeks in the undergraduate press. Not for the first or last time Mosley's manner and remarks touched a raw nerve.

The storm at Cambridge was a brief foretaste of what he would encounter in the House of Commons in the coming months. The vigour of his denunciation of General Dyer had undoubtedly been influenced by the revelation of ' Prussian frightfulness ' being practised much nearer home. That autumn, a neighbour of the Curzons had brought him evidence of torture being used by the British Military in Ireland. ' Still the swine won't talk ' were the words reported to him. With mounting disgust he realised that these tactics were actually being condoned by the Government in an effort to bring the Irish rebellion to an end. The Army, with whose honour he strongly identified, was being used by a cowardly government for despicable ends. Here was a cause for a humane and gallant aristocrat! Eagerly Mosley plunged into the fray.

The background to the Irish troubles can be briefly told. The seventy-three Sinn Fein M.P.s elected to Westminster in 1918 had constituted themselves a separate parliament and declared Ireland a republic. Soon afterwards the Irish Republican Army (I.R.A.) had been organised by Michael Collins to gain independence from the British by force. For a year the British did nothing as the Sinn Fein Government and the I.R.A. between them took control of much of the country, the Dublin Castle régime being gravely undermined by the boycott and intimidation of the Irish police (the Royal Irish Constabulary) whose members resigned in large numbers. Not till the spring of 1920 did Lloyd George, under pressure from the Conservatives, decide to reconquer Ireland by force. The method adopted was not to wage open war, which would have been unpopular and probably impracticable, but to counter terror with terror. Whether this was a conscious decision taken in advance, or whether the Government drifted into it because it could think of nothing better, has been debated to this day. The likely answer is that the Government condoned rather than sanctioned the actions taken in its name.

The undeclared war opened on the fourth anniversary of the Easter Rebellion of 1916 when the I.R.A. raided the income tax offices in Dublin, destroying the Government's tax-collecting machinery, and burnt 315 R.I.C. barracks. The British Government's riposte was to recruit unemployed English ex-servicemen for duty with the Irish police. These became known as the Black and Tans from their uniform. (Since there were not enough R.I.C. uniforms to go round, they dressed in surplus khaki with black belts and dark green caps.) In addition the Government recruited a mobile corps of Auxiliaries – mainly ex-officers of the gentleman-adventurer, Freikorps type. Many of the ' reprisals ' loosely attributed to the Black and Tans were the work of this group, whose habit of charging round wildly in open lorries brought them many casualties.

Ireland provides one of the first examples of the modern guerilla war. It is a war in which conventional military operations are ruled out by the nature and tactics of the guerillas who, indistinguishable from the civilian population, strike in small groups where least expected: the unseen enemy before whom the morale and discipline of even the most seasoned troops break down. It is a war without morality. On the one side are dedicated fanatics who believe that the end justifies any means, however vile. On the other side one finds a much smaller group of idealists with the same philosophy, plus a larger group of adventurers, often organised into

' special ' forces, who will only accept risks which ordinary troops reject by being given licence to murder and wreak vengeance. Torture of prisoners to get information and murder of ' loyalists ' become primary instruments of warfare; and that side succeeds which can in the end fool, bribe, inspire or terrorise the anguished population more successfully than the other.

It is not surprising that two aristocrats should have taken it upon their shoulders to uphold the cause of ' honourable ' warfare and to protest against the murder of women and children in the name of a knightly code of war. Nor was Mosley's protest confined to the victims of the Black and Tans. When the Irish peace settlement was made he condemned as criminal Lloyd George's refusal to give the Southern Irish Loyalists the option of evacuation with compensation prior to the withdrawal of British troops.[7] The idea of the ' proper ' way to wage war is permanent in Mosley's thought and led to repeated outbursts against atrocities. From this strain of thought, or tradition, we can trace his temperamental dislike of the political guerilla, of which the Sinn Fein ' murder gangs ', as he called them, was his first experience. For the guerilla is forced by his situation to break the rules of war, he is a creature of the underground using the weapons of the ghetto. This aristocratic distaste, not for the underdog, but for the methods of the underdog in revolt, was greatly to colour Mosley's future attitude to the Communist Party and to the East End Jews when he himself came into conflict with them.

But there was another equally significant strand in Mosley's revolt against Lloyd George's Irish policy which makes it something more than the protest of a Don Quixote against ' progress '; and that was its realism. Reprisals were not just dishonourable; they were the ' child of inefficiency '. By developing a proper Intelligence Service it should be possible to round up the ' murder gangs ' without recourse to terrorism of one's own, he told a reporter in December 1920.[8] Of course, this neatly sidestepped the question of how it was possible to get intelligence without the torture of captured prisoners – a problem which has confronted all ' counter-insurgency ' operations ever since. Reprisals were also odious because they swelled the guerilla ranks with all the maltreated innocent: here again honour and efficiency could be shown to go together. Finally, although his main onslaught was directed against the methods of warfare, he did not entirely neglect the political aspect. In the middle of 1920 before the fighting became acute he circulated a memorandum advocating what he called a ' Cuban ' solution for Ireland – complete internal independence with certain safeguards for defence and foreign policy.[9] Although Mosley never used the phrase, he firmly believed that ' freedom is the acceptance of necessity '. Britain could not hold Ireland against the wishes of its people: therefore it should give way generously, of its own free will, in advance of humiliation. As he remarked in another context: 'We are all in favour of "scuttle" in the end. The difference between us and hon. Gentlemen opposite seems to be that we advocate a policy of "scuttle" before the row begins, and they pursue a policy of "scuttle" after the row has begun.' We shall encounter the same attitude towards eastern Europe in the late 1930s.

Even granting that Mosley was partly misled by clever Sinn Fein propaganda and that the issue was not as simple as he portrayed it (at the ripe old age of twenty-four), nevertheless his assault on the policy of reprisals was by far the finest stand of his early political career. His anger at the butchery of women and children and at the use to which the Government was putting its servants blazed forth fiercely and forced the tongue into an eloquence that was the real beginning of Mosley's reputation as an orator. Moreover his parliamentary and extra-parliamentary activities had an importance which historians have not yet recognised. T. P. O'Connor, the pre-war Irish Nationalist leader, later wrote to Cimmie: ' I regard him as the man who really began the break-up of the Black and Tan savagery.'[10] It is a claim which students of this unsavoury episode will no doubt one day wish to explore.

It was on 20 October 1920 that Mosley put the first of those annoying questions to Sir Hamar Greenwood, a Canadian temperance lecturer, now Irish Chief Secretary, which in the following months were to wring some damaging admissions out of the Government. How many attacks on the lives or property of civilians had been carried out by the British authorities since January, Mosley wanted to know?[11] In the House the previous evening he had denounced the policy of reprisals in a powerful speech, the more notable, according to the *Sunday Times* of 24 October 1920, for the ' reserve, moderation and almost shyness with which he put his points '. The Government, he said, was ' confusing the right of men to defend themselves with the right to wander around the countryside, destroying the houses and the property of innocent persons, and depriving them of any possible means of earning a livelihood'. This 'promiscuous devastation of whole communities' was reminiscent of ' the pogrom of the more barbarous Slav '. ' You will not restore order in Ireland by pulling old women out of their beds and burning their houses.' The only way to break down the murder gangs ' is to catch them ... you must obtain information of their movements ... you must act upon it.'[12] Significantly he was cheered by the Opposition but jeered at by the Coalition Unionists among whom he still sat. The jeering got worse as he and other M.P.s persisted in their interrogation of the blustering Chief Secretary. ' Shut up, you old golliwog ' the hard-faced men shouted at the Liberal Lieutenant-Commander Kenworthy, a swarthy ex-pugilist. For the first, but not the last, time in his political life Mosley was finding it almost impossible to gain a hearing. Did the young Disraeli's challenge – ' The time will come when you will hear me ' – flash through his mind?

A day after the ' golliwog ' incident, on 3 November 1920, Mosley and Lord Henry Cavendish Bentinck ' crossed the floor '. The reason, Mosley explained, was that he preferred to face his critics and interrupters rather than remain amongst them. To his constituency association, who on 22 November gave him a unanimous vote of confidence, he explained that his action had ' no political significance '. In fact he was never to resume his place in the Coalition ranks; and the loyalty of the Harrow Executive was to be sorely tested in the months ahead.

From his new position among the Wee Frees, Lord Curzon's son-in-law answered the ironical jeers of his erstwhile confrères with his own brand of satire. Had the Chief Secretary devised any more efficient system for bringing the Irish assassins to justice than encouraging his subordinates to burn the houses of other people in the vicinity of the outrage, he innocently enquired?[13] On 24 November he spoke in support of Asquith's mildly phrased censure motion on the Government's Irish policy. It was an explosive parliamentary occasion. The previous Sunday twelve British officers had been murdered in cold blood in Dublin. The feeling of the House was running high against the Sinn Fein, and Greenwood exploited it in a hard-hitting speech. Everyone was getting very worked up about the so-called reprisals, he said, but no one had bothered to protest against the callous murder of over a hundred policemen since the troubles started. The Opposition had relied almost entirely on sources supplied by the I.R.A. Most of the creameries and houses which had been destroyed were centres of the I.R.A. murder gangs. The Sinn Fein was engaged in a plot to smash the British Empire. Every speech made in the Commons which did not explicitly condemn the murders was a direct encouragement to murder. The House cheered him to the echo. A few mild remarks by the Labour leader, Clynes, did nothing to dispel the effect of Greenwood's speech.

Then Mosley rose, eight days after his twenty-fourth birthday. He made no attempt to pander to the mood of the House. Taunted by the Coalitionists, he threw off his shyness and launched into a full-blooded attack on the Government. Sir Hamar Greenwood had appeared before them, he said, as the saviour and protector of the British troops in Ireland. Yet it was the gross inefficiency of his administration ' which has been largely responsible for the death of many of these gallant men '. Officers were allowed to sleep unarmed in hotels in the middle of Dublin; police and troops were allowed to drive around in open lorries. ' Overwhelming evidence ', he continued, existed that ' this policy of reprisals is a deliberate policy carried out by the Government with a deliberate purpose '. (Opposition cries of ' No ' and ' Nonsense '.) Turning on the interrupters Mosley snarled: ' The position of certain hon. Members appears to be, not to take part in a reasoned argument, but rather to howl down any hon. Member whose views are not acceptable to the Treasury bench.' Reprisals were completely ineffective. The one thing that they achieved was to give the murderers ' propaganda against this country all over the world '. Lloyd George's Government, he declared amidst mounting hostility, ' had obliterated the narrow, but very sacred line, which divides justice from indiscriminate revenge '.

> They tore into shreds the elaborate growth of centuries, that sense of justice which separates man from the animal. . . . As a consequence, we see today the government of civilisation in Ireland . . . charging wildly like a wounded bull in the arena against the first mortal object that crosses its infuriated vision, whether innocent or guilty of the injuries that afflict it.[14]

He sat down to jeers and catcalls. ' Pearls before swine,' hissed his friend Kenworthy. Liberal leaders hastened to congratulate him, Wedgwood Benn writing to Cimmie: ' I must tell you that I have just listened to one of the best speeches I have ever heard in the House.'

Despite Greenwood's parliamentary triumph, the Government's Irish policy came under increasing attack from liberal opinion: the home front started to crack before the Sinn Fein did. The Labour Party set up its own committee of enquiry into the atrocities; early in November 1920 a Peace with Ireland Council was formed with Lord Henry Bentinck as chairman and Mosley as secretary, and a galaxy of eminent supporters: Lord Bryce, Sir John Simon, Lord Buckmaster, Lord Parmoor, Hilaire Belloc, G. K. Chesterton, Leonard Woolf, J. A. Spender, Gilbert Murray, Ramsay Mac-Donald, G. D. H. Cole, Ben Tillett, Generals Gough and Maurice, and a bevy of bishops. Its purpose was to acquire and disseminate information on Irish conditions, to protest against the ' lawless policy of reprisals countenanced by the Government ' and finally to assist the victims of that policy. On 16 March 1921 it adopted an Irish Peace Policy calling for the immediate withdrawal from Ireland of the Black and Tans and the Auxiliaries; an immediate peace conference with representatives of the Sinn Fein; and a military truce.[15]

In the months that followed, the Committee acquired a mass of information on individual atrocities perpetrated by the Black and

Tans, as well as on miscarriages of justice; on the basis of this Mosley and Bentinck were able to ask damaging questions in the House and often secure the release of wrongfully imprisoned men, or investigations into outrages. On 16 March 1921 Mosley received a letter from James O'Donnell, ' H.M. Prison, Londonderry ', which started: ' May I venture to appeal to you to help me and find out why I have been here now for almost nine weeks without charge or trial.' On 22 March Mosley put a question to the Irish Chief Secretary, who replied that O'Donnell had already been released. In fact he was released two days later. ' Please accept my sincere and heartfelt thanks for getting me out of prison,' O'Donnell wrote on 9 April. Others were not so lucky. One Connor Clune was shot by drunken Auxiliaries as he was attending an annual audit of his firm in Raheen, County Clare. James Murphy and Patrick Kennedy were taken to a disused field in Clonturk Park, Dublin, old tin cans placed over their head, and shots fired at them. A Mrs Norah Healy of Cork was raped in her back yard. Drunken soldiers ' shot up ' the town of Balla in County Mayo, attacking even the local police barracks.[16]

As news of these and other ' reprisals ' began to spread, disseminated by the Peace with Ireland Council as well as directly by the Sinn Fein, protests came flooding in, especially from American politicians and leaders sensitive to the Irish vote. The burning of Cork by the Black and Tans on 11 December 1920 seemed a particularly flagrant and indefensible action. Although he loudly claimed to have ' murder by the throat ', in face of this pressure Lloyd George began to look for a way out. In December 1920 he sent Archbishop Clune of Perth, Australia, as an unofficial emissary to Arthur Griffith, acting president of Sinn Fein. But his efforts to make a truce were frustrated by his Conservative colleagues and also by Sir Henry Wilson, the Chief of the Imperial General Staff, who assured him that the war could be won.

Meanwhile in the Commons the questioning went on. A key point at issue was the nature of ' reprisals '. The Government always maintained that such reprisals as had taken place had no official sanction and were the hot-headed response of the troops to intolerable provocation. Mosley, as we have seen, took the view that reprisals were ' a deliberate policy carried out by the Government with a deliberate purpose ', that is, to coerce the Irish population into withdrawing support from the I.R.A. ' I know it will be quite inconceivable to hon. Members who have not devoted themselves to a very special study of the subject ', he declared in March 1921, ' that a policy of this sort should have been initiated and carried through by an English Government. It appeared equally inconceivable to myself at first.'[17] He and other Liberal and Labour Members pointed out that the *Official Summary*, a document issued from Dublin Castle and circulated to the troops, encouraged them to acts of reprisals.* Although the truth is difficult to establish, it seems clear that Mosley's version was nearer to it than Greenwood's. This is strongly suggested by a confidential report compiled for the Peace with Ireland Council by General Sir Henry Lawson, son of an Irish judge, who visited the country in December 1920:

> I must say at once that there is no doubt in my mind as to the general accuracy of the Reports of Reprisals which have reached this Country through the Press, and there can be no question whatever that this form of remedy was extensively and generally carried out, especially by the 'Black and Tans' and the 'Cadets'.
>
> Reprisals appear to have been originally commenced by the troops at Fermoy, now many months ago, when soldiers wrecked portions of the town in revenge for what had happened to some of their comrades; on that occasion and on the few subsequent ones of reprisals on the part of the Army, the cause was genuine and spontaneous ebullitions of feeling aroused in young and somewhat undisciplined soldiers. . . .
>
> It is very different however with the Black and Tans and Cadets. It probably would have been impossible had I tried to find out to what extent the policy of Collective Reprisals so widely carried out by the Black and Tans and Cadets was suggested and approved from above. That it received something more than tacit approval is obvious from many public utterances.
>
> The plan adopted was, when the I.R.A. had committed some offence, generally a killing in a locality, to burn or destroy things which would hit the Community generally in the hopes that the fear of such punishment in the future would impel the Community to make the I.R.A. desist; in fact to terrorise the District into taking the needed steps.
>
> I understand that this system of Collective Responsibility and Collective Punishment has been adopted elsewhere and has even been recommended – it has never however received publicly expressed official approval in Ireland despite its extensive practice. . . .

---

*In the debate of 23 November 1920 Asquith referred to issue no. 12 of the *Official Summary*, which had quoted 'without disapproval' instructions issued by 'one of the most blood-thirsty' of the Federal generals in the American Civil War to shoot citizens on sight, innocent or guilty, if any harm came to his troops. In the light of such revelations, the *Official Summary* was hurriedly cleaned up, and the first thirteen copies became virtually unobtainable. The Government seems to have been not above quite a little line in forgery as well, according to the *Nation and Athenaeum* of 30 April 1921.

It has further to be remembered that the instruments of this policy have had as a whole no previous experience with Ireland, probably the vast majority had never crossed the Irish Channel before, they were specially enlisted for a repressive job, and in the eyes of most of them they were engaged in a campaign against the Irish people for the suppression of acts of violence against police and soldiery. So far as one can judge they have treated the whole population on the same lines, just and unjust, landlord, shop-keeper, farmer – and their point of view seems to be that of military forces operating in an enemy country against guerilla warfare – very much like the Germans in France in 1870, and in Belgium 1914–1918.

... Though they have terrorized some regions into quiet they have done more than has happened for centuries to increase the numbers who dislike English rule. In this way – a little dreamt of way – they have served the cause of Self-Government in Ireland.[18]

Although the Government never publicly approved – or even admitted – the reprisal policy, it was in a weak position to stand up to any really determined questioner anxious to get at the truth, and in March 1921 Mosley trapped the Prime Minister in the following damaging exchange:

MR. MOSLEY asked the Prime Minister whether between the months of June and October last, inclusive, any proposals for the initiation or continuance of the policy of reprisals in Ireland were laid before the Cabinet or any section of the Cabinet; whether any such proposals were discussed; and whether any decision upon the subject was given or any form of sanction extended to such a policy?

THE PRIME MINISTER: The Irish policy of the Government was constantly under consideration by the Government during the time named in question, and has been frequently explained in Debate in the House.

MR. MOSLEY: Does the right hon. Gentleman definitely state that no official sanction whatsoever has ever been extended to the policy of reprisals? ...

THE PRIME MINISTER: Statements have been made in this House repeatedly by the Leader of the House, the Chief Secretary, and myself as to the policy of the Government, and by those statements we stand.

[Opposition laughter and cries of ' Answer ']

MR. MOSLEY: May I ask for a definite answer from the right hon. Gentleman? Has any official sanction ever been extended to the policy of reprisals? ...

[Opposition cheers]

THE PRIME MINISTER: I can add nothing to what I have said.
MR. MOSLEY: Does the right hon. Gentleman admit official sanction?
[Opposition cheers]
No answer was given.[19]

Mosley had in fact received private information about these Cabinet discussions in the summer and had framed his questions accordingly. 'As [Lloyd George] leaned on the box to reply it was observed that one of the notoriously short legs of the "goat" was swinging in front of the other like a pendulum of a clock; this peculiar movement had long been legendary among us young Tories as a sure indication that he was lying.'[20] However, Lloyd George was not often embarrassed so easily. To Lord Hugh Cecil's question: 'Why should the Government always be so afraid to speak the truth?' he delighted his supporters with a swift reply: 'And why should the Noble Lord always be so rude?'*

As Mosley developed confidence, eloquent, disdainful phrases came tripping off his tongue. On 7 March 1921 he taunted the Government with having 'denials on its lips and blood on its hands.' Of the increasingly embarrassed and conciliatory Sir Hamar Greenwood he said: 'We may be assured of the sincerity of his repentance, for no penitent is ever so sincere as he who has discovered that crime does not pay.' The Liberal *Westminster Gazette* of 9 March commented, 'Mr. Mosley speaks fierce judgments in a soft voice, but the gentleness of manner does not turn away the wrath of the Coalition.' Mosley, 'unperturbed' as he put it 'by the monosyllabic interjections of the otherwise inarticulate', kept up his attacks. 'So, in the final resort, reprisals have proved, not only an unsuccessful, but a stupid policy, and that is the thing which astonishes me more than anything else. I am not astonished to find the Government and the Prime Minister committed to a

*In fact, the question of whether Lloyd George ever authorised reprisals, like the question of whether President Nixon authorised the Watergate break-in, will probably never finally be cleared up. According to C. E. Callwell's biography of Sir Henry Wilson (*Field-Marshal Sir Henry Wilson: life and diaries*, 2 vols (1927) vol. II, p. 263), in the summer of 1920 'Sir Henry Wilson began to argue in favour of full Government authorisation of reprisals. On 29 September, for example, he talked with Lloyd George: "I pointed out that these reprisals were carried out without anyone being responsible . . . . It was the business of the Government to govern. If these men ought to be murdered, then the Government ought to murder them. Lloyd George danced at this, said no government could possibly take this responsibility."' The problem, of which Mosley took no account, arose from the impossibility of obtaining convictions and the reluctance to resort to full martial law (Churchill had advocated summary executions of terrorists by military tribunals as in Soviet Russia) for reasons of domestic and United States opinion. For the most recent revelations, see *The Whitehall Diary of Thomas Jones*, ed. Keith Middlemas, vol. III (1971).

wicked policy, but I am astonished to find them committed to a thoroughly stupid policy.'[21] As for Garvin of the *Observer* who supported Lloyd George all down the line, Mosley contemptuously referred to him as the 'musical doormat which plays "See the Conquering Hero Comes" whenever Mr. Lloyd George wipes his boots upon it'.

The Peace with Ireland Council's attempt to set up a commission to investigate reprisals on the spot had less success. The plan was to get Lord Grey to head it, but the veteran Liberal statesman refused; attempts to secure the services of other eminent persons turned out to be equally fruitless.[22] By this time (summer of 1921), in any case, Lloyd George was on the point of capitulation. On 11 July a truce was arranged; negotiations with the Sinn Fein started in the autumn; and a peace treaty was signed in December setting up an independent Ireland within the Empire, minus Ulster which remained part of Britain. Lloyd George's retreat came at the moment when the Black and Tan policy seemed finally to have paid off. When the truce was declared Michael Collins said in amazement to Sir Hamar Greenwood, 'You had us dead beat. We could not have lasted another three weeks. . . . We thought you must have gone mad.'[23] Such was the ironic, but inevitable, conclusion of a ruthless policy pursued by unruthless men.

The contrast between Mosley's position in Ireland and some of his later, less liberal, stands becomes less marked if we remember that his attack throughout was mainly directed at methods of warfare. He has always believed in 'fighting cleanly' and throughout his life his bitterest taunts have been reserved for those who have used 'un-English' methods such as in his view the British themselves were doing in Ireland. (How far he himself was able to live up to his own high standards is something we shall consider later.) An equally fundamental characteristic that emerges from the Irish episode is his belief that most crime in politics is the result not of wickedness but of weakness, muddle, inefficiency. Had the British acted efficiently they would not have *had* to become criminal. This is a view of life which recurs time and time again. Against the Black and Tans he had nothing personally. Indeed, he rather admired them as types, just as he admired the buccaneers of the air whom they resembled. What he objected to were the uses to which these men were put, which brought out all their worst, rather than their best, qualities. What might not such men achieve if they were aimed in the right direction, under the right leadership? Not surprisingly a number of former Black and Tans and Auxiliaries joined his British Union of Fascists in the 1930s. So did many Irish Catholics attracted both by his early stand and his later politics. In the B.U.F. at least they seemed to find the union that continued to escape them in their unhappy, divided country.

There is a personal epilogue to the Irish story. In December 1943 just after his release from prison, Mosley received the following letter from a solicitor in County Kerry:

> I had the pleasure of meeting you in 1921 in connection with the ' Peace with Ireland ' Council. . . . It seems a long time ago but I remember with gratitude the noble work done by your colleagues and your good self during the reign of terror of the ' Black and Tans ' in this country. The people of County Kerry who were the most to suffer appreciate it too and I can assure you that your good name will be remembered here long after those who now try and belittle you will be clean forgotten.
>
> We are neutral in the present turmoil. . . . On my own behalf and on behalf of the people of this country I ask you both to come for the duration, and leave the present controversies about your release to subside. We in this country have been called nasty names and we have experience of internment camps so we understand your position.

Mosley eventually made his home in Ireland for ten years, though not in County Kerry and not till 1952. As the one country in Europe for whom British, rather than German, oppression was the living reality the Irish not only remained neutral in the struggle between British freedom and German terror, but could not withhold their sympathy from someone who had fought with some courage to secure their own freedom from terror more than twenty years before.

Chapter 6

The Very Independent Member

THE ATTACK on reprisals formally opened the ' liberal ' phase of
Mosley's career, which lasted for about three years, during which
time he was the blue-eyed boy of the *Westminster Gazette* and the
Manchester Guardian. This is the period of Beatrice Webb's famous
diary entry which starts, ' We have made the acquaintance of the
most brilliant man in the House of Commons' and ends: ' So much
perfection argues rottenness somewhere. . . . Is there some weak spot
which will be revealed in a time of stress – exactly at the very time
when you need support – by letting you or your cause down or sweeping it out of the way.'[1] This can be regarded as prophetic:
but since all Beatrice Webb's heroes had feet of clay she was bound
to score from time to time!

Though Mosley worked closely with the Liberals, he never took
the Liberal whip. His liberal ideas came from Cecil, not from
Asquith. Besides, he was sceptical, with good reason, of the Liberals' chances of regaining power. This makes it surprising that
Liberals regarded him as a member of ' our ' party. What made
him liberal was his preoccupation with preserving peace. Liberal
foreign-policy ideas led on to liberal economics. For it could be
shown by many subtle arguments, which Mosley's mind certainly
appreciated, that free trade not only maximised prosperity but
helped the cause of peace. Thus, for the first and only time in
his life, Mosley becomes a fully fledged internationalist. His quest
for peace and prosperity never faltered: what happened subsequently
was that he lost his early faith in the efficacy of liberalism in
bringing them about.

Thus we find Mosley giving a highly orthodox explanation of
the economic crisis which in the winter of 1920–1 had thrown two
million people in England out of work:

> What is the cause of the trouble today? The cause is that
> half the world has been ruined. Half the world is not wor-
> king. Half the world is unable to buy the goods which this
> country is in a position to offer. This is the first, the pri-
> mary, the fundamental cause of unemployment today.

The remedy followed logically: ' to set to work at once upon the
business of European reconstruction . . . good Christianity . . . is
good business '.[2] This was what we may call the ' international solution ' much canvassed by perplexed British governments in the

1920s, the ingredients of which at various times included League of Nations' reconstruction loans, currency stabilisation, attempts to lower tariff barriers, and more generally to bring 'tranquillity' to the fevered parts of the world. The trouble with the international solution was that the benefits it promised were almost entirely in the future, while the measures it demanded in the present all involved economy, deflation and hence, as we now know, the creation of unemployment. Mosley did not as yet see the connection between the two, and throughout 1921 and 1922 he advocated economy with all the fervour of a Gladstone: ' Until the Treasury revert to the sound old Gladstonian position of weighing every penny of expenditure and examining with meticulous care all proposals . . . we shall not restore our finances to a proper basis,' he solemnly intoned.[3]   It was not till the end of 1923 that he began to perceive the contradiction between the doctrine of 'sound finance' and the dream of a ' land fit for heroes '. The attempt to break the stranglehold of sound finance on the high hopes of the war generation was to occupy him increasingly from that point onwards.

In the same orthodox vein, Mosley defended free trade against the protectionist heresies of the Tories. For the first time, however, we find a spark of originality in his economic presentation, which lay in his argument that fluctuating exchanges – then the fashion in Europe – made nonsense of the fixed tariff. A country could always get through a tariff barrier by currency devaluation. ' It passes the wit of man to fix a tariff barrier that is effective,' he declared on 6 June 1921. As an argument for free trade this line is very shaky. For, if the tariff was no defence against currency fluctuation, much less was free trade. Mosley's attack on the old-fashioned tariff led not back to free trade but forward to state control of foreign trade, to the Import and Commodity Board proposals of the late 1920s and early 1930s.

Although liberal ideas gripped him intellectually, politically Mosley realised that something more than the Liberal Party was needed to mount a successful opposition to the Coalition. For those opposed to the Coalition the logical thing was to try to bring together all the anti-Coalition forces – Liberals, ' patriotic ' Labour and Cecilian Tories – into partnership. Cecil himself was eager for this move, the half blind Lord Grey of Fallodon was much canvassed as a possible leader ' above party ', Henderson for Labour was at least prepared to listen. On 17 April 1921 Mosley wrote as follows to Lord Robert:

[Mosley to Cecil, 17 April 1921]

My dear Lord Robert,
    I anticipate that you are already inspired with the thought that the psychological moment for an understanding with

moderate Labour has at length arrived! They should be a very easy catch on the rebound from this debacle!* The hour lends itself entirely to our purpose and especially to the reappearance of Grey. The Government has cut a ludicrous figure and Labour should be in a peculiarly malleable frame of mind. A real opportunity presents itself for a confederation of reasonable men to advance with a definite proposal for the reorganisation of our industrial system upon a durable basis and a concurrent revision of the financial chaos. The yearning of the electorate for any escape from the present sequence of muddle and irritation might be lashed to a white heat by a timely exposure of the Irish atrocities to crown the present disgust as you indicated the other evening. I really feel we should make a great effort in the course of the next comparatively uneventful Parliamentary week to pull the whole movement together and secure a definite basis. The trouble is we are so immersed in the detail of every day existence that we lose the *a priori* mind – the only attribute in the world that matters – while we wallow through the fog of lesser events and fluctuations of transient opinion. One loses entirely the vision splendid of politics within the four walls of the H of C. It was so much easier in the past with such long intervals for dreams! . . . If we face the present situation really honestly . . . it is evident that our whole mentality and our every sympathy is fundamentally at variance with the elements consolidated under LG and whether he survives personally is really a matter of detail. There are elements in the amorphous mass of coalition that are less remote and tend to obscure the issue but generally there is no doubt that we are anathema to the bourgeois profiteer who really *is* the present Government and no true reconciliation could ever take place while that element predominates on the other side. I am convinced it lies within your power to change the whole course of the history of this decade and I think the opportunity is rapidly approaching.

Yours ever,
OEM[4]†

Underlying the theatricality and immaturity of style is Mosley's continuing preoccupation with a 'confederation of reasonable men'

---

*A reference to the collapse of the Triple Alliance on Black Friday, 15 April 1921, when the moderate leaders of the railway and transport unions (Thomas and Bevin) had refused to support the 'extremist' miners in their resistance to wage reductions, and thus averted what might have been a general strike.

†So little is the 'early' Mosley now known to British history that this letter is wrongly ascribed to Lord Grey in the British Museum file.

and his striking impatience to get it accomplished – let's 'pull the movement together' this week! Nine years later he was to embark on exactly the same attempt again, with the same impatience, but this time as a prime mover rather than as a subordinate.

Cecil did his best. He appealed to his friend Lord Cowdray the newspaper proprietor and already a heavy subscriber to the League of Nations Union for financial backing, arguing that liberalism alone could never recapture its former position.[5] He approached the liberal editors – J. A. Spender of the *Westminster Gazette*, C. P. Scott of the *Manchester Guardian*. Scott's reply was discouraging: 'a new Coalition would be the worst fighting flag for an election, for the very name has become a by-word and a reproach – thanks to the performance of the present lot. . . . So I think our Liberals and Radicals must be left to fight under their own flag.'[6] Mosley recalls a dinner party with Cecil and Henderson at his house in Smith Square: clearly it did not lead to anything. Grey himself in a speech at Berwick on 10 October 1921 appeared ready to assume the leadership of an anti-coalition front, and Cecil immediately offered to serve under him. Asquith, on the other hand, had no intention of doing so; and it was on this rock, as well as on Grey's own lack of appeal to anyone but Cecil, that these intrigues foundered. On 16 October 1921 Curzon wrote to his wife:

> Ll.G. says that Grey would like to replace Asquith and there has been a distinct plot to that effect – but that old Squith absolutely declined to budge. All these new combinations with their new leaders, whether it be Asquith . . . or Eddy Derby or Bob Cecil or Grey gradually peter out and disappear: and the little Man [Ll.G.] somehow or other survives.[7]

Mosley subsequently blamed Cecil for putting his faith in Lord Grey, 'a peculiarly tedious figure'. This comment is more than the expression of personal dislike. Lord Grey embodied that breed of English statesmen vividly described by Churchill as the 'goody-goodies.' It became Mosley's profound conviction that the desirable things in life are rarely achieved by the conventionally 'good' men, and that it is the basic failure to recognise this that has led to 'one of the greatest tragedies of our time', the divorce of the good from the dynamic.

> The English aristocracy in this period [writes Mosley in his memoirs] detested Lloyd George, who in tragic paradox was the only man who might have realised their fine ideals. . . . His faults were obvious, and so to any insight was their origin. What did they matter in comparison with his extraordinary capacity to get things done, if he were under the right influence, aimed in the right direction?[8]

The capacity to get things done: this was the important thing, not the odour of sanctity. Lloyd George had it; Mosley felt he had it. Was he thinking about himself in this passage? It is more than likely.

Mosley's increasingly severe attacks on the Coalition, both in Parliament and in his constituency, were for long treated with surprising indulgence by the Harrow Unionist Executive.[9] Mosley took full advantage of the confused state of politics of the time to stake his claim to independent thought and action. Too late the officials of the Unionist Association discovered that, in the flush of war-time victory, they had saddled themselves with a brilliant youth who not only owed no allegiance to their party but also had never admitted to any. The question was: how to extricate themselves from the dilemma? For some time they lived in the hope that as he grew older Mosley would settle down into sound conservatism. It was only when this hope faded that they decided to force the issue.

Their difficulty was compounded by a number of local factors. Mosley and his family had succeeded in entrenching themselves in the constituency in a most remarkable way. It appears that Mosley largely financed the Association and was thus able, according to the 1922 Report of the Executive Committee, ' to retain the organisation in his own hands '.[10] When the hitherto friendly *Harrow Observer* started attacking him as the ' will-o'-wisp now sitting for the Harrow Division ' and advised him to form a new ' Conservative-Liberal-Labour Association with power to add any party that might arise at any time ', Mosley riposted by buying its rival, the *Harrow Gazette*, from which he launched a heavy broadside against the ' budding Napoleons of the press world who purposely dedicate their pens to the power of evil '.[11]* Besides being active and diligent in his constituency duties, Mosley was an extremely exciting member. His platform style was already magnificent; his meetings were packed, women being especially prominent; he was always in the news; he was controversial; he was backed by a glamorous and charming wife, and a formidable mother. Nor were his personal relations with the local unionist officials at first affected by his increasingly independent political stands. Mosley was as courteous in his private intercourse as he was sharp in his public polemics. To all friendly requests for clarification of his position he reacted with equally friendly generalities and reassurances. In this atmosphere of ambiguous cordiality and mutual incomprehension the moment of rupture was put off from day to day and month to month, so that when it came both sides

---

*He sold it, however, in July 1921 to the *Harrow Observer* after it had involved him in heavy financial losses (see above, p. 91). Perhaps his habit of printing his own speeches *verbatim* contributed to its declining circulation.

had got themselves into a false position.

With the Coalition clearly breaking up in 1922 demands for a clarification of relations between Mosley and the Executive grew in volume. If the Conservative Party resumed its political independence, would Mosley be prepared to declare himself a Conservative and accept the normal obligations of party membership? A. K. Carlyon, the President of the Harrow Unionist Association, began to press Mosley for a definite reply. ' These enquiries were put to him ', Carlyon later wrote,

> in the friendliest possible way. We were all his friends and supporters anxious to avoid a split in the Party, and to retain him as our member if he would give us a chance of putting him forward as the Unionist candidate. But as time went on we found it extraordinarily difficult to bring Mr. Mosley to the point. He could never be persuaded to give a direct answer to a direct question, and developed an unrivalled skill in qualifying any written or spoken statement he could be induced to make with some loophole, by which, if convenient, he could escape from the obvious meaning of his words. This feature in his conduct became so marked both in private discussions and at meetings of the Executive that we were gradually forced to the suspicion that Mr. Mosley was merely temporising with us and that he intended at his own time and in his own way to throw over his Party in his constituency as he had already thrown it over in the House of Commons.
>
> It would be tedious to enumerate the various stages of the protracted negotiations which were carried on with Mr. Mosley through the months of March and April [1922]. Suffice it to say that on May 4th a meeting was held at Caxton Hall to which Mr. Mosley promised to come and in a short speech state definitely what his political attitude would be at the next Election. It was not a well-attended meeting, for by this time members had become weary of Mr. Mosley's windy eloquence on the subject of what he invariably called his 'well-known principles', which never brought us any nearer to the one simple question we wanted him to answer. Mr. Mosley's short speech lasted 40 minutes, during which he discussed at great length every possible label he might adopt or that it had been suggested he should adopt, and finally sat down with the declaration that he disliked labels and did not see his way to adopt any. The tired and exasperated handful of members who had sat it out, asked me when the meeting broke up to write to the Member that they could not be played with any longer and that he must now without further equivocation state in half a dozen words his attitude

at the next Election. I did so, and was answered by the usual telephone message, would I come to his house and discuss it, the usual talk about his well-known principles which had not altered, and the other time-gaining and procrastinating devices of which he is past master. But they had by this time worn very thin. I refused to meet him or discuss anything else until he sent me the document the Executive asked for. At last, by previous appointment, he came to my house on May 24 and handed me an envelope containing the much-discussed document. I opened it and read it in his presence, and at once told him I was greatly disappointed with it . . . that I was certain the Association would disapprove it, that it contained claims on his side which would make it extremely difficult, if not impossible, for us to put him forward as a Unionist candidate. I begged him to take it back or amend it before it was submitted to the Association, but he replied that he had fully made up his mind and that the terms of his manifesto were the only terms on which he could agree to enter Parliament. We discussed the document at great length in an interview which lasted nearly two hours and finally I told him that it was useless to prolong the discussion. I had given him my own opinion about it, and would now submit it to the Association for their opinion.[12]

The ' document ' which Mosley finally gave Carlyon on 24 May affirmed his willingness to accept the label of ' Progressive Conservative ' but went on:

I cannot enter Parliament unless I am free to take any action of opposition or association, irrespective of labels, that is compatible with my principles and is conducive to their success. My first consideration must always be the triumph of the causes for which I stand and in the present condition of politics, or in any situation likely to arise in the near future, such freedom of action is necessary to that end.[13]

Although the Committee had been pressing hard for a decision, it now proceeded to examine the document in the usual leisurely fashion of committees. Copies were circulated round the local associations: there was much lobbying for support. It was not till 7 July that the full Council of the Harrow Unionist Association met to decide their verdict. Mosley made a personal statement in which he offered to withdraw the ' document ' and produce a written statement of his principles and policies on the basis of which the Council should decide whether or not to support him. He then withdrew. There was considerable discussion, in which a strong pro-Mosleyite minority urged acceptance of his proposal.

The majority, seeing this – rightly – as a further delaying tactic, refused and sent Mosley the following ultimatum:

> That any candidate seeking to represent the Harrow Division at the next Election to Parliament in the Conservative and Unionist cause, must, as a condition of receiving the support of this Association, pledge himself, if the next General Election results in the formation of a National Unionist Administration, to give that administration his loyal support. In any event, as a general rule, he must follow the National Unionist whip into the Division Lobby and, if unable to do so in important matters, he must take the Association into his confidence, explain his reasons, and seek their continued support.

On 18 July, the Harrow Member sent back his disdainful reply. ' A gramophone ', he wrote, ' would be more suitable to this requirement than a human being.' Rejecting the terms Mosley announced that he intended to ' appeal for support in these great causes, both to my old friends who are still willing to continue their valued assistance and to all who are animated by similar beliefs in face of the great new issues of our times '.[14]

He was as good as his word. He had held up his reply only long enough to prepare his campaign against the Executive. He now circularised the Executive Resolution of 7 July, together with his reply of 18 July, to all 4000 members of the Harrow Unionist Association, asking those who supported him to write to him personally. It was an early example of his favourite tactic of appealing to the people over the heads of their official leaders. In a covering letter he wrote: ' All my constituents are well aware of the main principles of my policy. I have striven consistently for peace in every sphere, and for economy, both in its negative and constructive senses, as the two paramount requirements of our day.' Over 700 favourable replies were apparently received with only 33 ' definitely against '. ' I send you this information ', Mosley wrote to Carlyon, ' as I am sure that no members of the Council, while continuing to speak in the name of the Association will desire to take any action in violation of the expressed wishes of the majority of the members of the Association, to whom they are responsible.'[15] Carlyon replied testily:

> I would point out that this card canvass was a private device of your own, carried out by yourself for your own purposes, without reference to or consultation with the Association, to whom the result has no interest or value. . . . Do you really suggest that an important Unionist seat like that of Harrow should be allowed to go by default to a candidate who has thrown over his former supporters and claims absolute freedom

to associate himself with the Liberal, Labour or any other Party to which his 'principles' for the time being incline him to attach himself? The great majority of the eleven thousand Unionist electors who returned you to Parliament in 1918 as their 'Coalition Unionist' representative, are Unionist still, and few of them it may be assumed have any intention of surrendering their lifelong political convictions in favour of the changeful and unstable 'principles' of a Parliamentary freelance.[16]

Mosley's life was dominated to a degree unique in modern English politics by the passion for achievement, hence his political career resolved itself into a never-ending quest for an instrument of achievement. The idea that there was something especially meritorious in being born and dying a Conservative or a Liberal in a rapidly changing world always struck him as completely absurd. In 1922 he saw no party that he particularly wanted to join. To his constituents Mosley explained his decision to stand as an Independent in a passage that is worth quoting at some length:

Periods of temporary confusion such as the present, are recurrent in English history, and invariably follow any great upheaval which obliterates old issues and creates new problems. . . . Some people imagine that it is possible to pass through an earthquake and still to find the old familiar landmarks standing. But it is mere blindness to reality to ignore the basic fact that the world of politics, for better or for worse, is new. *The war destroyed the old party issues, and with them the old parties. . . . The party system must, of course, return in the very near future, but it will be a new Party system.* The great new issues will shortly create new Party alignments, which will truly divide the lines of men and determine their permanent associations. Then, and not before, I am prepared to form my Party allegiance. In present conditions it appears to be unnecessary and inadvisable for a politician who is not bound to existing Party machines and personalities, to adopt a label which, in the mind of the electorate, must be associated with past controversies with which he is not concerned. This consideration is especially true in the case of a young man who is necessarily concerned not with the past, but with the present, and still more with the future. My intention not to wear a label which, at present may be confused with past controversies, *does not mean that I adopt the empty independence of men who can agree with no one. . . .* I am not a freelance incapable of such cooperation, and am prepared to work immediately with men who hold similar *opinions* in face of the great new issues of our day. [Italics in original.][17]

In this passage we have the key to Mosley's success – and his failure. Everything he said about English politics was true – yet it was not the whole truth. There were new issues – but the old issues had not been obliterated. There was a new party – the Labour Party – but it was three-quarters in the nineteenth century. The old system, like King Charles II, took an unconscionably long time in dying. The young politician has grown old, yet many of the familiar landmarks remain.

The break with Harrow Unionism had now been made, but still the sluggish Executive made no haste to bestir itself to find an alternative candidate. It was not till 20 October that Major Ward-Jackson made his first appearance in Harrow. By that time the General Election was almost upon them. The previous day, the Conservative Party had decided by 187 votes to 87 at the famous Carlton Club meeting to withdraw from the Coalition. It was at this meeting that Stanley Baldwin emerged for the first time into the limelight with his denunciation of Lloyd George: 'a dynamic force is a very terrible thing'. Following Lloyd George's resignation, Bonar Law formed his government of the ' second eleven ' and immediately went to the country.

Mosley was without an organisation. But he had powerful local support. Captain Henry Miles, the Unionist agent, resigned to work for him; his supporters also succeeded in capturing the local Wealdstone Unionist Association, retaining both its building and funds for the duration of the campaign. Of decisive importance was the decision of the local Labour and Liberal parties not to run candidates against him, and that of many workers from both parties to canvass on his behalf. The financial burden of the campaign, too, was considerably eased when Mosley, on Cecil's advice, succeeded in getting £10,000 from Lord Cowdray to support a few Independent candidates standing in the election.[18]

Mosley's election address ran to 5000 words and sixteen printed pages: a complete vindication of the stands he had taken in the previous parliament, an outline of his policies for the future, in short, a one-man party manifesto. It was also liberally sprinkled with tributes from the eminent – an early example of what was to become a characteristic practice. Mosley always felt himself to be unjustly maligned, and the frequent quotation of statements praising him was his method of redressing the balance. Lord Robert Cecil came down to speak for him, and his encomium must have been the most gratifying of all:

> I have known Mr. Mosley ever since he got into Parliament and I have learned to admire and esteem him. You know

something of his qualities, you know he is an excellent speaker, you probably also know that he is a man of unfailing and unquenchable industry, and I am sure you know he is a man of the greatest ability (hear, hear). He has shown by his actions, young as he is, that he is a man of patriotism. . . . But I have deliberately left one quality of Mr. Mosley to the last and that is his courage (hear, hear). Physical courage in our country and among our kindred is not uncommon, but it is a curious thing that political courage is a much rarer virtue. In these times of great difficulty to us all a man of political courage is an invaluable asset to the state.[19]

In fact, there was little of principle that divided the two candidates. The Conservative Party's break with the Coalition had left it free to criticise Lloyd George's policy. Even before the Carlton Club Meeting, Bonar Law had repudiated Lloyd George's Middle East imbroglios with the words: ' We cannot act alone as the policeman of the world ' – a sentiment which was in complete harmony with the thrust of Mosley's own criticism. Baldwin, the new chancellor of the exchequer, had pledged himself to rigid economy. Taking his cue from his leaders, Ward-Jackson too came out in favour of peace and economy. But in general he preferred not to discuss policy: this could be left to his wordy opponent. ' I appear before you simply and solely as a life-long Conservative and a follower of . . . that great Statesman, Mr. Bonar Law.' Unlike Mosley, Ward-Jackson, it was clear, would always play his master's tune.

Mosley made a valiant effort to stick to policy. But the Harrow election was not about Mosley's policies, but about Mosley, for or against. Both he and the members of the Unionist Executive devoted considerable portions of their speeches to giving their own versions of the events which had led to the rupture, Mosley at one point referring cuttingly to the ' Tin Gods who reside on Harrow Hill ' – a sentiment calculated to appeal to the Labour and Liberal voters he was now so ardently wooing. Ward-Jackson went further. He felt, not unreasonably, that his only hope of success lay in discrediting Mosley with the Harrow electorate. He attacked his fickleness and instability: his campaign against ' our boys ' in Ireland, his disloyalty to those who had secured his election. But the climax was reached early in November.

But that is not all. My opponent also opposed the Government's Indian policy and at a meeting of the Cambridge Union on November 2 1920, he delivered a speech which, according to a correspondent of the ' New Cambridge ', was distinctly disloyal. After an attack on General Dyer, his peroration, according to a correspondent, amounted to this:

' Indian undergraduates, I address myself to you. The
English have in the past always exploited you and have now
adopted German brutality in repressing you, subjugating
you, murdering you, terrorising you. Therefore revolt,
revolt, revolt, against the Englishman who slaughters your
wives.'[20]

Mosley immediately issued a writ for libel. Ward-Jackson, though
admitting he had not read the text of Mosley's speech but had
relied on information supplied by Central Office, stood his ground,
announcing that if he were elected and lost the libel action he would
resign his seat; he challenged Mosley to do the same. Mosley
rashly accepted. The sequel, some four months later, was a
complete withdrawal and apology by Ward-Jackson, plus the
payment to Mosley of £200 for 'legal expenses'.*

Most local pundits expected Mosley to hold his seat. The size of
his majority, however – he polled 15,290 against 7868 votes, a
majority of 7422 – surprised even his most optimistic supporters.
It was a personal triumph. But it had not solved the problem of his
political future. He might be able to go on holding Harrow for ever,
but he could scarcely expect to make his mark on his time as an
eccentric Independent of mildly left-wing opinions. The election
results had to some extent clarified the confusing political situation.
The Conservatives with 345 seats had maintained their position, and
Bonar Law remained prime minister; but the most significant fact of
the election was the continued failure of the Liberals and the dramat-
ic rise in the Labour vote from $2\frac{1}{4}$ millions to $4\frac{1}{2}$ millions and the
increase in the number of Labour M.P.s from 63 to 142. The party
battle-lines were more clearly forming on a new basis of Conservative versus Labour. For conservatism the twenty-six-year-old
Mosley had little time: Labour was becoming the only logical
alternative.

Back in Parliament he was soon severed from his old political
mentor, Lord Robert Cecil. Cecil, too, had drawn his conclusions
from the failure of the Liberal Party, and on Bonar Law's retirement
in April 1923 accepted office from Baldwin as Lord Privy Seal,

*Mosley gives the following account of the events that led to the withdrawal
of the libel suit: 'some weeks [after the election] my Conservative opponent
sent in his card to see me at the House of Commons. . . . He told me that the
Conservative Central Office had supplied him with his account of my speech as
the actual words I had used, but on subsequent enquiry he had discovered that
I had said nothing of the kind and he was now advised by his experienced solicitors that he risked damages so large that he would be a ruined man. On
enquiry at the Central Office he had been told he must look after himself. I
was sorry for him and allowed him to escape with a public apology and payment
of a modest sum to a local charity.' (*My Life*, p. 163.)

with special responsibilities for the League of Nations.   He invited Mosley to accompany him ' into some post in that administration ',[21] but perhaps Mosley already realised that his future lay with Labour.   He declined the offer, and chaffed his former patron with the impossibility of having ' one foot in the Bastille and one in the League '.[22]   The Liberals also wooed him with ardour, and apparently with some success, for Asquith in a letter of 29 May 1923 refers to ' a really brilliant speech from Tom Mosley, who is one of our best recruits '.[23]   But, despite agreeable weekends at the Wharf, Mosley refused the Liberal bait.   For the time being he was content to remain, in Attlee's words, ' the very independent Member for Harrow '.[24]

The break with Cecil had not changed his interests, his attacks on foreign entanglements losing nothing of their pith or fervour. Early in 1923 the House retrospectively debated the Chanak crisis which had brought Britain to the point of war with Turkey the previous September.   By the Treaty of Sèvres of 1920 Britain and France had declared the ' internationalisation ' of the Straits of Constantinople, and it was the British force guarding the Straits that Kemal Ataturk, the Turkish leader, encountered at Chanak in his victorious advance of September 1922.   War was only averted when General Harington refused to communicate to the Turks the ultimatum calling on them to withdraw decided in London. Mosley ridiculed the whole argument for internationalising the Straits in a striking passage which would have borne repeating at the time of the Suez crisis in 1956:

> What is this freedom of the Straits?   I shall be happy if the hon. Gentleman can justify this part of the policy which was responsible for these Estimates.   I believe the ' freedom of the Straits ' to be an entirely meaningless phrase – one of those many meaningless phrases with which eminent statesmen delight in deluding themselves and the public.   In times of peace the Straits were always free.   In time of war they will always be at the mercy of the strongest army in their immediate vicinity. . . . Paper guarantees can be rendered entirely worthless – not worth the paper they are written on – and yet for this so-called freedom of the Straits, which has not been achieved by our diplomacy, which cannot be achieved except under impossible conditions, the Government were . . . ready to plunge mankind back into the holocaust of war.

' The freedom of the Straits ', Mosley concluded, ' is of no more interest or importance to this country than the freedom of the canals in the moon.'[25]

Once more the argument for non-intervention in the Middle East is linked to domestic needs.   The emotion and reasoning behind this are well brought out in the following passage:

> What are we to think of the myopic vision of statesmen
> whose eyes . . . are not open to the seething miseries of their
> cities, but are fixed upon the spectacle of Eastern deserts?
> It may be a pleasant pastime for a well-educated man to
> educate the Arabs in the art of government, but the pastime
> is purchased at the expense of the continued ignorance of his
> fellow-countrymen in the art of life. It is all very well to
> elaborate these grandiose schemes of Imperial domain . . .
> but these schemes are founded upon the degradation of
> Englishmen. They show but scant sympathy with those who
> in these harsh times have to live with starvation, who are fami-
> liar with sorrow and anguish. Far remote, I fear, are the
> thoughts of statesmen who go forward with such proposals,
> who resist with such indignation any suggestion of withdrawal
> from these far-flung territories and refuse to devote our re-
> maining resources to the maintenance of a proper standard of
> life among our own people. After all, the alternatives in this
> matter are very clear. You may have some disorder, you may
> have some suffering, you may even have bloodshed in Iraq,
> but if we have to choose between two evils, it is better to risk
> disorder in Iraq than in a city like Manchester, and if you go on
> squandering the resources of this country and burdening
> industry with these colossal commitments, you are running
> some risk, if not a great risk, of a collapse of the finances of this
> country, bringing in its train infinite suffering and despair
> to millions of our fellow men.[26]

Not that Mosley thought Britain was in Iraq for purely altruistic,
law-keeping reasons. Behind the rhetoric of bringing good government to primitive peoples he discerned the sinister scramble for oil.
' If we go to war in the Near East,' he warned, ' it is a commercial war and nothing else . . . the world will again be plunged
back into an immense catastrophe for commercial, money-
collecting reasons.'[27] Already he was beginning to see the unchecked operations of international finance as a potent source of
conflict.

The French occupation of the Ruhr, in January 1923, following
a German default on reparation payments, gave Mosley a further
opportunity to elaborate his views. He still put his faith in League
intervention (moral and financial) to bring France to heel, but
with a significant addition. If the League policy failed, Britain
should withdraw into ' complete isolation '. Above all else, we
must not get involved in another Franco-German war.

> Statesmanship should lay down in advance, and be careful to
> observe, one fundamental maxim, that not another drop of

British blood is to be spent in the European quarrel. We should proceed thus far and stop short of any appeal to arms. I think it is a fact – unpalatable it may be, but none the less a fact – that the generation which bore the brunt of the last war has had enough of war. I do not think they are going to lift another finger to cleanse the Augean stables of European diplomacy. I do not believe they will consent to the pouring of another drop of British blood down the gaping drains of its seething animosities, its racial hatreds, its atavistic prejudices. I do not believe they would consent to any such course. I do not believe that generation would fight again except in defence of their own homes, and I think it is perfectly useless for any Government in this country to appeal for an armed intervention in European affairs. Before we come to that point we must pursue the policy of withdrawal and isolation. In such a position ... we should suffer the loss of our trade, but we should preserve from loss precious lives, too many of which we have already sacrificed.[28]

This theme was to be consistently pursued in the 1930s. In the 1920s many liberal heads nodded in agreement, but ten years later a new generation had arisen for whom the war was ' old hat ' and for whom the evils of Nazism were starting to outweigh the evils of sacrificing precious British lives.

Mosley's early speeches on foreign policy introduce most of the themes he was to develop and elaborate in subsequent years. Britain should avoid all foreign entanglements. She should go to war only if she herself were attacked. All other disputes should be settled by an effective League of Nations. If the League could not be made effective Britain should pursue a policy of ' complete isolation '. It was a simple and attractive policy – too simple and attractive for the real world. It ignored the existence of empire. Should Britain defend India? If the answer was ' no ', Britain should clearly give India immediate independence. Mosley did not advocate this. He also ignored the extent to which British involvement in the Middle East was dictated by the Indian connection; and the ' scramble for oil ' by strategic necessity. Again, the option of complete diplomatic isolation might be attractive to a country like the United States, economically self-sufficient and protected by huge expanses of ocean. But no country as dependent on world conditions as Britain was for its security and livelihood could afford to ignore what went on outside in quite the cavalier way Mosley was advocating. The truth is that the violence of Mosley's recoil from the war-time slaughter had landed him in an untenable position. He came to recognise this in time. The concept of isolation was never to be abandoned. In fact it remained at the centre of all Mosley's thinking. But it was to be broadened and deepened in time to embrace the idea of a group of nations, extracted from the ' chaos ' of world conditions, building within itself ' the highest civilisation the world has ever seen '.

Mosley's polemics, delivered with a new poise and wit, were starting to captivate a House of Commons from which most of the ' hard-faced ' men had by now departed. Sympathising with Lord Robert Cecil, who had been reproached with a lack of firmness in his utterances at Geneva, Mosley asked, ' How is it possible to express a perpetual wobble in firm language? . . . His foundation is the British Cabinet and their policy. You might as well ask him to build a pyramid on a jellyfish.' In equally vivid language he attacked what he considered to be the prime failing of contemporary British statesmanship. ' There is nothing in the world so detrimental to national prestige as being full of bluff and bluster until you get into difficulties and then having to climb down. It is possible to walk down stairs of one's own free will with grace and dignity. It is impossible to be kicked downstairs either with grace or dignity.' For one of the rare intervals in his life he basked in the approbation of the Press. The *Sunday Express* compared him to the young Churchill; he reminded the *Morning Post* of the ' young Disraeli before he had got his bearing '; while the *Westminster Gazette* remarked, ' Although only in his 27th year, Mr. Mosley is spoken of by old and skilled Parliamentary hands as composed of the stuff of which Prime Ministers are made.'[29] A speech on the French occupation of the Ruhr[30] brought a warm note from Sir John Simon (2 August 1923): ' May a great admirer express his great admiration. Your speech was really splendid and said in the best language just what a real Liberal feels.' Thirteen years later, as Home Secretary, Simon was an admirer no longer.

Mosley's brilliant interventions on foreign affairs had attracted the attention of the Labour Party leader, Ramsay MacDonald, and a warm relationship had developed between MacDonald and the Mosleys. A rather cloying effusion survives from MacDonald to Cynthia dated 17 August 1923:

Thank you very much for your letter inviting me to stay with you in Venice when I am passing through. Sidney Arnold is with me and the two of us would I am sure be too big a handful for you. But in any event let us have a feast together. We shall not get to Venice, however, till the *end* of September, the newspapers as usual being wrong. Will you still be there? We shall be but a day and half. Is that barbaric vandalism?

I hope the little person, who I saw had come to smile on you both, gives you much happiness. My young folks – alas! not all young now exactly, run wild with me here.

I hope your husband is having some real holiday. He is filling a difficult position gloriously well. He is one of the redeemers of that dear old place.

But Mosley's now inevitable alignment with Labour was to be delayed a few months more. Baldwin's sudden dissolution on 13 November 1923 to seek a mandate for Protection as a cure for un-employment gave Mosley his third and last fight at Harrow. As a Labour candidate he would stand no chance, and so he was obliged to retain his ' independence ' a little longer. This time the Conservatives put up against him Hugh Morris, a thirty-year-old ex-President of the Cambridge Union. There was none of the bitterness of the previous campaign. It was as if the re-emergence from its mothballs of the great issue of Free Trade versus Protection had banished all meaner thoughts. Mosley was supported by Harold Laski of the London School of Economics (not yet become the ' little Jewish professor ' of the 1930s), while Hugh Morris brought down Leo Amery, dismissed by Mosley as ' that busy but ineffective drummer-boy in the Jingo brass-band '.

Mosley's speeches in defence of free trade, packed with facts and figures, were approvingly noted by the liberal and left-wing press. But onto them he added two arguments which his audiences were to hear a great deal more of in the future. ' Almost alone among candidates', noted the *Sunday Express* of 25 November 1923, ' he points out that the insanely exaggerated deflationist policy of the Cunliffe Committee is one of the principal causes of unemploy-ment.' Already, then, he has started to read Keynes. Keynes's influence, too, may be seen behind his advocacy of a big programme of public works.[31] The elaboration of these themes was to occupy him for the rest of the decade.

Mosley held Harrow on 6 December 1923 with a reduced majority of 4646 (he received 14,079 votes, his opponent 9433). This decrease, despite the Labour and Liberal current running through the country, was attributed by local observers ' to the fact that a large number of traditional Conservatives . . . who remained faith-ful to Mr. Mosley on personal grounds last year, returned . . . to party alignments '.[32]

Baldwin's gamble had failed. The electorate rejected Protec-tion and the Conservatives lost almost a hundred seats. (They were down from 345 to 258.) The Liberals, reunited under Free Trade, had come back with 159, but once more the real gainers were the Labour Party, up to 191. Having just fought a free-trade election, Asquith refused to put Baldwin back into office to keep out Labour, and so on 18 January 1924 Ramsay MacDonald became the first Labour Prime Minister.

Mosley's speech in the Debate on the Address found him at the top of his form. From the Conservative benches, he said, had been heard ' the loud lamentations of panic-stricken plutocracy'. They had tried to ' dress up the Red bogey' by suggesting that ' behind Labour Members who make statesmanlike speeches there are great masses of subversive and bloodthirsty savages. . . . It is time that honourable Gentlemen opposite realised that any Government formed in this country will be composed of British men and women.' Baldwin's policy had been one of ' drift buoyed up by drivel' replete with ' little sanctimonious sermons about his duty, his admirable intentions, the policy that was always about to be initiated '. ' Tonight ', Mosley concluded, ' the army of progress has struck its tents and is on the move.'[33]

Would he join it? In April of the previous year he had expressed some of his doubts about Labour:

> These men are worthy of every respect. . . . I do wish, however, that they would abandon, at any rate for the time being, their habit of discussing ultimate issues and advance in a concrete and concise form an immediate programme to deal with immediate issues.[34]

No doubt there was also a reluctance to attach himself to a party which had not yet shown it could win power. If the first doubt remained, the second had been conclusively dispelled. On 27 March 1924, Mosley formally applied for membership of the Labour Party. From Margot Asquith in Paris came an anguished letter of reproach:

7 April 1924

Dear Tom,
    I am too fond of you and Cimmy to let you leave our Party without a line of regret. Personally I think you have done an unwise thing at a foolish time, but after all this is your own affair and not mine. You had a very great – if not *the* greatest chance in the future of leading the Liberal Party. I don't believe in changing more than once nor do I believe in Labour. You need courage and conviction to achieve anything big in politics and above all patience and a certain amount of education. Till now I have seen none of these qualities in the new Government.*

*Margot Asquith concludes the letter with the sentence ' I had a wonderful time with Mussolini who is a really Big Man ' – an interesting comment for the wife of the Liberal leader.

But Mosley had decided that his future did not lie with the increasingly exiguous Liberals. To MacDonald he wrote expansively: 'The battle array of the future is determined. You stand forth as the leader of the forces of progress in their assault upon the powers of reaction. In this grave struggle ... I ask leave to range myself beneath your standard.' MacDonald replied warmly:

My dear Mosley

Although I have welcomed you into the Party by word of mouth, I would like to tell you in writing how pleased I am that you have seen your way to join us, and to express the hope that you will find comfort in our ranks and a wide field in which you can show your usefulness.

I am very sorry to observe in some newspapers that you are being subjected to the kind of personal attack with which we are all very familiar. I know it will not disturb you in the least, and I assure you it will only make your welcome all the more hearty so far as we are concerned.

With kind regards

I am, yours very sincerely,

J. RAMSAY MACDONALD

Chapter 7

Revolution by Reason

' And then after that, mind you, he suddenly went over to Labour.'
' To Labour!' repeated the girl, mildly surprised. ' Why?'
' Vanity', answered Lady St. Aubrey succinctly. ' He thought there would be less competition.'
Amabel Williams-Ellis, The Wall of Glass (1927)

FOR YEARS this was the 'smart' view of Mosley's 'class betrayal'. It is held to this day by septuagenarian colonels of extreme right-wing disposition: ' More chance of promotion in a line regiment than in the Household Cavalry, you know.' The implication that the Conservative Party was so stocked with talent that Mosley had no chance of a successful career there was of course a pure figment of imagination of those accustomed to equate talent with support for their own particular prejudices.

In public the Labour leaders made a great fuss over their rich young recruit, showing him off round the provinces like a prize exhibit. MacDonald, the party leader, attached great importance to the adherence of aristocrats. They made Labour respectable. Like most upper-class recruits Mosley joined the Independent Labour Party, one of the affiliated organisations, and to the left of the main party. His speech to the I.L.P. Conference in April was well received and the stipulation of a year's membership before being allowed to fight a seat was specially waived in his case.* From the beginning he established excellent relations with the Clydeside leaders, Jimmy Maxton and John Wheatley. Others were less sure. ' He'll need watching, he's oot o' a bad nest,' remarked the veteran Lancashire leader Willie Stewart. With two men of his own age in the Labour Party, who later came almost to symbolise British social democracy, Mosley never got on to terms at all. They were Herbert Morrison and Hugh Dalton. They were naturally jealous of a rich recruit who entered with such a fanfare of publicity and felt that their own years of patient toil

*Mosley's speech is worth a passing mention in view of his later Europeanism. A motion calling for ' an amalgamation or federation of all the European countries ' was challenged by an amendment calling for world federation. Mosley supported the amendment as revealing ' a more thorough-going international spirit, beyond the rather narrow conception of the European confederation '. (I.L.P. Annual Report, 1924, pp. 135-6.)

in the cause had been undervalued by comparison. This was an understandable feeling which Mosley's arrogance did nothing to lessen.

The rank and file appeared to have no such reservations about their new champion. In April 1924 Egon Wertheimer, London correspondent of the German socialist newspaper *Vorwärts*, attended his first Labour Party meeting at the Empire Hall. ' Suddenly ', he writes,

> there was a movement in the crowd, and a young man, with the face of the ruling class in Great Britain, but the gait of a Douglas Fairbanks, thrust himself forward through the throng to the platform, followed by a lady in heavy, costly furs. There stood Oswald Mosley . . . a new recruit to the Socialist movement at his first London meeting. He was introduced to the audience, and even at that time, I remember, the song ' For he's a jolly good fellow', greeted the young man from two thousand throats. . . . But then came something unexpected . . . from the audience there came calls; they grew more urgent, and suddenly the elegant lady in furs got up from her seat and said a few sympathetic words. . . . 'Lady Cynthia Mosley', whispered in my ear one of the armleted stewards who stood near me, excited, and later, as though thinking he had not sufficiently impressed me, he added, ' Lord Curzon's daughter '. His whole face beamed proudly. All round the audience was still in uproar. . . .[1]

When he joined the Labour Party, Mosley made it clear that he would not fight Harrow again: he could hardly have failed to notice that the further left he moved the smaller his majority became. Besides, he wanted to win his spurs in the Labour Party by a dashing act. Offers of seats poured in from all over the country. In July Mosley made his choice. Dr Dunstan, the Labour candidate for Ladywood, Birmingham, had just been expelled from the Party in line with its decision to exclude individual communists from membership. Mosley was invited to address the Ladywood party. The bait was Neville Chamberlain, the sitting Conservative Member. Mosley had fought Chamberlain's Rent Act, removing war-time rent-controls, clause by clause through Parliament the previous year. The great Chamberlain dynasty was still unbroken in power in Birmingham. What more spectacular feat could there be than to defeat a Chamberlain in his own fortress?

And so Mosley came to Birmingham. ' It was a large and enthusiastic meeting which met at Clark Street Council Schools on Monday evening last for the purpose of adopting a Labour candidate for the Ladywood Parliamentary Division,' began the report in Birmingham's Labour weekly, the *Town Crier*. After stressing his belief in party and party unity – a necessary precaution in view of his flighty record – Mosley announced 'with calm deliberation' that ' he was in the advanced wing of the Labour Party. . . . He wanted to see progress ever more rapid, reforms ever more effective. . . . That was why Birmingham had drawn him as a magnet. . . . Pouring scorn upon the notorious Birmingham caucus whose wooden effigies of greatness had been set up like images, Mr. Mosley said it must be their business to shatter the citadel to its foundations.' ' The speech', concluded the *Town Crier*, 'roused the audience to great enthusiasm, and was greeted by volley after volley of applause. . . . The Chairman then moved a resolution proposing the adoption of Mr. Mosley as Labour candidate for the Ladywood Division, which was carried with complete unanimity.'[2]

The fight for Ladywood was on sooner than anyone expected. That summer, when MacDonald's prestige as European concilia- tor stood high, Mosley had urged the Prime Minister to appeal to the country for a proper mandate. ' No, my boy,' MacDonald replied, ' that is what Lloyd George would do, much too opportu- nist. I know a trick worth two of that; we will carry on and show them what we can do with a long spell of steady work.'[3] Now on 8 October 1924 MacDonald's minority Labour Government was voted out of office after scandal and mismanagement had wrecked its reputation and drawn the Conservatives and Liberals into tem- porary alliance. MacDonald's evasive replies over the issue of the Campbell prosecution had been the final straw and had given the Conservatives their cue to exploit the Red Bogey which they were to do with devastating effect.*

Mosley campaigned on the full I.L.P. programme of nationalising railways, mines and banks. The strongly pro-Tory Birmingham press gossiped about the Mosleys sunning themselves at Biarritz. For years this was to be the standard line of attack on the ' rich Socia- list.' Stung by this charge, Mosley dubbed Chamberlain the ' landlord's hireling' – a reference to Chamberlain's Rent Act. Chamberlain took him literally. He indignantly denied that he was in anyone's pay and called upon Mosley ' as a gentleman ' to withdraw. Mosley withdrew nothing: he never did.

Despite the *Birmingham Post*'s complacent prophecy of an in- creased Conservative majority (it had been 1554 in 1923), it soon became apparent from the enthusiasm of Labour meetings all over

---

*The attorney-general, Sir Patrick Hastings, had decided to prosecute the com- munist J. R. Campbell for an article in the *Daily Worker* urging soldiers not to fire on fellow-workers. This was held to be an incitement to sedition. The prosecution was withdrawn because of left-wing pressure. The vote of no confidence actually took place on the withdrawal of the Campbell prosecution. (See *Whitehall Diary of Thomas Jones*, ed. Keith Middlemas, vol. i (1969).)

Ladywood that Chamberlain was facing defeat. ' It was a joyous day ', Mosley recalls, ' when in the courtyards running back from the streets in the Birmingham slums we saw the blue window cards coming down and the red going up.'[4] A new radical Joe had come to Birmingham, with all the fire and enthusiasm so conspicuously lacking in the original's desiccated successors.

' None of us who went through that fight with him will ever forget it,' wrote the editor of the *Birmingham Town Crier*. ' His power over his audience was amazing, and his eloquence made even hardened Pressmen gasp in astonishment.' But Mosley's Birmingham triumph was not yet to be. On 25 October, four days before polling day, came the Zinoviev Letter bombshell. The Foreign Office published a letter purportedly from Zinoviev of the Communist International to British communist leaders urging them to infiltrate the Labour Party and the Army. According to the Conservatives this proved that the Labour Party was under communist influence. The fact that MacDonald as foreign secretary had apparently authorised a protest to Russia against this interference in British affairs undermined the instinctive, and almost certainly accurate, Labour defence that the letter was a forgery.

The Zinoviev Letter stunt* persuaded many Liberals to switch to the Conservatives; on the actual polling day itself many Birmingham Labour supporters, without transport, were kept indoors by a massive thunderstorm. Even so, the voting was desperately close. When the first count was completed Mosley was the victor with a majority of 2. Chamberlain immediately asked for a recount, in which 60 votes shown for Mosley on the first count ' disappeared ' leaving Chamberlain with a majority of 77.† ' All the Labour officials ', wrote the *Town Crier*, ' believe that the final figures given do not agree with the total votes cast. '[5] Although bitterly disappointed at having failed to pull off what would have been a spectacular upset against the national trend, Mosley put a bright face on his defeat. ' A downpour of rain ', he said, ' washed the lifeless body of the last of the Chamberlains back to Westminster. ' Nationally, the Labour Party lost fifty seats and Stanley Baldwin formed his second Conservative Government. At Harrow Mosley's successor was Isidore Salmon (of the Joe Lyons family), who heavily defeated Kenneth Lindsay, the Labour candidate, and restored the Tory seat to its traditional alignment.

The two years following Mosley's defeat for Ladywood formed the first of the creative periods of his life. Politicians, he says, should have time for reflection, learning and recuperation. He and Cim-

*This was Britain's ' Watergate '. The Conservative Party machine was heavily implicated in the forgery.

†The final figures were: N. Chamberlain (Conservative), 13,374; O. Mosley (Labour), 13,297; A. W. Bowkett (Liberal), 539.

mie travelled to India at the end of 1924: a journey agreeably recalled in his memoirs. At Port Said he picked up a copy of George Bernard Shaw's *The Perfect Wagnerite*: did he already see himself as the revolutionary hero Siegfried? In Bombay he declared: 'Indians must create their own system of Government within the Commonwealth'; but privately he circulated a report on his return saying that political independence was less pressing than a 'mogul with a tractor and a deep plough'.[6] Western liberties were less important than economic reform – an attitude that he was soon to recommend nearer home. Before his departure for India he had revealed an ambitious plan to his Ladywood supporters. Birmingham was the home of 'unauthorised programmes'.* It was time to have another. 'Birmingham must be to the Labour Movement what Manchester has been to Liberalism,' he declared.[7] This was the origin of the Birmingham Proposals, the first of Mosley's great plans for realising his dream of a land fit for heroes.

Mosley's decision to apply himself to the economic problem shaped the course of his life. He became a man with a message, a prophet crying in the wilderness. It tells us a great deal about Mosley himself. The brilliant playboy was desperately serious. This mixture baffled his contemporaries. High thinking and frugal living was the Webb formula for achievement. When Mosley went fascist in the 1930s people came to the conclusion that he was power-mad. The power theory is as wide of the mark in its simplistic form as is the earlier playboy theory. Mosley wanted power but for a definite purpose: to solve the economic problem. And he trained himself to do so by applying himself to that least congenial of subjects, economics. By 1930 he had a firmer grasp of what needed to be done than any other politician in Britain. How did he achieve this feat?

Mosley always thought of himself as a pragmatist, a 'fact man' responding to the new facts of the new age. Yet these facts were by and large available to everyone. The malfunctioning of the world economy was a fact; the war was a fact; mass unemployment and bad housing were facts. But the majority of those in politics continued to ignore them, and plan their activities on the assumption that they did not exist, or were purely temporary deviations from normalcy. Clearly these facts did not define for them the age in which they lived. For Mosley they undoubtedly did.

---

*A reference to Joseph Chamberlain's 'unauthorised programme' of 1885. A more apposite reference might have been to Thomas Attwood, the Birmingham banker and ironmaster who opposed Peel's return to the gold standard in 1819 and put forward proposals for cheap money to revive industry at a time when a fifth of Birmingham was on relief following the Napoleonic wars. He later joined up with the Chartists.

The question is: why? ' Pragmatism ' offers no explanation. It is merely reality viewed from a standpoint that offers a challenge to existing interpretations of it. The interesting question is how a person comes to this standpoint. To answer it is to uncover the sources of originality.

Remarkable in Mosley was his almost complete freedom from nineteenth century orthodoxies. He did not have to rebel against *laissez-faire* and free trade: he did not believe in them. Partly, this was because he had never been to university where such wisdom was part of the atmosphere. But the deeper reason was that his background was in the nineteenth century, but not of it. Mosley took the straightforward view that it was the function of government to secure full employment and decent conditions for the people. Today this sounds like the merest commonsense, except perhaps to the supporters of Mr Enoch Powell. Yet it flew in the face of some of the deepest intellectual convictions of the time. These benefits were supposed to be secured by the market. The function of government was to secure the freedom of the market. Classical economists proved that interference in the market would only make things worse. It would also destroy individual liberty. Even socialists quailed before this apparently unassailable logic, however much they sniped away at it from the wings.

Mosley's whole background rebelled against the dogma. His family had been interfering with the market to protect the livelihood of its dependants for 300 years. For Mosley socialism was the modern expression of the feudal idea of community; he was an aristocrat in politics fulfilling the old function of his family in a wider sphere and under different conditions. He made this perfectly clear in 1928:

> Feudalism worked in its crude and inequitable fashion until the coming of the Industrial Age. Today the Feudal tradition and its adherents are broken as a political power and in most cases are ignobly lending their prestige and their abilities to the support of the predatory plutocracy which has gained complete control of the Conservative Party. In modern times the old regime is confronted with two alternatives. The first is to serve the new world in a great attempt to bring order out of chaos and beauty out of squalor. The other alternative is to become flunkeys of the bourgeoisie. It is a matter of constant surprise and regret that many of my class have chosen the latter course.[8]

There was nothing to impel Mosley to view the twentieth century as a continuation of the nineteenth. He had no reason to love the nineteenth century. It had destroyed his family's position and function, overturned its values. No one in English politics so frequently expressed his conviction that he was living through the birthpangs of a new age – with himself as midwife. Here he is in the great tradition of nineteenth century rebels like Carlyle and Nietzsche who developed a cyclical view of history, in which periods of decadence are followed by violent renewal. In the Nietzschean hero 'the transition from decadence, through conflagration, to health is made flesh'.[9] Phoenix arises from the ashes. For Mosley that conflagration was the First World War; the Phoenix was the war generation, ravaged, betrayed, ennobled. The continuity was not to be found between these 'new men', hammered into shape ' on the anvil of great ordeal' as Mosley put it, and the nineteenth century world with ' its little artificial life, its meanness, its stupendous selfishness'; but between them and an earlier, aristocratic, epoch. This whole picture of discontinuity was greatly overdrawn. Yet it contained an important element of truth. It was the conventional order of politicians who were wrong in believing that nineteenth century methods could cope with twentieth century problems. Mosley's particular relation to his age enabled him to grasp this central fact; and thus to view himself as an agent of ' becoming '.

Originality cannot, of course, be explained by background alone. To challenge the conventional wisdom of an age requires enormous self-assurance. Mosley had it in generous measure. From his earliest years, as far as one can tell, he had what George Eliot called ' the spontaneous sense of capability'. Perhaps his ' man-child' relationship with his mother contributed to this. There was also his aristocratic temper – 'high spirits', courage, contempt for 'shibboleths'. 'Such men are dangerous,' noted the Berlin *Tagen-blatt* of Mosley a little later, 'for to them possibilities are open that remain for ever closed to the middle-class caution of their opponents.' But here it is important to couple the 'spontaneous sense of capability' with effort. Mosley trained himself thoroughly for all the roles he played in his life. He was a complete professional in everything except the winning of power.

A second aspect of temperament relevant to his policy-making was his love of order and efficiency. Like the Webbs, he could not bear to see social machinery working badly. A Birmingham colleague Wilfred Whiteley recalls, 'I always felt with Mosley that he was the type of man who was never satisfied to see anything working ordinarily along. He must be planning and re-organising.'[10] He frequently likened himself to a mechanic repairing a broken car: it was the dirty hand, not the invisible hand, that had to do the job. His plea for a 'mogul with a tractor' was the Saint-Simonian vision of the technician as hero. Mosley was born into an age of technology which really believed – or at any rate paid lip-service to the idea – that man could control his destiny. The view that unemployment and depression were phenomena outside human control struck him as entirely unacceptable. In his *Revolution by Reason* he defined socialism as ' the conscious control and direction of human resources for human needs'. The belief in the possibility of controlling economic life was the necessary starting-point of any attempt to do so.

But we must not suppose Mosley to have been gripped by merely technocratic enthusiasms. He was moved by strong humanitarian feelings. If any single thing converted him to socialism it was the impact of the slums of Britain's great industrial cities with their stunted, undernourished, ragged, disease-ridden, vermin-infested inhabitants. They were the unbearable negation of everything the modern world was about – the negation of science, of intelligence, of community; an insult to the sacrifice of the war generation. They epitomised the helpless or selfish acceptance of disgraceful industrial conditions.

The slums started a train of thought which led directly to the Birmingham Proposals. They were the product of poverty. Yet for the first time in history the economic system was capable of eliminating poverty. Together the machines and the men were available to produce the goods and services the people needed. But they were standing idle. In May 1924 a journalist had taken Mosley round the Liverpool slums. ' This is damnable,' Mosley said. ' The rehousing of the working classes ought in itself to find work for the whole of the unemployed for the next ten years.' This was an exceedingly acute and perceptive remark. It brought together two things sundered in orthodox socialist economic thought: unemployment and poverty. For socialists unemployment was an incidental hazard of a self-regulating market economy. The real problem was poverty, which was caused by maldistribution of wealth. What Mosley was saying was that poverty was primarily caused by lack of demand. If you could increase production you could largely eliminate poverty. It did not eliminate the argument for redistribution, which exists both independently and, as we shall see, as part of the mechanism for increasing production. But it put the emphasis squarely in the right place. It is an early but significant example of Mosley's ability to relate apparently disconnected phenomena and habits of thought. This synthesising aptitude was perhaps the chief mental quality Mosley brought to bear on economic policy-making. It is the main characteristic of all his successive plans to realise his land fit for heroes.

In formulating his first plan, Mosley had the help of an outstanding collaborator. He was Evelyn John Strachey, son of St Loe Strachey, editor of the *Spectator* and a nephew of Lytton Strachey. (On his mother's side he was descended from that austere exponent of the ' dismal science ' Nassau Senior.) Born in

1901, Strachey was educated at Eton and Oxford; at university, he was an aesthete and Tory, much given to writing indifferent verse and bad melodramas. He read history, but did not take a degree, joining his father on the *Spectator* in 1922. When Mosley met him two years later – probably at the Webbs' – he had already joined the Labour Party and started working for the I.L.P. Mosley helped him get a constituency at Aston, Birmingham, for the general election of 1924.

What drew the two men together? First, and most obviously, a common interest: both had, quite independently, started thinking about economic problems and their minds were moving along parallel lines. Both men were, as Hugh Thomas writes, ' refugees from the upper class ' in a largely proletarian or lower-middle-class world.[11] Both had a very similar *cast* of mind: cold, logical, rational. However, the quest for reason had a special emotional significance for Strachey which it did not possess for Mosley (or perhaps the clues are less obvious in Mosley's case). This helps to explain both Strachey's attachment to Mosley and his later break with him.

Strachey was one of the generation in revolt against repressive puritanism. He was, according to his biographer, ' intoxicated ' by the ' heady mixture of racial and sexual freedom ' he found in the bohemian milieu in which he, like Mosley, lived his private life. At the same time he was revolted by it, obsessed by an acute sense of guilt, of loss of a vanished order. Introspective, he worried about his motives, and the disorder of his private life (which was considerable). Like others in his situation he was powerfully affected by Freud. Had he embraced socialism perhaps as an act of rebellion against his father? Did he unconsciously wish his father dead? Freud confirmed his own experience of an underlying world of destructive forces; of the fragility of civilisation. Reason was the only defence against barbarism; reason raised to the level of a faith. If Mosley's *Revolution by Reason* were not implemented Strachey foresaw an ' abyss of chaos, social regression and catastrophe – a dark age of unreason '.[12] Mosley lived in the same world, but operated differently. He was not introspective; somehow he had escaped the influence of ' vile, vile English puritanism ' as Strachey called it. His attitude to life was much more pagan: he accepted ' nature ' as it came. He felt no guilt about the ' lower self ' and lacked entirely the moral compulsion to strangle it in the ' higher ' interests of civilisation. The later clash between the two men was at bottom the clash between the moral and the pagan attitudes to life. Mosley, who in the 1920s stood for reason and order against the ' dark age of unreason ', later came for Strachey to symbolise the forces of barbarism; while communism, which Strachey had earlier denounced as barbaric (see below, pages 303-4) now represented the ' eternal cause of human culture, of science and of civilisation. . . .'[13]

Together they made a highly formidable intellectual team. Who contributed more? Mosley claims the major credit for himself; Strachey's role was essentially ' analytic and critical '.[14] Mr Thomas thinks that 'Strachey was the thinker, and Mosley the interpreter '.[15] When two minds meet and sparks fly who can say which one started the blaze? Nevertheless, Mosley's view of the matter is nearer the truth. Strachey's mind instinctively sought the security of doctrine. In the 1930s he tried to refute Keynes with Marx. In the 1950s he tried to refute Marx with Keynes. The Birmingham Proposals, by contrast, attempt to synthesise socialist and Keynesian economics. This is the Mosley approach, and it seems right to regard *Revolution by Reason* (the title itself is suggestive) as an authentic Mosleyite document, however great Strachey's contribution to it. Certainly, Mosley's commitment to its basic propositions was lifelong.

One wonders when Mosley had the time to work out the new policy. He had no formal background in economics. In Parliament he had latterly concentrated on foreign affairs. Yet by March 1925 the Birmingham Proposals were fully hatched. An important part of the explanation is Mosley's sheer quickness of mind. His ability to grasp the main point of an argument was little short of phenomenal. Many have said he would have made a brilliant lawyer; and the lawyer's ability to master a complicated brief rapidly is the nearest analogy to this particular mental talent. Again it was his habit to read and think about a problem in short, intensive, bursts. The sea journeys to and from India gave him six weeks of necessary seclusion. Although he rarely read long books, he was an avid reader of articles: he was one of the few beneficiaries of Keynes's unavailing efforts to educate the British public through the medium of journalism in the 1920s. Mosley relied heavily on efficient research assistance. From 1924 this role in his entourage was increasingly filled by Allan Young whom he had met in Birmingham. The son of a ' bookish ' railway clerk from Glasgow, Young had served in the war and knocked about the far east before coming to Birmingham as agent for the borough Labour Party in April 1924. Young was a brilliant constituency organiser. He soon fell under Mosley's spell and in 1927 resigned his job to become Mosley's full-time political secretary.* At a time when few Labour M.P.s had access to research assistance, or read more widely than the standard socialist literature or journalism, Mosley's money and wider range gave him an important advantage. But none of this would much have mattered had he not had the knack of spotting the right people (Keynes) and concentrating his

* His personal secretary for many years was Claud Sutton.

energy on the right problem (unemployment). Mosley's contribution was made possible by rigorous exclusion. This is what
appears to give his socialism such a narrow range. In fact it was
broader than it seemed. He was greatly interested in the ideas
of the guild socialists – and these reappear both in the 1930s and
in the 1950s. But for the moment he concentrated on the interlocking aspects of poverty and unemployment. This was exactly
the right focus for the 1920s.

To return to orthodox discussions of unemployment in the 1920s
is a depressing business. Unemployment, the experts insisted, was
due to temporary war-time dislocations in the world trading and
monetary system. The remedy was to recover lost export markets
by cutting costs at home and restoring ' stability ' to the world's
exchanges. The centrepiece of this restoration was supposed to be
Britain's return to the gold standard at the pre-war parity. The
process would promote the reduction of costs at home; the achievement would symbolise the end of abnormality and the return of
the City of London to its position as the premier financial centre.

There were two things wrong with this analysis. In the first
place, it ignored the extent to which the liberal world economic
order had started to disintegrate *before* 1914. The issue raised
by Joseph Chamberlain in 1903 was that, in a world of competing manufacturing giants, free trade meant trade war, not
harmony. This was the mercantilist position. The process of
local industrialisation had been carried further by the war, with
the burgeoning of the Indian and Japanese textile industries and
the switch from coal to oil: its major fruits were unemployment
in the British textile and mining industries. These factors presented Britain with a major problem of readjustment irrespective
of ' temporary ' war dislocations. The reason they were ignored by
British policy-makers was in part at least due to the temporary
elimination of Germany as a serious industrial rival.[16] The problem was also largely (but not entirely) ignored by Mosley in his
Revolution by Reason. It became the central point of his economic
thinking from 1930 onwards.

The second thing wrong with the orthodox analysis was that
the attempt to restore the pound to its pre-war parity involved
deflating an economy already under-employed owing to the factor
just mentioned, and thus increasing unemployment.* This became

---

*The process is well described by W. Ashworth:

> In order to bring back the exchange rate to par it was necessary to lower
> the British price level relatively to the American as a means of decreasing
> Britain's international expenditure relatively to its earnings. . . . To bring
> [these reductions] about a drastic restriction of credit was applied, mainly
> by means of high interest rates, despite the adverse repercussions this
> must have on business activity and employment. This restrictive policy

the subject of intense debate in 1924 and early 1925 with Keynes,
backed by Reginald McKenna, Sir Josiah Stamp and Sir Alfred
Mond, and more cautiously by the Federation of British Industries,
urging stabilisation at a lower parity in order to avoid deflation.
This was the point of departure of Mosley's Birmingham Proposals.
In his *Tract for Monetary Reform* (1923), Keynes explained the
connection between deflation and unemployment:

> During the lengthy process of production the business world is
> incurring outgoings in terms of money – paying out money for
> wages and other expenses of production – in the expectation
> of recouping this outlay by disposing of the product for money
> at a later date. . . . Whether it likes it or not, the technique of
> production under a regime of money-contract forces the busi-
> ness world always to carry a big speculative position; and if
> it is reluctant to carry this position, the productive process
> must be slackened. . . . If prices are expected to fall, not enough
> risk-takers can be found . . . and this means that *entrepreneurs*
> will be reluctant to embark on lengthy productive processes
> involving a money outlay long in advance of money recoup-
> ment – whence unemployment. The *fact* of falling prices
> injures *entrepreneurs*; consequently the *fear* of falling prices
> causes them to protect themselves by curtailing their ope-
> rations. . . .[17]

From this it followed that stable, or even slightly rising, prices,
not stable exchanges, ought to be the chief object of economic
policy. The attempt to restore the pre-war value of the pound
by deflation (Keynes was writing in 1923 before the return to the
gold standard) ought to be abandoned. But Keynes went further.
In the spring of 1924 he advocated a big programme of government investment to get the economy ' moving ' again.[18] He was
already convinced that government action was needed to break
down business pessimism. This fortified Mosley in his own view.

Keynes was important to Mosley for another reason. The
message of the *Tract* was that economics was about choices and the
need to make choices. The orthodox spokesmen all spoke and
acted as though there was only one possible thing that Britain
could do – deflate and cut costs. Keynes pointed out that this was
in fact the economic policy of particular interest groups – the *rentiers*
and the bankers. For example, deflation ' involves a transference
of wealth from the rest of the community to the *rentier* class . . .

---

continued even in the depths of the slump in 1921 and 1922, when every
other consideration would have suggested the opposite policy. Such was
the prestige of the gold standard, however, that hardly anyone of authority or influence questioned the rightness of the policy. [*An Economic History of England, 1870–1939* (1960) p. 387.]

from the active to the inactive '.[19]   Curiously enough Keynes did
not include the class struggle (between capitalists and workers)
in his account of interest conflicts.   He tended to assume an identity
of interest between workers and manufacturers against their common enemies – the *rentier* and banker.*   This notion of the conflict
of interest within the capitalist community and the identity of interest between the workers and one section of that community –
the manufacturers – was to have a profound influence on Mosley's
thought.   It was to give him both a strategy and a philosophy quite
different from the standard socialist conception of a struggle in
which the workers were all on one side, and the wicked capitalists
all on the other.   Henceforth the producers' state would be the
goal; and finance the enemy.

Underlying this switch in emphasis from the orthodox socialist
class-struggle between workers and capitalists to the struggle between producers and bankers was an important theoretical distinction between ' Keynesianism ' and underconsumptionism.   In the
underconsumptionist model savings were automatically transformed
into investments: excess savings led to excess production.   Hence
the remedy for unemployment and depression lay in reducing the
amount of saving, which involved transferring wealth from the
' accumulating ' to the ' consuming ' classes – that is, from capitalists to workers.   In the Keynesian account of depression quoted
above the problem was that savings, owing to a restrictive credit
policy initiated by the financiers, were not being offset by new investment.   Rather they were not being spent at all.   The solution
to unemployment, then, was not so much to redistribute wealth
from savers to consumers – though this might have some effect in
stimulating spending – as to increase investment by policies of
' cheap money ' or if necessary by direct government enterprise;
in other words, to substitute a producers' policy for the restrictive
financial policy aimed at restoring the position of the City of London
in international finance.   Mosley's plan was more Keynesian than
underconsumptionist in inspiration.   As we shall see, it concentrated
in the first instance on increasing total demand, not in redistributing
demand from one section of the community to another.   In that
sense the Birmingham Proposals were entirely independent of
J. A. Hobson, E. F. Wise, H. N. Brailsford – the underconsumptionist theorists of the I.L.P.   Where the Hobsonian influence is felt
is in his proposal that the new demand should be directed towards
satisfying working-class necessities rather than capitalist luxuries.
This, as well as the general emphasis on planning, gives his proposals
their socialist form.

*See the *Tract*, pp. 27–30.   Keynes assumes that in a period of rising prices
workers' remuneration can keep pace with profits.   Both benefit at the expense
of the *rentier*.

The first results of the new thinking were apparent at the I.L.P. Conference at Gloucester in April where Mosley moved a composite resolution from Ladywood and other Birmingham branches calling for the nationalisation of the banking system – ' that consecrated combination of private interests and public plunders' as Mosley called it. The new strategy was to issue ' consumers' credits ' to the unemployed and ' producers' credits ' to manufacturers in order to get demand moving again. The banking system, Mosley explained, lay at the heart of capitalism. Through its control socialists could ' dominate the whole field of capitalism, and with one stroke break the vicious circle ' of destitution. ' Every capitalist must come to you and you can dictate the conditions under which he will carry on.' Control of banking would make possible the ' qualitative ' control of credit. It would give government the power to choose between one industry and another. ' Let us join to our cry for the minimum wage the battle cry " the banks for the people ".'[20] Whether Mosley realised it or not, his strategy was in fact implicit in the Leninist analysis. Lenin had stressed the primacy of banking in the capitalist system. Banks controlled industry because they provided the credit necessary for it to carry on. If the Government controlled the banks, it would control industry without the need for wholesale nationalisation. Commented *The Times*, ' Of course under Mr. Mosley's scheme, no one would have any inducement to work. To obtain what one wanted, all that would be necessary would be to fall out of employment and obtain consumers' credit without stint from the Socialist bank.'

The Times now opened its sedate columns to a lively correspondence between Mosley and the banker R. H. Brand. Brand's main charge was that Mosley's proposals were inflationary, and would therefore reduce England's competitiveness.[21] Mosley denied this. ' If . . . it remains at all true that manufacturers will increase production if markets are provided, no danger of inflation would arise until unemployment had declined to a point at which the maximum productivity of the nation had nearly been reached.'[22] But how would an increase in internal purchasing power help England sell goods abroad, Brand wanted to know? There was in fact an obvious answer to this which Strachey was to give a few months later: an increase in domestic demand would also increase British demand for foreign goods; and thus would enlarge foreign demand for British goods. This was not an answer that Mosley gave; and the fact that he failed to give it pinpoints neatly the source of what was to become his major economic ' heresy': the belief that domestic trade is better than foreign trade.

A fortnight after Mosley's speech to the Gloucester Conference, Winston Churchill, the chancellor of the exchequer, carried the policy of deflation to its logical conclusion by putting Britain back onto the gold standard at the pre-war exchange rate. In a typical sally at Churchill's expense Mosley remarked, ' Faced with the alternative of saying goodbye to the gold standard, and therefore to his own employment, and goodbye to other people's employment, Mr. Churchill characteristically selected the latter course.' In his cele-brated attack, *The Economic Consequences of Mr Churchill*, Keynes argued that the British currency had been overvalued by ten per cent. This meant ten per cent on the price of British exports which could only be met by further wage reductions and more un-employment. Keynes' prophecy was almost immediately fulfilled. On 30 June 1925 the coal-owners served notice of their intention to reduce miners' wages; a general strike was only averted by the Government's promise on 31 July 1925 to pay the industry a subsidy pending the report of a royal commission of enquiry. Mosley's comment was, ' " All the workers of this country have got to face a reduction of wages," murmurs Mr Baldwin between a sermon and a subsidy.' In a bitter speech at Southport he argued that even if wages came down it would not save the mining industry. ' The German and the French mineowners would go to their men and say, " The British have undercut us in the world's markets. If you will accept lower wages and longer hours, we can regain our trade." And then the British mineowners would, in turn, make the same plea again, and so the mad, suicidal progress would go on, beating down lower and lower the wages of the mineworkers of this and other countries.'[23] Where in all this was the harmony of interests which the liberal economists had preached?

On 3 May 1925 Mosley introduced his ' unauthorised pro-gramme ' to Birmingham. Over 5000 people queued for seats in the Birmingham Town Hall which seated only half that number. ' Send the money to the necessitous areas,' Mosley cried. ' Give it to the poor whose demand is for the things which matter to this country and will stimulate employment in the great staple indus-tries; do away with the poor law and the " dole ".'[24] On 11 June Mosley and Strachey laid their plan before the delegate meeting of the Birmingham Labour Party. The president, A. E. Ager, explained that if the proposals were approved they would be em-bodied in a resolution for the Labour Party Conference in the name of the Birmingham Labour Party. Strachey explained that it was necessary by vigorous state action to break the vicious circle of destitution. ' The cause of poverty was that not enough necessaries were being produced; and when employers were asked why they did not produce more, they replied that it was because there was no effective demand.' The State would have to get control of the banking system and force up wages, thus creating the demand which manufacturers would then supply.

A vigorous discussion followed. ' No mere tinkering with credit ',

said one speaker, would remedy the evils of private enterprise.
' There were no short cuts to Socialism ' was the view of Fred
Sharkey, one of Birmingham's ' cryptos '. Replying to the discussion, Mosley attacked the ' strange view that Socialists could do
nothing until Capitalism had collapsed '. His policy was an ideal
policy for the transition to socialism, for it gave the State power over
the capitalist economy. Rejecting the policy of a mere redistribution of wealth, Mosley said that the fundamental problem was
' the need to create new wealth by drawing upon all the latent
power of production in the country '. Three weeks later when the
debate was resumed, Mosley's resolution calling for the nationalisation of the banks and the use of the national credit to break ' the
vicious circle of poverty and unemployment ' was carried by 65
votes to 14, and so became the Birmingham Proposals.[25]

The campaign of persuasion continued. On 11 August Mosley
presented his plan in a paper read to the I.L.P. Summer School at
Easton Lodge: it was later published under the title *Revolution by
Reason*. In December John Strachey's full-length exposition, dedicated to ' O.M. who may some day do the things of which we
dream ', appeared as a book under the same title. Strachey wrote
it in Venice in September where he stayed as a guest of the Mosleys.
Another guest, Bob Boothby, recalls: ' Every morning Tom Mosley
and John Strachey . . . discussed *Revolution by Reason*. . . . This was
the period when Mosley saw himself as Byron rather than Mussolini;
and to me was infinitely preferable. He was certainly a powerful
swimmer, and used to disappear at intervals into the lagoon to
commune with himself.'[26] Would either Byron, or Mussolini, one
wonders, have spent those sunlit mornings studying economics?

Let us turn briefly to some of the striking novelties of *Revolution by
Reason*. Deflation ruthlessly pursued had reduced demand below the
level necessary to achieve full employment. Therefore the prime
necessity was to expand demand ' to evoke our unused capacity
which is at present not commanded either by the rich or by the
poor '. Mere redistribution was explicitly repudiated.[27] It was a
' minor ' operation to be postponed till the stimulation of demand
had gone a great way. The ' practical results ' of redistribution,
argued Mosley, echoing Sir Josiah Stamp, would not help the
working class nearly as much as the expansion of demand.[28]

But Mosley made a distinction between a ' capitalist ' and a
' socialist ' credit expansion. A socialist credit expansion would be
planned. There appear to be three motives for this. The first was to
direct the new money into the hands of the poor. This would
create a demand upon the staple industries and thus guarantee
steady employment. The flow of credit would be decided by an
Economic Planning Council which Mosley described as a ' general

staff of union and business experts '.[29] The second motive was
to counter capitalist ' sabotage '. Mosley's great fear, echoing that
of his manorial ancestors, was that speculators would use the new
money to corner commodities, creating an artificial scarcity which
would force a price rise and thus cancel out working-class gains.
It was to guard against this that he adopted the proposals of E.M.H.
Lloyd, Lloyd George's war-time controller of food, for the state
purchase of foodstuffs and raw materials direct from the foreign
producer, thereby eliminating the middleman.[30] The third motive,
and in some ways the most interesting one, was to avoid inflation.
Mosley wrote:

> We propose first to expand credit in order to create demand.
> That new and greater demand must, of course, be met by a new
> and greater supply of goods, or all the evils of inflation and
> price rise will result. Here our Socialist planning must enter
> in. We must see that more goods are forthcoming to meet the
> new demand.[31]

This appears to be a retreat from the position he adopted in his
controversy with Brand that no danger of inflation would arise
until ' unemployment had declined to a point at which the maximum productivity of the nation had nearly been reached '. Mosley
had quailed before that formidable bogey the Quantity Theory
of Money, which held that a given increase in the quantity of
money will produce an equivalent increase in the level of prices;
his national planning of production was intended as an answer to
this criticism. The strong supposition that Mosley never read, or
never properly understood, Keynes' later *General Theory* is reinforced
by the fact that he never abandoned the Quantity Theory; and in
the 1960s attacked President Kennedy's ' unplanned ' budget defi-
cits to mop up unemployment on the grounds that they were inflationary. It is only fair to Mosley to point out that lately the
Quantity Theory has, in modified form, come back into fashion;
and that no one has yet managed to solve the problem of inflation;
so that this argument for planning effortlessly spans the intervening
decades of depression.

Since socialism was the ' conscious control and direction of
human resources for human needs ' it was incompatible with the
automatic gold standard or any system ' which makes our vital
medium of exchange dependent upon chance discoveries of gold
fields or upon the whimsical movements of world demand for an
attractively coloured but otherwise useless metal '.[32] If the home
recovery programme led to a drain on gold, the pound should be
allowed to float. Switching from his lecture-room to his platform
manner, Mosley asked, ' Is the employment of the British worker
to be dependent upon a nigger digging up a lump of glittering metal

in far-away Africa, or upon the gold jugglery of foreign statesmen
and international financiers?'[33]

Finally Mosley attacked the ' export fetish '.   Here a sharp difference appears between his *Revolution by Reason* and Strachey's.
Strachey argues that there is no point in increasing the proportion
of home trade to foreign trade, since ' in no conceivable circumstances can there be a net gain of real wealth '. This is the old argument for free trade.   Contrast it with Mosley's pronouncement on
the same subject:

> This process [of switching production to the home market]
> might go very far without any danger to the import of neces-
> sary foodstuffs and raw materials.   By no means all our
> present imports represent foodstuffs and raw materials.   We
> import completely manufactured articles to the value of
> £300,000,000 per annum, most of which could be made at
> home.   Our essential supplies can be purchased by far less
> exports than are at present sent abroad.   The natural revul-
> sion from the crude fallacies of Protection has resulted in a
> fetish worship of the present dimensions of our export trade by
> minds which have just succeeded in grasping the elementary
> fact that we must export in order to import certain necessaries
> which cannot be produced at home.[34]

Mosley already sensed intuitively that hopes of expanding the
export trade were illusory and that each country would have to do
far more for itself in the years ahead.   As a temperamental *dirigiste*
he also disliked the idea of leaving human welfare to ' invisible
hands ' especially when many of them were located outside the
country and the control of national government.

Above all, the Birmingham Proposals were designed as an immediate policy.   Their message was: we cannot wait for a hundred
years of evolutionary socialism, with a couple of industries being
nationalised each time a Labour government was fortunate enough
to be elected.   The pamphlet began with Mosley's usual vision of
disaster if its proposals were not immediately adopted, and ended
with some truly embarrassing rhetoric about ' the steel machine
of a ruthless realism ' driven forward by the ' lash of great ordeal '
stinging ' a historic race to action . . . in the spirit of rapturous
sacrifice ' to wrest the ' supreme sceptre of economic power ' from
the ' final turmoil of a bankrupt and brutal epoch '.

Mosley's education in the realities, rather than the myths, of
twentieth-century economics was by no means over. Early in 1926
he and his wife sailed for America to study labour conditions, in
true Fabian fashion.   Perhaps like the Webbs in Russia eight years
later, they went in search of a new civilisation.   First impressions
were not ecstatic:

[Mosley to Strachey, 15 January 1926 (dictated)]

Dear John,

We arrived here a day late after one of the worst crossings the ship had ever experienced. We suffered a terrible press ordeal on the ship and after landing. We were paraded on the top deck and cameras and cinemas were turned on us for a solid half hour. The reporters were a pleasant surprise, very courteous, almost old-fashioned. . . .

The city itself and the general life is in many respects rather contrary to expectation. The hustle which we were led to anticipate seems largely superficial and the rate of life is really not much in excess of our own. In banks, etc. our people seem to move a good deal quicker. Of the labour conditions I have not yet seen much, but spent yesterday going round the slums of New York which were pretty bad, but of course not so bad as our worst. The interesting thing from our point of view was that the rents have all increased in proportion to wages . . . it seems as long as rent and interest survive, the proportionate toll is taken of the workers whatever wages they may draw. They are of course better fed and were all cooking excellent meals. I will send you a photograph of our slumming for the next issue of *Forward*. You might draw a moral on the rise of rent to take the due proportion of the increased wages.

[By hand]

Forgive rather colourless epistle due to presence of American stenographer and steam drill outside which drives me quite demented. . . .

They are all mad – a seemingly normal and perfectly charming bank clerk has just wandered into the room – kissed both our hands and announced that after renouncing all other religions he had come to worship the living deity! Some people these Yanks. Unless the door is well-bolted Hearst's young women will interview me with perfect *sang froid* while seated on the rear!

Yours ever
Tom

From a fishing trip off the coast of Florida in Franklin Roosevelt's *Larocco* a few weeks later came some more scattered impressions:

The South Seas
15 February 1926

Dear John,

You are a rotten correspondent but forgiven because the Socialist Review must be weighing heavily upon you to judge

from your note in the New Leader. We are at peace at last
being away in a House boat with Franklin Roosevelt fishing
for ferocious and enormous reptiles which have not yet materialised.   Our host is a very charming and remarkable person
who was assistant-Secretary to the Navy in the war and ran
as vice-Presidential candidate in 1920 for the Democrats –
They say he will be next Governor of New York and may
eventually be President. In Washington we met all Presi-
dents past and prospective – a plentiful crop, but not the
present incumbent. . . .

   We were rushed round at an amazing pace to meet all celeb-
rities – heard the World Court including Baruch's speech
(a tissue of absurd and unchallenged inaccuracies delivered
in a stentorian bellow) and finally were taken to a small
dinner party at the Penguin Club where we found a large
room packed with the progressive elements of American
public life and to my intense surprise and discomfort was
compelled to deliver a lengthy speech which seemed very well
received.   Cimmy spoke charmingly in her best ' I am a little
soldier ' style and was amused by her neighbour observing
' you vamped them proper! ' . . .

   (A considerable diversion at this point – we have been out
fishing and caught 12 baracuda – a fish about the size of a
salmon but much more powerful and the fiercest animal in
the water – Legend has it they go for the balls and a nasty
mess results – We swam off the House boat with the crew
beating the water with poles to keep off the sharks – while at
dinner a 5 foot shark has just been hooked with dead bait.
I have shot it on the water with a revolver – really a most
amusing trip.) To return to the sharks of the political variety,
they were a most unimpressive crowd surpassed only by the
business ' brains '.   I had some long talks with the ' brain '
of Morgans (God help them) who is convinced our troubles
are over now we are ' walking on a sound metal floor '* and
much more of the same stuff.   The only interesting people
in the financial line were some pupils of Irving Fisher [Irving
Fisher was a prominent American monetary reformer] together with a very well known engineer who said America
was not producing at 25% of capacity. . . .

   Strong [Benjamin Strong, Governor of the Federal Reserve
Bank of New York] was going to see me but in the interval
saw Norman [Montagu Norman, Governor of the Bank of
England] and became evasive!!   It is impossible to go into
details of industrial impressions etc. – they must keep for when

---

*A reference to the restored gold standard.

we meet – The greater part of these experiences are still to come in Chicago and the Middle West – I am looking forward most to seeing the organisation of ' mass distribution ' in Chicago – any order guaranteed delivery within 24 hours – an extension only asked in case of a house or baby.   I believe this is the best thing in the country and a fine example for Socialist organisation.   We have already seen machinery years ahead of our own in point of general efficiency and health protection. ... Their public services are amazingly inefficient – telephones as bad or worse than Paris – Street cleaning a disgrace and innumerable instances of their total lack of any collective genius such as we possess. . . .

Florida ... was a delightful rest – Palm Beach a great relief . . . except for one or 2 large hotels, Petit Trianon complex out in small cottages and studied rusticity!   Of the land boom and the very interesting complexities more when we meet – a Smash is now *necessary* before Florida is really developed and will come – there are few better instances of capitalist mania.   However we had a glorious time, bathing and sunshine, quite free from Press persecution.   Cim found Palm Beach less stimulating than she anticipated for the same reasons that left so painful an impression on our Mr. Boothby!!

                                                                TOM

To Roosevelt, Mosley wrote from the Long Key fishing camp:

We shall long remember the happy time you have given us and will carry back to the dust and turmoil new strength. . . . Every good wish for your fights ahead – you who fight for Progressive causes in this country carry a vast burden and our eyes will always follow you with hope and well wishes.

Mosley, like so many other visitors, was fascinated by America's vitality.   He had evidently not yet been to Detroit when he wrote to Strachey. A trip to the Ford works there left a lasting impression. He encountered for the first time the conveyor-belt system capable of being worked by the least-skilled labour.   He immediately sensed that here was a most potent instrument for the ruin of any free-trade economy; for of what use was all the accumulated know-how of Lancashire when an equivalent article could be produced by these methods in India and Japan for a fraction of the cost? ' Yellow Peril ' ideas of this kind were to reinforce his later arguments for a self-contained system.

The conduct of American business gave him much to think about as he encountered the first stages of what was later to be called the ' managerial revolution '.   In the Metropolitan Life Insurance Company of New York, Mosley felt he had discovered a new-model

capitalist corporation, run by salaried managers with no direct
interest in the profit margins of their undertaking, men who saw
themselves as technocrats rather than as private profiteers. The
divorce of production from the personal profit motive – the fundamental point of socialism – was here taking place within the very
framework of capitalism. The same philosophy he saw at work in
the Federal Reserve Board system which he described on his return
as a ' semi-socialist banking system '. Hire-purchase too, then
almost unknown in England, he interpreted as a haphazard form
of his own more scientific consumer-credit proposals.

What disturbed him about America was precisely the haphazard,
piecemeal way in which all these new ideas were being applied,
without that ' collective genius' which he strangely imagined to be
a British characteristic. It was capitalism rampant; and Mosley
foresaw that ' a Smash is now *necessary* '. On the English left there
was a lot of theorising but no action, in America there appeared
to be a lot of action but no theory. Franklin Roosevelt seemed to
embody this weakness. ' Too much will and too little intellect '
was Mosley's verdict on him. It was his summary of his whole
American experience.

But the fundamental lesson of America was that high wages could
go hand in hand with private enterprise. Ford had produced
' the cheapest article and paid the highest wages in the world '.
From 1926 the idea of a ' managed capitalism ' began to take root
in his mind. He was not the only left-wing politician to see America rather than Russia as a model for the working class. ' If this
is capitalism,' wrote H. N. Brailsford, the leading I.L.P. theoreti-
cian of the 1920s, ' it is a variety which has discarded the fundamental principle on which Marx based his prediction. The case
against it is no longer that it makes poverty by its very success.
The case against it rather is that it is an unchecked autocracy.'

The return to the ' dust and turmoil ' of socialist politics was a
depressing experience. In the Labour Party, the great socialist
abstractions ruled, seemingly unrelated to the concrete task of
modernising an antique economy and providing a decent standard
of life for all. This was true even of the I.L.P., the most left-wing
and militant of all the Labour Party groups. In terms of structure,
the I.L.P.'s policy of the Living Wage was very similar to Mosley's.
It even provided for the nationalisation of the banks and the use of
credit policy to keep up the price level: an indication that H. N.
Brailsford, like Mosley and Strachey, had been reading his Keynes.
The idea of planning, too, was well understood by the ablest minds
in the I.L.P., like Wheatley, who advocated replacing the ' competitive system of fixing wages ' by ' State control of incomes'.[35] What
was entirely lacking was any notion of dynamic state effort to stimulate growth. As Brailsford told the same conference, ' If there is

poverty, if there is unemployment, the primary reason is that too much of the product of industry has gone into accumulation, and too little into consumption '. There is little hint of the new vistas being opened up by Keynes here.

The failure of the radicals to get together is one of the tragedies of the inter-war period. With the typical arrogance of the Cambridge economist, Keynes regarded the I.L.P. as hopelessly out of date (a view he was to revise with his generous praise of Hobson in his *General Theory*).* From their side, socialist radicals with a few exceptions preferred to remain uncontaminated by progressive capitalist thought. The two sides pursued their speculations without reference to each other, leaving the middle ground to be occupied by the vacuous goodwill of MacDonald and Baldwin. Mosley's attempt at bridge-building between the monetary radicals and the socialist planners and Hobsonians was thus doomed to frustration.

His proposals had even less success within the main body of the Labour Party. Hugh Dalton accused Mosley and Strachey of following Keynes in ' exaggerating the evil effects of falling prices ', attacked their cavalier attitude to the gold standard, and in general argued that in nationalising the basic industries ' we shall have our hands full for several years at least '.[36] Mosley clashed again with Dalton in 1927 when he championed an I.L.P. proposal to use the proceeds of a surtax to increase social services rather than pay off the national debt as Labour's financial experts wanted to do. ' I do not agree', Dalton wrote, ' with his policy of abandoning any serious attempt to pay off the debt.'[37] To the Webbs Dalton complained that Mosley was ' very uninstructed '. At the Labour Party conference at Blackpool that year Mosley clashed with Herbert Morrison on the same issue, Morrison remarking bitterly that the national debt was ' a crushing burden round the necks of the working-class ' and that to get rid of it was good socialism. Pethick-Lawrence, another Labour expert, agreed.[38] Other party intellectuals were equally unsympathetic to the new thinking. Beatrice Webb wrote of Mosley's schemes: ' they are as impracticable as they would be mischievous if carried out ';[39] of the I.L.P.'s Living Wage, ' a combination of conceit and ignorance '.[40] By 1926 she was prepared to concede that Keynes was both brilliant and humane, but there is not a hint that she was influenced by him. The Webbs, like most of Labour's intellectuals, inhabited closed systems which had no point of contact with the contemporary economic debates. Their generous social attitudes were built on a financial outlook that was even then coming to seem antediluvian.

This is even more obvious with Philip Snowden, the Labour

*On the other hand, Keynes wrote a sympathetic note to Strachey on the appearance of the latter's *Revolution by Reason*. (Hugh Thomas, *John Strachey* (1973) p. 52.)

Party's chief financial spokesman, and a fervent supporter of the policy of returning to the gold standard. Though Mosley conducted his currency controversy with Snowden with scrupulous fairness, avoiding personalities, the two men never got on close terms. ' I was always suspicious of a rich man who came into the Socialist Movement and at once became more Socialist than the Socialists,' wrote the ex-socialist Snowden in his autobiography in 1936.[41] Nor did Mosley fare any better with Snowden's wife, the social-climbing Ethel Snowden, who once remarked that she needed no friends in the Labour Party as she was so intimate with the royal family. At a commonwealth fête in Hampton Court Mosley teased her by saying, ' Mrs Snowden . . . after the revolution we must live here together.' ' Oh, Sir Oswald,' the humourless but loyal Ethel replied, ' we can't do that – this palace belongs to the King and Queen.'

Throughout 1927 Mosley urged the Labour Party to endorse a policy of credit expansion, adding significantly that soft-pedalling on nationalisation and concentrating on credit policy would attract ' neutral minds '.[42] One of these was Reginald McKenna, chair-man of the Midland Bank, who in his annual address to the share-holders in January 1927 had called for credit expansion, citing the American Federal Reserve Board's policy in support.   Mosley wrote, ' The ranks of the City are now divided.   The advanced section, headed by Mr McKenna and Mr Keynes, face the orthodox and reactionary ranks which are led by Mr Montagu Norman and the heads of the Treasury.   To the uninitiated it . . . seems a little unfortunate that the ex-Labour Chancellor should appear . . . to be an ardent supporter of Mr Montagu Norman.   It will be little less than a disaster if in this struggle Labour support is accorded to the reactionary elements in the City.   It will certainly be a fantastic negation of the purposes of our party.'[43] Writing in the *New Leader* on 30 September 1927 Mosley summed up the effects of government policy:

> The declared object of deflation was the restoration of the gold standard at pre-war parity.   Its actual effect has been to create unemployment by the restriction of industrial credit. By the lever of unemployment it has forced down wages and has thus facilitated the return to gold through the reduc-tion of prices.   An incidental effect has been to transfer pur-chasing power from the workers, whose wages have been reduced, to the bondholders, whose interest has remained the same.   It has also doubled the real burden of Debt since 1920, and was largely responsible for the mining lock-out last year, by the reduction in terms of sterling of the money which we receive for coal sold abroad.   Deflation, in fact, has been responsible for a sinister catalogue of disasters which

can be substantiated in detailed argument that has never yet been rebutted.

The argument now seems overwhelming; it did not appear so at the time. The key to Snowden's attitude is to be found in his fear of inflation. ' The microbe of inflation is always in the air,' he told the general council of the T.U.C. in 1927. Efforts to win the Labour Party over to a more modern monetary policy were greatly hampered by the lower middle-class puritanism represented by so many of its leaders. For Snowden deflation rewarded thrift and foresight; inflation penalised it. If virtue went unrewarded and vice unpunished what incentive would remain for people to behave virtuously? These views are not without point: what seems so odd in retrospect is the fervour with which they were espoused at a time when so many people were unemployed. It is a melancholy example of how easily the human mind slips into an ' either–or ' position, losing track of the valid point in an opponent's case in its determination to extirpate error. Arguments like Snowden's united *rentiers* and moralistic socialists in an unholy alliance against the spendthrifts.

MacDonald's attitude was more open. What determined his approach was a dislike of programmes such as the I.L.P. had tried to foist on him, a fear of antagonising respectable opinion, and a habit of interpreting all policy criticisms in personal terms. However, his weakness for the aristocracy led him to make a distinction between Mosley's proposals and the ' flashy futilities ' of the I.L.P. Up to a point he was prepared to use Mosley as a stick with which to beat Snowden whom he cordially detested. It was MacDonald's relatively permissive attitude to his ideas that gave Mosley grounds for hoping that the party leader might be won over to a bold policy.

The attitude of the trade union leaders was also ambiguous. The Mond–Turner conversations between leading unionists and employers in 1928 suggested that the union leaders, too, realised that a national effort had to be made to overcome the economic problem. These conversations in fact marked the first industrial approach to a producers' policy. Soon afterwards Ernest Bevin, the powerful general secretary of the Transport and General Workers Union, was to become a convert to the Keynesian approach. But what the unions were utterly opposed to was state interference in collective bargaining. As Henry Pelling has pointed out, workers tended to regard the State ' as an organisation run by and for the benefit of the wealthy '.[44] So the unions fell back on an attitude that has been well described as ' collective *laissez-faire* '. National planning of production, including the planning of prices and incomes, meant state interference with wage bargaining; and the unions were not prepared to have anything to do with it.

Underlying everything was the inability of the Labour leaders to look at the problem in national terms. When the Fabian elder statesman Sidney Webb was put in charge of a cabinet committee to examine unemployment in 1924, all he could prescribe as a remedy was ' a revival of trade '.[45] C. T. Cramp, a member of the National Executive Committee, told the Labour Socialist International meeting in Brussels in 1928 that ' the primary British requirement is the restoration of international trade '.[46] We have here a sudden glimpse of the awful price the Labour Party – and the millions who put their hopes in it in the inter-war years – were to pay for British socialism's marriage to nineteenth century liberalism.   L. T. Hobhouse had written in 1911: ' Free Trade finance was to be the basis of social reform.   Liberalism and Labour learned to co-operate in resisting delusive promises of remedies for unemployment and in maintaining the right of free international exchange.'[47] From this learning process came the seeds of the disaster of 1929–31; and it largely explains why Mosley's *Revolution by Reason* remained, in the words of Professor Pollard, ' an isolated *tour de force* '.

Chapter 8

The Dandy of the Revolution

I

IF MOSLEY's aims were moderate and reasoned, his methods were populist; the exact reverse of Labour's intelligentsia whose projects were as limitless as their contact with the masses was peripheral. It was this combination of thinker and demagogue that made Mosley such a puzzling, and frightening, person. Those who never credited him with any thinking saw him simply as an adventurer. Those who appreciated his intellectual worth could never understand why he wanted to associate with the mob – whether it was the Smethwick mob of 1926 or the fascist mob of the 1930s. Right policies, but wrong crowd, was their sad, but inevitable, lament. To this Mosley had a ready answer. The 'right crowd' never wanted to do the right thing. So from where was the motive force for change to come except from the masses? He would have said with Virgil, 'If I cannot move the Gods, I will stir the lower world to uproar.'

Underlying this 'rational' argument were two contradictory emotions which were probably fused successfully for Mosley only in fascism. On the one side, there was the whiggish desire to introduce necessary reforms from above in order to preserve existing society. On the other side, there was a pronounced alienation from that society, once the glamour of high politics had worn off. This alienation was rooted in background and in the impact of war. The First World War had destroyed the flower of Mosley's generation. It is doubtful whether he ever really forgave liberal England for having sent the bravest and the best to their doom. It had also produced the 'war generation' of survivors – new men, a new social ideal, a new set of personal values, all far removed from the old-style politics of Westminster. They had important points of contact with the Labour Party but were not satisfied by its sectarianism, its unheroic, repressed, political style. Displaced as he was from contemporary political values by a special kind of experience, Mosley turned, as others have done before him, to the people. Somewhere 'out there', far away from Westminster, beat the true heart of England. The people would restore his country to health – led, of course, by such members of the old ruling class as had managed to escape the bourgeois blight. Thus Mosley found himself locked in a contradiction. Intellectually he wanted to preserve; emotionally he wanted to destroy. This tension was to dominate his political career.

It emerges clearly for the first time in the course of 1926–in the events surrounding the General Strike and his return to Parliament as M.P. for Smethwick. Mosley had mixed feelings about the strike, called on 3 May 1926 in support of the miners' uncompromising stand of ' not a penny off the pay, not a minute on the day '. He opposed the principle of the General Strike for a number of reasons. First, if it was serious, it was revolutionary, and he had already given his opinion, in a debate with the communist Gallagher, that any revolutionary uprising would be crushed by the Army. As an old army man, he preferred to have the Army on his side.[1] Secondly, as a challenge to the elected government it was unconstitutional, and Mosley always had an innate respect for the law. Thirdly, although he loved the common man, he did not admire plebeian solutions, which offended his sense of order and intelligence. Mosley made a clear distinction between power and the men in power. He wanted not to destroy the State, but to use state forces for socialist ends. For these reasons, he was glad when the strike was called off after nine days and the emphasis swung back once more to the political solution which had always been his preferred alternative to industrial confrontation. The answer to the miners' grievances, he wrote, was to elect a Labour Government which would reverse the disastrous policy of wage-cuts.[2]

Nevertheless, Mosley was ' passionately on the side of the workers '.[3] He took a leading part in the Birmingham Strike Committee, financed a Strike Bulletin edited by John Strachey, spoke unwearyingly to keep up the strikers' morale, and narrowly escaped arrest when most of the Strike Committee were rounded up on charges of stirring up disaffection (he was out of town at the time). But his most active work was on behalf of the miners' strike which went on well into the autumn. He was happier in this phase of the struggle, since the miners' position was ' legally unimpeachable '. He spoke in mining villages all over England and helped the starving miners with lavish donations. (The attitude of the coalowners was brutally summed up by Lord Hunsdon: ' We did not feed the Germans, I cannot see for the life of me why we should feed the miners'.) The miners' struggle, he wrote, would ' awaken the working-class '. It would spearhead Labour's victory at the next election when ' retribution will overwhelm the present oppressors '.[4] In other words, he saw it as the first shot not in the revolution, but in the general election. An awakened working class was to be Mosley's guarantee against a cowardly leadership. The Party's chief flaw, as he saw it, was the continuing divorce between theory and practice. Committed in theory to extreme measures, Labour's leaders yet shrank from any conflict with their opponents. Mosley's strategy was to promise less, but fight more.[5]

The fight for the miners was to give him, alone of the left-wing

Labour ' intellectuals ', a power base within the trade union movement. From 1927 onwards he was a regular speaker at the great
Northumberland and Durham miners' galas; it was the support
of the miners that got him onto the National Executive Committee
of the Labour Party in 1927, 1928 and in 1930.*   He and John
Strachey (who edited the *Miner*) formed a close personal friendship with Arthur Cook, the fiery miners' secretary, then skirting
the fringes of the Communist Party.   Nothing is more typical than
Mosley's espousal of the cause of Cook in the teeth of bourgeois
Labour opinion.   Compare his assessment of Cook – ' an English
figure, a true product of England if ever there was one ' – with
Beatrice Webb's contemptuous dismissal: ' an inspired idiot, drunk
with his own words, dominated by his own slogans '.   But Cook
was not just admirable to Mosley as a fighter and mob orator of
genius; he was a symbol of the desperation of a particular set of
losers – a nineteenth century working-class aristocracy beaten down
and degraded by ' progress '.   Their anger would fuel Mosley's
crusade.

The switch to the political arena made it imperative for Mosley
to get back into Parliament.   The problem was how to do so without abandoning Birmingham.   In June 1925 the Birmingham
Labour Movement had brought heavy pressure on him to withdraw
from a by-election at the Forest of Dean.†   There seemed nothing
for it but to fight Chamberlain again in 1929.   But in July 1926
Chamberlain, seeing the writing on the wall, had shifted his own
candidature to Edgbaston, Birmingham's Belgravia.   Having thus
accomplished his primary aim of driving Chamberlain out, Mosley felt free to leave Ladywood. An opportunity to contest neighbouring Smethwick arose at the end of the year and Mosley decided
to take it.   It was a by-election that was to earn him a national
reputation for dangerous extremism at precisely the moment he

*Until 1937 constituency party representatives were elected to the N.E.C. by
the vote of the whole conference.

†On the death of the sitting Labour M.P., James Wignall, the executive of the
Forest of Dean, a mining constituency on the Welsh borders, invited Miss Margaret Bondfield to contest the seat.   The full party meeting, however, demanded
Mosley instead – though he had not been before the selection conference.   After
visiting the constituency on 22 June 1925, Mosley decided to accept; he was
endorsed by the N.E.C. the next day.   But the Birmingham and Ladywood
Labour parties refused to let him go 'even temporarily'.   Hurriedly Mosley
withdrew his acceptance, explaining to the N.E.C. ' that he had no alternative
after . . . finding the whole of the Movement in Birmingham strongly opposed
to it '.   (N.E.C. Minutes, 24 June 1925; for Birmingham's opposition to Mosley's
departure, see Minutes of the Birmingham borough Labour party, 23 June
1925.)   This demand for Mosley's services aroused considerable jealousy among
well-established, but less popular, Labour personalities: Miss Bondfield was not
thereafter a notably warm admirer.

was seeking to establish his credentials as a moderate. Smethwick revealed Mosley to the Conservatives as a dangerous and
unscrupulous demagogue playing shamelessly on the passions and
cupidity of a moronic electorate. To the Labour movement on
the contrary he became the symbol of the fight back from the defeats
and humiliations of the General Strike. For the first time he
started to be talked about as a future leader of the Labour Party.

Initially, Mosley's trouble came more from his own party than
from the Opposition. His wealth, arrogance and radicalism had
made him anathema to a powerful section of the bourgeois leadership. Thus when John Davison, an official of the Ironfounders'
Society and the sitting Labour Member for Smethwick, announced
his resignation on 22 November 1926 on grounds of ill-health, and
Mosley was hurriedly selected in his place, the National Executive
Committee refused to endorse him because of a ' technical irregula-
rity '. After much trundling of Labour politicians to and from
London this little local difficulty was sorted out and Mosley was
officially adopted on 4 December 1926.* Tory press attacks were
only to be expected, but attacks from his own party were harder
to bear. It was suggested that Mosley had bribed Davison to
retire; in fact the poor man was mortally ill and died three months
later. The real objections to Mosley were revealed when at the
height of the by-election Philip Snowden warned the Labour Party
not to ' degenerate into an instrument for the ambitions of wealthy
men ' and referred to candidatures being ' put up to auction by
the local Labour Party and sold to the highest bidder '.[6] Herbert
Morrison wrote sententiously in the *New Leader*, 'it all goes to show
how careful well-to-do people should be in their relations with a
political party which cannot and will not have its constituencies
handled in the way the Liberals and Tories handle the constituencies which they control '.[7] We may also detect an N.E.C. desire to
prevent Mosley from establishing a Labour equivalent of Chamberlain's Birmingham caucus. In fact the charge that Mosley had
' bought ' Smethwick was ludicrously wide of the mark. He was
chosen to fight Smethwick as he would have been to fight dozens

*The technical ground for withholding endorsement was that Mosley's adoption
had been steamrollered by the Smethwick Executive. Although he had been
adopted by the full party meeting, sufficient time had not been allowed for considering the claims of alternative candidates. The N.E.C. thus demanded a
new conference ' of all affiliated organisations to receive the local Executive's
nomination and to make other nominations if desired . . . '. The Smethwick
Executive claimed that it had followed the procedure laid down for emergencies.
Eventually it gave way and a new selection conference on 4 December ' elected
Mr. Mosley nem. con.', the two local candidates Aldermen Willetts and Betts
receiving no support. (See N.E.C. Minutes, November–December 1926, *Town
Crier* and *New Leader*, 3 December 1926.)

of seats all round the country because he was a brilliant, exciting and dangerous campaigner, a candidate with rare charisma and an exceptional electoral record.

Georg Brandes has written of Ferdinand Lassalle, the founder of the German Socialist Party, ' An intellectual aristocrat and a social democrat! The phenomenon that here meets us is, in the world of thought, precisely that contrast which was outwardly apparent when Lassalle, in his dandified clothes, his fine linen, and his patent-leather boots, spoke formally or informally among a number of grimy, horny-handed mechanics.'[8]

It was this outward contrast between the accoutrements and life-style of the wealthy aristocrat and the role of champion and leader of the proletariat that provided the theme of most of the attacks on Mosley in the 1920s. This campaign, led by the press-lords Beaverbrook and Rothermere, reached its climax during and immediately after the Smethwick by-election. The initial handle was provided by the fact that Mosley's two opponents, John Pike (Conservative), a former railwayman, and Edwin Bayliss (Liberal), son of a miner, could both be represented as genuine ' working-class' candidates in contrast to the aristocratic *poseur* fighting them on behalf of the working class.*

In the theme of the *faux homme* the Press thought it had hit upon a sure winner. The *Daily Mail*'s account of Mosley's opening meeting set the tone of much of Conservative press reporting. There was no mention of his speech; much of his and Cimmie's clothes. Mosley was 'immaculately dressed'. Cimmie was 'elegantly gown-ed', removing her ' magnificent fur coat' to display a 'charming dress' glittering with diamonds. (As Cimmie later explained, she had on a dress she had bought in India with little bits of looking-glass stitched into the sleeves.) The chairman of the meeting announced that for the duration of the campaign Cimmie would be known as 'plain Mrs. Mosley ... Lady Cynthia blushed and looked confused'. How Mayfair must have loved these sallies!

The Press could never quite decide whether the Mosleys were flaunting their wealth or adopting heavy proletarian camouflage – and which was the more reprehensible. One moment Mosley was preaching socialism ' in a twenty guineas Savile Row suit'. The next he was 'playing his part well' in an 'old overcoat and a battered hat and calling Lady Cynthia " the missus"'.[9] One moment the Mosleys were supposed to be driving around in their Rolls-Royce, drinking champagne and putting up in Birmingham's most expensive

---

*Cynthia Mosley found herself in the same position when she was adopted prospective Labour candidate for Stoke-on-Trent in 1927. Her opponent, the sitting Conservative, Col. John Ward, had once been a navvy. During the Smethwick election one newspaper poked fun at Cimmie's 'Hyde Park senti-ments delivered in a Park Lane accent '.

hotel; the next driving round in a hired Ford, drinking beer and living in a boarding-house. The papers were full of gossipy items about the wealthy socialist couple frolicking on the Riviera, spending thousands of pounds in renovating their 'mansion'* and generally living a debauched aristocratic life.[10]

To give its readers a more vivid impression of what the real Mosley world was like, the *Daily Express*, which with the *Daily Mail* took the lead in this brand of journalism, routed out Mosley's father and persuaded the no doubt alcoholic Tory squire to pour out his grievances against his son:

> He was born with a golden spoon in his mouth – it cost £100 in doctor's fees to bring him into the world. He lived on the fat of the land and never did a day's work in his life. If he and his wife want to go in for Labour, why don't they do a bit of work themselves?... My son tells the tale that he does this and that but he lives in the height of luxury. If the working class... are going to be taken in by such nonsense – I am sorry for them. How does my son know anything about them?[11]†

This interview gave the Press a new theme for attack. Now it was 'Mr. Mosley, who on his father's own admission, has never done a day's work in his life...'. The *Daily Mail* started headlining him 'Mr. Silver Spoon Mosley'.

This line of attack aroused all Mosley's fighting instincts. Turning savagely on the local press which followed the national line Mosley retorted, 'No one could go before a working class audience with a better certificate round his neck than the hatred of the *Birmingham Mail*.'[12] The words were prophetic, for the blatant bias of the Press gave him a new prestige in the eyes of many working-class voters. In his acceptance speech at the selection conference of 4 December, Mosley had said, 'While I am being abused by the Capitalist Press I know I am doing effective work for the Labour cause.'[13] His Smethwick supporters took him at his word and worked with redoubled enthusiasm for his cause.

Even without Mosley's special ability to raise the political temperature, it would have been surprising had an election in a work-

---

*The Mosleys that autumn had acquired a house and estate at Denham, just outside London, which was to be the Mosley home till it was sold in 1946.

†Sir Oswald's grievance against his son had been brought to life by a press report from America that the Mosleys had talked about relinquishing their titles. In a letter to the *Daily Mail* of 12 April 1926, Sir Oswald had written that ' more valuable help would be rendered to the country by my Socialist son and daughter-in-law if, instead of achieving cheap publicity about relinquishing titles, they would take more material action and relinquish some of their wealth and so help to make easier the plight of some of their more unfortunate followers '.

ing-class constituency under those circumstances not produced a good deal of passion. Some rowdiness was inevitable. In fact it was surprisingly small, and was by no means all the fault of Labour. On one occasion early on, Pike was howled down by communists singing the ' Red Flag ' – a strange foretaste of Mosley's own experiences in the 1930s.[14] But after this he was not troubled till the eve of poll. Pike accused Mosley of ' stealing ' his pitches outside factories: the local Liberal paper reported that in fact Pike was stealing Mosley's pitches.[15] At one of Mosley's meetings for Labour women, a group of 'Socialist Amazons' tried to manhandle a reporter in the press box. Their entrance was prevented by the simple expedient of locking the door, though Mosley's attempts to restore order by appealing to the ladies not to attack the ' wage-slaves of capitalism ' was adjudged ' mischievous '.

These incidents were built up by the Conservative press into a portrait of Pike battling valiantly against screaming mobs of socialist hooligans inflamed by Mosley's rhetoric of class hatred. The *Morning Post* of 18 December 1926 condemned ' Mobocracy at Smethwick '. Its special correspondent felt that he was witnessing ' the birth of a new era in electioneering . . . it is no longer a political struggle; it is an experiment in mob psychology of a kind that has never been attempted before '. After the election, *The Times* claimed in a leading article of 1 January 1927 that Mosley was seeking ' in civil troubles the readiest way to power ', that he 'delighted in the applause of the streets '. The stereotype had long ago been suggested by Burke: ' When men of rank sacrifice all ideas of dignity to an ambition without distinct object, and work with low instruments and for low ends, the whole composition becomes low and base.'[16]

The main answer to this is Mosley's *Revolution by Reason*. No soldier of fortune spends his time working out detailed economic blueprints. The real objection to Mosley was that he was stirring up trouble. His methods were contrasted unfavourably with the ' reasonable' approach of MacDonald and Henderson. Yet with the political élites wedded to the *status quo* how was a radical party to get support for change? It has recently been argued that the British working class in the 1920s was basically conservative and defensive, thus weakening Labour's punch at Westminster.[17] There may be something in this. But, if it were so, it cannot be considered in isolation from the quality of leadership and political education the working class was being given. As Tawney succinctly put it, How can followers be Ironsides if leaders are flunkeys?'[18] Both in their scepticism about the possibility of creating full employment and in their awe of their opponents, Labour leaders were flunkeys – slaves to dead economists and to the restrictive conventions of British public life. Smethwick briefly opened up an alternative road to power and the use of power. But this road could be tra-

velled only by fighters – and they were in short supply in Labour
politics.

It was central to the press image of Mosley as a shallow demagogue who had never done a day's work in his life that he should
have no policy.   He was indulging in promises of *panem et circenses*.[19]
In fact, Mosley fought on the official Labour and I.L.P. programmes,
but with special emphasis on the charge that Conservative policy
meant wage reductions.   This was the so-called ' wages lie' which
rankled with the Conservative press.

Mosley claimed that Baldwin had told Arthur Cook that wages
would have to come down.   Baldwin denied he had said any
such thing.   Mosley's announcement ' I withdraw nothing' led to
a scathing editorial in the *Birmingham Post*.   ' Apparently when he
abandoned the " political privileges " of his class he abandoned also
the ordinary decencies of political life.   Starting to win Smethwick
by gross misrepresentation, he has now committed himself to winning
it . . . by an audacious falsehood. . . . To speak quite plainly, a man
with such standards is out of his element in British politics.'[20]   A
few days later the *Post* charged Mosley with being ' devoid of any
sporting instinct, of any regard for the ordinary conventions of
political controversy, of any desire to " play the game " '.[21]   Mosley's
reply was characteristic: ' This is not a kissing match, but a stand-
up fight.'[22]   In his special message to Pike, Baldwin wrote, ' For
Socialists who pose as leaders of the people without having a shred of
qualification for that position we can have nothing but contempt.'[23]
Mosley's retort was swift.   In his attempts to weaken the trade
unions Baldwin's aim was ' to make working class bees without a
sting, who were to gather honey for the rich but be deprived of
the right to defend themselves '.[24]

As polling day (21 December) approached it became increasingly
clear that the Conservative campaign had heavily misfired.   Davison's majority against Pike in 1924 had been 1253.   By 13 December
the *Daily Herald* was already forecasting a Labour majority of 3000.
As ' Watchman ' remarked in the *Town Crier*, ' [Beaverbrook and
Rothermere] created such a position in Smethwick that if on the
eve of poll Oswald Mosley had committed bigamy or murdered
his wife, nobody in Smethwick would have believed the story '.

In anticipation of a Labour victory, the leading London dailies
framed their excuses.   ' He has descended to the lowest level of
electioneering that has been reached in this country for many a
long year,' wrote the *Daily Telegraph* on 20 December. His tactics,
it went on pompously, had ' excited in the public bosom a lively
feeling of disgust which Mr Mosley will find it hard to live down'.
' No antic has been too foolish, no mis-statement too petty or trans-
parent, no tactics too contemptible for the Socialists to adopt in
their grovelling appeal to all that is most stupid and most deplorable

in human nature,' thundered the *Morning Post* on 21 December. In a last-minute effort to turn the tide, the Rothermere and Beaverbrook press discovered a 'Red plot' when the communists Gallagher and McManus turned up in Smethwick urging the workers to support Mosley and a mysterious Chinaman, studying elections, appeared in his entourage.

Mosley's majority of 6582 on an eighty-per-cent poll surprised even his most optimistic supporters.* To a crowd of 8000 outside the Town Hall he said: 'This is not a by-election, it is history. The result of this election sends out a message to every worker in the land. You have met and beaten the Press of reaction.... Tonight all Britain looks to you and thanks you. My wonderful friends of Smethwick, by your heroic battle against a whole world in arms, I believe you have introduced a new era for British democracy.' The *New Leader* saw Smethwick as the 'Waterloo of the Press Lords'. Pike, attributing his defeat to rowdiness and Mosley's 'wages lie', thought that Smethwick marked the beginning of the conquest of the Labour Party by rich demagogues. Surprisingly reversing its earlier hysterics, the *Morning Post* in a sober analysis blamed the Conservative defeat on the efficiency and zeal of the Labour organisation and the discontent and suffering caused by the decay of industry.[25] The *Derbyshire Advertiser* of 24 December was one of the few to make the obvious point that 'Mr. Mosley, whatever we may say or think about him, made a good candidate.' Everyone now agreed that the press campaign against Mosley had caused a revulsion in his favour. 'Left to himself', the *Birmingham Post* declared ungraciously, 'he would have fouled his own nest. As it was, he reaped advantage from the extravagance of his opponents.'[26]

II

With his return to Westminster in January 1927, Mosley began the ascent to the peak of his parliamentary career. His political reputation was far from secure. Most Conservatives had not forgiven him for his 'class betrayal'. Most Labour leaders had not accepted him as one of them. On the other hand, he was something of a hero to a small group of younger politicians, not all of them in the Labour Party, and he possessed an unmistakable power of mass appeal. People were starting to argue furiously about his qualities and his future.

To conventional politicians – the overwhelming majority – Mosley was a perpetual affront. There was, first of all, his unparliamentary good looks, suggestive of the dark, passionate, Byronic gentleman-villain of the melodrama, in whose presence young ladies develop

*Mosley received 16,077 votes, Pike 9495, Bayliss 2600.

unaccountable palpitations and sedate husbands itch for their riding-whips. To Ellen Wilkinson he was 'The Sheik'. His type, she remarked, 'is not that of the nice kind hero who rescues the girl at the point of torture, but the one who hisses "At last ... we meet." '27 The fatal attractions of the sheik were not appreciated by the par-liamentary good husbands.

Then there was his arrogance, embodied in his whole demeanour. Black wavy hair swept back from a high forehead; huge hawk's nose; disdainful mouth curling contemptuously beneath a dark moustache; head tilted upwards to avoid the bad smells of the sur-rounding political countryside: this was the way the cartoonists saw him. The general view was that he had far too high an opinion of himself and needed to be taken down 'a peg or two', rather as prefects at a boarding school regard the precocious new boy. Certainly no one who later wrote – and obviously felt at the time – 'After eleven years of experience of politics I had complete confi-dence in my own capacity to solve any problem confronting the nation' can be regarded as a modest man. Mosley clearly believed that, unlike Lord Attlee, he had plenty not to be modest about. He actually did have better ideas than anyone else in politics. The trouble was that few people paid any attention to what he was saying, and when they did they misunderstood it. Mosley com-pletely lacked the art of pretending to be as uninspired as others—a necessary art for success in democratic politics. He knew he was cleverer and showed it. Few loved him in consequence.

He had the peculiar knack of infuriating his opponents. Partly it was his physical presence. Partly it was a certain look, expressive of extreme fatigue, that he was wont to assume in the presence of well-meaning but boring people, which could shrivel up their self-confidence. Partly it was his habit of subjecting loose arguments to relentless cross-examination, in the manner of a prosecuting counsel. Partly it was his facility for the clever, but cutting, phrase. In Parliament he referred to interruptions as 'zoological noises striving to attain the heights of human speech'. He sympathised with Winston Churchill – 'a racehorse with a donkey strapped to its back.' The donkey was the Conservative Party – 'sublime medio-crity at the head of inveterate prejudice'. Of Stanley Baldwin he remarked, 'He may not be a good companion for a tiger hunt, or even for a pig hunt, but every time he runs away, he proves afresh the honesty of his convictions.' Mosley's obvious enjoyment of his own *mots* prompted the Conservative Sir Reginald Banks to remark, 'I never listen to the orations of the hon. Baronet* the Member for Smethwick without thinking of the famous lines of Pope on Addison

---

*Mosley inherited the title and full control of an estate of £250,000 on the death of his father in September 1928.

Gives a little Senate laws,
And sits attentive to his own applause.'

Cimmie was a transparently ' good ' and ' sincere ' person.   By
contrast, Mosley, to most people, seemed to be an enigma wrapped
up in a mystery: all artifice, a series of roles carefully put on for
different occasions, so that people wondered where the real Mosley
was, or if he even existed.   He practised a highly stylised form of
politics.   The sudden raising of the eyelids, the studied movements
of hands and body, the polished phrases, even the elaborate courtesy,
all suggested a conscious attempt to give style to his character.
Here is how Hore-Belisha describes the finished parliamentary
product in 1927: ' When I gaze on Mr. Oswald Mosley speaking
I feel I know what Chatham was like.   The elder Pitt was an actor.
He acted in the closet, he acted in the Commons.   Natural only
in his unnaturalness, he cannot be imagined off-stage.   Nor can
Mr. Mosley.   Dark, aquiline, flashing; tall, thin, assured; defiance
in his eye, contempt in his forward chin, his features are cast in a
mould of disdain.   His very smile is a shrug.   His voice is pitched
in a tragedian's key.   His sentences are trailed away.   He is the
only man in the House of Commons who has made an Art of
himself.'[28]

Mosley himself would regard this as high praise.   He has always
rejected the view that the individual is a fixed collection of qualities
determined by genes or early upbringing, seeing him rather as a
process directed by will, a self-conscious instrument of the tasks he
sets himself.   To be a politician one had to learn the part from the
masters of action.   His earliest model, as Hore-Belisha suggests,
was Chatham.   In his early socialist days he saw himself as Lassalle.
In the later 1920s he became fascinated by Julius Caesar and even
planned a biography of the aristocratic tribune of the left who re-
established a new aristocratic state on the ruins of the bourgeois
one, of the youthful libertine of Mommsen's portrait who nevertheless kept his qualities of mind and body unimpaired for his encounter with destiny.   From Shaw's *Caesar and Cleopatra* Mosley
learnt the importance of dissimulation, the doctrine that for a man
of action people and ideas are not right or wrong, good or evil,
but useful or useless.   Mosley was often to remark that the ability
to assume as many shapes as Proteus is an indispensable requirement for political leadership in the modern age.   His own ability
to do so helps explain his immensely wide political and social range.
Uprooted himself, he was a perfect politician for a mass society.

In the end it is impossible to say how far Mosley fitted his character to his conception of his role, or his conception of his role to
his character: there was obviously a process of mutual adjust-
ment.   That he was genuinely indifferent to class distinctions and

to those externals of manner and style by which different groups separate themselves from each other is indisputable. What interested him were qualities of mind, skill and character. Here perhaps the war experience was crucial. If your life depends on someone, you are not concerned with his accent, school, or political opinions, but only with whether he can do what the situation requires. Mosley's politics were always based on situation, not class or doctrine. This attitude never failed to shock those wedded to ' normal ' peace-time distinctions. People wondered whether he had any deep attachments at all. He seemed to be someone with a great soul, but little heart.

One can also view Mosley's public artifice as an elaborate defence of his privacy. He always tried to maintain the old English distinction between public and private life. The aristocrat must put on a good show for the people; what he did in his own time, in his own home, was his own business. Inevitably the two spheres overlapped to some extent. Cimmie was both a wife and a political partner. John Strachey was a personal as well as a political friend. Nevertheless, the Mosleys' private world remained a very different place from their public one.

There were two main circles of personal friends. The first was connected with the arts: Oliver Messel, Cecil Beaton, Sacheverell Sitwell and less frequently the Barrymores were all guests at Denham. Mosley's own real interest in this world was centred on the cinema. He greatly admired Fritz Lang and one summer even directed a horror film based on his expressionist techniques, featuring among others John Strachey and Cecil Beaton, the latter dressed up in drag as Margot Asquith, with long pointed claws. The film having been completed, the whole party rushed down to the Riviera, where an irate chambermaid finally gathered up the strips festooned round the bedrooms and firmly consigned them to the rubbishbin of history. One reel survives as testimony to a talent lost to politics. There was also a small circle of men-friends of roughly Mosley's age and social background: Bob Boothby, Harold Nicolson, Esmond Harmsworth (with whom Mosley ran a shooting syndicate), Charles Baillie-Hamilton, Brendan Bracken and Hore-Belisha. This group formed a continuing link with the other side which was to be very useful in 1930.

Mosley lived his private life at a fast pace. There were jaunts to Paris and Berlin (where Harold Nicolson took him on the rounds of the bisexual night-clubs) as well as longer annual sojourns in Venice or in the south of France. Mosley was attractive to, and attracted by, the opposite sex and apparently took full advantage of his opportunities. A French journalist wrote, ' Paris has often seen him thus, driving too fast in too big a car, trailing after him many entangled hearts, many sarcasms, and a few confidences.'

High-spirited larking perhaps best describes the atmosphere of the Mosley milieu. Films taken by Cimmie show her husband as a comedian in the style of Charlie Chaplin – eyes rolling outrageously, acting out melodramatic opera duets, scampering along the banks of the river on the Denham estate, legs flailing in all directions. There are endless stories of his practical joking such as when he served an omelette filled with tobacco to a particularly boring guest, or when he arranged a mock burglary at a sedate dinner-party. His rather priggish sisters-in-law, Irene and Alexandra, were favourite butts; as was John Strachey's wife, Esther Murphy, a very tall lesbian with a squint who used to talk non-stop (Mosley was best man at Strachey's wedding in 1928).

Many found it hard to reconcile all this frivolity with Mosley's self-professed seriousness; hence the widespread impression that politics to him was simply another diversion, like the rest. Beatrice Webb, whose tried and tested formula for achievement was high thinking and plain living, was terribly disapproving. ' Deep down he is a cynic. He will be beaten and retire,' she wrote of him. Mosley himself explains his frantic quest for excitement as an attempt to escape from the memories of war as well as a product of intense frustration. He was the classic case of someone who could not settle down again to ' normal ' peace-time life; and the temptation to live life outrageously, even to the point of self-destruction, seems to have been growing stronger in the later 1920s. This is, of course, what actually happened in the 1930s. It is easy to read into the earlier decade the signs of later instability. Interestingly, such a dénouement was foreseen in A. P. Nicholson's novel, *Who Goes Home?*, published in 1930, in which the career of Sir Richard Garriock (Mosley), the brilliant, rising, young politician, is ruined by a murder charge arising from a fencing match with his mistress's husband. ' They say I killed a man; they made a holocaust,' Garriock remarks bitterly as he prepares to go into exile. ' What will you do now?' his friend Strange asks him. ' Ah, that is not easy, when you find the world is a trap in which you are caught.'

Shrewd though the insight is, Nicholson failed to emphasise sufficiently the strength of Mosley's underlying commitment to the ideals of the war generation. This is what was to give his 'suicide' its political, rather than personal, character. Try as he might, there was no way Mosley could escape the obligation to his dead comrades. They summoned him from their Flanders grave to win the future they had died for; and Mosley's life was a continuous rededication to their memory. The secret of his advance in the Labour Party according to Egon Wertheimer was 'that he is a much harder worker than even his closest friends realise'. He was an indefatigable public speaker, and there was nothing slapdash about his speaking methods. It is a tribute to his seriousness that he gra-

dually but surely schooled his flamboyant parliamentary style to
the demands of the oratorically unrewarding subject of economics.
'Mr. Mosley made a good speech to an empty House on the subject
of currency and credit – clearly the only thing worth talking about,'
remarked the *Spectator* on 16 April 1927.   His contributions to the
unemployment debates in November 1928 and March 1929 were
foretastes of his great speeches in 1930.   The *Spectator* of 17 November 1928 commented: ' Mosley delivered the single good speech
from the Labour benches during these days of debate.'   It was
' interesting, and along socialist lines, constructive. . . . To the amazement of Unionist members who had never before heard him in a
more or less reasonable mood, he was quietly effective.' (By contrast,
Ramsay MacDonald ' meandered about in his usual way, long-
winded and vague and as illogical as ever '.)   It was this hard
work that made possible Mosley's achievements in 1930.

III

Despite Mosley's unpopularity at Westminster, he was rapidly
becoming a force to be reckoned with in the Labour Party. For his
first three years in the Party his main national political base was
the I.L.P.   At its Leicester Conference in 1927 he was elected to
the National Administrative Council as a national member – that is,
by the vote of the whole I.L.P. It was an astonishing achievement,
for the three other national members – David Kirkwood, Emmanuel
Shinwell and Robert Wallhead – were all veterans of long standing.
He remained on the N.A.C. for two years before being defeated by
Fenner Brockway in 1929.   It was frequently suggested in the press
at this time that Mosley could have become chairman of the I.L.P.
This is doubtful.   In any case, by the time he became a real power
in the I.L.P. it was becoming less important for him.

   Mosley had little time for the sectarian politics and ideology of
the Clyde group.   By the late 1920s there was a strong grass-roots
movement in the I.L.P. in favour of disaffiliation from the Labour
Party.   Mosley would have none of this.   The Party must stay
united, he insisted, to win a majority at the next general election.
This view placed him on the ' sensible' wing of the National Administrative Council, together with Shinwell and P. J. Dollan.   The
crisis came in June 1928 with the publication of the Cook–Maxton
Manifesto.   Ostensibly a protest against industrial collaboration,
it was intended by Wheatley and Gallagher to be a sounding-board
for a new political party.   Ironically, in the light of his later
views, Mosley moved to heal the breach.   He 'wondered what all
the fuss was about.   It requires all types and personalities to make
a great movement, and the duty of leadership was to blend them.
So far from losing elections, different appeals to different sections
helped to win them.   MacDonald made an appeal to one section

of the community with incomparable skill, and Maxton and Cook appealed to the working-class as no one else could.'[29]   What Wheatley and Mosley might have done together had Wheatley lived is a fascinating speculation.   Wheatley had a high regard for Mosley, describing him at the Smethwick by-election as ' one of the most brilliant and hopeful figures thrown up by the Socialist Movement during the last 30 years '.   In his memoirs, Mosley describes Wheatley as the 'only man of Lenin quality the English Left ever produced'. In this period, though, their political hopes and interests pulled in different directions.   Wheatley, from long experience, knew that nothing could be expected of a MacDonald administration.   He was even prepared to break with the Labour Party.   Mosley still believed in the possibility of action within the Party.   By the time his belief in Labour had vanished, Wheatley was dead.[30]

As we have seen, Mosley was elected to the National Executive Committee of the Labour Party in October 1927, once more by a vote of the whole party.*   This for the first time brought him into close working contact with Labour's leaders.   He soon came into conflict with them on the question of the Party's manifesto for the next election.   Appointed to the N.E.C. Programme Committee, Mosley, in collaboration with Wilkinson and Trevelyan, prepared a couple of pages of short, snappy sentences, full of pep. MacDonald, refusing to be intimidated, as he put it, by the ' hectic rattle of machinegun prose', wanted a much longer statement full of socialist aspirations but vague on details – ' more of a running buffet than a set meal ', as John Scanlon remarked.   Eventually Mosley reluctantly agreed that the form of the programme was irrelevant, writing in the *Daily Herald* on 25 July 1928:

> In the end both the ideas and the personalities of the Labour Movement must be tried by the test of action.   That test can only properly be applied by Parliamentary power.   Preliminary criticism is mostly beating in the air.   It rests on words and speculations.   To many of us it will be a merciful moment when the Labour Movement passes from the test of words to the test of deeds.†

*He came fourth in the constituency section.   The figures were: G. Lansbury, 2,183,000; C. P. Trevelyan, 1,675,000; J. H. Hayes, 1,644,000; O. Mosley, 1,613,000; Herbert Morrison, 1,562,000.   In 1928 the figures were G. Lansbury, 3,071,000; Herbert Morrison, 2,823,000; O. Mosley, 2,153,000; C. P. Trevelyan, 1,882,000; H. Dalton, 1,774,000.

†Further details of this controversy are provided in the N.E.C. Minutes of 29 February, 28 March, 2 May 1928; and 25 March 1929.   The Mosley–Trevelyan–Wilkinson line received considerable, though minority, support.   According to the Minutes of 2 May 1928, ' Mr. Trevelyan and Mr. Mosley stated their opinion that there should be some statement as to the attitude of the minority, who desired a shorter and different form of Programme, presenting in unmistakable

Although Mosley clashed with MacDonald on this issue, it did not affect the noticeably warm relationship which had grown up between them. At first sight the radical, clear-headed Mosley and the respectable, woolly MacDonald would seem to have had little enough in common. MacDonald, the cynics sneered, was cultivating his taste for the aristocracy, while Mosley had sold out to the Labour establishment in the hope of office. There was something in this, but not much. MacDonald certainly had a weakness for the well-born. As Snowden remarked with his usual acidity, ' An intimate social relationship was established [with the Mosleys] such as never existed between Mr. MacDonald and the plebeian members of the Labour Party.'[31] As for Mosley, he was never as worried about his associations as is the pure doctrinaire who would rather die chaste than cohabit with sin. (For the true I.L.P.-er even entry into a Labour government was a betrayal. ' We felt he had left us,' Kirkwood wrote when John Wheatley took office in 1924.) Mosley would have supped with the Devil to get a vigorous unemployment policy. Frugal weekends with MacDonald at Lossiemouth scarcely came into that class.

But then Mosley was never a doctrinaire in the I.L.P. sense. His non-ideological activism attracted rather than repelled MacDonald. For MacDonald was an activist *manqué*. In many ways Mosley was the sort of person he would have liked to be had he been well-born, had he been less inhibited, had he not been obliged to sell out socially to overcome the psychological stigma of being illegitimate, had he not been saddled with the Labour Party, had he been less tired, less old, less confused. Where Snowden and others were simply blind to Mosley's qualities, or only paid them lip-service, MacDonald was perceptive enough to see in Mosley the makings of a great party leader, a worthy successor to himself, someone who might some day do the things which he himself had once dreamt of doing. Nor was MacDonald a complete Victorian like Snowden. He understood enough about the contemporary problem to realise that something more than Gladstonian budgets was required.

---

terms the actual measures upon which a Labour Government would at once embark, and which was the kind of document they considered Conference had in mind when instructing the Executive to prepare a Programme.' Eventually the compromise reached was that the Sub-Committee should issue the long document drafted by MacDonald and Tawney (*Labour and the Nation*), but should prepare a crisper one for the actual general election manifesto. But even the second one which emerged in 1929 was far too vague for the activists. On 26 March 1929 Miss Wilkinson pleaded for a crisper statement with ' only four or five important items '. ' Sir Oswald Mosley enquired as to the position of the Old Age Pensions. Was the pensionable age to be 60 or 65 and had the financing of the Scheme been worked out in any way?' This inconvenient query was predictably referred to a committee.

Harold Nicolson found his socialism rather synthetic – ' like Harris tweed made in Bavaria,' he once said. This is unfair. The real trouble was that, like so many other progressive reformers bred in the tradition of parliamentary ritual and compromise, MacDonald had long since lost the will or clarity of purpose to make change effective. Nevertheless he still liked to play the part of the radical leader, open to new ideas, and a few actual radical associates were necessary stage-props to these fantasies. Mosley was one; even Keynes was admitted to the magic circle. Occasionally MacDonald would astound those who had long since given up any hope of action from him by exclaiming, ' Something must be done.' New advisers were brought in; enquiries would be set on foot; there would be a hum of activity. Then just as suddenly the advisers would go home, the reports would be shelved, the activity would cease and the weary Titan would animadvert on the difficulties of life, the consolations of art, the simple joys of the countryside.

In October 1928 the Mosleys took MacDonald on a Continental motor-car tour, covering Prague, Berlin and Vienna. It was on this occasion that Mosley first encountered MacDonald's mistress, a mid-European lady well known at international socialist gatherings. Her later appearance in England was to cause MacDonald, then prime minister, some embarrassment. The European journey led to rumours that MacDonald was introducing a future Labour foreign secretary to European statesmen. (Mosley's seconding of MacDonald's foreign-policy resolution at the Labour Party Conference at the beginning of the month seemed to point the same way.) In Berlin the *Daily Mail*'s reporting of the socialists' European holiday took a familiar turn as MacDonald prepared to address the Reichstag. ' Lady Cynthia, the famous champion of the proletariat, looked more lovely than ever. She was in an evening frock of grey tissue with a rich grey cloak, and round her neck she wore a string of pearls. Slowly and with an air which a great actress might envy, she went to the place assigned to her, followed by her husband and Mr. Ramsay MacDonald. . . . As she sat down her shawl of snowy white ermine fell from her gracious shoulders. . . . '

In Birmingham, it was Mosley, not MacDonald, who ruled. To a small circle of friends in the Birmingham Labour Party he was a hero. They included John Strachey, Dick Plummer (manager of the I.L.P.'s *New Leader*), Allan Young and Sydney Potter, I.L.P. candidate for Sparkbrook till 1928. Mosley was best man at his wedding that year to Ursula Spicer. In a letter to the author, Potter has described the impression made by Mosley:

I was undoubtedly a hero-worshipper of Mosley in those days. It seems odd now looking back that he was only a few

months older than me.   He was a man of extraordinary maturity of mind, I think certainly the most mature-minded man
that I had encountered. . . . Of course, gifts of speech you can
be born with as undoubtedly he was, but where he acquired
his immense range of knowledge is beyond me.   He hadn't
been to university and he had had no theoretical training . . .
it was just natural genius.   His great height and his splendid
voice and range of language and his striking presence combined to set him apart.   Also, of course, he was an arch-
flatterer and you can get away with that sort of thing when
you are tall and handsome and a famous man and a baronet
to boot. . . . I remember a meeting, in the Smethwick by-election . . . a pretty turbulent, cheerfully riotous affair.   I was
what is called holding the fort . . . that wearying, exacting
business when you are up on the platform and the main speaker is late in arriving and they all want to hear him and it is
your duty to keep them going until he arrives. . . . I kept the
fort until Mosley came and then made way for him amidst
vast excitement and applause . . . he grasped my hand between
both of his and said: ' Sydney, old boy, they tell me you were
superb.'   But I recall now that when he uttered this . . . he
wasn't looking at me at all, he was looking over my shoulder
at the hungry mob longing to see him. . . .

Admittedly in his early days he made on the ultra-critical
and ultra-discerning an impression of insincerity.   Partly
this was because of the old offence known in others of being
too clever by half. . . . Mosley did tend to envelop himself in
melodrama.   He once said to me with a grin: ' We aren't the
modest type Sydney, are we?'   My wife's family who were all
liberals and non-conformists and people of the most worthy
kind all found him rather grating.   He was flamboyant, a
swashbuckler.   But if you have such staggering gifts, if you
are painted on so broad a canvas and in such brilliant colours
it must be very hard to be at the same time a person of modest
mien.   This is no day for eagles – and Mosley was, alas for
himself and in a way alas for all of us, an eagle.

Mosley was the key figure in Labour's advance in Birmingham
and the Midlands.   He took an impoverished, sluggish party by
the scruff of the neck, infused it with his own dynamism (and money)
and used it to break the hold of the Chamberlain dynasty.

To the ordinary Labour militant Mosley's outstanding quality
was his fighting spirit.   As a local correspondent put it, ' When
Mr. Mosley gets up he seems to suggest that if anyone wants a
scrap – well, he isn't going to be far away.'[32]   How admirable such
a quality seemed in the champion of Labour – how reprehensible

when the black shirt was put on! Mosley's speeches were full of fighting rhetoric. ' They would fight the Tories, they would break them and crush them, and subject them to the greatest disaster ever meted out to a political party.'[33] Wilfred Whiteley, who won Ladywood in 1929, considered that ' Grayson and Mosley were the two best mob orators I've ever known '.[34]

Nor were his efforts confined to the public platform. It was he and Allan Young who spearheaded Labour's campaigns in the municipal elections of 1924 and 1927, Mosley hammering home the point that a Labour majority was needed so that a Labour government would not be hampered by local-authority obstruction. His herculean canvassing, largely on foot, left his aides prostrated and probably brought on his first attack of phlebitis in 1927. Yet on May Day 1928, just up from his sickbed, he walked three miles in the Labour parade. It was this continual campaigning, plus superb organisation, that made possible Labour's successes in 1929.

With the local Labour newspaper, the *Town Crier*, and its editor, W. J. Chamberlain, Mosley established excellent relations (fortified by substantial subsidies). Chamberlain wrote after the 1929 election: ' He can flame with anger as quickly as the rest of us. But his anger is short-lived, and his smile predominates. He is ambitious – and rightly so. His ambition is to serve the common people, to do all that one can do to abolish poverty and to bring gladness and hope where there is now sorrow and despair. He is a gentleman in the highest sense of that much-abused term.'[35]

Although officially the struggle was between socialism and capitalism, Labour and Tory, Mosley interpreted it in personal terms: himself versus the Chamberlains and the press-lords. This personalisation of the conflict heightened its drama and bound working-class voters to Mosley (and through him to the Labour Party) in a way which more orthodox methods would never have done (or at least so quickly); at the same time it left something of a bitter taste in the mouths of some of the eclipsed, plodding, local Labour officials. It also led Mosley seriously to underestimate the extent to which modern political allegiance is institutional, not personal. Mosley's fault to these Labour activists was that he identified the Labour movement with himself, rather than the other way round. He was the new socialist lord of the manor of Birmingham. He had given the party a policy – his Birmingham Proposals. He financed it. He was the dynamic force behind its successes. ' Oswald is merciful; Oswald will save us,' Smethwick's children used to sing.

Nor was playing the *grand seigneur* confined to Birmingham itself. Once a year hundreds of Smethwick Labour supporters (and Cimmie's followers at Stoke) would depart by charabanc for Denham, there to have their socialist faith fortified by luncheon in the hay

barn, impromptu sports, funfairs, dancing and singing, not to mention a speech from Ramsay MacDonald on the theme that socialism
is not just a matter of wages but of soul.   Beauty spots like Denham,
said the party leader, must be available to the whole people.   But
to cynics the excursions to Denham looked less like practical experiments in socialism than lavish exercises in feudal patronage.   Thus
had old Sir Tonman Mosley held open house for the tenants, farm
labourers, gardeners and servants at Rolleston in the nineteenth
century.

IV

Three articles give an insight into Mosley's political thinking on the
eve of the general election of 1929.   The first sums up his impressions of Baldwin's Parliament:

> Unemployment, wages, rents, suffering, squalor and star-
> vation; the struggle for existence in our streets, the threat of
> world catastrophe in another war; these are the realities of
> the present age.   These are the problems which require every
> exertion of the best brains of our time for a vast constructive
> effort.   These are the problems which should unite the nation
> in a white heat of crusading zeal for their solution.   But these
> are precisely the problems which send Parliament to sleep.
> When not realities but words are to be discussed Parliament
> wakes up.   Then we are back in the comfortable pre-war
> world of make-believe.   Politics are safe again; hairs are to
> be split, not facts to be faced.   Hush!   Do not awaken the
> dreamers.   Facts will wake them in time with a vengeance.

' No institution of Government can long survive ', Mosley concluded,
' when it is completely divorced from reality. '[36]
      Mosley's reference in his parliamentary speech of November
1928 to the possibility of enlarging empire markets through the
creation of state buying and selling agencies – a favourite I.L.P.
device – caught the eye of the imperial crusader, Lord Beaverbrook,
who wrote to him warmly.   Despite the previous attacks on him by
the Beaverbrook press, Mosley responded in the same spirit and
by December Beaverbrook was writing to him about ' our personal
relationship '.   The first fruit of this was an article by Mosley in the
Daily Express on 19 February 1929 entitled ' Why I am a Socialist '.
The essence of the Tory creed, wrote Mosley, quoting Baldwin, was
that government should steer clear of industrial problems.   But
what was the function of government if it had no concern with
industrial problems?   Every major issue in politics was an industrial
one.   The old issues of liberty, conscience, Irish Home Rule,
Welsh Disestablishment and others had ' vanished from the scene '.
Socialism believed in active state intervention in the economy.

It was better to have intervention by those who believed in it than by those who were driven to it ' too late ' by the pressure of events. Mosley concluded on a characteristic note: ' These pleasant sleepy people are all very well in pleasant sleepy times, but we live in a dynamic age of great and dangerous events. In such an age we summon all classes to a united effort of the whole nation in the war against poverty.'

On 23 April 1929 Mosley wrote an article for the *Daily Herald* under the title ' Who is Unfit to Govern?' The Liberals had claimed that Labour lacked administrative experience. Mosley asked, ' Because a man has failed before is that a good reason to try him again?' History provided no evidence that a man with long administrative experience was best at responding to new challenges. ' His energies are sapped and his mind stereotyped. It is much nearer the truth to say that everything great has been achieved by new men. They come fresh to the situation which has created them. They are the children of their age.' Did Mosley already sense that the Labour Party might not be that ' new party ' which was needed? Were MacDonald and Snowden ' new men '? They had certainly been around a very long time.

Parliament was dissolved on 10 May 1929 and the General Election fixed for 30 May. The campaign was dominated by unemployment. Unfortunately for the activists on the N.E.C., the shorter Labour Manifesto was as vague on details as the rambling *Labour and the Nation*, which had appeared in 1928. Labour was to undertake housing and slum clearance, land drainage, electrification, railway reorganisation, road building, afforestation. There was no indication, however, of how these schemes were to be financed, or what their scope would be. A Labour government would ' increase the purchasing power of the working-class '. But the means were not specified. In fact the ' minutely detailed schemes ' which Mosley had claimed for Labour in his *Daily Express* article were being provided by the Liberals who, in a desperate effort to recover power, were offering a big programme of public works, financed by loan. Mosley, in common with other Labour leaders, dismissed the Liberal plans as mere borrowings from Labour's programme. The tragedy was that Lloyd George's unsavoury reputation derived from Coalition days now besmirched a really distinguished policy, drawn up by Keynes and brilliant Liberal intellectuals. In his one good joke of the election Mac-Donald said that Lloyd George's policy reminded him of a religious tract sub-edited by Satan. Lloyd George's riposte that Mac-Donald sounded like a broken gramophone-record was perhaps more apposite, but MacDonald's melodious phrases carried more conviction. For the Conservatives, Baldwin managed to think up the particularly uninspiring battle-cry of ' Safety First '.

Mosley galvanised Birmingham into action for the last time. In 1924, Labour had just squeezed into one of Birmingham's twelve seats. This time the target was nine. John Strachey was standing once more at Aston. Allan Young had taken Sydney Potter's place at Sparkbrook. Wilfred Whiteley was standing in Mosley's old constituency, Ladywood. Once again Mosley oratory and money were poured into the fight: C. J. Simmons, an ex-serviceman who had lost a leg at Vimy Ridge, got £100 at Erdington; Whiteley £150 at Ladywood; Young £250 at Sparkbrook. Mosley made it possible for the Labour Party to produce a series of four-page election-sheets throughout the city all through the campaign.[37]

The oratorical highlight was undoubtedly Mosley's debate with Commander Oliver Locker-Lampson (Tory M.P. for Handsworth) at the Rag Market on 13 May. Ten thousand attended. Locker-Lampson's speech, both silly (' the General Strike was manufactured in Moscow ') and insulting (' I shall call him " Comrade" Mosley because of his Communistic leanings '), led to repeated booing from Labour supporters, with Mosley repeatedly appealing to the audience to give Locker-Lampson a fair hearing. In his own speech, Mosley made mincemeat of his opponent. Where would we be today, he asked, if Drake, Disraeli and Gladstone had cried ' Safety First '? As for the Commander with his anti-Red obsession ' when anything goes wrong, from influenza to the Albion being beaten, he attributes it to Moscow '. Cimmie's sister, Irene Ravensdale, who was present, remarked that ' Mosley could dominate a frenzied audience with a mastery of voice and technique that should have made him one of the most memorable orators of our time.'[38]

At Smethwick, Mosley roused his supporters to new heights of enthusiasm:

When he came on to the stage the audience stood up and cheered and cheered again, and waved hats and handkerchiefs. Then somebody started singing ' For He's a Jolly Good Fellow ' and it went with a swing I can tell you. And after they had given him three rousing cheers they began to settle down to business once more.

When Mosley had been speaking for a short time he suddenly thought of something. ' I have a confession to make ' he told the audience, and they chuckled with mirth. ' I have got the wind up ' he added, and everyone roared. ' I am really afraid that my wife will get a bigger majority in Stoke than I shall in Smethwick ' he said in doleful tones. ' I appeal to every woman in this audience ', he said, ' you know what a dog's life I shall have if that happens.' And while most of the women were wiping their eyes in sympathy –

and laughter – he extended his arms, and in tragic tones declared ' that only the women of Smethwick could save him.'[39]

Alas, the women of Smethwick failed him.   His majority was up to 7340, but Cimmie romped into Stoke-on-Trent with a majority of 7850.   In Birmingham the years of campaigning finally paid off.   Six seats were won: Strachey was in at Aston, though Allan Young just failed to unseat Leo Amery at Sparkbrook.   Sir Austen Chamberlain only scraped home by forty-three votes at West Birmingham.   But the biggest upset was Jim Simmons' victory over Sir Arthur Steel-Maitland, Baldwin's minister of labour, at Erdington.   Mosley was overjoyed.   Simmons' election agent recalled Mosley ' running across Victoria Square, easily outstripping the crowd at his heels, with his huge strides, throwing his hat in the air and nearly breaking the back of our little four seater car . . . as he jumped upon it to congratulate us '.[40]

Nationally, Labour's advance, though not nearly so spectacular, was enough to make them the largest party in Parliament.   They had 287 seats, the Conservatives 261.   The Liberals managed only 59: they had made the running, but the race was not for them. ' For the Conservatives ', Mowat has written, ' the setback was much less serious.   They had suffered both for their pugnacity in 1927, their flabbiness since, especially concerning unemployment and disarmament.   They offered safety, but so did Labour which, since the general strike, had cold-shouldered its extremists and grown eminently respectable.   Why not have a change after five years?   But not to Lloyd George and his dynamic spirit.   So let it be Labour, but Labour still hobbled.   If this was the country's mood, it was certainly MacDonald's also.'[41]

Mosley, the ' ambitious young Alcibiades ' of *Echo de Paris*'s ' Pertinax ', expected office and got it.   He had hopes of the foreign secretaryship and MacDonald considered him for the post.[42]   But the new prime minister had too many senior men to satisfy.   The party manager Arthur Henderson got it, while Mosley became chancellor of the duchy of Lancaster, outside the Cabinet.   It must have been a disappointment, but it had its compensations.   He was to work with the new lord privy seal, J. H. Thomas, on the unemployment problem, a job for which he felt himself uniquely qualified.   Although Labour lacked a majority, its position was much stronger than in 1924 and it could count on Liberal support for bold measures.   The unemployed were crying out for salvation and the new men who would secure it for them had at last arrived in power.   The years of talk were over.   The hour of action had come.   In an eve-of-poll message to the Labour movement Mosley gave exalted expression to his hopes:

Before we leave this mortal scene, we will do something to lift
the burdens of those who suffer.   Before we go, we will do
something great for England.   Through and beyond the
failure of men and parties, we of the war-generation are
marching on and we shall march on until our end is achieved
and our sacrifice atoned.   Today we march with a calm, but
mighty, confidence, for marching beside us in irresistible
power is the soul of England.[43]

Chapter 9

The Day of Judgment

THESE FEVERED expectations were remote from the minds of Ramsay MacDonald and his leading colleagues as they tried on their dusty morning-coats for presentation at the Palace. While Mosley was keyed up for the Day of Judgment they looked forward to Business As Usual. While for him the moment had come for the ' new movement' to show its mettle, for them it was a matter of carrying on the king's government. If their hearts throbbed a little, it was with the excitement of having arrived, rather than in anticipation of the struggle ahead. For most of them office was the reward for honourable ambition, rather than an opportunity for action. Within certain limits, and provided not much thinking or doing were required of them, the Labour leaders were prepared to help their clients – the poor and unemployed. But the pace and scope of their ambitions were worlds away from Mosley's frantic urgency to get things done.

During the general election MacDonald had spoken grandiosely about setting up an ' Economic General Staff' to cope with the unemployment problem.[1] Out of his mountainous verbiage on the subject there issued a mouse in the shape of J. H. Thomas, who was made lord privy seal with ' special responsibilities for unemployment '. He was given half a dozen civil servants, headed by Sir Horace Wilson. Mosley, George Lansbury (first commissioner of works) and Thomas Johnston (under-secretary of state for Scotland) were deputed to help him in their spare time. Churchill was soon to describe Mosley as ' a sort of ginger assistant to the Lord Privy Seal and more ginger than assistant I have no doubt'. He was given a room in the Treasury and a Treasury official, Dudley Ward,* as his private secretary. Thomas also presided over an inter-departmental committee of civil servants inherited from the previous government. It had done nothing then, and it would do nothing now. The advisory ministers were only reluctantly invited to attend its desultory discussions.

Harold Nicolson has written: ' The exuberant dynamism of the Chancellor of the Duchy was ill-attuned to the cheerful lethargy of the Lord Privy Seal.' Cheerful Thomas may have been, but

---

*Dudley Ward had been one of Keynes's assistants in the ' A ' Division of the Treasury during the First World War. Ward also succeeded Keynes as the Treasury representative at the Paris Peace Conference.

lethargic he was not.   It is easy to forget that for most of the 1920s
he was regarded as one of the shrewdest brains and coolest heads
in the Labour movement.   He was freely spoken of as MacDonald's
successor.   His notorious lack of enthusiasm for socialism was considered an asset in winning support from the business and financial
community.   As an experienced trade unionist he was expected to
show that practical grasp of the problems of industry which eluded
colleagues intoxicated with socialist generalities.   He reminded
Thomas Jones of Lloyd George: ' His brain is full of plans and he
has energy, like L.G. getting busy himself and sending for the big
people who can co-operate.'² His régime got under way with a
burst of activity.   ' The projects that seethed in his mind ranged
from a bridge over the Zambesi river to a traffic circus at the
Elephant and Castle.   He saw civil servants, businessmen, local
government authorities, trade unionists, engineers, scientists, post
office officials . . . railway directors.   He was the chairman of an
unending succession of meetings, thrashing out the feasibility of
railway schemes, harbour schemes and road schemes, of drainage,
forestry, electricity and slum clearance schemes. . . .'³ To MacNeill
Weir, MacDonald's parliamentary private secretary, Thomas
appeared as ' a brilliant chairman . . . with the adaptability of a
Jack-of-all-Trades and the versatility of a one-man band '.   Most of
this early activity was talk, but there was just enough hint of action
to suggest more in the future.   A £37½ million five-year road-
building programme was announced.   A ' Home Development Bill '
was introduced on 15 July 1929 making it easier for railway
companies to borrow money (Thomas was secretary of the National
Union of Railwaymen); £1 million was allocated for colonial
development.   In August Thomas set off for Canada in pursuit of
a great scheme for expanding imperial trade.   Certainly there was
nothing lethargic about him in these early months.

      Yet frustration and failure were inherent in the organisation
set-up as well as in the character of the man appointed to the job.
Thomas's ill-fated career as ' minister of employment ' arose out of
MacDonald's flair for showmanship, as well as from the prime
minister's desire to develop a counterweight to Snowden and the
Treasury: a 1929 version of the 1964 D.E.P. (Department of Employment and Productivity) with its ' creative tension ' theory.*
But typically the concept had not been properly thought through.
The only reason for setting up a new piece of machinery is that you
have a policy or objective that cannot be fulfilled by the existing
machinery.   There was little enough evidence of any such new
strategy for dealing with unemployment.   The king's speech of 3
July 1929 promised merely schemes ' for the stimulation of the

---

*The comparison between the two organisations might with profit be extended
to their political chiefs.

depressed export trades'. Like its predecessor the Government would continue to rely on the 'international solution'. This was the set and unalterable policy of Snowden and the Treasury who, in Churchill's words, 'embraced one another with all the fervour of two long-separated kindred lizards'. The one concession made, if not to socialism, at least to the need to create the impression that something was being done, was to expand somewhat the local-authority public-works and road-building programmes. No one at Whitehall believed that such 'relief works', as they were contemptuously called, could make any major contribution to the unemployment problem, which was an 'export' problem. Right at the start Snowden and Thomas 'agreed that there was to be no inflation, no "subsidies to inefficient industries", no departure from the most stringent free trade principles'.[4] There was thus never any chance of Thomas's organisation developing a separate un-employment policy unless Thomas himself changed his mind. But, though that mind may have been seething with projects, they were not related to any central theoretical or practical conception opposed to Treasury orthodoxy. Hence, if at any moment Snowden chose to call a halt to the public-works expenditure on the grounds that it was diverting capital from the export recovery programme, Thomas had nothing with which to come back at him. His one economic heresy – Protectionism – he never pressed against Snow-den's free-trade dogmatism, although it later helped to ease his passage into the National Government. A lifetime spent in wage negotiations within a fixed framework had given Thomas an inti-mate knowledge of industry as it actually functioned but left him unable to envisage any practical alternative to the existing system.

Thomas's intellectual failure was compounded by a moral failure. It is this which makes him a less reputable figure than either Philip Snowden, the chancellor of the exchequer, or George Lansbury, his other main assistant on the Unemployment Committee. Snow-den was a man of complete integrity; his tragedy, which was also a tragedy for the country, was that he could never transcend a puritan culture which he represented with distinction, but in the wrong century. George Lansbury's intellectual failings were of a different kind. In charge of ancient monuments and, at seventy, almost one himself, he was one of the 'Great Hearts with Weak Intellects' brigade. 'No brains to speak of . . . certainly no capa-city for solving intellectual problems' was Beatrice Webb's charac-teristically brutal verdict. His own constructive ideas were limited to a romantic ruralism. On the other hand, unlike Thomas and MacDonald, he was prepared to support a constructive policy pro-posed by others, because at seventy the passions which had moved him all his life still burned brightly.

By contrast, all that survived of Thomas's proletarian zeal was

an ostentatious proletarian manner which pandered to the suburban Tory's sense of social superiority.   Thomas anecdotes were
enjoyed by everyone. ' I've an 'ell of an 'ead,' he remarked one
morning after an alcoholic night. ' Take a couple of aspirates,'
Lord Birkenhead advised him. His salty humour had King George V
laughing so heartily that he opened an abscess in his back. ' A
bloody hawful 'ole, more Privy than Seal,' Thomas grumbled
when he saw the offices assigned to him in the Treasury. To cries
of ' Jimmy's selling you ' at N.U.R. meetings he would invariably
reply, ' I've tried hard enough, but I couldn't find a bloody buyer '.
In fact Thomas was heavily involved with stock-exchange gamblers,
associations that were eventually to bring his public life to a premature close in 1936, but which in the meantime made him a
warm advocate of City interests.   He was the classic case of the
Labour leader for whom arrival and acceptance have become ends
in themselves.   As he himself put it in his inimitable fashion, ' To
think that I was once a carriage councillor and am now a privy
cleaner.'

Mosley, Lansbury and Johnston were not invited to attend the
Interdepartmental Committee of Civil Servants till the third
meeting on 27 June.   By then all the key decisions had been taken.
At the first meeting on 11 June Thomas, true to his bargain with
Snowden, had announced that it ' was no part of the Government's
Unemployment policy to undertake schemes of relief work pure and
simple '.[5]   This left the Committee free to chase the innumerable
hares Thomas produced from his conjurer's hat.   Like Churchill,
he found it hard to let go of an idea that temporarily occupied the
centre of his mind, however marginal it was to the main operation
on which he was engaged.   And his ideas were pretty marginal.[6]

Right from the start the public were made aware that co-ordination between those responsible for unemployment policy was not
all that it should be.   Making his first speech from the Front Bench
on 4 July 1929, Mosley astonished his listeners by announcing that
from 75 million to 100 million pounds would be spent on the electrification of Liverpool Street Station.   Apparently Thomas had told
him to announce that figure just before the debate.   Thomas later
explained suavely that his colleague must have been referring to
the total amount of all possible electrification schemes under consideration.   In his memoirs Mosley writes, ' It was the only time in
my life I ever gave to the House of Commons a fact or figure which
was not valid . . . and I did not forgive the deception.   My relations
with Thomas deteriorated.'[7]

He had better luck on subsequent occasions.   Put in charge of
piloting the Colonial Development Bill through the House, he
positively purred through the committee stages taken on 18 and
19 July, under considerable provocation from the Conservatives.

' His skill, tact, good temper and grasp of detail ' earned general praise, according to the *Sunday Express* of 21 July 1929. Fenner Brockway of the I.L.P. expressed particular appreciation when Mosley accepted a left-wing amendment guaranteeing conditions of native labour. ' His name will live ', commented the *New Leader* of 23 July, ' as the Minister responsible for the first Act laying down these important principles to protect native labour from exploitation.'[8]

Of more immediate moment were his exchanges with Churchill on the subject of the Treasury view. Speaking on 16 July Churchill had referred to ' the Treasury argument ' that money spent on public works was money taken away from private enterprise and could not therefore increase the total of employment. Mosley strongly objected to Churchill sheltering behind the Treasury. ' I have always been taught that when a Minister issues a statement of policy he should accept responsibility for it, and that it is highly improper to talk about it as Treasury policy when in fact it is his own policy.' Reverting to this theme a day later Mosley argued, ' After all, the activities of the Treasury are governed by the policy of the Government of the day. The Treasury becomes obstructive and restrictive if it is the policy of the Government of the day to obstruct and restrict, but, if it is the policy of the Government of the day to pursue a forward policy, then the views of civil servants . . . coincide with the views of the Government. . . . ' Still later Mosley said, ' I would like to mobilise the Treasury for these great development works '.[9]*

Here was contained a clear warning to Snowden. Financial policy, like every other type of policy, was a matter for political decision. There was no such thing as a ' correct ' policy which all governments, irrespective of political complexion, were bound to follow. This point is really fundamental to Mosley's philosophy of government. He has consistently rejected attempts to blame civil servants for the failures of ministers, insisting that the failures of government are failures of political will, not of administrative competence. It was up to ministers to make policy. The function of civil servants was to criticise it, to be sure, but ultimately to carry it out. His own instinctive respect for the ' expert ' was to be reinforced, rather than diminished, by his experience of government.

At the end of July Mosley made his now traditional appearance

*It is interesting how Mosley's views on the subject of the Treasury and econo-mic policy echo Lloyd George's on the subject of the generals and the conduct of war in 1916. Criticising Haig's claim to conduct military operations without political interference, Lloyd George remarked in the War Committee ' [Haig] talked about his responsibility – to whom was he responsible? He was respon-sible to them, to the Government and through Parliament to the people.' (Quoted in *Lloyd George, twelve essays*, ed. A. J. P. Taylor (1971) p. 120.)

at the Durham Miners' Gala. Calling his audience ' the storm-troops of Labour ', he concluded an emotional speech with the words ' I would rather see the Labour Government go down in defeat than shrink from great issues, because [from] such defeats men rise again with strength redoubled.' How different this was from the philosophy of Ramsay MacDonald and his colleagues the following months were to reveal.

Meanwhile Mosley had at last been given some work to do. Labour's one distinctive ' cure ' for unemployment was removing the old from industry by giving them better pensions. This would create vacancies for large numbers of unemployed. It was brought into Labour's programme at the insistence of the miners; and this made Mosley its warm advocate. On 29 June 1929 Thomas appointed a sub-committee to produce a scheme, consisting of Lansbury (chairman), Mosley and Johnston, together with civil servants and the government actuary. It was a curious arrange-ment, the civil servants being used not just to service the Committee but to sit on it themselves – a device probably intended to curb the enthusiasm of Lansbury and Mosley, who had reputations as spendthrifts. (Lansbury's appointment as first commissioner of works had been accepted by Snowden only when MacDonald pointed out that he could do ' a good many small things ' without the ' opportunity for squandering money '.)[10]

Here was an opportunity to redeem a specific Labour pledge. Mosley set to work in a ' semi-dungeon high up in the Treasury ', as Lansbury recalled it, with a poignant reminder of that pledge in a letter signed by ' 14 Smethwick Workmen ', aged sixty-five and over: ' We all have the greatest faith in you, that you will do your best for us in this matter, and anxiously looking forward to good results.' The first plan considered by Lansbury, Mosley and Johnston was to increase old-age pensions from the existing level of 10s a week (under the 1925 Act) to 30s a week for married couples over sixty-five. This, it proved, would cost the Exchequer £60 million a year, a prohibitive amount. On 24 July, therefore, Mosley proposed a ' temporary ' scheme offering pensions at sixty to those in employ-ment in certain depressed industries, conditional upon their retire-ment from work. The industries suggested were coal-mining, iron and steel manufacture and shipbuilding. (The textile industry had its own method of coping with its labour surplus – short-time working.) On 17 September, after the summer holidays, it was decided to drop this temporary scheme as ' insuperable difficulties ' of definition would arise and only a ' comparatively small number of vacancies would be likely to be created '. Instead the Committee decided to offer all insured workers (plus railwaymen) who had reached the age of sixty by a certain date a pension of £1 a week for a single man and 30s a week for a married man on condition that they retired from work within six months. This turned out to be the final proposal. Much argument took place on how much the plan would cost, how it should be financed, how many workers would accept the pension, how many vacancies would be created. The civil servants were unenthusiastic. ' I do not fancy we shall get away with our Pensions,' Lansbury was writing to Mosley on 25 September 1929. On the other hand all three ministers were determined to press forward. As Johnston remarked to Lansbury, ' It is one of the ways out. If it be not accepted – it, or something like it – there will be big trouble in our own Party. And rightly so.' To by-pass the civil servants Lansbury suggested to Mosley ' that we should ask the officials to agree to draft a colourless statement of facts, leaving you, Johnston, and me to make a definite proposal to the Privy Seal '. He added, a little doubtfully, ' I think we are entitled to do this because we shall be dealing with matters of policy ' – so timid were even the most radical Labour ministers when faced with the awesome responsibilities of office! Lansbury's suggestion was finally adopted on 4 November, and Mosley was directed to draft the ministerial report. On 26 November Thomas submitted it to the Cabinet with a noticeably cool covering note.

In his diary of 22 November 1929 Thomas Jones mentions reading ' an addendum ... written by Mosley in a rhetorical Second Reading style '. This impression may well have been conveyed by Mosley's insistence that the Retirement Pensions plan ' was in the forefront of our programme for dealing with unemployment, and was approved as a legitimate unemployment measure by our supporters '. Such plain hints of obligations incurred to the electorate no doubt struck this experienced civil servant as out of place in a state document. However, Mosley's case did not rest there. His report is a closely reasoned defence of the ministerial scheme.

Basing himself on civil-service estimates, Mosley assumed that 390,000 persons out of a possible 677,000 would take the pension. This would create job vacancies for 200,000. ' At one stroke ', he declared, ' we reduce by one-third the wholly unemployed.' Moreover it cost £250 to employ a man for a year on public works schemes, only £50 or so to retire his older workmates. It was, Mosley continued, by far the cheapest and most rapid method yet devised for reducing the numbers of the unemployed.

More from the heart was his plea that if, pending reconstruction, some workers had to be kept in idleness better it should be the old than the young. ' A man of 60 who has worked all his life will not suffer much demoralisation through living in idleness, but a man of 20 may suffer irreparable harm. By keeping the young in idleness we destroy the human material upon which the future prosperity of reconstructed industry must be built. ... Idleness may be a boon to the old, but it is a damnation to the young. By this measure we are obeying both the dictates of nature and of economics. . . .'

A cabinet committee of A. V. Alexander (first lord of the Admiralty), F. W. Pethick-Lawrence (financial secretary to the Treasury) and W. R. Smith (parliamentary secretary to the Board of Trade) was set up to consider the plan in the first fortnight of December. They riddled it with objections. The costs were much too high – £22 million in the first year; the benefits – reabsorption of the unemployed and consequent saving on unemployment insurance – were problematic. Mosley worked out an ingenious scheme for averaging the costs over fifteen years which, with the saving on unemployment insurance, would reduce the Treasury's net annual liability to £2½ million. But this did not convince sceptical treasury officials wedded to annual budgeting. The plan was also unfair. In 1928 some 80,000 workers had retired on a pension of 10*s* a week offered by the Conservative Government's Contributory Pensions Act. ' Are these persons ', asked the civil servants, ' to see their neighbours who remained a little longer in industry now pensioned off with thirty shillings a week?' And what about the claims of men and women who reached the age of sixty after the appointed day and had only the 10*s* pension to look forward to at the age of sixty-five? Mosley attempted to meet this argument by suggesting that in five years the increased pension should be made available to all workers over sixty-five as part of a comprehensive pensions policy. In the meantime, the limited scheme could be defended on the ' clear principle ' that it was an emergency unemployment measure. Any action, he continued, was bound to be unfair to someone. Such arguments as the civil service produced ' if accepted would lead to the complete paralysis of Government. . . . It is the function of Government to adopt proposals which are at the time . . . practicable and to resist those which are not.'

The Cabinet Committee was unimpressed. On 19 December it recommended that the Cabinet reject the plan (Smith dissenting). It was probably right. There would have been a political outcry which it was beyond the resources of a minority government or leaders of the calibre of MacDonald to withstand. In any case, the whole idea of ' curing ' unemployment by artificially diminishing the labour supply was hopelessly defeatist. It ran contrary to Mosley's deepest convictions on the subject. His support for retirement pensions rather illustrates the seriousness with which he took Labour pledges, and his eagerness to get something concrete accomplished.[11]

His real enthusiasm was reserved for public works. But here, too, he fared little better. Despite the war and all the notions which had grown up about the role of the State, government in 1929 was still largely ' liberal ' government. Public works – mainly road-construction and various types of building – were entirely in the hands of the local authorities. This meant endless delays in getting programmes started: in February 1930 less than 4000 men altogether were employed on road schemes; and some of these were schemes approved by Lloyd George in 1920. The Government's role was limited to giving financial assistance through the Unemployment Grants Committee and the Ministry of Transport. This assistance usually took the form of paying a proportion of the interest and sinking-fund charges on loans raised by the local authorities for the purpose of providing work. The Treasury disliked the whole idea. It believed that recovery had to be sought mainly in the export trade. Money was best spent re-equipping and modernising these industries. Loans raised for public works would divert capital from those much-needed activities. Moreover, Snowden had laid it down as a principle that ' no scheme should cost more than it is likely to bring back into the national purse '.[12] Thomas had stated firmly in his first speech to the House on 3 July that he was not going to pay men money to dig holes and then fill them up again: only works that improved the national efficiency would qualify. On these criteria, the scope for public works was limited indeed. How could the building of municipal cemeteries and wash-houses be said to improve the national efficiency? It was even difficult to justify larger schemes like road-building, on the criteria demanded by Snowden, for as Morrison, the minister of transport, was to argue it was impossible ' to get specific proof of immediate help to productive industry in respect of particular lengths of road improvement and constructions '.[13]

Mosley was instinctively attracted to public works. They represented something government could do immediately to help the unemployed. They expressed the philosophy of the strong, paternal state in which he and, he thought, the Labour Party believed. Mosley had little faith in local works. They took too long. Besides, local authorities assured him that they didn't have the money to start them. This was particularly true of the depressed areas like the Rhondda Valley. The answer to this was more money. But the answer to the delay was that the Government itself should take responsibility for starting schemes.

This was the view Mosley urged on the other departments in the summer and autumn of 1929. He found an ally in Thomas Johnston, the under-secretary of state for Scotland. One of the chief problems revolved round the ' transfer ' dilemma. In 1928 the Conservative Government had adopted a policy of encouraging the removal of unemployed workers from the depressed areas. Its method was to offer a ' bait ' to the more prosperous local authorities in the form of higher grants if they would accept fifty per cent transferred labour on their municipal schemes. But this meant that the grants to really depressed authorities had to be kept artificially low in order to preserve the differential – lower than required to evoke local schemes. And the wealthier authorities did not want to add to their labour supply, despite the higher grant.

Now Mosley saw a way out of this tangle. In a letter to J. H. Thomas of 3 September he had said, ' I am inclined more than ever to the view that some national effort in road construction, on top of the Local Authority effort, will be necessary if we are to secure any great acceleration of work.' He added, ' I will discuss this with Morrison [Minister of Transport] directly he returns from his holiday.' Now in a memorandum of 24 September he proposed national road-schemes as a way out of the transfer tangle. ' If in addition to local Authority schemes the Ministry of Transport or other State Authority would carry out some schemes at its own cost and on its own responsibility, transferred labour to almost any extent could be employed on such schemes '.

Mosley's memorandum of 24 September was savaged by the departments to which it was circulated. National schemes would involve ' a duplication of highway staffs and organisation all over the country '. The Road Fund would fall into debt. ' If mention is made at this stage of " national schemes ",' wrote the Ministry of Transport on 5 October, ' there will be a tendency on the part of the more deliberate local authorities to stand back, in the hope that the Government itself will start work in the locality, and . . . find the whole cost.' National schemes would be bad for local government, agreed Arthur Greenwood, minister of health – a complaint that was later to be echoed by Herbert Morrison.

Mosley and Johnston stuck to their guns (17 October 1929):

We thus come to a deadlock on the basis of the present transfer policy. After making every effort within the limits of our instructions we find it impossible, in fact, to combine the policy of the Labour Party with that of the Conservative Party. The present transfer policy is the policy of the late Government, which was vigorously opposed by our Party. . . . Conservative policy rejected the whole conception of national schemes and strove to throw as much as possible of the burden of unemployment policy on the Local Authorities. The declared policy of the Labour Party was the exact contrary: – ' It will treat unemployment as what it is – a national, not a local issue, and will transfer the present responsibility for unemployment from local rates to a national scheme. . . .' We remain of the opinion that we have consistently expressed since the inception of the present Government, that on the lines of declared Labour policy alone can any substantial extension and acceleration of work plans be secured. For months we have pressed the Ministry of Transport to initiate national road schemes. *On such schemes the transferred labour from the depressed areas should be carried.* Local authorities in non-depressed areas could then be relieved from the obligation of transfer which . . . is at present postponing and impeding work plans in those areas. At the same time more generous terms could be given to local Authorities in depressed areas, without any of the complications involved in such action while the transfer premium is maintained.[14]

The Ministry of Transport was in fact a major stumbling-block. Mosley and Morrison were enemies of long standing, Morrison never hiding his dislike of the wealthy socialist. Mosley's efforts to win Morrison over to national schemes were not as tactful as they might have been. He first tried to win from the minister an admission that the Labour Government's road programme did not represent any significant advance on that of the Conservatives. In cross-examining the Ministry's figures he adopted the style of a prosecuting counsel. 'He spoke to me', Morrison later complained, 'like a landlord addressing his peasantry.' One feels a certain sympathy for Morrison. As he wrote to Snowden on 9 December 1929, ' I am expected to solve everybody's problems and I do my best to gratify those expectations.' He was fighting a battle on three fronts – against Mosley's demand for national schemes, against Snowden who was holding up money for the larger road-programme that Morrison was advocating, and against his pessimistic departmental adviser Sir Henry Maybury, who claimed that no more roads were needed.[15] On national schemes Mosley was up against a brick wall. To start with, Morrison, himself a product of local government, was not prepared to abandon it at the behest of a rootless national politician like Mosley. Secondly, ministry officials pointed out that, even if the Government undertook to build roads itself, progress would not be much quicker, since the interests would have to be accommodated just as before. Indeed, one of their main objections to the Lloyd George trunk-road programme which had promised to employ 100,000 men a year for two years was that it would require a dictatorship.[16] Writing to Thomas a little later on the 'interesting but rather wearisome debates and cross-examinations on the Committee on National Schemes', Morrison observed, ' Clearly Mosley suffers somewhat from L.G.'s complaint: the road complex. A road is a means of transport: road works can assist, but cannot possibly be a principal cure of immediate unemployment.'* As a railwayman Thomas was equally opposed to

---

*In the 1929 election Lloyd George had proposed a £145 million road-programme to be carried out by the State (*We Can Conquer Unemployment*, pp. 13-16). Although Mosley never referred to the Lloyd George plan in support of his own, it seems reasonable to look here for the source of Mosley's ' complex '.

Mosley's ' complaint ', and so he did not receive any help from that quarter either.

These fruitless negotiations vividly expose the flaw in MacDonald's administrative arrangements. It only made sense to set up a special unemployment organisation if unemployment was generally accepted as an overriding priority to which departmental interests would have to be subordinated. As it was, Mosley was given *carte blanche* to make himself a general nuisance, but no power to do anything. He must have felt rather like Kafka's land-surveyor confronting the village representative: ' You've been taken on as land-surveyor, as you say, but unfortunately we have no need of a land-surveyor. There wouldn't be the least use for one here. The frontiers of our little estates are marked out and all neatly registered. . . . So what would be the good of a land-surveyor?'

It was only gradually that he came to realise that the main obstacle to his attempts to secure a vigorous domestic unemployment policy was the Government's continued reliance on the export solution. Government aid was justified only by the help it gave to improving the competitive efficiency of industry. Thus road and railway works might cheapen the costs of transport. The employment they gave directly was an incidental effect of the policy, for which credit might be claimed, but whose relevance to the basic unemployment problem was negligible. To spend state money ' wisely and fruitfully for the benefit of the export trade', as Thomas put it in a memorandum to the Cabinet (23 October 1929), was one thing; to sanction large expenditure just to ' provide work ' was something to be resolutely rejected.[17] Until early 1930 it was not realised that the Wall Street crash of October 1929 had destroyed the uncertain post-war prosperity of the western world and was ushering in the worst depression of modern history. The assumption was still that trade revival was just round the corner. British export industries must be put into a position to take advantage of it when it came. Committees of enquiry had already been set up for the cotton and steel industries. Early in January Thomas announced that the Bank of England and the City of London were ready to 'give financial advice and backing' to the rationalisation (or modernisation) of the basic industries.[18] This whole strategy was directly opposed to everything that Mosley and the left wing of the Labour Party stood for. Ever since 1925 Mosley had been arguing that what was needed was a home-market unemployment policy. To his horror he realised that the Government had not the slightest intention of trying anything of the kind.

The fragility of Thomas's hopes had already been cruelly exposed on his return from his six-week journey to Canada. Even his optimism could not hide the barrenness of his accomplishment.[19] As the autumn session of Parliament opened without any new unemployment measures, relations between Thomas and his three advisory ministers sharply deteriorated. Discussions at the inter-departmental committee became increasingly acrimonious. Mosley and Sir Horace Wilson did most of the talking with Thomas invariably mumbling, ' I agree with 'Orace 'ere. ' Attacked by his colleagues in committee, and by the two Oppositions in Parliament (Lloyd George dubbed his policy ' timid, pusillanimous, unintelligent '), and with the unemployment figures starting to mount ominously, Thomas turned to drink for consolation. On 2 December Arthur Henderson told Beatrice Webb that Thomas ' is completely rattled and in such a state of panic, that he is bordering on lunacy. . . . The PM fears suicidal mania.' On 21 December Beatrice Webb wrote, ' For years he imagined himself as a future PM; today the question is whether he will drink himself into helpless disablement.' The pathos of the situation was that Thomas was being completely loyal to the policy of the chancellor and the Government. It was the policy, not the man, that was at fault. The ever-deepening tragedy of the Labour Government is the tragedy of leaders whose conceptions were completely inappropriate to the conditions of their time and in whom the character and determination which might at least partly have bridged the gap had been eroded by the belated achievement of respectability.

It was with these experiences behind him that Mosley decided to write yet another memorandum, this time not to urge some parti-cular measure but, much more ambitiously, to advance an alter-native unemployment policy. He told MacDonald about the plan on 13 December – one of the rare opportunities of renewing his previously intimate relationship with his party leader. Whether MacDonald listened to what Mosley was saying is doubtful. What seems clear is that he encouraged him to go ahead. This is not as surprising as it sounds. We have already remarked on MacDonald's penchant for toying with radical ideas. Mosley was clearly having some thoughts. This was all to the good, provided they were not too adventurous. Besides, it would be useful to have some ideas to put before the Economic Advisory Council which he was then just in the process of setting up;* and to have a little ammunition to cut the detestable Snowden down to size. Mosley, for his part, interpreted these vague murmurs of approval

*On 2 December MacDonald held the first of a series of lunches with economists and businessmen to discuss the general economic situation. These resulted in the formation on 12 February 1930 of an Economic Advisory Council, an en-larged version of the earlier Committee of Civil Research which had been in existence for a number of years. Characteristically, neither Mosley nor the other advisory ministers were invited to these discussions nor told anything about them. (For the best account, see Thomas Jones, *Whitehall Diary 1926–1930*, vol. II, pp. x-xii, 219-28.)

as promises of support when his document came before the Cabinet. Nor was Arthur Henderson entirely discouraging. Thomas
should be sent away for a long rest and Mosley put in charge of
the unemployment programme, he was telling the Webbs in December. Mosley felt sure that there was sufficient support in the Cabinet and in the Party to force the Government to live up to its pledges
and go beyond the limits laid down by Snowden and the
Treasury.

The feeling that events were on his side must have grown in
the early months of the new year as the unemployment figures
mounted even higher and the Government's policy of relying on
a trade revival lay palpably in ruins. By March the 'economic
blizzard', as MacDonald called it, was raging all over the world.
Everywhere commodity prices were collapsing, thus reducing the
purchasing power of the customers of the industrial nations, whose
own export prices were forced downwards in turn as they fought
for ever-shrinking markets. Unemployment rose throughout the
western world. In Britain, the unemployment figures for March
instead of going down to just over a million as in previous years
shot up to 1,700,000. In July they would reach 2 million. The
Government's only response was to call for tariff reductions. With
every passing month Mosley's conviction that exports offered no
immediate help for unemployment was strengthened. It was more
than ever necessary to press ahead with huge schemes of public
works to absorb the unemployed, pending a world recovery.
Seven months of working with Thomas's committee had convinced
him that an entirely new executive and administrative machine
was needed to direct the fight. As early as 25 October Lansbury
had complained to Mosley, ' I am really in despair about the whole
business of unemployment. We all seem to be working in such
an unco-ordinated way. . . . ' Much more concentration of
thought and energy was necessary. These were the considerations
that went into shaping the famous Mosley Memorandum.

He worked furiously on it over the Christmas recess. Thomas
certainly knew what was afoot. Early in January Mosley 'casually'
told him that he ' had jotted down a number of new proposals on
"our special problem" ' and added, ' Some of these ideas you will
agree with and some you'll probably turn down; but, in any case,
Jim, I'd like you to see them.'[20] Whether Mosley told him on this
occasion that he definitely intended to appeal over Thomas's head
to the Cabinet is not clear. He was determined that his new proposals should not be stalled in Thomas's department as all his
previous ones had been. Lansbury and Johnston were kept more
fully in the picture; and in part the memorandum embodies the
joint experiences of the three advisory ministers in the summer and
autumn. John Strachey and Allan Young no doubt helped more

actively with its preparation; but the style alone suggests that Mosley was the sole author.

The memorandum was initialled on 16 January 1930. Mosley immediately sent a copy to Keynes: ' The enclosed document ', he wrote, ' is of course very confidential but I should greatly value your opinion upon it. You can show it to Henderson* in confidence if you care. We might discuss it . . . if you are in London next week – I am getting near to my " last word "! ' There is no record of a written Keynes reply, and the supposition is that the two men discussed it over lunch as Mosley suggested. Keynes did, however, show it to Henderson, who wrote on 22 January, ' I am very glad to have had the chance of reading the enclosed. It is, as you say, a very able document – and illuminating.' He did, however, criticise Retirement Pensions, which Mosley had included under his short-term proposals. ' I always felt certain ', Henderson wrote, ' that doles . . . . would serve in practice to dock the money allowed for development schemes. . . . Personally, I put the Retirement Pensions idea under the heading of doles: so I'm glad Mosley has been turned down on that.'[21] There is no evidence that any of the memorandum was rewritten on Keynes's advice.

On 23 January Mosley sent a copy of his memorandum to MacDonald. In a covering note he said that he had already sent a copy to Thomas and that Lansbury and Johnston would write to the prime minister expressing their general agreement. ' The policy suggested in the paper ', Mosley went on, ' is not advanced in any dogmatic spirit and certainly not as any cast iron formula. I am more than open to any alternative suggestion which can be shown to be superior. I have reached, however, the very definite conclusion after mature consideration that it is impossible to continue as at present.'

The memorandum came before the Cabinet on 3 February, when unemployment was discussed in the usual desultory manner. A committee consisting of Snowden, Arthur Greenwood, Margaret Bondfield and Tom Shaw (minister of war) was set up to consider the memorandum, which was thereupon dispatched to the Treasury for examination.

While the supposedly serious work was going on at the Treasury, MacDonald, Thomas and Mosley became involved in an elaborate comedy of manners. Thomas was already aggrieved that he had not been shown the memorandum before MacDonald received it. Now, early in February, the press was suddenly filled with reports of a ' mutiny ' of the advisory ministers and ' inspired ' complaints about Thomas's incapacity. These leakages were discussed at the Cabinet of 12 February. MacDonald saw both Mosley and Mosley's

*Hubert Henderson, the economist, soon to be secretary to the Economic Advisory Council.

parliamentary private secretary, John Strachey, in the following few days and reported the results of his investigations to the Cabinet of 19 February. 'My colleagues', MacDonald wrote to Mosley later that day, 'were greatly surprised by the story which I had to tell. . . . I was given to understand that the Memorandum was sent to me as, in the first instance, a private document putting me, as the head of the Government in possession of views which I ought to know and consider. That, however, was not what had happened, as I found out afterwards. It had been, in reality, communicated to other Ministers and also to some who were not Ministers, and had been left lying about quite openly in the house of Mr. Strachey. The whole procedure was a most grievous fault.' He urged Mosley to ' see Thomas without delay and try to remove the impression made by these unfortunate incidents '.

Thomas, however, was determined to extract the last ounce of sympathy from his predicament. He handed MacDonald a letter of resignation. The prime minister would recognise ' how reluctant I am to take this course after so many years of personal friendship with you – a friendship I will always cherish '. It was a sad end for one ' who for 34 years had worked in the Trade Union and Labour Movement '. His personal admiration for 'the great work you have done . . . work that will live for all time ' remained undimmed. But there was only one course open to a man of honour, etc., etc. The last thing MacDonald wanted was to have Thomas crying on his shoulder. ' We have to consider national interests; none of us are in a position now to follow our own feelings; we must endure however hard the road may be', etc., etc. Thomas dried his tears and prepared to endure a little longer.[22]

Mosley replied imperturbably to MacDonald's note of 19 February. Strachey should not have been so careless in leaving the memorandum lying around: for that Mosley tendered his profound apologies. He would certainly see Thomas and explain the situation to him. He could not, however, accept the prime minister's view that he wasn't entitled to consult with experts in preparing the memorandum since that would bring all policy-making to a standstill. There had been nothing personal in his attack on Thomas, and the only way to restore proper working relations was on the basis of an agreed policy. The best way to secure that was to expedite the work of the committee set up three weeks previously to consider the memorandum; this had not yet met. ' If my efforts to secure the formulation and discussion within the government of an effective policy appear to have given offence', Mosley went on, ' I regret that it should have arisen, but the only alternative was dishonest acquiescence in a policy that I am convinced is ineffective.'[23]

MacDonald's reply was characteristically convoluted. ' The circulation of the Memorandum ', he wrote,

> was more than a consultation, but, even in consulting, a
> Minister has to be careful that what he does does not develop
> inevitably into both an internal and external attack unless
> and until united responsibility has been carried to the utmost
> and every step taken to make differences of opinion the means
> of influencing government policy from within the organisation
> set up.[24]

In his reply of 28 February Mosley merely contented himself with
asking once more for an early meeting of the cabinet committee
as ' the situation has meantime become more serious '.

MacDonald and Thomas certainly had a point.   The revelation
of dissensions within the Ministry had proved highly embarrassing
to the Government.   On the other hand, it may be doubted whether
under modern conditions anything like the submission of the dissenting memorandum could have been kept secret from the Press: since
1930 leaks, of course, have become common.   For his part Mosley
felt justifiably aggrieved not only at having been excluded from
any share in the decision-making process on unemployment, but
also at being kept in ignorance of much of the information on which
government unemployment policy was supposedly based.   (His
exclusion from the Economic Advisory Council was a case in point.)
Beyond this, however, he was determined to force to a decision the
issues which had arisen between him and Snowden and Thomas.
This strategy of forcing differences to a decision was entirely foreign
to MacDonald's conception of government, in which events decided
and governments followed in their footsteps.   For MacDonald the
memorandum was merely another idea, thrown into the general
pool, to be discussed *ad infinitum* with all the other ideas floating
round.   MacDonald wanted the appearance of activity.   Mosley
wanted the reality.   This was what divided them.

The cabinet committee to consider the memorandum met for
the first time on 14 March 1930.   Before it was a draft report
submitted by Sir Frederick Leith-Ross rejecting every single proposal
which Mosley made.   After comments of unbelievable banality from
Miss Bondfield, Tom Shaw and Arthur Greenwood, Snowden ' promised to modify the report so as to cover points which had been
made in the course of the discussion '.   Mosley, Lansbury, and Johnston were then given one meeting to argue their case.   Snowden
chided Mosley for his pessimism: ' You are a young man who cannot remember previous depressions; they have often occurred in
my lifetime, and have passed away.   All those things to which
you refer, such as the rationalisation of industry and the displacement of man's labour by machinery, have been going on for long
past.   They were met in the past by a gradual raising of wages

which increased the power to consume, and by a gradual shortening
of hours which reduced the power to produce. Above all, in due
time fresh markets opened overseas to absorb our surplus production. For instance, when I was a boy, negroes did not ride
bicycles; now they do ride bicycles, and workers are employed
in Coventry to make those bicycles'.[25] It took the committee till
1 May to produce a final report, almost identical with the one considered on 14 March. This came before the Cabinet on 8 May.
Another cabinet committee, this time headed by MacDonald, was
formed to discuss the report with the advisory ministers.

In public Mosley continued to go through the motions of unemployment minister. In the House he did his best to defend a
policy in which he no longer believed, though not in words that
could have brought the Government much comfort. On 21 January he admitted candidly, ' I do not think anyone would suggest
that any measures taken by the present Government are affecting
the unemployment situation materially one way or the other, bene-
ficially or adversely.' The Government could not be accused of
breaking their pledges, he went on blandly, because they had never
made any. Touching on one of the main themes in his memorandum
he argued that rationalisation was necessary – ' in any State, Socialist
or Capitalist ', he pointed out, ' you have to be up to date; Socialism
is not a device for the maintenance of obsolete plant '[26]–but that in
the short term it was bound to lead to unemployment. That is
why it was essential to have a ' short term programme of constructive
and useful works '. He repeated the same point at the London
School of Economics in a speech to the League of Nations Union
conference on unemployment when he said that the existence of
large-scale unemployment 'should be regarded as the opportunity
to give England the clean-up which it has long lacked'.[27] In the
House on 3 February, he opened another window into his
memorandum in answering an attack from Leo Amery that
Thomas was confined to making 'representations' to other departments. That, Mosley said, was the cabinet system.

> Either you work through those Departments or you duplicate
> the whole machinery of Government. . . . The only way to sur-
> mount that dilemma is to have in supreme control a Minister
> who controls nearly all the major Departments of State. That
> would mean a change in the whole machinery of Govern-
> ment . . . which has not so far been contemplated by any
> party.[28]

It was precisely such a revolution in government that Mosley
was advocating.

In private, his utterances were clearly less restrained. In January, Curzon told Harold Nicolson that ' Oswald Mosley is

anxious to leave the Labour Party and to reconcile himself with his old friends '.[29] ' There are constant rumours that Tom Mosley is about to retire from the Labour Party,' Nicolson noted on 12 March.[30] One should not give too much credence to these stories, but clearly Mosley's disillusion with the Labour Government was starting to run deep. The Party itself was growing restive. At party meetings on 19 February, 12 and 19 March and 9 April 80 Labour backbenchers demanded a discussion on the Memorandum. They were told the Cabinet were considering it. From two Labour journals came slashing attacks on government unemployment policy. Thomas's reliance on the City, the Bank of England and the traditional export industries was ' perilously mistaken', wrote H. N. Brailsford of the I.L.P.'s *New Leader* on 14 February. It was to the home market the Government should look. ' For our part, we believe that . . . the main emphasis ought to be put on the provision of work ' rather than the doles, wrote the *New Statesman* the next day. ' Let Mr. Thomas be left to get on with rationalisation and other long-run measures for industrial revival. But let us have also another department, under a Minister of its own, with the sole mission of working out a big scheme for employing the unemployed at useful work. If this is the outcome of the Lansbury–Mosley memorandum, both the Labour Party and the country will have good cause for satisfaction.'

Had that been the outcome, Mosley would probably have stayed in the Ministry. But the seemingly innocent *New Statesman* suggestion involved a decisive breach with orthodox finance, a decisive breach with the past. The removal of Snowden as chancellor would have been the first step. It could have been done. A resolute Labour prime minister could have broken with Snowden on this issue with the support of his party both in Parliament and in the country and with the backing of at least half the Liberal Party. But MacDonald could not do it. He did not understand sufficiently the questions involved. He lacked the strength of character to fight on this terrain. He was old and he was tired. And so the field was left to the man who had no doubts, the Old Testament prophet hurling his anathemas on anyone who dared challenge the nineteenth century.

Chapter 10

The New Deal that Wasn't

THE MOSLEY memorandum falls into four sections, also followed in the treasury reply.[1] The first deals with the machinery of government; the second with long-term economic reconstruction; the third with short-term work-plans; and the fourth with finance and credit policy. It is only with regard to the third section that Mosley acknowledges a collective inspiration for his memorandum, writing that ' these proposals will be largely a summary of suggestions which Mr. Lansbury, Mr. Johnston and I have advanced at various times during the last six months, and which have been largely rejected or suspended '.

Underlying the complicated details of Mosley's revolution in government was the clear conception of a powerful executive committee headed by the prime minister and consisting of leading ministers concerned with economic policy, informed and advised by a high-powered ' think tank ' of economists and scientists; the whole to be serviced by a secretariat of twelve higher civil servants. The rationale behind it was the assumption that unemployment was the over-riding problem facing the nation requiring the mobilisation and concentration of all the resources of government, as in war. In it was reflected Mosley's experience of working with Thomas, who had no executive authority, and with an interdepartmental committee which in the absence of its political chiefs was largely negative and obstructive. His frustration at having to work out unemployment policy in Whitehall, cut off from the best thinking going on outside, emerges clearly in the importance attached to the research organisation, ' a body of experts employed on a full-time basis by the State. . . free from all distraction for the pure work of research ', as he called it. His admiration for the ' expert', stretching back to his Winchester days when he had avidly learnt fencing under Sergeant-Major Adam, was later to issue in a favourite dictum that ' statesmen must learn to live with scientists as the Medici once lived with artists'—an expression of faith in that union of doers and thinkers which would bring the new world to maturity.

To the treasury officials who examined the memorandum this was all highfalutin nonsense. ' We do not see how the Prime Minister', they said, ' could add to his burden so great and so intricate a responsibility.' Nor could other ministers spare time from their ordinary duties. Mosley's proposals would ' cut at the root of the individual responsibilities of Ministers, the especial responsibility

of the Chancellor of the Exchequer in the sphere of finance, and
the collective responsibility of the Cabinet to Parliament'. His
only practicable proposal – to set up a research organisation – had to
some extent been met by the formation of the Economic Advisory
Council.

These criticisms were largely beside the point. They could just
as easily have been advanced against Lloyd George's proposal for
a Supreme War Council in 1916. Mosley's assumption was that
economic reconstruction was a task like winning the war, and requiring a similar organisation. The broad outlines (as opposed to the
details) of his proposed organisation could be validly challenged
only by questioning the assumption on which they were based.
The treasury report did not even bother to discuss the assumption.

Turning from machinery to content, Mosley insisted on the importance of distinguishing between (1) long-term planning for permanent economic reconstruction and (2) short-term schemes for
the immediate relief of unemployment. The Government was holding out the hope that rationalisation would relieve unemployment.
In fact it would increase unemployment. ' That condition of weakness must be expected before the benefits of the surgery can be
realised. It is idle, therefore, to believe that we can dispense with
short-term schemes for the immediate relief of unemployment unless we also believe that any Government can face steadily increasing unemployment for at least three years, or would be morally or
economically justified in [so doing].'

The main point Mosley made in the eight pages of the memorandum devoted to long-term reconstruction was the need to establish
a rational order of priorities for the development of the British
economy as a whole. 'We are embarking', he wrote, ' upon a long-
term programme for a great transition of our industrial life from a
pre-War to a post-War basis. It really verges on the frivolous to
confront such a task with our present machinery. . . . It can only be
solved by scientific thought and the scientific method.' The chief
questions on the agenda were (1) ' the relationship of the Home and
the Export trade in our future economic equilibrium ' and (2) the
balance between the old staple industries and the newer industries
in the future British economy.

On the first, Mosley asks a series of questions which indicate
his doubts about the future of the export trade:

> Can we restore at all our economic position by an increasing
> struggle for competitive world markets, in which the develop-
> ment of other countries has naturally robbed us of our initial
> advantage? . . . Do these economics of the last century, which
> still find expression in speeches emanating from all political
> parties, in fact coincide with the economic facts and economic

possibilities of the post-War situation? Is the policy of all
Governments still to be dominated by the belief that employment in the steel trade to build a railway in Iraq or the Argentine is of necessity better for the people of this country than
employment for the building of a road in Britain?*

In an addendum to the memorandum dated 3 April Mosley
argued that even if, through rationalisation and the development
of newer industries, Britain succeeded in recapturing its pre-war
percentage of the world's export trade there would still be a substantial labour surplus which could find employment only in an
enlarged home market. This attack on the 'export fetish',
obviously influenced by the spread of the world depression in the
first few months of 1930, was to be developed more fully in his
resignation speech.

Consideration of the relationship between the traditional and
the newer industries led Mosley to attack the existing mechanics
of rationalisation. In essence his argument was that it was un-
safe to leave rationalisation to the banks (as envisaged by Thomas)
because (1) British, unlike German, banks had never played 'a big
and consciously formative part in the industrial development of the
country' and were unfitted by tradition and machinery to do so
(Mosley was getting a lot of his information about Germany from
Robert Boothby), and (2) that they 'approach the situation with
heavy existing commitments' to the basic industries. Quoting some
supporting arguments from Henry Clay, Mosley asked, 'Is there
not at least a danger that any effort of the Banks uncontrolled and
undirected by the State will tend to make the first objective the
salvaging of existing commitments rather than the development of
new, more economic, but possibly competitive industries?' In an
addendum dated 29 March 1930 Mosley suggested that the Government set up a state finance corporation with a large capital directly
to undertake rationalisation schemes and also to provide long-term
credit for newer industries. (This foreshadowed both the Istituto
Ricostruzione Industriale (I.R.I.) set up by Mussolini in 1933, and
the Industrial Reorganisation Commission set up by the Labour
Government of 1964.)

In its reply the Treasury rejected Mosley's distinction between
long-term reconstruction and short-term schemes, which involved
'an acceptance of non-remunerative and wasteful' expenditure which
would simply 'postpone and render more difficult the reorganisation of the national economy'. Short-term schemes could be justified only by the contribution they could make to 'reducing the

*In September 1929 he had sent a note to the Cabinet advising against a loan
for the building of a railway in Iraq on the grounds that this would divert
resources from the domestic unemployment programme. The loan went through.

cost of production and adding to the economic . . . capacity of the
country '. The report admitted that rationalisation would add to
unemployment but argued that the Government must be prepared
to 'face the temporary unpopularity that the realisation of this fact
may cause' and to 'wait for a justification of our policy until its
effectiveness is shown in . . . an increase in the competitive power of
British industry '. The overriding priority was to 'restore prosperity
to the four staple industries of cotton and wool; iron, steel and engi-
neering; coal; and ship-building '. The report entirely ignored
Mosley's question about whether the export trade would ever be
able to reabsorb the unemployed, and the consequent need to
rethink the relationship between the home and export market.

The Treasury had admittedly hit upon a weak point in the memorandum. Mosley was insisting upon a rational allocation of
priorities; but, assuming limited resources, surely it would be more
rational to concentrate money on the long-term export-recovery
programme than to squander it on emergency schemes? Mosley
might have met this in two ways. He might have argued
that an enlargement of the home market at the expense of
the export trade was a good thing in itself – especially in existing
world conditions. In this way large domestic programmes suitably
directed could be justified in terms of building up the home market
and therefore incorporated into the general recovery strategy. The
other way Mosley might have tried to justify his big public works
schemes was by reference to the extra demand they would generate.
Surprisingly absent is any hint of the notion of the *cumulative* effect
on employment and demand of any initial outlay – a thought
already present in the Keynes–Lloyd George programmes of 1929.
In the absence of any such insights his public works proposals are
robbed of any dynamic function in the recovery programme. The
argument for them is moral, not economic, inviting the inevitable
rejoinder that morality was temporarily too expensive.

Mosley's attack on the existing machinery of rationalisation
is met by a classic example of the familiar argument that new
things must not be done because they would prevent other things
from being done:

> Whatever might be the ultimate effect of such action by the
> Government on the process of rationalisation, there can be
> no doubt that its immediate effect would be to stop all acti-
> vity at present in progress.[2] On the one side it is practically
> certain that if the Government announced their intention to
> control, by executive and financial action, the process of ratio-
> nalisation, the efforts which are now being made by the City
> to set up an organisation for this purpose would cease. On
> the other side, it is equally plain that such efforts as are now

being put forward by industries to set their house in order
would slacken, indeed, would be quite likely to die away altogether.

(Notice the way that phrases like 'there can be no doubt', 'it is
practically certain', 'it is equally plain' and 'indeed would be quite
likely' are insinuated into this piece of special pleading.)

The third section of the Mosley Memorandum on short-term schemes was largely a recapitulation of the arguments and proposals
which the advisory ministers had urged on the Government in the
previous seven months. The road programme, Mosley claimed,
'shows little if any increase on the road programme of the late
Government'. It should be expanded to the 'maximum possible'
over three to five years without regard to expense or the claims of
the railways. The State should do the work itself, handing over
the finished roads for maintenance to the local authorities. Grants
for local-authority works should be uniform throughout on the
most favourable basis (about sixty-three per cent of the cost of the
works) though authorities with less than six per cent unemployment would still be required to use transferred labour. All other
workers transferred from depressed areas would be employed directly on the state road-schemes (Mosley suggested a 'mobile labour
corps'). Finally, the State should make hundred-per-cent grants
for approved works in distressed areas. The whole public works
programme of the Mosley Memorandum was astonishingly modest.
It would involve spending £200 million raised by loan which, he
reckoned, would employ 300,000 men for three years. This was
substantially smaller than the Lloyd George scheme which reckoned
to employ 600,000 men over two years. It was only by adding to
these works retirement pensions and the raising of the school-leaving
age that unemployment would be reduced by the 700,000 which
Mosley claimed in his resignation speech. Even in his memorandum,
though, he made it clear that there were other possible works which
he had refrained from considering only because they fell outside
his own immediate concerns – such as massive slum-clearance and
land-drainage programmes, once more to be undertaken directly
by the State. The concluding passages of the third section reinforce the plea for a proper allocation of priorities:

If it is to be replied that such a programme has its merits,
but that we have already mortgaged all resources available
for such purposes, an argument of exceptional force supports
the suggestion for more forethought and coordination in the
planning of the Government's programme. . . . For instance,
if the question of expenditure dictated a deliberate choice
between the Widows Pension Bill and constructive measures
[to reduce] unemployment who would choose the former?

Under the present system, not only of the present government, but of all governments, departments 'are like a crowd of bookmakers jostling through a turnstile on the race-course. The man who can push hardest and make the most noise gets through first and takes the money.'

The treasury report found this section of the memorandum 'very disappointing'. Mosley had suggested the figure of £200 million 'without advancing a single concrete scheme. He might just as well have put the figure at £1000m. Either figure is equally divorced from the practical considerations governing road schemes.' The real reason for the delay in the road programme was not the lack of money but ' the need for consultation and negotiation as to routes and the inevitable delays in the acquisition of many small parcels of land '. To these would be added difficulties in obtaining ' sufficient skilled staff and competent contractors ' if the programme were to be greatly expanded. ' If such delays are to be obviated ', the report continues, 'not only the rights of Local Authorities and the whole machinery of local government will have to be overridden, but a very drastic policy would be necessary in dealing with the rights of private individuals.' The threat to the rights of local government produced a particularly pained reaction.

The final section of the memorandum consists of three pages on monetary policy in which Mosley reverts to some of the ideas of *Revolution by Reason* and for the first time seems to link his short-term plans to a definite policy for developing the home market at the expense of the export market. America, he argued, had created a full-employment, high-wage economy, on the basis of a large home market and easy credit. ' An easy credit policy in this country, combined with a development policy which gave employment on a large scale might well reproduce here conditions on which prolonged American prosperity has rested. By natural and gradual progress we might pass from a low wage basis of production to a higher wage basis of production, the greater rate of which in response to a larger demand more than offsets the increase in labour costs. Once that awkward transition is achieved our future employment can rest increasingly on the growing Home Market.' Characteristically Mosley added, ' It is not in the successful countries that suggestions for wage increases and high purchasing power are regarded as immoral.'

Mosley, the treasury reply said, ' appears to have swallowed, without properly digesting it, the Keynes–Lloyd George programme of internal development loans.' On America: ' It is quite absurd to compare the conditions prevailing in the United States – a self-supporting country, with vast internal resources and a high protective tariff – with the competitive conditions under which the population of these islands must live and work if the standard of living to which we are accustomed is not to be radically altered.'

A big internal loan would hinder conversion operations, and deplete the private capital market; more fundamentally Mosley's policy would shatter confidence:

> ... what would be the effect of a sudden reversal of our present policy and the announcement that we were going to embark on a campaign of unrestricted expenditure financed out of loans, with its inevitable concomitants of special powers to coerce labour, landowners, etc, and its attempts to force capital into unremunerative channels or to attract it at the cost of subsequent increases in taxation? The combined effect of all these factors, ably fomented by all the resources of political partisanship, might well be to create a very serious shock to confidence not only in this country but abroad.

For these reasons the ' only practicable course is to continue the policy of long-term reconstruction which the Lord Privy Seal has adopted and to make a definite and considered pronouncement that we reject retirement pensions and the grandiose loan policy '. The report concluded: ' However much we may be criticised, we must not be rushed into shovelling out public money *merely* for the purpose of taking what must inevitably be a comparatively small number of people off the unemployed register *to do work which is no more remunerative and much more expensive even than unemployment.*' (My italics.)

Mosley's memorandum was far from offering a comprehensive alternative to the Government's policy. Much of it seemed to be calling only for a comprehensive enquiry. To the modern reader it seems embarrassingly free of the weighty statistical matter that would have sharpened and supported its main thesis. Nevertheless, the point at issue with the Treasury emerges clearly enough. Mosley believed in state intervention. His proposals for reorganising government, setting up a state finance corporation, mounting a central public works programme, all reflect his view that the State must assume responsibility for economic welfare. The Treasury believed in the free market. All its arguments against Mosley's proposals were restatements of classic objections to state intervention in the economy. It would create inefficiency. It would impede the normal forces working for recovery, etc. Mosley knew all about these arguments. They were the arguments of Labour's *opponents*. He could hardly expect the Party to take them seriously since, in his view, it had arisen to challenge them. Had the free market been employing the community's resources profitably and wisely there would have been no slump, no unemployment, no need for government interference and no need for socialism. The Labour Party had arisen precisely because the system defended

by the Treasury was breaking down. Mosley did not feel the need
in the memorandum to make a philosophic case for the state intervention. He took it for granted that all its readers already accepted
that case. The memorandum was simply an attempt to force the
Government and the Party to live up to its frequently declared
policy. This is why the Government's acceptance of the treasury
arguments destroyed Mosley's faith in the Government. On the
basis of the treasury document there was no need for a Labour Party,
certainly not for a Labour Government. By accepting it the Government was denying its own *raison d'être*. Hence the bitterness of
Mosley's rejoinder to MacDonald: ' I perhaps misunderstood you
when I came into the Labour Party.'

In this at least he was right. The Labour Party was not the sort
of party he imagined it to be. Ideologically it was; psychologically
it was not. The Labour Party's dream-world was particularly
luxuriant in utopias. However, its dreams were the fantasies of
the impotent. It was terrified of either acquiring or using power.
And without power there could be no utopia, not even the first
halting step on the way. To cover up the fear there was an attractive rationalisation: Labour Government lacked a majority. But
as Élie Halévy remarked, not unfairly, after the 1931 débâcle:
' I tell you frankly that I shudder at the thought of the Labour
Party ever having a real majority, not for the sake of capitalism,
but for the sake of socialism.'[3] This fear of power was rooted in the
psychology of the underdog. Although they dreamed of being
on top, the working class were in fact on the bottom; and the whole
of their struggle was directed not towards acquiring power for which
inwardly they felt themselves unfitted but towards limiting the power
of those who had it.

The Labour Party existed not to govern but to attack government, whether it be government in industry, or government in
Parliament. Power was for others – Tories, landlords, employers.
What Labour wanted was to tear down the mighty from their seats
and exalt the humble and meek. Hence arises the paradox that
in the inter-war years the party of state power was the least willing
of all to use state power. While Lloyd George Liberals and young
Tories preached the philosophy of state intervention, the Labour
Party practised the philosophy of small government. From this
irony was born in Mosley's mind the idea for a new type of movement which combined the passion for social reform with the
Übermensch psychology that could alone bring it about.

But this was still some time in the future. Snowden's report,
as we have mentioned, was not submitted to the Cabinet till 8
May 1930. A committee headed by MacDonald, and including
Thomas, Greenwood and Miss Bondfield, was appointed to discuss the points at issue with the three advisory ministers. Thomas

Jones, its secretary, wrote of Mosley in these discussions, ' He is too " logical" and if he had his way would attempt presently to " Russianise " . . . our Government.'[4]   This curious remark recalls *The Times*'s comment in 1843 on the resignation of Edwin Chadwick, the pioneering civil servant who had proposed health controls: ' We prefer to take our chance of cholera and the rest than be bullied into health.' *The Times*, as we shall see, had not changed its view; the trouble was that the civil service evidently now agreed with *The Times*.

At the two meetings between the cabinet committee and the advisory ministers, on 13 and 19 May 1930, the discussion centred on the difficulties in getting a public works programme going. Mosley claimed that basically the size of the public works programme was determined by the availability of money. Though willing to concede that the ' transfer ' condition was holding up work in the more prosperous areas, Thomas and Morrison argued that the difficulty was not getting money from Snowden, but getting schemes submitted, and, even once submitted and approved, getting them started. As Morrison put it, ' When money is voted, there are no plans in being.' Lansbury made the same point: ' You've got a hundred million pounds and you spent 15 million pounds. Where are your schemes?' Mosley retorted: ' A Napoleon could spend 200 million pounds in three years.' Thomas restated the conventional view in his parliamentary speech of 28 May: ' I am going to challenge anyone to show that schemes have been held up merely because of lack of finance. The difference between my hon. Friend and myself and the Government on that point is, that it is sheer madness merely to talk of any sum of money, and after you have raised the money to see how you are going to spend it.   The business way is to set about finding the scheme, to examine all the proposals, to test them in the light of practical experience and when you have done that, to see how you are going to find the money.'[5]

The point at issue was really fundamental. Mosley was arguing that the dimensions of the public works programme should be fixed not by some business-accounting estimate of the potential volume of useful work available in the country, but by the dimensions of the unemployment problem. The reason Mosley had asked for £200 million was that he wanted to provide work for 300,000 men for three years. (The Unemployment Grants Committee worked on the assumption that £1 million gave employment to 4000 men for one year.) The view of Thomas and Morrison seemed to be that, even if this sum were allocated, no schemes up to the value of £70 million a year would be forthcoming from the local authorities. Mosley's reply was that, in that case, the State must produce the schemes itself. But he was by no means convinced that local authorities could not find schemes to that amount. Unless the local authorities knew in advance that their big plans would be sanctioned they would not bother to draw them up. Their attitude was still governed by the restrictive policy towards public works of the late government. It was only by fixing a high, definite allocation of money that the psychological barrier to the submitting of large schemes would be broken down. In the discussions with the advisory ministers Morrison seemed to pooh-pooh this line of reasoning. Yet it was precisely the line he himself had adopted in his attempts to get more money out of Snowden for the road programme.*

A further issue in the discussion was the timetable of any such programme. Thomas, Morrison and Greenwood took the view that even if a £200 million public works programme could be organised it was madness to suppose it could be compressed into three years, and that consequently the amount of employment afforded in the three-year period would be very much less than Mosley claimed. Here is Morrison on the typical problems that arose in mounting a road scheme:

> Take Shooters Hill by-pass. It was found there was a railway in the way; houses on the route; tramway being built. There are always physical difficulties. Plant has to be shifted about. Negotiations must proceed with churches, allotment holders, residents – on the ground, local authorities fail to insist on proper detail. . . . If you bring in consulting engineers, the County Surveyor kicks up rough and will not delegate.

When Lloyd George had produced his own plan for building roads in the election of 1929, the civil servants had argued that to compress a road-building programme of 'at least a decade' into two years would require dictatorship. Once again we have a clear conflict of priorities. On the one side, business-accounting methods, Business As Usual procedures; on the other side the determination to put the solution of unemployment on an emergency, war footing, abrogating normal peace-time rights, riding roughshod over normal peace-time susceptibilities.

The discussions revealed a gulf of spirit that could not be bridged. What about the feelings of the County Surveyor? asked Morrison. There is less suffering than ever before, Thomas reminded them. MacDonald floundered around in his usual hopeless fashion.

Mosley was deeply depressed when he dined with the Webbs on

---

*Snowden's argument was that there was no point in sanctioning expenditure till schemes were drawn up. Morrison replied: ' We know by long experience that local authorities will not allow time and money to be spent in elaborating detailed proposals unless they are assured that the execution of the works, if they came to be agreed in principle, would fall within the scope of such a programme approved by the Government.'

the evening of 19 May.   The incomprehension of his colleagues, the invincible orthodoxy of Snowden, above all the lack of any will to overcome difficulties weighed heavily on his mind.   The strain of fighting a completely solitary battle within the Government, too, was beginning to tell.   Keynes, whom he needed more than any-one else at his side, was not available.   Even Hubert Henderson, secretary of the Economic Advisory Council, was never called in for these discussions.   Mosley in turn had been excluded from the meetings of the Economic Advisory Council, which on Keynes' insistence was even then beginning to discuss the very questions raised in the memorandum. (At the first meeting of the E.A.C. Keynes had offended MacDonald by describing himself as 'the only socia-list present'.)   There was a complete lack of co-ordination.   How could one get a decent unemployment policy when it was even im-possible to have the relevant issues properly discussed?   The only course of action that seemed to hold out any prospect of success was to resign from the Government and appeal directly to the Labour Party.   What advice the Webbs gave on this critical occa-sion is not recorded.   Beatrice found the Mosleys 'sincere and assiduous in their public aims' which from her was high praise indeed.   At any rate, the decision to resign was taken sometime that evening. Boothby, who visited Mosley in his room in the House of Commons, well remembers ' his relief and satisfaction, his deter-mination to go forward and "bring these grave matters to the test"'.[6]

Mosley handed in his letter of resignation to MacDonald at lunchtime the following day.   Ministers made a last effort to get him to change his mind.   Mosley was adamant.   He wanted to build a 'machine for a vast programme' but Snowden would not find the money.   It was a choice between him and Snowden and plainly he must go.   The only 'clean thing' was to submit the issue to the test of party opinion.   MacDonald begged Mosley to 'consider what he is doing to us'.   Mosley replied that it was Snow-den's policy, not his resignation, that would destroy the Govern-ment.   Thomas Johnston defended Mosley.   He 'had been tram-pled on; his talents ignored. . . . We, Lansbury and I, feel he should be used.'   It was too late.[7]

Of the sixty-odd ministers who have resigned their offices this century, Mosley was the only one to do so over un-employment.   Should he have stayed on?   In favour is the fact that certain concessions were offered and later implemented by the Government.*   Against this, Mosley had not been

*MacDonald took personal charge of the unemployment problem as chairman of a panel of ministers.   The transfer condition was dropped, and Morrison was able to squeeze a little more money out of Snowden for road works.   There was some attempt to galvanise local authorities.   (See R. Skidelsky, *Politicians and the Slump* (1967) ch. 9.)

met on his two main points: a big loan to be fixed not by the number of 'remunerative' schemes, but by the dimensions of the unemployment problem, and a centrally directed public works programme. Had Mosley been given a real job of work to do he would have stayed on. But the Government's policy did not call for anyone being given a real job of work to do. It was to keep the unemployed standing by, use the Unemployment Insurance Fund, and hope for better times round the corner. MacDonald may have had his doubts about this as a recipe for electoral success, but he was not equipped and not prepared to stand up to Snowden. This was the crux of the situation. As long as Snowden remained at the Exchequer there could be no Mosleyite – or Keynesian – unemployment policy. And no one in the Government was prepared to stand up to Snowden, because in the end they were all trapped in Snowden's assumptions, however hard they tried to kick against them.

An alternative argument is that Mosley should have delayed his resignation until the position worsened. He would then have been in a far stronger position 'both hierarchically and morally' to challenge Snowden.[8] The decisive argument against this is that for Mosley to have stayed on in face of the rejection of his policy would have been to remove the ground for resigning later – as George Brown found out to his cost after July 1966.

Mosley's resignation was an important political event, but it did not become overwhelmingly so till his parliamentary speech of 28 May 1930. Liberal and left-wing papers were on the whole sympathetic. The *Manchester Guardian* of 21 May thought it would be good for the Government to be harassed by a 'critic of the left-centre'; the *Daily Herald*, which had always been friendly to Mosley, thought his resignation 'courageous' and predicted that he would do 'big things for democracy'. In its columns of 24 May 1930 Harold Laski produced an interesting assessment of Mosley at this break in his career. As a speaker he had 'real charm and rhetorical gifts of a very high order'. He had 'courage and energy and enthusiasm'. He was a hard worker, who drove himself relentlessly. He had undeniable charisma, 'great gifts of leadership'. 'At Harrow and Birmingham and Smethwick people gave effort to him for his own sake far beyond what even the Labour Party can normally command.' Yet to counterbalance these qualities there were 'grave faults [which] constitute a real menace to his future'. He was impatient of opposition, rash and impulsive. He tended to jump at an idea rather than think deeply about it. He didn't appreciate the importance of time: 'He wants what he wants at once.' He could not plan a long way ahead, got angry too easily. 'He is, too, so anxious to realise his ambitions that he often leaves the impression of using both men and ideas for his own ends.'

Living on his nerves, he was unsparing of the nerves of others. 'What Mosley needs is a break in his success. He has been the wonder-child too long.'

The critical side of this assessment was echoed by *The Times*, which dismissed Mosley as an ambitious careerist, a man on the make who was deserting a sinking ship. *The Times*'s relentless hostility to Mosley is one of the features of these months. It saw not the slightest virtue either in the man or in his policies, reflecting to a degree unusual even for it the views of the most self-righteous sections of the British Establishment. Only in its correspondence columns did it allow an occasional breath of life. On 27 May it published a letter from Harold Macmillan. Mosley had broken the rules of the game by advocating adherence to his party's election programme. 'The mere suggestion that election promises ought to be implemented seems to have fluttered the dovecotes of more than one political party. . . .' Macmillan concluded, 'I hope some of my friends will have the courage to applaud and support his protest.' The next day a reply appeared signed by four Conservative M.P.s. When the rules of the game were criticised, it said, 'it is usually the player, and not the game that is at fault. It is then usually advisable for the player to seek a new field for his recreation and a pastime more suitable to his talents.' One of the signatories was R. A. Butler, the present Master of Trinity College, Cambridge. Like Sir Austen Chamberlain, he always played the game and he always lost it.

An even more interesting letter of support appeared on 6 June. In its editorial of 2 June, *The Times* condemned Mosley's 'panic policy of reckless extravagance'. Professor Pigou of Cambridge replied as follows:

> When industry is in equilibrium. . . there is a presumption that State action designed to stimulate employment in any particular field will be injurious. It will, in general, merely divert labour from more productive to less productive occupations. . . . There is also a presumption that men set to work in 'artificially created' occupations will not be worth their wage, for if they had been, these occupations would have been filled spontaneously – and that, therefore, the 'artificial creation' of employment is a waste of resources.
>
> Both these presumptions. . . would provide good reasons for deprecating State action designed to reduce unemployment. . . provided there was no unemployment to reduce! When, however, as at the present time, there is an enormous mass of unemployment, their virtue and their relevance are lost. If employment is 'artificially created' in these conditions, men are available to come into it, not merely from more useful occu-

pations elsewhere, but from soul-destroying idleness. It may
well be that, when they come in, they will not be worth the
wage paid to them. But this does not now imply a waste of
national resources. So long as they are worth more than the
excess of their wages over what they would otherwise have
received in unemployment benefit . . . there is not a loss to the
rest of the community, but a gain.

Pigou's reply is important in showing that the conventional economic wisdom trumpeted out by politicians and leader writers was
not representative of contemporary economic thought.

One cannot feel that at this period of crisis in its economic life
the country was well served by its press. Editorial discussion of
economic questions reached a depth of banality hard to credit,
with *The Times* leading the way. From the quality press, with the
notable exceptions of Garvin's *Observer* and the *Manchester Guardian*,
one gains the impression of a society in the last stages of *rigor mortis*.
And as far as official England is concerned this impression is largely
true: the Press merely reflected the great blight, the revulsion
against adventure and new ways of thought which had set in
with Baldwinism. Baldwin himself was its great exponent. He
boasted that ' one of the reasons why our people are alive and
flourishing and have avoided many of the troubles that have fallen
to less happy nations is that we have never been guided by logic
in anything we did '. One writer has observed that ' from 1922 to
1939 England's affairs were managed in accordance with Baldwin's
view that the country was best served by men of second-class brains,
on the ground that men with first-class brains had second-class
characters '.[9] Under this régime, *laissez-faire* was firmly back in
the saddle. New ideas in economics and politics found it almost
impossible to get respectful attention, much less acceptance: when
taken up at all by the commentators they appeared as hideous paro-
dies of their original, from which all sound men would rightly avert
their eyes. The reasons for this intellectual and psychological decay
have never been properly explored. Perhaps, as George Steiner
says, ' decisive reserves of intelligence, of nervous resilience, of political talent, had been annihilated' in the war. The result was
that England remained suspended between two worlds, one dead,
the other powerless to be born.

On 22 May 1930 Mosley appealed to the Parliamentary Labour
Party against the Cabinet's verdict. His speech in moving the
motion that ' this Party is dissatisfied with the present unemployment policy of the Government and calls for the formulation of
an alternative policy more in accordance with the programme
and pledges of the Party at the last election ' was by all accounts
a brilliant performance. However, Mosley's eloquence was largely

offset by Arthur Henderson's shrewdness.   In his most disarming
vein he appealed to Mosley to withdraw his censure motion and
'allow his proposals to be discussed in detail at various party meetings'.   As long as we can all keep talking, Henderson was saying,
what need have we to part company?   It was the exact opposite
of Mosley's determination to 'bring these grave matters to the test'.
Nevertheless, according to Sir George Catlin, it was Strachey who
gave Mosley the decisive push.   When Henderson produced his
compromise formula Mosley 'turned to his satellite moon (whom
some would hold to have been his evil genius) John Strachey . . .
to consult him about acceptance.   Strachey's counsel was to refuse.
"What the people want is Action." '   So Mosley declined to withdraw.   Twenty-nine M.P.s supported him; 210 supported the
Government.[10]

Mosley had made only a brief formal statement to the House
on 21 May 1930, reserving the major justification for his resignation for the debate on unemployment scheduled on 28 May.   The
House was packed when Stanley Baldwin, leader of the opposition,
rose at 2.30 p.m. to move the Conservative motion to reduce the
salary of the lord privy seal – equivalent to a motion of censure on
the Government's unemployment policy.   Suddenly the parliamentary situation had become extraordinarily fluid.   It was not
just because a junior minister had resigned.   It was rather because
the resignation symbolised at that moment a feeling in all parties
that the first phase of the Government's policy had ended in failure
and that something new was required.   Who would provide it?
MacDonald?   Baldwin?   Lloyd George?   Or Mosley himself?
The House was filled with that peculiar atmosphere of tension
which always accompanies the realisation of a possible political
crisis in the making.

Baldwin led off in his usual good humour, with a few jokes at
the expense of MacDonald, Snowden and Thomas.   Safeguarding,
he declared, was the only remedy that would meet the situation,
so that England could bargain with other countries for tariff reductions.   Just as he seemed on the point of saying something, Baldwin sat down – a tactic to which he was to be driven with increasing
frequency in the months ahead.

MacDonald was greeted with loud cheers from his own supporters.
There were none when he sat down.   The Government had sanctioned £103 million for public works.   Over how many years was this
to be spread, by how much did it exceed that of the late Government, Lloyd George wanted to know?   That was a matter for the
departments, MacDonald replied.   Churchill persevered: 'We
want to know what are the extra amounts over and above the
normal?'   MacDonald started to bluster.   How dare they query
the accuracy of the figures supplied by the departments!   Any

explanation as to how the figures were composed were, as they well knew, a matter for the departments. He as prime minister could not be expected to have these details in his head! Incredulous murmurs rose. MacDonald tried to pick up the threads. The crisis was only temporary. A boom was round the corner. Meanwhile the municipalities might be encouraged. Pensions would have to be co-ordinated. ' We have to face new conditions, and produce schemes and ideas . . . organisation, cooperation, co-ordination, rationalisation and national views.' The empty polysyllables, trumpeted, almost shouted out, produced a stunned vacuity.

During his leader's fumbling performance, Mosley had been sitting with folded arms in a corner seat above the gangway ' grand, gloomy, peculiar. . . wrapped in the solitude of his own originality '. After a few further exchanges between Philip Snowden and Sir Robert Horne, he rose, black-coated, striped-trousered, debonair, correct, a sheet of paper in one hand.

He would not indulge in any dialectics, he said, ' because I believe the purpose which this committee desires can best be served if, as directly as possible, I proceed to the actual facts of the great administrative and economic questions which are involved '. His one general comment was that the aggravation of world conditions should act as a spur to doing more, not as an excuse for doing less.

Following the general plan of the memorandum, Mosley then outlined the existing structure for dealing with unemployment and his own suggestions. The existing structure left all the initiative in the hands of the civil servants instead of in those of the Government. His admiration for the civil service had greatly increased, but to achieve results ' it is absolutely necessary that the whole initiative and drive should rest in the hands of the Government themselves '. A new machine was needed to grapple with the problem. ' After all, it was done in the War; there were revolutions in the machinery of government one after another, until the machine was devised . . . by which the job could be done.'

He then turned to his familiar distinction between long-term and short-term schemes. Rationalisation would throw people out of work; therefore it was necessary to have short-term schemes to provide employment in the interval. Even rationalisation, though, would not solve the permanent problem, because it was an 'illusion' to believe that there would be any increase in the export trade. 'It is to the Home Market that we must look for the solution of our difficulties.' (Hon. Members: 'Hear, hear!'). He continued: 'We have to get away from the belief that the only criterion of British prosperity is how many goods we can send abroad for foreigners to consume.' Tariffs were an inefficient instrument for securing the home market – his old point about them being useless against currency fluctuations was repeated here. Instead the I.L.P. policy of the import board to regulate trade was the best approach. Only in this way could the country be 'insulated' against the 'electric shocks of present world conditions'.

Mosley then described his short-term policy of constructive works, retirement pensions and the raising of the school-leaving age, going over once again all his difficulties with the departments, local authorities, etc. Large sums of money would be needed. 'How is it to be raised, out of revenue or out of loan? £100,000,000 out of revenue! Who will suggest it in the present situation? It is 2s on the Income Tax. It must be raised by loan. If the principle of a big loan is turned down then this kind of work must come to an end.' Here was Mosley's big break with the I.L.P.'s policy of financing extra wages and social services out of taxation.

It was argued that state expenditure would divert money from private spending. Mosley's reply to this was characteristic:

> I admit that there is some force in that view in a period of acute deflation. Given, however, a financial policy of stabilisation, that Treasury point of view cannot hold water. It would mean that every single new enterprise is going to put as many men out of employment as it will employ.... If it is true it means that nothing can ever be done by the Government or by Parliament. It means that no Government has any function or any purpose; it is a policy of complete surrender.

The Government, he noted, had no objection to loans being raised to finance foreign investment. 'Why is it so right and proper that capital should go overseas to equip factories to compete against us, to build roads and railways in the Argentine or in Timbuctoo, to provide employment for people in those countries while it is supposed to shake the whole basis of our financial strength if anyone dares suggest the raising of money by the Government of this country to provide employment for the people of this country?'

Mosley had been speaking for almost seventy minutes. Pale and exhausted, he came to his close:

> This nation has to be mobilised and rallied for a tremendous effort, and who can do that except the Government of the day? If that effort is not made we may soon come to crisis, to a real crisis. I do not fear that so much, for this reason, that in a crisis this nation is always at its best. This people knows how to handle a crisis, it cools their heads and steels their nerves. What I fear much more than a sudden crisis is a long, slow, crumbling through the years until we sink to the level of a Spain, a gradual paralysis, beneath which all the vigour and energy of this country will succumb. That is a far more

dangerous thing, and far more likely to happen unless some effort is made. If the effort is made how relatively easily can disaster be averted. You have in this country resources, skilled craftsmen among the workers, design and technique among the technicians, unknown and unequalled in any other country in the world. What a fantastic assumption it is that a nation which within the lifetime of every one has put forth efforts of energy and vigour unequalled in the history of the world, should succumb before an economic situation such as the present. If the situation is to be overcome, if the great powers of this country are to be rallied and mobilised for a great national effort, then the Government and Parliament must give a lead. I beg the Government tonight to give the vital forces of this country the chance that they await. I beg Parliament to give that lead.[11]

He had referred to the sheet of paper just twice, to read brief quotations, yet his speech had never faltered, every argument was in sequence, every thought and phrase in place. When he sat down there was a moment of silence. No one had stirred from his seat during the speech. Cimmie, who had never once taken her eyes off him, was crying with pride. Then the cheering broke out, loud and prolonged, from every section of the House and galleries. For those minutes he was the undisputed leader of his generation.

Rarely can a parliamentary speech have been greeted with such unanimous critical acclaim. 'Has MacDonald found his superseder in OM?' asked Beatrice Webb.[12] Even the unfriendly *Times* agreed that it had made a 'profound impression'. 'Whatever may be thought of the matter of it, nothing for the occasion could have bettered the manner.' The remainder of the press was even more fulsome.*

*For the *Morning Post* Mosley had 'stood forth with the argument of his career, a feat of coolness accomplished so masterfully and with such patrician ease as to subdue the House to admiration'. 'A tremendous personal triumph,' declared the *Daily Mail*. The speech had 'made the occupants of both front benches seem second-rate'. 'The most memorable one-man effort to grapple with unemployment which has been achieved in any . . . debate in recent years,' echoed the *Daily Express*. The *Daily Herald* wrote, 'Sir Oswald entered a brilliant defence of his own attitude, followed by a vigorous and sustained offensive. . . . Rarely, if ever, has a junior Minister, resigning under such circumstances, received such a remarkable personal triumph.' Mosley's speech, according to the *Evening Standard*, was 'one of the most notable Parliamentary achievements of recent times . . . the triumph of an artist who has made his genius perfect by long hours of practice and devotion to his art. It was too, the genuine reward of labour. There is no politician who works harder or who takes more pains to master his problems.' Encomiums continued to flow. 'Delivered without affectation, with perfect command of temper . . . here was evidence of hard

Parliamentary congratulations poured in: from Philip Noel Baker, Robert Boothby, Brendan Bracken, Clement Davies and many others. 'You are a great man now,' wrote Bob Boothby. 'But don't entirely forget a friend who sometimes stood by in darker days which will now never recur.' From Violet Bonham-Carter came a chatty letter:

> My dear Tom – I must write a line to congratulate you on a really great Parliamentary performance. I was enormously impressed by it and I don't believe there is anyone else in this House who could have done it.
>
> I must say your Front Bench did everything they could to create a 'favourable atmosphere' for you! The sensation of *terror* one received from hearing the Prime Minister say *he did not know* whether the 103 millions were being spent this year – or spread over 5 – was like being told by one's chauffeur that he didn't know where the wheel was – It was a *terribly* revealing debate – and a *really* alarming one – laying bare the emptiness of all Party minds.

From Mosley's mother came a letter that must have pleased him more than all the others:

> My darling Tom,
>
> So many better judges and abler folk must have congratulated you on your masterly performance of last night, my congratulations are almost absurd. But oh! my dear lad, I can never tell you what it meant to your old mother. I was so full of pride and joy in my man-child it almost choked me. It was wonderful. People of all shades of opinion were thrilled and staggered by the 'finest speech heard in the House for 20 years.' I was only sorry not to be able to stay and hear J.T's feeble effort to reply to an unanswerable case. You have certainly vindicated your resignation and are in a stronger position today than you have ever been. How I hope I may live to have the joy of seeing 'all your dreams come true' for the good of the country and your own honour and glory. . . .
>
> Your loving old Mother

---

work, of independent, concrete, thinking, and of a rare political conscience . . . must be regarded as a candidate . . . for the highest honours' (*Daily Telegraph*). 'The outstanding feature of the debate . . . as an intellectual performance it was one of the best made in the House for some time' (*Daily News*). 'Delivered with perfect clearness and faultless taste' (*Spectator*, 31 May 1930). 'We have seldom read a more lucid, cogent, or sustained argument' (*Nation*, 7 June 1930). 'Brilliant and powerful, without rhetoric, which left the majority of the House of Commons more than ever convinced that by one means, or another national policy must be boldly changed' (J. L. Garvin, in the *Observer*, 1 June 1930).

How good was Mosley's programme? It was an attempt, as Mosley himself was to say many times, to reduce Labour's own unemployment policy to administrative practice. Regarded as a whole, therefore, it suffered from the defects of a policy which itself lacked any coherence. Mosley was completely on target with his plan for a public works programme to be financed by loan, even though he failed to support it with its strongest economic argument: namely, its effect in keeping up the level of demand. On the other hand, the pension and school-leaving-age proposals were criticised at the time by Keynes and Henderson, and would be so today, as diversions from the need to provide more jobs. They were inheritances from the party programme, and Mosley soon dropped them.

The other questionable feature of his approach was his long-term analysis, leading to the proposal to 'insulate' Britain from world markets. The temperamental bias against leaving national well-being to the 'sport' of world conditions led him to an autarchic outlook which was to prove permanent. Whereas Keynes was prepared to go 'homespun' as a second-best solution, a self-sufficient area became for Mosley a permanent concept, an alternative system, designed to avoid the possibility of anything like the Depression from happening again. At this stage, though, it had not yet hardened into a dogma: and the emphasis on the home market was a salutary and necessary corrective to the Government's obsession with an export revival.

Indeed, Mosley's pessimism about the export trade was, within weeks of his resignation, to be reinforced from an unexpected quarter. On 30 May 1930 Sir Richard Hopkins, controller of finance and supply at the Treasury, wrote to Sir Horace Wilson, head of Thomas's secretariat: 'The Chancellor of the Exchequer has asked me to produce a very full report on Mosley's speech. . . . I should be very glad for your help . . . '—a significant commentary on the effect of Mosley's performance.

Sir Richard Hopkins circulated a draft for consideration by the relevant departments. With one exception, all returned approving replies. The exception was the Board of Trade. The departmental head, Sir Horace Hamilton, was not directly involved; but three Young Turks in his department had come to the astonishing conclusion on the basis of their own calculations that Mosley was right in his argument that the export trade would not absorb the unemployed. Their names were W. B. (later Sir William) Brown, Graham's private secretary, Percy Ashley, head of the Industries Department, and A. W. Flux, a statistician. They now proceeded to rewrite those sections of Hopkins' draft dealing with the export trade in such a way as to support the arguments of the ex-chancellor of the duchy.

In his resignation speech Mosley had declared himself much more positively on the export question than he had in the memorandum, adding new arguments and facts. The Board of Trade commented:

> There is perhaps some prima facie reason for the doubts expressed by Sir O. Mosley as to the extent to which a recovery of our world trade position can be expected, even if the policy of rationalisation be extensively applied. Among the factors which have operated to the disadvantage of British trade since the war not the least important is the growth, without and within the Empire, of local manufacture carefully fostered by protected tariffs. The consequences are two – reduction in the extent of the open market and intensified competition for the market still left open. There are no indications of any real check to this movement. . . .

(Before ' There are no indications ' Hopkins added in his own hand, ' Sir Oswald would argue no doubt that'.) ' In this connection', the Board of Trade note continued,

> it must be pointed out that in many of the more important industries knowledge of processes, methods and management is international; improvements are broadcasted; machinery is becoming continuously more and more automatic and more effectively usable by less highly skilled workers.

These were arguments that Mosley himself had used in the resignation speech. They were not welcome to the treasury knights. ' This doesn't help the argument very much. Will have to be altered, I think,' one of them wrote in the margin. Another scribbled: ' The Board of Trade should be asked to adduce evidence to the contrary. . . . '

> The tendency might seem, therefore, to be for international trade in manufactured goods . . . to play a relatively decreasing part in the world's economy. Though there may be an actual extension of that trade, the pace is likely to be slower than in the past; and for the reasons given above it may be increasingly difficult for the United Kingdom to maintain, and still more difficult for her to increase, her share of the trade, given the incidental advantages which some of her competitors enjoy.
>
> These seem to be the considerations which Sir O. Mosley has in mind *and on a short distance view – even if that distance be one of several years* – there is considerable force in them. But he appears to underestimate the potentialities in economic development, and especially the possibilities in the regions where for a very long time to come manufacturing industry of an advanced order is unlikely to establish itself. The economic development of Africa, for example, is only beginning. . . .

But admittedly such development can only be gradual.   [My italics.]

All these passages were incorporated into the final draft, with a few modifications.   These views may seem, from today's perspective, unjustifiably pessimistic.   The process of local industrialisation on which both Mosley and the Board of Trade lay stress clearly had much further to go before it was likely to put the export trade of the industrial nations out of business in a properly functioning world economy. Almost completely ignored were the possibilities inherent in the development of new industries – in the ongoing of that very scientific revolution which in Mosley's opinion had brought much of Britain's troubles upon it.   Yet it must never be forgotten that it took another world war and the establishment of an American hegemony to re-create something approximating to the nineteenth century world-market.   In the 1930s there was no single power strong enough to impose order on the rapidly disintegrating liberal world structure.   In these circumstances, Mosley's instinct that Britain must seek a way out of the crisis on its own stands extremely favourable comparison with the facile optimism of the orthodox rationalisers.

Sir Richard Hopkins, as we have seen, had gone to the lengths of including the Board of Trade's doubts about the export trade in his final report. He had followed Sir Oswald all the way to the edge of the shore.   But he shrank, as he himself put it, from that final plunge into ' an uncharted sea'.   However, he had already gone too far for Snowden's liking.   Scribbled on the first page of his final report of 16 June 1930 is the extraordinary note: ' Written for the Chancellor alone.   Copies not to be distributed without the Chancellor's permission, e.g., P.M. has been refused a copy, also Graham and Hartshorn.'[13]* In this way the evil spirit of the Mosley Memorandum was finally exorcised from Whitehall.

*W. Graham was president of the Board of Trade. Vernon Hartshorn was Thomas's successor as lord privy seal and MacDonald's deputy dealing with unemployment. The way in which both he and the prime minister were deprived of essential papers on the economic situation provides an instructive commentary on the working of British government and the role of the chancellor in it.

Chapter 11

Workers of the Empire, Unite!

IN RESIGNING from the Government Mosley had no intention of retiring unobtrusively to the back benches. He had told Mac-Donald that he intended to ' appeal to the judgment of our party '.[1] The first appeal, at the parliamentary party meeting of 22 May, had gone against him; the next goal was the Labour Party Conference scheduled at Llandudno for the autumn.

Mosley's political position was not nearly as strong as the Press made out. His dramatic resignation had created a situation, captured a mood. Exploiting it was a much more difficult task. In the parliamentary Labour party, his only consistent political ally – apart from Cimmie – was John Strachey. Beatrice Webb noticed Mosley's lack of roots in the Labour Party. He lacked MacDonald's strongest point – genuine puritanism. He was

> entangled in a smart set and luxurious habits – he is reputed to be loose with women – he arouses suspicion – he knows little or nothing about Trade Unionism or Cooperation – he cannot get on terms of intimacy with working men or with the lower middle-class brainworker, he is, in fact, an intruder . . . [he] will be a great success at public meetings – but will he get round him the Arthur Hendersons, the Herbert Morrisons, the Alex-anders, the Citrines and the Bevins, who are the natural leaders of . . . the proletariat? Hitherto they have had little use for Mosley . . . and it is they who will decide who shall succeed or supersede JRM – not the John Stracheys and Fenner Brockways – and Wises – all of whom like Mosley are intruders into the world of manual workers.[2]

Henderson at least was reasonably sympathetic. He had taken a conciliatory line at the party meeting and in an interview with Mosley after it had pressed him not to be too severe on the Govern-ment in his resignation speech. In the next few months he gave Mosley the impression that he regarded himself as ' residuary legatee ' if the Party revolted against MacDonald.[3] But Hender-son, a party man first and foremost, would only act at the behest of the Party.

Mosley was soon able to recruit a small body of Labour parlia-mentarians of varying quality. The two most important were W. J. Brown and Aneurin Bevan. Brown, the son of a Battersea plumber, had entered Parliament for Wolverhampton West in

1929, aged thirty-four.   Founder of the Civil Service Clerical Association, he had soon become a stern critic of Snowden's deflationary
policy.   An able, fiery man, burning with indignation, he wanted
Mosley to leave the Labour Party and start a new movement with
the I.L.P.*   The ex-miner Aneurin Bevan, a ' bold and brilliant
youth ' of thirty-three as one journalist described him, was M.P.
for Ebbw Vale.   Following Mosley's resignation, he organised
a petition signed by sixty Labour M.P.s, calling for a more active
unemployment policy.   Ellen Wilkinson saw him as a possible
bridge between the ' intellectuals ' round Mosley and left-wing
unionism.   ' To Bevan ', writes Michael Foot, ' the Mosley programme appeared as a better defined, more practical prospectus
than that which Maxton enumerated, one well suited to the urgen-
cies of the hour. '4

The fair-haired Oliver Baldwin also joined Mosley's standard.
M.P. for Dudley he was, at thirty-one, spoilt, unstable, homosexual,
naïve; but, as the son of Stanley, was an important name.   The
' Mosley Group ' was completed by Robert Forgan, M.P. for West
Renfrewshire, a medical man.   All four had entered Parliament for
the first time in 1929.   In Strachey, Bevan and Brown, Mosley
had the three ablest young men in the Labour Party.

Most of the rest of the Party remained suspicious.   To Rhys
Davies, a Lancashire M.P., Mosley's plans savoured too much of
compulsion.   ' Our people have always preferred freedom with
poverty to affluence under tyranny,' he wrote fatuously.5   ' Internationally knitted economic systems are much more powerful than
Minority Governments or little coteries of supermen,' observed
John Clarke, a Glasgow M.P.6   When Bevan's motion calling for
a more active unemployment policy came before the parliamentary
Labour party meeting on 10 July 1930, less than half the Labour
M.P.s bothered to turn up.   And then it was weakly referred back
to the consultative committee by 80 votes to 38.   It was this spirit of
negation, more than anything else, that was to break Mosley's faith
in the Labour Party.   To all efforts to arouse them from their inertia
they reacted, in Jennie Lee's phrase, ' like a load of damp cement '.

The reasons for it are highly complex and have less to do with
suspicions of Mosley's motives than with the structure and psychology of the Labour Party itself.   The chances of a successful rebellion within the Labour Party are never as high as in the Conservative
Party.   The Labour Party itself was a party of rebellion – a movement of the weak against the strong.   But the one hope of the weak
lies in their numbers; and numbers are useless without discipline.
That is why when the crunch comes the Party tends to close its
ranks and follow its leaders, why appeals to ' solidarity ' nearly

*He was secretary of the I.L.P. parliamentary group of sixteen M.P.s.

always succeed. Once we can see that the perpetual problem of the Labour Party – as of social democracy generally – is to make the weak strong, that its perpetual, ever-present fear is that of being broken by the strength of the forces opposing it, we can begin to understand the difficulties facing a brilliant rebel like Mosley, trying to rouse it from its torpor.

Ideologically, the need for strengthening the solidarity of the weak expressed itself in commitment to a collectivist creed, a creed that at once embodied the experiences and psychic needs of an oppressed class and projected them onto a higher level. Socialism, as Samuel Beer has pointed out,[7] was functional to the politics of class independence: the ideological cement of class solidarity. Failure to carry out socialism could be forgiven, for leaders must take account of the ' facts of the situation '. But renunciation of socialist belief, of socialist rhetoric, was unforgivable, for this heralded the dissolution of class solidarity.[8] Here we have an important explanation of why it proved so difficult for the Labour Party to ' connect ' with the radical Keynesianism represented by Mosley, and at the same time so easy for it to forgive the ' betrayals ' perpetrated on it by MacDonald, Snowden, etc. The Labour Party had not yet perfected the mental gymnastic that was later on to enable it both to accept the mixed economy and continue to proclaim its faith in the common ownership of production, distribution and exchange.

Organisationally, the need to make the weak strong can be seen in the emphasis placed on institutions at the expense of individuals. As the *New Statesman* remarked, ' Persons with no inside knowledge of the Labour movement find it hard to understand how little the influence of any individual counts against the sentiment of collective solidarity.'[9] Collective solidarity in the parliamentary party was buttressed by the phalanx of elderly trade union officials for whom safe parliamentary seats in industrial areas were equivalent to union pensions for a lifetime of hard service. It was this solid group which held the fort against the ' unreliable ' intellectuals, just as the union bloc votes did at party conference. The most that the Labour Party would tolerate – and it tolerated a great deal of it – was ' loyal grousing ', preferably directed at the leadership's failure to achieve socialism faster. But as soon as the grousing threatened to become disloyal the ranks would close, the big guns would be aimed at the rebels, and loyalty would be insisted on, on threat of expulsion.

The Labour Party was (and remains) so constructed that it is virtually impossible for any but the top leadership to take the initiative. This places a very high premium on good leadership from above; but bold leadership – the kind that takes advantage of favourable opportunities; that turns possibilities into achievements – is the one thing that the Labour Party finds it virtually impossible to

produce. Greatness of spirit cannot breathe in the mediocre atmosphere of social democracy. ' I recollect ', John Strachey wrote,
' the spectacle of Mosley sitting silent and alone, brooding with an
indescribable bitterness, as the elderly, portly Trade Union officials
and nervous pacifist intellectuals filed out of a party meeting at
which they had demonstrated their undiminished confidence in Mr.
Ramsay MacDonald.'[10] The attitude of these officials to Mosley's
revolt has been well described by W. J. Brown:

> Come to think of it – who is Mosley, anyway? He isn't really
> one of us! True, we have drunk his wine and smoked his
> cigars, and been flattered by an invitation to his house. But
> there you are! He doesn't really ' belong '. In any case,
> what's he getting at? Is it unemployment he's really con-
> cerned with, or is he playing a subtle game for his own advan-
> cement? Got too good a conceit of himself! – he has! Pro-
> perly considered, a bounder. Why, even the Tories couldn't
> stand him.[11]

For the first time, Mosley was starting to understand the inexorable
limitations of the Labour Party as a party of achievement. There
would be no path by that route to the Promised Land.

Most of the demand for action, he saw all too clearly, was coming
from outside the Labour Party – from the young Tory ex-officer
M.P.s, like Mosley radicalised by the war, from frustrated senior
politicians, from the press-lords. An evening at the Stanleys' in
February had been a typical gathering of the dissatisfied young –
Oliver Stanley himself, Mosley, Walter Elliot, Moore-Brabazon,
Terence O'Connor and Bob Boothby. ' They talked about the
decay of democracy and of parliamentarism. They discuss whether
it would be well to have a fascist coup. They are most disrespectful
of their various party leaders. . . .'[12] Captain Harold Macmillan,
temporarily out of Parliament, looked forward to a Mosley Government of young men with a place for himself in the Cabinet;[13] while
Henry Mond, thirty-two-year-old son of Lord Melchett (formerly
Sir Alfred Mond), wanted Mosley to ' free himself from the trammels
of party politics '.[14] Sir Archibald Sinclair (Churchill's adjutant in
the war) and Leslie Hore-Belisha were two young Liberal M.P.s who
shared the discontents and hopes of the young Tories. These
young men were not only eager for action, they were also tired of
the ' old shibboleths ' and ready for a spot of extra-party adventure.*
Their attitude to Mosley was summed up by Robert Boothby, who
wrote, ' he is the first of my generation to strike a blow against the
old men who have for so long battened themselves and their obsolete

---

*Boothby, Loder, Macmillan and Stanley had written a book, *Industry and the
State* (1927) which consciously sought an industrial ' middle way ' between
doctrinaire socialism and *laissez-faire* capitalism.

laissez-faire on the body politic . . . '.[15]   But for the ' missing generation' there may have been many more of them, and the history of
England might have been very different.   Were these men to be
brushed aside?   Or could they somehow be welded together
with Mosley's Labour collaborators into a revolt of the young men
against the old?

Then there were the two famous frustrated senior politicians,
Lloyd George and Churchill, old in years but young in heart and
mind.   Had the moment come for reviving that elusive centre party
of early post-war dreams?   Finally, there were the kingmakers of the
Press – Beaverbrook, Rothermere, Garvin – uncertain as yet which
way to jump, but conscious, as in 1916, that a palace revolution
might be there for the making.   There were almost too many
possibilities, too many options to be kept open.   As *Time and Tide*
shrewdly surmised, everything depended on ' conditions, opportunities, circumstances.   A man makes use of them and rises upon
them or is dashed to pieces in the trough of their waves.   Sir
Oswald has set his bark afloat upon these waters and no one quite
knows where he is going. . . . '[16]

In his first published statement after his resignation – an article
in the *Sunday Express*, where Beaverbrook had with characteristic
generosity provided him with a platform – Mosley reverted to one
of his earliest political themes: that the real division in politics
was not between parties, but between the ' modern mind ' and
the ' pre-war mind '.   The modern man, he went on,

is a hard, realistic type, hammered into existence on the
anvil of great ordeal.   In mind and spirit he is much further
away from the pre-war man than he is from an ancient Roman,
or from any other product of ages which were dynamic like his
own.   For this age is dynamic and the pre-war age was static.
The men of the pre-war age are much ' nicer ' people than we
are, just as their age was much more pleasant than the present
time.   The practical question is whether their ideas for the
solution of the problems of our age are better than the ideas
of those whom that age has produced.   The types which have
emerged from the pre-war and post-war periods are so different
that they can scarcely understand each other's language when
they face the economic and administrative problems of the
present time.   From this great difference arises many of the
difficulties of modern politics.   It is certainly responsible
for many of my own personal troubles.   I have belonged to
two great parties of the State, and in each party have differed
considerably in mind, method and spirit from its senior members.   However great my personal respect, or even affection
for them has been I have always been painfully aware

that our outlooks and methods ... were those of different
planets.[17]

Here was an unmistakable plea for the union of the 'young minds'
of whatever age against the 'old gangs'. But it would need more
than a common desire for action to bring them together. There
must be a programme. Could one be discovered?

In his resignation speech Mosley had called for the 'insulation'
of the home market from the 'electric shocks of present world
conditions'. The method he advocated was the 'import control
board' worked out by the I.L.P which he now suggested 'can
and should be extended to other trades'.[18]

But insulation went beyond the I.L.P notion of regulation, designed to eliminate middlemen and price fluctuations. The purpose
of the Import Board machinery was to arrange for bulk purchase
between governments or their agencies on long-term contracts at
guaranteed prices. Insulation suggested something more than a
planned foreign trade: it suggested a greatly reduced foreign trade.
This nationalistic strand in Mosley's economic thought can be
traced back to the Birmingham Proposals of 1925. But it was open
to a crucial objection from both free traders and international socialists. How could a country as dependent on international trade
as Britain simply 'insulate' itself from world conditions, however
full of unpleasant electric shocks they might be? Within a few
days of Mosley's resignation, Henry Mond publicly came out with
a tempting suggestion: 'If Sir Oswald Mosley ... could broaden
his vision from these islands to the Empire ... his fears for the future
would be dissolved.' Mosley clutched at the idea.

He first publicly revealed his 'new line' in an article for the
Daily Herald on 7 July headed 'Empire Unity – But No Food Taxes'.
The immediate occasion was a report issued by the Economic Committee of the T.U.C (26 June 1930) which pressed for 'as full a development as possible of the economic relations between the constituent parts of the British Commonwealth'. Bevin was strongly
behind it. Mosley commended the report as 'one of the most important contributions made to the constructive thought of the
Labour Movement'. It recognised that socialism was contrary
to *laissez-faire*. It recognised that Britain could not 'go it alone'.
It was forced inescapably to the conclusion that 'we should seek
conscious control and direction of the united economic resources
of our Commonwealth for the benefit of the Commonwealth as
a whole'. The Import Board machinery would get round the old
problem of food taxes. 'By the fixing of steady contracts it should
be possible to give the Dominions the steady market they desire
and yet by the economies of bulk purchase to supply the British
consumer at a price as cheap, or even cheaper than at present.'

Mosley followed this up by intervening in the Commons debate on imperial policy on 16 July. ' When I last addressed this House ', he observed, ' I suggested that we should strive to insulate these islands from the electric shocks of new world conditions. . . . It would be a better policy with far greater prospects of success if you could extent your area of insulation to embrace the whole common-wealth of nations within whose borders can be found nearly every resource, human and material, which industry requires.'[19] From Beaverbrook came a warm letter of appreciation: ' I congratulate you on your speech. It was a very fine achievement. I am ready at any moment to make overtures in your direction in public, if you wish me to do so. On the other hand I will be glad to organise a Committee to work with you and your colleagues in the hope of hammering out an agreed policy.'[20]

Imperialism was one point of departure: parliamentary reform was the other. At Leicester on 20 July 1930 Mosley called for a new parliamentary ' machine ' to replace the nineteenth century one. Parliament, he said, must become a workshop not a talkshop. Over the next few months he was to stress the need for a strong executive, free from detailed criticism and obstruction. The rela-tionship of government and parliament should be like that of a board of directors to shareholders. The shareholders could dismiss the board if they lost confidence in it; not interfere with its conduct of business.[21]

Disillusion with Parliament and its practitioners was running deep – at least verbally. Aldous Huxley wrote to Cimmie in Septem-ber, ' Wouldn't it be possible to bring in a Bill of Impeachment against a few of the old politicians who have landed us in this mess by their criminal negligence? . . . And if only one could get one or two shut up in the Tower, how it would encourage the rest!' A young journalist, Ward Price, wrote in Lord Rothermere's *Sunday Pictorial*, ' Can this imposing, antiquated Parliamentary machine of ours be made to move fast enough for days of deadly national danger?'[22] Oliver Baldwin has summed up the common contemporary left-wing reaction to Parliament: ' The House of Commons is a heart-breaking place. The wasted hours; the old-fashioned machinery . . . the opposition for opposition's sake; the interminable talking that has not the slightest effect, and the pile of legislation that need never come to us. . . . The deadening effect of the comfort and warmth so easily enable one to forget the pur-pose of one's presence. . . . '[23] The best-argued case for structural reform was put by Churchill in his widely discussed Romanes Lec-ture at Oxford on 19 June 1930. Parliament, he asserted, was supreme in handling ' political questions ' which had dominated the nineteenth century. It was much less successful in handling economic issues which had come to dominate the twentieth century.

These should be handled by an economic sub-parliament ' free altogether from party exigencies, and composed of persons possessing
special qualifications in economic matters '.   Here was an outline
sketch of the Corporate State.   In time Mosley would fill in the
details.

On the basis of these two propositions – an empire policy for
unemployment and a strong executive capable of rapid action –
conversations began with the younger Tories and Liberals at the
Mosleys' home in Smith Square to pave the way for a young
man's party. Hugh Massingham has recalled: ' In those days Mosley's
drawing room was an exciting place.   The gay Bob Boothby flitted
in and out.   There was John Strachey who could be relied upon
to give the talk a Marxist twist. C. E. M. Joad, a philosopher of
sorts, could be discovered cowering in a corner occasionally letting
out a squeak of protest whenever the necessity of violence was mentioned as it usually was.   Harold Nicholson gave a final blessing
with some irrelevant remarks about the views of Talleyrand.   Walter Elliot was there and so was the sad and brilliant Oliver Stanley.'
' Macmillan's association with Mosley ', adds Massingham ' had a
decisive influence on his early thinking.'[24]

The decision to start informal discussions with the younger
Tories vastly increased suspicions of Mosley's intentions within
the Labour Party.   If the discussions failed, he would be left without a political base.   Other well-publicised activities did not help
his reputation with Labour M.P.s.   He addressed audiences of
City men and advertisers.   He and Cimmie were seen far more
frequently at parties and other social events than at any time since
they became socialists: obviously old fences were being mended
in the traditional way.   The rapid evaporation of the goodwill
produced by his resignation speech is shown by Mosley's failure
to get elected to the Consultative Committee in July.   Suspicions
of the ' rich socialist ' were to be revived by photographs of Mosley
surf-riding at Juan-les-Pins in August.*

These intrigues were fully known only to the inner circle of
British politics: to a large section of the Labour rank and file
Mosley was still the hero who had resigned over the Government's
failure to carry out its election pledges.   And it was to the rank
and file that his next appeal was about to be directed.

The thirty-first annual conference of the Labour Party assembled
in the Welsh sea-side resort of Llandudno on 6 October 1930.   On
Wednesday morning, MacDonald opened the debate on unemployment with ' a wonderful speech.   He said nothing, but he said it
so eloquently that the delegates were deeply moved.'[25]   The after-

*Perhaps they would have been allayed had equal publicity been given to Cim-
mie's visit to Russia with John Strachey in September: she met Trotsky in
Istanbul.

noon debate meandered on in desultory fashion for a couple of hours. The effects of MacDonald and lunch had started to wear off, and the feeling of dissatisfaction with an unemployment total of just over two million had returned. Wise and Bevin had been politely critical, but somehow had failed to grip. The Labour Government had admittedly not done terribly well, but was there any real alternative to the diet of 'sober, steady, quiet work' which MacDonald had offered in the morning? In a thrilling quarter of an hour Mosley offered the meatier fare that many were looking for.

His speech, on the resolution from Doncaster calling for an N.E.C. report on his Memorandum, started off quietly enough with a sober account of the differences which had arisen between him and the Government. A hundred and twenty-two million pounds had been allocated to public works – an impressive-sounding total until it was realised that this was to be spread over four or five years, offering a maximum employment in any one year to little over 100,000 men and women. 'In other words, the "ambulance work" only put one man in employment for every ten put out of employment since they came into office.' The long-term programme of permanent reconstruction had been left largely to the banks. The conference must realise that rationalisation would inflict great hardship on the working class unless it was subject to government control and organisation. The Government relied on an expansion of the export trade, but this was illusory. The home market, the 'purchasing power of their own people,' alone offered any real hope for permanently absorbing the unemployed. But this market must be insulated from the shocks of world conditions by a combination of tariffs and import boards which might be extended to embrace the whole Commonwealth. 'The principle was to have an organism planning, allocating, regulating their trade rather than leaving these great things to the blind forces of world capitalistic competition. There they had a policy of organisation with which to meet and defeat the Tory policy of taxation, a scientific and modern policy to meet the cruel Protectionist devices of the last century.' Unless the Labour Party did it, capitalism would undertake it with all the chaos and suffering that would follow.

Mosley now came to the heart of his challenge. In place of the MacDonald policy of imperceptible evolution, he offered a bold and daring programme of action, a blueprint for a new political psychology.

If they could develop a great policy, the lesser things would follow. Relief works were difficult. If they said that relief works were the only things that could solve the problem, they would get very little public support; but if they could say:

'Here is a great policy of permanent national reconstruction, the building of a great national civilisation' ... then they could say relief works were necessary and vital to bridge the gulf between the present time and the time when that policy would be realised.... If they could develop any such policy... the difficulties of their minority situation would not be so over-whelming. He knew something of the House of Commons, having been there 12 years, and he did not believe that if the Movement had a ... great policy, any party in the House of Commons would dare throw it out. If they did, what better issue could they have to fight them on and beat them in the country? They would have mobilised behind them all the forces demanding action, which were liable to be against them if they let the situation drift.

He might be told that it was not the throwing-out of their proposals that they feared; it was the day-to-day obstruction in Parliament that wore them down. He agreed ... but it was no good complaining about Parliament unless they had proposals to deal with Parliament. He agreed that the present machine was hopeless. They would never carry a great policy with that machine.... They must go to Parliament with an unemployment policy. If they were obstructed in Parliament, then let them bring proposals before Parliament to reform it, so that they could get business through ... if their proposals were thrown out, they must go to the country and fight their oppo-nents on the question of unemployment and a revision of Parliament. At best, they would have their majority, at the worst they would go down fighting for the things they believed in. They would not die like an old woman in bed; they would die like a man on the field – a better fate, and, in politics, one with a more certain hope of resurrection.*

He did not believe the great national crisis they were living in was a menace to their Movement. It was their supreme opportunity. When, within the memory of any man or woman in that Hall, was the nation demanding action as it was demanding it then? They could get measures carried through Parliament ... which they would never get in a lesser age. With courage, vigour, decision, and a policy, they could use that situation to remodel the whole structure of the country. Let them not shrink before a great opportunity; let them not snrink in fear before it; let them seize it and use it and give the country a lead.

*Compare this simile, a favourite of Mosley's, with Brailsford's at the 1926 I.L.P. Conference: 'Let them go into it ... with something of the devotion of a monastic order' (I.L.P. Conference Report, p. 79) – the difference between the aristocratic and the priestly ideal.

The effect was electrifying. A Conservative journalist wrote:

> It was a hot, steamy afternoon, for the hall was crowded.
> There was stillness save for Mosley's voice gathering in power.
> Boldly, challengingly, he gave his own plan to restore stabi-
> lity. . . . I'm sure the throng, representative of all the Socialist
> organisations in the country, was not able to keep pace with
> his propositions. It was hypnotised by the man, by his auda-
> city, as bang! bang! bang! he thundered directions. The thing
> that got hold of the conference was that here was a man with
> a straight-cut policy. It leapt at him.[26]

Fenner Brockway wrote that Mosley got the greatest ovation he
had ever heard at a party conference.[27] From his seat on the floor
of the hall to which he had returned he had to get up to acknowledge the cheering that refused to die away. ' There were many to
say that here was the Moses to lead them out of the wilderness,'
wrote the *Morning Post* the following day. One delegate, with
more contemporary parallels in mind, was heard to shout, ' The
English Hitler '.

Had the delegates voted for themselves alone, it is almost certain
that the Doncaster resolution would have been carried by a large
majority. As it was, the union bloc votes ensured its defeat –
but only by a hair's breadth (1,046,000 votes were recorded for;
1,251,000 against), and only after Lansbury, put up by the platform to reply, had virtually conceded Mosley's case. An interesting story went round afterwards that the vote was lost because
A. J. Cook's taxi broke down and his number two switched the
miners' votes against Mosley. This is not true: the Miners' Executive decided to oppose the Doncaster resolution by a narrow majority, against Cook's advice. However, they supported Mosley on
the vote for the National Executive Committee, to which he was
elected for the third and last time.[28]*

At Birkenhead two days later Mosley appeared on the platform
with Ernest Bevin. His thrilling peroration completely eclipsed
Bevin's performance:

> There is too much today of the spirit of lethargy and surrender,
> as though unemployment were some visitation from above,
> beyond the wit of men to control. . . . We can see in sight a Socia-
> list society with its ideal of no unemployment, but the man
> who is hungry and unemployed today is saying: ' We put you
> into office . . . to do something now and at once!' (applause.)
> That is the question of the hour. (Loud applause.) We are a

*Mosley came fourth in the constituency section with 1,362,000 votes, behind
Lansbury, Morrison and Dalton, and ahead of George Dallas. Thomas lost his
seat on the Executive, coming bottom of the trade union section.

party with our eyes on the stars, but let us also remember that our feet are planted on the earth, on muddy soil, where men are suffering and . . . looking at us with eyes of questioning and anguish, saying ' Lift us from the mud; give us practical remedies here and now!' (Cheers.) That is the question of our time. This is not an age of dreams and fancies; it is an age of iron, in which an iron spirit and an iron will are needed by men to cut their path through to victory. Let us have no sentiment. We know of the agony of the country, of the tears of women and the misery of men, but we must steel ourselves, and organise, plan and fight to cure these things. Don't let's talk about them. Let us do something. (Loud cheers.) You will meet storms, and troubles, and dangers, but sooner or later, in this country, if the job is to be done, that battle must be fought, and the vital forces which have built our movement must face that battle and go through with it and win. (Cheering and applause continued for several minutes.)

Although Llandudno had been a personal triumph, it was, like his resignation speech, one of those triumphs that did not seem to lead anywhere. Some politicians had the knack of succeeding without any triumphs at all: here was Mosley with two to his credit as far away from power as ever. In these circumstances, he started once more to work on the dissatisfactions of the young Tories.

The immediate result was an agreement between Mosley's Tory and Labour supporters to make ' converging' speeches in the debate on the Address scheduled for the end of October.[29] The convergence seemed more like a stampede to the Right. Dropped from Mosley's speech was any mention of public works, pensions or school-leaving age. The emphasis was on ' insulation' and empire.

The economics, too, had hardened into dogma. Gone was the spirit of earnest enquiry which had characterised the Memorandum. England's old position had entirely gone, Mosley declared categorically. Local industrialisation, new competitors, sweated labour, great producers' organisations dumping goods at a fraction of their cost had all drastically reduced her export prospects. The main outlet for the ' enormously increased productive capacity' must be found in the home market. Yet 'we are asked still further to reduce that market by a reduction in wages, to be undertaken in the illusory hope of maintaining our competition in the export trade '. An empire policy was needed to stabilise the remaining export trade. Forty-five per cent of existing trade was with empire countries. Bulk purchase would enable Britain to discriminate in favour of those countries willing to extend reciprocal advantages; and the

likeliest to enter into such arrangements were the primary producing empire countries. Eventually Mosley hoped it would be
possible to 'allocate and plan future production as between the
component parts of the commonwealth and [thus] secure a far
higher standard of life than prevails in . . . the rest of the world'.
He denied that this meant breaking off trade relations with other
countries. Finally he advocated a pooling of the gold reserves of
the Commonwealth – the first political suggestion for what later
emerged as the Sterling Area. People might say that these arrangements would give too much power to a nation or to a government.
' You might as well say that it would be dangerous to place a man
in charge of a steam-roller because he might use it to knock down
a house instead of for the making of roads. It would not be a conclusive argument against the use of a steam-roller. Simply because
the power I have suggested might be used by some foolish or misguided people for a totally different purpose is no argument against
the use of . . . power.' Mosley always insisted that modern conditions required the exercise of power. It was too late for well-
meaning liberals to deplore power. The problem was to make
men fit for it.[30]

Oliver Stanley (Conservative), H. T. Muggeridge and W. J.
Brown (Labour), John Buchan (Conservative) and Morgan Philips
Price (Labour) all aligned themselves with Mosley's 'brilliant'
analysis.[31] It was left to Strachey to attempt to make that analysis
palatable to socialists. Mosley's policy was not socialism, Strachey
frankly admitted. It ran counter ' to the internationalist principles to which many of us very firmly adhere '. But it was the only
alternative to an immediate attack on the workers' standard of life.
Besides, in a collapsing world economic nationalism was ' no more
than a measure of self-preservation ', which might make other countries change their own policies for the better. Finally, it had one
element – national planning – which could be adapted to socialist
purposes.[32] Terence O'Connor (Conservative) thought that half
a dozen men ' of commonsense and prudence . . . selected from all
parties, could draw up between them . . . an emergency programme
on which there would not be much difference of opinion . . .'.
Boothby (Conservative) thought such a policy would consist of (1)
an empire monetary union (2) protection of the home market with
suitable safeguards for consumers and (3) the development of a
sheltered export market within the British empire.[33]

Yet agreement was not so easy as these young parliamentarians
supposed. A central ingredient of O'Connor's package was ' Gladstonian finance '. Aneurin Bevan, on the other hand, wanted Mos-
ey's public works. Far from wanting an alliance with the Tories
ne rather hankered after ' convergence ' with the Lloyd George
Liberals.[34] 'All the workers will get from that lot', remarked Bevan

of the young Tories, ' are epigrams and reductions of wages.'[35]

Other speeches converged in a different direction. Sir Donald Maclean (Liberal) thought Mosley and Stanley were much ' too pessimistic'.[36] Frank Owen (Liberal) accused Mosley of preaching ' the crudity of economic nationalism in a world in which the predominant features are the interlocking of finance and banking and industry'. He ' takes us right away from the responsibilities of civilisation and hides behind the barbarity of economic isolation '. Far from bringing peace, a division of the world into great economic blocs would be a prelude to a ' new and a more frightful world conflict'. Mosleyism was ' Birminghamism . . . rampant ', the old ' Jingo Imperialism ' of Joseph Chamberlain unleashed in more virulent form.[37]

What distressed critics like Owen was Mosley's emphasis on ' insulation ' and ' Imperialism '. This was, of course, the reaction to the breakdown of the world economic liberal order. Where Mosley struck a distinctive, though not a unique, note, was in his view that that breakdown was permanent. Many analysts stressed the breakdown of the world monetary system. Such a breakdown could be repaired provided people still accepted the basic assumption that economic liberalism was harmonious. This was the assumption Mosley rejected. He was aware of the monetary dimension, but it was entirely secondary for him. He took his stand on the 'facts'. The first fact was that Humpty Dumpty had broken into pieces, and there was no one to put him together again. There was therefore no practical alternative to economic nationalism. Many would have agreed with Mosley on this: even Keynes did. Mosley's deeper heresy was his conviction that this breakdown was inherent in the development of 'finance capitalism'. With capital mobile, the latest technology could be harnessed to cheap labour in the poorer countries. This meant that, even with an improved monetary system and ' rationalisation ', basic British export industries would be priced out of the market. As the home market shrank through an increase in the jobless, capital would try to recoup its losses, not by switching to new enterprises at home, but by setting up new industries abroad where labour could be more effectively exploited. But this would merely destroy even more British jobs. The only way to break out of this vicious circle was to construct a permanent new system. On this line of reasoning Mosley was three-quarters of the way into the Communist Party. They, too, believed that a new system was required – a world communist state, with the power to plan production for need rather than for profit. Mosley rejected this for many reasons. Here it is only necessary to mention one: he regarded it as entirely illusory. The lion would not lie down with the lamb. Rather than surrender their own independence, powerful national states would carve out their own autarchic systems. They were already doing so. Britain must do the same. That is what empires were for. The argument, as Frank Owen rightly noted, was Joseph Chamberlain's. It was the alternative both to international finance and international socialism.

We can see how far removed these considerations were from the economic 'logic' which pointed towards a single, increasingly inter-locked world economic community. For the Labour Party, espe-cially for its thinkers and idealists, these dreams of empire made no appeal. Their dreams lay elsewhere – in a world purged of exploi-tation, including imperial exploitation. Whatever reservations they may have had about Lenin's description of imperialism as the stage of monopoly capitalism, Labour ideologies firmly believed that im-perialism was the cause of war: Hobson's critique *Imperialism* (1902) was the bible with which many of them had grown up; and the First World War seemed to confirm its teaching. As early as July Fenner Brockway was taking note of Mosley's ' dangerous leaning towards a Labour Economic Imperialism '.[38] After the November debates the battle with the I.L.P. on this question was well and truly joined. For the *New Leader* of 7 November this was the ' fundamental difference ' between the I.L.P. and the Mosley Group. Apart from its impracticability, imperialism ' involves an economic rivalry in the world which will inevitably find express-ion in rival foreign policies and armaments, and perhaps in war itself. Any policy in line with the internationalism of the Socialist faith must be based, not on the rival grouping of nations, but on the principle of world co-operation.' The ultimate aim was ' the distribution of the world's goods according to the world's needs, through some international authority. *In seeking to establish a mini-mum standard of civilisation here we must not outrage this principle.*' (My italics.) The I.L.P. would therefore utilise import and export boards to enter into contracts with all countries, irrespective of their connection with Britain. The I.L.P. also objected to Mosley's increasing emphasis on a ' national ' solution ' above party '. The Labour Party ' is not concerned merely in securing a living standard for our workers. It aims at getting the full product of their labour for those who create wealth and this means Socialism. . . . ' Trade unionists like Bevin, even John Strachey under Mosley's influence, might just be prepared to swallow imperialism as a business arrangement in a world that seemed to offer few immediate alter-natives. But as a passion, as a vision of development, it had no place in the Labour Party.

On the other hand, Mosley's approach was by no means unwel-come to that section of the Tory Party in which imperialist senti-ment and mercantilist economics went hand in hand. Neville Chamberlain gave it particularly warm praise in the November debate;[39] while Stanley Baldwin was interested in the fact that Mosley after ' much seclusion and thought' was ' now producing ideas which I remember giving voice to in 1903 '. ' If I happen to fail in my task and my life is prolonged', Baldwin continued, ' I hope that when I am sitting by my fireside in my old age I shall read of the hon. Member for Smethwick carrying out all the things which I believe are necessary to-day for the welfare of this country.'[40]

The support of the younger Tories was no doubt very welcome to Mosley; that of the two leaders of the Tory Party much less so. For it suggested that the Tory Party was in favour of the very policy which he was advocating, which would greatly weaken his appeal for the young Tory rebels. A spate of appalling Labour by-election results suggested that Baldwin would soon be in a position to implement it – and award offices for good behaviour. To set against this was the continuing weakness of Baldwin's own personal position, the intrigues of Beaverbrook, the general atmosphere of crisis and conspiracy, and above all the continuing frustrations of young men, matured early by the war, who found themselves starved of the scope and responsibility they craved. These things were sufficient to keep Mosley and the young Tories talking – not enough to get them to come tiger-shooting with him. ' The disquieting thing about the younger men', noted the *Sunday Express* disconsolately, ' is that, with the exception of Sir Oswald, they seem to have none of the boldness of youth.'[41]

The lack of progress with the young Tories threw Mosley back on the Labour Party. Making a belated effort to get on better terms with the trade union leaders, he accepted the presidency of the newly formed National Trade Union Club. ' The Hotspur of the Labour Movement' was how Ben Tillott described him at the inaugural gathering of this elderly company. The party leaders had little time for Hotspurs. All his attempts to get a radical unemployment policy pushed on the N.E.C. foundered on Henderson's endless reassurances.[42]

By the autumn of 1930 Mosley had reached his highest point in conventional English politics. He had become a major political personality in his own right, with a wide, and almost unique, range of support and goodwill across the political spectrum.* No political calculations could leave him out of account. But, like Enoch Powell after his Birmingham speech of 1968, Mosley was no nearer power. Since the Labour Government did not propose to change

---

*This new status was recognised in a characteristically English way by his election to the Other Club on 27 November 1930, on the proposal of Winston Churchill. The Other Club had been founded by F. E. Smith and Churchill in 1911 as a dining club for men prominent in British political life. Mosley continued to attend till 1935; then he tactfully withdrew and has never been back. (See Colin R. Coote, *The Other Club* (1972) pp. 67-8.)

its policy, there was no way back into office. He had already sampled the Tory and Liberal parties and had no desire to repeat the experience. He was one of the men 'in reserve', waiting for the next turn of events. His obvious line was to stay in the Labour Party and wait for the inevitable débâcle which would deliver the party into his hands. The forthcoming crisis would give him his big opportunity. Had he been a man of ordinary aims and ambitions this is surely the course he would have adopted. But Mosley saw in the forthcoming crisis bigger opportunities than that. He had already written off the Labour Party as part of that pre-1914 world of easy times and parliamentary make-believe. The forthcoming crisis would at last give the frustrated and impatient war-generation its chance to make its own independent impact on politics. The 'modern mind' would take over. The old 1919 vision of a young man's party beckoned strongly. Young men in all the parties looked to him as their leader. The country, everyone said, was crying for a lead. Something surely could be attempted. The risks were great; but the rewards must be even greater.

It was in this mood that Mosley took the first tentative steps that were to lead him to fascism. The first decision was to form a Mosley group in the parliamentary Labour party. The method chosen was to invite signatures to a definite statement of policy. Mosley's first draft of a 'Manifesto' was rearranged, amplified, purged of some characteristic Mosley rhetoric and generally slanted leftwards by Strachey, Bevan and Brown. In its final form it was a collective enterprise in the truest sense of the word – a tribute to Mosley's capacity to subordinate his own ideas to ideas of others. Indeed, judged by Mosley's own evolution since his resignation the most striking thing about the Manifesto was its dropping of the imperialist theme. This was the price he had to pay for the attempt to acquire a definite following.

The Mosley Manifesto, published on 13 December, was put forward as 'an immediate plan to meet an emergency situation'. Significantly it invited 'any in our party *or the nation* who agree with [it] to state their agreement'. (My italics.)

It was impossible to meet the crisis with a 'nineteenth century parliamentary machine'. Mosley's repeated attacks on the Westminster 'talkshop' now crystallised into a definite proposal for a Shavian cabinet of five Ministers without portfolio, armed with 'power to carry through the emergency policy' subject only to the 'general control' of Parliament.

A national plan was proposed to 'adjust the balance of British production to the new conditions prevailing in the world', to develop new industries, and to secure the modernisation and re-equipment of others. The basic premise of any plan should be that the home market was the future basis of prosperity. For agriculture

MOSLINI.

The Duce (to Sir Oswald Mosley). "FIVE DICTATORS! WHY WORRY ABOUT THE OTHER FOUR?"

the Import Control Board, 'long advocated by our Party', would guarantee the farmer a 'stable and economic price' and the consumer 'that prices shall not rise'. For industry a tariff might be granted by a Commodity Board representing producers and consumers 'on conditions as to the efficiency of the industry protected, the price of the article supplied by that industry, and the wages of the workers employed in that industry'.* Such a

*The model here was Australia's New Protection policy when tariffs were made conditional on minimum working-standards. (See *Britain Pre-eminent*, ed. C. J. Bartlett (1969) p. 97.) Australia seems to have been very much of a model for Mosley's group.

producers' policy would benefit both employer and worker against the financier who for ten years had imposed a policy 'which benefits the bondholder and handicaps production'.

This Import Board machinery would help trade 'with all nations' by giving Britain powerful leverage to 'secure acceptance of our exports in return'. Although the best opportunity for making such agreements was clearly with the Commonwealth, it was emphasised that this would 'not conflict with the maintenance and development of trade with all other nations'.

While this grandiose reorganisation was going on 'a short-term policy of constructive works' financed by loan was needed. Emphasis was shifted from roads to a massive housing programme to rebuild the slums. 'The State should constitute a public utility organisation to turn out houses and building materials as we turned out munitions during the war': a reversion to the theme of Mosley's very first election address in 1918.

'We surrender nothing of our Socialist faith,' the signatories loudly proclaimed (as if trying to convince themselves), but pointed out realistically that 'the immediate question is not a question of the ownership but of the survival of British industry'. What was needed was an emergency programme to meet a critical situation: 'afterwards debate on fundamental principle can be renewed'.

Who were the signatories? Fenner Brockway describes how the manifesto was hawked round Labour politicians in order of anticipated willingness to sign. He himself was approached sixth in the I.L.P. Group (by W. J. Brown) and was the first refusal from that quarter. G. D. H. Cole also refused to sign, viewing it as a 'conspiracy against the Government'.[43] Bevin's refusal to have anything to do with it probably stemmed from the same reason. 'Ideas for dealing with the present situation must be separate from ambition,' he declared.[44] The document was shown to about half the parliamentary party. Apparently there were numerous offers to sign with reservations, but only wholehearted supporters were encouraged to do so.[45] Altogether seventeen Labour M.P.s signed, plus the Miners' Secretary, Arthur Cook.*

*The signatories were: Oliver Baldwin (Dudley, Worcs.), Joseph Batey (Spennymoor, Dur.), Aneurin Bevan (Ebbw Vale, Mon.), W. J. Brown (Wolverhampton West, Staffs.), William Cove (Aberavon, Glam.), Robert Forgan (West Renfrew, Renf.), James Horrabin (Peterborough, Northants), James Lovat Fraser (Lichfield, Staffs.), John McShane (Walsall, Staffs.), John McGovern (Shettleston, Glasgow), Sydney Markham (Chatham div., Rochester, Kent), Cynthia Mosley (Stoke-on-Trent, Staffs.), Oswald Mosley (Smethwick, Birmingham), Henry Muggeridge (Romford, Essex), Morgan Philips Price (Whitehaven, Cumb.), C. J. Simmons (Erdington, Birmingham) and John Strachey (Aston, Birmingham).

In a party of the elderly the Mosleyites stood out by their youth –
they were young both in age and parliamentary experience.   Nine
of them were in their twenties or thirties, five more (including Cook)
in their forties.   All of them except Mosley, Batey and Cove had
entered Parliament for the first time in 1929: hence their impatience with the parliamentary game.   Their educational qualifications were much above average for the parliamentary party,
seventy per cent of whom had only had elementary education.
Eight of the seventeen came from the Black Country complex,
thus justifying Frank Owen's description of Mosleyism as 'Birminghamism rampant'.   Six sat for mining constituencies: three –
Batey, Bevan and Cove – were former miners; McShane's father
was a miner on the Clyde.*   The mining connection was of course
emphasised by Cook's signature.   Mosleyism in the Labour Party
therefore drew its strength from two sources – the Black Country
and the coalmines.   'My constituency', Morgan Philips Price
recalls, 'was the very hard-hit mining area of Whitehaven, in
Cumberland, and I remember the absolute despair there was
over the Labour Government's policy. . . . A lot of us, including
myself, supported Sir Oswald for a time. . . . I still think that it
was the best thing under the circumstances that could have been
done. '[46]

The Manifesto got good press coverage and much discussion,
mostly contemptuous or critical, though the Tory press was disposed to admire its 'spirit'.   Politically, it was generally agreed
that it would get nowhere.   The reason was its 'wonderful eclec-
ticism. . . . There is something in it to satisfy all tastes and attract
every floating straw of current opinion.'   Designed to grip everyone,
it would grip no one.[47]   The Liberals were for public works, against
protection.   The I.L.P. approved of import boards but objected to
the 'anti-socialist' setting in which they were placed.[48]   The Tories
welcomed protection but abhorred public works and repudiation
of the war debt.   Most saw the five overlords as a proposal for
dictatorship.

There was expected and unexpected support.   Walter Elliot,
Bob Boothby, Moore-Brabazon and Harold Macmillan fired off let-
ters of generous praise to the national papers.[49]   Harold Nicolson
applauded in a B.B.C. broadcast on 12 December.   Garvin in the
Observer lauded Mosley for his 'brilliant fearlessness'.[50]   The
Manifesto had a surprisingly good press from religious journals.[51]

Apart from the signatories, the Labour Party would have nothing
to do with it, once they had interpreted it as an attack on the leader-

---

*' I grew up near the " Red Clyde " with Wheatley, Maxton, Kirkwood, etc. . . .
in a one roomed house, with 2 built-in beds, one for father and mother, and the
other for six sons, 3 at the top of the bed and 3 at the foot ' (McShane to author,
30 October 1962).

ship. Praise from Tory imperialists did not help make it more palatable. Henry Muggeridge's defence of it as ' applied Socialism ' led the *Manchester Guardian* to wonder why in that case it had had such a warm reception ' from such a progressive and open-minded thinker as Mr. Amery '.[52] Had the *Guardian* already forgotten the Coefficients (the dining club of imperialists and Fabians in the 1900s)? To the *Daily Herald* (8 December) it reinforced the ' insidious propaganda ' for a Coalition with the Tories which would ' mean the defeat of everything for which Labour stands '. Morrison attacked ' swell-heads not of working-class origin ' with ' Tory blue blood running in their veins '. In their abhorrence of any intellectual compromise with the other side – be it Tory or Liberal – the I.L.P. were at one with MacDonald and Co. W. J. Brown, who had worked tirelessly to get the Manifesto modified to suit I.L.P. taste, was bitterly disappointed at the Maxtonites' negative reaction. ' I should like to see the world one economic and political unit,' he wrote. ' But is it seriously argued that because of this we should do nothing within the unit in which we work?'[53] Attacking his critics in Manchester, Mosley accused them of producing the ' parrot cry ' of dictatorship as an excuse to prevent anything being done. ' If, in England, it is impossible to get things done,' he said, ' then England is done.'[54]

The chief criticism of the Manifesto was that the ideas in it did not ' hang together '. Hardly anyone noticed that the Manifesto represented a new *approach* to the economy; that the individual items – whatever their source – implied in combination a new economic philosophy. One of the very few to get the point was Keynes. The central debate in politics, he wrote, was between planning and *laissez-faire*. The details of the Manifesto were less important than its grasp of the fact that ' there is no design but our own, and that the invisible hand is merely our own bleeding feet moving through pain and loss to an uncertain future '. Socialism had nothing to offer ' our generation ' unless ' it makes much of the manifesto its own '.[55] Gerald Barry of the *Weekend Review* (soon to join with Sir Basil Blackett and Israel Sieff in founding Political and Economic Planning) gave the Manifesto his warm support for similar reasons.

Immediately, the ' New Labour Group ' (as it called itself), tried to organise a campaign against the cut in wages and public spending foreshadowed in the rising clamour for ' economy '. Its second (and last) manifesto saw the pressure for economy as ' the inevitable consequence of the failure to deal with mass unemployment. . . . The national standard of life cannot be maintained if two and a half million pairs of hands are prevented from producing.'[56] In the Economy Debate of 11 February 1931, Mosley launched a striking attack on Snowden's declared intention of reducing public expenditure. ' These suggestions to put the nation to bed on a starvation diet are the suggestions of an old woman in a fright,' he declared. ' The exact reverse is needed – a policy of manhood which takes the nation out into the fields, and builds up its muscles and constitution in effort.' The speech was noticeable for Mosley's first public attack on MacDonald whose ' complacency is, perhaps, one of the most serious dangers with which the country is faced '.

But Mosley chafed at the role of Labour critic. He was convinced that the time had come to realise his dream of a new party of the war generation. Soon after his resignation from the Government he had been introduced to Sir William Morris (later Lord Nuffield) by Colonel Wyndham Portal, a soldier turned businessman. The motor-car manufacturer knew little about politics, but was convinced the country was in a mess and that something needed to be done about it. In September he called for a ' strong Government . . . a real leader '. Mosley, he decided, was the leader the country needed. In December he praised the Manifesto as a ' ray of hope ', seeing it as the nucleus of an ' industrial party ' to bring the country out of its ' slough of despond '.[57] Now, in late January 1931, he handed Mosley a cheque for £50,000 to form a new party. ' Don't think, my boy, that money like this grows on gooseberry bushes,' he told him. ' The first ten thousand took me a lot of getting.'[58] Further support was promised – from others as well as Morris – if Mosley looked like getting anywhere. The chief obstacle to political independence had now been removed. On 4 February Cimmie told Harold Nicolson that ' Tom is about to found a new party '.[59]

Mosley immediately informed his closest Labour associates of his success. The moment for the great adventure they had been discussing for months had now arrived. So eager was Mosley to go ahead that he decided not to wait for the young Tories. They would no doubt join in time – as would others – if he looked like succeeding. In the febrile atmosphere of Westminster crises, maverick dinner-parties and audience applause up and down the country he had come to believe that the country was ' demanding action ' and he had only to stand forth as the young standard-bearer of hope for the people in their thousands to start flocking to him. His enthusiasm made a deep impression on his friends. As he told it, the political wilderness to which they were being asked to consign themselves appeared as a fertile pasture. And if the seed took some time in ripening there was always Morris's money to sustain body and soul in the interval.

By Friday, 20 February, six members of the New Labour Group had decided to resign from the Labour Party – Mosley and his wife, Strachey, Brown, Oliver Baldwin and Forgan. But all

Mosley's earnestness had failed to produce similar agreement on what to do after that. Mosley wanted to start a 'New Party'. Brown supported him. He had become more bitterly anti-Labour than any of the others except Mosley himself, accusing the Government of lacking 'either the guts to govern or the grace to get out'. Strachey and Baldwin would have preferred to become Independent Socialists for the time being, though Strachey was eager for the break. To many Labour M.P.s who refused even to consider leaving the Party prudential considerations were probably uppermost. Mosley and his wife, Strachey, Baldwin, even Forgan all had means or careers outside politics. They could afford to gamble. Most of the other signatories of the Manifesto could not. Bevan was unhappy about Mosley's financial backing: 'Where is the money coming from. . . . You will end up as a fascist party,' he is supposed to have said.

Having agreed to resign, it would have been better had they all resigned there and then. Instead they concocted an ingenious plan to resign by instalments – one a day for a whole week. Brown was to resign first on Monday the twenty-third. He did not. All efforts to contact him failed. He was apparently indisposed. Eventually he resigned on 5 March, but claimed to be too unwell to appear on the New Party platform. The reason – suggested both in Mosley's autobiography and in press reports at the time – is that he was threatened by his union executive with the loss of his job if he linked up with the new organisation.* With the loss of Brown, the plan for daily resignations was abandoned. Strachey and Forgan left the Labour Party on Tuesday, 24 February. Oliver Baldwin resigned on 26 February. He styled himself an 'Independent' but agreed to appear on the new party's platforms. Cimmie left six days later. On 9 March Mosley was joined by

*In his memoirs (*My Life*, p. 283) Mosley describes being taken to Brown's house in an ambulance (he was already ill) to plead with him to honour his undertaking. 'After being carried into his living room on a stretcher, I asked his reasons for not attending the opening meeting. Then something occurred which I had only seen rarely before; his face seemed to be pulled down on one side like a man suffering a stroke and he burst into tears. He said he would lose his trade union job and his family would be ruined. His fears appeared to me exaggerated because he knew I had already obtained a guarantee from Lord Nuffield to cover his salary for several years. He had never previously voiced these apprehensions, and had always posed as a man of decision, of iron will and resolution. I had myself carried back to the ambulance.' According to the *Daily Herald* of 10 March 1931, Brown 'reserved his decision as to whether he will join the Mosley New Party till after the annual Conference of the Civil Service Clerical Association of which he is secretary.' The *Daily Mail* of 12 March 1931 stated that his Union Executive had 'taken exception to his quitting the Labour Party and has reminded him that it was as a member of that party that they supported his candidature'.

W. E. D. (Bill) Allen, a mild-mannered, thirty-year-old Conservative M.P. for West Belfast – the only young Tory to come in.
Allen was the wealthy director of David Allen & Sons, a Belfast
poster firm. Mosley himself never resigned from the Labour Party.
He was expelled for ' gross disloyalty ' on 10 March and the New
Party was declared a proscribed organisation. The child promised
to be sickly.

While all this was going on, Mosley was involved in the painful
task of disengaging himself from Smethwick. As late as mid-Feb-
ruary he had given his constituency executive ' emphatic denials '
that he was planning to break with Labour.[60] A meeting had been
arranged with the Smethwick Trades and Labour Council for
Wednesday, 25 February. However, on Tuesday, following the
press leaks, Mosley asked Lawrence, the Council's president, and
Stonier, its secretary, to come to see him in London. Lawrence
asked Mosley whether the press reports of his activities were true.
Mosley said they were, but that the publicity had not been of his
own seeking. He told them that he intended to form a new political
party and expected that other groups in the Labour Party, including the I.L.P., would later join him. Lawrence begged him to
reconsider. As long as he stayed in the Labour Party, Smethwick
would loyally support him in his quarrel with the Government.
Mosley replied that the Labour Party was going to ' rack and ruin '
and that he had to try to organise an alternative to chaos. Lawrence
responded that as long as the ship was afloat it was everyone's duty
to keep it so. Stonier, on their way out, told Allan Young that he
was ' a bloody fool ' to have anything to do with Mosley's plan.
They both agreed, however, to take no action till Mosley had had a
chance to come down and explain himself. Mosley still believes
that had health permitted him to ' come to Birmingham as I intended I could have carried much of the Labour Party over with
me '. Instead he retired to bed with a temperature and a seven-
year association was ended without a word of explanation.[61]

Michael Foot has delivered a harsh verdict. Mosley ' had no
love for [the Labour Party], no roots in it, no compunction at the
breach with old comrades. He could leave as easily as he had
joined, without a twinge of conscience or regret.'[62] Against this we
may set Mosley's defence: ' I had become convinced that the
Labour Party was incapable of decisive action . . . that in a real
crisis Labour would always betray both its principles and the people
who had trusted it. . . . It was not that I had a poor opinion of the
rank and file of the party; on the contrary, I thought them the salt
of the earth. Yet any body of men and women with such leadership
and with the long habit of discordant chatter instead of collective
action will break into futility in such a test. . . . I was deeply convinced that sooner or later a situation would arise in Britain which

would require not only new policies but a different order of character and resolution.'[63]   With such expectations his course was clear. As he put it in 1955, ' Either get in and serve loyally, or get out and fight the lot; that surely is the way of the man.'

Michael Foot was right in his judgment that Mosley's primary loyalty was not to the Labour Party.   It was to his conceptions, which in turn were fired by the sacred memory of the trenches. The Labour Party had seemed to Mosley the best instrument for realising the dreams of the war generation.   It had never been ideal, because it was sectional.   It was the union of the men against the officers, rather than the *union sacrée* which war had evoked.   Its psychology was that of the underdog, not the achiever.   Mosley had always realised this; but had hoped that its commitment to social change would overcome these inhibitions.   Once he had failed to carry the parliamentary party and the rank and file against the timid leadership, there was nothing left to hold Mosley in the Labour camp.   He should not have given up so easily.   We all know the Labour party of today.   Had Mosley carried on the fight inside it, it might have developed into something very different. This is not to say that he would have won: no single man can ' win ' in any ultimate sense in a great coalition.   But he might have achieved a great deal.   And, above all, he would have provided a style and philosophy which would in turn have become part of the Labour tradition, an inspiration to those to come in their never-ending fight against all that is timid, weak, defeatist, ' respectable ' in the Labour psychology.   Personal impatience stood in the way. But, perhaps even more important, the times were impatient. The two came together in 1931 and decided his course.

Chapter 12

Exit John Strachey

MOSLEY'S New Party was surely the most bizarre episode in modern British politics. It started on 28 February 1931 when Mosley staggered to his office with pneumonia, appealed briefly for voluntary workers and funds, promised to run 400 candidates at the next election and then went to bed for a month with pleurisy. Instead of being born in an appropriate Futurist structure of glass, steel and ferro-concrete, the ' modern movement ' first saw the light of day in a beautiful old Georgian house overlooking St James's Square. Here I.L.P. workers, Oxford hearties and delicate intellectuals mixed uneasily in Cimmie's tastefully furnished rooms.

Flaming scarlet posters advertised numerous appearances by the Leader and W. J. Brown. But Mosley was genuinely, W. J. Brown diplomatically, ill. The audiences of the bemused, curious and interested who had assembled to hear the new faith were instead instructed and entertained by Cimmie, Strachey and Oliver Baldwin, whose ' act ' became the subject of considerable, if sometimes ribald, comment. 'Lady Cynthia contributes intensity, Mr Strachey states the case, Mr Oliver Baldwin adds the comic relief . . . while the choir from Stoke provides the harmony that may be lacking in the rudely hostile audience.'[1] In addition the audiences were handed personal letters from Mosley thanking them for their attendance and urging the converted to write to New Party headquarters. ' Rarely, if ever before, in English history can the formation of a political party have been essayed by means of a correspondence course,' commented the *Manchester Guardian*.

Cynthia's part in these anxious, bitter days, when Mosley lay dangerously ill and she herself was in indifferent health, approached the heroic. As Bill Allen wrote, ' There seemed something symbolic and supremely noble in her as she faced the angry audiences of disappointed Labour supporters in the North, and filled the place, not only of her husband, but of all the clever men who had been clever enough to keep out of the New Party.'[2] From the very first London meeting at the Memorial Hall, Farringdon Street, disruption pursued the New Party team through the country. The disrupters were always a small minority and in only two cases – at Dundee (19 March) and at Hull (23 March) – did they succeed in breaking up meetings. If the country was not ' demanding ' action, as Mosley thought, it seemed very curious to meet those who were: 3000 at Aston, Stoke and Liverpool, 2000 at Leeds, 2 consecutive meetings of 2000 each at Glasgow. From the first, then, there emerged a pattern which hardly varied throughout the 1930s: vast audiences of the curious come to hear the prophet, groups of angry Labour militants and communists determined to prevent him from being heard.

The ' case ' stated by the New Party's earliest orators was the *National Policy* written by Allan Young, John Strachey, W. J. Brown and Aneurin Bevan and published at the end of February. The decline in Britain's traditional export industries would have to be offset by an expansion of the home market ' insulated ' and ' scientifically ' protected against international chaos. Domestic planning by means of a National Investment Board would be co-ordinated with the planning of imports to be undertaken by import boards for agricultural products and ' commodity boards ' for industrial products on which workers and consumers would be represented. Although inter-imperial trade should expand, so should trade with Russia[3] – the main compromise in the document between the Right and Left in the New Party. The programme was to be supervised by a cabinet of five, freed from detailed parliamentary supervision.

Mosley's hope of making a dramatic impact on the political scene was disappointed. Unfortunately for him, starting new parties appeared to be the height of fashion just then. Beaverbrook was running a candidate against Baldwin at the St George's by-election; Churchill had just left the opposition front bench over India; Sir John Simon had removed a dozen or so Liberals from the Lloyd George fold; the I.L.P. was hovering tremulously on the brink of leaving the Labour Party. The tiny New Party got somewhat lost among all these splinters. Where they could claim to be unique was in taking their appeal directly to the people. They were the crusaders for the new gospel of Action.

The gospel was not without its adherents at Westminster, though they preferred to keep their allegiance quiet for the time being. Macmillan ' takes the usual young Tory view that his heart is entirely with the New Party but that he feels he can help us better by remaining in the Conservative ranks '.[4] Hore-Belisha has ' joined us in spirit and hopes to bring with him a group of Liberals. He will remain in the Liberal camp for the present and work for us there.'[5] Moore-Brabazon almost joined, but not quite. Keynes said he would undoubtedly vote for the New Party, but felt that Mosley should have stuck with the Labour Party: so did Beaverbrook and Garvin.[6]

At the grass roots the earliest recruits came from the I.L.P., the New Party's open bid for I.L.P. support being facilitated by the initial willingness of many I.L.P. branches to tolerate membership of both organisations.[7] W. J. Leaper of Bradford, Bill Risdon and Stuart Barr from Birmingham and Leslie Cuming were all I.L.P.

officials. Leaper, Risdon and Cuming were to follow Mosley into fascism. The important Welsh Liberal Sellick Davies became New Party treasurer. A little later came an influx of young aesthetes and Tory hearties from the ancient universities, who found in New Party politics a surprising, if temporary, meeting-point. The New Party appealed to Youth: perhaps it did not expect them as young as the precocious twelve-year-old nephew of Winston Churchill, Esmond Romilly, who campaigned for Mosley at his exclusive preparatory school. Unemployed professional men queued up outside party headquarters in Great George Street looking for paid jobs: some were taken on as organisers or speakers, usually with disastrous results.

Of the recruits Mosley was able to secure, the most prestigious was the Hon. Harold Nicolson, whose diaries form much the most important source for the history of the New Party. The third son of the diplomat Sir Arthur Nicolson (later Lord Carnock) Harold Nicolson was then forty-five. Educated at Wellington and Balliol, Oxford, he entered the Foreign Office in 1909. Four years later came his marriage to Victoria (Vita) Sackville-West. For the next fifteen years Harold Nicolson combined a conventional career as a diplomat with a growing reputation as an author from literary biographies and the amusing autobiographic sketch *Some People* (1927). He resigned his appointment in Berlin at the end of 1928, and joined Beaverbrook's *Evening Standard*. It was through his contributions to ' Londoner's Diary ', his book-reviews in the *Daily Express* and his B.B.C. broadcasts on ' People and Things ' that he became nationally known.

But journalism failed to satisfy him. An extremely fastidious man, he found it degrading. He was attracted to politics and hankered for adventure. In his diary of 19 October 1930 he wrote: ' I find myself having day-dreams of power and youth.' Mosley's enterprise appealed to both. He was captivated by Mosley's personal power and the rewards which the adventure promised. In a movement of youth he sought an escape from the dismal realities of middle age that were starting to oppress him. Like Strachey he was another case of the weak being attracted by the strong: there was a germ of truth in Dalton's description of him as ' wetter than the wettest sponge in the fullest bath '. For Mosley he was not only an important ' name ' but was also a link with Beaverbrook, for whose support the New Party was angling.

On one level, then, Nicolson can be classed among the tiny group of exotic intellectuals and literary figures who adhered to the New Party – Cyril Joad the philosopher and admirer of Shaw and Bergson, the Sitwell family and the Anglo-Catholic writer Shane Leslie. But this does not exhaust his role. Nicolson was a homosexual who was attracted to virile and manly youths of the better classes.   His young Oxford friends comprised not just intellectuals like Christopher Hobhouse, but also undergraduates of a quite different type, like Peter Howard, ' charming and forceful but terribly immature ',[8] captain of the Oxford, and soon to be captain of the England, Rugby team.   It was Nicolson who introduced Howard and, through Howard, many of the heartier type of undergraduate into the New Party.   It is not least of the ironies of the Party's development that it should have been this fastidious, well-connected habitué of London's intellectual, literary world, with his dreams of youth and glory, who brought Mosley into contact with precisely that ' fascistic ' element that was soon to alarm John Strachey and Allan Young, and to give Mosley the reputation of commandeering thugs to support his political programme.

In order to translate political sympathy into support the New Party had to prove it could win votes, and this meant fighting by-elections.   The most promising of those impending was at Ashton-under-Lyne, once Beaverbrook's seat, but won by Labour in 1929 with a majority of 3407.   A Lancashire cotton conglomerate of unrelieved drabness, it was dominated by the ' dark, satanic mills ' of Blake's description.   Most of them were now silent: unemployment stood at forty-six per cent.   It was this fact that persuaded the New Party to appeal for its suffrages, and Allan Young was nominated New Party candidate on 16 April.   Mass unemployment also dictated the nature of its campaign, which was bound to be largely an attack on the Labour Government.

The facile nature of the New Party's hopes was soon to be cruelly exposed.   Disillusionment with the old parties may have been rampant, but even the more volatile Continentals might have hesitated to transfer their allegiance at ten days' notice to a new organisation they had scarcely heard of, one, moreover, which at the start of the campaign had not got the name or address of a single person in Ashton.   In Germany, the Nazis had had ten years to build themselves up as a movement of the last resort.   The New Party had been in existence for six weeks.   Far from starting too early, it had started too late to take advantage of the existing crisis.

Despite these difficulties, Allan Young and Dan Davies, Strachey's agent at Aston, did succeed in creating a scratch organisation in an astonishingly short space of time.   Five days after Young's arrival the *Evening Standard* reported ' young men with fine foreheads and an expression of faith ' dashing from room to room at the New Party offices, brandishing proofsheets and manifestos.   ' I have seldom seen so many young people so excited and pleased.'[9]   These local volunteers were soon supplemented by ' 14 strapping young men wearing plus-fours ' – presumably Harold Nicolson's contribution to the campaign.[10]   The New Party team of Young, Cynthia Mosley, Strachey, Cyril Joad and Captain Eckersley (formerly chief engineer at the B.B.C.) all spoke valiantly in the pouring rain: Cimmie, in particular, drew big audiences of wide-eyed girls, perhaps attracted more by her clothes than by her politics. Since there were not enough cars, helpers or days to organise a proper canvass, New Party loudspeakers blared out dance music to attract attention. But mass response to these appeals remained as bleak as the weather. It would take more than plus-fours or the latest hit to convert these dour Lancastrians to the new creed.

It was not till Mosley's arrival on 24 April, just up from his sick-bed, and six days before polling day, that the New Party campaign really caught fire. There was an immediate heightening of tension and drama. His two big meetings – at the Palais de Danse and at the Drill Hall – attracted over 7000 people and ended in scenes of considerable enthusiasm. ' He is certainly an impassioned revivalist speaker,' noted Harold Nicolson, ' striding up and down the rather frail platform with great panther steps and gesticulating with a pointing, and occasionally a stabbing, index.'[11]. The ' silly, fatuous, nonsense ' that depressions were ' like sun-spots ' must be ' dynamited ' out of the minds of the old politicians, Mosley thundered at the crowd. ' Our policy aims at building, by scientific shelter, with reorganisation behind it, the home markets, with purchasing power high enough to absorb the production of the modern machine.' The pretensions of the international socialist were savagely punctured: ' Is every worker in Ashton to wait for higher wages and employment until Socialism comes to Timbuctoo and every Hottentot has called Mr Henderson comrade at Geneva?' Churchill had criticised commodity boards as too complicated: ' Science to the old politician is so new-fangled: they don't hold with it at the Carlton Club.' On Parliament, ' If the country could hear and see a talking picture of Parliament, there would be no Parliament.' The audiences roared their approval at these sallies. They also enjoyed some lightning repartee. Hadn't he left the Labour Party, one interrupter wanted to know, because he wasn't made Viceroy of India? ' Certainly not,' flashed back the reply, ' riding on elephants always makes me sick.' As *The Times* of 29 April sedately remarked, ' Sir Oswald Mosley has developed an astonishing power of platform appeal.'

Had the exits from the halls led straight to the polling-booths, Allan Young might have swept in to Westminster on the strength of Mosley's oratory alone. But the New Party's attraction seemed much less potent the morning after, when old faiths and habits reasserted themselves. The Labour Party in particular acted massively to counteract any lingering effects of Mosley's stimulants, to the extent of making the New Party the chief target of its attacks. It imported a battery of political heavyweights into the constituency – Bevin, Tom Shaw, Johnston, Clynes and Greenwood –

to rally the faithful and denounce Mosley's treachery. ' He was the first rat to leave the ship when he thought it was sinking,' said Greenwood. An attack by Johnston on the New Party's hidden backers brought a prompt revelation by Mosley of the Labour Party's own ' secret fund' solicited from rich men like himself. Faced by the monolithic hostility of organised Labour, the New Party fished hard for non-Labour support. In the absence of a Liberal candidate, Mosley and Young praised the Lloyd George programmes; the sizeable Catholic vote was wooed with ardour. But even in these areas prospects were not promising. ' Insulation ', described by MacDonald in a message to Gordon, the Labour candidate, as ' Protection set to jazz music to appeal to the Bright Young People ', remained a barrier to traditional free-trade Liberals; while Protectionists would be more likely to plump for the straightforward Tory variety.

In the upshot the New Party made a creditable showing. On an eighty-per-cent poll, Lieutenant-Colonel Broadbent won the seat for the Tories with 12,420 votes, edging Labour into second place with 11,005. Allan Young saved his deposit with 4472, or sixteen per cent of the votes cast. ' It is more than was expected when the Election opened but not as good as was hoped after the success of the Meetings' was Harold Nicolson's verdict.

Outside the Town Hall where the results were announced Mosley and his party faced the disappointment and fury of hundreds of howling Labour militants. Shouts of ' Traitor ', ' Dirty Dog ', ' Judas ', ' You let the Tories in ' were hurled at the New Party group. Gordon's son ran up the steps of the Town Hall and denounced Mosley for wrecking his father's chances. As the crowd roared at him, Mosley turned to Strachey and remarked, ' That is the crowd that has prevented anyone doing anything in England since the war.' Strachey claimed that this was the moment when fascism was born. ' At that moment of passion, and of some personal danger, Mosley found himself almost symbolically aligned against the workers. He had realised in action that his programme could only be carried out after the crushing of the workers and their organisation.'[12]* Whatever thoughts passed through Mosley's mind his action was characteristic. Making arrangements for the ladies of the party to escape by a side exit, he turned to face the crowd. Then, with a nonchalant smile on his face, he led Strachey and Allan Young through them to the waiting car. It was a superbly

*Of Strachey's interpretation of his remark Mosley writes, ' . . . it is clear that I did not mean they were averse to change. What I meant then and mean now is that the long-experienced and entirely dedicated agents and warriors of communism always play on the anarchy inherent in the Left of Labour to secure confusion, disillusion and ultimately the violence which is essential to their long-term plan.' (My Life, p. 284)

insolent gesture to be repeated time and time again in the next thirty-five years, and by its sheer audacity compelling a grudging respect.

The fury of the Labour Party pursued Mosley far beyond the Ashton Town Hall. Labour leaders all over the country took up the local refrain. A. V. Alexander inveighed against the ' traitorous Mosley campaign '. To the president of the Scottish Labour Party ' Mosley, his money-bags and his minions ' were good riddance. Cecil Malone in a Labour May Day rally at Northampton tastelessly accused Cynthia of having been ' round the cow-heel and tripe shops, allowing the poor to stroke her pearls, and so persuading 4,000 to vote for the New Party '. ' What is new about the New Party,' asked the viperish Shinwell. ' Did not Brutus stick his knife into Caesar? The stiletto in the back is as old as the hills.'

Labour reactions to the loss of Ashton were understandable; nevertheless, they were based on a misapprehension. The New Party intervention did not hand the seat to the Tories: with average by-election swings to the Right throughout 1930 and 1931 of 8·4 per cent, Ashton would have gone comfortably Tory in any case. If anything, the New Party reduced the Conservative majority, by capturing a sizeable proportion of the Liberal vote which over the country as a whole was swinging heavily to the Conservatives.* We have here a classic illustration of the way in which fascist and pre-fascist parties were forced into a social straitjacket contrary to the expectations of their leaders. Mussolini had hoped to fight ' many a good fight still ' with the proletariat, but he later had to admit that the proletariat had remained in the hands of his enemies.[13] Similarly Mosley, who seems to have started with hope of winning substantial working-class support, even of linking up with the I.L.P., observed that the main response was coming from the younger Conservative group, clamouring for dramatic action.[14] In such circumstances the chances of the New Party being able to hold the centre of politics as Mosley hoped began to look distinctly unpromising. Both the mounting hostility of organised Labour and the nature of its grass-roots recruitment were combining to drive it to the Right.

These developments were starting to have a disturbing effect on the left-wing leaders of the New Party – Strachey, Allan Young and Cyril Joad. ' No harm was done,' Mosley later wrote of the violent scenes at Ashton, ' except to the psychology of John Strachey.'[15]

*One wonders whether better electoral analysis such as is now available would have modified the hostility of the Labour Party and actually induced it to encourage New Party intervention as a method of keeping down the Tory swing! Probably not: the way of the political scientist is a hard one.

Emotionally, Strachey identified with the workers. Unfortunately, on the evidence of Ashton, it did not appear that the workers identified with the New Party. As Mosley has rightly pointed out, Strachey was misled by appearances: Labour ' militants ' of the kind that gathered to howl down the opposition were not synonymous with the British working class as a whole.

But Strachey would not have attached the significance he did to the Ashton demonstration had he not already been moving apart from Mosley intellectually. Hitherto what had united the two men was a belief in the possibility of a middle way between socialism and *laissez-faire* capitalism. The New Party itself had started out as a ' utopian attempt at social compromise ', an attempt to break the intolerable ' class deadlock . . . in which neither side can move and nothing can be done ' by uniting workers and employers in a new ' industrial party '.[16] Essentially Mosley remained true to this vision throughout his life; for Strachey, however, it was never more than a second-best policy: the only hope of social advance in a situation in which capitalism was impregnable. What brought this barely hidden difference between the two men to the surface was their agreement in 1931 that the existing system was on the point of collapse. For Mosley this presented them with the opportunity for which they had presumably been waiting to inaugurate the National Policy drawn up by Strachey and others, and he saw the New Party as increasingly appealing to all the active and constructive spirits in the State as the only alternative to anarchy. But to Strachey what was this ' anarchy ' against which the New Party was supposed to fight other than the socialist revolution at last made possible by the collapse of capitalism? National Policies and New Parties might all be very well in a pre-revolutionary situation when nothing else seemed possible. But if the revolutionary possibility was there the true socialist ought to be on the side of the workers, not on the side of ' order ', which in practice meant being on the side of those wishing to suppress the revolution.

Strachey could not help reflecting that for a number of years now marxists had been predicting that when the crisis came big business would create and finance a political movement – fascism – to crush the working-class revolution and salvage capitalism – if only briefly – by intensified exploitation. On its road to power this movement would be decked out with attractive left-wing rhetoric designed to hide from the workers its true objective, which was to crush their organisations. To Strachey this was beginning to fit the New Party uncomfortably closely. Whether or not Mosley realised it, he was being used by big business for its own ends.

Such was the drift of Strachey's thought in the early summer of 1931. For a little longer he stuck to the New Party in the hope that Mosley could be got to change direction. Years of friendship, loyalty and, above all, faith in Mosley as a great left-wing leader could not easily be jettisoned. Even at this eleventh hour Strachey still hoped Mosley would emerge as Lenin. So he continued to fight to keep the New Party in the fold of left-wing politics – by trying to recruit as many left-wing elements as possible, by deliberately propagating policies that would cause big business to cut off its supply of funds.

'John Strachey has been seeing Cook, the Miners' Leader,' noted Harold Nicolson on 22 June. 'He is entirely in favour of the New Party. He can't openly come out in favour until the Miners' Federation have definitely broken with official Labour....' Perhaps it was through Strachey's efforts that the Press about this time carried a story that Arthur Horner, the communist miners' leader, was also on the point of joining the New Party.

Although Mosley was by no means averse to Cook's adhesion, he, Forgan and Nicolson were assiduously wooing a different type of potential recruit. On 30 June at the Cannon Street Hotel, Mosley addressed a lunch-hour meeting in the heart of the City of London. Soon he was reporting that the Prince of Wales was sympathetic and that his name might be used to get money out of Lady Houston, the snobbish, eccentric, right-wing millionairess.[17] There was even a suggestion to send that impoverished but well-connected hostess, Sybil Colefax, hunting for subscriptions on a commission basis. Mosley wondered whether William Randolph Hearst might be prepared to put money in the paper which the New Party was starting up. 'This money cadging', Nicolson wrote, 'is a most humiliating and unpleasant necessity.' At the same time Mosley was seeing a great deal of Lloyd George, Churchill and Rothermere in an effort to organise a 'national opposition' against the clearly foreseen impending alliance between MacDonald and Baldwin.* These were not the kind of allies to which Strachey looked to advance the cause of the worker.

The first battle in this fight for the soul of the New Party took place over the related questions of the stewarding of meetings and the youth movement. Communist-organised disruption of New Party meetings was not invented by Mosley. It was a deliberate tactic of the Communist Party designed to stimulate the revolutionary enthusiasm of the workers and at the same time expose the

---

*Harold Nicolson recounts a weekend with Lloyd George, Churchill and Mosley at Sinclair's house on 21-2 July:

[After dinner] Ll.G. begins at once: 'Now, what about this National Government? We here must form a National Opposition. I have every reason to believe that Baldwin and Ramsay at the slightest drop of the pound will come together in a Coalition. That moment must find us all united on the front opposition bench, and' (this very significantly, tapping on the table) 'we shall not be there long....' (H. Nicolson, *Diaries*, p. 81.)

fascist potential of the New Party, thus making explicit the historical dialectic of revolution and counter-revolution. In this task it could hope to utilise the anger felt by Labour militants at Mosley's 'betrayal' of the Labour Party, and also the class prejudices of Mosley's young Tory supporters.

As we have seen, two of the first dozen New Party meetings were broken up. A meeting in Hammersmith addressed by Cimmie in April ended in considerable disorder. As the *Acton Gazette* of 24 April put it, ' What should have been a meeting of outstanding interest and importance was turned into chaos for most of the time by the local unemployed. These have organised well under the Communist banner, and have attended the more important meetings with the express purpose of breaking them up by pre-arranged shouting, interruptions, and streams of irrelevant questions. Heckling is not in itself objectionable, in fact it is usually welcomed by the old campaigner; but organised interruptions, such as have gone far to ruin the Labour mass meetings, at which Herbert Morrison spoke earlier in the year, and last Friday's meeting, are altogether different.'

At that time public meetings were the chief means of getting the New Party's message across. Mosley's own prowess as an orator was the Party's chief drawing-card and Ashton seemed to confirm the effect that could be produced by a couple of successful meetings. Mosley has often been accused of cynically welcoming disorder at his meetings as a way of publicising his readiness to deal with 'Red' disruption. That he deliberately sought to identify himself in the public mind with the forces of 'order' against 'Red' chaos is undeniable. At the same time public meetings always retained for him a very traditional propagandist function. They were the means of getting across a policy which he had spent many years in working out by methods of persuasion which he had spent his whole political life perfecting. The importance of the public meeting was heightened by the press boycott of which John Strachey complained so bitterly at the beginning of June.* It therefore became a matter of urgency to secure a fair hearing for New Party speakers.

These matters were thrashed out at a 'secret' conclave (immediately fully reported in the press) on 14 May 1931. Mosley, Strachey, Allan Young and 'Bill' Allen were among the leaders who attended.

*'Indeed I have definite evidence of a boycott; explicit instructions have been issued in certain quarters that no mention must be made of the Mosley Party. We're on the political correspondents' black list,' said Strachey in an interview for *World's Press News*, 4 June 1931. Earlier in the year a scheduled B.B.C. discussion on the future of Parliament between Mosley and the Conservative Lord Eustace Percy had been ' postponed ' at the last minute. It never took place. (See *Sunday News*, 15 Feb 1931.)

Oswald Mosley, 1915.

Newly-weds : Oswald and Cynthia Mosley at Hackwood, 1920.

HON. DRESS SUIT (checking the Unemployment figures)
"— 1,739,497 — 1,739,498 — 1,739,499 —
1,739,500 — GOOD LOR! — 1,739,501 !"

HEARTBREAK HOUSE

REJECTED MEMO[RANDUM]

AN EXTRA ONE.

Above, Mosley resigns, 19 May 1930. *Below,* New Party chiefs at Denham, June 1931. From left to right: W. E. D. Allen, Robert Forgan, Cynthia Mosley, Oswald Mosley, and John Strachey.

The sporting life. *Above*, fencing. *Below*, 'Prof Mosley's Boxing Academy'.

INTIMATE MOMENTS WITH THE GREAT.

(Copyright in all countries.)

Above, first B.U.F. rally, Trafalgar Square, 15 October 1932. *Below,* Cable Street, 4 October 1936.

Left, Oswald and
Cynthia Mosley, 1921.

Below, Mosley and supporters
in an East End London pub,
2 January 1954.

Above, first press conference after the war, 1947. In the centre is Frederic Mullally, the anti-fascist journalist. *Below,* march to Trafalgar Square, 1961. At Mosley's left is Jeffrey Hamm.

Left, Diana Mosley.

Below (left), family group at Crowood, Wiltshire, 1947; Max is on the left, Alexander on the right. *Below (right),* Oswald and Diana Mosley at the Parthenon, 1969.

They all agreed that meetings must be protected from organised disruption and that young recruits should be enlisted, trained (through judo and boxing) and disciplined specifically for this purpose. (Mosley was particularly keen on the Party being 'fit' and 'in training': he himself had just taken up fencing again after a lapse of many years.) This led on to the question of whether the Party should formally develop a youth movement. Strangely enough the strongest support for this came from the left-wingers who were anxious to recruit 'young workers' to counteract what they considered the pernicious influence of the strapping Oxford hearties in their plus-fours and sports cars.[18] It was Mosley's further thoughts on the function of this disciplined young force that disturbed the Left:

> The Communist Party will develop a challenge in this country which will seriously alarm people here.
>
> You will in effect have the situation which arose in Italy and other countries and which summoned into existence the modern movement which now rules in those countries.
>
> We have to build and create the skeleton of an organisation so as to meet it when the time comes.
>
> You have got to have an iron core in your organisation around which every element for the preservation of England will rally when a crisis of that kind comes, but that is a matter for considerable delicacy and skill.*

In other words, the New Party was to organise not just to keep order at its meetings (or for that matter to put an emergency programme before the electorate) but to take control in a revolutionary situation. This was to be its reserve function, its long-term purpose. Strachey himself did not object to the organisation of force. But he wanted it to be exerted on the workers' side.† The fact that both men had come to think in these doom-laden terms shows how far they had drifted from that rational search for economic consensus and social compromise which had earlier united them.

Rumours that he was recruiting 'storm troopers' to attack the workers forced Mosley into hurried denials. 'We are simply organising an active force of our young men supporters to act as stewards,' he explained to reporters. He tried to undo the damage of the comparison with Mussolini and Hitler. 'The only methods

---

*'Office short-hand report' of Mosley's remarks, released to the Press by Strachey and Young after they had left the New Party. (*Daily Herald*, 29 August 1931.)

†The *Daily Worker* was at this time advocating a Workers Defence Corps against Fascism. (29 May 1931). The Communists and Social Democrats in Germany both had para-military units.

we shall employ will be English ones. We shall rely on the good old English fist.'[19] Unfortunately for Mosley's publicity the ' good old English fist ' had rather gone out of fashion since the good old days of punch-ups on the hustings when candidates had hired prize-fighters to defend them against the good old English crowds. Nor were suspicions of Mosley's intentions eased when two New Party officials left for Munich apparently to study Hitler's methods.[*] The ' Biff Boys ' as his young recruits were dubbed were regarded as a definite challenge to opponents to do their worst. ' Unless very discreetly kept in the background, the brawny peace-preservers would probably have a provocative rather than a tranquillising effect,' predicted the *Edinburgh Evening Dispatch* on 18 May 1931. To Strachey and Young these plans for a ' physical force ' to deal with left-wing interrupters marked a significant stage in the development of the New Party's anti-worker alignment.

At a giant ' Congress ' held at Denham on a rainy weekend early in June – a mixture of country-house party and I.L.P. summer school – the New Party tried to thrash out its various differences. The active young men based on London wanted more action, the regional organisers wanted to build up the regional organisation first, a policy which Mosley endorsed, ruling out any further by-elections for the time being. John Strachey delivered a ' good old-fashioned Marxian speech ', heartily applauded by Allan Young, Cyril Joad and others. In a suitably attic barn a Mr Peter Winkworth discoursed learnedly on the Attic State. The New Party, he said, must attract people with the heads of thinkers on the bodies of athletes. ' Be careful you don't attract men with the heads of athletes on the bodies of thinkers,' quipped the waspish Cyril Joad. Mosley remarked that the trouble with the Labour Party was that it had the heads of communists on the hearts of social democrats. ' The Youth Movement swam,' Harold Nicolson noted laconically.

> Cynthia Mosley looks troubled, so does Mrs. Strachey. Harold Nicolson smokes his pipe diplomatically, and later speaks like a diplomat. . . . Dr. Robert Forgan, MP, speaks non-committally – for they are all his friends. . . . Mr Box[†] stands in the background with a smile on his face as he watches Allan Young squirming impatiently while Mosley is speaking soulfully of the Corporate State of the future. . . . Denham is a charming little place in which to differ.[20]

[*]Mosley denied that their visit had anything to do with politics.

[†]F. K. Box, appointed New Party chief agent early in May. He was ' for nearly a quarter of a century . . . one of the most popular of the highly-placed Liberal-Unionist officials ' with considerable experience of organising industrial constituencies (*Daily Herald*, 5 May 1931).

The scene of the struggle shifted briefly to the House of Commons. Since February the New Party had been conspicuously absent from Parliament. This was deliberate policy. Wrote John Strachey and Cyril Joad, ' The endless futile speeches have all been made – and re-made. To those who care for the future of Great Britain nothing is more horrible than to sit through those debates. In the ornate and hideous Chamber the nation's breath seems to grow fainter, speech by speech.'[21] The New Party's remedy was to arm government with the power to legislate by Orders in Council, Parliament at the same time retaining the right to dismiss the Government and acquiring a new right to pass ' admonitory resolutions.' As Mosley put it to the Select Committee on Procedure in June 1931, ' The original, and as we conceive it, the proper function of Parliament was to preserve liberty and to prevent the abuse of power. . . . That essential function we propose to retain.'[22] Till changes had been carried out the New Party proposed to attend as little as possible.

But on 18 June 1931 the Government, under heavy pressure from Conservatives and Liberals, introduced its Anomalies Bill designed to exclude certain classes of the unemployed from benefit. What was the New Party's attitude to be? ' We presumed ', Strachey and Young later wrote,

> that the New Party would not dream of allowing to pass this opportunity of demonstrating that its whole policy was to oppose such ' economy ' efforts, designed to solve the economic crisis by cutting down the workers' standard of life. Our astonishment was therefore very great when we found that Sir Oswald Mosley was strongly against opposing the Bill. This astonishment was modified, however, by the receipt of an urgent telephone message from one of the principal City supporters of the New Party politely threatening us with the loss of financial support if we acted against the Bill.

It was only when faced with ' definite threats of resignations ' from Strachey, Young and Bill Allen that Mosley agreed to oppose the Bill, insisting, however, that the New Party do so from the Opposition benches.[23] This story, while doubtless true, is unfair to Mosley. He had never been interested in unemployment insurance, regarding the whole system as an appalling tribute to the Government's failure to provide men and women with jobs. As he pointed out in his Commons speech of 18 July 1931, the Bill, like most things undertaken by the Labour Government, made little difference to demand one way or another. Nevertheless, he managed to work up some sort of passion: ' By this little Measure you buy until the Autumn another short lease of your own miserable lives. You buy it at the expense of the poorest of your supporters who

voted for you in more lavish days.   You buy it at the expense of
British industry which your continued existence in power places
in ever-increasing jeopardy.'[24]   He left detailed New Party opposition to the Bill, though, to his wife and John Strachey who harried
it unmercifully in an all-night session with the people they really
enjoyed working with – the I.L.P.

The actual breaking-point between Mosley and Strachey came
on 20 July when Strachey, at Mosley's request, submitted a
memorandum defining the New Party's attitude towards Russia.
He wrote it to force the question of the New Party's place in
the political spectrum.   The key point was contained in the
following sentence:

> . . . a New Party Government will enter into close economic
> relations with the Russian Government and will endeavour to
> conclude such trading contracts between suitable British and
> Russian statutory organisations as will rapidly develop the
> controlled interchange of goods between the two countries.

An economic partnership with the Soviet Union, Strachey admitted, was 'inconsistent with a political policy hostile to Russia'.
Rather it demanded a 'progressive break' with the United States
and France and a dismantling of Britain's imperial system: so
much for the New Party policy of building up an empire economic
system.*   Mosley was not wrong when he accused Strachey of
advocating in effect 'an economic and military alliance with Russia
which would admittedly antagonise nearly every nation in the
world. . . .   It is difficult to conceive that anyone but a communist
could possibly support on the public platform such an extraordinary
proposition.'   The New Party executive rejected the Strachey Memorandum by five votes to two (the two Mosleys, Forgan, Nicolson
and Allen against Strachey and Young).

Nicolson has provided a vivid account of the sequel three days
later:

> I am working at the *Evening Standard* office when, at about
> 11 a.m., Tom rings me up and says will I come round at once.
> He had at that moment received letters from John Strachey
> and Allan Young resigning from the Party.   I go round at
> 12.30 and find the Council gathered together in gloom.
> We try to get hold of our two delinquents but they are out
> and will not return till 6.   As 6 is the hour at which they

---

*It is true that Strachey could appeal for support to a couple of sentences in
A National Policy (p. 29) advocating greater trade with Russia.   But the clear
emphasis of New Party external policy had always been on increasing trade with
the Empire.   At the same time, Strachey as early as 1929 had been advocating
more trade with the Soviet Union (Hugh Thomas, *John Strachey* (1973) p. 80).

announced their intention of communicating their resignation to the Press, that is not of much value. We adjourn
for luncheon.

Back to the office. I begin drafting statements to the
Press in order to meet John's impending announcement.
While thus engaged, a letter comes in containing that announ-
cement. It says that they have resigned because Tom, on
such subjects as the Youth Movement, Unemployment
Insurance, India* and Russia, was adopting a fascist tendency.
On all these points except on Russia (where John's memo
was idiotic) they have had their way.

At 5.30 we at last find they have returned to 7 North Street.
Bill Allen and I dash round in a cab. Allan Young descends
to the dining room looking pale and on the verge of a nervous breakdown. We say that Tom suggests that they
should not openly resign at this moment, but ' suspend ' their
resignation till 1st December, by which date they will be able
to see whether their suspicions of our fascism are in fact justified. Allan might have accepted this, but at that moment
John Strachey enters. Tremulous and uncouth he sits down
and I repeat my piece. He says that it would be impossible
for him to retain his name on a Party while taking no active
direction of that Party's affairs. He would feel that in his
absence we were doing things, with his name pledged, of which
he would deeply disapprove. He then begins, quivering with
emotion, to indicate some of the directions in which Tom
has of late abandoned the sacred cause of the worker. He says
that ever since his illness he has been a different man. His
faith has left him. He is acquiring a Tory mind. It is a reversion to type. He considers socialism a ' pathological condition'. John much dislikes being pathological. His great
hirsute hands twitched neurotically as he explained to us, with
trembling voice, how unpathological he really was. They
both mind dreadfully severing this link with old associates.
Poor old Allan Young is on the verge of tears. . . . I feel a
pain in my soul.[25]

Two days later Cyril Joad also resigned having, he claimed,
detected the ' cloven hoof ' of fascism. Only a month before, he
had written to Mosley demanding ' to take direct part in shaping
the policy of the New Party '. It was perhaps as much Mosley's
rejection of this demand as the drift to fascism that determined
him to take up the university appointment in the provinces which
he had just been offered.

*A reference to Mosley's meetings with Churchill, suggesting a Diehard alliance
on India.

Although Mosley's 'caustic tongue', which Nicolson mentions as a cause of the break, may latterly have contributed to the embitterment of relations between him and Strachey, it is clear that the break came over policy, not over personal relations. Although Mosley has often been accused of aiming at a personal dictatorship, the inner story of the New Party as revealed in Nicolson's diaries does not reveal the temperament of a dictator. Mosley's style of leadership consisted not in imposing policy, but in allowing the maximum of discussion until agreement emerged and then insisting on absolute unity behind the agreement reached. What he abhorred was endless inconclusive discussion leading nowhere. A second element in his theory of leadership was a belief in the value of creative tension. This can cynically be interpreted as a stratagem of divide and rule. But it is really basic to Mosley's whole concept of how truth is reached, not just by discussion, as in the liberal model, but by the deliberate juxtaposition of opposites. That is why he wanted the New Party to consist of 'Left' and 'Right', of intellectuals *and* 'toughs'. This is something that Harold Nicolson and John Strachey could not understand. For them certain people, attitudes, philosophies were simply 'beyond the pale' – on aesthetic grounds for Nicolson, on political grounds for Strachey.

As a personality, the most striking thing about Mosley that emerges from Nicolson's intimate account is both his own sense of euphoria and the euphoria which he generated round him – a euphoria which made life seem eminently worth living. ('Yet in spite of all this – what fun life is!' declared Nicolson after reviewing the unrelieved catalogue of personal misfortunes which had followed his association with the New Party.) This sense of exhilaration tended to come on most strongly on the rebound from disaster. On 24 July, following the defection of Strachey and Young, Mosley opened a new Regional Office at Dalston in London.

> Tom makes a fine speech. Then on again to the Edgware Road office where there is a large crowd. Also an overflow meeting in the Hall. Hecklers are bad – very bad indeed – silly loons. Exhausted we all go to the Savoy Grill where we have hock and beer. . . . We are a happy band and my wounds seem healed.

Chapter 13

Hold High the Marigold!

On 15 July 1931 the executive of the New Party had decided to contest fifty seats in the next election and to disband any organisation outside those fifty seats. It was a typically authoritarian decision, taken over the heads of local organisations which were never allowed any real share in policy-making. As such it was easier to take than to implement.

It was not easy to find fifty suitable candidates. Harold Nicolson went up to Manchester with Forgan to interview applicants on 22 July:

> Pritchard the Organising Secretary has got a list of people and shoots them in to us, one every half hour. They vary from an old lunatic called Holden to a boy of 21 called Branstead who scarcely knows what the House of Commons is. Only one of the many we interview – a wild-eyed nymphomaniac of the name of Miss M. . . . is at all a possible candidate, tho' some of them may be possible workers. It is a depressing business as the Party has quite clearly not as yet attracted the better class of manual worker. . . .[1]

Nor were efforts to construct an electoral machine helped by the masterly inactivity of the New Party leaders. While their posters screamed CRISIS and ACTION, the Party itself went into virtual hibernation between the Ashton by-election and the summer recess. Mosley had not yet fully recovered from his illness. His only major appearance was at a giant New Party rally at Renishaw Park, the Osbert Sitwells' estate near Sheffield, at the beginning of August. He referred to the financial crisis which had just hit central Europe. 'For two years you have had a crisis in Britain, and what has British statesmanship done about it? Nothing at all. But when you have a crisis in Germany, MacDonald, Henderson and the rest of them rush to Berlin to save Germany. . . . Why all this interest in other nations? Why this rush to lend money to other countries? Why rebuild Germany before you have begun to rebuild England? You can't get anything done to-day unless you are a foreigner. Why, if a man were drowning to-day he would have to shout for help in German.' On the May Report* which had just come out Mosley was characteristically scathing: 'The only econo-

---

*The Government had set up the May Committee on 17 March 1931 ' to make recommendations to the Chancellor of the Exchequer for effecting forthwith all

mies demanded are from the workers. No economy from the bond-holders whose bonds have doubled in the last ten years, because Snowden is a flunkey of the bondholder and the banker. . . . ' Having delivered himself of these judgments to the acclamation of the faithful, Mosley, like the other party leaders, promptly went off for his holidays to France; while Cimmie, for the second year running, departed for Russia.

At the end of May the Party had taken the important decision to beat the press boycott by starting a weekly paper of its own. On 16 June Mosley asked Nicolson to edit it, offering him £3000 a year – what he was getting from Beaverbrook. After a further conversation with Sir William Morris Mosley was able to guarantee *Action* (as it was to be called) £15,000 a year for two years, plus £5000 initial promotional expenses. After some hesitation, Nicolson accepted the editorship and set to work at the end of July. First he hired ' an active and intelligent Jew' Hamlyn as general manager. Noel Josephs became sub-editor: ' an embittered I.L.P. inferiority-complex man who should be able to give me the acid I require '. The first issue of *Action* was planned to appear in October, together with a propaganda film on which Nicolson also worked. His notes on the scenario were as follows:

> Shots of unemployed to a background of Land of Hope and Glory. Rotting cargoes, railway trucks full of coal with captions: Looking for work? There is None. Why? Because the Countries of the world Have Produced Too much!
>
> Cut to somnolent old gentlemen sitting on front benches in Parliament filmed in slow motion. Shots of M.P.s half asleep talking about Ancient Monuments and Grey Seals Protection Bill, or advocating policy of Wait and See.
>
> At Trafalgar Square. One of the lions on Nelson's Monu-ment goes to sleep. Crowds very restive and jeering – rush forward shouting England Wants Action – placards torn and destroyed. . . . Final shot of the paper *Action*, with newsboys on street shouting the word.

From the Leader at Cap d'Antibes came a stream of encouraging letters.

[Mosley to Nicolson, 16 August 1931]

My dear Harold,
    The Foreign Policy Memorandum is a brilliant piece of

---

possible reductions in National Expenditure. . . .' Its report, published on 1 August, recommended £97 million worth of economies, £67 million to come out of savings on unemployment benefit. It was the implementation of this report that was demanded of the Labour Government when the financial crisis hit England in the first week of August 1931.

work – Exactly what is needed.   I would like to see it published by Macmillan with a note that it was offered by yourself
as a statement of our policy. . . .

On *paper* – delighted to hear that you are so far ahead – if
this situation develops the sooner it is out the better.*   Everything is moving towards us – few movements have been so spee-
dily or so dramatically justified.

One word to you and Box alone – I postponed my departure
in order to have an interview at Oxford – As a result I have
every reason to believe that more money will be available.
This is not a certainty.   But to act on the assumption is a
more than legitimate gamble.   Therefore I would not stint
to a crippling extent. . . .

Nicolson had meanwhile written to ask authority to engage the
economist Rupert Trouton as New Party economic adviser for
£400 a year – 'brilliant and honest . . . I am not certain whether he
is very lucid.   Economists never are.'†

[Mosley to Nicolson, 17 August 1931]

My dear Harold,
    . . . He is a bargain at £400 p.a. and if you and Box agree
I would suggest turning him on at once.   He should read all
our literature and every speech I have made in the House
since resignation. . . . He might in particular study the question of a rentier tax in relation to crisis. . . . Bill Allen is good
on that subject – Our main line, however, should be 'build up,
do not cut down' with assault on all parties for their failure to
build in time.
    . . . I shall now return at end of month unless things are
different.   It is a joy to have you on the job – do not kill yourself. Tom.

The crisis moved rapidly to a climax.   Unlike the major party
leaders, however, Mosley remained on the Riviera, no doubt judg-
ing correctly that it was more dignified to be absent and aloof than
present and not consulted.   However, with the formation of the
National Government on 24 August (Ramsay MacDonald and
four members of the Labour Cabinet had joined forces with the
Conservatives and Liberals to save the pound as Lloyd George had

*The English financial crisis had finally broken in the first week of August.
The leading Labour ministers hastily reassembled on 12 August to work out the
'economies' required to balance the budget and 'save' the pound.
†Rupert Trouton had been one of Keynes's protégés in the Treasury during the
First World War.

predicted), he cut short his holiday, landing at Dover on 26 August.
He declined to say whether he would support the National Government; to the *Daily Herald* he said that it 'consists of the very men
who have failed most conspicuously in English politics in the past. ...
The attack on working-class standards which is being led by Labour
leaders arises inevitably from the failure of the Labour Party when
in office.'[2] A day later Mosley defined what was to remain the
official New Party attitude to the crisis: its root cause was industrial, not financial, and no financial expedients could meet it unless
a constructive policy was adopted to meet the industrial situation.[3]

The New Party's political position was not enviable. The crisis
which it had been predicting for so long had at last arrived, but
not in a form of which it could take advantage. What Mosley
had been banking on was a combination of all the ' old gangs ' in
a policy of ' cutting down ' the standard of life, leaving the field
clear for the New Party plus a few mavericks to campaign as a
' national opposition ' on a policy of ' building up '. This strategy
was foiled by the decision of the Labour Party under Arthur Henderson to go into opposition to its own leaders. Immediately the
intellectual issue – whether to contract or expand – was swamped in
an emotional class-issue. On the class-issue Mosley was with Labour.
If more taxation was needed, he said, it should come from the rich,
not the poor. But for Mosley this was a side issue: he wanted to
' build up ' not ' cut down '. And he knew perfectly well that the
Labour opposition had no real alternative to the National Government's policy: it was just that in the end even the worm turned
at the prospect of the final betrayal being demanded of it. This is
why Mosley could not take the easy way out and simply rejoin
the Labour Party, claiming credit in the process for being the first
to spot the treachery of MacDonald and Snowden. For it was
not just a question of MacDonald and Snowden, but of all those
who had sustained them for years in their policy of betrayal, and
had spurned all efforts to secure an alternative policy. What
he did recognise, however, was that the ' present crisis has somewhat
altered our target. The Labour people will no longer respond
to our appeal since Henderson and the machine have transformed
the crisis into a class conflict.' Hence the New Party would have
to readjust its appeal temporarily to the upper and lower middle
classes.[4]

But was there any reason for such groups to support the New
Party rather than the National Government? As Nicolson saw
it, just as the Labour Party would rob the New Party of the anti-
cut platform, so the National Government would take from the
New Party the slogans of unification, patriotism, insulation, planning, etc. The result would be that the New Party would have

no platform left on which to appeal to the electorate, as 'I told you so' was no platform. The alternative to swift annihilation was to try to do a deal with either the Labour or the National party and Nicolson advised the New Party to enrol under the National label.[5]

For a short time this seemed possible. When Parliament re-assembled on 8 September Mosley delivered two powerful speeches which in political terms were thought to have helped the National Government if only by virtue of the savage attacks they contained on the Labour Party. To the modern reader it is less this aspect that commands attention than the Keynesian spirit which breathes through them, especially the first which Mosley as a party leader who had just squeezed on to the Opposition Front Bench was called upon to deliver after Stanley Baldwin. 'Perhaps my views', Mosley said,

> can be briefly summarised if I say that I believe it is vastly more important to deal, and deal quickly, with the industrial situation, than it is to deal with the Budget. And for this reason: the continual decline and collapse of the industries of this country makes completely illusory any attempt to bal-ance the Budget. You may balance the Budget on the present basis of revenue, but there is no one in the House who can say with any confidence that this basis of revenue will be long maintained. . . . That is why the one thing I want to urge upon the House is the immediate adoption of some construc-tive industrial policy. I do not care who does it. I do not so much care what the policy is, as long as someone gets busy. . . . I put forward my suggestions for an industrial policy over 18 months ago. I also put forward an analysis of the position leading to the present crisis which has since proved correct. So perhaps the remedies might be looked at now with a little more favour than they received at the time. . . .

Dealing with official socialist explanations of the crisis, Mosley turned upon the Labour Party with a controlled fury:

> In face of this decrease of our industrial position it is really idle to talk about the recent crisis as a bankers' ramp. . . . If the Labour Party had said that it was the banking policy of the last 10 years, a policy which they supported, that was responsible for this situation – [Interruption] – a policy which their Chancellor of the Exchequer supported and which they supported him in supporting, then they would be getting at the root facts of the present situation. [Interruption] Over and over again, in party conferences and meetings and in this House, some of us challenged the policy of the Chancellor of the Exchequer. Over and over again the solid ranks of

Labour closed up behind him, supported the policy of deflation, supported the policy of the Cunliffe Committee to
which he adhered, supported the policy which led to the
wage reductions in 1921 and 1926, which led to the doubling
of the burden of the National Debt, which led to the doubling
of the interest of every debenture holder, rentier and bondholder, and which placed upon British industry and trade
a burden which no other industries in the world had to
carry. The Labour Party again and again . . . supported the
Chancellor of the Exchequer. They did not walk out of the
bankers' palace till it fell about their ears. They were as
fatuous in supporting the bankers' policy for the last two years
as they are now in denouncing the bankers' ramp.

Mosley then outlined his own suggestion for dealing with the
financial crisis:

Suppose that we adopted the view that it is far more important
to have industrial recovery than to balance our Budget. . . . We
should then adopt the method of balancing our Budget advocated by Mr. Keynes and other economists which is simply
to continue to borrow – I know that it shocks hon. Members
– to continue to borrow to provide for the Unemployment
Insurance Fund, or I would prefer to say, borrow to
provide constructive works to give employment in place of it,
to suspend the Sinking Fund and to raise the remainder by a
revenue tariff or, as I should say, a protective tariff.

If this policy produced a run on the pound, Britain should boldly
mobilise its foreign assets – should have threatened to do so in fact
already rather than gone crawling cap in hand to the bankers:

We could have said to Wall Street or to any other stock
exchange, ' We have £400,000,000 of dollar securities and
unless we get the loan we want, they go on to Wall Street
to-morrow morning and you will get the biggest bear raid
in your market that you have known for the last two years.'
And you would have got your loan. If you want a policy
of vigour and virility to face world finance, there it is.*

The conclusion was authentic Mosley:

It seems to me that Britain in her crisis is being asked to turn
her face to the wall and to give up like an old woman who
knows that she has to die. I want to see this country at least
make an effort. I do not believe and never have believed
in the cure of fasting, but in the cure of effort. I believe

*It is odd that Mosley, like Keynes, never advocated devaluation.

that the way out is not the way of the monk but the way of
the athlete. It is only by exertion, it is only by endeavour,
by a great attempt to reorganise our industries, that this country can win through and I venture to suggest that the simple
question before the House in this Debate is whether Great
Britain is to meet its crisis lying down or standing up.[6]

Next day Mosley found himself once more in opposition to the
Labour Party. The Government had asked for powers to curtail
parliamentary discussion and private members' bills – a demand
which Mosley, true to the New Party doctrine of executive initiative,
warmly supported. Jim Simmons of Birmingham had got up
to ask the Government to allow through a private member's bill
dealing with ex-servicemen. Mosley, who felt himself rather than
Simmons to be the authentic representative of the war generation,
somewhat snootily observed that Simmons' request would have
been more appropriately addressed to the previous Labour Government which had blocked that particular bill for two years. Uproar followed, with a Labour member angrily shouting ' Liar ' – 'an
observation', Mosley darkly observed, ' which the hon. Member in
question would not address to me twice outside this House . . . '.[7]

Mosley's constructive criticisms as well as his clashes with the
Labour Party considerably increased his prestige in those younger
National circles which were looking for some constructive policy.
A Mosley luncheon group at the House of Commons on 12 September included Lord Melchett, Brendan Bracken, Randolph
Churchill, Bob Boothby, Hore-Belisha and Terence O'Connor.
Soon they were joined by Leo Amery and William Jowitt, former
Labour attorney-general, who had joined the National Government. ' Jowitt wants Tom to assist the National Government by
eliciting from the Socialists what cuts they themselves, when in
power, did actually recommend. The fact that he should creep
into our luncheon room and try and lobby Tom in this way to
do his own work for him shows what prestige the latter has now
acquired.'[8]

Wishful thinking perhaps, but there is no doubt that many of
the younger Tories, while even less willing than of old to join Mosley
in the political wilderness of the New Party, were extremely anxious
to have him inside the National Coalition. For his part, Mosley
certainly toyed with the idea of joining, if only to secure the return
of a few New Party candidates to Parliament. But at the back of
his mind there was always the conviction that the National Government would fail to solve the economic problem and that the New
Party unsullied by contact with it must hold itself in reserve for
that day. His line was ' The movement is more important than
the Party.'

With so little time left before the general election the New Party would have done better to concentrate on getting a few M.P.s elected, leaving the national 'movement' till afterwards. In practice it attempted to do both, with a consequent dissipation of effort.   True, it cut down its fifty seats to twenty-five; while the dates for the autumn speaking campaign and the first issue of *Action* were brought forward.   At the same time Mosley decided to go ahead with plans for a nation-wide network of athletic clubs to attract youth[9] and with the rapid build-up of the 'active force' of stewards under the direction of Edward ('Kid') Lewis, a White-chapel Jew (born Gershon Mendeloff) who had been welterweight boxing champion of the world.   From this moment onwards the New Party started to have the dual character associated with its successor, the British Union of Fascists.   On the one hand it was a political party organised to seek power in elections; on the other hand it was a para-military force organised to fight communism in a revolutionary situation.

In the New Party the split was more marked than in the B.U.F. because it retained the considerable high-brow element which its successor lacked.   While Nicolson went round recruiting leading young intellectuals to write for *Action*, 'Kid' Lewis was training the 'active force' in fisticuffs, and Glyn Williams was busily intro-ducing the whole Boy Scout paraphernalia of uniforms, badges, saluting, flags, etc., into the youth movement. Mosley was charac-teristically complacent about the possibilities of combining these elements into a marvellous new political synthesis:

[Mosley to Nicolson, 4 September 1931]

Re the Youth Movement, yes, I think Williams is a very remarkable man with an extraordinary flair for working-class movement and organisation.   He realises what the bourgeois never can realise – that the working-class have practically no sense of being ridiculous in the way that we have, and that their very drab lives give them a thirst for colour and for drama: hence the excesses of the cinema.

At the same time recognition of those facts must not lead us into discredit and ridicule with the sound elements, intellec-tual and otherwise, from whom we are at present drawing sup-port and should draw increasing support.   If Williams is let loose without check this might well occur and apart from the laceration of our own feelings, might lead to some damage.

It should not be impossible to hold the balance now that we are rid of the pathological element [Mosley's description of Strachey, Young and Joad] and can settle the question by inquiring not whether the Germans, Italians or Russians have done the thing before, but whether the said thing is likely to

attract the average Englishman or to make him laugh at us.
I agree very much with you than Williams' line is much less
likely to excite ridicule if it is introduced under cover of clubs,
sporting and otherwise. . . .

On the whole, however, I think that Peter Howard is just
the man to hold the right balance. He must see that Mr.
Kid Lewis is invariably accompanied on his tours by Mr.
Sacheverell Sitwell – in a Siamese connection they might
well form the symbol of our Youth Movement!

The issue between the New Party's 'highbrows' and 'lowbrows'
was soon to be dramatised by a series of happenings that captured
press headlines. The Party's autumn campaign opened quietly
enough with a rally in Trafalgar Square on 12 September. The
weather was too damp for the rumoured communist opposition
to materialise, but not for Mosley to get in one of his best cracks
at the Labour Party. The element of farce in the political tragedy, he said, was provided as usual by the spokesmen of the late
government who claimed that the present crisis was the collapse
of capitalism which they had long prophesied with religious fervour. When the great moment arrived, Labour had the unique
advantage of being in office. The day dawned, but the Labour
Government resigned. 'What are we to think', Mosley exclaimed,
'of a Salvation Army which takes to its heels on the day of
judgment?'

Good humour was not a marked feature of the New Party's
next meeting. 'The papers are full of a razor attack made on
Tom at Glasgow,' noted Harold Nicolson on 21 September. Mosley
had addressed a giant open-air rally at Glasgow Green the previous
day (*The Times* estimated the crowd at 40,000). Heckled severely
by a group of about 500 communists, Mosley and his 'bodyguard'
which included 'Kid' Lewis and Peter Howard were attacked with
stones and razors as they made their way through the crowd after
the meeting and were only saved from serious injury by the police.
Back in London, a meeting of the New Party executive was hurriedly summoned. 'Tom says that this forces us to be fascist and we
need no longer hesitate to create our trained and disciplined force.'
They then discussed uniforms. Nicolson, in one last effort to preserve English middle-class respectability, suggested grey flannel
trousers and shirts. Since it was on his advice that the New Party
had previously adopted the orange marigold as its official 'colours'
he could claim the major credit to date for the New Party's sartorial
arrangements.[10]

If Mosley's reaction to the Glasgow incident, and Nicolson's
acquiescence in it, seem rather exaggerated, one must not forget
the extent to which, under the impact of economic catastrophe,

imaginative people of all political persuasions were starting to
flee from the liberal centre of politics.   The movement of a section
of the young liberal left towards communism had already started.
'Stephen [Spender] is going bolshy like most of my friends,' noted
Nicolson on 24 September.   For others, like Nicolson himself, a
form of fascism appeared the only answer.   For many this conviction of impending liberal collapse came as a liberation – from parents,
from sexual taboos, from old hypocrisies.   They felt free for the
first time in their lives.   Mosley shared this feeling of exultation.
At last the new world, Phoenix-like, was starting to rise out
of the ruins of the old.   At last they could sweep away all the
bogus cant of the dreadful old gangs and get down to the
things that really mattered.   The difference between Mosley and
Nicolson was in the quality of response to the situation which they
both believed was developing.   Whereas temperamentally Mosley
welcomed it with all the eager courage of a cavalier, Nicolson shrank
from it with all the sensitivity of a hot-house plant exposed to a
storm.

On the very same day that Mosley was going ' fascist ' the National
Government was forced to a step which at any rate greatly
lessened the need for either fascism or communism.   On 21 September Britain went off the gold standard, thus bringing to an
end a decade of deflationary finance.   In his last speech in the
House of Commons Mosley recognised that the main obstacle to
recovery had now been removed.[11]   The last obstacle to a general
election was also gone, since the Government could now go to
the country with 'reconstruction' rather than 'economy' as its
main plank.   Parliament was duly dissolved on 8 October 1931
and an election called for 27 October.

Had Mosley by this time been primarily interested in ordinary
party politics he would surely have attached himself to the National Coalition.   The leadership of the Young Tories was still his for
the asking – if he returned to the fold.   The National Government,
which by no means anticipated the runaway victory it in fact
achieved, would have welcomed his assistance in the anti-socialist
crusade.   In fact Mosley saw Neville Chamberlain, and Box negotiated with Central Office, to try to get New Party candidates a
clear run against Labour in a few seats, but without success.[12]   In
the end Mosley was not prepared to give up the ' vision splendid '
to rejoin the old parties.   As he wrote in the first number of *Action*,
' the fundamental task of new creation . . . is far more relevant to
the modern age than the transient labours of a nineteenth century
Parliament'.[13]

In terms of the electoral politics of October 1931 the New Party
was a complete irrelevance.   There was an emotional stampede
towards the vacuous MacDonald and the comforting Baldwin, a

panic flight of the middle classes from Bolshevism Run Mad (as Snowden vitriolically described the absurdly respectable Labour Party programme), drawing after it a section of the working class bewildered and disappointed at Labour's failure in office. In intellectual terms, the whole election was a meaningless farce – ' the most fraudulent campaign of modern times ', as the *Manchester Guardian* described it. But as a political stratagem it was superb. The two in combination go far to explain why Britain in the 1930s remained economically stagnant and relatively free from political disturbances. This picture must not be overdrawn. There was a moderate recovery helped by the tariff policy, by cheap money, and by the gradual revival of business confidence in a government that balanced its budgets. Walter Elliot was a successful minister of agriculture. On the other hand the economy continued to function well below full capacity: the unemployed, whose total never fell below a million and a half, were allowed to languish in what were euphemistically called the ' special areas '; despite the private-housing boom, little progress was made in clearing the slums; and up to twenty million people, according to Sir John Boyd Orr, remained seriously under-nourished. Intellectually, official England remained dead, displaying a nauseating air of self-superiority towards political and economic experiments abroad. Roosevelt's note – ' if private enterprise does not provide the jobs, government will take up the slack: I will not let the people down ' – was entirely absent. To all varieties of ' new deal ', whether emanating from Russia, Germany, Italy, America or Sweden, official attitudes were like those of Burke to the French Revolution: ' If it be a panacea, we do not want it. We know the consequences of unnecessary physic. If it be a plague, it is such a plague that the precautions of the most severe quarantine ought to be established against it.'

All this was decided on 27 October 1931 when the electorate gave MacDonald and Baldwin a ' doctor's mandate ', by an unprecedented margin. The New Party had entered twenty-four candidates. Harold Nicolson's wild-eyed nymphomaniac was not among them; even so, they were mostly a scratch lot – politically raw, and when not raw distinctly unimpressive.* This meant that virtually

*The New Party fought five London seats, five Scottish ones, six in the Midlands, three in the North, a couple in Wales, a couple in the South, and a university seat. Their candidates were Stuart Barr (Gateshead, Northumb.), Capt. E. J. Bartleet (Yardley, Birmingham), Ronald Bradon (Hammersmith N.), Leslie Cuming (Battersea S.), Sellick Davies (Merthyr Tydfil), Marshall Diston (Wandsworth Cent.), Maj. Randolph Dudgeon (Galloway), Robert Forgan (W. Renfrew), W. W. Gilmour (Coatbridge, Lanark), Christopher Hobhouse (Ashton-under-Lyne), H. L. Hodge (Limehouse), W. J. Leaper (Shipley, Yorks.), ' Kid ' Lewis (Whitechapel), William Lowell (Pontypridd), Joseph Mellick (Cathcart, Glasgow), Sir Oswald Mosley (Stoke-on-Trent), Harold Nicolson (Combined English Universities), Sir John Pratt (Hulme, Manchester), E. Copeland Snellgrove

the whole burden of public propaganda fell on Mosley himself, who at a critical moment was deprived of Cimmie's assistance. Three months pregnant and suffering from nervous exhaustion, she was ordered by her doctors to take a complete rest. Cynthia Mosley was the one New Party candidate (apart from Mosley himself) who might have got elected, since her following was very strong at Stoke. Her withdrawal saved Mosley an awkward decision whether to fight at Smethwick again, and he stood in her place at Stoke against Conservative and Labour opposition. His prospects of holding his wife's seat were not improved by his inability to spare his new constituency more than five days.

Mosley's national campaign on behalf of the New Party presents an extraordinary study in contrasts, scenes of enthusiasm being matched by scenes of wild disorder. At the Manchester Free Trade Hall on 24 October Mosley swept a great audience off its feet:

> In his 35th year Oswald Mosley is already thickly encrusted with legend. His disposition and his face are those of a raider, a corsair; and his place in the history of these times will be won, if at all, by the sword. We speak metaphorically; but who could doubt, when Oswald Mosley sat down after his Free Trade Hall speech in Manchester on Saturday, and the audience, stirred as an audience rarely is, rose and swept a storm of applause towards the platform – who could doubt that here was one of these root-and-branch men who have been thrown up from time to time in the religious, political, and business story of England.

This same report gives us a vivid glimpse of Mosley as a speaker:

> There was a tepid welcome when Sir Oswald Mosley came. He has a lithe and catlike figure, and as he sat down smiling one thought of M. Rigaud in ' Little Dorrit ' whose ' moustache went up under his nose, and his nose came down over his moustache.' The moustache is trim, the nose shapely, the teeth very white and perfect. The profile is aristocratic.

(Brightside, Sheffield), William Stevenson (Shettleston, Glasgow), Rider Troward (Reading), A. Williams (N. E. Derbys.), Jesse Williams (Duddeston, Birmingham), Martin Woodroffe (Chatham, Kent). The candidates included three sitting M.P.s, Mosley, Forgan and Dudgeon (who had come over from the Liberals at the last moment); one ex-M.P., Sir John Pratt, who had been a junior Coalition Liberal minister (1916–22); five ex-I.L.P.-ers, Stuart Barr, Leslie Cuming, Marshall Diston, Robert Forgan and W. J. Leaper; two twenty-one-year-olds, Christopher Hobhouse and Martin Woodroffe; and a taxi-driver, H. L. Hodge. They fought on a five-point programme of (1) reform of Parliament, (2) scientific protection, (3) national planning, (4) imperial co-operation and (5) a General Powers Bill for government.

The whole air of the man is that of a soldier on parade.   His suit is well cut, with a double-breasted waistcoat.   The grey flannel shirt is set off with an amber tie, and in his lapel are two rosettes: a small one of black and amber, and under that a big one of amber.

When he begins to speak we find that he has a powerful, harsh voice that would carry well on a parade ground.   There is a microphone before him, and after a moment's experiment he has it disconnected, explaining: ' I hate these machines '. Certainly it is unnecessary.   They must be hearing him perfectly at the back of the gallery.   He begins very smilingly with some references to his legend, but he has not got very far before the smile disappears and the face says clearly ' into battle'.   It is an earnest, gripping mood.   First that apathetic audience is arrested, then stirred, and finally . . . swept off its feet by a tornado of a peroration yelled at the defiant high pitch of a tremendous voice – a peroration denouncing the old men 'who muddled my generation into the crisis of 1914, who have muddled us into the crisis of 1931 – the old men who have laid waste the power and glory of our land ' – 'men ' from whose tired old hands, stained with blood and disasters innumerable ' our flag is slipping down into dust and dishonour.

His illustrations are striking.   He told how he stood in the Ford works at Detroit and watched a man who earned £6 a week for working six hours a day at nothing but turning a screw with a screwdriver.   Any illiterate oriental could learn the job in half-an-hour, and then he would work not for six but for eight, ten, twelve hours a day, and not for £6 a week but for 5s. a week or for a bowl of rice.   The threat to artisanship of the vast machine is one of the dangers, and he brings all the dangers home with vivid imagery.   To safeguard our home market he would give us protection, but once the tariff wall was up he would not leave to chance, as the Tories would, the things that happen behind it.   He envisaged a sort of Civil Service carried out by the industries themselves, but supervised by Parliament, for the prevention of price raising, wage-cutting and other tariff evils. . . .[14]

At the Birmingham Rag Market a few days earlier, the other side of the Mosley legend had been on view: the howling, organised opposition, Mosley jumping down from the platform and advancing at head of his ' bodyguard ' in fighting attitude into the centre of the disturbance, women screaming, Mosley and his party, some injured and bleeding, forced back to the platform under a barrage of chairs and bottles, a flash of a smiling Mosley and party surveying the scene of desolation from the platform after the audience had departed, the final escape through a side exit on police advice. According to the *Birmingham Post* of 19 October the cause of the fiasco was the failure of the loudspeakers (the wires had apparently been cut). But it also blamed the appearance of the stewards which 'immediately set up a militant feeling on the part of the few who were out for trouble'. The sequel was the first of Mosley's legal battles of the 1930s – he was unsuccessfully charged with assault. The defence offered by his counsel Sir John Hutchinson has remained the basis of his own defence ever since on charges of provoking disorder at his meetings: 'The case against my client is indeed remarkable. He is charged with having hired at considerable expense the largest hall of the City and with having persuaded many thousands of people to enter it, for one purpose and one purpose only, that he might assault the lot of them.'

Mosley was not unique in having his meetings broken up: the same fate befell other Labour 'Judases' like MacDonald, Thomas, etc. Where he was unique was in organising and training a large body of stewards to accompany him on his meetings, and in reacting extremely vigorously to the disturbances themselves. The question of how far the presence of the stewards contributed to the disorder which they were supposed to quell has been debated ever since. Sober opinion in 1931, while deploring 'Red hooliganism', advised Mosley to leave the stewarding of his meetings to the police. Whether by accident or design, this is exactly what Mosley did on the second day of a flying visit to the Red Clyde just after the Birmingham fracas. The entertaining sequel is described by a local newspaper:

> For five minutes yesterday I thought that Shettleston would be Sir Oswald Mosley's burial place.
>
> Shettleston Town Hall, Glasgow, was packed. The voice of the people was loud and angry. 'Bring us Oswald' they chanted, and when the leader of the New Party arrived they swarmed round him breathing into his face the cheerful promise – 'We'll hang Oswald Mosley by the neck in the Gallowgate.'
>
> Then the bravest of the brave, and certainly the most articulate among the acrimonious, jumped up on Oswald's platform and threw out a challenge –
>
> 'There's fifty polis hidden here. What chance have we against them? . . .'
>
> Fifty polis. A woman in the front row screeched, and brandished a length of red ribbon. Her amiable friend squirted the engaging term, 'Traitor' at Sir Oswald.
>
> Then someone settled the issue.
>
> 'Hey Oswald' he cried. 'Send awa' yer polis. Come

ootside and see what'll happen. Fair's fair.'

Even to my innocent ears this did not seem the most pleasing invitation. But Britain's all-round champion smiled blandly. . . .

' I never asked for police protection ', he declared: ' I never asked for police protection in my life.'

Quite definitely there were fifty ' polis ' whom nobody wanted. So outside we went, and the people's champion parked himself on a proletarian chair, while the proletariat itself surged round him.

' Hey Oswald!'

How they loved to yell ' Hey, Oswald '.

' Is it true you pay super-tax. . . ?'

' Well, whit'll ye pay us to jine yer party?'

' Hey, Oswald, whit aboot the Royal Family. . . ?'

' Hey, Oswald, ye dirty dog, whit made ye desert?'

' Ach, ca' the . . . aff his chair.'

And they did. Then Glasgow spoke up, or rather down. At a window ' three stairs up ' a champion appeared for Oswald.

' Hey, you MacGreigor ' she screamed, ' Whit d'ye ken aboot politics? Lae the man alone. He's daein ' his best. Ye wee. . . .'

' Aye, that's right. Speak up, Oswald. You're gem anyway, we'll say that for you.'

That finished any prospect of bloodshed . . . a hundred voices chanted ' Hey, Oswald ' and then they swept him forward to his car.

Sir Oswald left Shettleston smiling. Behind him, men who had sworn deep oaths to let Oswald see what Glasgow thought of him, stood speechless and amazed. What had happened? Why did they let him go? . . .[15]

Mosley's only other intervention in Scottish politics at this time brought a characteristic note from George Bernard Shaw. Cimmie had solicited Shaw's support for Mosley's candidature for the rectorship of Glasgow University. Shaw replied on 25 October:

For some months past I have been in one of those recurring crises – a real one, not a MacDonald one – in which the only way out is to go at my professional work first thing in the morning and hammer away at it until I am incapable of writing another syllable. Which leaves me, of course, friendless: nothing left but neglected, insulted, and estranged correspondents in all directions.

I have long lost all interest in these silly university contests for rectorships and the like. They only shew that our seats

of learning and culture are the only places where representatives of learning and culture are invariably at the bottom of
the poll, and the vulgarest available party careerist at the top.
Webb, Wells, Chesterton, Gilbert Murray have been booted
out in this fashion. Only the young and innocent take the
affair seriously. Support from me, though a guarantee of
failure, is quite superfluous. Defeat is certain without it. . . .
    Oh, if Oswald had only waited – if only he had known that
MacDonald was contemplating political suicide!

Shaw was right: Mosley came bottom of the poll.

The national press were only interested in those few Mosley
meetings that ended in disorder: indeed, by a curious inversion of
political values, the meetings that passed off peacefully were referred
to as ' anti-climaxes '. Since these were the vast majority little of
the New Party leader's tour appeared in the newspapers. Efforts
to compensate for the press boycott were unsuccessful. Mosley
was refused B.B.C. time; he tried unsuccessfully to buy time on
French radio. The New Party's film *Crisis* was banned by the
censor on the ground that shots of snoring M.P.s were calculated
to bring parliamentary institutions into disrepute – one of the very
rare examples in England this century of political (as opposed to
moral) censorship.

Apart from the public platform, the only vehicle of propaganda
was the New Party's highbrow weekly *Action* whose first issue
appeared on 8 October. *Action* was not supposed to play a direct
part in the general election. Its task, as conceived by Mosley, was
' to imbue the nation with a new idea and a new faith '.[16] Even so
Nicolson interpreted his brief more broadly than Mosley would have
liked. While the leader tramped the constituencies in search of
converts, Eric Muspratt tramped Six Countries on £15; while 'Kid'
Lewis arranged the stewarding of meetings, Vita Sackville-West
arranged Your Garden. Mosley must have wondered how far the
new faith was being advanced by Harold Nicolson's own sensitive
review of William Plomer's *Sado* – a novel of homosexuality set in
Japan. But the editor was not entirely unmindful of the purposes
on which Sir William Morris's money had been so profusely lavish-
ed. ' We believe that the old world is dead,' he exclaimed ex-
citedly. ' We believe that from its ashes will rise a new world,
more scientific, more human and far more enjoyable. Week by
week we shall put before you new vistas into the future. Week by
week you will see the sunlight glimmering at the end of this dark
forest.' Unfortunately an ever-diminishing number of readers
waited for the sunlight.

At Stoke, too, the auguries were unpromising. Nicolson found
Mosley ' strained ' and ' tired ' there on 21 October and ' not

really optimistic' about his prospects. Despite the enthusiasm of the meetings, the tide was running too strongly in favour of the National candidate, Mrs Ronald Copeland, for Mosley to reverse in five days' campaigning. Perhaps it was this realisation of impending defeat, as well as the strain of carrying the whole New Party campaign on his shoulders, that gave to Mosley's last meetings at Stoke that impression of hysteria noted by one observer. From his ' very subordinate ' position as the New Party chief's canvasser and bottle-washer at Stoke, Mosley's cousin James Lees-Milne has left an unflattering portrait:

> It became clear that he was in those days a man of overweening egotism. He did not know the meaning of humility. He brooked no argument, would accept no advice. He was overbearing and overconfident. He had in him the stuff of which zealots are made. His eyes flashed fire, dilated and contracted like a mesmerist's. His voice rose and fell in hypnotic cadences. He was madly in love with his own words. . . . The posturing, the grimacing, the switching on and off of those gleaming teeth, and the overall swashbuckling, so purposeful and calculated, were more likely to appeal to Mayfair flappers than to sway indigent workers in the Potteries. I did not then, and do not now, think that the art of coquetry ought to be introduced into politics.[17]

As soon as the first results came through it became apparent that the New Party had done disastrously. Christopher Hobhouse got only 424 votes at Ashton where six months previously Allan Young had got over 4000. ' Vote for Hobhouse, the Children's Champion ' might have appealed to the children: unfortunately they lacked the vote. The long and gloomy trail of lost deposits was relieved only by Sellick Davies who, standing at Merthyr with Conservative support, collected 10,834 votes and by Mosley himself who, though bottom, polled 10,534 against the 13,264 for Ellis Smith (Labour) and the 19,918 for Mrs Copeland. The New Party polled 36,377 votes in 24 constituencies, as opposed to 70,844 for the Communists in 26 constituencies. Eighteen candidates polled fewer than 1000 votes, including ' Kid ' Lewis who got a derisory 154 at Whitechapel. To compound the misery of the New Party group at Stoke, Cimmie, who against doctors' orders had travelled north to attend Mosley's final meeting, was taken ill, with the threat of a miscarriage, on the day of the election.

In a statement to the Press Mosley put the question to which before long he would have to give his own answer:

> The fate of the National Government, of the New Party, and of all parties depends upon the development of the situation.

Is it a passing storm which will be weathered without great effort, or is it a storm which can only be weathered by the greatest effort this nation has ever known? Upon the answer to that question depends the fate of old parties and new parties, and whether this country in the future must be governed by men like Baldwin and MacDonald or by men like we in the New Party.[18]

Following its electoral débâcle the New Party virtually ceased to exist as a political party. The central office in Great George Street was closed down; the regional organisations were disbanded and their officers retired. Of the paid staff Mosley kept only Box, Forgan and Peter Howard. All that was left of the Party was the embryonic NUPA (Nu-Party), or Youth Club, organisation which had been started in September.

The electoral débâcle also brought to light the extent to which the New Party had been infiltrated by adventurers, incompetents and crooks. The first to go was Hamlyn, *Action*'s general manager, who had botched up advertising: he was sacked on 5 November. Two days later Mosley told Nicolson that 'Sellick Davies has taken £270 from the till and will have to be sacked.... He takes it sensibly. We feel sorry for him in a way and know that it was all due to vagueness on his part rather than to iniquity.' It transpired that the New Party candidate for Reading, Rider Troward, was wanted by the police under several aliases. Just before the election the Party had been joined by the novelist Peter Cheyney, 'a Jew fascist – a most voluble, violent and unpleasant type. He thinks in terms of a gangster and talks in terms of a soap-box politician. I took a violent dislike to him. And told Tom on the way back.'[19] A few weeks later a pained Nicolson wrote: 'He is to do articles on the NUPA organisation. I dread them.' Despite the protests of Nicolson and Forgan, Mosley was characteristically tolerant about the activities of Cheyney and his friend Bingham. He eventually got rid of them, but not till Nicolson's feelings had been considerably 'lacerated'.

Mosley's tolerance extended to Nicolson's own enterprise, *Action*. He made little attempt to interfere with editorial policy, and even submitted to the drastic cutting of his own articles. Despite this, the paper did not prosper. An initial circulation of 160,000 fell rapidly to 60,000. By the beginning of December it was 20,000. With losses running at £1500 a month, with Morris refusing to put any more money into it, and with the remaining money needed anyway to cover the debts of a collapsing organisation, Mosley had no option but to close it down as well. The decision was taken at a party meeting on 22 December. The last issue of *Action*, number 13, came out on 31 December.

Action was a victim of a combination of bad luck and bad management. It was started in the depth of a depression when money was scarce: it was tied to a political party whose own fortunes had reached their nadir. For neither of these two things can Harold Nicolson be blamed. On the other hand, there is little doubt that a lot of money, advertising revenue and probably circulation was lost through sheer incompetence. For this Nicolson must bear chief responsibility. Mosley never reproached him, though Nicolson felt guilty at having let him down.[20]

As a literary and journalistic enterprise *Action* suffered from one major defect. It was the organ of a party whose own profile had as yet not been defined – suspended between a vestigial socialism and an incipient fascism as C. E. M. Joad described it. As a result it suffered from precisely that vague and eclectic modernism which was the bane of the New Party itself. It was ' trendy' without being coherent. This would have been an admirable recipe for success forty years later. At a time, though, when the centre was starting to disintegrate into its various ideological components, *Action* was too all-embracing in its enthusiasms to keep a politically conscious readership satisfied for long. For young left-wingers like Ian Mikardo, as well as for those who later joined the British Union of Fascists, the columns of *Action* provided merely a temporary common halting-post on their diverse intellectual pilgrimages.

Reading *Action* today one is still struck by the range of its enthusiasms. Gerald Heard fervently preached the utopian gospel of science: ' If we human beings can only keep our heads with each other, there seems no limit to our power of making the world we live in what we will' (no. 8.). Robert Forgan, who had interested himself in the ventilation system of the House of Commons, wrote on the importance of correct breathing. From the youthful Christopher Isherwood came a theme that effortlessly spans the intervening years: the revolt of the young against industrial civilisation, against the demand that they become ' useless screws in a broken-down machine' (no. 10). Le Corbusier, the contemporary cinema and Jacob Epstein found in *Action* warm admirers, while from Rupert Trouton came a stream of Keynesian articles on economics: ' The sooner the shibboleth of savings and their imaginary ethical value is exploded the better,' he wrote. The time for saving was when there was full employment and rising prices. To cry ' save ' with idle capacity ' is merely to give voice to the blind spirit of panic ' (no. 8). Incipient fascist economics make their appearance in Christopher Hobhouse's review of Major Douglas' Social Credit theory: ' He has found a distinction, to which all Socialism seems blind, between those who lend capital and those who borrow it. He has attacked Shylock and defended Antonio, while the Tawneys and G. D. H. Coles, in their vicarious solicitude for the wage-earner, have been raving at both' (no. 9). There were contributions from L. A. G. Strong, Alan Pryce Jones, Peter Quennell, Raymond Mortimer, Eric Partridge, and E. Arnot Robertson. Less distinguished, but unfortunately equally characteristic of the New Party, were effusions from Peter Cheyney urging 'the establishment of a country-wide system of Nupa-Shock Propaganda Controls by June, 1933, and the completely organised Political-Shock-Youth Movement by June, 1935'.

On the central issue of fascism, *Action*, like the New Party, refused to commit itself. Nicolson was convinced that the 'corporate State' was the answer to the impending 'proletarian revolution' (no. 1). But did this make the New Party fascist? Certainly not, Nicolson replied, horrified: 'We do not believe in formulas. . . . We shall take from all . . .' (no. 11). To prove his point he published articles praising communism and Soviet planning. Mosley gave a some-what different answer: the New Party was fascist in theory, but not in method. But this was then further qualified when he said that the New Party's theory came from the commodity boards worked out by him and his friends in the Labour Party (no. 12). With these rather unsatisfactory prevarications, the New Party followers had to be content for the time being.

Chapter 14

Part-time Saviour

IN THE aftermath of the New Party's defeat, what was Mosley to do? 'We shall win; or at least we shall return upon our shields,' he had written in the last issue of *Action*. A few months before, his reaction had been different: in the event of defeat 'he would retire from public life for ten years'. 'After all,' he said, 'I have never led a civilised life at all since I entered politics as a boy. I can well afford to wait ten years, to study economics, and even then when I return I shall be no older than Bonar Law was when he first entered politics.'[1]

Several lives, several careers, beckoned in the aftermath of defeat. He could simply have enjoyed himself. He had, as he admits, an almost unlimited capacity for pleasure. Another possibility was to work his passage back into the National Coalition. Friends suggested that he should go on a world-wide tour, write a book and come back as National Government supporter in a convenient by-election. Lord Rothermere on the other hand definitely urged him to go forward with fascism, promising to put the *Daily Mail* behind it.[2]

'Everything depends upon the development of the situation,' Mosley had declared after his defeat at Stoke. There were two possibilities. Either England would recover without too much trouble, in which case there would be no need for the new movement: such valid ideas as it had could be introduced in that 'more evolutionary, more scientific, and less political' form that Harold Nicolson wanted. The other possibility was that the economic crisis would intensify, in which case, as Mosley put it in the *Political Quarterly* of January-March 1932, 'Communism will quickly supersede the woolly-headed and woolly-hearted Social Democrats of Labour, and Communism's inevitable and historic opponent will arise to take the place of a flabby conservatism.' Mosley himself inclined to the second possibility. If some form of fascism was inevitable, he would argue to his friends, it was better for him to get in on the ground-floor and make sure that the movement took a reputable English, rather than a more violent Continental, form.

No one in Mosley's immediate circle shared his belief in the coming crisis (Strachey meanwhile having drifted far away to proclaim the same belief from the marxist standpoint).* Keynes

*Allan Young's marxism had cooled sufficiently for him to take the job of Harold Macmillan's secretary in February 1932.

came to dinner on 11 December. Despite the appalling incompetence of the National Government he thought that Britain would
come through all right and that things would start to get better.[3]
He could see no point in organising for crisis. Neither could
Beaverbrook. Neither could any of Mosley's friends.

Yet on Mosley their arguments seemed to have precisely the
opposite effect. Something in him was irresistibly drawn not so
much to fascism as to the idea of a politics half-civilian, half-military, a 'mobilisation of ex-servicemen for the achievements of
peace', as he put it in a speech in November. Nicolson and Forgan
were becoming alarmed by the extent to which he was starting
to share the fantasies of Cheyney and Bingham. 'They really
are the devil,' wrote Nicolson on 16 November, blaming Mosley's
increasing involvement with fascism on their pernicious influence.
Cimmie had another theory. 'She talked about Tom – about his
incurable boyishness and *joie de vivre*. She welcomes his fencing
as it serves as a safety valve for his physical energy. That in fact
is what is wrong with Tom. His energy is more physical than
mental.'[4] Cimmie was frankly terrified of where Mosley's restlessness would lead him. She hated fascism and the Harmsworths.
She threatened to put a notice in *The Times* dissociating herself
from Mosley's fascist tendencies. They bickered constantly in public, Cimmie emotional and confused, Mosley ponderously logical
and heavily sarcastic. Since she was also mostly unwell with a
difficult pregnancy and they had just lost a small fortune in yet
another expensive lawsuit over the Leiter millions, it was not a
happy personal time for them.

Immediately, Mosley's excess energy took him, together with
Harold Nicolson, Bill Allen and Christopher Hobhouse, to Rome
to study fascism at first hand. He saw Starace, secretary-general
of the Fascist Party, Mussolini whom he found 'affable but unimpressive' and Mussolini's biographer, Margherita Sarfatti. She told
him that Mussolini was the greatest worker ever known: he rode
in the morning, fenced a little, then worked, and in the evening
played the violin to himself. 'Tom asks how much sleep he gets.
She answers "Always nine hours". I can see Tom doing sums in
his head and concluding that on such a time-table Musso cannot
be hard-worked at all. Especially as he spends hours on needless
interviews.'[5] Mussolini advised Mosley to call himself a fascist, but
not to try the military stunt in England.[6]

Mosley found Rome invigorating, Milan 'Greek and bracing'.
He was by no means put off by the regimentation of the Press and
people, which Nicolson found painful. 'Tom cannot keep his
mind off shock troops, the arrest of MacDonald and J. H. Thomas,
their internment in the Isle of Wight and the roll of drums
around Westminster. He is a romantic. That is a great

failing.'[7]*   Back in London, after a brief stop in Munich, Mosley wrote an enthusiastic article praising Italy and its leaders in the *Daily Mail*.   His views on Mussolini had evidently undergone considerable change in the interval:

> A visit to Mussolini ... is typical of that new atmosphere. No time is wasted in the polite banalities which have so irked the younger generation in Britain when dealing with our elder statesmen.   The talk is neither of the beauty of the Italian sunsets nor of the sweetness of the birds singing in the gooseberry bushes [a reference to MacDonald]. . . .
>
> Questions on all relevant and practical subjects are fired with the rapidity and precision of bullets from a machine gun; straight, lucid, unaffected exposition follows of his own views on subjects of mutual interest to him and to his visitor. Every moment possible is wrung from time; the mind is hard, concentrated, direct – in a word, ' Modern '.
>
> The great Italian represents the first emergence of the modern man to power; it is an interesting and instructive phenomenon.   Englishmen who have long suffered from statesmanship in skirts can pay him no less, and need pay him no more, tribute than to say, ' Here at least is a man.'

The great constructive achievements of fascism in his view far outweighed the loss of the ' right to blather ' which English liberals so deplored.[8]   Previously Mosley had promised Nicolson to go to Russia before making up his mind about fascism and dictatorship.   But the pilgrimage to Moscow was never made; in Rome Mosley had evidently found what he was looking for.

Mosley had still not decided what to do.   The mavericks were starting to get together once again in an embryonic ' national opposition ': Lloyd George was in touch; Churchill wanted him to stand at a by-election with his support;   Lord Lloyd, the ex-imperial proconsul, was intriguing with all three; Beaverbrook wanted Mosley to attack the National Government at meetings in the provinces.   On the other hand, David Margesson, the Tory chief whip, was urging him to come back into the National fold.   So was Nicolson, whose own thoughts were increasingly tending in that direction.   There were even overtures from the Labour Party.†   This widespread demand for Mosley's services is a tribute to the

---

*Mosley insists he was ' pulling old Harold's leg again.   I was very fond of him but it was always an irresistible temptation when young to tease [him] on points on which he was rather absurdly sensitive. . . .   Later I strove hard to develop the requisite *gravitas* and *pietas*, more successfully perhaps in the former than the latter.'

†Kenworthy wanted Mosley back in the Labour Party (Nicolson, *Diaries*, 19 Apr 1932, p. 115).

public prestige he still commanded. Most serious people on the non-Labour side, and perhaps even a few in the Labour ranks, while agreeing that the New Party had been a terrible mistake, were prepared to write it off as a young man's folly. Few at this point thought Mosley was finished politically. His appeal to the young was universally acknowledged. Elderly crusaders like Lloyd George, Churchill and Beaverbrook were anxious to acquire him for that very reason.[9] The National Government which, till the emergence of a substitute Mosley in Anthony Eden, had a very senile appearance about it also wanted him in order to give it a face-lift. Mosley was attracted by the idea of a ' national opposition ' backed by the Harmsworth press. But he suspected, with good reason, that he would have to wait till Doomsday for it to materialise. He never seriously thought of Labour again. He was tempted by Margesson, but was held back by the stronger temptations of a new style of politics and the conviction that a crisis was coming which would sweep away the old politicians. At luncheon at the Carlton Grill he held forth expansively on these themes. Every country before a revolution produces its Giolittis and Kerenskys, he said. The National Government was nothing more than a series of Kerenskys – row upon row of eternal Kerenskys sitting side by side. Raising his eyes Nicolson was perturbed to see the original and only Kerensky sitting at the next table.

At a party meeting on 5 April 1932 Mosley announced his decision to close down the New Party, but to keep on with NUPA on a reduced scale.* Nicolson welcomed the former decision, as freeing Mosley to stand for Parliament as an independent, but strongly objected to the latter. ' I quite see that that organisation may have its uses as a militant branch. But I am not militant in the least, and if we are too closely identified with these fascist bands, not only I, but other... intellectuals, will become alien and even adverse to the whole movement.'[10] He made the same point in a letter to Forgan a few days later, arguing that it was impossible for Mosley to ride two horses simultaneously – ' the young filly of the King's Road and . . . the old cab-horse of intellectualism '.[11] Forgan's and Nicolson's plans for Mosley at this stage were for him to scrap the New Party, and get back into Parliament as soon as possible. Meanwhile they would try to organise a series of symposia on the New Party philosophy, drawing in men like Keynes, Arthur Salter, even T. S. Eliot.[12] Both Forgan and Nicolson, in other words, wanted a respectable fascism – the corporate state idea introduced under the benevolent dispensation of the National Government and leading intellectuals, without recourse to revolutionary violence. ' You are right in your sentiment, but you have

*Finance for the NUPA clubs was apparently coming from the 'Cousins Group', a commercial firm with sporting connections. (Nicolson MS, 5 Jan, 1 Feb. 1932.)

picked the wrong crowd' was Nicolson's line.   It was the complaint
intellectuals have made against Mosley ever since.

Mosley on the other hand was on the point of coming down in
favour of the fascism of the streets.   On 19 April Nicolson attended
his final New Party meeting.

> Tom . . . wishes to coordinate all the fascist groups with
> Nupa and thus form a central fascist body under his own lea-
> dership.   I say that I think this is a mistake.   He says that
> it would be impossible for him to re-enter the 'machine' of one
> of the older parties.   That by doing so he would again have
> to place himself in a strait-waistcoat.   That he has no desire
> for power on these terms.   That he is convinced that we are
> entering a phase of abnormality and that he does not wish to
> be tarred with the brush of the old regime.   That he thinks,
> as leader of the fascists, he could accomplish more than as a
> party-backbencher, and that in fact he is prepared to run the
> risk of further failure, ridicule and assault, rather than allow
> the active forces in this country to fall into other hands.   I
> again say that I do not believe that this country will ever stand
> for violence, and that by resorting to violence he will make
> himself detested by a few and ridiculed by many.   He says
> that may be so, but he is prepared to take the risk.   I see that
> on such paths I cannot follow him.
>
> The argument, though painful, is perfectly amicable.
> The ice cracks at no single moment.   Nor do I think that Tom
> was hurt or imagined for one moment that I was deserting
> him.

It was in fact Mosley's continued amiability that made desertion
such a difficult process.   He politely listened to all Harold Nicolson's arguments, and then ignored them in a way that was most
exasperating.   Then, to make up for any distress that he might
have caused, there would be playful little reconciliatory gestures –
' Sending you a little grey shirt with flame and black tie for wear on
gala nights at the Savage Club,' he scribbled to Nicolson a few
days after this meeting.   But Nicolson's disengagement from the
New Party was now almost complete.   To Mosley he wrote on
20 May 1932:

> In a few months, not more than eighteen, you will become
> essential.   I wish I could convince you that until that moment
> comes you should lie low. . . . What makes it so distressing is
> that I should like to be able to encourage and support you in
> everything you do and feel.   You have had a bloody time:
> and all of us who believe absolutely in your future would like
> to stick close to you now that things are so complicated and

obscure.   Yet I cannot make myself feel, until a crisis arises, there is any chance at all of making headway . . . as a New Movement.

[On NUPA] You know, that the thought of young Bermondsey boys with *gummiknüpfel* makes me sad.   I do not see, moreover, how it will be possible to disassociate the New Movement from these grey shirts.   In such combinations it is always the more active element which colours the whole.   I do not think that in practice you will succeed in keeping distinct the ideology of fascism from the violent and un-truthful methods which the fascists have adopted in Italy. I think there may well be a future for the corporate state idea in this country.   But I do not think . . . there is any possible future for direct action: we have, by training and temperament, become possessed of indirect minds.

You will think I am defeatist with a weak and wobbly mind. I may be.   And you know, Tom, that whatever happens I wish you success and power from the depth of my soul.*

Although Nicolson was still to give Mosley advice, and the two men met from time to time, this was really the end of their part-nership.   Cecil, Strachey, now Nicolson – they had all been left behind as Mosley blazed his lonely trail to glory or oblivion.   Peter Howard had gone too; Forgan and Bill Allen still hung on by a thread – Bill Allen the wealthy adventurer with nothing to lose, Forgan still in receipt of a New Party salary.   As in 1920, 1924 and 1930–1, the quest for new friends, new allies, had to start all over again.   With each sortie, however, Mosley was drawing a little further away from the centre of politics, a little nearer that abyss where dark spirits, unknown to Westminster, luxuriated in an underworld of fantasy and frustration, and from which, once drawn in, there could be no escape unless society itself exploded.

There was still time to hold back; time for reflection and study; time to join forces with the elusive young Tories; time even to work his passage back into the Labour Party.   Yet Mosley strode for-ward into fascism.   Why, oh, why, has been the despairing cry ever since of those who recognised his brilliance and his potential for greatness.

The decision to go fascist was made for a variety of reasons, some of them rational, others rooted in Mosley's temperament and out-look.   At the core of his rational justification was the notion of the ' crisis '.   The liberal economic system was doomed.   The exis-ting élites lacked the character and mentality to create a new system in time.   Therefore the system would collapse into desti-

*In his novel, *Public Faces*, published later in the year, Nicolson forecast a Chur-chill–Mosley Government in 1936 and a Mosley Government in the 1940s.

tution and disorder. This would give communism its historic opportunity. Communism was unacceptable, both philosophically, and because its inauguration would involve a large-scale destruction of the productive forces. Since the ' old gangs ' could not avert the situation from which communism would benefit, the challenge to communism would have to come from a new movement with an alternative faith and an alternative system capable of winning mass support. Such movements had already arisen on the Continent. It was necessary to organise a similar movement in England.

Although it was widely ridiculed at the time, the analysis which led up to this conclusion was far from negligible. What Mosley was attacking was the application of the parliamentary doctrine of evolution to the dynamic pace of modern life. The revolutionary changes which were needed would be enabled only by a crisis produced by the failure of existing men, ideas, and institutions. If we apply this analysis to the question of how, in fact, the Keynesian Revolution came about, we can see that Mosley was not altogether wrong. For the economic ' revolution by reason ' which Mosley had campaigned for in the 1920s was not to be achieved by ordinary political evolution. It took another world war to ' dynamite ' some at least of the nonsense out of the heads of the politicians. In this sense, Mosley's more sombre view of the conditions of change compares favourably with the facile optimism of the ' inevitability of gradualness ' school.

However, the fact that war, fascism and communism have all, in their different ways, been powerful agents of modernisation does not imply that they are the only possible ones, or that politicians should necessarily embrace them as alternatives to less extreme courses. For outcomes to a large extent depend on the responses of men. The argument that the existing political order is bound to fail becomes a self-fulfilling prophecy if all the outstanding men forsake it, leaving the duffers in charge. This is not to say that all political systems can be made equally effective or deserve to be preserved. Some may be so impervious to change, so corrupt and oppressive, that revolution is the only rational (and moral) response. The question is whether this was true of the British political system in the 1930s.

Those who felt Mosley was taking the wrong turning could (and no doubt did) advance three powerful practical arguments which lose nothing in retrospect. The first was that the British political system was not nearly so impervious to change as Mosley made out. There were groups in all parties clamouring for a British ' New Deal '. By rejecting Parliament, Mosley was surrendering his existing political base and cutting himself off from his natural political and intellectual allies; in short, losing the opportunity to mobilise that 'national opposition' to *laissez-faire* which Lloyd George had talked about in 1931. The second argument was that the prestige of British political institutions was so much higher than that of the fragile Continental parliamentary régimes that simplistic comparisons with 'new movements' elsewhere were well beside the point. At the very least, the degree of crisis would have to be much greater in Britain to produce a political collapse comparable to those in Italy or Germany. The third argument was that even if crisis came it might easily not be the kind of crisis from which a 'fascist' Mosley could benefit. (The war proved this to be the case). To emphasise the strength of these considerations is not to argue that there was no royal road to the realisation of Mosley's aims within the political system of the 1930s. Complacency, inertia, stupidity were rampant. Nevertheless, the rapidity and relief with which Mosley gave up the struggle to influence events from inside suggest that his alienation from the normal political process ran much deeper than the 'rational' argument for fascism would indicate. It is one thing for a politician to abandon normal politics when society is visibly collapsing. To do so when substantial possibilities of reform still remain suggests that what is being rejected is the whole conception of social life on which the political system rests. And this was clearly so with Mosley.

Mosley's alienation from parliamentary politics was rooted in his disgust with contemporary social values. At heart he was not preparing for catastrophe, but rebelling against a diseased normality. He came close to admitting this in an article he contributed to the *Political Quarterly* of January-March 1932 when he envisaged a 'slow and imperceptible decline, until in the course of a generation or two, Britain has degenerated into the position of a Spain. . .'. What attraction could conventional politics under those circumstances have for 'spirits which are dynamic'? Despite his conventional successes, the bonds holding Mosley to ordinary politics had always been fragile. They might have been strengthened had he been given a real job of work to do. When that failed to materialise, they snapped. Strachey's remark about a 'reversion to type' gives an important clue to what then happened, though not quite in the sense that Strachey meant. Mosley was a product of his landed background and his war experiences. Both combined in revolt against the flabbiness of politics and the sham values of bourgeois life. This was the psychological dynamic of his fascism, not his rational economic policy or even his 'rational' argument about the inevitability of collapse. The 'crisis' was not a prediction but a 'necessary myth' to justify a movement of 'renaissance'. Rational calculations of success or failure were basically irrelevant to the mood in which Mosley embarked on his new adventure. No doubt he was heavily influenced by the rapid growth of the

' new movement ' elsewhere, and no doubt he felt he was living in an age of violent convulsions rather than smooth transitions. But these considerations would never have weighed so powerfully with him had he not felt such a violent hostility to the old world. Such nausea would normally lead, and clearly in countless cases has led, to a withdrawal into private life, private pleasures. But the nature of the times, the intellectual and emotional capital Mosley had already invested in politics, and his continuing conception of himself as fighting for the ideals of the war generation all combined to suggest a different solution. He and those who felt and had experienced as he had done would re-create that alternative society previously incarnated in the trenches and use that as a base for the political conquest of England. If the Gods smiled, they would succeed. If they failed, they would at least go down fighting like men for the things they believed in. Above all, they would no longer have to *pretend*.

If the vision of Phoenix rising from the ashes was truly life-enhancing, the task of giving it a political form proved unedifying. In his search for new allies Mosley entered the world of fringe politics for the first time. There were two fascist groups already in existence. The first was the British Fascists, jocularly known as the ' B.F.s ' by Mosley's Birmingham friends in the 1920s. Started in 1923 by Miss Rotha Lintorn-Orman, ' a forthright spinster of thirty-seven with a taste for mannish clothes ',[13] it was an extreme right-wing group with a disproportionate number of generals and admirals, and dedicated to unrelenting struggle against the powers of evil represented by bolshevism. It had achieved a certain notoriety in the mid-1920s, but by the end of the decade was in full decline, and what remained of its active membership was mostly eager to join Mosley. The motion for a link-up with NUPA was in fact defeated by the ' Fascist Grand Council ', but most of the members, headed by Neil Francis-Hawkins, went over to Mosley anyway, leaving as Mosley contemptuously put it ' three old ladies and a couple of office boys '. The Imperial Fascist League had been founded by a retired veterinary surgeon and specialist in camel diseases, Arnold Spencer Leese, in 1928. ' One of those crank little societies . . . mad about the Jews,' Mosley not unfairly dubbed it. Yet he chaired a meeting of 27 April 1932 when Leese and his lieutenant Beamish spoke to NUPA on ' The Blindness of British Politics under the Jew Money-Power '. For his part Leese refused all co-operation with Mosley, believing him to be in the pay of the Jews. This rejection of his overtures did not discourage Mosley too much. The ' Fascist Legions ', as Leese's followers called themselves, numbered about three dozen members.

The New Movement already had a policy: the big question was what it should call itself. ' New Party ' was no good. As Nicolson had pointed out, 'it is no longer new and no longer a party'. What remained was fascist. Mosley was quite explicitly setting out to lead the British equivalent of the fascist movements in Italy and Germany. Should the British movement therefore be called fascist as well? Forgan and Allen strongly advised against, arguing that nothing 'foreign' would ever succeed in Britain. The NUPA militants urged him to adopt the name as well as the idea. Mosley hesitated, but in the end decided to call his movement the British Union of Fascists, 'union' standing for that rallying together of the best elements in the British nation which had always been his dream, 'fascist' for the creed that would animate them. For its emblem he adopted the *fasces* carried by the lictors of ancient Rome, the bundle of sticks symbolising unity, the axe the power of the State.*

Mosley's decision to call himself a fascist has often been criticised. He would have encountered less opposition and got more support, people say, had he called his movement something else. This is doubtful. It was the style, not the name, that identified the beast. But it is symptomatic of Mosley's hostility to the old world that the name was intended to repel as much as to attract: to repel the kind of fair-weather friends who had thronged the New Party; to attract the true representatives of the 'new age'. The barrier of name would be crossed only by the dedicated; and on their dedication the movement would be built.

Much the same reasoning lay behind the decision to allow, and indeed encourage, a uniform – initially a simple black shirt, modelled on a fencing-jacket. The black shirt was to be the symbol of fascism, 'the outward and visible sign of an inward and spiritual grace' as Mosley put it. To nail one's colours to the mast was to take a risk; and Mosley wanted men and women who were prepared to risk something for their faith. The appeal of uniform to youth was also a factor. In opting for a uniform Mosley was adopting the tradition of a more colourful and passionate period of British politics even then not entirely dead (Maxton's followers wore red shirts; Major Douglas's green shirts) and which he deemed appropriate to a period in which, as he wrote, 'form and expression become continually more emphatic.'

The uniform was also a means of discipline, and Mosley wanted a movement that would pull in one direction. But he had two particular motives for wanting a disciplined force. The first was to steward his meetings against interrupters. The uniform enabled his stewards to recognise each other in a *mêlée*. In addition, the uniform was a symbol of authority, and as such his uniformed squads would not only be a rallying-point, but also a striking-force in any battle that might develop with the communists for the control of

*The *fasces* were abandoned in 1936, the new emblem being a flash of lightning in a circle: action in unity.

the State. It was this last motive that led many to allege that Mosley was seeking to parallel state powers. This fantasy of civil war, of course, was shared by Strachey: it was when he and Mosley saw themselves on opposite sides of the barricades that they parted company.

The third reason for the black shirt was to break down class barriers. ' To us it is a very real and vital reason,' Mosley wrote. ' In the Blackshirt all men are the same, whether millionaire or on the dole. The barriers of class distinction and social differences are broken down by the Blackshirt within a Movement which aims at the creation of a classless brotherhood marked only by functional differences.' It is interesting that Mosley also refers to his family's Rolleston estate as a ' classless society '.

May and June saw him at work on his book, *The Greater Britain*, his exposition of the policy and philosophy of the new movement. The British Union of Fascists was formally launched on 1 October 1932. Thirty-two founder-members attended the inaugural ceremony in Great George Street. To them Mosley said, ' We ask those who join us to march with us in a great and hazardous adventure. We ask them to be prepared to sacrifice all, but to do so for no small and unworthy ends. We ask them to dedicate their lives to building in this country a movement of the modern age. . . . Those who march with us will certainly face abuse, misunderstanding, bitter animosity and possibly the ferocity of struggle and danger. In return we can only offer them the deep belief that they are fighting that a great land may live. . . . '[14]

Had Mosley yet grasped the full implication of all those decisions – of cutting himself off from the Establishment, of seeking out those who had nothing to lose and everything to gain, of adopting a name, a style and a livery that he knew to be particularly abhorrent to a section of his fellow-countrymen – with all the opposition and violence that this was bound to mean? Few of his friends at the time were prepared to believe that he had, or that fascism was to be anything more than a passing folly, a gesture of defiance, like many another. He had left the Lloyd George coalition after two years; the Labour Party after seven. The New Party had lasted just over one; there had been a spell as an Independent. Each career had been embarked upon with the same enthusiasm, the same dedication, the same fine words. To many who refused to see the thread running through Mosley's life – the unceasing quest for that perennially elusive land fit for heroes to live in – his career seemed nothing but a series of adventures, the escapades of a rich, spoilt young man with too much money and far too high an opinion of himself. Fascism was just the latest ' trendy ' thing, soon to be dropped like all the others.

Nor were the pundits being entirely unreasonable in prophesying a brief career for Mosley as a fascist leader. Intellectually he might accept the need for fascism; emotionally he was on the rebound from the bitter disappointments of 1930–1; nothing in 1932 suggested he was psychologically prepared for a long, hard, unyielding struggle. Indeed, in reaction against socialism and the tensions of the previous years, he had started to indulge to the full his taste for the gay life, and the playboy once more seemed to overshadow the politician. His Continental journey to study 'the modern movement' in January 1932 was typical. In Paris, Nicolson visited him at his hotel in the late morning. 'He is still in blue pyjamas having only just arisen from sleep. He had spent *réveillon* at the Fabre-Luces and had been kept up doing the *jeux de société* till 8 a.m. He looks pale.' May found him and Cimmie at the magnificent Villa d'Este in Como; August and September were spent on the Venice Lido. Nor was life in London devoted to unremitting political toil. Strachey and Young had complained that it was impossible to get Mosley to transact important New Party business because he was so busy fencing. To have returned with a gammy leg from a twenty-year lay-off to become runner-up in the British épée championship in 1932 was a formidable achievement. It also took up a formidable amount of time. Throughout 1932 he was fencing all over England. Fencing was not the only sport that claimed him. Early in 1932 he became a fan of the new craze of all-in wrestling, and a snap at this time shows him, in the somewhat incongruous company of Lady Margot Asquith, intently watching one Norman the Butcher performing at David Tennant's Gargoyle Club.

The Mosleys, separately or together, once more became good copy for the gossip columnists: Sir Oswald and Lady Mosley at a private view of modern French paintings at the Curtis Moffat gallery; Sir Oswald and Lady Mosley at the première of *Frankenstein* at the Tivoli; Cimmie 'well on the gold standard in a glittering sequin coat' at a ball given by Princess Arthur of Connaught. There were escapades of a less reputable kind. 'Tom really ought not to go to the parties given by Valentine,' Beaverbrook told Nicolson early in February.* The egregious Chips Channon also appeared in his circle in this period. He was frequently seen in the company of the Marquise de Causa Maury, an ex-mannequin over whose beauty London society swooned. Another beautiful companion was Diana Guinness, wife of the Hon. Bryan Guinness. The Guinnesses were guests at the Mosleys' 1932 New Year's Eve party, together with Brendan Bracken, the Sacheverell Sitwells and Major 'Fruity' Metcalfe and his wife Alexandra, Cimmie's younger sister, subsequently nicknamed Ba-Ba Blackshirt. Éclairs were hur-

---

* 'Valentine' was Lord Castlerosse, a well-known *bon viveur*.

led round, and according to the *Tatler* ' one fair lady caught one in the eye ', which led the *Daily Worker* to remark humourlessly that the ' above picture of Fascists at play should remove once and for all any lingering doubt as to the superman nature of Mosleyini self-cast for the role of future dictator of Britain '.[15] The *Worker* might have reflected that the above picture of Mosley at play suggested rather that he would go on playing for a great deal longer.

Nor was it possible in the early days to take fascism entirely seriously as a revolutionary force. Indeed, the opening fascist rally at Trafalgar Square on 15 October had a positively festive air about it: Cimmie turned up with the children, Brendan Bracken and Randolph Churchill looked in. Nor was there much hint in the coming months of political or social ostracism. Cimmie resumed her luncheon parties for the famous and well-born at Smith Square; Mosley found no shortage of reputable platforms. On 13 October he was guest at the annual dinner of the Manchester Sales Managers Association, speaking before the lord mayor and local M.P.s. On 10 November he spoke on the principles of fascism at a Foyles literary luncheon, subjecting the lady novelists, in the *Daily Herald*'s words, to a ' Duce-like look of determination '; two days later he shared the toast-making with the former Australian prime minister, Stanley Bruce, and the writer E. F. Benson, at the annual dinner of the Institute of Journalism. He accepted an invitation to address the Anglo-Palestine Club; he won 218 votes against Attlee at the Cambridge Union on 21 February 1933 (' probably the finest debating speech that the Union has been privileged to hear,' declared *Granta*, the undergraduate magazine); and on 16 March 1933 he debated fascism with Megan Lloyd George on the B.B.C.

The highlight of this phase of respectable fascism was the encounter between Mosley and Jimmy Maxton under the benign chairmanship of Lloyd George at the Friends' Meeting House, Euston Road, on 24 February 1933. ' All Mayfair turned out to watch,' wrote Irene Ravensdale.[16] Lloyd George congratulated Mosley later on ' that brilliant debate which I was privileged to hear. It was to me an unflagging treat; the swordsmanship was superb.'[17]

Nor was the black shirt at all prominent in the early months of fascism. It was publicly worn only by stewards at fascist meetings – and at first there were few such meetings. Mosley himself appeared in a grey shirt and amber tie (New Party colours) under an ordinary suit. By the spring of 1933 he was starting to wear a black shirt with his suit. In an article headed ' Savile Row Fascism ' the *Evening Standard* of 17 April 1933 called Mosley ' one of the best dressed men and the worst dressed Fascist in the world. Pictures from Rome show Sir Oswald's blackshirt incongruously swathed in a double-breasted waistcoat. The beautiful cut of his coat is ill-attuned to the violence of the Fascist salute. And I do not wonder that the Italians who welcomed him to Rome averted their eyes from Sir Oswald's trousers, which were in elegant but startling contrast to their own breeches and leggings.' If this sort of fascism could bring an ovation from the lady novelists at Foÿles, there was certainly nothing in it to put Mosley beyond the pale of the English Establishment.

Mosley still kept up his private contacts with parliamentary politicians. There survives a letter dated 5 March 1933 from Cimmie to Franklin Roosevelt, just after his inauguration.

Dear Mr. President,

We were staying with Lloyd George last night at his place in the country. It was an extraordinary party consisting of us 2, Ll.G & his son, the Soviet Ambassador and his wife, Oliver Baldwin (Stanley's son), a Labour and a Tory MP. We all listened in to your speech which came over the wireless magnificently and completely bowled us all over–Ll.G. was terrifically excited about it and said it was the *most remarkable* utterance by a man in your position (*not* on the eve of an election but on taking up his job *after* the Election) that he had heard. We were also tremendously thrilled.

It seemed to me it might just interest you to hear of the universal effect you created among our small but very varied group.

All the good wishes in the world and God speed you in your colossal task.

Affectionately,
CYNTHIA MOSLEY

Three months before Roosevelt had written to Cimmie to acknowledge her congratulations on his election:

12 December 1932

Dear Lady Cynthia,

If answering your letter is a nuisance, I hope I may often be 'bothered' in this way!

I was happy to have your good wishes and appreciate the confidence which you and that fine husband of yours have in me. You may be sure that I recognise both the great opportunities and the grave responsibilities of the days that lie ahead. However, there will still be occasional chances for fishing and I hope we may have a repetition of that jolly trip some time soon.

Mrs. Roosevelt and my mother join me in warmest personal regards to you both.

Yours very sincerely
FRANKLIN ROOSEVELT

Cimmie's health had been causing concern ever since 1929, when just after the election she had suffered a miscarriage. In 1931 Mosley had been the more seriously ill, but Cimmie was undoubtedly worn down by the strain of carrying on the New Party, the bickering with Strachey and old associates and her own inner doubts about the wisdom of her husband's actions. She became pregnant once again at the end of July 1931. It was apparent that it would be a difficult confinement, and from September she spent much of her time in bed, with the unfortunate exception of the Stoke interlude. There is a gloomy entry in Nicolson's diary for 13 January 1932: ' Cimmie comes to see me. She has not been v. well. She faints. She even faints in bed. She talks about Tom and Fascismo. She really does care for the working-classes and loathes all forms of reaction.' And on 8 March 1932: ' Cimmie has been v. ill. She has kidney trouble and they want to do a caesarean operation. Unfortunately the child is too young to survive and Cimmie wants to hang on for a fortnight. Tom is faced with the awful dilemma of sacrificing his baby or his wife.' Fortunately this crisis was surmounted, and on 25 April 1932 Cimmie gave birth to her third child and second son Michael. Harold Nicolson and Robert Forgan were godparents. The long convalescence took place at Como.

Thereafter Cimmie's health recovered. She opened up Smith Square again; she was even reconciled to fascism sufficiently to search for designs for a fascist flag* and to accompany Mosley to Rome in April 1933, where he made a spectacular appearance with Mussolini on the balcony of the Palazzo Venezia, and they both took the fascist salute in a light drizzle at a huge parade – one of the very rare occasions when she publicly showed any sympathy with fascism. ' My tragic sister, on returning, expressed the hope that the man she worshipped and adored had finally pegged his creed to a pattern that he could serve without any more deflections,' wrote Irene Ravensdale.

Back in London, Cimmie fell ill once more with appendicitis. She was rushed to the London Clinic and operated on. The operation was successful. She and Mosley laughed and joked, and talked of their plans for the future. Two days later, on 16 May 1933, she was dead. Peritonitis had set in. There was nothing the doctors could do. Her sister Irene wrote: ' So passed a woman of supreme courage, who was the model of a noble political figure, and stood always by the man she loved. She never failed him in her loyalties, and people of all sorts and kinds to this day remember her warmth, her goodness, her lovely face, and her gallant heart.

*Mosley wanted to make a Sousa march into a fascist anthem, with words by Osbert Sitwell! (Lady Ravensdale, *In Many Rhythms* (1953) p. 141.)

Perhaps God in his great wisdom preserved her from greater suffering in the years ahead.'

Mosley was completely shattered by Cimmie's death, not least because of its unexpectedness; shattered and filled with remorse, at the pain inflicted, and the things left unsaid. His response was to hurl himself furiously into his movement. Henceforth he would live only for his faith. ' He now regards his movement as a memorial to Cimmie and is prepared willingly to die for it.'[18] Mosley's mother emerged from retirement to take up fascist work. To reporters she said, ' When my son married Lady Cynthia, she took her place by his side. Now she is dead there must be someone to help him in his work, and I am doing my best to fill the gap.'

If the movement was to be Cimmie's spiritual memorial, Mosley and others planned memorials of a more solid kind. For almost a year Cimmie lay in the chapel at Cliveden while a pink sarcophagus set in a sunken garden to designs by Sir Edwin Lutyens was prepared to receive her at Denham. Meanwhile an appeal for a Cynthia Mosley Memorial Fund to build a children's nursery in the poorest part of Westminster went out over the signatures of Ramsay MacDonald, Stanley Baldwin, George Lansbury and Lloyd George. Robert Boothby and Brendan Bracken were the joint treasurers. It was built and stands today in Lambeth.

Cimmie's body was transferred to Denham in May 1934, where the dedication service was conducted by the Reverend Dick Sheppard. Etched into the marble was the simple inscription: ' Cynthia Mosley 1899–1933.' Beneath it were the two words:

MY BELOVED

Chapter 15

The Return of the Demons

FASCISM WAS an extraordinary explosion whose reverberations are felt to this day and will go on being felt in the years to come. It is already possible to write about it without the heavy additions of what Eric Bentley calls 'ritual exorcism' which disfigured the work of earlier scholars. Eventually someone, remote from the sectarian passions of the inter-war years, will essay the task of relating it properly to the great forces which have moulded the modern world, and of integrating it into the mainstream of European civilisation whose product it was.

This is not a chapter about fascism in general. It is about Mosley's fascism. Nevertheless we must try to set it in the context of the wider fascist movement where it belongs.

To the historian fascism is Janus-faced. One face looks forward, in the spirit of the Enlightenment, to the rational control and direction of human life; the other face looks backwards to a much simpler, more primitive, life when man struggled to live and express himself against the incalculable buffets of fate. The two dynamics appear quite incompatible: the one grounded in objective processes and objective tasks; the other springing out of the horror of a contemporary atavism (the First World War) and consuming itself (and almost consuming mankind) in its purposeless striving.

It is idle to deny that this tension existed in fascism. In fact it constituted its basic contradiction. It is the existence of this contradiction which makes it such a difficult and, at the same time, such a fascinatingly modern, phenomenon. For this is the contradiction that lies at the heart of modern life. George Orwell summed it up in the 1930s:

> The truth is that many of the qualities we admire in human beings can only function in opposition to some kind of disaster, pain or difficulty; but the tendency of mechanical progress is to eliminate disaster, pain and difficulty. . . . In tying yourself to the ideal of mechanical efficiency, you tie yourself to the ideal of softness. But softness is repulsive; and thus all progress is seen to be a frantic struggle towards an objective which you hope and pray will never be reached.[1]

Fascism arose from the confrontation and attempted fusion of the two impulses – the quest for modernization and the revolt against its consequences – at a particular moment in time when alone that

synthesis could have been attempted. The objective disasters of
war and economic collapse had once more brought the problem of
economic and political organisation to the forefront of politics.
The historic parties of the left, however, could not solve it. The
dynamic proletariat of marxist imagery was no longer dynamic, if
indeed it ever had been. Hence the social dynamic needed to
tackle the economic problem had to come from the largely middle-
class revolt against modern life itself, a revolt which had not yet
run itself dry in the sands of privatism or escapism. In this attempt
it could draw upon a certain equivalence between the objective
and subjective needs which had not existed before and which was
not to reappear after the Second World War. For the construction
of the new economic civilisation in the conditions of twentieth
century collapse seemed to require the very values which had been
declared obsolete by the economic progress of the previous hundred
years. The subjective, patriotic, yearning for a distinctive national
community received its objective justification in the programme of
economic nationalism or autarchy. The anti-bourgeois, anti-ratio-
nal, ' heroic ' psychology elaborated by the nineteenth-century critics of liberal civilisation seemed appropriate to the epoch of struggle
that had replaced the ' automatic progress ' of the nineteenth
century.

What, then, can one say about Mosley's relationship to the fascist
explosion? He himself emphasises that fascism took ' an entirely
different form in different countries '.[2] For reasons which will later
become apparent, Mosley deliberately underplays the affinity between the various national fascisms. Without it, as Nolte notes,
' Hitler would not have found convinced and fanatical collaborators all over Europe, from Quisling to Mussert, from Szalasi to
Doriot '.[3] Nevertheless, it is perfectly true that fascism was highly
modified by national traditions and circumstances.

The most damaging charge levelled against the B.U.F. was that it
was ' un-English '. Its reply was to represent itself as the heir to all
that was finest in the ' true ' English tradition. Strangely enough
it did not search for its own immediate antecedents in the late
nineteenth century. It has been left to a modern historian, Bernard Semmel, to make the obvious point that ' British fascist doctrine was firmly rooted in [the] home soil ' of Joseph Chamberlain's
social imperialism, in the national socialism of Robert Blatchford's
Merrie England, in Karl Pearson's Social Darwinism.[4] For fascists
this, the newest branch of their family tree, was largely unknown.
There were a few tributes to Keir Hardie and the late nineteenth
century socialist pioneers; but the pre-war figure who really fired
the fascist imagination was not Joseph Chamberlain* but Lord

*As Semmel perceptively suggests, Mosley's ' struggles with the Chamberlain
family in Birmingham were perhaps too recent for him to do anything but de-

Carson. 'In bearing, will, act and thought, Carson was a Fascist'; his Ulster Volunteer Movement, not just a precursor of fascism, but 'the first real and tangible resistance that Liberal Plutocracy had to encounter in Britain'.[5]

For their true British antecedents, fascists went back to the Tudor state. This identification first appeared in W. E. D. Allen's book, *B.U.F., Mosley and British Fascism* (1934). By the time Mosley came to write his *The Alternative* (1947) it was firmly established. The Elizabethans were 'the first to recognise the responsibility of the State towards the poor'; their spirit was 'almost Greek in its hard Hellenic gaiety and passionate admiration of the great and vital qualities in nature and in men'. The Tudor age was the dawn. The tragedy, according to Mosley, was the absence of the high noon, except for one ray in the eighteenth century when, under Chatham, 'the gay, but purposeful stride of the Elizabethan was felt upon the earth in the winning of the British Empire'. 'What cut across the further developing of that extraordinary burgeoning of the English genius? What inhibited the full efflorescence?' Mosley had no doubt about the answer – 'Puritanism – that cold dark sickness of the mind and soul. Puritanism bent, twisted and deformed for generations, the gay, vigorous and manly spirit of the English. Puritanism turned even the Empire, which their invincible energy and courage had won, from what might have been a Parthenon of human achievement and constructive beauty into a counting house concealed in a monastery.'[6]

From the early seventeenth century to the First World War, with the single exception of Chatham's age, the vista was black with only a few centres of resistance to the deepening infection. The landed gentry was one, fortified 'by their great addiction to hard and dangerous sports', but in the end even the land, with Lord Shaftesbury dissenting, sold out to the counting-house. Fascists were particularly interested in the early nineteenth century rebels, seeing a parallel between the post-Napoleonic age and their own. Bill Risdon, who had joined Mosley in the I.L.P., saw him as the heir to Robert Owen. According to the B.U.F.'s agricultural expert Jorian Jenks, in Mosley 'another Cobbett has come to life, but one with twice Cobbett's intellect and none of Cobbett's bigotry'.[7] E. D. Hart was attracted by Charles Western, the architect of the Corn Laws, and Thomas Attwood, the Birmingham banker and currency reformer.[8] According to William Joyce Thomas Carlyle was 'the first National Socialist'.[9] From the standpoint of precursors, then,

nounce Conservative protection' – despite the presence in the B.U.F. of the old Coefficient Carlyon Bellairs, and the sympathy of other old Chamberlainites like Ralph B. Blumenfeld, former editor of the *Daily Express*. In the same way, Mosley never tried to get together with Lord Beaverbrook, who was running a rival 'empire crusade'.

fascists found modern England distinctly barren and it is hardly surprising that many of them were drawn to the rather more heavily populated Continental terrain. Here was the root of that conflict of loyalties that ran right through the B.U.F. in the 1930s and which was only resolved after the Second World War when Mosley announced his new creed of Europeanism.

In one important respect, though – and this is the one which immediately concerns us – Mosley's fascism was distinctively English. It is a paradox, but not perhaps a surprising one, that out of the heart of economic liberalism should have come its most sustained and brilliant critique: that body of economic doctrine associated with the name of Keynes. Mosley was a disciple of Keynes in the 1920s; and Keynesianism was his great contribution to fascism. It was Keynesianism which in the last resort made Mosley's fascism distinctively English, though it was not an Englishness which most English pundits were then prepared to recognise, being as remote from the Keynesian thinking as they were from the problems which gave birth to it.

In terms of economic understanding, the programme expounded by Mosley in *Greater Britain* was far in advance of anything produced by Continental fascism. In both Germany and Italy state control over the economy derived not from an economic, but from a political logic, and was geared not to managing demand but to preparing for war.[10] By contrast, Mosley's demand for a strong state was largely (though not completely) built on his economic proposals.

Analysts of the economic crisis fell into two schools – those who were fundamentally critical of the system of *laissez-faire* capitalism and those who supported it. Analysts of the second school did not believe there could be such a thing as mass unemployment caused by a lack of effective demand, since according to Say's Law of Markets an economy always provides demand sufficient to buy its own output, provided it is not interfered with. The *fact* of mass unemployment was explained by these theorists in terms of interferences by government and unions with the laws of the market. Provided workers were prepared to accept a lower wage, it would once more become profitable for manufacturers to expand production and thus restore the system to full employment.

Mosley, as we have seen, never accepted this view. He saw clearly enough that cuts in wages destroyed the market which manufacturers had to rely upon to sell their goods. A single firm might solve its problems by reducing its wages bill. But the aggregate wages bill was the purchasing-power of the community. If it were reduced the demand of the whole community for the goods and services of industry would fall. Indeed, the trouble in Britain was that it was already too low: hence the problem of idle capacity and unemployment that had persisted ever since 1920.

Mosley therefore was identified with those who regarded the poverty of the workers as the real cause of capitalist crisis. The first question, then, is why, having decided to break from orthodox politics, he did not join the revolutionary left. The decision to go fascist, rather than communist, was fateful, for it proved far easier for ex-communists than for ex-fascists to reintegrate themselves into political life later on. The issues between Mosley and marxism were serious. They also help to elucidate what Mosley meant by his fascism. Three areas of conflict may be identified.

First, Mosley rejected the marxist doctrine that individual and social actions are determined by material conditions. To read the writings of Strachey and Palme Dutt in the 1930s is to be presented with a picture of a capitalist society riddled with insoluble contradictions, lurching towards a bloody demise. Every mechanistic strain in marxist thought is heavily emphasised in order to show the impossibility of improvement within the capitalist system. Twist and turn as they may, capitalist statesmen, economists and businessmen are doomed by inexorable economic laws. Now for Mosley the iron laws of marxism were no more palatable than the economic laws of liberalism. He had not left the Labour Party, which said that nothing could be done till capitalism recovered, to join a party which said that nothing could be done till capitalism collapsed. He believed that the private-enterprise system could be made to work properly provided the men in charge of government were determined to make it work. The First World War had proved this.

Secondly, Mosley never accepted the moral basis of marxism which underpinned its economic analysis. The radical argument that 'property is theft' was extended by Marxists from landed to industrial property. Mosley's argument that property can be justified by duty was rooted in the landed tradition which he extended to industrial ownership. The marxist view, grounded in a burning sense of injustice, led to the egalitarian society. Mosley's, grounded in a burning sense of inefficiency, led to the functional society, one in which each group performed its proper duty. This view was perfectly compatible with meritocracy; indeed Mosley's own thought demanded it. It was not compatible with an egalitarian system.

Thirdly, Mosley had the technician's horror of needless destruction. Early in 1931 he had rejected the 'mad Communist faith in revolution following economic collapse' aiming to 'wade cheerfully to its objective of the Soviet state through the blood and starvation of a disintegrated society.'[11] Strachey had used the same argument in supporting Mosley's original *Revolution by Reason*: '[the Soviets] knew of no way of acquiring economic power except by revolution and the destruction of the entire fabric of the life of the community. (And this of course led to almost irreparable damage to its wealth-producing resources.)'[12] Both Lenin and Bukharin acknowledged that the 'victory of the workers' would entail 'an extremely steep decline in the productive forces'.[13] Such a solution to the economic problem deeply offended Mosley's constructive mind; he also regarded it, as we have seen, as completely unnecessary. Mosley was the mechanic who wanted to get the car moving again, not scrap it and replace it by a different model.

How, then, did Mosley think that the marxist laws could be circumvented within the private enterprise system? His basic answer was the changing nature of capitalism. From America he had taken away the fundamental idea that the overriding concern of large-scale industry is security, not profit maximisation. If a small firm is faced with a fall in demand it can lay off workers. But a big firm cannot lay off machinery. Rationalisation had enlarged productive capacity, but it had also proportionately increased the cost of not working at that capacity. ' The more effectively an industry is rationalised ', wrote Mosley, ' the smaller is the recession in demand needed to turn profit into loss, and the more rapidly does that loss become unmanageable. The more, therefore, that industry is rationalised, the greater is the need for a stable and established market. . . . '[14] The process of ' trustification', which to socialists meant the development of unfettered power to exploit workers and consumers on an increasing scale, Mosley saw as a system of market-sharing which removed the old economic need to keep wages low. It was a new feudalism with markets instead of land being parcelled out among the barons. What the new system required was not expropriation, but state direction of resources to their most socially useful employment and state control of the operations of the few ' robber barons '.

This was not only an important economic, but also an important sociological perception, for it established not just the desirability but also the *possibility* of a managed capitalism. This was the decisive break with marxism. Marxists said: Those who preach high-wage capitalism are either foolish or dishonest. Capitalists cannot live with such a system. This was the economic underpinning of the class war. Mosley replied: Not only can modern capitalists live with such a system; they cannot live without it! A buoyant market has become as essential to the big firm *in its individual capacity* as to the economy as a whole. In that fact lies the possibility of the State so managing demand as to introduce a high-wage economy with the support of capitalism, and also the possibility of bringing unions and employers together as joint directors of industry rather than as opponents in the class war. But *only* if a ' stable and established market ' could in fact be secured. How could this be done?

The first requirement was to eliminate low-wage competition from abroad. Mosley was by no means the first visiting English politician to have discovered that America combined a higher level of technology with a higher standard of life than any other country in the world. But he was the only English politician at the time to consider seriously the conditions under which American prosperity had been achieved and how far they could be reproduced in England. The key to American prosperity Mosley found to be the existence of ' so large and so assured a home market '.[15] The ' happy accidents ' of geography had given America virtual self-sufficiency in foodstuffs and raw materials. This meant that it hardly needed to trade with the rest of the world. High protective duties ' afforded comparative immunity from the competition of foreign low-paid labour '.[16] Stringent immigration laws ' created a shortage of labour in relation to demand, and afforded labour a strong bargaining position on the market '.[17] Thus an insulated American economic system was able to raise wages ' to heights dizzily above the subsistence level . . . in defiance of all Marxian laws '.

It was from this perspective of a successful capitalism that Mosley turned to the problems of an unsuccessful capitalism. In the nineteenth century, he argued, Britain had what amounted to the whole world as its market. Free trade was simply another name for British monopoly. Britain owned the means of production and could therefore extract ' unpaid labour ' from all the other countries. However unfair, free trade could be justified by the conditions of the time. With the growth of populations, progress out of this stage in the infancy of the industrial revolution required specialisation: ' any barrier to the thin trickle of international trade was obviously bad . . . [and] liable to result in distress and starvation in a world community whose resources barely satisfied the needs of life '.[18] In the 1930s, by contrast, the problem was one of plenty, which recognised that ' modern nations can produce any goods they require with present machinery. Variations in production costs between nations in modern conditions are negligible in an age of potential plenty.'[19]*

*Keynes made the same point, though more moderately, in his article ' National Self-Sufficiency ', New Statesman, 8 July 1933. ' But I am not persuaded that the economic advantages of the international division of labour to-day are at all comparable with what they were. . . . Over an increasingly wide range of industrial products, and perhaps of agricultural products also, I become doubtful whether the economic cost of national self-sufficiency is great enough to outweigh the other advantages of gradually bringing the producer and the consumer within the ambit of the same national, economic and financial organisation. Experience accumulates to prove that most modern mass-production processes can be performed in most countries and climates with almost equal efficiency.' This article produced a correspondence between Keynes and Mosley, in which

Thus science had turned full circle. It enabled the restoration of the largely self-sufficient economy of mercantilist times. Nor was this just a hypothesis. With the growing emphasis on security great nations were deliberately constructing autarchic systems. Former British markets had industrialised and were now increasingly producing for themselves the goods that Britain had formerly sent them. In the remaining markets (including the home market) Britain faced intensified competition from cheap, semi-mechanised labour (textiles) and from dumping. These processes had been greatly accelerated by the economic collapse as each major industrial nation strove to cut itself loose from what had become an ever more suicidal struggle. 'In such circumstances,' Mosley wrote, ' we ask the old parties a simple question ':

> How can any international system, whether capitalist or Socialist, advance or even maintain the standard of life of our people? . . . None can deny the truism that to sell we must find customers and, as foreign markets progressively close . . . the home customer becomes ever more the outlet of industry. But the home customer is simply the British people, on whose purchasing power our industry is ever more dependent. For the most part the purchasing power of the British people depends on the wages and salaries they are paid. . . . [Yet] wages and salaries of the British people are held down far below the level which modern science, and the potential of production, could justify because their labour is subject to . . . undercutting competition . . . on both foreign and home markets. . . . The result is the tragic paradox of poverty and unemployment amid potential plenty. . . . Internationalism, in fact, robs the British people of the power to buy the goods that the British people produce.[20]

Yet it was on the revival of the export trade that the Old Gangs pinned their hopes for creating that ' large and assured market ' which could alone absorb the product of the modern machine.

It was by this process of reasoning that Mosley reached his own solution of a self-contained economic system 'insulated' from low-wage competition. The unit was to be the empire. Why the empire? Because it was the most obvious unit of life for Mosley's ' Greater Britain ', the area carved out by its history and sustained by kinship and sentiment. Mosley hoped to arrange complementary trading arrangements with the White Dominions leading in time to a planned imperial economy; his military adviser, General Fuller, advocated an Imperial Council to plan and co-ordinate im-

---

Mosley wrote to him congratulating him on his ' fascist ' economics, and Keynes replied that he wrote as he did ' not to embrace you but to save the country from you '.

perial defence.[21]   Both saw economic and military arrangements
as a strategic whole.   India was to play a crucial role.   In the
late nineteenth century it had been the main market for British
textiles.   The key to Lancashire's recovery, therefore, was the exclusion of Japanese textiles from the Indian market and the suppression of India's own textile industry developed in the First World
War.   This in turn meant suppressing the Indian nationalist movement and holding India down by force.   This entailed a considerable reversal of Mosley's earlier attitude.   In 1925 Gandhi was
' one of the great world forces, not by the power of his considerable
intellect and personality, but because alone amongst statesmen he
appears to have conquered in himself the ordinary weaknesses of
humanity '; Pandit Nehru was the ' Parnell of Indian politics, whose
cold resolution of purpose blends effectively with the Celtic ardour
of the passionate Bengalee '.[22]   In fascist days such figures became
babbling ' babus ' in the grip of a ' few great interests [who] exploit the Indian masses '; to be kept under control by the strong
hand of British government.
Within the area secured, it would be the task of government
acting with employers and unions deliberately to plan incomes as
science increased the power to produce.   It may be asked why
Mosley attached such importance to planning, the socialist comple-
ment to autarchy. Having ' insulated ' the economy – the precondition as he saw it of an assured market – why was he not content to
let capitalism get on with it ? Mosley gives the reason in his interpretation of what went wrong in America between 1929–32:

> The ' philosophy of high wages ' succumbed to its first serious
> test.   It failed chiefly because it was never a philosophy, nor
> yet a conscious policy. . . . The credit which should have been
> used for industrial development and the financing of reason-
> able consumption was devoted to the uses of Wall Street. . . .
> The Federal Reserve Board . . . were able only to check credit
> expansion in *a quantitative rather than a qualitative manner*. . . . No
> machinery existed for discrimination between social and anti-
> social use of credit, only for a general policy of restriction.
> By restriction of credit, the genuine producer was hit long be-
> fore the Wall Street speculator, who summoned European
> short-term credits to his aid.
>   In an effort to check the frenzy of a few irresponsible indivi-
> duals, the whole great structure of American industry was
> shaken to foundations which did not rest on the reality of Cor-
> porate organisation.   Had private enterprise been acting in
> accordance with a reasoned national policy, the trouble might
> well have been avoided.   In the stress of internal competi-
> tion on a sagging market, and in the absence of any State

machinery for the maintenance . . . of wages, the high wages
and the hire-purchase system began to crumble. . . . Never
was more notable the absence of a coherent national plan . . .
to check forces inimical to the stability of the State, and to encourage the genuine forces of production and exchange in
which national welfare must rest.   America made a god of
unregulated anarchy in private enterprise.   This, she falsely
believed, was the only alternative to Socialism.   Both in
her success and in her failure, in her dizzy prosperity and
in her cataclysmic depression, there is an instructive lesson.
Throughout the boom she achieved, on a basis purely
temporary, what organised planning and Corporate institutions
can set on a permanent footing. The very energy of American
libertarianism is the best argument for Fascist institutions.[23]

Apart from the autarchic bias, which only hardened into dogma
after 1934, there was nothing in the economic analysis or programme
of *Greater Britain* to repel the ' men of goodwill '.   Had not Keynes
himself advocated going ' homespun '?   Harold Nicolson believed
that *Greater Britain* would ' impress all clear thinking people ' and
as we have seen advocated an educational campaign on the fringes
of the National Government.   To Walter Elliot it seemed to be
' courting failure to tell people that they have first to dress themselves in black shirts and throw their opponents downstairs in order
to get the corporate state. . . . This new economic order has already developed further in England than is generally recognised.'[24]
To the *Spectator* fascism was ' a canto of quotations from ideas put
forward by others '.   All its points had been met by Elliot's agricultural policy, Roosevelt's New Deal, Beaverbrook's Empire policy,
Sir Stafford Cripps' parliamentary proposals, Churchill's India
policy, etc.   But the real issue was ' whether the methods of Fascism are the only or the best way of realizing whatever is useful
in any or all of them. . . . If fists are to be used to cure . . . faults are
they better used thumping the Treasury-box . . . or the faces of
their opponents ?'[25]

Mosley's answer to this was that behind every ' fault ' there was
a vested interest.   As long as governments and parties failed to arm
themselves with the popular support to challenge the interests, so
long would the interests determine policy, despite all the enlightenment pouring out from thinkers, despite the actual needs of the
major producers.   The right idea had to have behind it the
force of popular passion before it could triumph.   Thus Mosley
laid down his programme of action.   ' The rebirth of a nation
comes from the people in a clear and ordered sequence.   The People, their Movement, their Government, their Power. To create their
Government . . . the people have first to create their Movement.'[26]

The chief vested interest which the new radical movement would have to challenge and overcome was not ' capitalism ' but the City of London. This was the force preventing the construction of a national economic system. The traditional business of the City was foreign lending. The only motive of foreign lending was to derive a higher rate of interest on investment than could be got at home. ' That interest ', Mosley wrote, ' can only be drawn annually from foreign nations in the shape of gold, services, or goods. As few of them have either gold or services to offer the annual interest on foreign loans is derived almost entirely from the import of foreign goods. Consequently the business of finance depends on foreign imports, because without such imports it cannot draw usury from abroad. Therefore, the interest of finance conflicts directly with the interest of the producer. . . . For it should further be noted that the entry of foreign goods representing interest on foreign loans is not balanced by any corresponding exports of British goods. They are tribute from one country to another in respect of a past transaction without any countervailing payment.'[27]

This is the key passage. In economic thought finance is simply the handmaiden of production and trade. For Mosley it was the master. The whole system of international trade is kept going in order to maintain the ' almost unlimited mobility of finance ' and to guarantee the profits of the City of London. At one time, he was prepared to concede, such a system may have served the interests of the producer in opening up markets. But under existing conditions its effect was destructive of the interests of home producer and worker alike (a) by preventing the substitution of home production for imports and (b) by exposing the British staples to competition from sweated labour equipped by finance to undercut British goods – especially textiles – in third markets. This was not the sole consequence. Finance vastly increased the system's tendency to instability. Speculation was life to the financier but death to the producer. The inherent instability of the system gave tremendous opportunities to the ' quick jumping financier ' to gamble in commodities, stock markets and exchanges – to gamble, in other words, with the prosperity of whole industries and nations.[28] And why was this allowed? 'Solely because the British Government and our economic system are debt collectors for the City of London.'[29] This meant that finance could 'break' any government whether it was the Labour government of 1931 or the Blum government in France simply by cracking the whip of a financial logic to which all parties in the state subscribed. In a graphic simile Mosley likened the ' giant rogues of international finance ' to the ' robber barons' of the Middle Ages whose power centralised monarchy and Parliament were developed to combat. Against the twentieth century robber-barons the people must organise 'collectively their own

police force to deal with the enemy and the exploiter '.[30]   This
police force was fascism.

Why was the existing political system unable to master the force
of predatory international finance?   Like many other radical reformers in the aftermath of 1931 Mosley diagnosed as a major cause
of the trouble the feebleness of parliamentary government.   At no
time was the orthodox view that party government was strong
government more widely challenged than in the 1930s.

> What is the historical function of Parliament in this country?
> It is to prevent the Government from governing.   It has never
> had any other purpose. . . . Bit by bit it broke the feudal Mo-
> narchy; it broke the Church; and finally it even broke the
> country gentleman.   Then, having broken everything that
> could govern the country, it left us at the mercy of our private
> commercial capitalists and landowners.   Since then we have
> been governed from outside Parliament, first by our own em-
> ployers, and of late by the financiers of all nations and races.

The words were Bernard Shaw's (1933), but the message was the
same as that preached by Mosley: the abdication by government
to the vested interests through the fear of entrusting to the people's
representatives the necessary power and knowledge to overcome
the predatory forces of capitalism.

Inevitably Mosley directed the question of why the existing
political parties were unable to master the force of predatory
finance at the Labour Party, the ' people's party ' formed for that
express purpose.   It was out of the answer Mosley gave to this
question that the argument for fascism developed.

Mosley tried to explain the problem of Labour's weakness in
face of its opponents on a number of levels.   Socialists were handi-
capped by obsolete ideas.   Gripped by the vision of the international Socialist Commonwealth – the legacy of their nineteenth century
past as well as of Britain's own unique free-trade tradition transposed into the language of idealism – they shrank from any hint of
national organisation that might hinder or hurt anyone else. ' Prate
of world brotherhood from the Socialist opens up the way to
world exploitation by the financier,' Mosley tartly observed.[31]

For the ' international system. . . relies on the financier to supply
credit for the international transit and sale of goods and capital. . . .
The supply of these facilities by the great finance houses makes
utterly dependent upon them . . . any Government which supports that system of trade.'[32]   Thus the Labour Party had been
reduced to seeking ' to secure benefits for the British working-class
by kind permission of international financiers, within an international system which makes these benefits impossible '.[33]   But it would
be wrong to suggest that Mosley saw these inadequate ideas as the

prime reason for Labour's failure. It was the will to act that was lacking; and the lack of a will to act was in the last resort a feature of character rather than ideas.

For Mosley, the politician was the archetypal Impostor. Parliamentarians he saw as talkers not doers. Even if they entered public life with a genuine urge to do something, this was rapidly drained away and reduced to charlatanry by the requirements of party politics and the corroding atmosphere of the House of Commons:

> Many a good revolutionary has arrived at Westminster roaring like a lion, only a few months later to be cooing as the tame dove of his opponent. The bar, the smoking room, the lobby, the dinner tables of his constituents' enemies, and the ' atmosphere of the best club in the country,' very quickly rob a people's champion of his vitality and fighting power. Revolutionary movements lose their revolutionary ardour as a result long before they ever reach power, and the warrior of the platform becomes the lap-dog of the lobbies.[34]

The manner of life of democratic politicians produced a type of man for whom action and decision have become impossible – a favourite theme: ' To divide life ', Mosley wrote in 1937,

> between the meaningless function such as the public banquet and the idle chatter of the House of Commons is no life for a man. What is worse, it entirely unfits man physically, mentally, and spiritually for any serious executive task. Mere talk for the sake of talk replaces the aptitude for decision and action. The life of undeviating purpose fortified by the habits of an athlete becomes impossible. In such an existence men must either eat or drink too much [and] . . . sit up too late and talk too much or labour beneath that damning indictment of modern Democracy that they are 'inhuman'. . . . In fact the system is devised to turn a man into a windbag in the shortest possible time. If the public desires to maintain the system they [sic] must pay the price in executive futility. . . . If they desire executive men to represent them in the modern world they must vote for a system in which executive men can function. In fact, if the people want a public leader they must cease to expect a statesman to be a private clown.[35]

But the decay of character was not just caused by the practices of an institution. It was grounded in the whole 'softness' of modern civilisation, which had rendered the hard, heroic character, forged and tested by the adversity of earlier times, obsolete. The aristocrat had given way to the financier; the warrior to the clerk; the creator to the intellectual; the doer to the talker. This was Mos-

ley's vision of decadence, powerfully influenced by Spengler's
The Decline of the West. According to Spengler, 'Faustian' civilisation was approaching its predetermined end: 'we cannot help
it if we are born as men of the early Winter of full civilisation instead
of on the golden summit of a ripe Culture'.[36]   The only possible
attitude was one of stoicism.

Mosley was no stoic.   Impressed as he was by Spengler's ' colossal
contribution', his whole spirit rebelled against his 'massive pessimism'.   That pessimism, Mosley suggested in a lecture in 1933,
'arises from his entire ignorance of modern science and mechani-
cal development . . . which for the first time places in the hands
of man the ability entirely to eliminate the poverty problem'.[37]
The only relevant question was whether or not 'in this epoch of
supreme scientific achievement, man is armed with the weapons,
and possesses the will, to challenge and to alter the very course
of mortal destiny'.[38]

Thus the task of regeneration was a double one: not just to inaugurate the new economic order which science made possible, but
to re-create the heroic psychology by which alone that task could
be achieved.   Hence the critical importance of the concept of the
'new man'.   This new man had already emerged in the First World
War, but Mosley specifically and insistently rejected war as an
instrument of renewal.   His moral equivalent to war was the fascist struggle.   The struggle was instrumental to the creation of
the new order.   The values of a vanished heroic age would be
utilised for the attempt to realise the heroic possibilities of the
present age.

The difference between fascism and the old parties was thus

> not a difference of method or points of policy, but a differ-
> ence of spirit.   And this difference of spirit expresses itself in a
> different type of man – Blackshirt man.   Fascism excluded
> the possibility of collaboration with any old party because the
> psychologies of the old parties are irreconcilable with revolu-
> tionary Fascism.   Fascism can only take members of the old
> parties and mould them into Blackshirts through the furnace
> of the struggle for power.   The making of Blackshirts and the
> making of the Fascist Movement is the preparation in embryo
> of the new Britons and of the new Britain.[39]

What was this 'new man' to be like?   For W. E. D. Allen he
was the aristocrat reborn.   Fascism was a reversion to a pre-
bourgeois morality:

> Out of the night of history old shadows are appearing which
> menace their [bourgeois] complacency. . . . Growing groups of
> unknown men out of the streets are laughing the unbeliever's

hollow laugh at all those things the democrat has taught the
people to hold dear.   Worst of all, a figure appears that they
had thought was gone for ever over the great scaffolds of the
Reformation.   Sir Herbert Samuel, a Liberal of singular pers-
picacity, believes that Europe is returning to the conditions
of the twelfth century.   Professor Laski wails against these
new men, who have ' no inhibitions '.   The oligarchs and
the democrats dread this classic figure more than anarchy –
for it is the figure of the Leader, the natural aristocrat, whom
they had thought long dead and buried in the obloquy of
whig history. . . . Now it comes out into the stark day – in the
grim serenity of Mussolini, in the harsh force of Hitler.   And
behind them stride the eternal *condottieri*. . . . These men move
the people – as no democrats can ever do – to rise up from the
dreary life of the machine.[40]

For Captain Gordon-Canning, a descendant of the great Cann-
ing, fascism expressed a ' certain barbaric splendour ', the ' warrior
spirit ' opposed to ' that of the night club '.[41]   E. D. Randall, the
B.U.F. song-writer, declared: ' Our belief has as its basis the reaffir-
mation of natural and normal things.   To this extent we are
reactionary: we react decisively against a demented and degrading
trend of thought – against mind run mad and intelligence gone
rotten.   To this extent we are atavistic and barbaric.   We accept
the validity of human and heroic values, the pride of tradition and
the voice of blood.'[42]   ' Foul City ', cried *Blackshirt* in echo of
Spengler, ' with its scheming and gambling and lending, prostrated
before the Golden Calf, led by criminals too respectable for gaol!
Pray heaven that the cleansing fire of Fascism shall soon destroy
this festering moral slum.'[43]

Mosley's personal ideal was Shavian rather than barbaric.   He
saw himself acting out in real life the central dramatic situation
of Shaw's plays: the vital man, with ideas and impulses, confronting the inert creature of ideology and habits.   His model was Caesar and he once described fascism as ' collective Caesarism '.   Mosley's
own view of Caesar and his great antagonist Brutus is captured
in this striking description of the nineteenth century literary critic
Georg Brandes:

Caesar was descended from Venus; in his form was grace.
His mind had the grand simplicity which is the mark of the
greatest; his nature was nobility.   He, from whom even today
all supreme power takes its name, had every attribute that
belongs to a commander and ruler of the highest rank. . . .
His life was a guarantee of all the progress that could be accomplished in those days.   Brutus's nature was doctrine, his dis-

tinguishing mark the narrowness that seeks to bring back dead conditions. . . . His style was dry and laborious. His vice was avarice, usury his delight. . . . And on account of a dagger-thrust, which accomplished nothing and hindered nothing of what it was meant to hinder, this arid brain has been made a sort of genius of liberty, merely because men have failed to understand what it means to have the strongest, richest and noblest nature invested with supreme power.[44]

Unlike Marx (or for that matter Mussolini or Hitler), Mosley described in some detail the structure of his fascist state of the future. Government was to be given the power to inaugurate the new economic system by an Enabling Act freeing it from detailed parliamentary obstruction. Parliament would still at this stage have the right to dismiss the government by vote of censure. This was the system to apply in fascism's first parliament. However, the permanent system would be different. In place of a parliament elected on a geographical basis, there would be a parliament elected on an occupational franchise – doctors would vote as doctors, miners as miners, farmers as farmers, etc.[45] Its functions would be purely advisory – to ' assist on the technical problems of a technical age '. On a separate franchise, the people would vote for or against the government of the day at least every five years.[46] If the government was defeated, the monarch would send for new ministers ' who in his opinion have a good chance of receiving the support of the country at a fresh vote ', thus restoring to him his traditional prerogative.[47] The House of Lords would become a second advisory chamber representing the ' proved ability and experience of the nation '. It would apparently have been the only political forum for the discussion of non-technical subjects such as foreign policy, religion, etc.[48] The Press would remain free, but subject to the ' revolutionary principle that it shall tell the truth '. This principle was to be enforced by the right of government to sue newspapers through the courts.[49]

The political proposals were clearly designed to give the government complete freedom from parliamentary control. At the same time, Mosley proposed to set up a parallel industrial structure which, in theory at least, was to be self-governing. This was the Corporate State. A National Council of Corporations would preside over corporations formed from the employers, trade unions and consumer interests of the various economic sectors. (These were an outgrowth of the New Party's Commodity and Import Boards.) Within the guide lines of a national plan, each corporation would work out its own policy for wages, prices, conditions of employment, investment and terms of competition. Government would intervene only to settle deadlocks between unions and employers. Strikes would be abolished.[50] The marxist critique is obvious. Mosley's state would enshrine the freedom of capitalists to exploit a working-class deprived of both its industrial and political weapons. Mosley's reply was that the inauguration of an economic system that made possible full employment and uninterrupted growth would remove the causes of class conflict. The traditional class configurations would dissolve into functional categories within a rational industrial system. Problems of profits, wages, conditions, etc., would become technical questions to be settled by experts in the light of national priorities drawn up by all the major interests in the state.

Like Marx, Mosley believed that the solution of the economic problem would mean the end of politics. The basic idea of his Utopia is not the one-party state, but the no-party state. ' In such a system ', he wrote, ' there is no place for parties and for politicians. We shall ask the people for a mandate to bring to an end the Party system and the Parties. We invite them to enter a new civilisation. Parties and the party game belong to the old civilisation, which has failed.'[51] The Fascist Party was simply the instrument for bringing about the new civilisation. The ' strange and disturbing ' men of fascism were the means ' by which the world shall pass to higher things '.[52] Once the new viable area was established, once the machinery had been set up for getting problems decently discussed and effectively tackled, then the technocrats could take over. Thus the ultimate paradox in Mosley's proposals was that only the victory of fascism would make fascism unnecessary. Mosley's state, too, would eventually ' wither away ' and the ' administration of things ' replace the government of men.

Yet it is doubtful whether this vision of the technical society would have satisfied fascism's contradictory cravings. Contrast W. J. Leaper's view of the fascist state as the ' statistically ruled State ' with the notion of fascism as ' an orgasm of the soul of modern man which will bring forth in the end a new life, strange and beautiful and strong '. The central problem remained: after the orgasm what? The statistical state? A depressing prospect! It was a dilemma which fascism never resolved.

Chapter 16

The Anatomy of a Movement*

WE REALLY know very little about British fascism. Certain aspects have been covered with varying degrees of accuracy and insight: its organisation, its anti-semitism, the violence to which it gave rise. However, we know next to nothing about its mass support. There has been only one regional study, for Yorkshire, undertaken by a group of enterprising sixth-formers.[1] There has been no study of the East London movement. There have been no investigations of the various occupational groups that were drawn to fascism: their trade journals, which contain a mass of information on their particular problems and how they saw the world, have remained unread. These gaps in the evidence make it very difficult to estimate the progress of fascism in its six years of peace-time existence. In a biography of its leader it is not possible to attempt anything more than an impressionistic survey, the details and conclusions of which may well have to be modified in the light of later research.

Mosley founded a movement, outlined a policy, and appealed for support. Since he was well known, he got a lot of publicity. Members enrolled at recruiting offices in all the major urban centres, paid their monthly subscription of a shilling (fourpence for the unemployed), and bought their black shirts. A big Mosley meeting would be organised as soon as possible, preceded by a parade through the main streets of the town. Who joined? There were university graduates and ex-public schoolboys; unemployed pugilists and unemployable professional men with useless classical educations. The 'serious' ranged all the way from ex-communists to crackpot and obsessional anti-semites. With the exception of the young of all classes, the early B.U.F. was heavily middle-class. Its following in the industrial areas was middle-class. It picked up support in London and the southern coastal towns. Its headquarters in Chelsea seemed to symbolise its place in the political spectrum: the *Morning Post* dubbed the blackshirts 'Boiled Shirts'. This is not perhaps what Mosley wanted. But it was what he got.

The most striking thing about active blackshirts was their youth. This remained true throughout the history of the movement. With

*Mosley's party started off as the British Union of Fascists. In 1936, its name was changed to the British Union of Fascists and National Socialists, or more shortly British Union.

the exception of old retired career-officers most of the fascist leaders (including, of course, Mosley) were in their twenties or thirties: the movement's two best orators after Mosley, William Joyce and 'Mick' Clarke, were twenty-nine and twenty-four respectively in 1935. This pattern was followed all the way down. Statements taken from B.U. officials imprisoned in 1940 show district leaders to have been typically in their late twenties or early thirties. Youth was characteristic of the later mass following, especially in East London.

It might be said that anything that is radical and exciting attracts the young; also that a new movement obviously gave more chance than older parties of promotion to young people. The uniform, too, was attractive to a certain type of youngster. But fascism's appeal to youth obviously went deeper. It claimed to stand for the new world against the old, for the future against the past. The division of politics between the pre-war and the post-war mind was central to Mosley's appeal. *Theirs* was the generation that had muddled the nation into war and depression; *theirs* was the world of mediocrity and respectability, of the pot-belly and the bowler hat. Arise and come into your own was Mosley's message to the youth of England and it evoked a response. One of the first reputable public-opinion polls organised by Dr Gallup in 1937 asked: ' If you had to choose between Fascism and Communism which would you choose?' Fifty-six per cent gave fascism and forty-four per cent gave communism. Seven out of ten respondents under thirty preferred fascism.[2]

Mosley's appeal to youth broke through class barriers from the start. However, among middle-and upper-class recruits certain types predominated. They were, typically, ex-soldiers, marginal professional men dissatisfied with what life had to offer, and sportsmen. These, of course, are not discrete categories. Of a leadership sample of 103 selected by W. F. Mandle, 62 had served in the armed forces (the proportion is much higher among those chronologically eligible), not just in the war, but as career soldiers.[3] Here again we must distinguish between different kinds of motivation. Many ex-officers found themselves unemployed in the Depression. Fascism offered a number of them jobs. Moreover, they were jobs of the sort they liked and could do well. The B.U.F. was organised on military lines and the ex-officers felt quite at home with all the 'sirs', saluting, order papers, etc. As Ian Hope Dundas, ex-naval officer son of an admiral and Mosley's 'chief of staff', remarked, ' You get the same spirit in the B.U.F. as you get in the Navy – without the sea-sickness.'

The military atmosphere was deliberate. Mosley wanted to create an efficient instrument of action. ' Armies will in the future take the place of parties,' wrote Spengler in 1933. The army was the best instrument of action man had devised. Mosley sought to apply its principles to the winning and using of power. He wanted a movement that would stand united and firm in the face of the enemy, a Prussian Guard, not a collection of ' portly trade union officials and nervous pacifist intellectuals ' as John Strachey had described Labour parliamentarians.

The military organisation of British fascism was not just a method, but a social ideal: the B.U.F. was the fascist state in miniature, just as the old parties were microcosms of *their* states. Those who identified with the ' war generation ' expected the values of war, the comradeship, the disciplined life, the responsibility, the danger and excitement, the freedom from the usual sexual inhibitions, to be carried over into civilian life. It has often been noted that the war promoted collectivism. What is not so often emphasised is the connection between the military and the collectivist ideal, which had appealed so strongly to Robert Blatchford even before the war. Fascism was the ' soldier's socialism ', the political form through which he could express the social idealism generated in the war and betrayed by the politicians. The tank expert, Major-General J. F. C. Fuller, Mosley's most eminent military supporter, justified fascism's military conception of social organisation on strategic grounds. Since war had become a total activity, involving not just soldiers but whole populations, the distinction between peace-time and war-time politics had lost its validity. In the modern age, prevention of war, preparation for war and waging of war all required the same economic and political organisation. Fuller's aim was to realise through fascism what the war had temporarily created – a social engine under unified political–military direction.[4]

The category of ex-soldier merges into a more general category of displaced professional men. Mandle has noted an ' alarmingly high degree of restlessness ' among B.U.F. activists. Most of them had ' knocked around ' a great deal, generally around the Empire, trying their hand at one thing or another, feeling dissatisfied and unused. Time and time again in the biographies of fascist parliamentary candidates we come across ' rubber planting in Malaya ', ' sheep farming in Patagonia ', ' farming in Kenya ', ' gold prospecting ', ' travelled extensively in Africa ', ' continental courier '. This was in addition to those whose regular careers in Army, Navy, or Imperial Civil Service had kept them out of England for long stretches. Of course, the war itself does not alone account for this displacement. Mosley himself, and perhaps other upper-class recruits, had also been uprooted from the land with the post-war sale of landed estates.[5] William Joyce was a southern Irish loyalist. A contracting labour-market and a classical-cum-athletic education made it genuinely difficult for many ex-public schoolboys to get jobs after the war.   Opportunities for imperial service – that vast system of outdoor relief for the upper classes – had also become more restricted.   But the restless wanderlust was there, independently of these things, not just in England but all over Europe, and reflects the shattering of the psychological frame that had held liberal civilisation together.   Long sojourns abroad also produced a highly unreal picture of England to add to more imme- diate grievances.   Absence certainly made the heart grow fonder, and it evoked an image of the loved one that had little connection with reality and which was rudely shattered when world depression forced these unhappy imperial wanderers back to the unemploy- ment queues in their own homeland.   Reynell Bellamy returned in 1931 to find ' the country in a mess '.   With relief he answered Mosley's call to the colours.   It was a typical reaction.

Sportsmen figured prominently in the galaxy of fascist types. There was a strong link between fascism and aviation with its ' fascist ' combination of individual daring and futuristic technology. Mosley of course had a personal interest and proposed that ' every suitable boy, at an appropriate age, if he and his parents were willing, would receive air training.   We would soon be a nation of potential air pilots.'[6]   There was great alarm when fascists started forming flying clubs in 1934; two B.U.F. pilots, K. G. Day and G. T. Brocking, appeared in the first R.A.F. casualty list in the Second World War.   The journal *Aeroplane* was sympathetic to fascism; its editor, C. J. Grey, was a supporter; its sub-editor, Geoffrey Dorman, who had first met Mosley at the R.F.C. Flying School at Shoreham in 1915, was a prominent B.U.F. member, editing *Action* for a time in 1937.   Sir Alliott Verdon Roe, first Englishman to fly in 1908 and designer of the Avro aircraft, was also an eminent sup- porter.   Speed on the ground attracted fascists almost as much as speed in the air.   Sir Malcolm Campbell's *Bluebird* carried the fas- cist colours when it broke the land speed record; Vernon Pickering, winner of a hundred racing trophies, was identified as a supporter.[7] ' Fabulous ' Fay Taylour, the first woman to drive on dirt track, joined in 1938.   Boxing was represented by Joe Beckett, former middle-weight champion of Great Britain, after the Jewish ' Kid ' Lewis had been ' frozen ' out soon after the B.U.F. was formed.

The public-schoolboy flavour of the early B.U.F. won encomi- ums from the right-wing press and helped build up a pervasive myth.   This was that it started off by attracting the better class of person but that after the events of 1934 all good men shunned it and that thereafter it became the home of toughs and hoodlums. The B.U.F. certainly did become more proletarian after 1934, and there may be an unconscious class-bias in conventional accounts of its fall from grace, right-wingers being by no means alone in identifying virtue with a middle-class accent. (It is noticeable how the stock of British communism rose the more middle-class it became.) But this decline in social status did not have the implication middle-class commentators gave it. In many ways, the B.U.F. was at its worst when it was most upper-class. The stewarding was at its most excitable. Members were always getting into scrapes (the 'panty raids' on rival fascist organisations are one example; allegations of the ' castor-oil ' treatment being given to unpopular recruits are another).[8] District treasurers would abscond with the funds; and some local headquarters were more like bawdy houses. It was in its earliest period, too, that the B.U.F. was most obviously organised as a military force, ready to seize power in a revolutionary situation.

In the autumn of 1933 it acquired the lease of Whiteland Teachers Training College in the King's Road, Chelsea, which became known as Black House. It was a cross between an administrative headquarters, social club and army camp. Other Black Houses in the main urban centres were formed on the same model. In the original one, hundreds of members of I Squad or the London Defence Force slept, ate and lived to the sound of the bugle summoning them for reveille, meal-times, parades and lights out. They trained in gymnastics, boxing and judo. They roared out in their military-looking vans to defend speakers or rescue them in trouble. From Black House, a thousand stewards marched out for their epic battle with the ' Reds ' at Olympia.

The Black House episode seems to come from an earlier period of English history. It recalls the great lord and his ' men at arms '. Far-fetched as this parallel might seem, it corresponds to the facts and fantasies of the early 1930s. The facts were a return to a more violent, passionate politics of which both fascism and communism were manifestations. A miniature civil war had broken out between two private groups – at meetings, in the streets. The fantasy of both was that this war might escalate into a half-political, half-military, struggle for power over the stricken body of liberal England and the disintegrating authority of the liberal state. This belief was apparently shared by Mosley. ' When the [Labour Party]', Mosley declared in his debate with Maxton in February 1933, 'have led us more rapidly to the situation which comes anyhow, but which they precipitate, behind them will emerge the real man, the organised Communist, the man who knows what he wants; and if and when he ever comes out, we will be there in the streets, with Fascist machine-guns to meet them.'[9] This was the moment for which fascists all over the country trained to keep fit.

Under the headline IS IT PROGRESS? the *Star* of 25 February 1933 reported that ' Sir Oswald Mosley warned Mr. Maxton that he and his Fascists would be ready to take over the government with the aid of machine-guns when the moment arrived. Mr. Tom Mann was recently thrown into prison on the mere suspicion that he might say something ten times less provocative than Sir Oswald's words.' Mosley immediately brought a case for libel against the Daily News Ltd alleging that the words suggested that he was planning to use machine-guns against the Government in order to take control of the State. A galaxy of legal talent was assembled by both sides for the High Court hearing in November 1934: Norman Birkett, K.C., and Valentine Holmes for the *Star*, Sir Patrick Hastings, St John Hutchinson and Gerald Gardiner for Mosley. Mosley himself sparkled under Birkett's three-hour cross-examination, Lord Chief Justice Hewart in his summing-up referred to him as ' a public man of no mean courage, no little candour, and no mean ability '[10] and the jury awarded him damages of £5000. Yet when sixteen months later Mosley sued John Marchbanks, general secretary of the N.U.R., for the rather worse slander of accusing him of assembling a political party ' in the guise of a military machine with the object of overthrowing by force the constitutional Government of the country' Mr Justice Finlay summed up much less favourably for Mosley and the jury awarded him one farthing damages.[11] No doubt there are intricate legal arguments that can be adduced to explain both decisions, but to the layman it seems that in the first case both judge and jury were too impressed by Mosley's recent credentials as an ex-minister of the Crown, and in the second case too much impressed by the extremely unfavourable publicity the B.U.F. had received since 1934. The legal stereotypes of 1934 and 1936 have impressed themselves on the minds of historians ever since.

Lord Rothermere's article in the *Daily Mail*, ' Hurrah for the Blackshirts ', on 8 January 1934 opened the second phase of the B.U.F.'s history, one which suggested an alternative future for it as a right-wing ally of the Conservative Party.* This was the period when Lady Houston of the *Saturday Review* praised it in hysterical editorials and execrable verse; when the January Club was formed to permeate the Establishment (guests included Lord Lloyd, Liddell Hart, Philip Magnus, Sir Charles Petrie and Ralph Blumenfeld); when Baldwin described it as ' ultra-montane Conservatism '. Perversely, this period, too, is regarded as more reputable than that which followed. In fact, Mosley was forced to compromise his radical policies in deference to Rothermere for whom blackshirts stood for ' sound, commonsense, Conservative doctrine ';[12] and the ' Rothermere fascists ', who joined in droves, got the movement into great trouble with their ignorance and lack of discipline. The Olympia meeting of 7 June 1934 brought this phase of ' respect-

*The most obvious parallel to the Mosley–Rothermere alliance was the Hitler–Hugenberg one.

able' fascism to a close. Although fascist stewarding on this occasion was, as we shall see, more violent than Mosley had intended, the real significance of Olympia was to reveal the incompatibility between 'blackshirt man' and 'Rothermere man'. In a formal exchange of letters with Rothermere, ending their association, Mosley insisted that he was leading a revolutionary, not a conservative, movement.

The fascist bubble was pricked and the B.U.F. shrank to its proper dimensions – that of an infant movement trying to establish itself in conditions of economic recovery against a hostile political culture. This moment of truth would have had to come at some point in the career of any serious fascist party. But the way in which it came about left its peculiar scars on the B.U.F. psychology. As one of Mosley's followers, Reynell Bellamy, put it, 'Those who were worthy of the cause stuck it out, and found that the almost universal hostility put more iron into their souls. . . .' The role of Jews at Olympia also brought the anti-Jewish forces to the fore in the fascist party. For the first time, Mosley found himself isolated with a shrunken following, as perhaps he had always wanted to be. There was a new emphasis on élite, struggle, persecution, heroism. W. J. Leaper, *Blackshirt*'s editor, noted an 'improved tone' in the movement. 'Its spirit . . . is more powerful, the character is more steel-like, the determination of the Movement to keep itself unsullied is stronger than ever.'[13] Mosley began to talk privately of a struggle lasting thirty years.

The end of the Rothermere (as well as the civil-war) fantasy forced the B.U.F. to work out a proper strategy for winning power. 'During 1935', writes Colin Cross, 'Mosley carried through an extensive reorganisation, centralising control of branches through a system of headquarters inspectors, inaugurating strict financial controls and turning the bias of the Movement away from semi-military training, designed to suppress a Communist revolution, towards a more conventional plan for winning power at a general election'.[14] National Headquarters were gradually built up to a staff of 140 officials, headed by a director-general. For the first time, the two central principles of fascist organisation – leadership and team spirit – were fully applied. 'Give a man a job to do; sack him if he fails' became the fascist motto for party and state. Activities were closely defined and responsibility allocated for them at each level of the organisation. From the leader at the top down to the humblest follower stretched a chain of command unbroken by committees, party conferences, grand debates on principle. 'Expression of collective opinion' was firmly discouraged.[15] Equally important were the ward and action units, the skeletons of constituency organisation. 'The unit will be the basis, not only of Blackshirt organisation, but of Blackshirt life,' wrote Mosley.[16] He was particularly pleased to read in the report of one branch: 'Saturday night: unit went to the cinema.'[17]

In line with this new austerity of spirit, the 'social-club' approach came under heavy fire. Headquarters had sprung up in all the main provincial centres 'elaborately equipped with bars, gymnasia, lounges, dining-halls and suites of administrative offices'.[18] There were fascist weddings, funerals and football teams. B.U.F. members could take language courses and smoke fascist cigarettes. There was a Blood Transfusion Corps. Mosley put an end to it. 'The social club idea is Social Democratic and is not Fascist,' he declared.[19] A local headquarters should consist of the barest necessities only – an office and a room in which political activities could be organised. Blackshirts should be on the streets canvassing and selling the newspaper. Comradeship should be developed in work, not play. The London Black House was given up in the summer of 1935 and the Central Defence Force disbanded. New offices were acquired on three floors of Sanctuary Buildings, Great Smith Street, Westminster, overlooking the House of Commons, jocularly known as the 'gas works'. A. K. Chesterton, one of the national inspectors, 'struck down' two fascist clubs in Coventry and Stoke, expelling 300 members at the latter in one go.[20]

Another organisational innovation of this period had less happy consequences. Mosley was determined to combine the creation of a blackshirt élite with the drive for mass membership. The solution he hit on was to offer the privilege of a superior uniform to those who gave superior service to the cause in selling the newspaper, stewarding, canvassing. Members were divided into three categories. Division 1, who guaranteed to give a minimum of two nights' service a week, were regarded as the flower of the movement, alone entitled to the full uniform. Division 2 members had to give a minimum of one night's service a month. Division 3 consisted of members under no obligation to serve. They were expected to contribute money. The idea of using the uniform as a reward for service was organisationally sound, but politically naïve. For an irresistible tendency developed to add to the uniform as a spur to further service. The more copies of fascist journals a member sold, the more uniform he was entitled to wear: he could look forward to belt, special trousers, mackintosh, boots, breeches and greatcoat.[21] This naïveté was to cost the B.U. dear in 1936. What the military mind inside the movement regarded as a solution to an organisational problem, the political mind outside it regarded as a menace to civil society. At the moment when the B.U.F. in fact stopped acting like an army, it started looking like one.

Electoral organisation was only one side of the problem. Electoral strategy was the other. When the B.U.F. started, Mosley's closest political friends, Bill Allen and Robert Forgan, urged him to concentrate on potentially 'good' fascist areas like the depressed regions and East Anglia in order to build up strength from a regional base, and thus get himself and if possible a group of M.P.s back into Parliament as quickly as possible. They never saw fascism as winning power independently. Mosley insisted that it must be a national movement or nothing. Possible short-term successes must be sacrificed to long-term building. However, by the end of 1934 he recognised that the movement must concentrate its resources on certain regions and economic groups rather than spread its propaganda like thin jam all over the country.

In the autumn of 1934 the B.U.F. launched a big campaign in Lancashire under the direction of 'Bill' Risdon, an ex-miner and former Birmingham I.L.P. leader. Lancashire was promising in that it was the regional base of the once proud, but now declining, textile industry, and also because a large section of the Lancashire working class had always voted Conservative. Early in 1935, Mosley himself spoke to packed meetings in Blackburn, Accrington, Darwen, Oldham, Earlestown, Ormskirk, Ashton, Preston and many other cotton centres, explaining how the B.U.F. policy of excluding Japanese goods from India, removing the Indian tariff against British cotton goods, and excluding foreign textiles from the Crown Colonies would give employment to 65,000 Lancashire workers. There was another campaign in 1936. Reynell Bellamy, who was in charge of the North West Division, claims that the B.U.F. managed to establish a strong branch in Blackburn under Bill Sumner. The Nelson and Colne branch was run by a young girl weaver called Nellie Driver. Burnley was organised by a Catholic working man, John Naughton. In other areas the B.U.F. made less impact – mainly, he feels, because of the legacy of adventurers and misfits who had signed on in the Rothermere period. It was impossible to get the movement re-established in small, compact, self-contained communities, respectable and church- or chapel-going. Nevertheless, by 1937 the B.U. was prepared to fight sixteen Lancashire seats.

Yorkshire had already been penetrated in 1933–4, and under the impact of Rothermere's publicity the Leeds branch had expanded to 2000 members by the middle of 1934, mainly from the middle-class residential areas of Roundhay and Headingley. Following Olympia, upper middle-class support fell away, and fascism had to re-establish itself on a more modest basis. This it did mainly in the West Riding area of wool towns, as well as Hull. By 1938 the B.U. had selected twelve seats to fight in Yorkshire, nine of them with Tory majorities. The exceptions were Leeds South, where anti-semitism attracted some working-class support (Leeds had the highest Jewish percentage in any British town), Barnsley, and Normanton where a lively, if short-lived, fascist branch had been established in strongly socialist Featherstone. In the 1930s Mosley had good receptions in the smaller towns: Leeds and Hull, however, gave him some of his stormiest meetings. There are some interesting membership figures for Yorkshire. The membership of the Leeds branch fell from 2000 to 500 by mid-1937, the banning of uniforms at the end of 1936 estranging the younger elements. The recession of 1937–8 and the threat of war produced a recovery and by 1939 membership was up to 1000 again. Total fascist membership in Yorkshire was about 5000 in 1939, a figure to be kept in mind when assessing total fascist strength in England at the war's outbreak.[22]

With the other depressed industry, coalmining, the B.U.F. had less success. Mosley hoped to recapture his earlier following among the miners, and 'Tommy' Moran, ex-miner and former navy cruiser-weight boxing champion, was sent to open up South Wales late in 1935. By the end of the year the B.U.F. was campaigning strongly in Merthyr, the Rhondda Valley, Pontypridd and Tonypandy: there were already branches in Cardiff, Newport and Swansea. There was plenty of violence, particularly in the open air, thirty-three communists being convicted of breaking up one of Moran's meetings at Tonypandy in June 1936. Outdoor meetings were also broken up regularly on Tyneside, where John Beckett fought hard to establish a fascist foothold. The B.U.F. fared even worse in the third mining area, Clydeside, and indeed in Scotland as a whole; lively, but isolated, branches in Edinburgh and Aberdeen being Mosley's sole representatives north of the border. He also made little headway in his old stamping-ground of the Black Country round Birmingham where heavy industry started booming once home-market recovery got under way.

The rural areas provided more promising soil for the fascist seed. Mosley's first rural campaign had been launched in East Anglia in 1933, when fascists took a prominent part in the tithe war. Throughout the 1930s he campaigned continuously there and in Lincolnshire, Worcester, the West Country and south and south-east England. Here the meetings were more relaxed and informal. Sometimes Mosley would be invited to address meetings of the National Farmers' Union. Often he would speak at garden parties organised by wealthy supporters or prominent agriculturists, such as Dorothy, Viscountess Dorne, who became B.U.F. candidate for North Norfolk, Lady Pearson, sister of General Page Croft, who ran the Canterbury branch, and Jorian Jenks, farmer and author who played an active part in Surrey. The black shirt would be abandoned, or worn under a suit, and at most places no more than half a dozen stewards would be needed. Most of those meetings, and there were several hundred of them, were never reported in the national press, and so a completely distorted picture grew up of the 'typical' Mosley meeting. Outside East London, these were perhaps the meetings which Mosley liked best. This was his England, and it responded to him without hysterics.

East London appealed to another side of his character. Here Mosley was with an entirely different type of people, voluble, excitable, feckless and intensely sentimental. Here he drew his largest and most enthusiastic crowds of the 1930s and indulged his most emotional and flamboyant rhetoric. In the East End he could talk his head off about Drake and Raleigh, about decline and regeneration, about all the great themes of war and peace, and his audiences listened spell-bound. The East London movement, with its particular feature of anti-semitism, will be discussed later. It is actually quite a separate episode in B.U.F. history. It is the one fascist movement that sprang to life without the direct stimulus of a Mosley speech or campaign. It ran itself almost autonomously under 'Mick' Clarke, and had little connection with the rest of the B.U.F., almost the only direct link being Mosley himself.

Fascism concentrated not only on certain regions, but on certain occupational groups. Its problem here was that the trade unions and the Labour Party claimed to look after the interests of the workers, while Conservatism claimed to safeguard the interests of business. It might try to detach workers in declining industries by its emphasis on the joint interests of managers and men in face of foreign competition; it might hope to gain business support by playing on fears of Red revolution. But its main hope of immediate conversion lay with those intermediate groups which fell outside the labour–capital confrontation.

All over Europe it was the 'small men', the *petite bourgeoisie*, who gave fascism its initial social space to grow. In Britain the archetypal small men were small shopkeepers, craftsmen (tailors, cabinet-makers, small bakers), and other small owners (cinema, restaurant and hotel proprietors, barbers, taxi-men): those offering individual services who eked out a proudly independent and (in depression) precarious living in the interstices of an increasingly mass-production and mass-service economy. These were the Britons who felt most neglected and unloved in the 1930s. They were typically the people who in previous ages had been protected by the guild system, but whose independence precluded effective trade-union organisation. In the course of industrial evolution they had managed to escape the division of the mass of the population into workers and capitalists, and thus clamoured for two things that neither *laissez-faire* capitalism nor orthodox socialism could combine: protection *and* independence.

From 1935 onwards the B.U.F. made a determined play for their support. It analysed their problem. 'In general business life', wrote Raven Thomson, 'the small man with his independent firm is caught between the upper millstone of trustification and the lower millstone of socialisation.'[23]   It flattered their ' manly striving for independence' and proposed a distributive Corporation to limit competition by eliminating ' alien' chain-stores, preventing overlap, and spreading out units more widely.[24]   To the accusation that such remedies would hinder efficiency, it replied easily that ' we can afford to put human values before economic values'.[25]   In these ways the ' nation of shopkeepers which smashed Napoleon can inflict yet another Waterloo [on] . . . the chain-store octopus'.[26]   From 1938 onwards Peter Heyward ran a ' 'gainst Trust and Monopoly' column in *Action* and in 1938 organised a British Traders Bureau to draw shopkeepers into fascist politics.   This interest paid off hand-somely.   Fascism received sympathetic coverage in a number of trade journals – the *Dairyman*, the *Green Badge* trade journal (cab-drivers), the *Bakers Record*, the *National Newsagent, Bookseller and Stationer*.   Four hundred taximen attended a meeting at B.U. head-quarters in June 1938 when Mosley promised to abolish private car-hire services which cut prices, and eliminate part-time cabbies who ' stole the cream from the hard-working British man who devoted his entire energies to the taxi-trade'.[27]   Over a thousand shop-keepers attended a Mosley address at the Memorial Hall, Farring-don Street on 7 February 1939, giving him a thundering ovation. ' I was impressed, not only by his earnestness, but by his command of details as connected with Retail Trade – an accomplishment not always found in speakers of his calibre,' wrote a trade journalist.[28] Alex Gossip, general secretary of the Furnishing Trades Association, confirmed that an ' extraordinary proportion of those who took part in Fascist propaganda had some occupational connection with the furniture trade'.[29]   This was truest in East London, with its host of jostling small businesses, and where the B.U.F. was able to develop its anti-alien line to greatest effect.

The B.U.F., as we have seen, hoped to appeal to industrial workers as well: there was an Industrial Section with its slogan ' Power Action not Strike Action' and members were urged to form trade-union groups.   Mosley was reported as addressing a meeting of trade uni-onists at Denison Hall, London, on 3 April 1938.[30]   But, apart from its footholds in Lancashire and the coalmining belts, fascism's main contact with proletarian England was through the service sector of the economy.   A former I.L.P.-er, Henry Gibbs, ran a series of articles exposing the conditions of shop assistants, cinema ushe-rettes, barmaids and waiters.   *Blackshirt* claimed proudly that ' nearly every hotel and restaurant in the West End' had B.U.F. members,[31] and Oxford and Cambridge ' scouts' were said to be particularly pro-Mosley.   Efforts were made to win the support of seamen (whose union had a strong nationalist tradition), post-office workers and even busmen: a National Socialist Busmen's Group was formed

in July 1937 and fascists hoped to pick up support in the commu-
nist-led Busmen's Rank and File Movement.   However meagre the
rewards might have been, these efforts at any rate reveal the areas
in which Mosley hoped to make gains: among the non-industrial
working class, generally with weak unionisation and a 'deferential'
attitude; and where foreigners were most likely to appear as employers or job-competitors.

These, then, were the Mosleyite areas and groups.   In addition,
there were the national campaigns: the 'anti-election' campaign of
November 1935 which the B.U.F. fought under the slogan 'Fascism
Next Time' and the 'Mind Britain's Business' campaigns of 1935,
1938 and 1939 being the most prominent.   The shortest-lived was
the 'Stand By the King' campaign at the end of 1936 – an issue
which found Mosley, Churchill, Beaverbrook and the communists in
lonely agreement against the Establishment.   Edward VIII was
fascism's ideal king, young, unconventional, anti-Establishment who
stood for friendship with Germany and action on unemployment.
His famous 'something will be done' speech in South Wales came
only a month before his abdication.   Mosley urged him to fight
for his throne. 'The issue', he wrote after the abdication 'was never
whether or not we were pleased by the King's intention to marry
this American lady. . . . The issue was whether or not the King,
under our Constitution, had the right to marry whatever woman
he chose to marry, and the answer is clearly that he had.'   The
Cabinet had been guilty of the 'most flagrant act of dictatorship'
in hustling Edward off his throne 'without consulting the People'.[32]
Mosley felt from his tours in the north of England that 'the line
of division was broadly the line dividing the younger from the older
generation'.   Reynell Bellamy, who organised the northern campaign, and who received reports on scores of meetings, came to a
different conclusion: the middle class, particularly the lower middle
class, abhorred the marriage; the working class was solidly for
the King.   As Colin Cross notes, the heart went out of the B.U.'s
monarchism with Edward's departure.

The task of building up the fascist movement from the grass
roots was carried on in face of formidable obstacles which resulted
in severe internal strains.   The banning of the uniform by the
Public Order Act of December 1936 was a severe blow.   The
internal crisis came to a head in March 1937 when, following the
only partly successful East London municipal election results, Mosley purged his headquarters staff, reducing it from 140 to 30 in
one afternoon.   Though there were solid organisational reasons for
this act of decentralisation as it was euphemistically described (after
the war Mosley admitted that 'half the Movement was running
to Headquarters every five minutes'), the main reason was undoubtedly financial.   The economic recovery of the mid-1930s as

well as British Union's increasing unsavoury reputation, had dried
up funds.

The question of who financed fascism has been much debated. The Italians probably gave large sums at the time of
the Abyssinian crisis (see below, page 463–4). It was part of
the left-wing case that fascism was financed by Big Business, and
the Labour Party tried hard to uncover Mosley's secret backers.
Lord Inchcape, the shipping magnate, Sir Henry Deterding,
chairman of Dutch Shell, Lord Nuffield, and Courtaulds, the arti-
ficial-silk firm, were all mentioned in the early days. Guests at
the January Club included men connected with Siemens, Caxton
Electric, London Assurance, Vickers, Handley Page, and Morgan,
Grenfell & Co.[33] How much, if anything, they gave is not known.
It is known that Lady Houston almost gave Mosley £200,000 and
that Lord Rothermere did give him a much smaller amount.[34]
The movement was probably helped by rich members and supporters like Bill Allen, Gordon-Canning and Sir Alliot Verdon Roe.
The wealthy stockbroker Alex Scrimgeour, William Joyce's friend,
may have contributed till Joyce's departure in 1937. The over-
all impression is that, with the exception of the occasional lavish
handout, the amounts given were small, and mainly by small
businesses, wealthy individual supporters and family connections.
Mosley himself spent £100,000 of his own money to keep the
movement going in the two years before the war.

The drying-up of money was accompanied by the drying-up of
all British Union's effective propaganda outlets. The Public Order
Act gave police chiefs power to ban fascist processions. From
1937 onwards Mosley was denied most of the big halls in the urban
centres. In London he could get no big hall at all after 1936 and
the Earls Court booking of 1939 was made possible only by a sudden
cancellation. He was thus deprived of his two chief weapons – propaganda marches and meetings. This in turn meant that he could
not break the national press boycott.

Mosley realised that he had to break this stranglehold of poverty
and boycott or perish politically. He devised an ingenious scheme on
which he spent much of the last two years of peace. It was to build
up a big network of radio-advertising stations, on the model of Radio
Luxembourg. He planned to bombard British audiences from
three sides – Ireland, Germany and the Channel Isles – not with his
propaganda, but with light entertainment. With the profits made
from this undertaking, he hoped not only to finance his own movement, but also to purchase local newspapers. Everything was
kept very secret: Mosley's name was never used in the official
negotiations, nor would it have appeared in a case before the Privy
Council needed to crack the B.B.C. monopoly in England itself.
' One thing is certain, that but for the accident of war we should

have made an immense fortune. I should have achieved my ambition to be the first revolutionary in history to conduct a revolution and at the same time to make the fortune which assured its success. Our money would have been clean money, made by our own abilities and great exertions. We should neither have double-crossed nor capitulated to capitalism. We should have beaten it on its own territory with good clean weapons of relatively decent commerce, which at least provided the people with an entertaining alternative to the dreary schoolmasters at the B.B.C. Last but not least we should have had a good crack at the press Lords.'[35] This was not the only one of Mosley's projects to be frustrated by the Second World War.*

How much progress had Mosley made by the time war put an end to his chances? By 1936 he was claiming 500 branches, divided into some 180–200 districts (or constituencies). In 1937 he announced a list of 100 constituencies which the B.U. would fight at the next election, and when war broke out about 80 candidates had been selected. In 1937 the B.U. showed that it could win sizeable votes in East London. All this, however, could mean very little. The expansion of branches might mean only a redivision of existing branches to fit a ward organisation. Many of the candidates might never have fought.

Much ink has been spilt over the vexed question of B.U.F. membership, a reasonable index of the movement's progress. The conventional view is that fascism 'peaked' in 1934 and thereafter went into a slow but steady decline. The conclusions of a number of inspired guesses may be summarised as follows. The active membership reached its peak of approaching 10,000 in 1934, thereafter shrinking to a little over 1000 in 1940. The non-active membership shrank from 30,000 in 1934 to 7000 or 8000 in 1940. At its maximum in 1934, B.U.F. numbered 40,000 members; at its minimum in 1939, it numbered 9000–10,000.[36] A Home Office memorandum of 1943 'estimated' the paying members in 1939 'between 8000 to 10,000 persons'.[37] In the House of Commons on 25 July 1940, Sir John Anderson in reply to a question ' understood that the number of persons who had paid their last annual subscription was in the region of 9000 '.[38]†

*Mosley's other major business venture in the 1930s was started with a press-lord. In 1934 he formed a cigarette manufacturing company – New Epoch Products Ltd – with Lord Rothermere. It had bought a large factory and was ready to begin production when the break with Rothermere aborted the whole undertaking.

†There is some ambiguity about whether these figures refer to the membership at the time of Mosley's arrest or at the beginning of the war. If the former is the case, then British Union would have been considerably larger in September 1939, for by May 1940 only the hard core would be left. The Home Secretary's

This figure was almost certainly obtained from membership lists taken from fascist records following the raids on 23 May 1940. Both the timing of the statement and the pattern of the arrests in May–June 1940 suggest that Intelligence was working from the headquarters file. However, Mosley's headquarters kept lists only of division 1 or ' active ' members.* The inference is that the figure of 9000 represents British Union's active membership at the beginning of the war. This is at any rate not contradicted by the conclusion of the Yorkshire survey already quoted that total Yorkshire membership was about 5000 in 1939 – a figure that would be much too high if *total* membership in the same period was only 9000. Assuming at least three non-active members to one active member, we get a total membership in 1939 of about 40,000 or about the same as the peak period estimated for 1934 – a peak scaled only very briefly with the help of a highly transitory push from Lord Rothermere. This would make the B.U. about as large as the Communist Party at this time. To offset the fall in numbers following Rothermere's withdrawal, there was the East London movement which had grown up entirely since then and which seems to have been largely ignored by Benewick and Cross in making their estimates. There is also the evidence of the Earls Court meeting of July 1939 to which Mosley attracted a sympathetic audience of about 20,000 and of commentators at the time who felt his movement was increasing in strength.† It seems reasonably clear that Mosley's support came up rapidly in the first few months of 1934 and ebbed away just as rapidly after Olympia. The next big forward surge was the East London movement which was followed by another recession after the Public Order Act and the municipal election results of March 1937. By 1938 it was picking up again (helped by the economic recession) and may have regained its 1934 strength. In short, Mosley's claim that British Union was stronger in 1939 than at any other time in its history, if not convincing, is more plausible than the view that it was a

---

exchanges with Josiah Wedgwood on 25 July imply that the 9000 was at the beginning of the war, and my argument is based on that assumption.

*The reason for this emerged in the course of a private meeting between Mosley and his leading supporters shortly after the war: non-active members, often secret supporters, were afraid of having their names on a central file, and this practice was therefore discontinued once the organisation was decentralised in 1937.

†Cassandra writing in the *Daily Mirror*, 17 July 1939: ' There is no doubt that numerically the adherents to fascism are increasing. To have filled Earls Court, which I believe is about the world's largest meeting hall, is a considerable achievement. This strange young man, with his violent remedies and his uncompromising courage may yet serve to rock the smug conservatism that acts like a drag upon our political life. If so, he deserves a place in history.'

spent force.

The chief obstacle to accepting this claim has been the view of those who have written about British fascism that it was killed off by the civilised British political culture which abhorred violence and anti-semitism.[39] This fits in with the myth of a 'respectable' fascism that attracted early support and a 'disreputable' one which all good men shunned later on. Undoubtedly the contemporary British political culture was less hospitable to fascism than the contemporary German, or even French, political culture. But Mosley, one must remember, expected to win mass support in conditions of economic crisis, just as the Nazis had done. This was not an unreasonable assumption. It is, after all, in conditions of breakdown that new movements, however abhorrent and unnecessary they appear in normal times, get their opportunity. The argument that British fascism was a spent force by 1939 depends on the supporting argument that Britain and what remained of the liberal world had solved the economic problem which had produced the breakdown of 1929–33. Despite the fragile recovery of the mid-1930s, this is not plausible. In the absence of Keynesian techniques, with the world monetary system in disarray, the non-fascist and non-communist world was quite liable to relapse back into depression. Indeed the British and American economies were only floated off the rocks of a serious recession in 1937–8 by war preparations. Would British fascism, one wonders, have done so disastrously at a general election in 1940 fought in the trough of a new depression?

If any single factor killed off British fascism, it was the war, not the British political culture. The war defeated the fascist powers on the battlefield. It also brought to an end the economic horror that had made fascism a world force. It gave infant Keynesianism its chance to grow. It gave the Americans the power to reconstruct the shattered economic order. It temporarily re-created the heroic psychology and the conditions that enable problems to be tackled at their root. In this sense it was the decisions of Chamberlain and Hitler, not British traditions, that doomed Mosley in the 1930s. His gamble left out the possibility of war; and, even more importantly, the possibility of an anti-fascist victory in war.

MOSLEY BY LOW

Chapter 17

Leaders and Fellow-travellers

UNLIKE European communist movements, fascist movements have always taken on the personality of their leaders. Leadership was, of course, the central concept in the fascist theory of politics: Mosley was unusual among fascists in introducing an element of economic determinism into his plan for winning power.* It is quite possible to imagine a fascist movement in the England of the 1930s without Mosley. But it would have been very different: much nastier, and probably less effective.

What, then, was his contribution? We have already mentioned policy and money. In addition, Mosley was the B.U.F.'s chief, and most remarkable, propagandist. He carried a crippling load of speaking, more than any British politician has ever done. From 1933 to 1937 he made about 200 speeches a year: in other words, spoke every day for about eight months in the year, travelling thousands of miles by car round the halls of Britain. After the war he complained to his son Nicholas that incessant speech-making had given him 'a perfect nausea for words ... with the result that I detested conversation in which earlier I had delighted'. In addition to this speaking load, he wrote three books and over a hundred articles. He decided every major issue of policy and strategy. He bore the immense psychological burden of keeping up the spirit of the movement in its frequent periods in the doldrums. Perhaps worst of all was the sheer physical, emotional and mental effort of getting up on a platform night after night, facing a sea of faces, credulous, amused, hostile; trying to convince, persuade, inspire, humour; keeping calm when fights broke out. And the astounding thing is that all this was done by a man who had the money and the taste to enjoy quite a different kind of life. It was will and passion that alone drove him to these prodigies of exertion.

It was chiefly as a public speaker of rare and compelling power that Mosley appeared before the British public in the 1930s. The main effort of persuasion took place at public meetings. 'Never forget', he told a group of supporters after the war, 'that the basis of our Movement is the straight, direct propaganda and that the man

*One must use this term with caution. Mosley did not believe that all men and women were prisoners of their circumstances. But he believed that most people were—including his political opponents. Hence they would be unable to cope with conditions which could be overcome by superior men and movements. This is the Shavian doctrine.

who can stand up and say what he is and why he is there, is, and
always has been, the backbone of our Movement.' Mosley was
the last of the great English platform-speakers, just as the fascist
crusade was the last great attempt to rally the people against the
system by means of a popular oratory developed in the heyday of
nineteenth century Radicalism.

Although he used demagogic aids, Mosley was not a demagogue.
He always insisted that his speeches were serious speeches for serious
men and women.   There were all kinds of spectacle associated with
a Mosley rally, especially in the early days: drums, orchestra,
communal singing, flags, spotlights and, of course, the propaganda
march to arouse interest.   The speaker himself used every kind of
oratorical trick to get his message across the footlights – changes in
pitch and speed, carefully calculated movements, finger jabbing
straight ahead, arms flung apart, crouching low in attack.   But all
these were techniques for getting across a serious message.   The
standard Mosley speech would consist of an outline of the fascist
creed, its detailed application to the problems of the audience or
locality, plus the topical foreign policy of the day.   In the mining
districts he would expand on the iniquities of the system which
prohibited the extraction of oil from British coal, explaining how
the City of London had invested its money in oil-fields to the ruin
of British coalmining.   In rural areas he would outline his plans for
expanding British agriculture by excluding foreign imports and
increasing home purchasing power, explaining how under the
financial system Britain had to import Argentine beef to secure the
interest on foreign loans to the Argentine; in Lancashire he would
explain his plans for recapturing old markets by excluding Japanese
goods from Empire countries, pointing out that Japanese and Indian
competition did not spring up out of nowhere but was financed
also by the City of London.   To shopkeepers he would describe
his plans for reducing competition and eliminating the big chain
stores.   Much of the analysis was simpliste, but there was plenty of
meat for the audience to chew.

The secret of his success was a flawless speaking technique, an
exceptionally incisive, clarifying style of exposition, and an ability
to infuse passion into facts and arguments.   ' He must be the sort
of orator who could thrill a multitude by declaiming the explanatory
notes on an income-tax form,' a reporter of the *Leeds Mercury* wrote
in wonder.[1]   Mosley would habitually speak for up to an hour and
a half without a single note; there would then usually be an hour
for questions.   No one ever reported him at a loss for a word.
' He spoke . . . without a moment's hesitation and without a single
flaw in the structure of the speech,' noted the *News Chronicle*'s
A. J. Cummings, a hostile observer, after the Albert Hall meeting of April 1934.[2]   This virtuoso performance was consistently

maintained. Where Mosley was less consistent was in managing to convey an impression of spontaneity and freshness. Especially when he was tired – which must have been very often – a certain relentless, machine-like, quality would obtrude. The speech would still be fluent, but it would lack sparkle. ' It ran on unpausingly, word-perfect; at first compellingly, then just wearisomely, almost oppressively,' wrote the *Yorkshire Post*'s special correspondent of a Leeds meeting.[3] Mosley could – and can – be boring just because he learnt his lines so well. It needed him to be only a little below par for the impressive mastery of an argument to sound like a gramophone record.

Another critical comment which occurs from time to time in the 1930s is that his speeches lacked humour. Here again the virtue of careful preparation could turn into a vice when the surroundings were insufficiently stimulating. There is no doubt, too, that Mosley consciously reacted against the flippancy of the parliamentary tradition – the jokes and clever classical allusions, at which he had shown considerable promise in his early days. Humour was not a notable feature of the fascist struggle. Mosley hoped to project a stern, steely, virile image. He wanted people to support him not because he was likeable or charming, or could tell anecdotes, but because he would get things done that needed doing.

The seriousness of the struggle was of course reflected in the nature of the opposition. Much less frequent in the Mosley meetings of the 1930s was the old type of heckler eager to test his wits against the speaker's, show him up as illogical or ridiculous, or generally just cause a disturbance for the fun of it. Fascism aroused furious opposition, and the chanting and shouting it evoked were not the making, but the breaking, of a speech. With the old type of heckler Mosley could deal easily enough. At Grimsby, Lincolnshire, one heckler objected persistently to Mosley's references to fishermen. Mosley kept up a running commentary with him for much of the meeting. At the sixth or seventh interruption, he lifted a glass of water and said, ' Try a glass of this, it's a great experience '. In reply, the man produced a pint of beer. Mosley: ' I hope you will keep sucking away at that for the rest of the evening. You do your job, and I'll do mine.' After another interruption, Mosley said, ' I don't think you are interested in international finance. You go in for British produce. There is a very good bottle of it beside you.' And so it went on till the man staggered unsteadily towards the exit. Everyone including the speaker was in high good humour.[4]

It must not be supposed that even communist and Labour hecklers would generally be put out as soon as they opened their mouths. Often Mosley would conduct a running battle with them through the meeting, relying on his sarcasm to silence them or show them up as foolish before the audience. Newspapers referred to the ' rare adroitness ' with which he used his forensic skills to disarm heckling. Generally his technique seems to have been to ignore them as long as possible; when he saw an opportunity to turn the laugh on them, he would deliver his thrust leaning forward. He would then pivot back and smile broadly.[5] Mosley was expert in the rough and tumble with Labour supporters not positively bent on breaking up meetings. His proposal to exclude Japanese goods from the Empire provoked a roar of protest from one gallery. Mosley flashed out, ' Now the Labour leaders demand the exclusion of Japanese goods – not to save the markets of Britain, but to save the people of China. There you are, Englishmen, if you are ever in a mess find a Chinaman who can be pulled out first.' A less subtle, but equally effective, retort came at the Cambridge Union when a Socialist speaker accidentally knocked over a glass of water. ' The first blow ever struck for Socialism,' commented Mosley. To Labour interrupters in Edinburgh Mosley said that if they didn't like the idea of his speaking to them he'd send Ramsay MacDonald back up to them and he'd talk to them for ever and ever, whether they liked it or not. An attack on Sir Stafford Cripps in Mosley's old parliamentary style went down well with one audience: ' He is a novel revolutionary, because he always apologises the next day for the statements he makes the night before. . . . But there is method in Sir Stafford's madness, because when he does his revolutionary posturing he gets the support of the Left wing and then by apology next day he secures his seat in the next Labour Government.' Another effective retort was at the expense of the Liberal leader, Sir Herbert Samuel. ' Sir Oswald said that Sir Herbert had asked why no experts in the finance of the present system supported fascist economics. It would be equally relevant to ask why no committees of well-known burglars assembled spontaneously to help the police. Inventions to render safe breaking impossible seldom came from those who derived their livelihood from the cracking of safes.' On a lower level his humour was broad and schoolboyish. Sir John Simon was ' Soapy ' Simon; Lord Halifax ' Holy ' Halifax; Anthony Eden ' the tailor's dummy stuffed with straw '. One Labour leader who never felt the lash of Mosley's tongue was his old friend, George Lansbury. In the course of one attack on the Labour Party at Newcastle, he suddenly stopped short, saying with ' obvious sincerity ', ' I'm sorry, I won't say anything about Lansbury: he's had an accident and I sincerely hope that he will soon recover.'

Mosley could be a striking phrase-maker. He was expert in the imagery of battle: ' The slow soft days are behind us, perhaps for ever. Hard days and nights ahead, no relaxing of the muscle of mind and will. . . . The tents of ease are struck, and the soul of man is once more on the march.' ' This is our generation, not theirs,' he yelled defiantly at the Albert Hall in 1934, ' the epic generation which scales again the heights of time and history to see once more the immortal lights.'[6] Striking, too, was that imagery which welled up from the bottomless depths of his scorn for the old world and its practitioners. ' Supposing people had stood on the shore when the ships of Drake and Raleigh, or of Clive, set out to sea and said " Don't go. The sea is very rough and there will be trouble at the other end." There was no old wife on the shore then, whispering Mr. Baldwin's favourite slogan " Safety First".' [7] And on another occasion: ' Contrast such May Days of Elizabethan England with that shuffling procession to Hyde Park, where Labour leaders will declare that China and Spain must be saved by the dreary drip of their drivelling words. . . . Let us think, too, of the early leaders of Labour, marching on May Day in passionate protest against the conditions of the people of Britain . . . and contrast it with these little men who lisp of China and Timbuctoo, on the rare occasions when their mouths are not stuffed with high living at the luxurious tables of the oppressors of the British people.'[8] Mosley was famous for sweeping an audience off its feet in a thrilling peroration. In cold print, the Puccini-like effects he secured on these occasions appear less impressive. They are full of ' holy vows ', ' frail craft ', ' storm-tossed seas ', ' mighty spirits ', and ' sacred unions '. If the challenge of the peroration is to give fresh form to old and basic emotions, it is not one Mosley can be said to have surmounted successfully.

Mosley's public activities left him little time for his private life. Following Cimmie's death, the London house at Smith Square was sold, and he moved into a large single room in Ebury Street, Victoria. The growing children, Vivien, Nicholas and Michael, were left at Denham where they were looked after by Irene Ravensdale, Cimmie's elder sister, as well as by her old Nanny and French housekeeper. A full domestic establishment was kept up there, but Mosley only came back at weekends and even that infrequently. Public and private life were kept in rigidly separated compartments. No fascist lieutenants ever came to Denham. While Mosley lambasted Jews in public his son Nicholas played opposite Julian Mond (later Lord Melchett) in their preparatory school production of *Twelfth Night*. Nicholas still recalls with wonder the contrast between his father's stern public personality and his private self. ' My father', he says, ' was the funniest man I have ever known.' The old scampering down the chimney on Christmas Day was discontinued; but the private family joking with its litany of special names and signs went on unabated. Under the steely mask of the fascist leader still lurked much of the wilfulness of a child. Before the Earls Court meeting of 1939, Irene Ravensdale, a friend of Halifax, begged Mosley to let off the foreign secretary lightly in his speech.   The opportunity was too good to miss.   A slashing attack on Halifax followed.   At Denham that evening Mosley put his head timidly round the drawing-room door to meet Lady Ravensdale's frosty stare.   ' Naughty, naughty,' he said sheepishly as he edged into the room.

A journalist has given us a glimpse of Mosley's private life in this period, at any rate as Mosley himself liked to portray it.   He had dropped all social life, parties and eating out.   He drank nothing but a little beer, relaxed with a pipe, a little tennis, occasional horse-back riding and championship fencing (his last appearance for England was in 1937 at épée).   He explained that he preferred to live in ' bare, severe, but beautiful rooms.   I hate the junk of modern civilisation with which bourgeois people litter their lives and rooms.'   His office at N.H.Q. was certainly severe.   A black and chromium modern desk stood in one corner.   Over the fire-place hung a pencilled portrait of Mussolini; on the chimney-piece, a personally inscribed photograph of Hitler shared pride of place with a coloured picture of King George V.   There was one chair for visitors; no other furniture.   His one vice remained driving fast sports cars at an alarming speed.   At the B.U.'s holiday camp at Selsey in 1937, members presented him with an MG coupé, which he drove till the war.   To fascist meetings he would be driven by his chauffeur and bodyguard Perrott in a big black Humber, which sustained smashed windows on a number of occasions and at least one bullet hole.

Another area of Mosley's life was kept equally private. Mosley had known Diana Freeman-Mitford even before Cimmie's death.   After it, he saw her more frequently.   Diana was the fourth of seven remarkable children (six girls and one boy) of Lord and Lady Redesdale, the ' Muv ' and ' Farve ' of Nancy Mitford's early novels (her grandfather was the translator of Houston Stewart Chamberlain).   Born in 1910 she had married the Hon. Bryan Guinness (later Lord Moyne) in 1929, by whom she had two sons, Jonathan and Desmond, and whom she divorced in 1934.   Her younger sister Jessica described her in youth as a *Vogue* cover-artist's conception of the goddess of the chase, with her tall, rather athletic figure, her blonde hair, and perfection of feature. After her marriage she became a society beauty.   Photographs of her stared regularly from the covers of society weeklies.   She was painted by a dozen artists.   The face always looked the same, large, calm, gazing rather vacantly into space.   Diana explained to Jessica that if one kept one's face in a relaxed and beautiful expression when young one was less likely to succumb to the ravages of age later in life.   There seems to be something in the theory.   To this day Diana Mosley is an exceptionally beautiful woman, with a smooth, almost expressionless face which can suddenly and temporarily dissolve into a shriek of laughter.   At the time her looks and gaiety attracted a distinguished circle from diverse walks of life – Randolph Churchill, Lytton Strachey, the economist Roy Harrod, the painters Augustus John and Tchelichev.

In the 1930s the Mitford sisters came into prominence for different reasons.   Jessica ran off with Winston Churchill's rebellious nephew Esmond Romilly to support the Republican side in the Spanish Civil War and had to be fetched home in a destroyer.   Muv and Farve were less alarmed by their elopement than by their obvious communist sympathies.   An elder sister, Unity Valkyrie (Boud), went in the opposite direction.   She was attracted by Nazism and became a personal friend of Hitler.   She was a prominent guest at Nazi occasions and caused a scandal in sedate circles by appearing in public with Goering wearing a swastika.   On the outbreak of war, she shot herself in Munich.   German doctors saved her life, and Hitler sent her back to England through Switzerland; but the bullet was never removed, and she died a few years later.   Where Unity blazed the trail with youthful abandon Diana followed more discreetly.   She, too, fell under Hitler's spell, and to this day tends to idealise him.

In 1935 Mosley installed her in a beautiful, lonely house at Wootton, Staffordshire, where Irene Ravensdale found the portrait of Hitler 'particularly painful '.   Their friendship was never revealed, or known, to the Press.   More surprisingly, nothing leaked out about her marriage to Mosley in Berlin in October 1936, at which Frau Goebbels gave a luncheon which Hitler attended – one of the two occasions when Mosley himself met him. Mosley says that Berlin was the only place where he could get married without the Press hearing about it: an advantage of totalitarianism.   He explained that he could not expose Diana to the risks of his public life.   The secret broke only two years later, when their first son Alexander was born.   Max followed a year and a half later.   Later Diana identified herself publicly with Mosley's cause, writing review articles for his post-war journal, *The European*, in a style often as amusing as Nancy's or Jessica's, but betraying a bitterness lacking in their writings.   For Diana, as for her sister Unity, the supreme tragedy was the war between England and Germany, and this has marked her whole life.

It is often claimed that Mosley preferred to surround himself with mediocre yes-men so that his light could shine all the brighter in the surrounding gloom.   This is, to say the least, a great over-simplification.   At all stages of his career Mosley has captured the interest and support of remarkable individualists, and the B.U.F. period was no exception.   If he has quarrelled with many of them, the quarrels have been primarily political rather than personal. Mosley's human deficiencies were obvious.   He drove people hard and often thoughtlessly, though he drove himself even harder. He was much too impatient of mistakes, and did not hide it. He could be extremely sarcastic. He tended to take loyalty for granted. Outside a small circle of family and friends he was not cosy or intimate. On the other hand, he was loyal to his colleagues and supporters almost to the point of idolatry. Despite flare-ups, he would keep people on long after their frailties had been exposed, and they had become liabilities to the movement. In the movement, members knew that they could rely on him to come to their defence against any outside attack, and help them out in trouble, real or invented. He was a notorious ' soft sell ' for any adventurer or petty criminal hoping to use the movement for personal gain or satisfaction. This habit of thinking the best of those who joined him landed the B.U.F. and later the Union Movement in frequent embarrassments and disgraces, but paid a handsome dividend in reciprocated loyalty. It was also a considerable advantage in holding a team together. Because he paid so little attention to personalities Mosley was able to harmonise the personalities of others and keep a group of extreme individualists moving forward with some semblance of unity and common purpose.

It was from personal rather than political loyalty that Mosley's two ex-parliamentary New Party colleagues, Robert Forgan and Bill Allen, followed him into fascism. Although Forgan became first director of organisation and deputy leader, his heart was not in it and he retired in October 1934. Bill Allen served the early B.U.F. as a propagandist writer of great flair. In addition to his book *B.U.F., Oswald Mosley and British Fascism,* he contributed the ' Letters of Lucifer ' to the early *Blackshirt,* notable for their stinging attacks on the Tory plutocracy. Himself an ex-Tory buccaneer, he saw Mosley as an aristocratic adventurer in the Elizabethan tradition. After his early retirement from fascist politics, Allen concentrated on his family business and pursued his interest in Russian, particularly Georgian, history and art, on which he became a considerable expert.

A different type of adventurer was John Beckett, the I.L.P. M.P. for Peckham who ' stole the mace ' in a celebrated parliamentary incident in 1931, and joined the B.U.F. in March 1934. Like Mosley, Beckett was a product of the war and believed in a patriotic socialism. A courageous and effective propagandist, he edited the main B.U. weekly *Action* in 1936–7, becoming involved in a famous libel action when Lord Camrose sued him for calling him a Jew. In 1937, he broke off with William Joyce and Angus MacNab to form the National Socialist League; later he became secretary of the Duke of Bedford's People's Party.

His closest friend in the B.U.F. was William Joyce – an unlikely mixture of two completely different backgrounds and political histories. After Mosley, Joyce was the most remarkable personality in the Movement. Born in New York of Irish parents, he joined Mosley early in 1933 at the age of twenty-seven, after a varied career as a Black and Tan informer, brilliant English literature student (he obtained a first-class honours degree at Birkbeck College) and fanatical right-wing agitator. The guiding principles in Joyce's life were a highly abstract belief in British empire, coupled with a belief in a financial–Bolshevik world Jewish conspiracy that was destroying it. Diminutive, chain-smoking, dressed in a grubby raincoat, his face disfigured by a razor slash, Joyce appeared a frightening figure. For concentrated oratorical passion, delivered in a cold, clinical voice, he was in a class of his own. ' Thin, pale, intense, he had not been speaking for many minutes before we were electrified by this man. I have been a connoisseur of speech-making for a quarter of a century, but never before, in any country had I met a personality so terrifying in its dynamic force, so vitu-perative, so vitriolic. The words poured from him in a corrosive state.'[9] The source of Joyce's hatred seems to have been an intense feeling of betrayal. He and his family (who had returned to Ireland when he was two) were victims of the British withdrawal, the casualties of failing empire. Out of this experience grew a counter-revolutionary creed which was more abstract and consistent than that of anyone else in the B.U.F. ' The real struggle lies not between Conservatism and Socialism, not between Autocracy and Democracy, not between Capitalism and Communism, but between International Jewish Finance and National Socialist patriotism ', he wrote in 1937.[10] Joyce was one of the few in British fascism to carry this particular thought to its logical conclusion, for when the struggle between these two forces, as he saw it, was finally joined, no love of a country which had cut him off from his childhood roots prevent-ed him from joining Germany in the anti-Jewish crusade. And yet, when he was not ravaged by bitterness, he could be humorous, lovable and generous; and he went to his unrepentant death with dignity, a man of rare abilities twisted out of shape by one of the innumerable tragedies of our century.

Arthur Keith Chesterton, a cousin of G. K. Chesterton, offered another example of that passionate, abstract patriotism so characteri-stic of the B.U.F. His roots were in South Africa, where he lived half the year till his death. He had served with distinction in the war in the Durban Light Infantry, gaining the Military Cross at the age of twenty. In 1922 he had helped to crush the miners' up-rising on the Witwatersrand, leading one section of the final assault on Fordsburge, their last redoubt.* A journalist by profession, like

*The Witwatersrand revolt originated in a proposal by the coal owners to re-duce costs by introducing black labour to do skilled jobs at a lower rate of wage than white workers. The white workers struck in the name of the colour bar

Rex Tremlett, another South African who edited *Fascist Week*,
1933–4, Chesterton found it hard to settle down to civilian life
after these exciting experiences and drifted to England in the 1920s.
He edited a group of newspapers in Torquay.   When the call came
in 1933 he was working as a public relations man at the Shakespeare
Memorial Theatre, Stratford-upon-Avon.   Chesterton was the
B.U.F.'s best polemicist.   For him fascism was 'the passionate
revolt of the spirit of man against the lawless stampedes of greed and
treachery carried out by liberalism throughout the ages.'[11]   The
chief agents of this stampede were the Jews, whom Chesterton savaged vigorously and unrelentingly.   Jews parading in the uniform
of ex-servicemen particularly annoyed him and he became involved
in an undignified squabble with the *Jewish Chronicle* about the
proportions of Jews and Gentiles killed in the First World War.[12]
At the same time, Chesterton was by no means as uncritical of
Germany as many in the British Union were inclined to be, and this
was one of the issues which led to his break with Mosley in 1938,
soon after publishing a eulogistic biography, *Portrait of a Leader*.
In the Second World War he served with the British forces in the
Middle East and helped put Haile Selassie back on the throne
which blackshirts in 1935 had been so eager that he should vacate.
After the war he founded the League of Empire Loyalists, and
more recently was involved in the politics of the National
Front.

Beckett, Joyce and Chesterton, together with men like 'Bill'
Risdon, a Birmingham follower from I.L.P. days, later B.U.F.
chief agent, represented the political, propagandist wing of the
movement.   The chief organisation men were Neil Francis-Hawkins, the director-general from 1935 onwards, and Bryan Donovan,
his assistant. Francis-Hawkins, a fat surgical-instrument salesman,
with a British Fascist background in the 1920s, was a first-class
administrator and brought much-needed order to British Union's
affairs, following the Forgan régime. He drove himself unceasingly,
working twelve hours a day, expected others to do so, and thereby
caused much wife-trouble at N.H.Q. His loyalty to Mosley was a
byword.   Donovan, a former Captain in the Indian Army and

---

which they saw as a defence against a capitalist threat to both employment and
wage-rates. General Smuts ruthlessly crushed the strike with troops; but the
chief beneficiaries were not, as might be supposed, the Communists, but the
Nationalists, whose leading young lawyers, like Oswald Pirow, later Mosley's
friend, defended the strike leaders in the subsequent trials. There is clearly a
close link between this kind of Nationalism and the fascist defence of British
workers against Jewish undercutting in the 1930s and coloured immigration in
the 1950s. It is ironic that A. K. Chesterton should have been on the side of
'multi-racial capitalists' in 1922. (For the best account of this episode, see
Norman Herd, *1922: the revolt on the Rand* (1966).)

assistant director-general (administration) was one of the B.U.F.'s martinets.   According to Reynell Bellamy, a former official, he was ' too taut, inflexible, exacting'.

Between the politicals and the bureaucrats a perpetual battle raged in the Policy Directorate, a group of senior officials appointed by Mosley to thrash out major policy questions.   The central issue was whether the energies and resources of the movement should best go to building up the organisation or to mounting a more radical propaganda.   For Joyce, Beckett and Chesterton, Mosley was far too cautious.   They disliked the B.U.F.'s half-hearted anti-semitism, and wanted to make it a central issue.   They also intensely disliked its military aspects, the uniforms and saluting, which they saw as emanations of Francis-Hawkins' tidy, bureaucratic mind, as well as Mosley's megalomania.   Mosley tried to hold the balance, but he tended to come down on Francis-Hawkins' side. In return, he was rewarded with unswerving loyalty; and it is true to say that he kept the allegiance of the bureaucrats far better than that of the political individualists, for whom the B.U.F. in the end proved an inadequate vehicle for their ideas and ambitions.

Standing somewhat outside these power configurations was the Scotsman Alexander Raven Thomson, the philosopher of British fascism, who joined Mosley at the age of thirty-four in 1933 and remained with him till his death in 1955.   Thomson had studied philosophy and economics at Scottish, German and American universities.   He was one of the generation that fell under Spengler's spell.   But like Mosley he could not accept Spengler's conclusions. In his book *Civilisation as Divine Superman* (1932) Thomson argued that civilisation could avoid decay if it adopted as its model the communal organisation of Maeterlinck's insect communities, ' super-organisms ' in which individual differentiation took place within a ' communal spirit shared by every member of the hive '. In practical terms, decay could be arrested by substituting collectiv-ism for individualistic capitalism.   Such views brought Thomson for a time into the Communist Party, but his corporate analogy as well as his rejection of the materialist view of history made the association brief.   Man could attain the collectivist goal only under the inspiration of great leadership and an evolutionary faith.   In Mosley Thomson found the leader and in fascism the faith he had been looking for.   He was the B.U.F.'s main theorist of the Corporate State; but the fascist struggle brought him out of the study onto the soapbox where he acquitted himself with great courage in face of violent hostility.   Mosley wrote: ' He died young, and we his friends will always feel that the prison years and the decline of his country combined to curtail a life which would have been of brilliant service to the nation.'[13]

Raven Thomson was one of the few intellectuals to bridge the gulf between thought and action, thereby earning Mosley's rarest accolade 'thought-deed man'. Most hovered uneasily on the other side, emitting alternate signals of encouragement and distress. Not that Mosley attached much importance to bringing them over – far too little, he now admits. He launched his movement with the phrase ' I have finished with those who think; henceforth I shall go to those who feel.' His followers took him at his word. In fascist rhetoric, intellectuals were the 'pink pansies of Bloomsbury... sobbing away the Empire ',[14] the shrill word-spinners of Spengler's Megalopolis, the ' so-called gentlemen who will not fight for King and Country' as Mosley himself called them. For the average fascist, contemporary art and literature were unambiguous signs of decadence and exhaustion.

It is a matter of record that the English intelligentsia which came to political awareness in the 1930s tended to be pro-communist. According to J. M. Cameron, ' Marxism in the form approved by the Communist Parties was in the 'thirties a kind of cultural establishment with vast influence.'[15] The reasons for this are complex and have never been properly explained. It was not nearly as true on the Continent where fascism had a wide intellectual appeal. This suggests that the phenomenon must be analysed in English terms. Perhaps the key factor was the weakness in England of non-liberal intellectual traditions. The successful oligarchic struggle against the monarchy had destroyed any independent theory of the State. The completeness of England's Industrial Revolution had destroyed the land as a political force. Catholicism was always weak. The triumph of the factory system had greatly shrunk the artisan class. There were no nationalist grievances. These developments left liberalism as the only significant ideology and hence the only significant intellectual barrier to marxism (there were, of course, powerful non-intellectual barriers – tradition, deference, etc.). Once liberalism was weakened by its association in the 1930s with the ugliest face of capitalism, marxism seemed to young radicals to be the only available alternative. They largely accepted the marxist identification of ' state ', ' capitalism ' and ' fascism ', and never seriously considered the possibility that state power, properly used, might be capitalism's most dangerous enemy. It was not, indeed, till 1945 that the traditional identification of the State with Reaction was to be broken.

By contrast, those intellectuals who did sympathise with fascism tended to be marginal figures: some were not really English at all. Representative of what Robert Blake calls the ' buccaneering, adventurous, unconventional ' tradition in Toryism were Major Yeats-Brown, author of *Bengal Lancer* and editor of *Everyman* (' a Bohemian on horseback surviving into an industrialised age '[16]), the poet Roy Campbell, and the writer Douglas Jerrold, founder

and editor of the *English Review*. The first two publicly identified
with fascism. Jerrold wrote about Mosley with sympathy and
discernment:

> He is very un-English in his dislike of forms and red-tape
> and of the slow progress nowhere in particular which fills up
> the lives of Kensington and Belgravia. . . . Mosley is a great
> orator; among my generation, only John Strachey can even
> run him close, and the intellectual content of Strachey's
> effervescence is too thin even for the Albert Hall on a Sunday
> afternoon. Mosley is also, which most people deny, an
> important man. . . . He has no great chance of attaining a res-
> ponsible position in the public life of Europe. He is, however,
> telling the truth as he sees it, and he is one of the few people
> in England who are even trying to do so. . . . He has sacrificed
> the certainty of office for the certainty of a life in the political
> wilderness . . . to call [him] a careerist is itself impertinence
> of the most vulgar order.

Interestingly, Jerrold reported that Mosley ' does not believe that
he will succeed in his own chosen fashion. He does believe that it
is somebody's duty to keep alive in times of tolerable prosperity an
active distrust of the political machines, so that when adversity
comes, the people may not find themselves without hope.'[17]

Jerrold was linked to an important conservative literary movement in the early years of this century, whose aesthetic and social
credo – anti-romantic, anti-humanist – was expressed by T. E.
Hulme, Hugh Kingsmill and T. S. Eliot. Such writers occasionally
looked to fascism to defend civilised values against democracy in
both literature and politics: more frequently they sought to defend
civilisation on the aesthetic and religious, rather than on the
corrupted political, plane. ' The attempt to externalise the kingdom of heaven in temporal shape must end in disaster,' wrote
Kingsmill. It summed up his own, as well as Eliot's, attitude to
fascism.[18]

Unlike High Anglicanism, Catholicism had developed a social
and economic theory requiring action on the political plane; and
many Catholics saw in fascism the movement that corresponded
closest to their social ideals. *Blackshirt* of 17 May 1935 reported
that twelve per cent of leading B.U.F. officials were Catholics, a
substantially higher proportion than the Catholic percentage in
the country. In the late 1930s, the Catholic newspapers, the *Herald*
and the *Tablet*, were among the few journals that reported Mosley
and British Union sympathetically, the *Herald* of 10 June 1938
writing that ' its policy is the nearest approach to the social theory
of the encyclicals that we have yet been offered by any prominent
political party '. The Catholic solution to the social problem,

proclaimed by Pope Leo XIII in his encyclical *Rerum Novarum* (1891), and eloquently expounded in England by Hilaire Belloc and G. K. Chesterton, entailed the widest possible distribution of property. Rejecting class warfare, it favoured a corporative system modelled on the ancient guilds. Catholics, as the eminent theologian Father C. C. Martindale, S.J., explained in *Action* in November 1938, found it difficult to accept fascism's claims to total allegiance from the citizen; but Catholics and other Christians found these claims, unpalatable as they were, preferable to the equally totalitarian claims of atheistic, materialistic marxism. Opposition to the Red Peril made ' many clergy and ministers in Britain . . . among the most ardent advocates of Fascism' according to the ' fascist padre', the Reverend E. C. Opie.[19] The Reverend E. B. Nye was another cleric who harped on the bolshevik theme in his many contributions to Mosley's journals.

Two writers who did transfer Hulme's aesthetic theories to the political plane were Wyndham Lewis and Ezra Pound. Bereft of religious faith, they went further than the Catholic thinkers. Wyndham Lewis saw fascism as a defence against democracy; Ezra Pound as a defence against usury which ' thickened the line' of modern literature and modern life. Lewis initially praised Hitler and contributed to the *British Union Quarterly*: he only abandoned his support for fascism when he perceived that it ' had certain characteristics in common with what he called democracy'.[20] Pound divided his admiration between Mussolini, Mosley and Thomas Jefferson. His strange articles with their capital letters and American slang were a prominent and idiosyncratic feature of *Action* in the late 1930s. In 1939 he wrote, ' Usury is the cancer of the world which only the Knife of Fascism can cut out of the life of the nation.'[21]

Although these traditions are unthinkingly dubbed right-wing or reactionary, Pound's polemics against international finance and his support for the amateur monetary reformers Silvio Gesell, Major Douglas and A. R. Orage (the last also a theorist of guild socialism) bridged the conventional antithesis between right- and left-wing thought. Mosley and a substantial proportion of his following had come to fascism from the left in politics. The most famous example of intellectual sympathy from the left is George Bernard Shaw. It is worth recalling what Shaw said about Mosley in his Fabian lecture, ' In Praise of Guy Fawkes' (1933):

Sir Oswald Mosley – a very interesting man to read just now: one of the few people who is writing and thinking about real things, and not about figments and phrases. You will hear something more of Sir Oswald Mosley before you are through with him. I know you dislike him, because he looks like a

man who has some physical courage and is going to do something and that is a terrible thing. You instinctively hate him,
because you do not know where he will land you; and he
evidently means to uproot some of you. Instead of talking
round and round political subjects and obscuring them with
bunk verbiage without ever touching them, and without
understanding them, all the time assuming states of things
which ceased to exist from twenty to six hundred and fifty
years ago, he keeps hard down on the actual facts of the
situation. When you pose him with the American question,
' What's the Big Idea?' he replies at once, ' Fascism ' for he
sees that Fascism is a Big Idea, and that it is the only visible
practical alternative to Communism – if it really is an alternative and not a halfway house. The moment things begin
to break up and something has to be done, quite a number
of men like Mosley will come to the front who are at present
ridiculed as Impossibles.[22]*

Shaw's encomiums for Mosley, Hitler, Mussolini and Stalin have
been consistently misinterpreted as ' an eagerness to shock British
Liberals '.[23] Shaw saw fascism and communism alike as twin
expressions of the collectivist creed he had preached ever since the
1880s. The failures of democratic politicians had long convinced
him that this creed could be implemented only by heroic realists.
His collectivism and his doctrine of the Superman thus combined
to make him look with favour on the social experiments initiated
by Hitler and Mussolini. Mosley, of course, had been heavily
influenced by Shaw himself. Shaw reciprocated the esteem and
supported virtually the whole of the B.U.F.'s programme, down to
the occupational franchise.[24] He was no sentimentalist, and in his
play On the Rocks accepted the need for brutality and ruthlessness to
bring about necessary changes. But, like many who recognised
Mosley's ability and seriousness, he did not think that Mosley's
fascism would succeed in England. Also he had no sympathy
with anti-semitism.

Shaw is the outstanding, although highly idiosyncratic, representative of those who saw fascism as a legatee of the nineteenth
century revolt against capitalism. John Scanlon started writing
a regular industrial feature for Action in 1936 under the pen name
of John Emery. A former miner and shipyard worker, a close friend
of Maxton and a prominent I.L.P. journalist, he had written a

*Shaw annoyed his fellow socialists at another Fabian jamboree in 1937 when he
remarked, ' My friend, Oswald Mosley, is a much better Socialist than most of
them.' When a lady came up to ask him to lead the fight against fascism, Shaw
replied, ' Why do socialists fight each other and let the reactionaries in?'
(George Catlin, For God's Sake, Go!, p. 140.)

brilliantly mordant book, *The Decline and Fall of the Labour Party*, in 1932. Maxton, he wrote on 16 October 1936, ' should join with Sir Oswald Mosley in a great National campaign having but one object. The object should be to rouse the British workers against their warmongering leaders.' Another who came over from Labour for much the same reason was Hugh Ross Williamson, writer, playwright, editor of the *Bookman* from 1930–4. In his book *Who Is for Liberty?*, written when he was still Labour candidate for East Dorset in 1938, Ross Williamson rejected the marxist identification of fascism and capitalism. ' Marx predicted a final struggle of disintegrating capitalism: what, in fact, happened was the emergence of Fascism. Therefore Fascism must be the final struggle of disintegrating capitalism. That is the argument. There is no other.'[25] Ross Williamson concluded that fascism was ' a form of anti-capitalist Socialism ' and that ' the real genius of capitalism in its struggle for survival is that it has set its two opponents at each other's throats '.[26] ' Peace, civilisation itself may depend on uniting the Socialists of the Labour Party with the members of British Union,' he wrote in 1939.

For John Scanlon and Hugh Ross Williamson fascism was heir to the isolationist tradition that rejected British involvement in ' very foreign affairs ' (the title of another of Scanlon's books) as a diversion from the tasks of social reform. Mosley's combination of peace abroad and social reform at home attracted two other very dissimilar characters. The first was the novelist Henry Williamson, author of the prize-winning *Tarka the Otter* (1927). Williamson was the poet and chronicler of the war-generation. With Ezra Pound, he believed that wars were not made by ordinary people but by the ' usurial moneyed interests '.[27] The same interests were destroying the life of rural England. In 1935 he bought a derelict farm at Stiffkey in North Norfolk which he farmed according to the principles of ' Turnip ' Townshend. ' The spirit of the farm and what I was trying to do there was the spirit of Oswald Mosley. It was all part of the same battle.'[28] Williamson was a nature romantic. He was also a political romantic. His dream was to get his friend T. E. Lawrence to join Mosley in a great peace campaign: they were to discuss it when Lawrence was killed.[29] Mosley appears as Sir Hereward Birkin in *The Phoenix Generation* (part of Williamson's autobiographical saga *Chronicle of Ancient Sunlight*) leading the fight against international finance, that ' Minotaur which claims another generation of European youth to bleed to death on the battlefields.' What Mosley represented to Williamson (and still represents) is best summed up in the following passage in the same novel:

> Birkin is *my* generation, he is English of the English. I think it is a great pity that he resigned office from the Labour party.

But then all history is a pity. He belonged to the war generation, and we survivors all resolved to *do something*, to *be* something different when it was all over on the Western Front,
that great livid wound that lay across Europe suppurating
during more than fifteen hundred nights and days – torrents
of steel and prairie fires of flame, the roar of creation if you
like. Birkin should have remained in Parliament – that was
his platform – but what's the use of talking about should-haves,
or might-haves? Birkin remains the *only* man of prominence
in England with the new spirit. He limped away from the
battlefield determined that never again would it happen.
Perhaps such a spirit can only be acceptable to a new generation after another war. When he is dead. And I hope
I'll be dead too.

Beverley Nichols was also drawn to Mosley's campaign for peace.
President of the Oxford Union, editor of *Isis*, prolific author, his
book *Cry Havoc* (1933) had become the bible of the pacifist generation. This was the period when *Action* with its usual contempt for
the 'pink pansies of Bloomsbury' referred to him as La Beverley.
Nichols evidently did not hold this against Mosley, for in his *News
of England* (1938) he produced a highly sympathetic account of the
man, his peace aims and his movement. 'A million men may not
be forced, by the government, to wear the bright uniform of the
state, but they *are* forced to wear the drab uniform of poverty.
They may not be compelled to stand in a straight line on the parade
ground, but they *are* compelled to stand in a ragged line outside the
Labour Exchange. To talk about " freedom " in a country where
the doctrine of *laissez-faire* has come to mean simple criminal
negligence is as irritating as to talk about "oppression" in a country
where nine-tenths of the people heartily enjoy the " oppression ",
and only ask for more.' But Nichols would not wear the fascist
uniform. ' The reason is because I once saw a photograph of a
frightened Jewish child, standing outside the door of a school in
Germany, from which it had been locked out by the " Aryan "
authorities.' To Mosley he protested violently against an anti-
semitic article which had appeared in *Action*. ' This sort of thing
drags you down to the level of Streicher. I cannot believe that you
who have given proof of such high ideals can possibly have approved
it. Please say that you did not.' Mosley replied enigmatically:

I can so well appreciate the factors in our movement that
repel you. Anyone with innate kindness is at first spiritually
restrained from the harshness of the modern struggle. I have
seen it before and the final realisation of the hard necessity
is an experience sad to witness. Dynamic ages – like all great
things in nature – are in many respects brutal. Childbirth

itself and most wonders of life and death – to the inherently
good these things are tragic and instinctively they seek
another way.   They only come to our way when, in actual
experience, they find there is no other.   I will at least to the
utmost of my power reduce to the minimum the pain. . . .[30]

Nichols did not reply.   To Hugh Ross Williamson who voiced similar doubts Mosley said, ' I only wish that you could be put partly
to sleep and wake up when all you wanted to be done has been done.'
Here we come to the heart of the intellectual's difficulty not just with
fascism but with any revolutionary movement that involves them,
however remotely, in ' the harshness of the modern struggle '.
The intellectuals could share Mosley's ends; they could not approve
of his means, means which he regarded as essential to secure those
ends.   Were they deceiving themselves?   Or was he deceiving
himself?   It is to chief features of that struggle – violence and anti-
semitism – that we must now turn our attention.

Chapter 18

The Politics of Confrontation

THE British Union of Fascists got off to a rowdy start. To the *Daily Telegraph*'s ' Peterborough ' Mosley complained in December 1932 of being followed from meeting to meeting ' by an organised band of Communists whose object was to interrupt all his speeches '.[1] On 24 October at a meeting in the Memorial Hall, Farringdon, he had made his first recorded anti-Jewish remark, referring to hecklers as ' three warriors of the class war – all from Jerusalem '.[2] A typical early confrontation took place at the Battersea Town Hall in December. Communists, reportedly armed with razors and broken milk-bottles, attacked fascist stewards. Captain Godfrey, a member of the Battersea Borough Council, alleged that fascists used rubber truncheons in reply.[3]

The lag between action and reputation is never more clear than in the early history of the B.U.F. This was the period when its stewarding was at its least restrained. Yet it did not really acquire a reputation for thuggishness till the mid-1930s when its methods had been much improved. The most spectacular example of stewards getting out of hand (with the exception of Olympia, which we will consider separately) occurred in the Manchester Free Trade Hall on 12 March 1933. A man asked a series of questions on anti-semitism. He persisted in his observations, whereupon a steward went up to him and told him to sit down. Mosley from the platform could be heard telling the steward to leave him alone. But apparently the man then called the steward a ' lousy bastard ', the steward hit him and violence broke loose. A row of chairs was lifted in the air and used as weapons by the anti-fascists – a favourite device, to be repeated at the Oxford Carfax Assembly Rooms in 1936; the stewards retaliated with rubber truncheons, issued by Hamilton Piercy, the head of the Fascist Defence Force.

Manchester was one of the very few indoor meetings at which the police openly intervened, telling the stewards to remove themselves on the theory that this would quieten the crowd. This. too, had important consequences. For over a year after the Manchester meeting, Mosley refused to have the police in the building. He claimed they would take action against the stewards, not against the disturbers. Although his excitable Defence Force had caused all the trouble Mosley was resolutely loyal to them. ' When my men are asked to leave, I leave with them,' he called defiantly at the Manchester audience in closing the meeting.[4]

A different kind of confrontation occurred at Bristol on 27 March 1934. After a crowded meeting at Bristol's Colston Hall, 400 blackshirt stewards who had assembled to march away were attacked *en route* by a hostile crowd. In the House of Commons on 9 April Sir John Gilmour, the home secretary, blamed the disorder largely on the 'semi-military evolutions by the fascists', their marching 'in formation' and their 'provocative' behaviour. All these charges were to recur frequently in the 1930s. In his reply Mosley argued that marching away in formation was the only way to defend men 'who were well known to roughs'. Gilmour replied that if such men had not been wearing black shirts they would not be 'well known' to be fascists.

The Bristol affair was in fact the first example of a typical conflict situation in the 1930s, one which was to give the police some of their greatest headaches – the organised opposition outside the hall, and Mosley's determination not to be driven off the streets. Following a meeting at Worthing Pavilion on 9 October 1934, Mosley and leading lieutenants were tried for riotous assembly before the Worthing Police Court and later the Sussex Assizes. They were all acquitted. One of the accusations against Mosley was that he personally had strutted round outside a café after the meeting, thereby challenging the opposition to do its worst. To this he made a characteristic rejoinder. 'If any body of "roughs" intimated that they had chased him from the streets of his own country which, as a British citizen, he had a perfect right to walk upon, he should certainly at once walk down the street to show that mob law and terror did not prevail in this country.'[5]

These charges and counter-charges, each side claiming that it was acting defensively against the other's attacks, went on throughout the 1930s and have continued in the history books ever since. Truth, as Mr Baldwin once sagely remarked, is many-sided, and the side which one happens to be on depends largely on one's political preferences. One man's defence is another man's provocation. Here one can do no more than dispel a few of the more vulgar myths, and attempt to give some explanation of how these contests evolved.

In his thinly fictionalised biographical sketches, *Fellow Travellers*, T. C. Worsley describes the way in which a 'perfectly peaceful meeting organised by the Communists' was broken up by Mosley's blackshirted 'bully boys'. These 'horrible-looking toughs' arrived in four green vans fitted with wire over the windows. After putting on knuckledusters they charged the meeting ten abreast in two lines. They overturned the platform and smashed the banners, knocking over and injuring 'comrades' as well as their wives and children in the process. They then took off in their vans again 'laughing and grinning to each other'. Two policemen, who had been watching the whole scene ' did nothing, absolutely nothing. They just stood aside and let it happen '. When the upper-class communist ' Lady Nellie ' reported the disgraceful occurrence to her brother ' an Under-Secretary or something in the National Government ' his only comment was ' If you will attend street-corner meetings you must expect what you get.'

It fits in neatly with the left-wing myth of the 1930s – brutal fascists going around beating up ' peaceful ' opponents, with the complicity of the police and National Government, three-quarters fascist themselves. But as a historical snapshot of British fascism in action it is grotesquely misleading. Leaving the role of the police and the Government to one side, the facts were almost the exact opposite to those portrayed in this vignette. Blackshirts rarely interfered with the meetings of their opponents, and were in fact forbidden by Mosley to do so.[6] Rather it was communists who were encouraged and often organised to break up fascist meetings.* Whether they were justified in doing so is a debatable question. But to pretend that it happened the other way round is simply bad history.

Any serious account, then, of political violence in the 1930s must start with the actions and motives of the Communist Party in breaking up its opponents' meetings. Contrary to popular belief, communist-organised disruption of political meetings did not start with the formation of the British Union of Fascists in 1932. It had been going on all through the 1920s as part of the tactic of increasing class militancy. In an article in the *Evening Standard* of 30 February 1927 C. F. G. Masterman, the ex-Liberal cabinet minister, commented on the ' new phenomenon ' of ' organised rowdiness ' at political meetings and referred to an ' electoral reign of terror and intimidation ' organised by communists and socialists in the East End of London. In 1930, in obedience to the Comintern's ' Class against Class ' line which saw social democracy as the ' moderate ' wing of fascism, the new leadership of Pollitt and Palme-Dutt proclaimed an all-out attack on the Labour Government. There should not be a Labour meeting held anywhere', Pollitt said in January 1930, ' but that the revolutionary workers in that district attend such meetings and fight against the speakers, whoever they are, " Left ", " Right ", or " Centre ". They should never be allowed to address the workers. This will bring us into conflict with the authorities, but this must be done.'[7]

By these, and other, means, the Communist Party hoped, of course, to get the support of workers disgusted with Labour's capitulation to a disintegrating capitalism. But it was not the

In 1936 Mosley claimed that over 500 anti-fascists had been convicted for assaults on fascists or on fascist meetings (*Blackshirt*, 14 Nov 1936). This figure was not challenged at the time.

only contender in the field.   There was Mosley's New Party and
also the I.L.P.   These groups were even more dangerous to
communist hopes than the orthodox Labour leaders, since with their
'social demagogy' they could hope to win over the 'slum-
proletarian and demoralised working-class'[8] to their own brand
of social salvation.   Hence, in addition to a general opposition
offered to the Labour leadership, the communists paid particular
attention to the New Party and I.L.P. which were both thought
to show high fascist potential: indeed, for much of 1930 and 1931
the names of Mosley and Maxton were bracketed together in
communist propaganda as potential fascists.

Communist opposition to New Party meetings has already been
described; less well known is the systematic attempt to disrupt I.L.P.
meetings, especially in Glasgow.   The issue came to a head in June
1932.   ' You are a lot of dirty rats,' shouted David Kirkwood to his
communist tormentors at an open-air meeting, adding, ' If you
Glasgow communists ruled Britain I would join the Tory party.'
In the mêlée which followed, Kirkwood was reported by *Forward* as
' planting his foot on the nearest Communist face and pushing hard'.
On this occasion ' a few enthusiastic members of the I.L.P. had
volunteered for steward duty, but they had been given no definite
instructions and wore nothing to distinguish them from the rest of
the crowd.   One half did not know who the other half were.   As a
result they were quite ineffectual in maintaining order or protecting
the speakers. . . .'   The I.L.P. leaders were divided about what to
do.   John McGovern was in favour of physical force.   ' The I.L.P.',
he said, ' has conducted meetings in the square every Sunday
night for years and we intend to maintain our rights.'   John
Heenan, chairman of the Exchange branch of the I.L.P., while
admitting that ' the organised suppression of free speech . . . has
been going on for eighteen months now ', argued that it should be
met by ' moral and not physical force '.[9]   In fact, a shift in the
Communist Party ' line' back to co-operation with left-wing groups
absolved the I.L.P. from having to decide between these two alternatives: and hostile Communist attention concentrated entirely on
the B.U.F.   It must be remembered, however, that though the
I.L.P. as an organisation remained staunchly anti-fascist a considerable number of its militants joined up with Mosley and
brought into the B.U.F. both a hatred of communism and considerable experience of fighting it in the streets.

To anyone unfamiliar with the Communist Party it has always
seemed inherently implausible that a party with such a tiny membership (it was scarcely more than 5000 in the early 1930s) should be
responsible for all the mischief attributed to it.   The mistake arise
both from underestimating the numbers of people actually required
to whip up a disturbance and from ignorance of the Communis

Party's *modus operandi*. When Mosley claims that the bulk of the disturbances he faced in the 1930s were organised by the communists, he does not mean that only communists took part in them. What he is saying is that communist agitation was the crucial factor in activating opposition. It takes, after all, relatively few people to create disorder. Carefully calculated acts of violence on authority, provoking over-reaction, would inflame class hatred; rumours of 'atrocities' would complete the good work.[10] These were the classic methods of agitation, tested by revolutionary groups and secret societies in every European revolution since 1789.

Communist agitation was promoted by groups and organisations that had no obvious connection at all with the Communist Party. The Communist Party itself was, in Philip Toynbee's words, merely 'the iceberg peak above the submarine majority'. The open membership was always supplemented by a secret membership and a still wider circle of 'cryptos' and 'fellow-travellers' actively at work in a wide variety of groups. These were the 'satellite' or 'front' organisations in which, as Mr Pelling has written, 'members of the party [had] secured all or most of the executive posts ... although the honorary positions would be occupied by an array of non-Communist "figurehead" nominees for display purposes'.[11] The National Council of Civil Liberties appears to have been in this category. Ronald Kidd, its secretary, wrote to the *New Statesman* on 8 September 1934, ' My Council expresses no opinion as to the desirability of holding any counter demonstration to Mosley's meeting in Hyde Park. ...' In fact, the Special Branch reported that at this time the activities of the N.C.C.L. were directed, via Kidd, from Communist Party headquarters.[12] Another Communist Party front was the innocent-sounding Co-ordinating Committee for Anti-Fascist Activities. Both the N.C.C.L. and this group were prominent in the anti-fascist campaign; the latter in organising violence, the former in pinning the blame on the fascists. In addition, small 'fractions' of communists, open or secret, occupied strategic positions in factories or trade unions, enabling them to get anti-fascist resolutions passed by the small minority of active union members, and to organise agitation under official union auspices.[13] Further, from the early days of the B.U.F. the Communist Party was active in the East End, mobilising Jews in the anti-fascist cause: poor Jews to attack meetings, and rich Jews to give money. All of this activity may or may not have been meritorious and justified by the circumstances; but it was *organised* with the definite objective of winning support for the communist and revolutionary cause.

Of course, the game takes two to play. There are many ways of avoiding violence other than forming a fascist movement to meet it. Thus Mosley's bare description of the situation in the 1930s, ' They attacked; we defended ', is not really adequate to explain his response.

The very act of calling oneself a fascist in the inflamed conditions of the 1930s was a provocation to many. British fascism was bound to be identified with Continental fascism. Left-wingers interpreted Mosley in the light of what had already happened in Germany and Italy. Transnational passions were thus inevitably concentrated on national movements. In calling himself a fascist, in adopting the black shirt, Mosley was deliberately identifying himself with a movement which, rightly or wrongly, was regarded with peculiar abhorrence by all left-wing organisations. By forming a fascist movement he was giving the Communist Party a chance for growth and leadership which it did not otherwise possess in England, and above all a moral justification for acts of preventive violence. Someone whose main anxiety was to avoid violence (or for that matter to stop the growth of communism) would not have embarked on this course.

Mosley's own psychology and *modus operandi* is therefore very important in explaining the nature of the fascist response. Mosley was a fighter who attracted fighters to him: had he not been he would not have called himself a fascist. This does not mean that he went around looking for fights. It does mean that avoiding them was not his chief priority. This was reinforced by his contempt for the old gangs and their craven psychology. The fighter took over, the soldier came to the fore.

In projecting his own fascist appeal to the people Mosley adopted a style at once traditional and modern. Traditional was the big public meeting to get across policy, modern was the theatricality and bombast to sugar the pill. This was the tradition of popular politics on which Mosley had been brought up and to which he added its last innovations. It was already on the point of obsolescence, and the big main meetings of the 1930s were its last expression, just as Mosley was its last exponent.

The big public meeting thus performed a central function in fascist propaganda which it never did for the communists, who relied much more on 'agitation'; hence the problem that arose of protecting New Party and B.U.F. meetings from assault. This was the function of the Defence Force. It was not its only one. Its other function was to 'defend the State from Communist violence if the collapse of the State should ever create such a necessity'.[14] In his pamphlet *Fascism in Britain* (1933) Mosley amplified as follows: 'We must organise to some extent on a military basis in case we are called upon to save the nation in a condition of anarchy when the normal measures of government have broken down.' This attitude must have been intensely provocative to all those who did not wish to be saved by fascism and would have had the effect of encouraging hostile action against it. It is hard to disagree with the *New Statesman*'s view that the military organisation of the B.U.F. was an ' incitement to violent resistance ', designed to help bring about the very situation which fascism was intended to meet.[15] Behind all the charges and counter-charges of the 1930s lies the simple truth that both sides needed each other to create a situation from which each might hope to benefit.

Having formed a fighting force, it was necessary to fight to keep up the *élan* of units organised specially for that purpose. Thus the legitimate aim of securing a hearing for the speakers at public meetings co-existed with the aim of ' blooding ' the troops. Sometimes these two aims coincided; that is, there was no means of keeping order at the meetings without sending in the stewards to prise out the interrupters. At other times, fighting was not always avoided as it should have been. Reliance on stewards inevitably lessened reliance on charm and eloquence to win round hostile opinion. ' Given a courteous hearing, he responded courteously as befits a sixth baronet ', noted one reporter in 1935.[16] On the other hand, any suspicion of rudeness or malice was far more liable than of old to provoke a cutting response. Asked by one interrupter what his profession was, Mosley flashed out: ' I fought in France for Great Britain so that rats like you might live ' – which predictably caused a disturbance and ejections,[17] and which obviously would not have been said had not a force of stewards been present to protect the speaker from the consequences of the remark. The ejection or maltreatment of persons who refused to stand up during the National Anthem was another clear sign of the corrupting effect of reliance on force. After the war Mosley told a meeting of supporters, ' You win not by the punches you give, but by the punches you dodge.' Such wisdom came later in the day.

Here we come to another aspect of fascist propaganda – Mosley's ' provocative ' processions and marches through working-class areas. The accepted view is that these marches were designed to provoke conflicts with ' Reds ' and ' Jews '. In fact they were primarily designed to attract support. The march or procession had three main purposes. The first was to create publicity for a big Mosley meeting in a town – very necessary for a movement which relied on meetings and lacked a supporting press to advertise them. Its second function was as an activity to involve members and give them something to do. Its third function was as a colourful means of propaganda aimed particularly at attracting working-class support. Mosley always claims he learnt it from the Labour Party.

Mosley's break with Labour was made on the assumption that he

would gain considerable working-class support by appealing to
his old Labour Party following above the heads of the leaders who
had betrayed them.   Hence the appeal to the working class – in
the East End of London in 1936 and in the big northern centres.
To those who assumed that working-class areas must *by definition*
be inhabited by anti-fascists, these marches were of course bound
to seem nothing but provocations.   That Mosley with his background may have sought out a working-class following is generally
ignored.

Nevertheless, in this strategy lay the dynamics of conflict.   It is
easy to forget how much political peace in England – or anywhere –
depends on the tacit assumption that the parties do *not* make any
determined effort to win over the supporters of the other side.
Had Mosley confined his appeals to retired colonels, farmers and
suburban housewives he would have aroused far less opposition.
Indeed, the B.U.F.'s rural campaigns passed off peacefully.   It
was campaigns in working-class areas, and particularly those areas
where the Communist Party had succeeded in entrenching itself,
that produced violence.

Despite this, the view that somehow the fascists were trying to
impose themselves where they were not wanted does have some
basis, if not in fact, in the English tradition of political parties.   The
traditional pattern of party development has been from the roots
upwards: local parties existed before their central organisations,
which came as capping-stones.   To some extent this is true even
of the Communist Party.   The B.U.F. was unique in starting from
the top and then trying to strike roots lower down.   This is what
gave its propaganda such a flamboyant and relentless quality.   In
Mosley's concept (which fitted Continental politics much better)
the idea, the organisation came first, then the task of conversion.
In British politics it has always been the other way round: the roots
came first and the ideas and institutions grew up round them.
This is what gave to the B.U.F. the character of the eternal poacher
on other people's domains.

However, few things Mosley did in the 1930s were quite as simple
as he makes out.   There was always a rational reason; there was
also invariably a psychological reason, connected with the demands
of the ' struggle ': this corresponded to the dual nature of fascism
itself.   Take the fascist activities in purely or largely Jewish areas.
Far from fascists enjoying marching through Jewish quarters,
wrote Mosley, ' we march through some of those streets for the
simple reason that no other means exist of getting from East to
West London or vice versa '.[18]   The reality was often strikingly
different.   ' You'll never come down to Whitechapel,' Jews and
communists would taunt blackshirts.   And of course the blackshirt
spirit would demand that they did just that.[19]   Police files on East

London make it clear that if one pitch became too quiet or attentive fascists would soon transfer it to more ' stimulating ' surroundings.[20] ' Sport ', confrontation, excitement, were all necessary to keep up the spirit of the movement, and, of course, invaluable in gaining publicity. Fascism saw itself as the movement of challenge, and it was necessary to be always challenging someone. Exactly the same strategy operated on the communist side.

This whole complicated pattern of challenge and response makes it extremely difficult to assign responsibility for violence. Legally, the responsibility rests with the opponents of fascism. They attacked fascist meetings, processions, and occasions.[21] By and large fascists did no more than the law entitled them to do to defend those occasions. The basic reason why more communists than fascists were convicted in the courts in the 1930s is that communists broke the law more frequently than fascists. Morally, the verdict has gone against Fascism; and the Public Order Act of 1936 was certainly passed on the assumption that the fascists were the guilty party. To the Left the anti-fascists were right to attack fascism simply because it was a ' bad thing '. And even the moderate Right found it hard to sympathise with Mosley. Their attitude was very much that of the newspaper which remarked of him at the time of the Smethwick by-election, ' Mr. Mosley rather asks for it, as he is a very provocative young man.'

Uncritical acceptance of Mosley's sole responsibility for violence obviously owes a lot to the war. But the conventional wisdom was well established before the war. Mussolini's famous statement, ' War is to man what childbirth is to woman ', was taken to epitomise fascism's approach to political problems. In Spain José Primo de Rivera talked of a ' dialectic of fists and pistols '. Mosley's motives were clearly mixed. His argument that the B.U.F. acted in self-defence,.that it minded its own business, that it campaigned in opposition areas to gain support, not to provoke the opposition, is largely true. But it is not enough in politics or anywhere else to be *largely* law-abiding or largely honest. There was just enough truth in the opposition charges to stick.

The general context in which violence took place was also favourable to opposition propaganda. The B.U.F.'s use of force always appeared to be more calculated, visible, more obviously organised than that of its opponents. In fact, the communists organised just as thoroughly, with as much military precision, as did the fascists. But their use of force was largely concealed; they were the guerilla army; fascists the traditional army. In the actual conflicts it proved all too easy to portray the situation as one in which ' single ' and ' innocent ' hecklers were brutally manhandled by fascist ' bullies ' or in which whole neighbourhoods rose ' spontaneously ' against deliberate fascist provocations. Take

meetings. What the observer often saw was a 'squad' of
stewards moving in to prise out a 'single' heckler from the middle
of a row. What he could not know was that the heckler in question
had planted himself in the middle of the row to make ejection as
difficult and conspicuous as possible; that he was surrounded by his
'comrades' with heavy boots to kick the stewards on the shins as they
struggled to the spot; that the 'un-English' tactic of setting half a
dozen stewards on one interrupter was necessary because many
opponents violently *fought* ejection, which they were not entitled to
do, and it would obviously be disastrous to stage single combats all
round the arena. Similarly with processions: a fascist march through
a working-class area was a visible, open act. But when bricks were
hurled at it what did anyone know about those hurling them?
Who were they? Where did they come from? It looked like a
'spontaneous' expression of anger. But usually it wasn't. The
court and police records leave no doubt about the extent of communist organisation of disruption, the calculated use of violence as
a tactic to discredit fascism. At the time, these things were largely
shrouded in darkness, a darkness partly induced by the brilliant
left-wing propaganda of such bodies as the National Council of
Civil Liberties. 'It is fashionable to allege that we were starry-eyed
idealists, but we certainly knew where to put the razor blades in
the potato when it came to a fight,' says that veteran of many
battles, Claud Cockburn.[22] What he omits to add is that these
'allegations' were carefully fostered by himself and others at a time
when it was advantageous to do so.

Having said all this, it is important to keep violence in perspective.
No one is known to have died as a direct result of over six years of
fascist politics. On the whole fascists suffered more severe injuries
than their opponents, but even so there were neither fascist nor
communist 'martyrs' such as in Germany, Italy, France, Spain
and other Continental countries where politics were genuinely
violent even when fascist movements were small. Above all,
violence occurred at only a small proportion of Mosley's meetings
and demonstrations. He addressed a thousand meetings or more
in the 1930s. The vast majority of them were peaceful. The disturbances were confined to the large urban centres, and even then only
intermittently. Nor is it fair to brand the blackshirts indiscriminately as thugs, sadists and bullies. A minority were, of course –
and there were just as many on the other side. But on the whole
they acquitted themselves with aplomb in many difficult situations,
and often with conspicuous courage.

By the start of 1934 there was at least some reason to believe
that Mosley had got them under proper control. In April of
that year he held a big meeting in Leeds. 'Sir Oswald Mosley's
peroration was one of the most magnificent feats of oratory I have

ever heard', wrote the enthusiastic Randolph Churchill. He added, ' Whatever else [the fascists] may be able to do for British politics, they have at least learned the art of holding orderly meetings.'[23] Olympia was just six weeks away.

Chapter 19

The Beast Unchained?

FOR BOTH fascists and anti-fascists Olympia was the epic battle of the 1930s. Fascists looked back with satisfaction on the ' beating ' they had given the ' Reds ' and claimed that it restored ' free speech ' in Britain. Anti-fascists regarded it as the moment when they unambiguously exposed the brutal face of fascism and condemned it thereafter in the eyes of all decent Englishmen. Today it is clear that Olympia's notoriety owes less to the events of the meeting itself than to the context in which they took place.

Its essential background was Lord Rothermere's massive press campaign in support of the B.U.F. which suddenly thrust it from comparative obscurity into the limelight. Mosley determined to exploit it by organising three monster rallies in London, hoping to develop enough momentum to start a bandwagon in the B.U.F.'s favour. The first of these meetings, at the Albert Hall, on 22 April 1934, had been a great success, with a packed house, well-received and widely reported speech, and no disorder. Olympia, with a seating capacity of 13,000, was planned on an even more grandiose scale for 1 June. The summer campaign was to culminate with a huge rally at the White City in August.

If the established parties hoped to kill fascism by ignoring it, the Communist Party hoped to use it for its own ends. Unable to make any significant headway on economic issues, it hoped to enlist workers and intellectuals under its banner in an anti-fascist crusade. After the success of the Albert Hall meeting on 22 April, it decided on co-ordinated, militant opposition all the way down the line. The level of violence escalated sharply. ' Within the last month', reported the *Blackshirt* of 15 June, ' a Blackshirt at Edinburgh has lost the sight of an eye, following a cut from glass caused by a brick thrown through a bus window. A Blackshirt who was at a meeting at Derby is in grave danger of losing the sight of one of his eyes. At Newcastle two of our men were so seriously injured that they had to receive medical attention for over a week. Violent attacks have been made on the speakers in Finsbury Park, headquarters have been ransacked at Gateshead, and in almost every part of the country Blackshirts have been violently attacked.' What is more, the Communist Party was now openly encouraging the use of force against fascism. The *Daily Worker* reported with approval assaults on fascists;* on 24 April 1934 it printed a major article

*At Edinburgh ' The workers turned on the local Blackshirt group after their

justifying violence; on 15 May it published a statement by a prominent communist urging workers ' to use force . . . it is no use
talking about constitutional methods '.   Communist motives were
mixed.   Probably the Party took seriously enough the menace of
fascism for, with the Rothermere alliance, fascism and capitalism
seemed to be marching hand in hand according to the marxist
scriptures.   Left-wing intellectuals were in particular very alive
to the menace of fascism.   They saw it everywhere – in the National
Government, headed by the decrepit MacDonald, in the police, in
the armed forces, in the public schools.   Mosley's movement was
seen as the most militant variety, ready to take over when the
moderate fascism of Stanley Baldwin collapsed before intensified
depression.   On the other hand, the Communist Party's tactic
of militant opposition was designed less to smash fascism than to
help communism, by dramatising its role as fascism's chief opponent,
thus undercutting the appeal of the moderate Labour leaders.
As Springhall put it after Olympia, ' The success of the counter-
demonstration would provide a great stimulus for the future growth
of the anti-Fascist movement. . . .'[1]

It was on 17 May 1934 that the *Daily Worker* published the first
of many calls for a ' counter-demonstration ' at Olympia to meet
Mosley's ' challenge to the working-class '.   Fascism ruled in Italy,
Germany and Austria by murdering workers.   Mosley's call for
British rearmament was simply a device to give soldiers weapons to
shoot the workers.   Mosley's tune ' is the old capitalist one dished
up through new instruments – the knuckleduster '.   The workers who
come to Olympia ' will see . . . hundreds of Rolls Royces and fine
cars – showing the class who want more fascist action against the
workers – to maintain their dividends '.[2]

Special Branch* reports give a detailed picture of communist
preparations:

> 25 May: The leaders of the Communist Party have definitely
> decided that something spectacular must be carried out by
> members of the organisation against the fascists at Olympia.
> . . . They realise that for any protest to be effective they must
> mobilise as many communists and sympathisers as possible.
> They have accordingly issued instructions to their followers to

meeting in Prince's Street, who were only saved by the intervention of the police
. . . the Manchester contingent leaving the town by bus suffered a number of
attacks.   The bus they travelled in was almost smashed up . . . four Blackshirts
were taken to the infirmary. . . . At the hall . . . windows were broken and one
group of Blackshirts at the rear of the hall was cut off, and despite police efforts
at rescue, the workers gave them a good hiding.' (*Daily Worker*, 4 June 1934.)

*The Special Branch was that section of the Police Force charged with the sur-
veillance of political activities.

obtain as many tickets of admission to Olympia as they possibly can. . . . *

The Special Branch reported on 28 May that the Communist Party was providing members with black shirts so that they could get in more easily and disrupt the stewarding.

A copy of the Party's instruction to 'All Street and Factory Cells' shows that the counter-demonstration was planned with military precision. There was to be an 'organised opposition' inside Olympia as well as 'a monster mass demonstration' outside. Cell leaders were charged with utilising 'every means of approach and publicity' in persuading workers of the necessity of the counter-demonstration. They were to arrange for all cell members, friends and relatives to apply for tickets couching their letters of application so as to appear friendly to fascism. Members in trade unions should raise the question of Olympia at their branch meetings, get the branch to declare its support for the counter-demonstration and try to get a contingent from the branch or factory sent to Olympia. Numbers of tickets obtained and the names of 'comrades' who agreed to go inside the meeting were to be sent immediately to party headquarters. In addition, cells should organise the chalking of slogans and distribution of anti-fascist leaflets. Every cell was exhorted to 'plan and organise to bring a party of workers to Olympia', taking advantage of the group excursion rates offered by the London Underground.[3]

On 4 June the Special Branch noted that 'many of the Communists who are going to take part in the counter-demonstration have stated their intention of carrying missiles'. A final report of 7 June said that communists '*have been especially active among the Jewish elements in the East End*, from whom they hope to obtain a large number of demonstrators' (my italics). It also provided a summary of communist tactics inside the auditorium:

> The communists and sympathisers who have obtained tickets for the meeting will sit in groups in different parts of the hall. They will act in an orderly way during the opening of the meeting . . . but after Sir Oswald Mosley has commenced his speech slogans will be shouted by each group in turn, according to a pre-arranged plan. A few men have been told off to locate the main lighting switch, with a view, if possible to cutting off the light at a favourable moment.[4]

It all sounded very formidable and highly dangerous. But there was a considerable flaw lying at the heart of the campaign.

*One tactic was to write letters to the *Evening News* praising the B.U.F. Lord Rothermere's organ had offered free tickets for the best letters published on the theme of 'Why I Like the Blackshirts'.

Like Hitler in the closing days of the Second World War, the Communist Party manœuvred largely fictitious divisions. They were as yet in no position to mount monster demonstrations (though they were soon to be), especially not one both inside and outside Olympia. It is unlikely that more than 500 communists were able to get inside Olympia, out of an audience of 12,000; and the number may have been even less.

Unfortunately, nothing comparable is known about the B.U.F.'s plans to counter the communist assault. One would think that the Special Branch had sources of information within fascist headquarters. The fact that they had nothing of interest to report suggests that the B.U.F. took no special precautions beyond the routine – having a large body of stewards on duty, ready to eject any persistent interrupters. Certainly there is no evidence as Benewick claims of a deliberate switch from ' defensive ' to ' offensive ' violence.[5]

The Communist Party organised four columns to march to Olympia. The largest was from Stepney, which had a big Jewish population. It was led by Edward Bramley and Julius Jacobs. There were much smaller contingents from Mornington Crescent, Battersea and Edgware. The last two columns marched all the way to Olympia, the other two were dispersed and made their way separately. They arrived at about six o'clock. A thousand additional demonstrators came separately, mostly after work. A further sixty communists arrived at nine o'clock in two motorvans. If we include the 500 or so who got inside Olympia, the total number of men and women that the Communist Party were able to put into the field came to about 2500. Altogether 1150 fascists marched to Olympia in five groups from Black House in the King's Road, and another 900 men and women in black shirts made their way separately. There were 2000 uniformed fascists in Olympia, of whom 1000 were stewards.

The meeting was scheduled to start at eight o'clock. At 6.30 the first arrivals started to come. According to the police, the crowds milling outside Olympia ' manifested intense bitterness towards the fascists and others entering . . . shouting slogans and using offensive and sometimes obscene expressions '. The 500 police, both foot and mounted, had a difficult time ' in preventing breaches of the peace and keeping the anti-fascist crowd on the move '. The class nature of the confrontation comes out clearly in a letter which one member of the audience afterwards sent to Lord Trenchard, the police commissioner, complaining that he and his wife had been ' pushed by a gang of roughs ' at the entrance, that he had heard the phrase ' bloody murderers ' shouted at ticket holders of ' high rank in society '; while ' ladies and gentlemen of gentle birth ' had had ' horrible faces thrust in their carriage windows'. In fact Olympia was not a typical fascist audience. The enormous publicity had built it up into a social occasion; the startlingly rapid rise of fascism (more apparent than real) had made many people curious to see the new phenomenon. For the first and only time in the B.U.F.'s history Mosley was able to get into one of his halls a substantial percentage of Britain's Establishment. It did not like what it saw.

The crush and disturbances at the entrance meant that the audience of 12,000, which included 2000 free-ticket holders in the galleries, was not finally seated till 8.30. It was entertained by a band playing popular tunes, in the manner of big public meetings at the time. At about 8.40, preceded by fifty-six blackshirts carrying Union Jacks and ceremonial flags, Mosley limped down the central aisle to the rostrum, spotlighted by four searchlights. The National Anthem was played. At 8.45 Mosley began to speak. ' Ladies and gentlemen. . . . This meeting, the largest indoor meeting ever held under one roof in Britain, is the culmination of a great national campaign in which audiences in every city of this land have gathered to hear the fascist case. . . . '

At this point the first disturbance broke out in one of the galleries, with groups of men and women starting to chant ' Fascism Means Murder: Down with Mosley '. The speaker paused in his speech and warned them that if they did not stop they would be removed. The shouting continued, and Mosley then ordered the stewards into action. The interrupters were removed, but as soon as he had started to speak again further shouting took place from another quarter of the building. Again the offenders were removed. Sergeant Thompson of the Special Branch takes up the story: ' Then followed a series of interruptions and removals from all parts of the arena which lasted for about an hour. Opposition to the meeting had obviously been organised, for as fast as interrupters were removed others commenced to disturb the proceedings.'[6] The highlight came when two men climbed the girders and from a point high up above the audience shouted slogans and rained leaflets down at them. Two stewards followed them up, but Mosley called out that there must be no fighting, and eventually all four returned safely to the ground. Mosley's speech, scheduled to last for an hour and a quarter, was prolonged by all this to two hours. It consisted, according to the police report, ' in the main of an analysis of the present economic condition of the country, and an explanation of the policy his party would adopt if it came to power '. It was almost ludicrously unconnected with the events taking place in the hall, though on several occasions Mosley turned on his interrupters, which provoked even bigger disturbances. Eventually the meeting came to an end at 10.50 with the National Anthem.

Meanwhile, the hostile crowd outside, numbering some 1500, was kept on the move by the police. Twenty-three were arrested, of whom three were charged with carrying offensive weapons, and seven were known to be communists. Barnet Becow was a young communist charged with possessing an offensive weapon. This was apparently the first of a number of appearances in police courts in the 1930s following fascist occasions. The police also spotted thirty more known communists in the crowd outside Olympia, of whom nine had foreign names.* The fact that a significant proportion of his assailants was Jewish was later to be given by Mosley as one of the chief reasons for his attack on the Jews.

In view of the furore that was to erupt in the next few days, it is perhaps worth recalling the immediate police reactions. The log entry for that night at the Hammersmith Police Station simply states that the meeting passed off ' without any serious violence '. The police report to the Home Office of the next day noted that about thirty people had been ejected ' with a certain amount of violence '. These estimates were soon to be drastically revised, but they are useful in keeping the meeting in perspective.

While these somewhat complacent remarks were being penned, three Conservative M.P.s – W. J. Anstruther-Gray, J. Scrymgeour-Wedderburn and the lawyer T. J. O'Connor had rushed straight from Olympia to Printing House Square to hand in a letter which appeared in *The Times* the following morning. ' We were involuntary witnesses', they declared, ' of wholly unnecessary violence inflicted by uniformed Blackshirts on interrupters. Men and women were knocked down and were still assaulted and kicked on the floor. It will be a matter of surprise for us if there were no fatal injuries. These methods of securing freedom of speech may have been effective, but they are happily unusual in England, and constituted in our opinion a deplorable outrage on public order.'

This was the first shot in the war of words which followed the battle of fists – a war fought in the newspapers, on the radio, in Parliament, even in the Cabinet. ' The Blackshirts behaved like bullies and cads,' wrote Geoffrey Lloyd, Baldwin's parliamentary private secretary, the next day. If Mosley had been so keen on the right of free speech, why hadn't he simply used his battery of loudspeakers to drown interrupters? ' His tactics ', Lloyd continued, ' were calculated to exaggerate the effects of the most trivial interruptions and to provide an apparent excuse for the violence. . . . '[7]

The same evening Mosley and Gerald Barry, editor of the *News Chronicle,* and a former enthusiast for the New Party's economic programme, made statements on Olympia on the B.B.C. – the last

*Jack Cohen, Saul Schube, Ivan Seruya, Pincus Zinkin, Sonia Tomchinsky, Leonard Hine, Joe Jacobs, Harry Landsberg, Y. Papasolomontos. (Public Record Office: MEPOL 24319.)

occasion Mosley was allowed on till 1968. Mosley produced what was to become the standard fascist defence. The communists had organised to break up Olympia. They rose in ' highly organised groups' to 'shout down free speech'. They attacked his men with every kind of ' vile weapon '. ' Now I put it to you, to your sense of fair play: would you have handled these Reds very gently? – when you had seen your men kicked in the stomach and slashed with razors, and your women with their faces streaming with blood?' Gerald Barry had seen no weapons but had observed single inter-rupters ' being struck on the head, in the stomach, and all over the body with a complete absence of restraint'. Nor were these actions confined to the auditorium. The worst atrocities took place in the corridors running off the hall where he had been horrified to see ' a man lying on the floor, obviously powerless and done for, being mercilessly kicked and horribly handled by a group of . . . Blackshirts '. The violence of this and a similar incident was greater than ' anything I have seen in my life short of the war '.[8]

In the next few days, accounts of fascist brutality flowed in to the newspapers – often from writers and journalists like Naomi Mitchison, Storm Jameson, A. J. Cummings, Phoebe Fenwick Gaye, Vera Brittain, Aldous Huxley, Pearl Binder and Ritchie Calder. On 13 June the Cabinet discussed a proposal from the Home Secretary, Sir John Gilmour, for legislation to give the police right of entry to indoor meetings. Two days later, there was a notable parlia-mentary clash between ' those who hate the interruption of the right of free speech ' and ' those who hate still more the brutality with which the Fascists have been charged by many impartial members of the audience '.[9]

The main charge against the blackshirts was that they deliberately used unnecessary and sadistic brutality with the object of impressing interrupters, audience and England generally with fascist ' ruthless-ness '. In pursuit of this aim they worked out a strategy whereby on the slightest interruption Mosley would stop speaking, powerful searchlights would instantly swing round to focus their full glare on the offender, and squads of stewards armed with blackjacks and knuckledusters would leap on him and beat him up.[10] The eye-witness accounts collected and published by the Left[11] deny that the interrupters were organised or fought ejection. The Very Reverend ' Dick' Sheppard, who had officiated at Mosley's wedding in 1920, and who had just buried Cimmie at Denham, confirmed Barry's account of atrocious acts in the corridors in an interview with the *Daily Telegraph* on 11 June.

Defenders of the blackshirts, who included a number of right-wing Tory M.P.s, did not deny that violent incidents had taken place, but argued that they must be judged against a background of organised opposition, violent resistance to ejection, and frequent use of weapons. Dissenting ' entirely ' from the view of his three colleagues, M. W. Beaumont, M.P., argued in *The Times* on 9 June that ' while the forces of law and order make no effort to safeguard the rights of free speech in this country, the use of some such methods is the only way in which those putting forward an unknown and controversial case can obtain a hearing '. Patrick Donner, M.P., claiming a friend of his had seen a woman fascist with a ' razor cut across her face ', thought it hardly surprising that ' stewards, faced with organised and armed gangs, reached and passed the limit of human patience '.[12] Replying to the corridor charges, Douglas Jerrold commented, ' Before we can form a fair judgment we want to know the circumstances which led up to the incidents described by the Revd. H. R. L. Sheppard and Mr. Barry. These incidents are not to be defended, in any case, but our judgment on them will obviously differ enormously if these particular interrupters were armed.'[13] Mosley picked up some unexpected support. That curious maverick socialist, Hamilton Fyfe, former editor of the *Daily Herald*, wrote: ' . . . I feel free to say how unwise – and even unfair – it was to organise interruption at the Olympia meeting. It was organised; that is certain. I saw in Oxford Street, in the early evening, bands of young men, mostly Jews, on their way to the meeting. . . . They were clearly in a fighting mood – and they got what they wanted. . . .'[14] Lloyd George, though not at Olympia, wondered ' why the fury of the champions of free speech should be concentrated so exclusively, not on those who deliberately and resolutely attempted to prevent the public expression of opinions of which they disapproved, but against those who fought, however roughly, for freedom of speech '.[15] Lloyd George was perhaps unduly influenced by the break-up of his own meetings in his young Radical days. To Mosley he wrote privately, ' You are having a very exciting time and I envy you your experience. At your age I went through a period of riot and tumult in my endeavour to convey my ideas to a resentful public.'[16]

What, then, is the truth? There is no doubt that fighting took place inside Olympia, and that the blackshirts used very violent methods. The seven Special Branch men stationed inside the building agree on this (it is important to note, though, that none of them were stationed in the gallery where the worst disorder and the most strenuous resistance to ejection occurred). One policeman explicitly endorses the letter of the three Conservative M.P.s to *The Times*. Sergeant Hunt testified that he saw interrupters ' handled in a most violent manner and in some cases were punched unconscious and their clothing torn. . . . As the evening drew on, the Blackshirts grew more vicious at the interruptions, and as soon as a person shouted, he was pounced upon and felled to the ground. . . . I saw no weapon used.' It is interesting that, according to Sergeant Willey, the audience registered no protest against these tactics. At any rate the passivity of the bulk of the audience encouraged the stewards in their actions. ' Many of the stewards were very young and upon their return from some ejection some of them were seen to spit on their hands and remark " next one please ".'

Police on duty round Olympia reported on the condition of those ejected. Sergeant Rogers at the Empire Hall entrance reported

> at least 30 persons, of both sexes, ejected into the roadway. Almost every person bore some mark of violence and was in a state of semi-collapse. Several men were bleeding profusely. . . .

Inspector Rogers saw twelve ejections: ' Their clothing was torn and disarranged, their faces bruised and bleeding.' From the Beaconsfield Terrace exit one man was flung out ' minus his trousers. His private parts were exposed, and he was bleeding freely from a head wound.'[17] (A favourite blackshirt trick was to cut the braces or belts of interrupters so that, in the days before skin-clinging clothes, they had to hold up their trousers and could not use their hands for fighting.)

On the other hand, it is clear that interruptions were organised. On this point the eye-witness accounts presented by the Left are definitely misleading. Reference is almost always to ' single interrupters ', ' respectable looking people ', ' the most trivial interruptions ', ' one, still small voice ', etc. Ritchie Calder testified that he heard no interruptions at all! The *New Statesman* reporter, who did, dubbed them ' spontaneous exhibitions by a large body of English working-class men and women . . .'.[18] All this flatly contradicts the evidence already quoted of communist preparations for the meeting, and the manner in which the actual interruptions were carried out, according to a prearranged plan, with definite slogans and at definite intervals. What Mosley faced at Olympia was no ordinary ' heckling ' situation as Geoffrey Lloyd implied. Once it became clear from the frequency and numbers of interjections that there was a sizeable body of people in the hall determined to break up the meeting, the stewards had to act swiftly and decisively.

It is equally clear that interrupters *fought* ejection. According to Sergeant Willey, ' this no doubt accounted for a great deal of the violence used upon them '. Probably a number of interrupters were beaten up who would have been happy to retire peacefully – especially later on when they knew what their fate was likely to be. But the fascist tactics had been conditioned by the fact that the earlier interrupters did fight back – and fiercely. On the morning after Olympia, the *Daily Worker* reported with considerable pride: ' The Blackshirts went to deal with an interrupter, the workers hit back, man for man, and on many occasions were often getting the better of it until like a swarm of blackbeetles, the Blackshirts poured on the fighting workers until they were overpowered – then they were beaten up.' This is backed up by another plain-clothes policeman, who saw forty ejections ' and a struggle in every case '. It was, of course, precisely to prevent such ' man-for-man ' fighting that stewards moved in squads. But it was not even as simple as that. As one blackshirt pointed out afterwards: ' The " single interrupters " were in most cases surrounded by their own toughs. It was not possible to get the interrupters, in many cases, without coming into conflict with their bodyguards.'[19]   This was an aspect of handling opposition at indoor meetings not always appreciated by witnesses.

To what extent weapons were used in these fights remains debatable. Both sides allege use of weapons. Mosley produced a collection of them which he said he had captured from the ' Reds ' after Olympia, including a hatchet. Philip Toynbee and Esmond Romilly had knuckledusters.[20] Miss Pearl Binder, on the other hand, specifically states that she saw ' several Blackshirts using knuckledusters '. In proof of their allegations, both sides cited a formidable array of injuries. Mosley claimed that sixty-three blackshirts were injured, many from kicks in the genitals, stabbing and razor slashes. This is based on the testimony of medical personnel in charge of first-aid stations inside Olympia, one of whom found a girl fascist ' with a scratch, commencing under her eye and running down her cheek and neck and finishing on her back between her shoulder blades . . . some sharp instrument must have been used '. Fascist accounts of injured blackshirts were corroborated by the Press. The *Daily Express* reporter saw ' Bandaged Blackshirts . . . all over the hall . . . limping and bruised Blackshirts were seeking Red Cross attention, a score at a time '. According to *The Times* of 8 June, ' Men and women Fascists were seen going away after the meeting with bandaged heads '. On the other side, four doctors attending first-aid stations outside Olympia claimed a number of injuries on those ejected ' which could only have resulted either from a blow from some weapon or from the banging of the head against some hard object '. Colin Cross's view that ' the greater part of the fighting was with bare fists ' is probably correct.

That unsavoury incidents took place in the corridors is beyond dispute. However, we still do not know the circumstances which led up to them, or how serious they really were, since the one police report is curiously ambiguous. At one particularly wide passageway known as the Portcullis Avenue, leading into the Hammersmith Road, Inspector Carroll was on duty at about nine o'clock.

The police were not allowed to enter the building unless they actually saw a breach of the peace taking place. Inspector Carroll, however, went inside because he saw a man almost unconscious lying near the entrance. 'On looking down the Hall I saw six groups, each containing six to eight "Blackshirts" beating and kicking unmercifully a man in the centre of each group. In three instances the men assaulted were lying on the ground. In company with about 10 PC's who were on duty with me outside, I went to the rescue of the men who were being kicked and beaten. . . . When we had succeeded in rescuing all we could see, agonising cries came from the foot of the stairs and there we found four "Blackshirts" with a weak youth on his back on the stairs. He was being beaten in a brutal manner. When we rescued him he was scarcely able to walk and his friends whom we had previously rescued came to his assistance and partially carried him from the building.'

When this report reached his superiors, Carroll was immediately asked the obvious question: why had he not arrested the men committing these atrocious acts? Then a curious thing occurred. In an interview with the assistant commissioner, Carroll considerably modified his original statement. Perhaps, he said, he had been inaccurate in stating that he had actually seen anyone being beaten up. As for the weak youth whom he had described as ' being beaten in a brutal manner' Carroll now said that he did not actually see this and should have said ' he appeared to have been beaten in a brutal manner'. The assistant commissioner commented: ' I am inclined to think that Inspector Carroll's report gives a rather more serious impression of the assaults than was actually the case. None of the individuals whose rescue he effected had actually received any serious injuries: they were all asked whether they required attention and all declined. . . . Inspector Carroll frankly admits that he wrote the report having regard to the fact that his action in entering the building at all had been called into question by Fascists, and that he was consequently emphasizing the justification for doing so, with the result that his report laid stress on this aspect of the case. . . .'

There is a final question about fascist motives at Olympia. Did Mosley stage Olympia, not for the purpose of giving a speech, but ' for the purpose of overpowering the interrupters ' as T. J. O'Connor claimed in Parliament on 14 June? Or was it a case of the fascist Defence Force over-reacting to an admittedly difficult situation? In support of the former view is the charge that Mosley refused to have the police in the building although he knew that trouble was coming, and that his method of handling interruptions was designed to magnify the effect of every incident. Mosley admits that he refused to have the police in the building, though not for the reason alleged. It was because his experience at Manchester on 12

March 1933 had convinced him that the police would try to stop the stewards doing their duty.   Subsequently he changed his mind, and the police were present at all the big fascist meetings after Olympia, though to this day the law lays down that organisers of indoor meetings have the right and duty to arrange their own stewarding.   He denies that he stopped speaking at every interruption.   There was a break in his oration, he admits, but this was because the loudspeaker wires had been cut.   As for the famous searchlights, ' they were nothing whatever to do with me . . . they belonged to the newsreel companies, which were present in force.   Directly I was silenced they preferred to take pictures of the fighting.'[21]   In support of this, the *Manchester Guardian* report of 8 June does mention a period when Mosley's voice could not be heard, adding that later he ' went on speaking ' through the disturbances. It is known that the newsreel companies did come to photograph big Mosley rallies.   Possibly more significant, none of the press reports the day after Olympia mentioned the use of spotlighting as a deliberate anti-interrupter technique, though one or two do mention ' arc lamps ' being swung around from time to time.*

The whole theory of Olympia being set up to smash interruption has an incurably academic ring about it.   Mosley's meetings were organised to show off Mosley doing what he was best at – public speaking.   His purpose at Olympia, in this high tide of fascist respectability, with the Rothermere press in full support, and with a distinguished audience present, was to show how reasonable and logical the fascist programme was.   The speech itself fits the thesis that he wanted to present a logical case.   The fact that this plan was upset by unprecedented communist organisation is no argument for imputing to him a more sinister and infinitely less rewarding purpose.

More credible is the view that the fascists had deliberately decided to use maximum violence in order to *deter* interruptions at future meetings.   But even here there is a snag.   Sergeant Willey, one of the plain-clothes policemen inside, reports that ' at the commence-

*In the *Blackshirt* of 22 June Mosley said that the searchlights belonged to the Paramount Cinema Company.   ' I ordered them to be switched off after the first 20 minutes as they were even more trying to me than to the audience.'   In his book, *Political Violence and Public Order*, p. 90, Benewick alleges that at Belle Vue, Manchester, in October 1933 ' spotlights deliberately switched from Mosley to focus on the scenes of disturbance where the defence corps had converged – a tactic that was to be repeated at Mosley's future meetings '.   His reference is the *Manchester Guardian* report of 16 October 1933.   That report mentions spotlights being turned onto a confused fight which broke out at the back of the hall, adding ' and the cinema photographers busily photographed the scene ', an observation Benewick omits, but which is obviously relevant to the question of ownership of the spotlights.   Nor does he provide any references for his assertion that this spotlighting of interruptions was a tactic used at subsequent meetings.

ment of the interruptions, the attitude of the fascist stewards was uncertain . . . '. It was only later that they ' took a very decided line of action and proceeded to eject with some violence the chief interrupters '. Other accounts agree that the ejections grew more ' vicious ' as the evening proceeded. The implication is that the maximum force strategy was applied only after the scale of interruptions was appreciated. The impression one gets from the press and police accounts is that of an escalation of violence within the meeting itself, fed by fierce fighting, injuries and rumours, so that in the end a thoroughly jumpy and edgy collection of stewards are rushing around, almost out of control, pouncing on anyone who so much as dares stir out of his seat. Even so, some deterrent motive of a ' teaching them a lesson ' kind was probably present.

Olympia must be kept in perspective. Though Douglas Jerrold may have exaggerated in saying that ' you can see nearly as much toughness in a " Rugger " match in the Midlands or in Wales any Saturday in the autumn or winter ', it was hardly the atrocity it was made out to be. Altogether about fifty people were ejected. ' It will be a matter of surprise if there were not fatal injuries,' wrote the three Conservative M.P.s that night. In fact, a number of people, fascists included, were treated in the nearby hospitals, but only one anti-fascist, Jacob Miller, was detained for any length of time. This Sheffield university student, who claimed he had been bludgeoned with a formidable weapon over the head till ' half dead ' was sufficiently recovered and undaunted to attend a Mosley meeting at Sheffield three weeks later, and to engage the speaker in repeated altercation from the floor – without any harassment and without, apparently, any trace of injury.[22]

Why, then, all the furore? First, there is no doubt that many violent acts took place which were deeply shocking to those who witnessed them. Secondly, although political violence on the scale of Olympia had occurred in the nineteenth and early twentieth centuries, it had virtually disappeared by the 1920s. People relatively new to politics or those unconnected with politics were shocked at this echo from half-forgotten times which seemed so ' unEnglish '. Politicians with older memories, like Lloyd George, or those with more recent experience of violence, such as the I.L.P. or left-wing labour groups, were less shocked and outraged. There was little sense of outrage in the *Daily Worker* report after Olympia: the tone was very much that of the good fight well fought. It was only after Olympia that the communists fully realised what a valuable ally they had in the liberal conscience.

There was also something distinctly novel about the deliberate way in which Mosley chose to go through with this particular showdown. Most speakers in his position would have played it extremely gently, relying on winning the sympathy of the Press the

next day, even at the cost of abandoning the meeting. Such a
procedure would have been contrary to Mosley's temper and that
of his movement. His attitude was ' If they want a fight, they
shall have it.' In the movement, a climb-down would have been
interpreted not as a brilliant tactical manœuvre, but as a sign of
softness, as a social-democratic, not a fascist, solution. ' This is
not a kissing match, but a stand-up fight,' Mosley had said at
Smethwick eight years previously. Given his temperament he
took the only course at Olympia he could possibly have done.
The great flaw in his design was that his instrument – the stewards –
was not sufficiently disciplined to carry it through successfully. It
was more like the Black and Tans than the Prussian Guard.

The comparative lack of support Mosley received from the Right
shows that English conservatism was a very different animal from
the Continental Right: witness, for example, Poincaré's endorsement of the far more serious outrages of the Camelots du Roi in
1923.[23] The absence of Conservative endorsement was partly due
to the fact that the fascists in 1934 were not serving any patriotic
purpose. Indeed, the traditional Right would become ever less
sympathetic to Mosley as Germany superseded Bolshevism as the
main menace. The testimony of the three Conservative M.P.s was
crucial in destroying the credibility of the fascist defence. Lloyd in
particular was a disciple of Baldwin's politics of decency and accommodation. Liberal conservatism was as remote from Mosley's
methods as liberal socialism.

What people saw in Olympia was the future, not the present.
The fascist stewards for some became stormtroopers trampling on
liberty; the demonstrators for others became the vanguard of the
proletarian uprising. The future seemed dramatically confirmed
when the Roehm purges three weeks later added to the public
impact of Olympia by artificially associating the two events and
the two movements. Thus the circumstances in which it took place
conspired to magnify it out of all proportion. Thousands were
drawn to Olympia as to a bull ring. They came to satisfy their
prejudices, appetites, curiosity, hopes and fears; and they saw and
heard just enough to make out of it an epic.

Chapter 20

Who Was then the Englishman?

THE PROMINENCE of Jews in the Olympia disturbances brought to a head the submerged issue in British fascist politics: the Jewish question. To understand the origins of this conflict we have to go back to the New Party. In the spring and summer of 1932 Mosley started his negotiations with existing fascist groups with a view to uniting them under his leadership. This brought him into contact for the first time with the anti-semitic fringe of British politics. On 27 April 1932 he attended a lecture by Arnold Leese on ' The Blindness of British Politics under the Jew Money-Power '. This may be considered the beginning of his education in the ' realities ' as opposed to the ' surface appearances ' of modern life. The education of many of his new followers was much further advanced. Anti-semitism had flourished on the extreme right of British politics ever since the Russian Revolution and the English translation of the *Protocols of the Elders of Zion* in 1919. Henry Hamilton Beamish had started a Britons Publishing Society in 1920 to warn his country-men of the Judaic–Bolshevik conspiracy. ' Hidden-hand ' theorists like Mrs Nesta Webster enjoyed a certain vogue; John Buchan placed the ' hidden hand ' in the fiction where it always belonged in his *Thirty-Nine Steps*.[1] The modern anti-semitic movement, of course, went back much further on the Continent – to the great stock-exchange collapses of the 1870s and 1880s which ruined the reputation of Jewish financiers and shattered the security of the civilisation Jews had done so much to build up.[2] In England the B.U.F. was the first big opportunity it had had. Anti-semites joined the B.U.F. in order, as Mosley himself put it, to get into a ' bigger and better fight '.

Mosley himself had no previous anti-semitic history,[3] yet there is some evidence that he toyed with the idea of starting his movement with at least one anti-Jewish plank. On 29 June 1932, Harold Nicolson wrote him a letter commenting on the first draft of *Greater Britain*:

It seems to me that you sometimes shift the key or tone of your remarks from the constructive essay to the destructive platform manner.... Under this heading I would group that angle of approach which sees evil intention where there is only weak abstention. I dare say that the Jewish banking houses may have been a trifle international in their frame of mind. I am quite prepared even to believe that they have been the villains of the piece. But there is a Nazi note, a yellow press note in these denunciations which will cause many people to blink and to question your seriousness. It is so easy to tone down that sort of statement by a short qualifying phrase. English readers are always impressed by propagandists who take off their boots before they start kicking below the belt.

Mosley obligingly struck out the offending passages in the published version. ' He cut them out because I asked him,' wrote Nicolson to Cimmie.[4] Obviously Mosley had been flying a kite, but the idea of attacking Jewish finance had been implanted.*

The B.U.F. thus got under way without an anti-Jewish policy but with a number of anti-semites in its ranks – William Joyce was the most notable recruit in this category. Its intensely nationalist ' Britain-for-the-British ' line gained it further support among a group of people who were disposed to dislike foreign immigrants, of whom the Jewish community at that time formed the largest number, and to associate them with unsavoury crimes and anti-social practices: an approach typified by Colonel Lane's book, *The Alien Menace*, published in 1928. A certain type of youth who went in for ' Jew-baiting ' was also drawn in. It is the fringes of a movement who give it a bad name, and so it proved with the B.U.F. Even before it had started, a couple of anti-Jewish incidents were reported in the press. ' The facts are ', said a New Party statement issued on behalf of the leader in Antibes, ' that anti-Jewish propaganda is neither authorised nor approved by Sir Oswald.' But, as the *Jewish Chronicle* of 26 August 1932 pointed out, these assurances meant nothing unless Mosley took steps to rid his movement of those likely to associate it with anti-semitism. But this he refused to do, unless they specifically contravened party policy on the subject, and then only fitfully. A further statement issued by the B.U.F. in October said Jews had nothing to fear from fascism unless – significantly – they were associated with its two enemies, communism and international finance. In December 1932, Mosley was assuring Lord Melchett that ' anti-semitism forms no part of the policy of this Organisation, and anti-semitic propaganda is forbidden '.[5] A. K. Chesterton confirms that ' speakers who put over their personal views on the Jewish question were barred from the rostrum; some were expelled '.[6] Some Jews even joined. The party line had been settled and there it was to remain officially for almost two years.

*There is a curious story in Israel Sieff's *Memoirs* (pp. 170–1) that some time in 1932 he asked Mosley to leave his house for announcing to the assembled company that ' a new movement must find something to hate. In this case it should be the Jews '. Mosley denies the story. It sounds inherently implausible.

What started to change it was the attitude of Jews themselves, and they must take a large share of the blame for what subsequently happened. From the earliest days, according to Chesterton, a Jewish body calling itself the British Union of Democrats ' sent round van-loads of Jews all over the country to break up Blackshirt meetings '.[7] This may have been the ' organised band of Communists ' whom Mosley complained about to the *Daily Telegraph*'s ' Peterborough '. On 24 October 1932, it will be recalled, he made his first anti-Jewish remark – when he referred to persistent hecklers as ' three warriors of the class-war – all from Jerusalem '. ' The greatest danger to the Jews in this country arises from the Communist company some of them keep,' warned *Blackshirt*. These activities have to be considered in the context of the Communist Party's strategy of disrupting Mosley's meetings. Whether they deliberately used Jews as front-line troops in order to expose fascism's anti-semitic potential, or whether Jewish communists showed particular relish for this work, is difficult to say: probably a mixture of both. A Jewish malaise of this time was to be obsessed by fascism. If some Jews found it intolerably provoking they certainly went out of their way to be provoked. Fascist meetings drew them as a magnet. The very sight of a blackshirt in uniform was enough to make their blood boil.

A typical early confrontation took place in the spring of 1933. On 30 April seven fascists were arrested in Piccadilly Circus while selling *Blackshirt*. A police superintendent's report goes as follows:

> They had previously been advised to move away from Coventry Street owing to the unfriendly interest shown by Jews. On Sunday evenings Coventry Street is crowded with Jews who appear to come from the East End, and it has been the practice for a number of Blackshirts to sell their publication in the streets of the West End including Coventry Street. Since the Jewish persecution in Germany the Jews have taken objection to the selling of the Blackshirt publication *which gives great publicity to the German point of view.* [My italics.]

Six Jews were arrested at the same time, including two for assaulting a fascist lying on the ground. Appearing at the Marlborough Street police court on 1 May, the seven fascists were let off with a warning not to appear in the West End on Sunday evenings, the magistrate stating that Coventry Street was not a suitable place for them to sell their paper. The defendants were ' specially asked by Sub-Division Inspector Wells [of the Vine Street police station] to avoid Coventry Street owing to the Jewish attitude towards them.'

The following Sunday (7 May) twelve fascists appeared once more in Coventry Street to sell their paper. A scuffle broke out in which three of them received injuries, one being detained in

St George's Hospital with concussion and injuries to his testicles.
Eight men were charged with assault and disorderly conduct and
in the words of Inspector Satterthwaite ' all appear to be of the
Jewish faith '. Two of them, Fegenbaum and Goldstein, were
sentenced to five weeks' imprisonment. At the same time, Inspector Wells noted of the fascist news-vendors that ' their attitude
was extremely provocative '.

Clearly tension was building up on both sides. On 11 May
a report was received from the Commercial Street police station
in East London:

> At 11 a.m. Mr. Barlow of ———— informed Police at this station
> that he had received information from two of his employees . . .
> that about 20 Aldgate roughs, led by Mr. Robert Lazarus,
> alias Bobby Nark of . . . Stepney proposed on Sunday 14
> May 1933 to dress as members of the Fascisti and proceed to
> the West End for the purpose of causing a disturbance. . . . Mr.
> Lazarus is at present away from home but enquiries are being
> continued by the CID. . . .

On the same day, Mosley himself wrote to Inspector Wells:

> As you are aware, certain of our members were assaulted
> in the neighbourhood of the Haymarket when selling our
> newspaper ' The Blackshirt' last Sunday, in accordance with
> our usual practice. . . . I propose next Sunday personally
> to take charge of the Party selling newspapers in this area.
> I very much desire to conform in every way with Police regu-
> lations, to avoid any obstruction to the traffic and to preserve
> the peace . . . but I desire to affirm the right of Englishmen
> to pursue any legal and peaceful activity in this country with-
> out molestation and assault.

This produced much flapping in the Metropolitan Police all the
way up to the commissioner. Inspector Wells of the police station
most closely involved wanted Mosley to be told ' that in view of the
breach of the peace his proposed action is likely to cause, it cannot be
allowed '. He went on: ' If Sir Oswald is so keen on keeping the
peace he will prevent his followers from frequenting the West End
on any Sunday evening. Their presence is definitely likely to provoke a breach of the peace. . . . It is not to be expected that the enormous number of Jews visiting the neighbourhood will tolerate the
arrogance of the fascists.' On the other hand, Mosley's legal right
to sell his newspaper in the streets could not be denied. The deputy
commissioner minuted:

> I saw Sir Russell Scott (Home Office) and the Director of
> Public Prosecutions. . . . The latter pointed out that there

was no legal grounds for any proceedings against Sir Oswald Mosley, inasmuch as there was no expressed intention of doing anything unlawful, and it has long since been decided that a lawful act, e.g., selling newspapers, cannot be prevented on the mere ground that it is likely to lead to a breach of the peace.

Interestingly enough, it was Mosley who backed down, withdrawing his newspaper from Coventry Street on Sunday evenings. In a final gesture, he paraded through another part of the West End on 14 May, the result being the arrest of two Jews, one of whom, ' evidently a mental case ', had been trying to slash fascists with a razor. Arnold Leese, secretary of the Imperial Fascist League, provided a final note of comedy when he wrote to the commissioner protesting against his own removal from his Piccadilly pitch in view of the continued permission given to the B.U.F. to operate there. ' May I ask you to prevent this? It would obviously be unfair for pro-Jew Fascists to be allowed to sell their paper in Coventry Street when we cannot do so.' He concluded on the sinister note of the true believer: ' There is, as a matter of fact, far more at stake than meets the eye.'[8]

What attacks like this and the constant Jewish attendance at meetings were to do was to make a movement already prone to distrust of Jews ' Jew-conscious '. However, the immediate consequence was an effort by both Mosley and Jewish leaders to improve relations, Robert Forgan acting as Mosley's emissary. Mosley told a *Jewish Chronicle* reporter that he considered Hitler's anti-semitic policy a ' great mistake '. His most comprehensive statement came in a signed article published in the *Jewish Economic Forum* on 28 July 1933. Attacks on Jews in ' any shape or form were strictly forbidden '. ' Bias for or against the Jew is completely irrelevant to the issues involved in our political creed.' Jews associated with communism or finance would be attacked as opponents, not as Jews. The attacks on Jews in Germany ' do not rest on any Fascist principle but are the manifestation of an inherent quality in the German character '. ' Religious and racial tolerance ' would be guaranteed under fascism. For its part the *Jewish Chronicle* condemned as ' wicked and stupid ' Jewish attacks on fascists.[9]

Once again a dispute seemed to have been settled amicably. But, of course, what the *Jewish Chronicle*, organ of Anglo-Jewry, wrote had little influence in the ghetto from where the attacks were coming. And on the fascist side there were forces itching to get into the fray. They seemed to have won an important concession from Mosley in the autumn of 1933 when a couple of articles appeared in *Blackshirt* on the theme of ' The Alien Menace ' (echo of Colonel Lane) pointing out Jewish involvement in various rackets and threatening to deport the ' low type ' of foreign Jew

as well as the ' alien financier '.[10]   In themselves, the articles were
simply a plea for stronger powers to deport undesirable aliens.
But they were loosely and offensively worded, betraying an anti-
semitic pen eager to graduate to higher things.

An unsigned article in *Blackshirt* by Mosley himself on 4 November
1933 headed ' Shall Jews Drag Britain to War?' indicates the probable cause of his change of front.   Hitler's initial assault on German Jewry had transformed the Jewish communities of the world,
but particularly of America and Britain, into a formidable political
lobby against Nazi Germany and its foreign sympathisers.   Jewish
organisations had been set up in the summer of 1933 to organise a
boycott of German goods and to mobilise world opinion against the
Nazi régime.   The *Jewish Chronicle* had called for League sanctions
against Germany.[11]   Mosley's own sympathy for the German
experiment strengthened his anger at these threats, as he saw them,
to European tranquillity.   He felt strongly that no sectional interest
should be allowed to interfere with the overriding aim of learning
to live in peace with Germany, especially when that interest was
not British but Jewish, and not even anglicised Jews but foreign
Jews were leading it (50,000 East End Jews had demonstrated at
Hyde Park in July against the Nazi régime).*   He had just heard
a story–possibly from Lloyd George himself–that Isidore Ostrer,
the Polish Jewish owner of the British Gaumont Cinema chain had
objected to a newsreel film of Lloyd George speaking in favour of
friendship with Germany and had threatened to cancel Fox Movie-
tone's contract if further speeches of that character were shown.
There was certainly a case to be made out here against allowing
the terms of public debate on an important foreign-policy issue to
be unduly influenced by a minority ethnic interest.   Had Mosley
followed Harold Nicolson's advice about taking off his boots
before hitting below the belt, an effective and timely criticism
might have been mounted.†   What is startling and unexpected
about the actual article is its uncompromisingly anti-semitic
character.   Jewish finance controls the Conservative Party.   Jewish

---

*It is important to note that the Board of Deputies of British Jews did not give
the British boycott its official sanction.   (*The Times*, 24 July 1933.)

†The question of how much influence the Jewish lobby did actually exert on
British foreign policy in the 1930s has never been properly studied.   For the later
1930s Beaverbrook believed that Jewish émigrés in the professions and the ' big '
Jewish position in the Press made accommodation with Germany very difficult.
' The Jews may drive us into war ' (quoted in A. J. P. Taylor, *Beaverbrook*
(1972) pp. 379, 387).   Sir Samuel Hoare wrote: ' All Jews and Communists for
war ' at the time of Munich (Templewood Papers, Box 10; I am indebted to
Mr Kendall Myers for bringing this to my attention).   My own view is that the
Jewish lobby was more influential earlier in the 1930s and may have had some
permanent effect in conditioning the way people felt about the Nazi regimé.

intellectuals run the Labour Party. The Press is largely Jewish. The Jews thus effectively control the system, and they are using it to drag the nation to war in their ' racial passion '.

The *Jewish Chronicle* responded strongly to these ' stale and trashy oddments, taken from the rag-bag of the pedlars of Continental anti-semitism '. Only the ' bilious ravings of irresponsible agitators could suggest that Jews are anxious to see the whole world laid in ruins . . . for any sectional purpose, particularly as the supposed bene-ficiaries of their action would also be decimated, if not destroyed '. Under this barrage *Blackshirt* retreated to a more reasoned position. ' If Jewry in Britain is British, and places the interests of Britain first, then it is utterly unjustified in interfering with the internal affairs of Germany by declaring a boycott of German goods. It is not in the interests of Great Britain that certain of its citizens should use their money power to the detriment of a great and friendly nation.'[12] Raven Thomson followed this up in an interview with the *Jewish Chronicle* (2 February 1934) by stating that ' we are more interested in putting things in this country right than in interfering in the internal affairs of other countries '. The storm subsided as quickly as it had arisen – though not before Joyce had got in a nasty crack at the ' weed of Israel ' – but this and the continuing Jewish attacks left a legacy of bitterness. From now on the B.U.F. was pointedly to remind Jews that they must put Britain's interests first. In the same interview with the *Jewish Chronicle* Ian Hope Dundas said that Jews were now excluded from the London member-ship because of the ' physical opposition on the part of a certain section of Jews towards their movement '. In April, this ban was extended to the provinces as well. On the other hand, Lord Rothermere's influence ensured that references to Jews vanished completely from the pages of *Blackshirt* – a telling commentary on Mosley's later claim that he was unable to control what went into his journals.[13]

Jews were responsible for the next escalation. Police and other reports suggest that East End Jews formed a high proportion of the demonstrators at Olympia; and threats of a similar assault forced the B.U.F. to abandon its White City rally planned for August. In July, according to Mosley, Lord Rothermere was taken out of his alliance with him ' at the point of an economic gun '. Apparent-ly the press-lord had told Mosley that the pressure of Jewish advertisers made it impossible for him to continue not only the political, but a business, association.[14] Whatever Rothermere said to Mosley, it is unlikely that Jewish pressure was the decisive reason for the break. There were fundamental differences of policy and Rothermere's enthusiasms were notoriously short-lived. Nevertheless, it may have been a factor, and coming on top of Olympia it made Mosley a man with a grievance. At Hyde Park on 9 September he let fly at his tormentors: ' behind the Communist-Socialist mob were Jewish financiers who supply the palm-oil to make them yell ' – the suggestion being that people were being paid by Jews to break up his meetings.   This may have been true, though the word ' financiers ', suggestive of the anti-semitic connection between high finance and communism, is a curious choice: ' frightened small shopkeepers ' would be nearer the truth (see below, page 403).   Mosley showed even less restraint at Belle Vue, Manchester on 29 September, referring to hecklers chanting in a mixture of Yiddish and pidgin English as ' sweepings of the ghettos '.

At the Albert Hall on 28 October 1934, he marshalled his case. In his autobiography, he claims that the ' gravamen of my charge ' was his reference to the effort of organised Jewry ' in a racial passion ' to ' arouse in this country the feelings of war with a nation with whom we made peace in 1918 '.[15] Mosley now suggests this was the ' sole reason ' for the quarrel.   This is definitely misleading.   The ' gravamen ' of his charge at the Albert Hall was that ' the Jews more than any other single force in this country are carrying on a violent propaganda against us '.   In an obvious reference to Rothermere among others* he claimed that' big business men have come to me and said " I dare not come out for Fascism, or dare not remain with you, because if I did the Jews would ruin me and my business" '.   Big Jews were using their position in the press to attack him.   ' Little Jews ' were attacking his members and meetings. Mosley was particularly sensitive to the charge that his fellow-Britons were hostile to a British movement.   ' Ragotski, Schaffer, Max Levitas, Fenebloom, Hyam Aarons, Sapasnick,' he read out to the delight of his audience.   ' Old English names: Thirty-two of them out of sixty-four convicted since last June of attacks on Fascists. Thirty-two names of that character.   Spontaneous rising of the British people against Fascism!'

Mosley was right in claiming that he was being attacked by Jews, communists and intellectuals rather than by ' ordinary ' English men and women who regarded him as a colourful eccentric and fascist occasions as entertaining spectacles.†   But the fact that only

*Who the others were is unknown. It is suggestive, without being conclusive, that the *Jewish Chronicle* of 20 July 1934 carried a letter from Lord Nuffield denying he was anti-semitic or had ever supported fascism, and enclosing a cheque for £250 to Jewish charities. On 24 August 1934, the same journal published a letter from Appleyard of Leeds Ltd, denying they had ever supported Mosley or anti-semitism and testifying to ' the happiest relations with a very large and valued Jewish clientèle '.   At Cardiff in April 1934 Mosley alleged that Jews ' prevented our party from obtaining a large hall in the city ' (*Jewish Chronicle*, 20 April 1934).

†This interpretation is taken from the findings of Mass Observation: ' Attitudes to Oswald Mosley in the Thirties ' collated by Mr Tom Harrisson.

MEETING OF INDIGNANT BRITONS (INCLUDING BRITISH
SECTION OF RED ARMY) TO PROTEST AGAINST
IMPORTATION OF FOREIGN IDEAS, UNIFORMS,
SALUTES ETC., CONTRARY TO
BRITISH TRADITIONS. —

the fringes were attacking him cannot have brought undiluted joy, for it suggested that the B.U.F. was failing to make the larger impact for which it hoped. Rather, with the movement receding to fringe status after the knocks of the summer, Mosley was being trapped in a private war with other fringes, which had little relation to the big national issues with which he had started. The Jew was starting to loom so large because fascism was so small. And the B.U.F. was starting to acquire the persecution complex of any frustrated small group with a high sense of its own importance.

Although in its report on the Albert Hall meeting *Blackshirt* had looked forward happily to the commencement of a ' new battle in British history' between the ' great cleansing spirit of Fascism ' and ' organised Jewry ', Mosley had as yet done little more than complain about Jewish hostility. What possible reason could they have in disliking him so much? He is now prepared to concede that it might just have been because they saw some superficial resemblances between the B.U.F. and the Nazis, but was not at the time. A. K. Chesterton takes up the story:

> Genuinely puzzled (I have the clearest possible mental picture of him at the time) Mosley ordered a thorough research into the Jewish question, especially into the financial and political activities which the movement attacked, and it was then found that there was a very close identification between those activities and specific Jewish interests. Rightly or wrongly Mosley imagined that he had stumbled upon the secret of Jewry's bitter attack on his movement.[16]

Unfortunately the details of these thorough researches have never been published, but A. K. Chesterton, who conducted them, produced a summary which showed that Jews controlled the great foreign lending-houses which sent British money abroad to equip foreigners, that they controlled the 'great producer rings and combines', that they had 'invaded' and 'virtually captured' commanding positions in important branches of the retail trade, that whenever a 'corner' in essential commodities existed a group of Jews was usually to be seen 'rubbing their hands with satisfaction at the door', that the cinema industry was 'Jew-infested' and used politically to further specifically Jewish interests, that Jews 'burdened and debased' the British theatre, that the National Press was 'soaked' in Jewish influence which could dominate policy both through direct shareholding and by advertising pressure, that Jews influenced political parties by large subscriptions, and that the Communist Party was Jewish.[17]

No wonder the Jew hated fascism so much. 'He hates Fascism as the burglar hates the policeman,' Mosley declared. But by the same token the Jew was elevated into a worthy opponent for fascism. The Jewish domination of national life 'precludes the possibility of an economic square deal for the British people . . . until that power has been politically crushed', declared Chesterton. Jewish power as revealed in these researches enabled Mosley to link up his actual struggle with street-corner Jews and small shop-keepers and tailors in the East End of London with the great national issues with which he had started his movement; for these 'small Jews' were merely the lower echelons of a 'foul growth' that stretched right upwards to the City of London: 'the big Jew puts you out of employment by the million, the little Jew sweats you in Whitechapel'.[18] The little Jew attacks you with the big Jew's gold. They were all part of the same system of usury.

From the end of 1934, the B.U.F. switched its propaganda line to the Jew as the power behind the throne. The main theme which was worked into all Mosley's 'bread-and-butter' speeches is that at the root of all the proximate sources of distress lurks 'international Jewish finance'. One typical example, from his Free Trade Hall, Manchester, speech (as reported in the *Manchester Guardian*, 2 November 1934) will suffice:

An extremely serious threat to Lancashire was the employment of cheap Oriental labour against the cotton industry, and it was this fact which underlay the controversy about the Indian report and the White Paper. Directly modern methods of mass production and automatic machinery were introduced Oriental labour was for the first time able to compete with white labour, and a greedy capitalism – the usual elements of international finance – were only too willing to seize the opportunity of a higher rate of interest than they could get at home, and as a result we had had international loans advanced from the City of London to countries like Japan and Empire countries with backward peoples like India to exploit those backward peoples, to equip mills and factories where cheap labour could be exploited in competition with Lancashire.

For that purpose skilled men from Lancashire were employed to teach these people their job, and Lancashire itself exported the machinery which equipped the mills of Japan and India.   In the guise of international finance we were witnessing the tragedy by which Lancashire skill and talent are forging the weapons by which Lancashire industry was being destroyed.   (A Voice: ' That's capitalism.')

Capitalism [said Sir Oswald].   No, it is not the small man with a little capital who is developing industry and giving employment.   It is not the Lancashire millowner who is doing this thing to ruin himself.   No.   It is the force which is served by the Conservative party, the Liberal party, and the socialist party alike, the force that has dominated Britain ever since the war, and which ruins Lancashire – the force of international Jewish finance.   (Cheers and hooting).   Ah, I thought they would not like to hear their master's name. The Labour party squeals about capital doing it.   It is those who have accumulated great holdings in financial houses who sit in London, not developing British industry but exploiting foreign industry, not lending money to assist British industry and re-equip our mills but going where they can get quicker returns and profits, going into the Orient, where there is a great virgin field of labour unemployment, where women work in the foul slums of Bombay and Madras, for one purpose, and one purpose alone – that Lancashire may be destroyed in order that the City of London may wax fatter and fatter.

In the same way, Mosley would work the theme of Jewish finance into his anti-war line by adapting the radical, marxist, argument that international finance causes wars to the argument that Jewish finance was trying to destroy world fascism because it had challenged the dictatorship of that finance.[19] It is important to note, though, that this is not the same as the much more sympathetic explanation Mosley now gives for Jewish hostility to Germany – that the German Government was persecuting German Jews.   In the 1930s the argument was that Jewish finance was pursuing its ' implacable vendetta ' against Germany because Germany had ' suppressed the

great Jewish interests '.   Stories of persecution Mosley dismissed as
' lying Jewish propaganda '.[20]   The note of sympathy which he can
now summon up was entirely absent in the 1930s.   It would have
saved him from many bitter reproaches.

One can see that the new propaganda line, by identifying British
Union's actual opponents with a world force of unique malignity,
served to increase its own self-importance; one can see that to put
' Jew ' in front of finance was to remove its anti-capitalist sting and
thus serve the tactical purpose of uniting right and left; one can see,
too, that it served the purpose of enabling many fascists to project
their own foreignness *vis-à-vis* the English political culture onto the
Jew.   The real question is, how far did Mosley himself believe what
he was saying?   It seems probable that he believed it enough to
justify to himself using it for propaganda purposes.   He was working
closely with people who did believe it strongly; and it was inevitable
that once he himself started imagining himself an innocent victim
of Jewish malevolence some of the classic anti-semitic arguments
would start to rub off on him.   But Mosley was too intellectually
sophisticated to be entirely happy with it.   One gets the strong
impression that to him the Jew was a metaphor rather than a belief,
a word added to a pre-existing structure of thought to sharpen the
propaganda line, rather than a basic reassessment of the structure
itself.   This is supported by the extremely meagre and summary
way in which he deals with the Jewish issue in his speeches and
writing, as if he was afraid that to give it more space would expose
the fragility of his arguments.   Mosley never explained what he
meant by Jewish finance, never in fact explained what he meant by
Jew at all.   In his speeches, the Jewish problem *qua* problem is
invariably relegated to question-time; his most extended treatment
– in *Tomorrow We Live* – takes up three pages.   There is a striking
disproportion, in fact, between the implication of what he was
saying and the attention he devotes to it.

This becomes even more startling in his various proposals for
dealing with the ' problem '.   Slipped in almost as a footnote in 1936
is the proposal to deport Jews (undefined) for ' anti-British conduct '
(undefined).   By implication this would include the majority of
Jews resident in England.   The minority ' against whom no such
charge rests ' would suffer for the sins of their fellow-Jews by
being deprived of the rights of British citizenship.[21]   The only
justification Mosley ever vouchsafed for this drastic remedy was
that the Jew ' comes from the Orient '.   The ' final solution ' could
be to resettle Jews in one of the ' many waste places of the world
possessing great potential fertility ' (though not Palestine or the
British Empire) where they could recover the status of nationhood.[22]
Many Jews who have felt ' deformed ' by their diaspora have
longed to become an integrated nation once more; but once again

Mosley never gave any very clear reason for this enforced transport-ation. Presumably the export of capital and the sweating in White-chapel could have been controlled by laws; and if the Press were to be obliged by law to ' tell the truth ' there would be no scope for ' Jewish ' methods there either. Mosley might have attempted to justify the expulsion of a whole community by a religious or racial theory; but he never mentioned religion or race. And so we come to the dénouement – a ' final solution ' without an explanation.

What judgment are we to pass on Mosley's ' quarrel with the Jews ' as he now calls it? Mosley had a right to object to Jewish attacks on his meetings. He had a strong case against the Jewish boycott of German goods. And in East London (the subject of the next chapter) there was a case – and demand – for a political campaign along ethnic lines to redress the local balance of power. People might differ profoundly on all these questions; but here at least were the makings of genuine political argument. The spurious charges which Mosley brought to the quarrel were the claim that inter-national finance was Jewish, the claim that Jews were the main force driving Britain to war with Germany, the claim that the Jewish community could and should be treated and judged as a single entity, and the claim that Jews were the ' power behind ' the political system. The proposals for mass deportation were also a complete *non sequitur*. In short, he erected an anti-semitic super-structure on the base of a genuine, but limited, set of issues. His intellectual and moral carelessness in so doing constitutes the greatest blemish on his whole career. I believe he later came deeply to regret it. But it is the most difficult of all his offences to forgive – and by some will never be forgiven.

NOTE: Sir Oswald Mosley comments (1973):
You do not appear to understand that it is possible to be sincere in not being an anti-semite – by definition a man who attacks Jews on ground of race or religion – and to be sincere in attacking Jews for their drive to a Second World War which in my view was one of the greatest crimes of history. If I try to stop a man burning down a house, it is not because he is a Welshman or nonconformist. Let it not be forgotten that in this event over 54 million lives were at stake. What should be forgotten is a quarrel of over 30 years ago which today divides people who might co-operate to avert similar or even greater catastrophes. My method of conducting the quarrel is of course another question, and no doubt I made mistakes. When you are in a life and death struggle – literally – with a big and powerful man, you tend to hit him with everything you have got, and to use methods you would not normally employ, which may even be repugnant to your character.

[On the policy of deporting some Jews and depriving others of their citizenship:] The principle was that in the life and death matter of world war in which Empire and British Isles might be lost as well as thousands of British lives, an organised minority of recent immigrants should be deported if they were acting, often violently, not in any political quarrel, but in the service of an outside interest, namely their co-patriots in Germany. No one could reasonably think that men like Sir Herbert Samuel or Sir Alfred Mond would fall into this category; or thousands of Jews who had been for generations in this country, often since they were re-admitted. Such Jews, and also in many cases more recent arrivals, conducted their political quarrels in an entirely British fashion. . . . Passages on deprivation of the vote could possibly be read as applying to all Jews on the principle that in all communities some suffer for the mistakes of others . . . but in practice it is inconceivable that it would have been applied to any Jews who were not organised as a community for war agitation. . . .

Chapter 21

The Campaign in East London

FROM 1932–4 it would be true to say that Mosley regarded the Jewish issue as more of a liability than an asset, a diversion from his main task. In a curious way this always remained his attitude: hence the summary way in which he dealt with it in his speeches and writings, as if to give it more space would be to give it an importance it did not deserve. No doubt the eagerness of Jews to attack him made him more ready to ' have a go ' at them on suitable occasions, but what really turned the liability into a limited asset in his mind was the support he was starting to pick up in the East End of London. Here again conventional accounts err in suggesting that at the end of 1934, with the old movement petering out after the disasters of the summer, Mosley made a deliberate decision to ' invade ' East London and stir up hatred against the Jews. Rather what happened is that Gentile East Londoners sought out the B.U.F. in order to make it a vehicle for their local grievances. Mosley went to where his ' natural ' support lay. He sympathised with the East Londoners' grievances: Britain for the British was a theme going back to 1918. He established a strong emotional *rapport* with East London audiences. The campaign the B.U.F. fought there was anti-Jewish, but not anti-semitic. It was a political campaign along ethnic lines, the basic issue being whether local power should lie with the ' British ' or with the Jews. The nearest parallel is contemporary Ulster, though with nothing approaching the violence.

In East London congregated the largest number of Jews in Britain. Of the 350,000 British Jews, about 230,000 lived in London, 150,000 of them in the East End. (There were smaller Jewish communities in Leeds, Manchester, Cardiff, Bristol, New-castle, Hull and on the Clyde.) These were mainly foreign immigrants who had come in about the turn of the century and who remained largely unassimilated. Politicians talked about them as fellow-Britons, but to many of their Gentile neighbours they were foreigners: a small proportion, difficult now to determine, were still technically aliens, that is, they had not been naturalised. There were Yiddish newspapers, Yiddish shops, a Yiddish theatre. It was as if a piece of Jewish East Europe had been torn up and put down again in the middle of East London. Sixty thousand or so Jews were to be found in Stepney; another 20,000 or so in Bethnal Green; smaller numbers in Hackney, Shoreditch and Bow. The more prosperous Jews had spread north and west to Stoke Newington, Hampstead and Golders Green. In no metropolitan borough in London were Jews in an actual majority. This fact is important. Many at the time and since have alleged that Mosley marched and campaigned in Jewish areas to provoke violence and gain publicity as though East London were somehow a Jewish preserve. In fact most East Londoners were non-Jewish and the bulk of fascist campaigning was done in non-Jewish areas where its support lay.

The B.U.F. campaign was waged against a background of poverty, trade depression and unemployment, the last two particularly unsettling in the East End economy with its network of tiny businesses unsupported by effective trade unionism. Jews were accused of taking over British businesses and jobs and undercutting the native standard of life by paying lower wages. This was particularly felt in the tailoring and cabinet-making trades consisting largely of small-unit factories working small-power machines, which Jewish employers often set up in the back rooms of private houses. The great charge in the tailoring trade was ' sweating ', that is, working employees, chiefly girls, hideously long hours at miserable wages.[1] The fact that Jews were sweated just as much as non-Jews created no solidarity with Jewish workers who were looked upon as blacklegs of Jewish employers in accomplishing the ruin of British concerns. The small British shopkeeper was loud in his complaints against his Jewish competitors for price-cutting. He was subject to a double squeeze: from the ' chain store octopus ' on the one side and the cut-price store on the other. (The latter was often only the former in embryo: Marks & Spencers started life as a trestle-table selling penny goods in the Leeds market.[2]) Bakers complained that Jews got in an extra day's baking by working on the Jewish sabbath, whereas no Christian would work on Sunday. Costermongers said that ' Jew boy gangs ' were terrorising them out of their pitches.[3] British criminals complained that Jewish criminals were taking their living away from them: one fascist supporter with interests in prostitution plastered the walls with the slogan ' British Streets for British Cows '. Obviously many of the ' natives ' were incompetent and uncompetitive. Why should anyone owe them a living? asked the economist. Because they are British, replied the B.U.F.

They also felt strangers in their own land. ' Above all else the English working man valued his home, the character of his streets and shops, his friends and neighbours. He resented bitterly changes in any of these which disturbed the even tenor of his ways.'[4] This was particularly true in areas of East London such as Bethnal Green which possessed an especially deep-rooted and tenacious culture of its own, deriving in part from an earlier Huguenot immigration. The fierce village parochialism, symbolised by the tiny terraced houses facing each other across narrow streets where children would play safe from traffic, grandparents sit out gossiping, and neighbours constantly drop in for a chat, had long harboured deep resentments against a ' domineering, all pervasive Yiddish culture '[5] which had slowly squashed native Bethnal Greeners into the north-east corner of the borough. Harry Roberts, a doctor with thirty years' experience of the East End, had seen ' street after street in Mile End, which were even twenty years ago almost wholly occupied by " Gentiles ", progressively occupied by Jews until almost every house in the street, including every little corner shop, has come to be in Jewish occupation '. Jews, he added, stuck to each other, preferred to buy from each other, objected to intermarriage and ' when they have a post to fill prefer to fill it with a Jew '.[6] Another group which resented the alien influx was the Irish dockers, who were also trying to maintain a separate identity in the Whitechapel area. Much of the fascist support was to come from these earlier immigrant groups, contesting the rights of later arrivals.

The complaints against Jewish competition show surprisingly little variation over time. On the one side there is the native artisan or merchant, not very bright or enterprising perhaps, but solid, hard-working and competent (on his own valuation). On the other side, there is the pushful Jew, who comes in and steals the business by superior cunning and flagrant disregard of custom and etiquette, soliciting trade instead of waiting patiently for it to come to him, entrapping his customers by slick advertising patter, dealing with all forms of merchandise instead of sticking to one line, price-cutting shamelessly, and perhaps above all ' sticking together ' – at any rate until the Gentile has been driven out.

Equally explosive East End grievances were connected with housing. Immigration had greatly increased the pressure on existing accommodation – already grossly inadequate – forcing a sharp rise in rents. As Jews prospered they bought up derelict housing and were thus able to screw up rents even higher forcing the poorer non-Jews to ' herd together like swine ' to keep a roof over their heads. So once again a situation which had its roots in inadequate social control was turned into a hatred of the ' Jew landlords with the money bags '. Whereas to the outside world the Jews of East London and other cities like Leeds (where much the same conflicts arose) appeared as inoffensive and hard-working communities menaced by fascist thugs, to their indigenous and often indigent Gentile neighbours they seemed ' privileged guests and doing very well ' as John Beckett put it. It was the English who felt underdogs.

The B.U.F. was not the first anti-alien movement in the field. It was the successor of the British Brothers League, a Conservative group which had campaigned successfully there in the early 1900s to get Jewish immigration stopped.[7]   One particular feature which enabled the B.U.F. to pick up almost where the British Brothers had left off was the unchanging cultural patterns of so many isolated East London communities.   The turn-of-the-century patriotic, imperial rhetoric in which the B.U.F. specialised was a positive asset in the East End where one gets the impression that life had stopped altogether; with even proletarian speakers using the pre-war public-school jargon of ' white men ' and ' dagoes ', filtered down through the boys' weeklies.   (As George Orwell has pointed out, these magazines catered chiefly to working-class boys, and especially to the sons of shopkeepers and artisans.)   The East Londoner was a classic case of vicarious identification with the white man's burden.

The first blackshirt branch in the East End was established at Bow in the autumn of 1934.   A little later came the first foothold in Bethnal Green – a disused stable in Green Street at the southern edge of Victoria Park.   North-east Bethnal Green was to become Mosley's stronghold in East London.   A branch was set up in Shoreditch in the spring of 1935 and one in Limehouse in July 1936. Two local men, Owen Burke and Edward ' Mick ' Clarke, both in the furniture trade, spearheaded the blackshirt assault on Bethnal Green.   They spoke at street-corners to jeering audiences.   ' Night after night ', recalled John Beckett, ' squads of their comrades used to receive the riot-call, and from Chelsea the old vans would rush to extricate the venturesome speaker from a hostile crowd.'[8] Gradually they created interest and Mosley was able to make his first East London appearance at the Stratford Town Hall, West Ham, in July 1935.

' Mick ' Clarke, twenty-three years old in 1934, was the only really important grass-roots leader that British fascism threw up, just as East London was the first – and, as it turned out, the last – local base that it ever established.   It was the East End that finally put paid to British Union's Officer Training Corps image, giving it instead a reputation for proletarian roughness which it never lost.   In fact, East London fascism was a curious mixture of the two – a proletarian or *petit bourgeois* movement with a vicarious public-school ethos: a kind of political Boys Brigade, personified by Clarke himself with his neat, military appearance, his juvenile humour and working-class exuberance.   Mosley in turn came to establish a relationship with many East Londoners which was unique in English politics.

Fascist progress in the East End went largely unnoticed through 1935.   It was only at the end of the year that stories first began to appear in the Press that fascists were ' terrorising ' the area.   In the Commons, the icy Sir John Simon said he had heard things which had made his blood boil. On 5 March 1936 Herbert Morrison referred to a number of incidents in Shoreditch and Hackney, mainly of insulting words, but including two cases of assault on Jews, and the breaking of a shop window.[9] In the following three years stories repeatedly appeared of fascist atrocities, numerous delegations called on the home secretary imploring him to take action, and Jews were described as living in a state of panic and hysteria. ' Fascist terror ' became a press cliché and even a modern historian talks about a ' siege of terror '.[10]

What are the facts? From the beginning of January 1936 to the end of 1938 the police kept a complete file of all complaints of ' Jew-baiting ' reported in the metropolitan London area, that is, the whole of London not just the East End. Leaving aside the disturbances which arose at public meetings, which we shall consider in a moment, 260 incidents in all were reported. There were 60 cases of alleged assault on Jews, 100 cases of damage to property (very largely breaking of windows), 39 cases of insult, and 61 cases of offensive slogans chalked or stuck on walls and anonymous postcards – mainly of the ' Perish Judah ' variety. In connection with all these complaints thirty-eight persons were arrested, about one-half of whom were fascists.[11] The sixty assaults on Jews are clearly at the heart of the matter. A number of comments can be made. In the first place there were just as many if not more assaults on fascists in this period. The police files give twenty-nine instances of alleged Jewish assaults on fascists in the period August 1936 to December 1938, but there were many more which were not recorded in these files, because the police only included in them those incidents which definitely involved Jews either as victims or aggressors: the first was clearly much easier to establish than the second. In his survey of the East London ' terror ' in November 1936, the *Evening Standard*'s Dudley Barker reports that ' most of the back-street assaults appear to have been directed *against* Blackshirts. . . . There seemed no doubt . . . that East End Blackshirts are in some real danger of physical violence ' (my italics).[12] Moreover, there is no doubt that some local Jewish communists were more violent than anything produced by the East London or any other branch of British fascism. Sentencing Barnet Becow yet again, this time for an assault on the police, the Magistrate at the Old Street Police Court remarked, ' He is a man trading in violence and is more likely to lead to the destruction of the Jewish community in the East End than the Fascists are.'[13]

It is clear that the overwhelming majority of the incidents were what in any other context would be referred to as brawls between groups of teenagers. As far as can be established, there was no case of serious injury. Nor is it clear that most of them had anything at all to do with politics. Often when police investigated

complaints by Jewish youths that they had been beaten up by
fascists they found that there was no evidence to link the assaults
either with race or with politics.   One Jewish father reported that
his son had been knocked unconscious by fascists.   The police
found no evidence that he had either been attacked by fascists or
knocked unconscious.[14]   *The Times* of 20 October 1936 hit off the
true situation when it remarked that the intense political campaigning gave inevitable opportunities ' for the irresponsible and lawless
to enjoy themselves at the expense of others ' – the Montagues and
Capulets of East London as it called them.

How did these stories circulate and, what is more, come to be
discussed even in the Cabinet?   First, many, particularly older,
Jews were terrified, and read into every little injury sustained by
their children a foretaste of a frightful pogrom about to descend on
them.   D. Fraenkel, the M.P. for Stepney (Mile End), explained
that ' the Jews in the East End of London are only one generation
removed from those who were persecuted in Russia, Hungary and
Poland '.   These Jews saw the Blackshirts as the Black Hand of
Tsarist Russia.   ' Mr. X and his family are all highly excitable
individuals,' reported the police after investigating one hugely
exaggerated complaint, ' who appear to be obsessed with the idea
that they will be seriously injured by fascists.'   Jews brought
pressure on their M.P.s to protect them: hence the stream of
parliamentary delegations from East London that visited the Home
Office.   As one precocious seventeen-year-old pointedly reminded
Captain Hudson, Tory M.P. for North Hackney, ' the Jewish
community was instrumental in reinstating you in the present
House of Commons '.[15]

This understandable fear was whipped up into panic by interested
parties.   Douglas Hyde gives an entertaining example in his
exposures of communist tactics.   When the slogan ' Perish Judah '
appeared round his Maida Vale home, he noticed that ' the majority
had obviously been done by one hand '.   But the lady from the
National Council of Civil Liberties had been very impressed.   A
big conference of the N.C.C.L. was summoned.   Anti-fascist
resolutions were moved by (undercover) communist delegates and
passed by overwhelming majorities.   Soon the Labour and Liberal
press took up the tale: ' new members came rolling into the Party,
subscriptions from East End clothing and furniture manufacturers
sky-rocketed '.[16]

On 7 March 1937 a headline appeared in *Reynolds News*: ' Child
nearly killed in Cot by Fascists.   East End Terror Again.'   The
Jewish Chronicle carried an identical account.   According to the
father ' a brick was thrown through the window of my flat on the
Bethnal Green Estate.   The brick narrowly missed hitting my
nine-months-old baby sleeping in a cot in that room.   I am convinc-

ed it was thrown by Fascists who know me as being an Anti-Fascist, and a member of the Labour Party.' The National Council of Civil Liberties circulated M.P.s. A deputation called on the home secretary with this and other complaints. Sir John Simon ordered an investigation. The story receded dramatically. A small stone had been thrown through the window. The father had seen no one. He hadn't even thought of reporting the incident to the police. But a gentleman from the National Council of Civil Liberties had come round asking for instances of fascist violence. The father had mentioned a stone being flung through the window, though he denied he had ever said it had been flung by fascists. In fact he was ' very annoyed ' when he discovered that an ' exaggerated version ' had appeared in the newspapers. The police report concluded: ' The window alleged broken is about 40 feet from the ground, on the top third floor. . . . Examination revealed that only a small stone could have broken it. Whoever threw the stone could not have taken deliberate aim at the window '.[17]

The other main form of political violence in East London in the 1930s arose at public meetings and processions, particularly at fascist meetings and processions. Most commentators felt that this violence occurred because fascists flung insults at Jews in the audience. Ivor Jennings, in an article in *Political Quarterly* which appeared in January 1937, referred to the ' peculiarly fascist technique ' of ' incitement to violence ' by use of ' insulting words and gestures '.

The first question is: how prevalent was fascist abuse of Jews at meetings in the East End? It was an offence under English law to use threatening, abusive or insulting words or behaviour with intent to provoke a breach of the peace or whereby a breach of the peace might be occasioned. On 16 July 1936, following complaints of anti-semitic abuse, Sir John Simon ordered the police rigorously to enforce this law, and to that end most fascist meetings in the East End from the middle of 1936 onwards had police shorthand writers taking notes of what was said, as well as police inspectors charged with cautioning or arresting speakers contravening the law. In the period August 1936 to December 1938 inclusive the B.U. held 2108 meetings in East London. B.U. speakers were cautioned by the police on sixteen occasions. There were seven prosecutions and, as far as it is possible to ascertain, no more than three convictions, one before a Juvenile Court! Mosley himself was never cautioned or prosecuted for insulting language in a career of extremely controversial platform-speaking.

On this evidence it cannot be claimed that the B.U. in East London contravened the law as it then stood. In fact, in July 1936 Mosley insisted that the law be obeyed, which aroused great opposition from militant B.U. anti-semites like Joyce and Beckett,

who were urging a policy of courting arrests and imprisonment to
'intensify antagonism towards Jews'.[18] In an article in *Blackshirt*
of 3 October 1936 Mosley wrote, 'Mere abuse we forbid. . . .
[It] is bad propaganda, and alienates public sympathy.'

But the fact that fascists did not break the law does not mean
that they were not guilty of abusive language. 'Mick' Clarke,
in particular, led a charmed existence on the right side of the law.
The reason he and others got away with it was that abusive language
was not itself an offence. It only became one if police could show
an intention to provoke a breach of the peace or a likelihood of a
breach of the peace resulting. In practice this could only arise
when Jews were present. If no Jews were there, speakers enjoyed
a great deal of latitude. This position was not affected by the
Public Order Act to which we shall refer later.

The limitation of the law in this respect is shown on the occasion
when Clarke came before the magistrates' court charged with
using insulting words and behaviour at a meeting in Bethnal Green
on 23 June 1937. According to the police shorthand report
Clarke had referred to Jews from time to time as 'greasy scum',
'lice of the earth', 'untouchables', etc. The flavour of the
speech, and perhaps of fascist street-corner oratory in the East End,
is brought out by the following passage. Clarke is attacking the
banning of a projected fascist march through East London, supposedly under Jewish pressure:

> One of them thought that on July 4th we intended to have an
> unofficial pogrom in East London and persecute the undesir-
> ables from our midst and drive them down to the docks. Just
> fancy, a few British people, born in the East End of London,
> wanting to have a little walk round; and then they want to
> wind up in Trafalgar Square and hear the voice of a white
> man . . . to hear a white man speak and put forward a policy
> for the British people.
>
> I read that the Jews were going to demonstrate to the
> Commissioner and the Home Secretary with a view to getting
> the march banned and apparently they succeeded very
> well. . . . But I don't want people to be led away with the
> idea that it is our desire to walk through the land of the
> waving palm, because we can do that any night of the week
> we jolly well choose. What a funny thing it would be if we
> did organize an unofficial pogrom without Wobbly Willie
> [a favourite nickname for Sir Philip Game, the police
> commissioner] knowing about it. For my part, I have no
> desire to mingle with them whatsoever. The only time when
> I would visit the land of the waving palm is when the gas
> masks are issued.

In the meantime, boys, I have been trying to ascertain what part of this London of ours belongs to Englishmen. What part of England is Jew-land? You know, like the swine of the earth, the kangaroos are scattered far and wide, and now we find that Wobbly Willie has ticked it off very graciously in order that we can see the area of the East End of London which belongs to the Jews. . . . Gradually we are seeing the big drive of Jewish international financiers from the top of the tree down to the stalls and shops in our own local markets. We gradually see the boards with Smith and Brown taken away. In place of Smith and Brown we see another name (inaudible). Moreover, underneath we see kosher signs and ' Hot Salt Beef sold here '. Silently, do we see the Englishman driven from his stall because Jews have become real Englishmen and have got our birthright.

Clarke's defence was that the meeting was ' so orderly that the uniform police made no attempt to stop [it] at any time. Experienced police officers, who are the best judges as to what is likely to happen, thought there was no chance of there being a breach of the peace.' A police witness testified that there were no Jews in the audience. The magistrate was apparently much more affected by Clarke calling Sir Philip Game ' Wobbly Willie ', Sir John Simon ' Soapy Simon ' and Sir Philip Sassoon a ' rotter ' than by his references to the land of the waving palms. It was ' beastly conduct ' and he bound Clarke over to keep the peace for the next twelve months – a conviction quashed on appeal for the reason that Clarke had said nothing to insult the people actually listening to him.[19]

Even when insults were flung at Jews who were present it was almost impossible to get a conviction. Most of the insults arose out of the whole context of meetings. ' Whilst Jews and others attend the meetings and indulge in " Baiting " the speakers, such occurrences as this are almost inevitable ,' noted one Inspector. It was the familiar problem of interaction. The expressions ' You louse ', ' Yiddish scum ', ' Jew boys ', ' hook-nosed unmentionables ', or William Joyce's more comprehensive ' submen with prehensile toes ' do seem appallingly insulting when set down in cold print, especially nearly forty years later. They were certainly unparliamentary expressions. But they were used on unparliamentary occasions – at rowdy meetings, usually on street corners, in tough areas. Speakers had no control over who came. Jews would heckle and shout. ' Fascist murderers,' they would scream. ' Yiddish scum,' the speaker would fling back. And so it would go on. An interesting test-case arose when Raven Thomson was charged with using insulting language on 11 September 1936. In acquitting him, the magistrate said that ' if Fascists come down and make wholesale attacks on a law-abiding community they will be punished fully for using insulting words. . . . If, on the other hand, a coterie of Jews . . . challenges the [speaker's] remarks, Thomson is free to deal with the challenge and comment on Jews in the same way.'[20]

To represent Jewish and communist opposition as having come along to hear an argument and then being goaded beyond endurance by the speaker's insults is misleading. Opponents came along to prevent the speaker from saying anything. For much of the East London campaign fascist speakers were subject to organised opposition which coincided with the maximum disturbances. For example, in August 1936 ' at about 60 per cent of fascist meetings . . . organised opposition in the form of continuous heckling, singing, shouting of slogans, jeering at the speaker and generally attempting to prevent speakers from obtaining a proper hearing, had been actively conducted by the opponents of Fascism '.[21] In May 1937 police were again reporting that ' heckling and interruption of Fascist speakers has been persistent and organised '. A police report of a meeting which led to considerable disturbance on 16 June 1938 is worth quoting:

> Speakers: Mr. E. G. Clarke and Mr. E. G. Thomas.
> Subject: Fascism. No inflammatory language was used.
>
> The meeting was quite orderly until about 9.20 pm approximately 1,000 persons then being present the majority being of Fascist sympathies. A large number of Communists and Jews then came along Cambridge Road from the direction of Whitechapel and assembled a short distance from the meeting on the South side and began to shout abusive remarks towards the speaker and the audience. The opposition continued to increase, and it was apparent by their attitude, that it was their intention, when they reached sufficient strength, to raid and break up the meeting. Police reserves were sent for and a cordon was placed between the rival factions to prevent them making contact. The opposition continued their abusive remarks and as the Fascist supporters were getting restive Police pushed the opposition away along Cambridge Road with the object of dispersing them. Several of them then attempted to break through the Police cordon. . . .[22]

The police files make it clear that most political disturbances in the East End arose in the manner described above. Of the 1075 people arrested in the East End between January 1936 and December 1938 for disturbances arising out of meetings and processions, 352 were fascists and 723 were anti-fascists. The vast majority of the disturbances leading to these arrests took place at fascist meetings and processions. ' On the other hand,' the police noted, ' at only a very few anti-fascist meetings was there any interruption of any importance by Fascists or their sympathisers.' This was not because Fascists lacked support or sympathy in the East End, as we shall see in a moment, but because breaking up opponents' meetings was not a tactic of the B.U., whereas it was of the Communist Party.

Who organised the anti-fascist opposition in the East End? We may exclude at once the two respectable bodies set up to defend Jewish rights and interests – the Co-ordinating Defence Committee of the Board of Deputies and a prestigious Council of Citizens headed by the Archbishop of Canterbury. The former was created on 10 September 1936. Its first meeting on 6 October provoked so much opposition from more militant Jews that the police had to clear the streets after the meeting. It did much better in the wealthier areas: a meeting at Willesden which attracted Jews from neighbouring Hampstead raised £725 from an audience of 500[23]. The official Labour and Liberal parties also held aloof from street fighting, though no doubt some of their militants took part. Their tactics were to lobby the Home Office and Press. We are left with the Communist Party, its subsidiaries (Young Communist League, National Unemployed Workers Movement) and the various Jewish organisations. All of these had heavily overlapping memberships. The communists provided the leadership. ' Reliable information has been received ', reported Special Branch, ' that the Communist leaders are very apprehensive that their policy of *physical attacks* on the Fascists, if pursued too ruthlessly, might cause the Government to take steps which would affect them adversely ' (my italics).[24] The Jewish organisations had their ups and downs. There was the Ex-Servicemen's Movement, a Jewish–Communist group of which it was ' doubtful whether more than one-half were ex-servicemen ' dedicated to ' attacking Fascism in its strongholds and sweeping it off the streets of London '.[25] Then there were bodies of changing names under the control of Schwartz and Bateman – British Union of Democrats, Blue and White Shirt Legion, etc. Both Schwartz and Bateman, according to the police, ' are only concerned with monetary gain, to be obtained by exploiting more or less wealthy Jews . . . '.[26] The Ex-Servicemen's Movement, too, was apparently ' more concerned with collecting money than propaganda '.[27] A Stepney Citizens' Council, described as ' Communist inspired ' with close links with the National Council of Civil Liberties, was mentioned in July 1937. More genuinely political was the Jewish People's Council against Fascism and Anti-Semitism, also a communist front, which was ' behind many of the anti-Fascist demonstrations '. All these bodies were able to draw on a ' hooligan ' element which ' includes many foreign Jews [who] are far more anti-police than anti-Fascist '.[28]

Underlying most of the charges against British Union in East London as elsewhere was the simple notion that it had no roots in English sentiment and tradition and therefore no inherent right to exist or propagate itself. Mosley was coming into areas that did not want him simply to stir up trouble and possibly recruit a certain type of adolescent, weak in the head, but strong in his capacity for mischief. This misconception extended to the right of politics. For example, the *Spectator* of 9 October 1936 wrote, ' The Fascists have no desire to persuade or convince the East Londoners; they knew well enough that this was impossible. No one doubts the hatred and loathing of Fascism in the East End. . . . '

Mosley was determined to prove his right to a political existence there. On 16 July 1936 he announced that his movement would fight East London seats in the municipal elections the following March, while recognising that the municipal register was un-favourable to his hopes – it was confined to householders, which excluded not just his teenage supporters but young men and women in their early twenties who still lived with their parents, a not uncommon situation in a hugely overcrowded area.

He launched an intensive campaign. ' In the name of free speech Bethnal Green and Stepney are trapped in the toils of a by-election with no polling day,' lamented the *Times* correspondent as Mosley took his message ' into the streets and houses of the people '. He meant it literally. The amplification system used by British Union speakers meant that even walls of houses were in-adequate to keep out the blasts of impassioned fascist oratory, supplemented by drums and martial music as bands and processions wove their way through the narrow streets. To the tune of ' Daisy, Daisy ', fascist youths would sing:

> Abie, Abie, now that we've tumbled you,
> You'll go crazy before we are done with you,
> What with your cut price tactics,
> Secret meetings in your attics,
> It'll be grand, when you leave our land,
> On the barges we've made for you.

Another favourite refrain was ' The Yids, the Yids, We've got to get rid of the Yids '. Fascist leaders, Dudley Barker was told, discouraged such exuberance, but they either could not or would not stop it.

To many in the East End, in the pre-television and bingo era, these displays of speech-making and marching must have brightened the pattern of a dreary existence. Audiences for street-corner meetings were astonishingly large; both fascists and anti-fascists attracting hundreds at a time, while Mosley's appearances drew thousands. For others they must have been wearing, perhaps terrifying in their import. Mothers complained that they could not get children to sleep at night; and irate neighbours would bang pots and pans from their windows in an attempt to drown the speaker. At schools it was reported that ' Gentiles ' and ' Jews ' had replaced ' cops ' and ' robbers ' as a favourite game.

Mosley himself soon replaced Clarke as the centre of attraction. Thousands streamed to hear him at his big open-air rallies in Victoria and Finsbury parks. But he had an even more ambitious project. British Union ' planned to complete the summer propaganda season with a great march of London members through ten miles of East London streets, culminating with four great mass demonstrations on pitches where for the last twelve months the British Union has regularly held meetings.'[29] Part of the route lay through Cable Street, just north of the London docklands in Whitechapel.

On Sunday, 4 October 1936, while fascists, communists and police clashed bloodily in the streets of Paris, London staged its own heavily expurgated presentation of the same drama. The battle of Cable Street has been told many times. The fascists planned to march from the Royal Mint near Tower Bridge through Shoreditch, Limehouse, Bow and Bethnal Green, halting at each place for speeches by Mosley. Moderate Labour leaders had tried to get the procession prohibited or diverted. When this failed they urged their followers to stay away. However, the Communist Party and the I.L.P., viewing the march in the context of the Spanish Civil War, planned to prevent it by force. ' They shall not pass ' was their motto. When Mosley arrived at the Royal Mint in the early afternoon, 3000 fascists had assembled for the procession. However, much larger crowds had gathered in its path. No doubt many had come only to watch, but the activists erected barricades in Cable Street. The foot and mounted police (6000 of them had been drafted into the East End) charged repeatedly in an attempt to clear a passage for Mosley's men but without success. Meanwhile Jack Spot, ' king of the underworld ', armed with a chair leg filled with lead, headed a group which broke through the police ranks in an effort to reach Mosley, standing, tense, in his car surrounded by his bodyguard. A pitched battle developed in which many blackshirts were injured while defending their leader before the police regained control.[30] Eventually Sir Philip Game sent for Mosley. He said, ' As you can see for yourself, if you fellows go ahead from here there will be a shambles. I am not going to have that. You must call it off.' Mosley asked: ' Is that an order? ' ' Yes,' replied Game. Mosley complied. The fascists marched off and soon dispersed. They had not passed. In the fighting between anti-fascists and police, 83 demonstrators were arrested and almost 100 people (including police) injured. A. K. Chesterton on 10 October summed up British Union reactions. ' Put in briefest form [the facts] boil down to this – that the British Government is prepared to find an expeditionary force of twenty-five thousand British soldiers to protect Jewish lives in Palestine, but is not prepared to use a sufficient force of police to keep a largely Jewish rabble in order on the streets of London while British patriots march to places set apart for the holding of their lawful meetings.'

The general verdict has been that East London rose ' spontaneously ' against Mosley. A Special Branch report throws the events and the aftermath of the Battle of Cable Street in a rather unexpected light:

> The general cry of the anti-fascist press was that the ' entire population of East London had risen against Mosley and had declared that he and his followers should not pass ', and that they did not pass ' owing to the solid front presented by the workers of East London.' This statement is, however, far from reflecting accurately the state of affairs regarding fascism in the East End. There is abundant evidence that the Fascist movement has been steadily gaining ground in many parts of East London and has strong support in such districts as Stepney, Shoreditch, Bethnal Green, Hackney and Bow. (No attempt has been made by the B.U.F. to hold meetings or spread its propaganda in the immediate vicinity of Aldgate where the disorder occurred on the 4th October.)
>
> There can be no doubt that the unruly element in the crowd ... was very largely Communist-inspired. A number of well-known active communists were seen at, or near, points where actual disorder occurred, and Marks Barnet Becow, one of the most violent communists in London, was seen at the point where a lorry containing bricks had been placed as a barrier across the road and overturned, the bricks being used as missiles. (Becow was subsequently sentenced to 3 months imprisonment for assaulting a police officer.)
>
> The British Union of Fascists alleged that ' train loads of toughs and undesirables from all over the country were imported into London for the occasion ', but there is no reliable evidence to support this statement and it is significant that of the 83 anti-Fascists arrested ... only one gave an address outside London. ...
>
> While attempts by the Communist Party to raise enthusiasm over the ' Fascist defeat ' were comparative failures, the British Union of Fascists, during the week following the banning of their march conducted the most successful series of meetings since the beginning of the movement. In Stepney, Shoreditch, Bethnal Green, Stoke Newington and Limehouse, crowds

estimated at several thousands of people (the highest being 12,000) assembled and accorded the speakers an enthusiastic reception; opposition was either non-existent or negligible and no disorder took place. On 11 October, Sir O. Mosley addressed a meeting of 12,000 at Victoria Park Square, and was enthusiastically received, later marching at the head of the procession to Salmon Lane, Limehouse, without opposition or disorder. On the first he again addressed a meeting at Aske Street, Shoreditch, where he received similar treatment.

In contrast, much opposition has been displayed at meetings held by the Communist movement's speakers. On several occasions meetings of the Young Communist League have been accorded an antagonistic reception in different parts of East London; it has been necessary for the police to close some meetings to prevent breaches of the peace; on other occasions meetings of anti-fascist bodies have been abandoned owing to lack of support.

Briefly, a definite pro-fascist feeling has manifested itself throughout the districts mentioned since the events of 4th October.... It is reliably reported that the London membership has increased by 2,000.[31]

It was at the Salmon Lane pitch in Limehouse that Mosley on 14 October 1936 gave his own justification for being in East London:

The *Daily Herald* this morning – the paper that used to preach revolution – was saying that everything was peaceful and happy in the East End of London until the wicked *Blackshirts* came along. You were all living in Paradise until then. According to the *Herald*, before this troublesome Movement came down to the East End and opened your eyes to the facts of your existence you had always voted for the Labour Party, and having voted you suddenly became happy and contented; just because you had local Labour governments in office you began to imagine that your houses were quite perfect, your wages high enough, your hours and conditions of work as you would wish them to be, and no such thing as unemployment or poverty existed in East London. That is what the *Daily Herald* was saying this morning. Everything was perfect till a man like Mosley came down and stirred up trouble. And that is the Party which used to call itself a revolutionary party. Why, today they are more conservative than the conservatives.

They say the system is all right and there is nothing wrong with it. But how are we to judge any system? Surely, by the conditions of the people. Today we have in England low wages, long hours, rotten houses, unemployment and poverty – all absolutely *unnecessary!* With the vast Imperial resources which are the heritage of this country, in this age when scientific progress and technical advance has vastly increased production, the problems of poverty and want can easily be solved by a Government empowered by the people to carry out their will. While democratic Governments are giving away the Empire which our fathers won, our people are abandoned to poverty and unemployment.

Yet the Empire belongs to you, the people of Britain! Thousands of Englishmen won this great Empire which has been the glory of the world; their sacrifice and heroism gained it for us, and today modern science can take its resources, take its wealth, organise this mighty heritage. . . . The message of the Blackshirt Movement to the people of Britain is, Arise and enter your own, and be great, happy and wealthy once again!

Here tonight you have given me that loyalty and comradeship which I have come to love in East London. But if you believe in our cause, do not leave it at that; do not leave it just in saying ' They are right ', or ' They are good fellows '. Arise in your thousands, work with us, fight with us, and march with us to certain victory; and in days to come, among children yet unborn, you the pioneers of the British Revolution shall be remembered and honoured wherever English men and women are gathered together. In days to come your children shall call down the blessings of Heaven upon your heads because you had the courage in these days of our struggle to stand with us against all the forces of political corruption and all the hatred of the old world.

East Londoners could be roused to a pitch of great excitement, but rapidly sank back into their usual apathy. By the time the municipal elections came round, the situation was much calmer. Mosley himself formally opened the fascist election campaign at the beginning of February 1937. Raven Thomson and ' Mick ' Clarke were the candidates in Bethnal Green North-East; Anne Brock Griggs and Charles Wegg Prosser fought Limehouse; William Joyce and Jim Bailey, ' a Cockney . . . [with] a large personal following ',[32] were put up for Shoreditch. (Bailey, like many East End Mosleyites, was in the furniture trade.) The party in power in all three boroughs was the Labour Party which had, in fact, won control of the London County Council for the first time in May 1934 under Morrison's leadership. Conservatism was a small minority in East London; and Conservatives campaigned there under the title of the Municipal Reform Party – ' a coterie of hard-faced businessmen, younger sons, building contractors and profiteers ', according to Beckett.[33]

British Union's campaign theme according to the Special Branch ' has been to attack semitism. International financiers (alleged to be Jews), Jewish landlordism in the East End, shopkeepers, employers of labour, and Jewish members of the LCC, have all been strongly criticised.'[34] Mosley's own appeal to the electors to ' choose between us and the parties of Jewry ' and to ' give the Jews notice to quit ' was a reference not only to economic interests but to recent political events. One main factor had been the local Jewish efforts through the Labour and Communist parties to stop B.U. meetings in East London, either through denial of halls, or by organising street attacks. Mosley was asking the electors to show to the public at large which of the two sides was really ' alien ' and oppressive to the local people.

His own speeches were mainly devoted to attacking the Labour Party for its inability to solve the housing problem. Here he returned to his favourite proposal of slum-clearance by war methods. He would pull down houses, block by block in a three-year plan, find temporary accommodation for the occupants while it was being done, and then rehouse them, not right away from their locality, but in the place they had been born and lived in all their lives. Attacking the communists for the slogan ' Vote Labour and Save Madrid ' Mosley exhorted the electors to ' Vote British and Save London '. Wegg Prosser, the Catholic lawyer put up to attract the Irish vote in Limehouse, also ran a restrained campaign in harness with Anne Brock Griggs. Clarke, Joyce and Bailey had Jews on the brain, but even they were forced to diversify their interests: as Mandle has noted, ' it was perhaps more a Mosley campaign than a Joyce or Chesterton one '. Abusive language was absent, largely because Jews stayed away from fascist meetings. ' The attention of the audiences and the lack of heckling has been very noticeable. '[35]

The election results announced on 6 March 1937 failed to live up to Mosley's hopes, but justified his claim that he represented some-thing substantial in East London. Nearly 8000 ' dads and grand-dads ' as he called them, together with their spouses, representing an average of almost 18 per cent of the votes cast, voted for British Union candidates. Clarke and Thomson did best in Bethnal Green North-East with 23 per cent of the votes, or about 3000 apiece, as compared to the 7700 recorded for the Labour candidates; Mrs Brock Griggs and Wegg Prosser got 2000 (or about 16 per cent) in Limehouse; and Joyce and Bailey 2500 (14 per cent) in Shore-ditch.* This was not a bad result for less than a year of hard

*Full details may be found in W. F. Mandle, *Anti-semitism and the British Union*

campaigning. However, the verdict does not confirm the view that the fascists gained at the expense of Labour. The Labour proportion of the vote fell significantly only in Shoreditch; elsewhere it was the Liberals and anti-socialists who lost out. This strengthens the view that Mosley had as yet made little political headway among the ' ordinary ' working class of East London – dockers (non-Irish), transport men, shipyard workers. His local position may be likened to Enoch Powell's national one after the anti-immigration speech of 1968. He had become personally popular in much of East London and there was a definite sympathy for the B.U. point of view. However, this was not sufficient to get older voters to switch traditional allegiances. People may have disliked foreigners, but they still looked to the Labour Party, the party of the underdog, to remedy their economic grievances. Whether those allegiances had been broken among younger voters – the sons and daughters of the dads and granddads – we shall never know for certain because the general election of 1940 never took place.[36]

of Fascists (1968) pp. 57–8; also R. Benewick, *Political Violence and Public Order* (1961) pp. 281–2.

Chapter 22

The Government Steps In

In 1936, Mosley's tempestuous penetration of East London and the fears aroused by fascism's international successes combined to escalate militant opposition to British Union to the point of facing the Government with a serious problem of public disorder.

The question of giving the police the right of entry to public meetings, as well as the banning of uniforms, had first been raised in Cabinet just before the Olympia meeting in 1934.[1] Had there been another Olympia, legislation would certainly have been introduced. However, contrary to expectations, Olympia was an aberration, not a precedent. There was never again to be indoor violence on the Olympia scale. Partly this was achieved by the simple expedient of denying Mosley the use of halls. The fascists had planned a monster rally at the White City on 5 August 1934. The communists planned to be on hand with bigger and better demonstrations. But the police smoothly persuaded General Critchley, chairman of the White City Board, to cancel the letting.[2] This tactic was to be used with increasing frequency throughout the 1930s, so that in the end Mosley was denied the use of most of the large halls in the country, despite his manifest ability to fill them.[3] Olympia was the beginning of the end of the big public meeting in Britain, a process ratified by the final victory of the fireside chat over popular oratory. Mosley and the communists between them had combined unwittingly to establish a new principle: that the right to free speech would be maintained only if no one said anything sufficiently controversial to arouse militant opposition.

This was still for the future. Immediately, a typical British compromise had been set in motion which permitted the *status quo* to continue. Mosley cleaned up his stewarding methods. New instructions issued by Neil Francis-Hawkins stressed particularly that all interrupters were to be warned twice before action was taken and that on no account were stewards to leave their section of the hall, carry weapons or wear gloves. Interrupters resisting ejection were not to be flung onto the streets, but handed over to the police for prosecution under the Public Meetings Act of 1908.* Nor did Mosley stop there. Preparing for his Albert Hall meeting of 28 October 1934, he wrote to the Commissioner of Police, Lord Trenchard: 'We have no objection to the police entering the hall

*The Public Meetings Act of 1908 made it an offence for any person to act in a disorderly manner at a public meeting.

if you think it is necessary in the public interest for the maintenance of order.' Trenchard accepted with alacrity, and legislation to ensure a police presence was dropped – never to be revived.* In fact the police were not needed on that occasion. Springhall, a leading London communist, wanted to send his battalions into action once again, but he was overruled by his colleagues. Fascism, they decided, was in decline. They left the arena to Mosley and his supporters.[4] Thus the unobtrusive presence of the police, better discipline among the stewards and a greater disposition by the opposition to leave fascists alone all combined to ensure that Olympia would not set an immediate trend.

Admittedly the improvement was relative only. Left-wing forbearance was patchy, and could be shattered by new fascist ' scares ' of the kind that occurred in 1936. Fascist stewarding also remained extremely tough. Often it had to be. At other times it seemed that Mosley positively welcomed a showdown, taunting the opposition to do its worst. The ensuing battle would bring bad publicity in the next day's press (perhaps any publicity was better than no publicity), but a glow of satisfaction in the movement at another thrashing handed out to the ' Reds ', a hardened resolve and fresh bonds of loyalty forged in adversity. Certain sensitive issues could still bring out all the old savagery. At the Hornsey Town Hall on 25 January 1937, an ' unknown Jew ' stood up and said: ' Mr Mosley, do you mind if I ask you a personal question – is Mrs Mosley a Jewess? ' He was immediately ' pounced upon by persons sitting nearby and forcibly ejected from the Hall '. At the same time, widespread allegations of fascist brutality on this occasion were dismissed by a police enquiry as being largely without foundation.[5]

One notable indoor battle remained to be fought. This was at the Carfax Assembly Rooms, Oxford, on 25 May 1936. The number of future memoir-writers and Labour politicians in the audience alone ensured that it would be talked about for years to come.

The bare bones of the plot are that after Mosley had been speaking some time – between half an hour and forty minutes – to fairly continuous heckling he ordered an undergraduate to be put out. When a group of stewards attempted to do this, a free fight developed in which the metal chairs were used as weapons. Various well-known names then put in brief appearances. Richard Crossman, a don at New College, jumped onto the platform and pleaded with Mosley to remove his stewards. Mosley's response was to order the removal of Mr Crossman. Basil Murray (son of Professor Gilbert Murray), Philip Toynbee, a veteran of Olympia,

*The *right* of the police to enter indoor meetings under certain circumstances was established by a court case in 1935.

and Bernard Floud of Wadham College (a future Labour M.P.) were also ejected. Frank Pakenham (later Lord Longford), a fellow of Christ Church, complained of being ' horribly maltreated by a gang of Fascist thugs ' as he went to the rescue of one of the undergraduates; an experience which, it is said, transformed him from a Protestant Tory to a Catholic Socialist at one blow! Patrick Gordon Walker was also evidently at hand to provide a summing-up in *Isis* on 27 May. After a brief scuffle the police, who were present throughout, restored order. Whoever started it, one thing is certain. The fascists got the worst of the fighting, four of them being taken to the Radcliffe with broken heads and many others receiving minor injuries.

How did the trouble start? Gordon Walker and Crossman had no doubt at all that Mosley deliberately provoked his audience. The playing of the ' Horst Wessel Lied ' on the gramophone before the meeting started was not perhaps auspicious. But Mosley's opening remarks seem unexceptional enough. His first words, as reported by Gordon Walker, were that any interrupters would be ejected ' courteously and quietly '. It is interesting that elsewhere in his article in *Isis* Gordon Walker says that Mosley's speech was so dull ' that his audience evidently became bored, and even heckling came to an end '. It is difficult to see how a speaker could simultaneously succeed in setting an audience alight by insults and sending them to sleep with boredom. But this was evidently Mosley's achievement.

Both Gordon Walker and Crossman are agreed that the chief source of provocation was not anything Mosley said, but the presence of fifty or so uniformed stewards. Crossman refers to the ' steady advance foot by foot for the first hour of a Blackshirt phalanx down the main gangway '. This is not confirmed by other accounts, and indeed it is inherently implausible that any speaker who wanted to hold the attention of his audience would have a squad of twenty men (the number given) engaged in military manoeuvres up and down the central gangway. What seems to have happened, according to Gordon Walker and V. S. Hunter of Christ Church (*Oxford Mail*, 26 May), is that just before the first ejection a squad of blackshirts did advance to the centre of the disturbance. Indeed, according to the *Times* report of 26 May the undergraduate to be ejected was at first approached by two or three stewards and it was only when it became clear that they would not be able to handle the situation that the ' squad ' advanced.

What, then, was this situation which it required twenty blackshirts to handle? The police court proceedings a month later give some answers. According to the police evidence ' heckling and disturbances started whenever Murray and Floud turned round to give the signal '. Superintendent Webb said that the stewards only started moving up the hall when the order to eject one of the undergraduates had been given. Before they could reach him, the people surrounding him rose and began to rip up and throw the steel chairs at the stewards. The stewards were still some distance away.[6]

From Charles Fox, the chief constable at the time, comes further elucidation in a letter to the late Sir Maurice Bowra dated 22 February 1971:

> I was at the meeting. Murray was there in company with about 100 busmen who were on strike and with whom he acted. Immediately Mosley commenced to speak he and they flung out their newspapers to their full extent and at a given signal closed them, making as much noise as possible in the process. This was repeated time and time again, interspersed with foot shuffling. My deputy [Superintendent Webb] was with me and I remarked how long-suffering Mosley was. He stuck it for 20 or 30 minutes and then shouted ' Put that man out '. I cannot say if it was Murray he indicated, but this order was the signal for the metal chairs to be flung at the stewards and a free fight ensued in which many people received minor injuries, including Pakenham who went into it as in a rugby scrum, finishing with concussion.

Mosley himself remarks: ' The Chief Constable's account of the opening of newspapers is quite correct. I was however partly responsible for the subsequent irritation by then observing: " I am glad to see the young gentlemen have brought their lessons with them as I hear they are rather backward this term." The Cowley workers who had been prepared for the fray were then brought to the fore.' Fox is, however, wrong in thinking that it might have been Murray whose ejection Mosley ordered. It was another undergraduate, Robert Cook, who was ' with Mr. Basil Murray ', and only after ' repeated warnings ' to keep quiet.[7] Basil Murray was later prosecuted for assaulting one of the fascists. The anti-fascists had also slashed the tyres of the stewards' vans in Gloucester Green.

Dons, it seems, are just as prone to see only what suits them as ordinary mortals. It is surprising, to say the least, that not one of the three eminent scholars quoted mentioned the organised opposition of hand-and foot-banging which started immediately Mosley began speaking and had clearly been concerted between a number of undergraduates and workers on strike; or referred to the fact that it was the busmen who flung the metal chairs at the stewards, not the other way round (since it was blackshirts who were treated for broken heads and multiple scalp-injuries). As always the opposition to Mosley wanted to have it both ways: they were both heroic anti-fascist fighters and innocent victims of fascist brutality. The distortion arises from transferring all the blame for the disorders to the organisers of the meeting and omitting to mention that it was the opposition that was actually the first to resort to physical violence.

In the summer of 1936 violence switched to outdoor meetings and processions. Mosley's stewards were stoned as they marched away from a meeting at Hulme, Manchester, on 28 June 1936, Mosley himself escaping under a 'fusillade of bricks, pieces of mortar and coal'.[8]   At an open-air meeting in Hull on 12 July, six blackshirts were knocked unconscious by iron bars while defending Mosley as he tried to address a huge crowd at the corporation field: this time the window of his car was shattered by a bullet as it drove away, probably the only genuine attempt ever made to assassinate Mosley (but see below, page 417 n).   Trying to avert violence, the Manchester Watch Committee banned uniforms for a fascist procession and meeting at Albert Croft on 19 July: the meeting was stoned nevertheless.[9]   In August, an open-air rally was abandoned at Perth; a Bristol open-air meeting was stoned; three blackshirts, plus the chief constable, were injured at Merthyr in Wales. Finally on 27 September 1936 Mosley was himself assailed by a shower of missiles at a giant open-air rally at Holbeck Moor, Leeds, which attracted a crowd of 30,000.   Over twenty fascists were treated for abdominal injuries sustained while defending the platform.[10]   Hodgson was fined forty shillings on this occasion for throwing a stone at Mosley.   He said he had been goaded beyond endurance by the speech.   The stipendiary magistrate: What did he say to annoy you?   Hodgson: Well, he talked about Britain for the British.   Magistrate: Why should that annoy you? What nationality are you?[11]

Mosley was doing nothing illegal.   Yet the situation was rapidly becoming intolerable to an era which thought it had outgrown rowdy politics.   The Government was faced with the clear alternative of either enforcing or changing the law.   The first would have involved prosecuting left-wing groups for incitement to violence or unlawful assembly; and/or deterrent penalties for those actually arrested in connection with political disturbances.   To this course there were legal objections (a prosecution might not succeed), but the overwhelming ones were political.   Since it was the fascist meetings and processions that were being attacked, defence of the right of free speech and assembly would in practice mean defending the fascists against their opponents; and the Government was far too sensitive to the risk of being identified with fascists and making martyrs of the communists to contemplate this remedy. The alternative was to change the law so as to prevent or curtail the activities of the fascists.   But this might cause trouble with some of its supporters and with all anxious to preserve freedom of expression and propaganda for themselves: legislation directed against fascists might too easily be applied to others – Hunger Marchers for example. As the *New Statesman* of 24 October 1936 argued, a ban on demonstrations would 'invite a reactionary Government to make impossible genuine expression of public opinion in any industrial area whenever it thinks fit.' The Left drew a sharp distinction between its own right to propagate its views and Mosley's, but since it was never able to think up a method for enshrining this distinction in law it was generally suspicious of any interference with the right of dissent.

Coming on top of the provincial disturbances, the Battle of Cable Street in East London on 4 October 1936 was enough to decide a nervous government to prepare special legislation to call a halt to the succession of violent political clashes in the streets of Britain. On 10 November it introduced a Public Order Bill into the House of Commons. This became the Public Order Act the following month.

As we have seen, the Government had two alternatives. Either it could enforce the law by prosecuting those who broke it. Or it could change the law in such a way as to put hitherto legal fascist activities outside the law. It chose the second. The Public Order Act prohibited the wearing of political uniforms and proscribed what it called ' quasi-military organisations '. It gave to chief officers of police the power to ban processions for up to three months with the consent of the home secretary. It restated the law against insulting or abusive language likely to lead to breaches of the peace. Finally, it slightly strengthened the hands of organisers of public meetings in bringing charges against disrupters – the one concession to the 'right of free speech'.[12] Although the object of the Act was to keep the peace, it set out to do so by crippling British Union, thereby implying that Mosley was largely responsible for the disorder. To argue that it was aimed with fine impartiality at both fascists and communists is misleading. Its critical provisions were directed specifically at fascist activities. It was fascist activities that were being attacked by organised left-wing opposition, not the other way round. By passing a law to curtail those activities, the Government was in effect condemning those activities as illegitimate and endorsing the actions of those who had been trying to get those activities stopped. As such it was a value judgment against fascism and in favour of its opponents.* What is interesting is that it was passed by a Conservative government with a large majority.

*No one in the Commons debates on the Public Order Bill doubted that it was aimed at fascism – e.g. Lovat Fraser: ' I hope that the action that we take tonight may crush Sir Oswald Mosley's movement.' (*Parliamentary Debates, House of Commons*, vol. 317, cols 1433-4.)

Why was this kind of Public Order Act passed? The basic reason was political. The people who objected to fascist methods of political propaganda felt much more strongly about the matter than those who felt that the fascists had a right to those methods. No one was basically prepared to defend Mosley's right to hold processions in East London; many people were prepared to make a row to stop him doing so.

The question arises why Mosley received so little support from the large 'law and order' brigade on the Tory backbenches who might normally have been expected to favour a different kind of bill – one increasing the penalties for political violence, for example. There was a complex of reasons – some going back to Mosley's initial act of 'betrayal' in joining the Labour Party: the right-wing Oliver Locker-Lampson, who attacked Mosley with equal ferocity both as a socialist and as a fascist, is an example of this attitude. But the key to Mosley's defeat in this area of politics was uniforms. No one, except the odd right-wing eccentric (for example, Sir Robert Turton) was prepared to support Mosley's right to parade about in uniforms. The uniform definitely raised M.P.s' hackles. 'A uniform in politics symbolises force, to be used either now or in the future.'[13] In the Commons, Sir John Simon gave it as 'the unanimous view of the chief officers of police in the areas primarily concerned that the wearing of political uniforms is a source of special provocation.'[14] On the other hand, in his memorandum to the Cabinet, he doubted whether uniforms were 'the kernel of the mischief', pointing out quite rightly that un-uniformed parades would still evoke opposition.* Simon's chief complaint against the uniform was that it added to Mosley's 'power of appeal with a section of the public',[15] that is to say it was an effective means of propaganda. Whether or not the uniform was provocative and hence a source of disorder, there is no doubt that its use by fascists was resented, for different reasons, by both politicians and police. The Government was able to use this resentment to push through another prohibition – on processions – which deserved, and would otherwise have received, much more criticism; as well as to get away with a measure for maintaining public order which did

*In fact, the most violent outdoor clash in the 1930s took place *after* the banning of the uniform, on the route of Mosley's procession through Bermondsey, South London, on 4 October 1937. 'This scrubby crowd of weedy clerks', as a Labour M.P. described them without their uniform, was still sufficiently provocative to evoke an opposition which resulted in 113 arrests and many fights and injuries, although the march took place through entirely non-Jewish areas. (Public Record Office: MEPOL 2/3117.) The one occasion in the 1930s when Mosley was injured at a political meeting – in November 1937 when his head was gashed open by a brick – also occurred after the passage of the Public Order Act.

virtually nothing to safeguard the rights of free speech against those who organised to prevent them.

At the time, Mosley staunchly upheld the ' right of Englishmen ' to wear whatever clothes they liked without molestation. At a businessmen's luncheon in Manchester he asked: ' Are we really to have it laid down in Great Britain that a man might not wear the clothes he wishes to wear? If that is the view of Parliament then let Parliament have the courage to translate its opinion into law. Meanwhile, a Socialist has no more right to throw a brick at a Fascist whose clothes he dislikes than I have . . . to deliver a heavy blow on the jaw of Mr Baldwin for wearing . . . the detestable top-hat and frock-coat that symbolises a Victorian mugwumpery offensive to any decent-thinking Englishman.'[16]   Later he admitted that he had made a ' considerable mistake ' in allowing the development of a ' full military uniform. . . . I should have known that while we could have got away with the simple black shirt, the uniform made us much too military in appearance and would create a prejudice.   The old soldier in me got the better of the politician.'[17] (See above, page 324).

The banning of uniforms was supplemented by the right of police chiefs, with the consent of the home secretary, to ban all public processions in their areas for up to three months.   The question is whether this was the suppression of a genuine political right or of an intolerable public nuisance.   The two relevant common-law cases are *Beatty versus Gilbanks* (1882) and *Wise versus Dunning* (1902). In the former, Beatty, the leader of the Salvation Army in Weston-super-Mare, had appealed against a conviction for refusing to disperse his procession when it was attacked by a rival group.   In quashing the conviction, Mr Justice Field held the magistrates were wrong since the disturbance of the peace was not ' the natural consequence of the acts of the appellants ' but was caused ' by other people antagonistic to the appellants '.   He saw ' no authority ' for the proposition that ' a man may be convicted for doing a lawful act if he knows that his doing it may cause others to do an unlawful act '.   Wise, a rabid anti-Papist whose habit of speaking and dressing in a manner offensive to Catholics in Liverpool had led to disturbances at his previous meetings, was bound over to keep the peace after the police had prevented him from addressing a meeting.   On appeal, the magistrates' decision was upheld.   Both F. E. Smith and A. V. Dicey argued on his behalf that the judgment in the case of *Beatty versus Gilbanks* applied to him.   Disagreeing, Lord Alverstone and Mr Justice Darling held that the circumstances of the two cases were different.   The first was an example of a genuine attempt to convert people to a point of view; the second a deliberate attempt to provoke by insult.   In the first, an organised attempt had been made to break up a legal procession; in the second, the disturbances vere a spontaneous reaction to provocations. It followed that the illegal acts in the second case were a ' natural consequence ' of the appellant's acts, consequences he must be assumed to have intended. The whole question, according to Darling, was one of ' fact and evidence '.[18]

The question in 1936 was whether Mosley's circumstances in the East End were more like Beatty's or Wise's; whether he wanted to convert or insult; whether the opposition was organised or spontaneous. The question is complicated by the fact that his effort to convert some people entailed attacking others, but this is, after all, what political controversy is about. In a court of law Mosley could have advanced powerful arguments in favour of the following propositions: (1) that his movement was advancing a serious policy on national and local issues; (2) that his processions were intended to publicise that policy; (3) that in some hundreds of meetings in the East End there had been only one conviction (up to mid-1937) for using insulting language; (4) that the seriousness of his intentions was established by his decision on 16 July 1936 to contest the municipal elections; (5) that the size of his friendly meetings and the results of these elections showed that he had sizeable support; (6) that, far from being spontaneous, the opposition to him was largely organised; and (7) that this organisation was carried out by his direct political competitor, the Communist Party. Had these issues been thrashed out in a court of law, it is by no means clear that Mosley would have lost. As it was, the question of his right to campaign in East London was decided in the purely political context of preventing disturbances with the least trouble. Once the argument was switched from the question of Mosley's intentions – a legitimate subject of debate – to that of avoiding violence at all costs, then the opposition was given the whiphand because it could always provide the violence.

The powers given to government and police to prohibit processions must be seen as part of the general strengthening of executive powers to cope with dissent. One commentator has pointed to a ' fine variety of executive-minded decisions given by the Courts [during the 1930s], curtailing freedom of speech and of public meeting and extending the police powers of search and entry. The effect of these cases was to provide the State with a complete armoury of weapons for stopping the propagation of unpopular views.'[19] *Duncan versus Jones* (1936), giving the police the power to prohibit open-air meetings if they apprehended a breach of the peace, established beyond doubt that there was in Britain no right to free speech as such.[20] Mosley's ability to hold indoor meetings was dependent on his being able to hire halls owned either by municipal corporations or by private individuals. His ability to hold outdoor meetings depended on the courtesy of his opponents in not making a

disturbance.   The vaunted right of free speech became in Jennings'
words ' the right to hold a peaceful meeting on private property if
the necessary funds can be found or the necessary consents obtained.
Meetings in the Carlton Club are still lawful provided that they do
not put reasonable persons in fear that there will be a breach of
peace in the Reform Club.'[21]

The Public Order Act also raises the question of the attitude of
the police and government to the fascists.   It has become a standard
part of left-wing mythology that both were pro-fascist.   There is
not the slightest evidence for this.   Police chiefs were the earliest
and most persistent advocates of measures to prohibit the wearing of
political uniforms and suppress ' private armies ', as well as to
prevent controversial processions and public meetings.[22]   The first
two were directed against the fascists; the last two in principle
aimed at both socialists and fascists, but were likely to hit fascists
harder than their opponents, since disturbances were most likely
to occur on fascist occasions.   A further point is that the natural
police antipathy to left-wing demonstrators who attacked them and
slashed police horses was balanced by hostility to those who challenged their monopoly of the law-enforcement function, and in
particular their monopoly of *uniforms*.   The police insistence that
fascist uniforms were the cause of the trouble, which runs like a
leitmotiv through all the police proposals, stems in part from a very
natural jealousy towards what they saw as a rival organisation.
The police attitude, then, was not pro-fascist or pro-socialist, but
pro-police.   Their chief concern was to maintain public order
with the least expenditure of time and manpower; and the easiest
way to do so was to ban any activities likely to lead to a breach
of the peace, irrespective of the intentions of their organisers.   It
is because the police had little cause to love either fascists or their
opponents that their evidence is the most reliable we have of the
origins and causes of political disturbances involving both in the
1930s.

Nor was the National Government any more partial to Mosley.
Its general political orientation may have been right-wing, but it
showed no favour to Mosley's particular brand of fascism, which
it regarded as un-English.   If there was going to be fascism in
England, it would be introduced under the auspices of the National
Government, not by a grass-roots fascist movement.   In all the
Cabinet and Home Office papers dealing with fascist activities
there is hardly a remark to be found favourable to Mosley and
his movement; rather a great solicitude for the rights and sensibilities
of those he was attacking.   This was not true of a handful of right-
wing M.P.s like Lieutenant-Colonel Moore, Captain Ramsey,
Sir Arnold Wilson and A. C. Crossfield.   But it was certainly
true in ministerial and civil-service circles.   Such help as Mosley

received took the form of a certain reluctance to abrogate long-standing principles of free speech and assembly which helped him. But, even so, all the essential measures required to render him ineffective, in so far as that could be achieved by fiat of a liberal régime, had been taken by the end of 1936 – four years after he had started. By normal British peace-time standards that is not bad going.

It may be argued that no liberal régime need display undue solicitude for those whose declared aim is to destroy it. This is a complicated question, but a simple practical point may be made. No system or viewpoint has a monopoly of wisdom. Denying Mosley the use of halls, closing down his open-air meetings, forbidding his processions, refusing to distribute or review his writings or report his speeches, denying him the facility to write articles or broadcast, all had the effect of progressively excluding an original and distinctive voice from the political dialogue. This was a particular loss to the nation as the great issue was joined between peace and war.

Chapter 23

The Peace of Europe

I F M O S L E Y ' s attacks on the Jews damned him in the eyes of the intellectuals, it was his opposition to the Second World War which ruined him with the British people.   Many still believe that he was prepared to let Hitler take over Britain.   This is an unjustifiable slur.   But there is good reason for re-examining his foreign policy in the 1930s independently of his own reputation.   The origins of the war are once more becoming a subject of lively debate.   The view that Churchill was ' right all along ' has been challenged by a ' revisionist ' school which argues that ' appeasement ' of Germany was a much more realistic policy than its critics have allowed, given Britain's diminished strength and its awesome imperial commitments. As the process of re-evaluation continues, Mosley's own view that the real trouble with appeasement was that it did not go far enough, that had it been based on a consistently realistic estimate of Britain's possibilities and a conception of a genuine alternative peace could have been preserved, may well gain increasing assent.

Mosley was always prepared to fight Germany and Italy under certain circumstances.   Those circumstances were a direct attack on Britain or the British Empire.   His policy was more pacific than that eventually followed by the British Government because his definition of British interests differed from theirs.   Mosley's definition of these interests rested on his conception of a self-contained empire.   The traditional definition rested on a conception of Britain as upholder of the European balance of power.

Mosley's repudiation of the traditional balance of power stemmed from the First World War.   In the air and in the trenches he had seen his best friends killed, the flower of young Europe slaughtered. What advantage of maintaining the European balance could possibly justify such a fearful devastation?   Churchill, on the other hand, had seen nothing 'which has occurred to alter or weaken the justice, wisdom, valour, and prudence upon which our ancestors acted '.[1]   This was the basic difference between the two men. Mosley's strongly isolationist attitude to European politics dates from the early 1920s.   Admittedly, he championed the League of Nations as an alternative to the balance of power.   But he made it clear that, should the League fail, Britain alone could not take on the burden of keeping law and order in the world.   Such views at the time were almost orthodox, though practice fell far short of aspiration.   This was the era when Bonar Law declared that Britain could not be the world's policeman; when Austen Chamberlain, rejecting any thought of an Eastern Locarno, said that the Polish Corridor was not worth the bones of a single British grenadier; when Churchill refused ' to accept as an axiom that our fate was involved in that of France '. Nor, of course, was the ' appeasement ' of Germany in the cause of a durable peace the dirty word in radical circles that it was to become in the 1930s. Mosley's crime was consistency: he carried over the ideas of the 1920s into the 1930s. Where he differed from his former colleagues was in seeing fascism as their legatee, not as their destroyer.

By the early 1930s, Mosley's twin aims of preventing war and building a ' land fit for heroes ' had crystallised into the concept of a British imperial system, politically isolated and economically 'insulated' from the rest of the world. This policy was clearly stated in the 1932 edition of *The Greater Britain*, written *before* Hitler had come to power and before Mussolini had started expanding in Africa. ' The measure of national reconstruction already described ', Mosley wrote, ' involves automatically a change in our foreign policy. We should be less prone to anxious interference in everybody else's affairs, and more concentrated on the resources of our own country and Empire.' Britain would keep out of the ' tangled skein of European politics and animosities '. Already there was a clear statement of the connection between self-sufficiency and peace:

> It would be possible to end the anachronistic struggle for markets of an unorganised capitalism, leading again, as it has often done in the past, to the entanglement of governments in the commercial rivalries of their nationals. In place of that explosive chaos, rational discussion of the world economic problems could supervene. Nations which, in their internal organisation, were largely self-contained would find it a comparatively smaller problem to settle the allocation of the relatively small remaining area of raw materials which were subject to international competition, and the comparatively small remaining area of international markets. . . .[2]

Wars, Mosley was arguing, were caused by commercial and financial rivalries. Get rid of the rivalries by autarchy and you would have got rid of the most important single cause of modern wars. In the decay of the liberal system, Keynes took much the same view. ' I sympathise with those who would minimise rather than maximise economic entanglements between nations,' he wrote in 1933. ' I am inclined to the belief that, after the transition is completed, a greater increase of national self-sufficiency and economic isolation between countries than existed before 1914 may tend to serve the cause of peace rather than otherwise.'[3] The

problem, as the 1930s were to show, arose from the 'transition'.
Europe went to war over the transition.

How was isolation–the key to radical hopes for building a better
Britain–to be reconciled with British security which had involved
maintaining the European balance of power? This problem had
not arisen in the 1920s. It became acute with the resurgence of
Germany in the 1930s. Mosley offered a dual policy: a settlement
with Germany and rearmament.

In considering the possibility of a settlement with Germany,
Mosley started from the proposition that Germany's goals were
limited and not of a kind to conflict with the interests of Britain,
properly conceived. This derives from his general argument that
fascism stood for autarchy, and that autarchy removed the causes
of war. It followed that there was little connection between the
aims of the Kaiser's Germany and those of Hitler's Germany:

> The former regime was Financial–Democratic Imperialism
> and latter is National – Socialist; therein lies a difference which
> the old-world politician cannot or will not comprehend; but
> from that difference follows every modern possibility of
> European peace. The Imperialism of the Kaiser, operating
> from the basis of an export–capitalist system, expressed itself
> naturally in terms of a vast colonial Empire and concomitant
> navies which clashed at every turn with the British Empire.
> The Judaic–financial system of pre-war German economics
> could only think in terms of progressively expanding export
> markets because it could not envisage even the attempt to
> build an autarchic system. . . . The whole psychology of Nazi
> Germany . . . is precisely the opposite. . . . Her national
> objective lies in the union of the Germanic peoples of Europe
> in a consolidated rather than diffused economic system which
> permits her with security to pursue her racial ideals. In fact,
> in the profound difference of national objective between
> the British Empire and the new Germany rests the main
> hope of peace between them.[4]

From this analysis followed Mosley's 'world alternative'.
Germany should be given its free hand in eastern Europe, even if
this meant war with Russia.[5] Italy should be guaranteed its outlets in north and north-east Africa. Japan could have north
China. The eastward expansion of Germany was France's best
guarantee of security as well. And Britain would get on with the
job of creating its 'land fit for heroes' and developing its empire.
Such a settlement would remove the major causes of war. An
effective League of Nations could be re-created on the basis of a
Four Power Pact between Britain, France, Germany and Italy.

The moral justification of Mosley's policy rested on the fascist

doctrine of the ' leader ' nations. ' Nations must be either hammer
or anvil,' wrote the German geopolitician Karl Haushofer.   Mosley
agreed:

> ... we must recognise the existence of other ' leader Nations '
> who, like ourselves, had the natural duty to lead and to
> organise the more backward countries in their sphere of
> influence and thereby enrich not only themselves but the world
> by the production of fresh resources for civilisation.   If this
> natural leadership of other great Nations was denied by British
> interference, in regions where we had no concern, world ex-
> plosion became inevitable.[6]

Both requirements – economic self-sufficiency and leadership in a
defined sphere – were included in Mosley's conception of the ' satisfaction ' of the fascist powers.

Was Mosley's conception of German aims in fact realistic?
Even accepting that a Nazi land-empire in eastern Europe with its
' racial ideals ' would have been far from the idyllic picture of
' leader ' nations taking in hand the progress of backward peoples,
was Mosley's argument that the project was in essence limited to
that soundly based?

Historical debate about the nature of Hitler's ambitions has raged
furiously, especially since the publication of A. J. P. Taylor's *Origins
of the Second World War* in 1961.   Nevertheless, there is wide
acceptance of the view that in so far as Hitler can be said to have
had explicit long-term aims they were directed at eastern, and not
western, Europe.[7]   In *Mein Kampf*, which is often cited in support
of the thesis that Hitler's aims were unlimited, Hitler specifically
renounces ' an intoxicating Alexandrine campaign of conquest '
and argues that the future of the German people lies ' in the diligent
and persistent work of the German plough, to which the sword has
only given the soil '.[8]   The goal of German foreign policy as
enunciated in *Mein Kampf* is the acquisition of living-space or
Lebensraum at the expense of Russia where Germans could be
resettled on the land.

Alan Bullock has summed up: ' Hitler never looked to the West for
the future expansion of Germany, but always to the East. The conflict
with Britain and France arose not from any demands he had to
make on the Western Powers themselves, but from their refusal to
agree to a free hand for Germany in Central and Eastern Europe.'[9]

In *Mein Kampf* Hitler had argued that, in carrying out Germany's
eastern plans, an alliance with England was indispensable.   Whatever else he may or may not have intended, he tried very hard at
least till 1937 to get an English alliance.   This was the purpose of
Ribbentrop's appointment in London, however misguided it turned
out in retrospect.   As Bullock says:

Although Hitler's attitude towards Britain was modified later by growing contempt for the weakness of her policy and the credulity of her governments, the idea of an alliance with her attracted him throughout his life. It was an alliance which could only, in Hitler's view, be made on condition that Britain abandoned her own balance-of-power policy in Europe, accepted the prospect of a German hegemony on the Continent and left Germany a free hand in attaining it.[10]

In Keith Middlemas's view, Hitler's hope of being able to fulfil his eastern ambitions with Britain's consent and support waned after 1937; thereafter his policy was based on the assumption that although Britain would oppose his European plans it would not in the last resort intervene. The hope of an alliance with Britain, however, never completely faded away.[11]

There is thus considerable support for Mosley's view that (1) Hitler's explicit expansionist aims were confined to central and eastern Europe, and that (2) at almost any time in the 1930s an Anglo-German settlement or alliance could have been negotiated on this basis. The fact that it was not, and that in the end Britain went to war, clearly means only one thing: that this policy was not acceptable to the British Government and public opinion.

The question of why it was not is at the heart of the debate between Mosley and his opponents in the 1930s. The German programme of creating a ' consolidated ' economic system was unacceptable to the 'old parties', argued Mosley, because it challenged their conception of internationalism. As he put it in *Tomorrow We Live* (1938):

Certain countries have at once extirpated the control of international finance and the hopes of international Socialism. No reason exists in British interest to quarrel with these countries and every reason for world peace forbids the quarrel. Yet the feud of international finance and its twin, international socialism, thrusts the manhood of Britain towards mortal quarrel with these countries. Germany and Italy, despite a present poverty of natural resources have, at least, broken the control of international finance, and Germany in particular has offended this world power by summary dealing with the Jewish masters of usury. So every force of the money power throughout the world has been mobilised to crush them, and that power does not stop short of payment for its vendetta in British blood.[12]

In other words, western hostility to German aims was at root ideological. The western powers went to war for a principle – internationalism – which was in turn a ' superstructure ' (in the marxist sense) of financial interests hoping to preserve or re-establish the 'export–capitalist' economy. This remains Mosley's view today. The only concession he made, in the post-war years, was to allow that Hitler's methods may have frightened the democracies into believing that he aimed at world conquest which in fact was not the case.[13]

This, of course, is not the conventional view. The conventional view denies that Britain and France were motivated by anti-fascist feelings; rather the reverse: the ruling groups in both countries were pro-, rather than anti-fascist. Britain and France were driven to war because they realised, all too late that, Hitler's actions menaced their security. According to this argument, the question of Hitler's ultimate aims is irrelevant. His immediate, or intermediate, aims, if realised, would be quite sufficient so to alter the balance of power in Europe as to put Germany into a position to dictate future terms of existence to Britain and France. This was why, in the end, no settlement with Germany was possible on the terms which Hitler wanted.

Mosley was bound to take the balance-of-power argument seriously. Even though he believed that the character of German aims made it irrelevant, he had to meet the objection that he might be completely wrong, that after Hitler had consolidated his position in the east, won his war against Russia, used his conquests to create a military machine of awesome dimensions he would turn round and say to Britain and France: Do this or else!

To this Mosley countered with the second part of his policy: massive rearmament. The whole political idea of an isolated empire was linked to the current strategic doctrine that defence was stronger than attack. Throughout the 1930s he repeated one simple argument – that a properly rearmed Britain would be able to maintain its independence even against a Nazi-dominated Europe. At Earls Court in 1939 he insisted that ' if the wildest fears of our opponents were true, and Germany did attack Britain, provided that Britain had a Government and a system of the modern age, Britain has nothing in the world to fear even if she fought alone '.

The strategic doctrine underlying this was that Britain's defensive position was overwhelmingly strong:

> We are not dependent on these entangling alliances, because, under modern Government, we are more than capable of defending ourselves and, if necessary, of defending ourselves alone, with the sole aid of modern defence technique . . . we must combine, as never before, our natural gift for air power with our traditional naval power in defence of the arteries of Empire. Also from British land we must extract the last ounce of food by the system of steady but intensive agricultural production at home. . . .[14]

From 1934 onwards Mosley made rearmament in the air the central
plank of his defence policy.   Together with the mechanisation of
the Army and the strengthening of the Navy – the whole programme
to be financed by loan – Britain would be invulnerable.[15]   And
so in fact it proved: as Taylor writes, ' In June 1940 . . . [the]
policy of isolation and great armaments was forced on Great
Britain by events under the most unfavourable circumstances.
This policy enabled Britain to survive and get through the second
world war with far fewer casualties than in the first.'[16]

So Mosley's policy was thus an agreement to give Germany a
free hand in eastern Europe negotiated from a position of sufficient
defensive strength to render Britain invulnerable to attack if the
Germans turned on the West.   We will never know whether such a
policy could have avoided war, because it was never tried.   What
is clear is that it would have meant a very different world.   This is
what Mosley means when he says the objection to it was ideological.
This does not contradict the conventional view that it was rejected
on balance-of-power grounds, because the balance of power was
itself an ideological concept.   Its function in British history was
not to preserve security in the narrow sense but, as Churchill put it,
to preserve Britain's ' greatness and liberties '.[17]   By keeping
Europe divided Britain could create and maintain an empire and at
the same time preserve a free society – free politically, free economically – at home.

The basic objection to Mosley's plan was that it would have
destroyed the condition of Britain's ' liberties '.   It would have
meant heavy armaments over a long period and a centrally controlled economy.   Since the war, we have grown used to the first and
are moving towards the second.   They seemed alarming prospects
to most people in the 1930s.   The objection to Churchill's policy
was that a resolute attempt to uphold the European balance, quite
apart from its toll of lives, would involve the destruction of the
British Empire and of European independence.   This was because
under modern conditions no purely European combination could
defeat a German bid for hegemony.   It could be done only by
bringing in both America and Russia, who would be left as arbiters
of Europe's fate.   Mosley saw more clearly than Churchill that
the avoidance of a European war had become the condition of the
survival of the British Empire.   It could be argued that Churchill's
policy of allying with Russia was a peace policy because it would
have deterred Germany.   This is doubtful.   Most people saw it as
a return to the policy of armed camps which had led to the 1914
war.   In any case, by 1937 Churchill was no longer thinking in terms
of deterrence, only of getting Britain into the best position to fight
the coming war.

Churchill and Mosley represented the two logical choices facing

Britain in the 1930s. Mosley's offered the best hope of peace; Churchill's the best hope of winning a war. In the middle was the wobble known as appeasement. Appeasement was based on a military conception very close to Mosley's but on a political conception nearer Churchill's: in that contradiction lay its inevitable failure. The military conception pointed to isolation; the political conception to maintaining the balance of power. In practice, Britain pursued a policy of anxious interference which exasperated the dictators without earning their respect, and which brought neither durable alliances nor a durable peace. At the same time, the contempt with which Britain's feeble initiatives were treated created such a sense of shame and humiliation that the psychological pressure to make a firm stand, somewhere, anywhere, became irresistible.

The era of the feeble slap scornfully brushed aside opened with the Abyssinian crisis of 1935, which also gave Mosley his first opportunity to present his alternative policy to the British public. By late nineteenth-century standards Abyssinia, with its slavery and slave-trading, was a prime candidate for the white man's burden: had the Italians taken over the country in the 1890s as many of them wanted to, nobody would have much minded. At the same time, Abyssinia was a member of the League of Nations and part of the post-imperial order set up by the United States and Britain in 1919. The British claimed they were upholding the League system. But the First World War had a paradoxical effect. The ideologies with which the victorious powers (especially the Americans) justified their sacrifices were anti-imperialist. They were fighting for small nations, against militarism. This influenced the whole post-war settlement and mentality. At the same time the material and political conditions which could alone have supported a renovated liberal–capitalist order were further eroded by the war itself. The collapse of its economic props removed the necessary condition for the continuance of the League of Nations system. With self-help and autarchy the dominant economic ideologies of the 1930s, the economic arguments for empire, first mooted in their modern form in the late nineteenth century, were greatly strengthened. The British, having an empire, and one self-governing in some (though not all) of its parts, could go on preaching and believing in the League morality even as they tried half-heartedly to develop an imperial economic system. The thrusting 'have-not' powers had to try to grab empires in an increasingly autarchic world. In practice, British government was usually prepared in the end to concede to force what it would not concede to fascist reasoning. But because these concessions attacked head-on not only its own moral susceptibilities but also the whole set of moral expectations created in 1918 and continually re-created in the successive

crises of the 1930s the policy was bound to break down before the
anger and shame of public opinion.

The cabinet papers of the 1930s show how torn was Stanley
Baldwin's government between moral disapproval of Italy's aims in
Africa and its desire to keep Mussolini's friendship in Europe to
stop Germany (the Stresa Front); between its ideological commit-
ment to collective security, and its recognition that an Imperial
Britain could not afford a hostile Italy in the Mediterranean and
Middle East.   The first set of attitudes pointed to League action to
stop Italy; the second to the ' blind eye '.[18]   Unable to make up its
mind which to do, the Government characteristically did both.
The Mediterranean fleet was transferred from Malta to Egypt at
the end of August 1935.   At Geneva on 11 September, Sir Samuel
Hoare, the foreign secretary, proclaimed in ringing terms Britain's
determination to stand by the Covenant in resisting acts of un-
provoked aggression.   ' The ideas enshrined in the Covenant and
in particular the aspiration to establish the rule of law in international affairs have become part of our national conscience,' he
declared.   (It would be truer to say that they were the product of
Britain's national conscience.)   When Italy invaded Abyssinia the
following month, Britain took the lead in imposing economic
sanctions.   Liberal England was thrilled.   At the same time Hoare
was privately preparing to back down.   Sanctions were carefully
limited and excluded oil.   The Suez Canal was kept open.   In
December Hoare made his famous deal with Laval that would have
given Mussolini the fertile plains of Abyssinia.

Mosley responded to the first half of this programme with a great
' Mind Britain's Business ' campaign, launched at the beginning of
September.   The theme which he incessantly hammered home was,
as the campaign slogan suggests, that the Abyssinian quarrel was
no concern of Britain and that therefore Britain should stay out
of it.   Mosley attacked the integrity and impartiality of the
' collective security ' argument.   The motive behind sanctions ' is
the fear and hatred of the Old World for the New.   For long past
they have sought to use the idealistic conception of the League of
Nations as an instrument to encircle the resurgent fascist nations;
first Germany, then Italy.   To this end they have not hesitated to
use the vile weapon of the Soviet, whose shifty Litvinoff now presides
over the League.   This is not a League of Nations, but the old
Balance of Power in a more vicious and dangerous form, based not
on British interests, but on political prejudices.'[19]   Mosley emphasised the connection, little stressed in public debate at the time,
between sanctions and war.   ' Either sanctions are effective, in which
case they mean war, or sanctions are ineffective, in which case they
are humbug.'   Baldwin's ' more complex understanding ' of the
matter[20] earned Churchill's justifiable jibe: ' The Prime Minister

had declared that Sanctions meant war; secondly, he was resolved there must be no war; and thirdly, he decided upon Sanctions.'[21] Mosley's bitterest taunts were reserved for the Labour Party which demanded full support of the Covenant, yet consistently opposed rearmament. After the crisis had passed Mosley remarked that ' the spokesmen of the Labour Party proudly claimed that if they had been in office they would have pursued a policy that would have made war certain, with a deliberate deficiency of armament which would have made defeat inevitable '.[22]

The B.U.F. liked to claim that its great peace campaign had prevented the Government from taking the stronger measures that might have led to war with Italy.* Certainly Mosley attracted large and enthusiastic audiences–but then he always did. The usual verdict has been that most people would have welcomed a stronger stand against Italy. The Peace Ballot published at the end of June 1935 showed that over eleven million people favoured the idea of economic and non-military League sanctions against an aggressor; six million favoured military sanctions.[23] There was a great public outcry when the terms of the Hoare–Laval agreement leaked out in December, with the episcopal bench strongly to the fore. Against this two points can be made. First, the connection between sanctions and war was not clearly appreciated: confusion was compounded by Baldwin's misleading election slogan ' All sanctions short of war '. Secondly, it is one thing to keep out of a dispute; another to take up a strong moral position implying intervention and then back down, for then the elements of lost prestige and shame enter in. The great outcry against the Hoare–Laval terms stemmed in large part from the contrast between Hoare's performance at Geneva in September and the shabby deal he concocted in December; as well as from the feeling that Baldwin had just won an election on a League programme which he immediately jettisoned. In 1923 Mosley had said, ' There is nothing in the world so detrimental to national prestige as being full of bluff and bluster until you get into difficulties and then have to climb down. It is possible to walk down stairs of one's own free will with grace and dignity. It is impossible to be kicked downstairs with either grace or dignity.' This applied with particular force to the Abyssinian dispute. Drifting helplessly between ' its spite for fascism and its impotence to act ', as Mosley not unfairly put it, the Government got the worst of both worlds. The opportunity to vindicate the League was lost. Mussolini was driven inexorably into the German camp. And Hitler came to the conclusion that the British were degenerate and that he could do what he liked.

The first fruit of this revaluation was Germany's reoccupation

*The question of whether the campaign was actually financed by Mussolini is discussed on pp. 463-4 below.

of the Rhineland on 7 March 1936. The reason given was the Franco-Soviet Pact, ratified by the French Assembly on 27 February. Hitler claimed that this exposed Germany to a war on two fronts and was inconsistent with Locarno. Mosley took the common view that Hitler was simply walking into his back garden; he welcomed the reoccupation as helpful to peace by removing one of Germany's main grievances.[24] At the same time his demands for an understanding with Germany became more urgent.

' British policy must choose decisively between Germany and the Soviet,' he declared in May 1936.[25] In place of the ' virtual alliance of Conservative Government in Britain with Communist Government in Russia ',[26] Britain should seek ' peace and association with Germany and Italy '; should try to create ' a Bloc of Great Powers united in common interest and inspired by a new world ideal '.[27] The main obstacle to such understanding was ' the hatred of International Finance, and of International Socialism, for nations and systems which have thrown off the servitude which they jointly impose '.[28] In Berlin for his marriage to Diana, Mosley gave an interview to the *Lokal-Anzeiger* in November 1936. He urged the return of former German colonies now held as British mandates as a ' contribution to peace '. Nothing would then stand in the way of a close alliance between England and Germany.

How far was the policy of Anglo-German alliance dictated by the search for peace or by Mosley's Nazi sympathies? ·Certainly there was a strong pro-Nazi sentiment in British Union. An ' intelligent and reasonable critic ' wrote to *Action* on 26 December 1936: ' Many of your followers seem to regard Germany as a recovery of Eden, and I even know one young Fascist who always refers to Germany as the " Fatherland ".' Criticism of Germany in the fascist press was extremely rare (Catholics tended to be offended by Nazism's hostility to Catholicism and its Nordic paganism).[29] By 1936, the B.U.F. was defending the Nazi attitude towards the Jews and even describing it as ' similar ' to its own.[30]

But pro-Nazi sentiment alone does not account for Mosley's policy. The truth is that Mosley's quest for peace and his National Socialism alike propelled him towards Anglo-German agreement, just as Churchill's refusal to contemplate such an agreement sprang from his lack of commitment to peace and from his hostility to Continental ' tyrants '. Churchill has recorded how he was ' obsessed by the impression of the terrific Germany I had seen and felt in action during the years of 1914 to 1918 suddenly becoming again possessed of all her martial power . . . '.[31] Mosley was obsessed by the gruesome slaughter of those years. To Churchill the First World War had been a successful if costly operation to preserve the traditional balance of power. For Mosley it finally discredited the whole idea of the balance of power. For Churchill nothing had changed. Britain must continue ' to oppose the strongest, most dominating Power on the Continent ... '. For Mosley one purpose had replaced all others: to remove the causes of war.

But it is equally true that Churchill and Mosley were on different sides of the ideological divide of the 1930s. In Churchill's view Philip II, Louis XIV, Napoleon, Wilhelm II, Hitler were all tyrants endangering the liberties of others through their insatiable ambitions, and who therefore had to be ' struck down '. This was the main English tradition, the ideological basis of the balance of power as England has always seen it.[32] Democratic socialism, liberal capitalism and League idealism fitted into this tradition easily enough since all three were offshoots of the English ideology. Once Mosley had lost his belief that England's ' free institutions ' were the last word in civilisation, his commitment to this particular version of England's historic mission, already severely jolted by the First World War, disappeared altogether.

Neville Chamberlain became prime minister in May 1937, determined to halt the fatal drift towards war by reaching agreement with Hitler. He shared with Mosley a commendable horror of war. Unfortunately he was in no position to carry out his plans. Appeasement from strength was impossible owing to the previous neglect of rearmament. This increased Britain's dependence on the French alliance. The trouble here was the French commitment to its system of eastern alliances and the Franco-Soviet Pact. This was bound to involve Britain in the affairs of eastern Europe. Chamberlain never grasped this nettle firmly. Nor could he in view of the domestic position. Many in the Foreign Office, the Cabinet, and the Party were opposed to the search for agreement with Germany. Beyond them part of the Press was hostile to the idea.[33] In any event he never offered a clear alternative to Britain's traditional role. Czecholovakia might be a ' far-away country ', but although he was the son of Joseph Chamberlain empire development was even further away from Chamberlain's vision. Nor did he come to the British public with any bold domestic programme. The result was that his appeasement policy lacked popular appeal. Soon it was to become a byword for surrender.

Mosley put his finger on the fatal flaw in Chamberlain's methods when, following Eden's resignation (February 1938), he remarked, ' Eden's policy means war – Chamberlain's policy means humiliation.'[34] Chamberlain could not reach accord with Germany because the pro-French wing of the Tory Party would overturn him.[35] Commenting on the ' rape of Austria ' Mosley declared, ' What on earth does it matter to us if Germans unite with others of that race? If all Germans outside the Reich were added to Germany, their population would only increase from seventy to eighty millions.

Has British Empire sunk so low that we have to shut up shop if another ten million Germans enter their Fatherland? If not, what is the fuss about?'[36]   On this occasion at least the British Government managed to keep its fingers out of the fire. Similarly, its policy of non-intervention in Spain met with Mosley's approval. On this major issue for the British left, the B.U.F. had little to say. Although the fascist press supported Franco, Mosley confined himself to attacking the Labour Party for putting Spain above England.

Mosley's prophecy of humiliation was soon to be fulfilled. Czechoslovakia was the symbol of the whole Genevan order, now stretching from London to Moscow. More practically, it was the linchpin of the anti-fascist collective-security system, linked to the west through the Franco-Czech alliance, and to the east through the Soviet–Czech alliance. (The B.U.F. had its own way of describing these relationships. Czechoslovakia was the 'knot which links the two ropes of Red Russia and Popular Front France'; it was the 'central European outpost of Jewish communism and Jewish Finance.'[37]) The removal of this 'Western–Bolshevik dagger' pointed at Germany's heart became in 1938 the main goal of Nazi foreign policy. Hitler's instrument was the German nationalist movement in the Czech Sudetenland, roused to a frenzy of pro-German fervour by the *Anschluss*. Beneš, the Czech president, hoped to avoid looming client-status by getting the French and British to stand up to Hitler. Chamberlain, who saw the makings of a war, tried desperately to defuse the situation by concocting compromises designed to satisfy the demands of the Sudeten Germans. This met neither Hitler's aim of destroying the Czech system of alliances, nor Beneš's hopes of employing the west to resist Hitler. By showing that no compromise was possible, Chamberlain's well-meant efforts merely brought on the crisis he was trying to avert. As Taylor puts it, ' the Czechoslovak problem was not of the British making; the Czech crisis of 1938 was '.[38]

Mosley, who saw this coming, urged the one solution that might have met the German demands: a ' Swiss solution ' with a ' cantonal' system and permanent neutrality.[39]   But, of course, this would have involved precisely that decisive break with the French security system and hence with the Soviets that Chamberlain, for all his efforts to ' appease' Germany, could not bring himself to make. However, for the first time Mosley began to sense danger in the reckless haste with which German aims were being pursued. However logically sound Hitler's policy, it showed an alarming indifference to the need to avoid humiliating Britain. The ' skill of German statesmanship' had become a necessary ingredient of peace, Mosley wrote on 3 September 1938. 'If the skill of German statesmanship can present with persistence the strength of the German case, without any error which will assist her enemies, not only

peace will be won, but justice to oppressed Germans will be gained.'
Action the following week carried a major article urging the B.U.
to be more ready to criticise Germany when its foreign policy put
into jeopardy the hopes of fascists all over Europe.

At Hackney on 24 September 1938 Mosley described Chamberlain's flight to Berchtesgaden as an ' act of courage and commonsense'.   Three and a half million Sudeten Germans, he said, had
justice on their side; but, even if they did not, it was no concern
of Britain.   As always he harked back to the 'other war ':

> Give British Union its chance and we'll declare war–war
> on poverty and suffering.   Tonight I come to you and
> ask you to answer finance–answer the alien and say–We'll
> fight for Britain but we will not fight for you.   Break the
> system–smash the tyranny of money.   Endow our people with
> the wealth of modern science and let us dedicate ourselves to
> building the Britain of our dreams.[40]

The B.U. plastered London with a new slogan: ' The War
on Want is the War We Want '.

Berchtesgaden was followed by Godesberg when Hitler, not content with the transfer of territory which Chamberlain had already
conceded, demanded its immediate occupation by German troops.
With his previous pleas for ' skill' in German diplomacy, Mosley
could scarcely have approved the way in which Hitler had brutally
faced Chamberlain ' with an apparent choice between war and abdication as a Great Power '.[41]   In public his line was unchanged.
' I don't care if $3\frac{1}{2}$ m. Germans from Czechoslovakia go back to
Germany, I don't care if ten million Germans go back to Germany.
Britain will still be strong enough, brave enough to hold her own.'

Munich had averted immediate war, and had even raised muted
hopes of Peace in Our Time.   These hopes were soon dashed.   On
7 November Herschel Grynzpan, a German Jewish youth, shot
Ernst vom Rath, a secretary of the German Legation in Paris.   On 9
November vom Rath died from his wounds.   That night, the *Kristall-
nacht*, Jewish shops and synagogues were looted and burnt in Germany, apparently on deliberate orders.   With its usual insensitivity,
Action attributed the German action (which evoked world-wide
horror) to the ' simplicity of the German character.'[42]   Mosley set
his own comment in the context of his overriding quest for peace:

> Supposing that every allegation was true . . . supposing it was
> a fact that a minority in Germany were being treated as the
> papers allege, was that any reason for millions in Britain to
> lose their lives in war with Germany?   How many minorities
> had been badly treated in how many countries since the war
> without any protest from Press or politicians? . . . Why was it

only when Jews were the people affected that we had any
demand for war with the country concerned? There was only
one answer . . . that today Jewish finance controlled the Press
and political system of Britain. If you criticise a Jew at home—
then gaol threatens you. If others touch a Jew abroad – then
war threatens them.[43]

Mosley's fear that the Jewish Question would undo the Munich
achievement is understandable. It is difficult to forgive the unfair-
ness of his actual comment. For, moral considerations apart, the
unleashing of this pogrom at this particular time fell far short of
that 'skill' in presenting the German case which Mosley had earlier
described as a necessary ingredient of peace. It should have given
him an inkling of the fact that Hitler had contemptuously discounted further British intervention, relying either on blackmail
to win more concessions or on Anglo-French decadence to win
a war. Mosley should have known his fellow countrymen well
enough to know that Hitler was making a big mistake. A
consistent and reputable public line under these circumstances
would have been to warn Hitler that, while there were powerful
forces in England working for peace, the only chance they had to
succeed was if Hitler moderated his methods. The reckless flou-
ting of British susceptibilities and prestige would unite the British
nation in a war in which there would be no easy German victory.
Such a warning would have served the cause of peace better than
the policy of continued support for German actions.

Hitler's thoughts were far from such moderation. The collapse
of the Czech state in March 1939 may not have been his doing:
the German occupation of Prague on 15 March was a gratuitous
and calculated gesture of contempt, making a mockery of the recent
Anglo-French guarantee. Of course, Britain and France did nothing, Sir John Simon sagely pointing out that it was impossible
to fulfil obligations to a state that had ceased to exist. But shame
and humiliation exploded into a furious resentment against Germany. Chamberlain, abruptly switching round, pledged in his
Birmingham speech of 17 March Britain's undying resistance to
any attempt to dominate the world by force: the Polish, Romanian
and Greek guarantees followed. Mosley saw all this as the inevitable
result of ' umbrella politics '. ' It is to the eternal discredit of successive democratic governments ', he wrote in *Action* on 25 March,
' that their foreign policy has been one of everlasting bluster, innumerable foreign commitments, followed inevitably by . . . abject
humiliation.' And on the Polish guarantee: ' Note that the Polish
Government is the judge of when action should be taken. . . . Any
frontier incident which excites the light-headed Poles can set the
world ablaze. British Government places the lives of a million

Britons in the pocket of any drunken Polish corporal.'[44]   British
Union plastered London with a new slogan, 'Who the heck cares
for Beck'.

Mosley lucidly analysed the alternatives facing the Government
in an article written for *Action* on 1 April 1939.   The first possible
policy was British Union's: (1) disinterest in the east of Europe;
(2) disarmament in return in the west of Europe; (3) return of
the Mandated Colonies to Germany; (4) retention and intensive
development of the Empire 'which is now neglected for foreign
quarrels'.   He had 'not the slightest doubt that such a policy
would secure for the nations of the West both relief from the shadow
of war and the burden of armaments'.   The alternative policy,
based on the belief that Hitler aimed for world domination, was to
form a 'combination of the whole world' to resist him.   In concrete
terms this meant an Anglo-French-Russian military alliance.   This
would make war certain; but at least it was clear and understandable
and would enable Britain to enter such a war with some hope of
winning it.

In the aftermath of the Czech occupation the British government
wobbled between the two.   Appeasement was kept going in the
form of proposals for gigantic loans to Germany – 'Danegeld,' Mosley contemptuously declared.[45]   Unable to nerve itself for the Soviet
alliance on Russian terms, Chamberlain's government tried to
create a 'jelly front' (as Mosley termed it) in eastern Europe
through loans to Romania and Greece: 'Encirclement at 6 per cent,'
in *Action*'s phrase.   Finance, briefly and uselessly, took the place of
resolution.

On 15 April *Action* deployed a formidable argument against the
old balance-of-power politics.   The old balance of power, despite
the fact that it ended in 'wars of gigantic dimensions that left
Europe exhausted for generations . . . was justified . . . from the British point of view by the free hand it left to British sea power to
achieve a world empire external to Europe.'   The new factor was
that 'Europe has lost her unchallenged world domination.'   England could no longer hope to emerge victorious from a European
struggle.   The victory would be America's and Russia's – that of
international finance and bolshevism.   'It is no longer a question
of dividing Europe in order to conquer the world. . . . Today it is
a question of uniting Europe. . . . This is the task of our generation:
to find a new ideological basis of European union . . .' so that a
'united Europe' could play its part in a 'world balance' of powers.
Britain and Germany alone could unite the old Continent.   This
was a remarkably accurate diagnosis and, indeed, prediction of
what was to follow.   Its basic weakness was that in the 1930s there
existed no will to European unity or ideological basis on which
such unity could be constructed.   Europe could be united only

if fascism destroyed democracy or democracy destroyed fascism. And that meant another ' civil war '.

Mosley now saw war as virtually certain. His only remaining hope was to get the British people themselves to stop what he regarded as the suicidal and criminal policy of their government. All the big halls were denied him; but there were still the streets: ' My friends,' he declared in Attlee's constituency at Limehouse,

> you would think that at such a time as this Attlee would be leading the British people against war. You would think that he would be down here among you, doing what the Labour Party used to do, rallying the people against war. But where do you find the Labour Party? You find them hand in hand with Chamberlain. Sitting in Parliament and agreeing with the Government in its plans for capitalist war. . . . You find the Labour Party demanding military alliances. You find the Labour Party asking for world war in the service of capitalism, the capitalism they used to fight. . . . There are thousands of women living here in East London today with their husbands, their brothers, their children who may be doomed by this war conspiracy to the bitterest tears that a woman can shed. What good does it do to such a woman to know that German women, too, are doomed by us striking back at a foreign city?
>
> What consolation does it bring to that weeping woman of East London who has lost her husband, or has seen little children dying in the streets? Is that going to mend any broken heart in the world? Is that going to bring the broken body of a child back to life? War is a crime against the people of all lands.[46]

And he ended his speech at British Union's May Day demonstration with the words 'Let not our generation be dismissed with the contempt of posterity that history may write "Like dumb cattle they were driven to the slaughter because they had not the manhood, the wit and the will to live in peace and greatness ".'[47]

Belatedly he tried to rally a peace front. The *Catholic Times*, the *Catholic Herald* and the Peace Pledge Union all came out against the war policy. Lord Elton, Lord Alfred Douglas, Sir Thomas Jones, Lord Ponsonby, the Marquess of Tavistock, Yeats-Brown, Ethel Mannin, Dean Inge and others lent their support to the peace cause, Dean Inge writing, 'The danger of war comes not from Germany or Italy but from ourselves.'[48] The famous left-wing journal *Forward*, striking a radical theme of earlier times, attacked Jewish control of British foreign policy.[49] A few pacifists came into the B.U. from the left. Hugh Ross Williamson joined from the Labour Party. Henry Williamson wrote in *Action* on 15 July 1939:

' I have a little boy now, an innocent who with his friends in the village streets laughs in the sunshine; he sings and smiles when he hears the bells on the wind.   Must he, too, traverse a waste place of the earth; must the blood and sweat of his generation drip in agony, until the sun darken and fall down the sky, and rise no more upon his world?'   There was talk of an alliance with the I.L.P. On the right was Sir Barry Domvile with his pro-German *Link*. Here were the scattered forces of a peace army.   In the old days Mosley might have been able to rally them.   But too much water had flowed under the bridge.

Unexpectedly British Union managed to secure the Earls Court Exhibition Hall, the biggest indoor hall in England.   Here on 16 July before 20,000 people Mosley made his last great appeal:

> Fellow Britons, tonight the British people are here, and to-night from this great audience will be heard the voice of the British people telling Parliament, telling Parties, telling Government something it is time that they should hear.   This is a demonstration of *Britain First* and, therefore, is a demonstration of world peace.   This, the greatest gathering of the English under one roof assembled, tells the Government . . . 'At last we have had enough '.   We are here to tell them there is something for them to do here in Britain. . . . Enough we have had of alien quarrels, enough threats of foreign war, enough diversion from what matters to the British people, our own land, our own Empire and our problems.   We say to the Parties . . . tonight. . . .   ' If any country in the world attacks Britain or threatens to attack Britain, then every single member of this great audience of British Union would fight for Britain '.   But just as straight this too we tell them . . . ' We fight for Britain, yes, but a million Britons shall never die in your Jews' quarrel'. And before you drag a million Englishmen to doom, we of British Union . . . will sweep you by the declared will of the British people from the seats of power that you disgrace.

A revealing note from Major Yeats-Brown to Lord Elton shows why it had become impossible for Mosley to rally the peace forces under his banner:

> Last night I was at Mosley's big meeting – which is quite fairly reported in The Times, tho' briefly, and with no indication of the great enthusiasm his oratory aroused. He is as good as Goebbels as a speaker. His references to Jews and Lord Baldwin, were greeted with prolonged booing. He spoke for 2 hours, and kept everyone's interest.   Personally I agreed with $\frac{3}{4}$ of what he said, but the other quarter is a stumbling block. He declares that there can be no compromise or conciliation

with any of the old parties, and this is absurd in England.
He made much play with the young intellectuals who were
not prepared to fight for King and Country, and are now
wanting us to fight for King Carol . . . but I listened in vain
for any word that would have shown that if a crisis came
suddenly he would be behind the Government. I suppose he
wouldn't be, and that he would use the opportunity for
political ends.

There were a number of other interesting comments on the meeting
itself:

When we arrived at Earls Court there must have been 7000
people who had paid for seats. Another 2000 arrived – say
at the lowest estimate 9000 people who had paid. Say another 10,000 came in free, still it is an impressive audience
to gather to hear a speaker who is practically banned from the
Press and BBC.

I certainly think he should be asked to debate on the air
with Winston Churchill. The questions discussed would
interest the people of England. Why shouldn't we discuss
them? One thing I disliked was that there were 100 semi-
Nazi banners, and 40 semi-Fascist flags in the procession,
and mixed up with them 40 Union Jacks. I think he
shouldn't mix up the Union Jack with his movement's flags.[50]

Time had finally run out for Mosley and for peace. The
British government's neck was in the noose of the Polish guarantee –
and Hitler was tightening the rope. ' Any Englishman who will
not fight for Britain is a coward; any Englishman who wants to
fight for Poland is a fool,' Mosley had declared in May. Now,
after the German–Soviet pact of 23 August 1939, he wrote, ' War
for Poland was always a crime; now it is madness.' Lloyd George had
recognised the danger on 3 April: ' If we are going in [to help
Poland] without the help of Russia we are walking into a trap,' he
had told the House of Commons. Mosley coined a new slogan –
' Why cut your own throat today to avoid catching a cold tomorrow?'
War over Poland he regarded as a hopeless war. Britain could not
save Poland without defeating Germany. He did not believe
Britain could defeat Germany. Therefore the war was completely
pointless. He has not changed his view. ' It is always better to
have a war tomorrow with arms rather than a war today without,'
he wrote in the *Listener* on 21 September 1972.

Colonel Beck, secure in his assurances of Anglo-French help,
and placing exaggerated hopes in the Polish Army, refused all
German attempts to bring him to the negotiating-table. On 1
September Hitler, confident in his ability to handle the western

powers in peace or war, launched his armies across the Polish frontier. Although no Russian help was forthcoming, Lloyd George now
insisted that the government honour its rash obligations.   Another
climb-down had become unthinkable.   On 3 September Britain
and France declared war on Germany. 'They made these
promises because they believed the world was still living in an age
of words,' Mosley said.   Now the hour of action had come at last,
as Mosley had always said it must.   But it was Churchill's hour,
not his.

There were last-minute peace rallies in east and north London,
larger and more enthusiastic than any in the B.U.'s history.
Mosley's friend, Henry Williamson, had the wild idea of flying to
Germany to persuade Hitler not to make war.   'If I could see him,
as a common soldier who had fraternised, on that faraway Christmas
Day of 1914, with the men of his Linz battalion under Messines
Hill, might I not be able to give him the amity he so desired from
England, a country he admired. . . ?'   But it was already too late.
In London he saw Mosley:

> The sun arose above the warehouses along the Thames east of
> the bridge; but as morning grew, and the movement of men
> and vehicles impinged upon my eyes and ears, I felt a coldness
> growing upon me; and when just after noon I went before the
> man in whose ability and realistic vision I believed, I could not
> speak more than a few words.   With his invariable courtesy
> he rose to greet me, but the calm and aloof strength of his
> usual self was withdrawn, as though for the moment he had
> expended all his life, and was poor.   He held my letter half-
> crumpled in his hand, as though it had been thrust hastily
> into his pocket.
>
> 'I have been thinking about your letter' he said.   I wait-
> ed; I knew the answer.   He looked before him a moment
> before saying, 'I'm afraid the curtain is down.'
>
> I nodded.   There was little more to be said.   But I said,
> 'What will you do?'   He shifted his weight, from the leg
> broken in the aircraft crash, and permanently crippled after
> he had re-joined his Lancer regiment in the flooded trenches
> of the battle of Loos, before he had permanently recovered.
> With eyes averted, he said, 'They might shoot me as Jaurès
> was shot in Paris in 1914'.
>
> Then he said, 'I shall keep on, while I can, to give a plat-
> form for peace should our people want it.'   Then he said, 'I
> cannot see my country sink.'
>
> 'Goodbye, sir,' I said, and left his office.
>
> Outside the newsbills read *Nazis Seize Danzig Customs*.

In a message to all members issued on 1 September 1939 Mosley promised to ' continue our work of awakening the people until peace be won, and until the People's State of British Union is born by the declared will of the British people '.   He went on:

> To our members my message is plain and clear.   Our country is involved in war.   Therefore I ask you to do nothing to injure our country, or to help any other Power.   Our members should do what the law requires of them, and, if they are members of the Forces or Services of the Crown, they should obey their orders, and, in every particular, obey the rules of their Service.   But I ask all members who are free to carry on our work to take every opportunity to awaken the people and to demand peace.

Mosley had a dual motive in urging a swift peace with ' Britain undefeated and the British Empire intact '.   First, he regarded the war as completely unnecessary: ' a political war against the political system of a foreign country which our politicians do not like '.[51]   It was unnecessary in the double sense that Britain and Germany had nothing to fight about and that, if properly conducted by both sides, neither could win.   Britain could not restore Poland over German objections, and Germany could not win a decisive victory in the west.   This would be true, Mosley felt, if the war were efficiently conducted.   But he had no confidence that it would be on the British side, and this led to the second reason for wanting peace: he saw a real possibility of a British defeat under existing political management.   Mosley had no more confidence in the ' old gangs ' ability to run a war than he had in their ability to do anything else.   They had neglected rearmament.   They had fallen into Lloyd George's ' Polish trap '.   Why should their war direction be any more successful?   Mosley was not far wrong. Anglo-French planning had little contact with reality.   It lost all contact with reality when the British and French proposed to add Russia to their list of enemies in order to ' save ' Finland – a piece of insanity only prevented by the refusal of the Scandinavians to allow the hastily assembled expeditionary force to pass through their countries.

Had Mosley really been the traitor depicted by war-time propaganda, he could simply have sat back and looked to an accumulation of British mistakes to give Germany its inevitable reward, from which he could have hoped to benefit.   But this was not, and never was, his aim.   ' The defeat and destruction of British Empire is the greatest disaster which British Union can conceive,' declared Mosley on 2 May 1940.   Mosley's last six months of liberty were devoted to trying to avert that disaster.   In so doing, he developed a ' war policy ' which ran parallel with his ' peace policy ' and was in fact designed to extricate Britain from the war without defeat and without the loss of its empire. For the first and only time in his life, he applied himself seriously to high military strategy.

The central assumption of Mosley's war doctrine was that defence was stronger than attack. This was true for both Britain and Germany. Britain could no longer cut off German supplies with eastern Europe and Russia open; Germany could not cut off British supplies in face of British naval and air power, neglected though these had been. Similarly, Britain and France could not force a military decision in the west; while any British government ' with even a shred of efficiency could repel an attempt at invasion with consummate ease '.[52] The real danger to Britain lay in a dissipation of its resources in foreign adventures – such as mad expeditions to Finland and Norway, and garrisons in the Middle East, use of scarce foreign currencies to buy up countries that were destined to fall into Germany's orbit, etc. The biggest danger of all lay in the commitment of British land forces to the Continent. Had the British Government thought through how they were going to ' transport such forces to such theatres of war, and, still more important, how, in some circumstances, they are going to bring them back ' ? In a war of siege, he insisted, ' the first essential is to conserve supplies and develop the capacity to endure. . . . Air Power, Naval Power, Food Power; this is the Trinity upon which the security of Britain can be built.'[53]

The remarkable unity in Mosley's foreign policy and strategic thinking only really emerges when one reads the articles on strategy he contributed to *Action* in the first six months of the war.[54] The foreign-policy proposition that Britain should withdraw into empire and keep out of European quarrels was backed by the strategic proposition that Britain could successfully defend itself against a dominant Continental power but could not successfully impose its will on one. As *Action* claimed with considerable justice on 8 February 1940, ' It was inherent in the political ideas of British Union that the British Empire should be capable of defending itself. That political idea was related . . . to proved expert principles of current strategy.' And as Mosley himself wrote on 21 March, ' So the great dream of a self-contained British Empire . . . rests upon the great fact of what is practical and possible under modern conditions.'

It is perfectly true that this strategy renounced the goal of victory in war, just as the foreign policy which it supported renounced Baldwin's goal of ' making Britain's will prevail among the nations '. As expounded in the columns of *Action*, Mosley's strategy ruled out any hope of victory over Germany, thereby implicitly questioning the whole purpose of being at war with her. But victory was inconsistent with Mosley's aim of preserving Britain as an independent great power. In the state of equality which he postulated between the British whale and the German elephant, victory could be won against Germany only by calling in other elephants – America and Russia. But then this would not be a British victory, but an American–Russian victory, as destructive of Britain's world position as a defeat by Germany. Thus the strategic goal of fighting Germany to a draw was, too, consistent with Mosley's foreign-policy objectives.

A more serious criticism that might be levelled against Mosley's strategy is that it assumed that the French could hold the Maginot Line. This was part of the whole doctrine of the primacy of defence. From this Mosley went on to deduce that the Germans would also fight a largely defensive war in the west. Britain had therefore only to sit tight behind its defensive positions, risk nothing, and the logic of the situation would impose itself and force a war that ought never to have begun to peter out.

This was a clever and plausible argument and was not without its powerful advocates on the Axis side – notably Mussolini and the German High Command who also had a healthy respect for the French defences and wanted to end the war in the west as quickly as possible. But it ignored the logic of Hitler's position and also the new doctrines of land warfare developed by Guderian and von Manstein. The logic of that position favoured neutralising the west while the going was good, before turning to the east where his real ambition lay. He believed that he had the military means to do it by a massed armour-attack through the Ardennes. In one of his articles Mosley wrote that ' the most fatal blunder in war is to think out what course of action you would prefer your opponent to take and to assume that he will adopt your wishes '. Mosley fell into this error himself. He wanted Hitler to hold off in the west because he believed that would make the war peter out. Hitler's foreign-policy aims, by contrast, could now be achieved only by conquering France and bringing Britain by *force majeure* to the conference table.

Although Mosley invoked the Maginot Line to strengthen his argument, his strategy as it happened did not depend on it. He believed that a properly armed and led Britain could fight Germany to a draw without France and the Low Countries. Events vindicated him, and at the same time destroyed the rationale of the British Government's war policy. The only rational reason for going to war in September 1939 was to defeat Germany (since Poland could not be restored in any other way). The belief that this could be accomplished by Britain and France alone was illusory. It took a combination of Britain, America and Russia, plus the German war-mistakes which created that alliance, to defeat Hitler. At the same time the events of 1940–1 showed that even a Britain far less well prepared for war than Mosley's argument required, one moreover which had lost most of its military equipment through precisely the foreign adventure against which Mosley had warned, was nevertheless able to deter the Germans from attempting a landing.

This was exactly what Mosley had foreseen. 'Behind these three lines of defence [minefields, navy and air force]', he wrote on 9 May 1940, ' would rest a people entirely united at the disposal of their nation. . . . Therefore it is extremely unlikely that any such attack will be delivered.' If it was, he wrote in the same issue, ' every member of British Union would be at the disposal of the nation. Every one of us would resist the foreign invader with all that is in us. However rotten the existing Government, and however much we detested its politics, we would throw ourselves into the effort of a united nation until the foreigner was driven from our soil. In such a situation no doubt has ever existed concerning the attitude of British Union.' A week later, he wrote, ' Come what may, at all times and under any circumstances, the soil of Britain will be defended by every Briton'. A week after that he was arrested as a potential fifth-columnist and his long struggle for peace was ended.

Chapter 24

Churchill's Guest

ON 24 August 1939, as war became imminent, Parliament rushed through an Emergency Powers Act, empowering the Government to make Regulations by Orders in Council for the Defence of the Realm. By a strange irony, Mosley in 1931 had demanded exactly such powers to wage another war – against unemployment. On 1 September 1939, the Government promulgated Defence Regulation 18B, empowering the home secretary to detain ' any particular person if satisfied that it is necessary to do so '. This was so sweeping that the House of Commons protested and on 23 November the Government produced an amended Regulation 18B much narrower in its scope. The home secretary might now detain any person whom he had ' reasonable cause to believe ' to be of ' hostile origin or associations ' or to have been recently concerned in ' acts prejudicial to the public safety or the defence of the realm '. An advisory committee was set up to hear appeals by detainees and to make recommendations to the home secretary. The Defence Regulation in its amended form was aimed chiefly at enemy aliens and British saboteurs. Since Mosley was neither, he himself appeared to have little to fear from it. In fact, up to May 1940, only about fifty persons had been rounded up; including five comparatively minor members of British Union.[1]

What altered the situation was the explosion of the war in the west which by 21 May 1940 had brought German troops to the English Channel and Churchill to power in England. A wave of fifth-column hysteria swept the country, fomented by the popular press. On 15 May, Sir John Anderson, the home secretary, started pressing the Cabinet to intern enemy aliens, fascists and communists as security risks. Churchill thought that enemy aliens and suspect persons should be rounded up in large numbers to protect them from the fury of the population. As the Germans approached the Channel, fear of fifth columnists increased. On 18 May Anderson demanded the internment of all Italians who had lived less than twenty years in England. As regards the fascists he ' explained at length the difficulty of taking any effective action in the absence of evidence which indicated that the organisation as such was engaged in disloyal activities '. Under Regulation 18B as it stood the Government had no power to intern Mosley or disband British Union.

The critical cabinet discussion took place on 22 May when the

Germans seemed poised for an invasion of England. Anderson, who 'had been asked by the Prime Minister to raise the matter', reported

> . . . a long talk with two officers of M.I.5., who had devoted special attention over many years to the Fascist Organisation. They had been unable to produce any evidence, on which action could be based, showing that either the Leaders of the Organisation or the Organisation itself had anything to do with what might be called Fifth Column activities. There was indeed some evidence in the other direction, as, for example, Sir Oswald Mosley's recent instruction in *Action* to members of the Organisation. [See above, page 446]
>
> The two officers of M.I.5. to whom he had referred had given it as their opinion that a certain proportion of the members . . . say, 25-30 per cent, would be willing, if ordered, to go to any lengths.
>
> The Home Secretary said that his own view was that Sir Oswald Mosley . . . was too clever to put himself in the wrong by giving treasonable orders.
>
> The Home Secretary said that he realised that the War Cabinet might take the view that, notwithstanding the absence of such evidence, we should not run any risk in this matter, however small.

Neville Chamberlain, who presided in Churchill's absence, reported that Churchill's own opinion was that, 'if any doubt existed, the persons in question should be detained without delay'. This view met with unanimous approval. Anderson was instructed to amend Regulation 18B in order to make possible the immediate arrest of 25–30 leading fascists in order to 'cripple the Organisation'. Further arrests might be necessary later. Four men took this 'unanimous decision': Chamberlain, Attlee, Lord Halifax and Arthur Greenwood.[2]

That evening Defence Regulation 18B(1A) was published. The home secretary was now authorised to detain any members of an organisation which in his view was either subject to foreign influence or control *or* whose leaders 'have or have had associations with' leaders of enemy governments or 'sympathise with' the 'system of government' of enemy powers. The Regulation was deliberately framed to catch any member of a fascist or pro-fascist organisation the Government wanted to put inside: for any such person by definition could be held to 'sympathise' with the fascist system of government. The assumption of the Regulation was that anyone who belonged to a fascist organisation would automatically become a security risk in the event of a German invasion. Whether the Government actually believed this is doubtful. It would be truer to say that the internment of Mosley had become psychologically necessary to keep up national morale. 'The internment was, in one sense, Churchill's belligerent reaction to setbacks beyond his control. This was his first and perhaps his smallest victory, but one he could at least win at once.'[3]

Sir Oswald himself was arrested on 23 May at his flat in Dolphin Square: Diana was detained on 29 June. At least thirty-one and probably nearer seventy or eighty B.U. officials were arrested with Mosley in the first swoop. The big round-up, however, took place in June, as a result of which 747 B.U. members and sympathisers were detained.

For the historian and biographer the main question to decide is whether Mosley was in fact a security risk on 23 May 1940. Press and government fears of a fifth column were not entirely fanciful. Major Quisling, leader of the Norwegian Nasjonal Samling (or Fascist) Party had already given his name to the word traitor by proclaiming a puppet government the day after the German invasion of his country. In Holland, thousands of National Socialists under Mussert were believed to have collaborated with the German invader.* Up to a point it was natural to suppose that Mosley would be prepared to play a similar part if the Germans landed. On 3 and 15 July 1940 Mosley was cross-examined for a total of sixteen hours before the advisory committee headed by Norman Birkett, K.C., who had led for the *Star* in Mosley's successful libel action of 1934. The proceedings were a formality in the sense that the Government never had any intention of letting Mosley out. Also the transcript of these hearings is not available. However, from other government sources as well as from the notes Mosley himself prepared for his defence, it is possible to piece together the case against him, as well as his own replies to it. This case formed the basis of Morrison's allegation in the House of Commons on 10 December 1940 that Mosley was 'our own Quisling . . . ready to play his part'.

The Government's contention that the British Union was an incipient fifth column rested on the allegation that it was subject to 'foreign influence or control'. In support of this charge it alleged that Mosley had borrowed his creed, political style and choice of opponents from Continental fascism. It accused him of having accepted money from Italy and Germany and of having enjoyed close personal relationships with Hitler and Mussolini. Finally, it claimed that Mosley's foreign policy was in every way subservient to the aims of German and Italian foreign policy which, it was implied, involved the destruction of an independent Britain. In

*In fact there were far fewer traitors in these countries than was believed at the time. David Littlejohn, *The Patriotic Traitors* (1972), believes that Dutch collaboration was largely a myth.

sum, whatever Mosley's original aims, he had come to see that his only hope of obtaining power was through Britain's defeat by Germany, which he would do anything to help.

The central point in Mosley's defence was that his opposition to the war was a legitimate and legal expression of political opinion; that in neither speech nor writing had he indicated that he wished to see Britain defeated by Germany; that his policy was a negotiated peace settlement with Britain undefeated and the British Empire intact. He denied that British fascism was a foreign import.

He pointed to the Labour Party origins of his economic ideas and his proposals for reform of the system of government. His methods of political propaganda were based on his own abilities as a speaker and ideas he had picked up from the Durham miners' galas in the 1920s. British fascism did not ' choose ' its opponents: Jews and communists had attacked it. In general, such similarities as existed between the various fascist movements arose from similar conditions, not from imitation. ' It is perfectly true ', Mosley argued before the advisory committee, ' that the creed of our Movement is the Fascist or National Socialist creed. This does not, in any shape or form, imply foreign influence. For instance, the creed of the Labour Party is the Socialist creed. There are Socialists in all countries, but the freedom from foreign control is *a fortiori* stronger in our case because we are by creed and constitution a National Movement as opposed to an International Movement.' In a letter to the prime minister, written in October 1942, Mosley cited the historical cases of English Catholics who had fought against the Armada, and English Radicals who had fought against France in the Revolutionary Wars as proof of his contention that even where spiritual, ideological or other affinities existed with countries fighting England this had not stopped Englishmen from doing their duty to their own country.

Mosley denied ever having received money from abroad. Following his detention, M.I.5. carried out extensive investigations into the finances of British Union and its network of companies. These failed to come up with anything conclusive, though according to a Home Office memorandum of 14 April 1943 the ' inference ' was that Mosley had received Italian subsidies between 1934 and 1936.[4] Mosley made vigorous use of a second line of defence: even if it were true that his movement had been financed from Italy in its early days, what was wrong with this? There was no suggestion then that Italy and Britain would be at war,* nor was the transaction illegal. Lansbury had solicited Russian money for the *Daily Herald* and strikes had often been supported by foreign

*Nor when Mosley was detained were they at war.

funds in the name of workers' solidarity.*

Equally, there was nothing in the least bit sinister about his infrequent meetings with Hitler and Mussolini which had, in any event, stopped in 1936. These meetings had as their object, ' by personal contact or any other proper means, to make whatever contribution I could to the maintenance and building of world peace '. Lansbury and Lord Allen of Hurtwood, to mention just two, had been to see Hitler on similar errands.

Finally, Mosley denied absolutely that British Union's foreign policy was subservient to the aims of Germany and Italy. He had supported the right of Germany and Italy to expand in certain directions, but *not* at the expense of England or the British Empire. It was because he did not see German demands on Poland as a threat to British security that he opposed the present war. He personally claimed the right to oppose particular wars in a great tradition of English dissent, stretching back to Chatham, Fox, Cobden, Bright, and in the twentieth century Lloyd George and Ramsay MacDonald. Was every politician who opposed a war a traitor? In his notes for his defence Mosley wrote:

> It is apparently suggested that I want my country to be defeated. Yet for the last seven years I have spent much of my time demanding that Britain should be properly armed to resist any attack. In particular I have demanded air parity with the strongest other country – which was Germany. This is a curious policy to have been advocated by someone who is alleged to have wanted his country to be defeated
>
> My grounds for opposing this war may be considered right or wrong. The question is whether they are a legitimate statement of opinion or the attitude of a traitor. Very briefly I opposed this war on two grounds: (a) The members of my movement are ever prepared to fight in defence of Britain but we did not think that Britain should go to war for the sake of Poland or any eastern European question. (b) They were more than ever opposed to intervention in foreign war when Britain was not properly armed for war. . . . For a Government to go to war except in a British quarrel is criminal. To go to war without complete preparation for war is insane.
>
> If I am accused of treachery to my country may I enquire what was my motive? . . . Is it contended . . . that my motive is some overweening, inordinate, or insane ambition? If so, I ask ambition to achieve what? Is it really suggested that my ambition is to be the ruler of a country which is totally dependent upon a foreign power? Even my worst enemies

*For the whole question of foreign funds coming into the B.U.F., see appendix at end of chapter.

have not accused me of small ambitions. . . . I admit quite
frankly, and have always admitted, that I hold the high ambition to make a great country even greater.   It is not compatible with such ambitions to be the lackey of a foreign
power. . . . I cite my whole record and my whole caieer in
refutation of the charge as absurd as it is vile that any aim
which I have ever held can be achieved through disaster to
my country.

What conclusion is one to come to thirty years later?   It is
clear that no legal case against Mosley for high treason could
possibly have been sustained.   His policy was peace with Britain
and its empire intact.   At no point did he sabotage the war effort
or call on anyone to do likewise.   It is true that the very call for
peace without the defeat of Germany might cast doubt on the
rightness of being at war at all.   No doubt the fact that he continued
his campaign for peace in public gave the Government a popular
handle for detaining him.   But such a campaign, even had it been
illegal, which it was not, did not make Mosley a traitor.   In short,
Mosley never did anything treasonable.

The case against him rested, therefore, not on anything he had
done, but on what he might do under different circumstances.
It is important to be absolutely clear about what such circumstances
might be.   The only relevant ones were those in which Mosley
might have collaborated with the Germans before the outcome of
the war had been decided – such as in the course of a German invasion of England.   It is important to limit the concept of treason
to this single case for it is all too often assumed that one is a traitor
if one collaborates with the enemy *after* one's country has been
defeated.   On this definition Adenauer and the whole post-war
generation of German politicians would be ' traitors ' – which is
obviously absurd and quite unhistorical.   Once a war has been
decided, as it would have been had England suffered a decisive
defeat through successful invasion or blockade, the question of treason no longer arises.   Hence the question of whether Mosley would
have been prepared to take office in a Britain which had lost the
war to Germany is irrelevant to the issue of treason.   As a matter
of practical politics, it is highly unlikely that he would have been
called upon to do so, any more than were the French fascist leaders
after the fall of France.   There would have been sufficient numbers
in the old parties to make peace and to ensure that the king's government was carried on; and this would have been the best solution
from the German point of view.

Nor can the question of treason arise in all those possibilities
of settlement intermediate between victory and defeat expressed in
the concept of a negotiated or compromise peace.   Mosley was by

no means alone in advocating this course: his tendency always to claim a unique standpoint played into the hands of those who tried to prove him uniquely wicked. Mosley's uniqueness here consisted in saying publicly what a number in conventional politics thought privately, or semi-privately. 'Are we really content to bring our own civilisation to ruin in order that the Hammer and Sickle shall fly from the North Sea to the Pacific?' wrote Richard Stokes, Labour M.P. for Ipswich, to Lloyd George in October 1939.[5] Stokes, a wealthy Catholic, was chairman of a Peace Aims Group of twenty M.P.s which in November 1939 called for an armistice. Lloyd George, too, stood for a compromise peace. Some ministers hoped that the war would peter out of its own accord; others that it would somehow be diverted against Russia. There was a peace group in the Cabinet after Mosley had been locked up. None of these men were traitors. None of them wished for a German victory.

So we are left with the single case mentioned above – Mosley collaborating with, or aiding, the enemy in the event of a German invasion of Britain. Would he under those circumstances have taken up the attitude of Alcibiades betraying Athens: 'The Athens I love is not the one which is wronging me now. . . . The country that I am attacking does not seem to be mine any longer; it is rather that I am trying to recover a country that has ceased to be mine.'

Let us consider what kind of evidence would be needed to establish a reasonable inference that Mosley would play the part of traitor. Evidence that the policy and tactics of British Union had since 1933 been decided in Berlin would have been extremely damning. Had Britain gone to war with Russia in 1939 there would have been a strong case for detaining leaders of the British Communist Party; for the British Communist Party was under the 'control' of the Comintern which was itself a tool of Soviet policy. (In fact, when war broke out in 1939, the British Communist Party reversed its support for the war on instructions from Moscow.) The Government never produced the slightest shred of evidence of any such foreign control in the case of British Union; and all the ransacking of enemy archives since the war has failed to come up with any such evidence. Fascist parties all over the world operated as independent organisations. There was no central organisation controlled by Berlin or anywhere else. There remains a lesser case of 'influence'. Even without formal control, it might be argued that Mosley and the British Union were so 'influenced' by Germany that they might well have supported Germany's cause in a struggle with Britain. Here it is a question of relevant kinds of influence. German generals were influenced by the British military thinkers Liddell Hart and J. F. C. Fuller. This did not make them subservient to the aims of the British High Command. Most people are influenced by others in the sense of adopting methods or techniques that have succeeded elsewhere, without thereby becoming subservient to the aims of those who influenced them. There was much in British fascist tactics that was modelled on the successful Continental movements. However, the policy was Mosley's own. Far from looking to Rome or Berlin, he always believed that his own brand of fascism was far superior to theirs. The sole relevant question in this context is whether the attraction undoubtedly exerted by Germany on foreign fascisms was strong or general enough to make British Union likely to be subservient to German war aims.

Mosley was undoubtedly sympathetic to the aims of German, Italian and even Japanese foreign policy, but only in so far as they did not conflict with the maintenance of the integrity of Britain and its empire. Rightly or wrongly, Mosley decided that there was nothing in Hitler's published aims that conflicted with Britain's interest Quite apart from ideological sympathies, he favoured German expansion to the east and Japanese expansion in north China as a guarantee against ' explosions ' at the expense of Britain. At the moment when German expansion started to threaten Britain directly – when the Germans invaded the Low Countries – Mosley made his position clear. In the event of a German invasion of Britain, he and his fellow fascists would fight the foreign invader ' with all that is in us ' until the Germans had been expelled from British soil. It may be that he said this simply to put himself in the clear. But it was consistent with his whole line in foreign policy ever since 1932 and beyond that ever since 1918: Britons should fight only when the independence of Britain and its empire was at stake.

The Government furnished the advisory committee with evidence of Mosley's support for German, Italian and Japanese expansion, without giving it the evidence from innumerable speeches and writings throughout the 1930s and the phony-war period that Mosley would 'never surrender an inch of British territory'. Yet this second set of assertions is clearly critical in coming to any view on what Mosley's attitude was likely to be in the event of a German invasion or blockade of Britain.

What, then, about the Continental fascists who collaborated with the German invaders? In what way did Mosley differ from them? The critical difference was that he was a *British* fascist. ' I admit quite frankly . . . that I hold the high ambition to make a great country even greater. It is not compatible with such ambitions to be the lackey of a foreign power.' Here speaks not only a representative of fascism, but a representative of the greatest empire in the world. No Englishman, certainly no member of a British ruling class, could forget that fact, so long as any possibility remained of preserving that inheritance intact.

As a fascist, Mosley welcomed the attempt of Germany and Italy to create autarchic areas. As an Englishman, he could not accept the acquisition of such areas at the expense of Britain. For fascism and consciousness of Britain's greatness united to dictate that Britain itself would remain one of the great powers in an autarchic world. Here arises a fundamental difference between the outlook of someone like Mosley and that of a Quisling, a Mussert or a Degrelle. No small country could think of itself as an imperial centre. In a world of large units, a small country could only hope for a status of honourable subordination. Thus Belgian, Dutch and Norwegian fascism had no real alternative to incorporation in some larger area which they did not control. Increasingly the only possible unit seemed a German-dominated one; and so their aims crystallised into securing the best possible place for their countries in Hitler's New Order and trying to ensure that it would not be simply a fig-leaf for German exploitation.* Here was an extremely powerful motive for collaboration which did not exist for British fascism, and especially for its chief, who sprang from the oldest ruling class of what was still one of the greatest powers in the world. To assume that a common fascism made Mosley's motivations identical to those of the small-nations fascists is to make the cardinal error of assuming an identity in the situation and psychology of their respective countries. In the end no one can say with certainty what Mosley would have done. The country he loved was fighting against the system he believed in. But the evidence of his record and character suggests that in this crisis country would have won out over system by a handsome margin. It was because the Government knew that it could not establish even an inferential case that could pass muster that it, in effect, defined security risk as fascist; which, of course, left Mosley with no defence.

Mosley was held for over a year and a half at Brixton prison in 'F' wing. His next-door companion was a black musician who had played in the Berlin Philharmonic Orchestra: 'I found him a charming and cultured man,' Mosley later wrote. With him were other prominent 18B detainees – Captain A. H. Ramsay, Conservative M.P. for Midlothian and Peebles and founder of the Right Club, and also Admiral Sir Barry Domvile, founder of the *Link*.† Also detained at Brixton were a large number of Anglo-Italians, many of them teenagers. C. F. Clayton, the governor of Brixton, later wrote of Mosley, ' I found him co-operative, and, in his own

---

*It is interesting that the strongest impetus for the post-war programme of European unity came from the small countries who saw no independent place for themselves in a world of super-powers.

†On Ramsay and Domvile, see Ramsay's book *The Nameless War* (1952) and Domvile's *From Admiral to Cabin Boy* (1947).

peculiar way, a patriot. He followed the exploits of the R.A.F. in those early days with intense appreciation of their gallantry, and showed ardent anxiety for their success.   His conduct during the blitz was irreproachable, and he set an example of calmness and equanimity to his followers.' While the Italians screamed and yelled in panic as the German bombers passed overhead, 'the British prisoners stood at their cell windows and cheered the British fighter aircraft'.[6] Some of the warders had their own reasons for not panicking: they believed that Hitler would never allow German bombs to fall on Brixton!

Other detainees were interned at Ascot and York, and later at Huyton near Liverpool.   In May 1941 most of them were transferred to Peel Camp on the Isle of Man which became the main detention centre.   Diana Mosley and the women languished at Holloway in conditions of unbelievable filth, with food like something out of Dickens.   Conditions at Brixton were better.   The main horrors were bed bugs and hygienic facilities considered adequate for the 'criminal classes' but which came as a shock to middle-class B.U. detainees.   At the same time political prisoners, being held for 'custodial' and not 'punitive' purposes, were allowed a number of privileges – having food and a certain amount of drink brought in, being allowed to wear their own clothes and to associate with other prisoners at meals, labour and recreation (Cmd. 6162). There were a few unanticipated benefits.   To the telephone officer, Mosley's solicitors, Oswald Hickson & Collier, wrote in October 1940: 'I am instructed by Sir Oswald Mosley to return to you the enclosed account and to inform you that he is at present detained . . . at Brixton Prison and, in the circumstances, does not propose to attend to any business until he is released.'*

In the early days, privileges were largely on paper: the authorities made little effort to live up to them, and it was not till Mosley and others threatened to prosecute the prison governor for breach of statutory regulations that freedom of association was permitted: Mosley recalls spending his first months locked up in his cell for twenty-one hours out of twenty-four.

The popular press seized upon the 'privileges' of the 18B detainees to construct a totally fanciful picture of Mosley and his wife leading the 'high life' while the nation exerted its 'blood, sweat and tears'.   A typical example from the *Sunday Pictorial* of 4 August 1940 was headed 'Bridge and Bubbly':

Fascist leader Mosley, No. 1 'Guest' at the big house of Brixton Hill, pays £4 a week for his board and lodging.   In

*Diana Mosley writes: 'I had a very hard time with solicitors. Nobody wanted to act for us.   I finally found an old liberal, Oswald Hickson, who did his best in a fearless way. . . . People were badly frightened.'

his long leisure hours he plays bridge with Captain Ramsay and a few of his selected lieutenants. They play for several hundred cigarettes a week. . . . Every morning his paid batman delivers three newspapers at the door of his master's cell. Breakfast, dinner, and tea arrive by car. After his midday meal . . . Mosley fortifies himself with alternative bottles of red and white wine daily. He calls occasionally for a bottle of champagne. . . . Mosley still takes great pride in his appearance. He selects a different smartly cut lounge suit every week. His shirts and silk underwear are laundered in Mayfair.

From Eton, Mosley's sixteen-year-old son Nicholas wrote: ' We thought the stories of you playing bridge the whole time were very funny. You know how you used to grunt when anyone played it at Denham. Also the champagne.' As for the clothes, there is an actual request scribbled by Mosley to his solicitors on 12 July 1940: ' Please send corduroy trousers, thick blue polo neck sweater, two sets of winter underclothes, oldest country coat. Fetch washing and send no more clean clothes unless asked for.' In a particularly spiteful piece, the *Daily Mirror* asked why Diana Mosley had at first been left at large with her month-old baby, Max. ' Does the law act with such delicacy to ordinary women delinquents? It does not. Regardless of their unborn children, women convicted of serious offences get clapped behind bars with abrupt and impolite speed. Who pulls the wires? ' The fact that Mosley's wife had been convicted of no offence evidently escaped the writer. These and other articles led to actions for libel as a result of which ' the defendants had recognised that they had made a mistake, and they had met Sir Oswald fairly in the matter. . .'.[7]

With Britain fighting for its life, Parliament and Government had more important things on its mind than worrying about what happened to a few fascists in his majesty's gaols. But, with considerable courage, a handful of M.P.s headed by Richard Stokes and Irving Albery (Conservative M.P. for Gravesend) took up the highly unpopular cause of the imprisoned detainees. In a Commons debate on 10 December 1940, Stokes demanded a speeding-up of the advisory-committee procedure, the quick release of men flung into prison through little more than ' tittle-tattle and jealousy ' and drastic improvements in the conditions of those detained, including the right of husbands and wives to visit each other. Mosley, he argued, should either be allowed to stand trial for treason or be released.[8] This demand was taken up by many of Mosley's old friends, including Robert Boothby. In a chilly reply, Morrison dismissed Stokes's arguments as those of ' classic Liberalism ', quite inappropriate to war-time.[9] He brusquely refused to consider any

improvements. This negative approach did not altogether satisfy
Churchill who on 22 December minuted Morrison on the subject
of ' Mosley's present confinement ':

> ... would it be very wrong to allow a bath every day? What
> facilities are there for regular outdoor exercise and games
> and recreation under Rule 8? If the correspondence is cen-
> sored, as it must be, I do not see any reason why it should be
> limited to two letters a week. What literature is allowed?
> Is it limited to the prison libraries? Are newspapers allowed?
> What are the regulations about paper and ink for writing books
> or studying particular questions? Are they allowed to have
> a wireless set? What arrangements are permitted to husbands
> and wives to see each other, and what arrangements have been
> made for Mosley's wife to see her baby, from whom she was
> taken before it was weaned?[10]

As a result of Churchill's intercession, Mosley was allowed to
visit Diana once a month in Holloway. Mosley himself remained
fertile in schemes for improving conditions of internees. Permission
given in January 1941 for alien husbands and wives to be interned
together prompted a proposal, conveyed to Richard Stokes, that
the remaining ten B.U. couples should be lodged in a house in the
country where the men ' could spend most of the day working on the
land and spend the evening in decent conditions '.[11] Later he put
forward a ' Constructive Scheme' for self-supporting communes of
detainees, thus turning the prisoners ' from a liability into an asset
to the state with great benefit to their own physical, mental and
moral welfare '. All these proposals were ignored. Once more it
was Churchill who secured improvements: he was, as Mosley ruefully remarked later, ' a genial host'. An extraordinary, and typically British, feature of the situation is that the Mosleys, Churchills
and other leading personalities in this drama all came from a tiny
social and political class. They all knew each other very well, had
stayed in each other's houses and shared the same life-style. Indeed
the Mitfords and Mrs Churchill were cousins and they and the Churchill children had been more or less brought up together. Thus
it was intolerable to Churchill that Diana should be deprived of a
bath a day:* and no doubt had it fallen to Mosley to intern Churchill
he would have done his best to secure him an ample supply of
cigars. Even in war, the old English tradition of private friendship amid public animosity survived to soften the rigours of Mos-

---

*Diana Mosley writes: ' After I had been in the foul prison a few months I was
sent for by the Governor and he said "There's an order from the Government,
Lady Mosley is to have a bath every day "... . But of course the governor
knew, and I knew, that it was an impossibility. There were 2 baths between 60
women and one couldn't or wouldn't jump the queue.'

ley's imprisonment. Maxton, Boothby and Harold Nicolson, old friends, came to see him. So did Walter Monckton, to whom Churchill remarked sardonically: ' Still a prison visitor?' Dorothy, Viscountess Downe, the British Union candidate for North Norfolk, and a personal friend of Queen Mary, was able to put in a good word in royal circles. It is not at all surprising to find Diana's brother Tom Mitford having lunch with Churchill, or that following this lunch Churchill should fire off another minute to Morrison (15 November 1941):

> I shall be glad to know what action you have taken about enabling the twelve couples of married internees to be confined together. . . . Sir Oswald Mosley's wife has now been eighteen months in prison without the slightest vestige of any charge against her, and separated from her husband. Has the question of releasing a number of these internees on parole been considered . . . ?[12]

Morrison put up a barrage of administrative difficulties to cover his objections to ' appeasing' fascists,[13] but apparently Churchill insisted, and early in December 1941 the Mosleys were reunited in a disused wing of Holloway, thereafter jocularly referred to as Lady Mosley's Suite. The Governor of Holloway, Dr Matheson, said crossly to Diana Mosley, ' You are under the Cabinet now.'

Life was now more tolerable. Diana cooked, with Mosley assisting (' My favourite work at this stage is Simon's... Soups, Salads and Sauces – war-time fare for the fastidious,' he wrote to his son Nicholas at the beginning of 1943). He also cultivated his vegetable lot. Gardening would be accompanied by poetry readings: ' Racine is the school craze just now,' he wrote to Nicholas in June 1943. ' When I declaim the speeches of Achilles *à haute voix* in the garden, [Diana] is almost as embarrassed as when she hears the resounding strains of Aïda coming from the ' leafy forests' of our upper window.' The youngest children, Alexander (three) and Max (two) were also allowed to visit more frequently, though those occasions provided anguish as well as joy. ' Parting from them ', Diana recalls, ' became more and more sad and Ali in particular minded very much. I made up my mind not to let them come any more. . . .'

Mosley still continued to press for the right of reply to the charges being circulated against him. To Churchill he wrote in October 1942:

> . . . it is very wrong that our fellow-countrymen should be given any occasion to think that we have done something disloyal to our country during this war; while, in fact, during the private inquiry of the Government, nothing of the kind was suggested against us. No one can show that I or my friends

have ever done anything disloyal to our country, and, given the opportunity, I will defend myself at any time before the whole nation from any such suggestion. . . .

To hold political opponents silent in gaol while a gross untruth is circulated against them is a procedure that cannot be justified to History, even if the moment permits it. . . . If we, and through us our dependants, are to suffer not only the miseries, but also the slur of further imprisonment, I suggest that, in honour, the Government should state publicly whatever they have to say against us, and that I should at least have the right to make a public reply.

This course, was, in fact, considered, but rejected, by the War Cabinet.[14]

Failing unconditional release, Mosley's efforts were directed to getting the remaining B.U. 18B detainees (the number had been whittled down to about 200 by the end of 1942) released under supervision. To his solicitor he wrote on 23 December 1942:

Supervision,–not captivity; that is the fundamental difference. Without that difference most 18B's seem to have got to the point that nothing at present matters very much. For instance it appears certain . . . that colonies in the country, which I myself suggested two years ago, would not work now. The necessary cooperation would not be forthcoming, because the phobia against captivity and herding has gone too far. Prisoners will go on automatically following the prison routine to which they are accustomed; but that is all they will do in confinement. To change this condition of mind you have to restore them to something like normal life. . . . Supervision under the machinery of 18B can be made as stringent or as lax as the State thinks fit. That machinery seems to furnish the administrative solution, if it is desired. . . . All of this without prejudice, as you people say, to my fundamental position that the whole situation has been utterly wrong throughout, and that our imprisonment, in any case, should long ago have been brought to a clean conclusion.

It was Mosley's deteriorating health which finally brought his captivity to an end. Ever since the First World War he had suffered from occasional bouts of phlebitis, or a condition of blood-clotting, in his injured leg. These were particularly liable to occur when he was deprived of exercise. His phlebitis returned in both Brixton and Holloway. It did not become really serious till June 1943, when he rapidly started to lose weight. Diana Mosley recalls that ' his bones were sticking out. . . . I think he was like a wild creature of the woods shut up in a cage.' In July and August he was seen on three occasions by his personal physician Geoffrey Evans and also by the king's doctor, Lord Dawson of Penn.   Dr Methven, medical commissioner of prisons, examined him in September. There were further examinations in October and early November. By this time it had become bitterly cold, with the temperature in the cell dropping to freezing-point in the night.   In a report to the Home Office dated 9 November Evans and Dawson, with three other prison doctors concurring, gave it as their opinion that Mosley would suffer permanent damage to health and possibly even death if he remained 'under conditions of prison life'.[15]   Churchill, who, despite the impending conference of the Big Three at Tehran, had been following Mosley's medical case-history with surprising attention, immediately pressed Morrison for his release. So apparently did Beaverbrook.[16]   Opposition within the Government came mainly from Bevin: behind him was the general council of the T.U.C., which according to Beaverbrook mistook itself for a committee of public safety.   Enmities on the Labour side went back a long way: Labour leaders, too, were genuinely worried about the effect of Mosley's release on industrial relations, particularly in the handle it would give to communist agitation inside the trade union movement.

Apart from the personal feelings of Churchill and Beaverbrook for an old opponent, the basic reason for Mosley's release was a desire to avoid the embarrassment of having him die on the Government in prison.   Political calculation played its part in releasing him, just as it had in imprisoning him.   Prolonged detention with the slur of traitor had hopefully finally discredited the man and his movement; release on the point of death would prevent him becoming a martyr and fascism becoming, as one M.P. put it, 'a permanent factor in the political issues of this country'.[17]

It was for these reasons that on 17 November 1943 Morrison informed the War Cabinet that he intended to release the Mosleys on 'humanitarian grounds'.[18] They were smuggled out early on the morning of 20 November through the murderess' gate of Holloway and placed under house arrest instead.   He was obliged to report monthly to the police, undertake no political activities, make no attempt to communicate with his followers and not travel more than seven miles from his home.

Protest was largely, though not exclusively, organised by the Communist Party, whose Agit Prop department, as Herbert Morrison remarked at the time, was immediately galvanised into action. Deputations descended on M.P.s and the Home Office; a flood of resolutions poured in, 'representing' hundreds of thousands of workers.* Mosley's old friend Lady Astor received one delegation.

*The most substantial was a resolution by the executive of the Transport and General Workers' Union whose secretary was Arthur Deakin (*The Times*, 20 Nov 1943).

Her reply was characteristic: 'I don't want to hear what you've got to say. I want you to know what I think of you. You're the same lot as stabbed us in the back in 1939.' In the Commons a motion was tabled by two Labour M.P.s protesting against the decision as 'calculated to retard the war effort'. In the debate of 1 December, the vocal opposition came chiefly from East London M.P.s, spokesmen on this occasion for their Jewish constituents. Labour M.P.s tried to make it a class issue: Why, they asked somewhat illogically, should the Government be more solicitous for a rich man's phlebitis than the workers' varicose veins? Dr Haden Guest warned that the release would strike a powerful blow at the morale of the nation. The 'whole country' had been roused. The opposition was, on the whole, a mean and squalid little affair. The lowest point was reached when one M.P.–the obsessional Commander Locker-Lampson, who had never forgiven Mosley's triumph at his expense at the Birmingham Rag Market in 1929 – suggested that Diana Mosley be examined for phlebitis, and another pointedly enquired whether she was being given facilities for engaging nurses and maids to look after her sick husband and young children.[19] Altogether, sixty-two M.P.s voted against the release, fifty-five of them from the Labour side.[20]*

The storm in a teacup subsided as quickly as it had arisen. On Christmas day, Mosley wrote to Nicholas:

> One small amusement has arisen from the press howl (which now seems over). They roared that we were arriving here with a large domestic staff. Then, being only able to obtain a photograph of me carrying the coals, switched over to the line that no domestic would come to us. . . . The result was a stream of offers from all over the country of 'domestic' help – all from non-members. From these we selected a most excellent man – £50,000 worth of free advertisement to secure

*There is some evidence of public attitudes to Mosley in the war from Mass Observation. In the phony-war period there was little support for the punishment of Mosley. The day after he was interned Mass Observation was asked by Home Intelligence to do a snap survey of public reactions, which it carried out in three areas. The conclusions were: (1) very seldom have observers found such a high degree of approval for anything, (2) some people, however, objected to a person being arrested for what he might do rather than for what he had done, (3) the commonest comment was that it should have been done a long time ago, and a great many people mentioned this spontaneously (Wartime Report 135). Three surveys carried out after Mosley's release, the first just after the announcement of his impending release, the second just after his release, the third a few days after the Commons debate, found 8 per cent, 7 per cent and 11 per cent respectively approving of it, and 66 per cent, 87 per cent and 77 per cent disapproving. Mr Tom Harrisson notes: 'The British are a forgiving people, and attitudes to Mosley mellowed rapidly as the war went on and after.'

me a domestic is a favour the press confers on few!   However,
enough of these absurdities. . . .

Diana Mosley recalls: 'We spent Christmas at an inn at Shipton-
under-Wychwood with my four boys, who all got whooping cough.
Everyone was ill, including Kit [the family name for Mosley] but
it was heaven to be free.'

Appendix

The question of foreign funds remains impenetrably obscure.
Oswald Hickson, Mosley's solicitor, was asked by the advisory committee to get hold of the balance sheets of the Movement for the years
1934–6.   These disclosed no details of subscribers.   Barclays and
Westminster banks, British Union's bankers, also searched their records and were able to report that no foreign currency had been paid
into British Union's account.   On the other hand, according to
the Home Office memorandum of 14 April 1943 'the income in the
two years from February 1934 to February 1936 was shown as
£160,500.   As a result of the investigation of various banking
accounts, which was made after the detention of Sir Oswald Mosley
in 1940, it appears that the funds of the British Union for these
years consisted chiefly of moneys which were paid into a secret
account in the names of two of its members.   The greater part of
the sums paid into this secret account consisted (a) of the proceeds
of foreign currencies (Swiss francs, French francs, United States
dollars and Reichsmarks) and (b) of remittances from foreign sources, which were further concealed by being passed from a Swiss
bank into the account of an individual in this country before they
reached the secret account.'   Because of the 'elaborate steps taken
to shroud the financial arrangements of British Union in mystery'
there was no definite evidence that Mosley's movement had been
subsidised from abroad, but the 'inference' was that Mosley had
received 'large sums of money' from the Italian Government in the
'early days of his movement'.   Further light was thrown on the
matter when the Labour home secretary, Chuter Ede, revealed
in the Commons on 6 June 1946 that captured letters from Count
Grandi, the Italian ambassador, to Mussolini, showed that in 1933–5
the B.U.F. was receiving about £60,000 a year from the Italian
Government in monthly instalments of £5000.   Robert Forgan, the
deputy leader till October 1934, told Colin Cross in 1960 that from
1933 onwards the B.U.F. received parcels of mixed European currencies, each the equivalent of some £5000, at irregular intervals
and believed to come from the Italian embassy.[21]   This is consistent
with the Chuter Ede statement and also with the memorandum
of 14 April 1943.

Another significant pointer is the statement in *Action* of 25 April 1940 (repeated by Mosley in *My Answer*) that a ' well-known firm of Chartered Accountants ' had found that ' over a long period before the war ' only funds from British sources had come to the B.U.F. Had no foreign funds at all come in, the words would surely have been ' since the B.U.F. was started '.

The likeliest answer is that Mussolini invested money in Mosley's movement as one means of securing British public sympathy for his Abyssinian venture contemplated since 1933. In his letter of 1 March 1935, quoted by Chuter Ede, Grandi says to Mussolini, ' With a tenth of what you give Mosley . . . I feel that I could produce a result ten times better.' What possible result could Grandi be referring to except the creation of pro-Italian feeling on the Abyssinian crisis?

Chapter 25

The Faustian Riddle

PRISON WAS Mosley's fourth period of enforced retirement from active life, the longest, most complete and most frustrating. To his eldest son Nicky he wrote in June 1942:

> I have no news except of such things as the Jersey Beans, the third of which, to my intense emotion, showed above the ground this morning; while with the prognosis that others direct to the stirring events of this great age, I attend the arrival of my French Petit Pois.

However, the cultivation of the Petit Pois took second place to the cultivation of the mind and spirit. The vast bulk of Mosley's serious reading has taken place in short and intensive bursts, during forced intermissions from an active life. Mosley never sought knowledge for its own sake, but to help him fulfil his task. Invalided out of the First World War he avidly devoured biographies of great parliamentarians in preparation for the career on which he had set his heart. Ousted from Parliament in 1924 he equipped himself to tackle the economic problem. Following the New Party débâcle in October 1931 he read Spengler to prepare him for his new undertaking as leader of renaissance. In all this reading a progression is evident that parallels the evolution of Mosley's own career from brilliant political adventurer ascending the greasy pole of parliamentary fame to prophet of a New Order crying in the wilderness. Prison set the brutal seal on Mosley's estrangement from the English political culture. Forty-five years old, only just approaching the peak of his powers, he could not disguise from himself the bitter realisation of failure. All his high hopes and ambitions had crumbled into dust. These were not the ' stirring events ' for which he had been born. The child of a previous cataclysm, his destiny was not to send a fresh generation of heroes ' like Kings in pageant to their imminent death ' but to create a land fit for heroes to live in prosperity and in enjoyment of the arts of peace. What tasks were there left for Mosley in a hostile and uncomprehending world? Yet he never contemplated retirement. And, even if he had contemplated it, his physical and mental energy made any such prospect unthinkable.

Three things united to determine the content of Mosley's serious prison reading and reflection. Cut off by the prison walls and the prison censors from any direct involvement in, or discussion of, the 'stirring events' around him, he could only pose the problems which exercised him obliquely, on the level of abstract ideas.

Secondly, Mosley's prison reading came at a point in his life when for the first time he had a past to understand – and justify. Hitherto he had never seriously questioned the *rightness* of what he had done in life. Intellectually he had certainly grown up, but in attitude to life he remained very much a child of nature, not wicked so much as naïve. His choice of prison reading reflects for the first time a consciousness of moral complexity. It therefore marks not only an important stage in his own moral growth, but also in the revaluation of the causes and methods he has espoused. For the first time he can look ' beyond Fascism '.

Finally, we can see in Mosley's choice of prison reading a process of detachment from the particular problems of Britain that had consumed his political life. Partly this was a consequence of his physical incarceration; partly it was a product of his emotional detachment from the conflict between fascism and democracy engulfing Europe. In his own eyes he had nothing to reproach himself with in having striven mightily to avert this conflict. But he saw that the struggle had been waged on too narrow a front. Old national antagonisms reinforced by new ideological hostilities had driven the European nations into disaster. A new healing synthesis was required, drawn from the whole panorama of European culture and experience. Mosley set himself the task of ' learning to think and feel as a European '.

We can see, then, in his prison reading a conscious quest for a philosophy of life that, as he was to put it after the war, went ' beyond both fascism and democracy ', that is, could produce a synthesis of the two at a higher level. For Mosley the terms fascism and democracy were not simply contemporary catchwords. They stood for two opposing poles of the European temperament whose twentieth century rivalry had destroyed Europe. These poles of temperament might be differently designated – aristocratic versus plebeian, egoistic versus altruistic, spiritual versus material; but, however called, it was the same ' scarcely remediable cleavage ' that Schiller had diagnosed in the soul of European man.

Increasingly Mosley realised that this cleavage had its root in the problem of evil. In Christian theology man is portrayed as a fallen creature. Puritanism, the most radical version of Christianity, identified self-expression with sinful pride. The Puritan ethic was based on the repression of self for the sake of a later heavenly or, in the capitalist version, earthly reward. Humility and meekness were exalted. On the social plane much the same process of repressing the mighty and exalting the humble and meek took place. ' The Christian Utopia . . . looked forward to the ultimate triumph not of the rich and the powerful, but of the poor, humble and meek. . . .

The lion would lie down with the lamb.'[1] The causes of these developments are much disputed. In a brilliant flash of insight Nietzsche saw the growth of the moral outlook, the separation of nature and social phenomena into ' good ' and ' evil ', as the attempt of ordinary people to stop themselves being used, abused, exploited, savaged, killed by extraordinary people. What else is the purpose of the great moral injunctions ' Treat each man as an end, never as a means ', ' Do unto others what you would have them do unto you ', ' All men are equal in the sight of God'? The moral outlook was thus developed to control and suppress what ordinary people perceived as evil in relation to themselves. (All the great religions of mankind were in their inception popular mass movements.)

The trouble was that the efforts to destroy evil thus defined also posed a mortal threat to beauty, valour, strength: the heroic qualities. The reason is that man's creative possibilities are, as Nietzsche put it, ' insidiously related, knotted, and crocheted ' to his destructive ones. A society that has adopted the moral outlook is a society, according to Nietzsche, that has renounced genius, heroism, supreme achievement. It is a society, as Mosley would put it, that has lost its evolutionary urge. For not only can evolution be seen as a process of generalising humanity's peak experiences; but the instruments of that evolution must themselves be heroes, capable of breaking through the crust of convention, the force of habit and inertia, the power of the great interests built round life as it is. If goodness ever becomes the principle of life, then life stops.

Herein, according to Mosley, lies the central flaw of the democratic psychology. In its aversion to monstrous acts, it is prepared to tolerate monstrous phenomena. At root, the various objections to Mosley's policies and methods were moral ones: power must not be concentrated, for it leads to abuse; great men are more dangerous than lesser men; political passions must be exorcised for they lead to intolerance. Yet how, in face of these inhibitions, were the great potentialities which science made possible to be realised? What was required was a new attitude to life, or rather the revival of a much older attitude: yet one that at the same time took into account man's moral demands. This was Mosley's quest in his years of forced idleness.

The fruits of Mosley's reading may be studied in his book *The Alternative* which appeared in 1947. But some of the stages of this intellectual pilgrimage can be followed in a correspondence with his eldest son Nicholas. Nicholas, who had become head of his house in his last year at Eton, was soon to see action with the Rifle Brigade in Italy. In training in England in 1942, he was a frequent visitor at Holloway where father and son would stay up talking far into the night. Nicholas found his father a vivacious and stimulating companion; while Mosley was overjoyed to find his own son eager to be tuned in to his own particular Muses. ' Darling Nick,' he wrote soon after his release from prison, ' I can never tell you what a joy it was to know you as an adult and to find what a perfect community of mind and spirit we had in searching together through all the higher and lovelier things of life.' It was an idyllic father–son relationship – too idyllic to last.

In a typical gesture of contempt for his captors Mosley had immediately started to learn German. It was more than a gesture of contempt: it was the beginning of the attempt to think and feel as a European. He had been profoundly impressed and influenced by Nietzsche and Spengler who exhibited a range and depth of speculation unknown to English ' liberal ' literature.* He already knew that behind Nietzsche and Spengler stood the shadowy but towering figure of Goethe, whom alone both recognised as their master. Here was a great literature, largely unavailable in English. And behind Goethe himself was ancient Greece, which had influenced him so profoundly and where the great European adventure had started. Was it not here that one might find a key to the riddle of European man in all his splendid accomplishment and frightfulness?

Mosley's initial exploration of the Greek world was through the writings of the eighteenth century German neo-Hellenists, Winckelmann, Wieland, Goethe, Schiller. But he also read the Greek tragedians, Aeschylus, Sophocles and Euripides. Euripides' *Bacchae*, which he read in Gilbert Murray's translation, greatly moved him. ' I especially envy you your capacity for Euripides in the original,' he wrote to Nicholas in October 1943. ' I agree more and more with Goethe's verdict, translated by Browning, "I'd hang myself to see Euripides ".' Mosley also read the philosophers, Plato and Aristotle of course, but more interestingly those deeply obscure fragments of Heraclitus, whom he came to honour, as Lassalle had in the nineteenth century, as the father of all evolutionary thought. Mosley's letters from prison as well as later writings show that he had read some of the foremost modern authorities on ancient Greece – Maurice Bowra, Lowes Dickinson and in particular Werner Jaeger's classic *Paideia*. He also read Humphry Trevelyan's *Goethe and the Greeks*, which he exempted from his usual strictures on academic writing. 'Oh, these dons and commentators,' he once wrote to Nicholas in exasperation, ' the depths of their intellectual dishonesty are unfathomable – Let them by all

*After the war, Mosley would maintain, half-seriously, that a new idea might with benefit first be broached in German, the language of poetry, then clarified in English, the language of criticism; finally reduced to precision in French, the language of science.

means direct you to great subjects with the vast store of their erudition. But then always go to the original. In the end even genius should be allowed to speak for itself.'

It is agreeable to imagine Mosley at Brixton following Winckelmann and the young Goethe on their journeys to Italy, to the rediscovery of ancient Greece; an unravelling of civilisation to its childhood and youth. From Paestum, near Naples, came an ecstatic letter from Nicholas to his father:

> I came across the first temple quite unexpectedly plodding round a corner to find it straight in front of me, rising rather bleakly from the bushes and the long grass by the side of the road. In the first suddenness of the discovery, I think I was a little disappointed. It was such a cold and desolate ruin, the pillars being rather thin and forlorn under the golden heat of an Italian midday sun. But then as I wandered up beneath the gray portico I caught a glimpse of the second temple – the only temple that really matters at Paestum – a glimpse of gold more golden than the corn which clung about it, more serene and beautiful than any Italian sun. I rushed towards it in an ecstasy of wonder. . . .

Winckelmann's Greece was an idyllic society in which the exquisite nature of Greek life achieved its enduring memorial in the beautiful sculpture which represented the highest achievement of its plastic art. Winckelmann portrayed ancient Greece as a people with its eye trained on beauty; a land where climate brought all nature to its most perfect development; a society where ' no bourgeois respectability hemmed the free and natural outlet of all youthful joys '.[2]

This was the evidence of a civilisation portrayed in its plastic art. By contrast, Greek poetry exhibited a completely different view of that civilisation: one in which men cry, weep, rage and destroy each other, and in which the implacable Fates and Furies pursue their victims in an unceasing vengeance of the gods.

From these discordant elements of their existence, the very elements of Nature itself, the Greeks fashioned their aristocratic philosophy of heroic pessimism. Its keynote was what Mosley called the ' fierce acceptance of life as it is '. Nature was not something to be suppressed or overcome, as in the Judaic–Christian tradition; it was something to be fulfilled, its every power raised to a higher degree of completion. The gods were not moral beings; they were the personifications of natural (including human) powers and passions, Supermen who ' can do on an enormous scale what man can do only faintly and fitfully . . . '.[3] This conception of life left little room for a moral order, with rules for men to obey and according to which they would be judged. The gods being manifestations of power and energy were amoral: they set no standards, gave no guidance. Lowes Dickinson has pointed out that the Greeks had no sense of sin;[4] while from the fact that the blows of fate fell on worthy and unworthy alike the Greeks drew the conclusion that ' it was a divine privilege to refuse gifts without giving any explanation '.[5] This is not to say that the Greeks did not speculate about the purpose and place of suffering. They even detected a method in the gods' madness as when Homer wrote of suffering and evil that they are visited on humanity by the gods so that ' men in the ages to come may make of us stories for singing '.[6] Such transfiguration of sorrow into art made the Greeks less afraid, more determined to live greatly. It did not make them less pessimistic. Theirs was ' despair reconciled to life through Beauty '.[7]

It was, in fact, the overwhelming sense of life's precariousness that fed the Greek heroic ideal, that fierce determination to wrest the last ounce of beauty and achievement from the fleeting moment, ' to bid it stay because we cannot bear to lose it '. This ideal had little in common with humanitarian conceptions: a tragic view of life is incompatible with belief in social progress. Rather it leads to a cult of fulfilment, of individual greatness: a 'will to power' in the Nietzschean sense. Hence the Greeks showered their admiration and approbation on the great, the beautiful, the intelligent, however unbeneficent their effect on the human plane. (The heroic ideal was many-sided: Achilles was not just good at fighting, but the most beautiful man of his time, eloquent, courteous, generous.) The Greek ideal was aristocratic in a twofold sense: in the sense that the aristocratic qualities were obviously not possessed by everyone, and in the sense that the desire to excel inevitably fed on the humiliation of the majority, especially in the sphere of action which, for most of their history, the Greeks regarded as the great man's chief and natural calling, and in which humanity was simply the raw material from which the great soul fashioned his achievements. In the Sophoclean tragedies, Ajax and Heracles were both ' justified ', despite their crimes, for their nobility ' which redeems them from the taint of common clay '.[8] Defending Euripides' Admetus from Wieland's charge of unacceptable inhumanity in calmly allowing Alcestis to die for him without once considering refusing her sacrifice and dying himself, the young Goethe argues that such was his perfection that ' should he not wish to live for ever?' According to Goethe ' Admetus represented life in its highest form, and had therefore the right to expect other less perfect individuals to sacrifice themselves for him '.[9] It was to curb such excesses of the heroic ideal that the Greeks developed the concepts of *hubris* and the Mean; however, these were never more than very imperfect checks on that consuming quest for individual greatness that was the triumph and the tragedy of the Greek civilisation.

It was this ' fierce acceptance of life as it is ' that made the Greeks so attractive to Nietzsche, in revolt against the Protestant ethic. Nietzsche discerned that if the Greek cult of heroism was based on the denial of rights to the inferior, which in the end led to its destruction through the 'slaves' revolt', the alternative cult of humanitarianism was based upon a hatred or denial of self – stemming in the first place from the objective impotence of the downtrodden – which in the end would prove fatal to genius. Nietzsche unequivocally chose genius. For him the good life was the self-affirming life of fulfilment; the good society, one which deliberately cultivates the soil required for the growth of genius. The humanitarian ideal, by contrast, seeks the good life in self-denial, sublimated into moralism and good works; and sees the good society as one, where, according to the young Goethe, ' the world will be one great hospital, and each will be occupied in being the other's humane nurse '.[10]

Mosley could not accept Nietzsche's apparent antagonism between heroism and humanitarianism.* The rejection of this antagonism, indeed, forms the core of his philosophic position. To Nicholas he wrote on 25 March 1943:

> Nietzsche . . . plays his part in the triumphant affirmation of this life and his furious denunciation of the flight from it. . . . I pondered long before sending you any Nietzsche, but think you are now intellectually strong enough to take it. The great thing is not to swallow him whole but to see him in relation to the whole. To be repelled by the unbridled violence of his mind and exposition is as great an error as to become obsessed by the power of it – as many have been. In Christianity you have the thesis – in Nietzsche the antithesis. There remains the synthesis. . . .

It is evident that Mosley was deeply attracted by the heroic, Nature-affirming, amoral ideal held by the Greeks and, following them, by all those plentifully endowed with what Nietzsche called *Heiterkeit*, cheerfulness, high spirits. But he was unable to accept its background of a capricious, amoral universe, with the gods and men as supreme artists, recklessly creating, destroying, realising themselves indifferently in whatever they do or undo. To accept this was to deny progress. Heroism, with all its amorality, could be justified to modern man only in an evolutionary framework.

It was as a child of the Enlightenment who would not accept Divine values contrary to human reason that Mosley wrote to Nicholas on 25 March 1943:

*It is not clear how far Nietzsche did either: his highest type was 'the Roman Caesar with the Soul of Christ '.

Unless therefore the God-standard departs entirely from anything we can conceive, it would not appear that an all-power-
ful God afflicts [men with suffering] because he capriciously
dislikes them. We are therefore driven back towards a conception of suffering, of all the phenomena which are shortly called
evil in the experience of man, as fulfilling some creative purpose
in the design of existence – Back in fact to the Faustian
riddle. . . .*

The problem, then, that gave rise to Goethe's *Faust* was that of
reconciling two conventionally opposed attitudes to life: the heroic
and the moral, the one associated with self-expression, the other
with self-denial. Goethe's solution, the Faustian 'riddle', is to press
the first into the service of the second, the amoral into the service
of the moral. Life-improvement can take place only through life-
affirmation, for without the will-to-life there can be no will to an
improved life. Faust's desire to 'bid the moment stay' – the Greek
ideal – is only assuaged when he can live it 'in the light of
eternity'. Joy is renounced for Destiny.

The portrayal of evil as an instrument of the good was anathema
to the Christian ethic. It is one thing to recognize that evil in
fact has been the agent of progress† but quite another to articulate
a philosophy that consciously incorporates evil as an instrument of
progress. As Burckhardt noted, ' From the fact... that good may
come from evil, and from disaster relative happiness, it does not
follow that evil and disaster are not what they are ' – or, Burckhardt
might have added, that men should deliberately 'will the bad' to
work the good.[11] Yet this, as Mosley wrote to Nicholas, is ' I
believe . . . the main thesis' of Goethe's *Faust*'s 'innumerable pro-
fundities ' expressed with ' curious crudity ' in the Prologue in
Heaven when God sends Faust Mephistopheles with the words:

Man's active nature, flagging, seeks too soon the level;
Unqualified repose he learns to crave;
Whence, willingly, the comrade him I gave,
Who works, excites, and must create, as Devil.‡

*This particular section of the correspondence was evoked by Hugh Ross William-
son's remarkable little book *A.D. 33* (1941) in which he had attempted to overcome
the God All-Powerful/God All-Good dilemma by postulating an ' unfair ' God
who arbitrarily selects men for salvation and damnation.

†As in wars which bring about social and political transformations which cannot
be accomplished in peace: twentieth-century progress has been largely brought
about through the two world wars.

‡This is Bayard Taylor's translation of the original:
                    Des Menschen Thätigkeit kann allzuleicht erschlaffen,
                    Er liebt sich bald die unbedingte Ruh';
                    Drum geb' ich gern ihm den Gesellen zu,
                    Der reizt und wirkt, und muss, als Teufel, schaffen.

Of all the things he read in prison, Goethe's *Faust* made the most profound impression on Mosley: after the war, he published an English translation, with an introduction by himself. He identified his own destiny with Faust; which in turn made that destiny more conscious. At the beginning of the drama, Faust is portrayed as the dissatisfied intellectual who has shut out from his existence love, beauty, action. Mephistopheles brings him to life. Mephistopheles' conception of life is extremely limited: it is the life of the senses. He awakens in Faust the long-dormant fires of sexual passion. Faust lusts after the pawnbroker's daughter Gretchen. This is what Mephistopheles wants. Then he will win his wager with God for Faust's soul. The terrible consequences of unbridled lust are explored as Faust, a slave to Mephistopheles, encompasses Gretchen's death. But the Gretchen tragedy has an unexpected outcome. Lust has awakened Faust from his torpor, as God always intended. His craving for action takes an increasingly public turn in Part II. He is still in alliance with Mephistopheles; but the latter's role changes increasingly from that of tempter to instrument of Faust's creative purpose, as Goethe implies he was of God's creative purpose. Before Faust is ready for creative achievement he has to go through a further stage of personal development: the wild aspiring North has to be united with the balance of classical Beauty. 'It was by attaining to knowledge of Beauty symbolised by his mating with Helen that Faust was to transcend his blind desire to a state in which activity and creation could alone satisfy him.'[12] By evoking the monsters of the classic *Walpurgisnacht* Goethe again returns to his theme that Beauty arises from the elemental forces.* Armed with this vision, Faust embarks on his great life-work: the reclaiming of the marshes. The last tragedy of the drama is the murder of the old couple, Philemon and Baucis, symbols of all the innocent people sacrificed to progress. But this 'necessary' evil is the immediate prelude to Faust's redemption. His Destiny about to be fulfilled, he can at long last dispense with the services of Mephistopheles. 'Thus he perceives the Moment in a setting in which he had never known it before . . . and so he foresees how he could approve it and bid it " stay ".'[13]

> *Faust.*   A foul swamp stretches to the mountain's feet,
>   And poisons all the work that I have done:
>   If I could drain the marsh and make it sweet
>   Then my last deed would be my grandest one.
>   I'd open room for millions on the earth,
>   Not safe, not safe, I know, but free to work.
>   Green are the fields and fertile: herds could grace
>   And men live gladly on the new-found soil,

*This is the theme of Nietzsche's *Birth of Tragedy*.

> And on the great hill-barriers that they raise,
> Strong in the nation's valiancy of toil.
> Within the wall a land of Paradise,
> Without the fury of the flood may rise,
> For where it gnaws and threatens to devour
> The gap is closed by the People's thronging power.
> Yes, now this thought shall have my whole allegiance,
> This word high-throning Wisdom knows for true,
> That only he deserves his life, his freedom,
> Who wins them every day anew.
> Thus, compassed round with every danger here,
> Boy, man and greybeard fill the gallant year.
> That is the life and vigour I would see,
> Standing with free men on a soil that's free:
> Then to the passing moment I could say,
> 'Thou art so beautiful wilt thou not stay?'
> The centuries to come will keep the trace
> Of what I have accomplished in my place.
> Dreaming, I draw that far-off rapture near
> And win my highest moment now and here.*

Mosley writes: 'Faust falls dead at this instant of supreme realisation, as he swore he would so succumb if he ever became content. But the heavenly hosts bear him away from darkness to the empyrean of light because he has so greatly striven.'[14]   Yet Faust dies before his life's work is accomplished and so the drama ends on a final note of mystery. Is he redeemed by his own striving or by Gretchen's love? What is man's purpose on earth? Is it simply to strive greatly without hope of final achievement, without certain knowledge of direction? Or is it possible for man to discern God's purpose?

It is impossible fully to understand the fascination which the Faustian riddle had for Mosley without drawing attention to the central characteristic of his thought, his instinctive urge to reconcile opposites in a higher synthesis. The genius of the drama for Mosley lies precisely in the manner in which Goethe overcomes the age-old antithesis between man's 'lower' and 'higher' self – between egoism and altruism – by showing how the 'lower' is in fact an instrument of the 'higher'. As Lukàcs writes, 'The mastery of passion, its ennoblement, its orientation towards the really great goals of the human species – this is Goethe's ethic.' Mosley's approach is dialectical. It is only under static conditions that the laws of contradiction apply. They tend to dissolve automatically once a dynamic outlook replaces a static one, once action takes the place of pure thought. As Mosley's favourite Greek philosopher Heraclitus

*This is the translation of Stawell and Dickinson, pp. 244–5.

put it: 'Even the posset separates if it is not stirred.' Goethe's achievement for Mosley was to have shown how forces which appear contradictory when viewed in repose become complementary when viewed dynamically; and how man resolves his contradictions in action.*

Goethe's spiritual odyssey of Western Man answered a number of key problems which exercised Mosley in prison: the problem of evil and suffering, the problem of reconciling the heroic ideal with humanitarianism; problems which had an obvious relationship to his own life. But he was unhappily aware that the whole magnificent structure of *Faust* rested upon an unexamined premise: that man was in fact placed on earth for a definite purpose, to bring about higher forms of life. Without this assumption the whole scheme falls to the ground. For in that case what *moral* right did Faust have to act at all, with all the evil that such action brought in its train? This was the question Nicholas posed in his letter of 29 May 1943:

> I see everything as a possibility and have not the conviction to decide what is Truth and what is Right. I do not see how one can ever have this conviction, and even if one has it, why one should presume that one's convictions are right. My Reason tells me what theories are the most possible, the most likely, the most desirable, but it needs more than a Reason to put my theory across, it needs a great Faith. And my Reason tells me that it is dangerous to trust in Faith, for how does one know that one's Faith is Right? And so I am stuck. And am likely to remain so I feel, until I am old and wise enough to have Faith in my Reason.

To this Mosley replied on 1 June:

> I agree that one of the prime needs of the world today is a Faith . . . which can be believed by the modern and educated mind. Further agree that it is impossible for finite reason to elucidate all the mysteries. But come more and more to the conclusion that it should be possible to formulate a Faith (now

---

*Marxism, of course, accepts this dialectical view of progress, and *Faust* can be interpreted easily enough in marxist terms – e.g., G. Lukàcs, *Goethe and His Age* (1947), p. 215: ' It is precisely the practical activity with which Faust ends and in which is fulfilled his ideological longing for a unity of theory and practice and for the practical progress of the human species that is objectively impossible without the active assistance of Mephistopheles. The development of the productive forces in bourgeois society is possible only under capitalism.' Mosley's objection to dialectical materialism is twofold: (1) that the marxist laws of motion are overdetermined by material forces; and (2), connected with this, that the marxist dialectic moves towards one end – communism, which Mosley does not regard as a higher form.

largely felt but inarticulate) which draws the Spiritual in Life from the best of the thought, creeds and civilisations that the world has so far produced, weaving it into a coherent whole of conduct and attitude to human existence, and attuning it to the main tendencies of modern science. . . .

It is an indication of Mosley's essentially rational mind that he felt the need to establish the Faust allegory on some scientific basis: to derive it from the ' best of the thought, creeds and civilisations ' of the past (that is, from man's nature as revealed over time) as well as from the ' main tendencies of modern science ':

It we accept the seemingly unanswerable argument concerning finite mind it is plain that the last stage of the journey must be a matter for Faith.   But until that point Reason should guide us, Faith should only begin where Reason must stop. The trouble with the Churches is that Faith and Reason are proceeding so fast in opposite directions.   The trouble with so much philosophy is the ignoring of actual facts which can be observed in favour of a priori theorising . . . e.g, Hegel who lately has disappointed me so much.   Spirit can only begin when nature is overcome.   This is the Divine purpose – Why? What evidence has he concerning Divine Purpose, except as it is revealed in Nature?

Shaw had already given the answer in the Don Juan episode in *Man and Superman* and in *Back to Methuselah:* Creative Evolution, the evolution of the species to Superman, the movement of life from lower to higher forms.   But like Shaw – and Samuel Butler from whom Shaw drew his evolutionary ideas – Mosley rejected any materialist theory of progress, favouring instead the Lamarckian approach, that is, the evolution of the species through individual striving and effort, a doctrine that reinstated the outstanding individual at the centre of the evolutionary scheme.   In Shaw's view, circumstances pose the challenge: the exceptional man takes it up. This is the area of the Will.   Human action was stimulated by Nature, not determined by it.   (This corresponds to Spengler's distinction between Destiny and Causality.)

Such a view of purposive evolution necessarily involved a rejection of any materialist psychology or philosophy of history.   We have already noted Mosley's rejection of marxism.   In the field of psychology, he predictably found Freud, with his biological reductionism, less palatable than Jung.   ' Sexual determinism ', Mosley wrote in *The Alternative*, ' is not so very different in essence from economic determinism. '   The tendency of modern physics to dissolve matter into mind also seemed to point to an enhanced view of intelligence in the evolution of life, though the relation between human and divine intelligence was not altogether clear. Jeans and Eddington seemed in agreement with Jung that the religions of man, far from being manifestations of sublimated sexual desires, were symbolic attempts to reach out to an Ultimate Reality which science was approaching by another route.*

Mosley summed up his beliefs in *The Alternative*:

> When all illusions have been destroyed we still return to the basic question – is it likely that anything so complex as the Universe, and so purposeful as the evolution of man . . . can have lacked conception and design? To destroy what man thought in his less developed state is not to impair, let alone destroy, what God thinks and wills, or the evidence of his fundamental purpose which exists on earth. . . . For, we begin to see not only the necessity of design in the increasing complexity of the known Universe, not only purpose in the astounding achievement of the evolution of present man from the original lowest forms, but, also, something of the method by which that extraordinary result has been secured. . . . Even the paradox of evil, which long appeared to controvert the presence of any beneficent or creative providence, takes its place in the pattern of things as an agent which stirs from lethargy, and demands the answer of a new energy that carries men forward. . . . Nature drives man until he is sufficiently developed to advance under his own power, when the flame of the spirit is ignited.[15]

The end to which the whole process was directed must necessarily remain obscure for ' *ex hypothesi* it must be impossible for finite mind to comprehend the infinite '. Like Samuel Butler Mosley could only ' *bet* that my Redeemer liveth '. Yet some answer – based on the ' observed process ', Mosley hastens to add – might be attempted. It was, surely, the realisation of man's dreams, the universal reproduction on earth of that ' pattern of perfection ' in the Heavens of which Nature and previous pinnacles of human achievement had given some flickering indications; it was, as Mosley had himself put it as early as 1927, to ' wrest beauty out of squalor and order out of chaos '. Only in service to this high mission could the heroic ideal which had inspired the Greeks and the greatest achievements of European culture be justified in the contemporary world of the ' common man ':

> It is by service that man both develops his own character and aids this purpose of God. No conflict exists between individual development and service of humanity: that was the error

---

*In their war-time correspondence Mosley and his son discussed at length the theories of the ' metaphysical physicists ' Jeans and Eddington.

of the brilliant Nietzsche in posing a conflict between the character of his higher type of man and the interests of the people. On the contrary, the type beyond his ' Will to Power ', which is the Will to Achievement, finds his self-development under the impulse of the derided compassion in his long striving to lift all earthly existence to a higher level, at which the attainment of a higher form is possible. In this sense, the purpose of life is not self-development, *in vacuo*, but the development of the self in Achievement, as an artist in action and life, who creates, also, for humanity. The proud words, ' I serve ', are to such a man also the highest expression of self-development. He serves the purpose of God in assisting the emergence of higher forms of life. No mechanism of Society or of Government can function unless we can produce more such men: they are the lights of humanity.[16]

Such was the philosophy that Mosley was to offer the world in his book *The Alternative*. He returned to it a number of times in his post-war writings, particularly in a brilliant little critique of Shaw's *The Perfect Wagnerite* (an analysis of *The Ring*) when he takes his favourite sage to task for his lament at Siegfried's failure. Siegfried was for Shaw a Nietzschean figure: the anarchist destroying all values in order to clear the ground for fresh creation. To the youthful Shaw it was intolerable that Wagner should destroy him in *Götterdämmerung*. But to Mosley he was the one-sided Hellene who has to be transcended: ' he was capable of human heroism but not of divine love. . . . He had to set aside the human, even the superhuman, in service of the eternal; not because he lacked life but because he had so much, not to deny but to affirm, not for frustration but for a higher fulfilment. . . . Renunciation, not to deny life but to fulfil life, is to find a synthesis between life and love at a higher level. '

When a man aspires to be both philosopher and man of action, to write about Superman and to be Superman, the question of the relationship of his ideas to his life becomes of central importance.

At the impersonal level it is possible to present these ideas as the response of pure thought, not just Mosley's, but other thinkers' who influenced him, to the challenges of his age. The attempt to revive the heroic ideal and press it into the service of humanity was obviously a response to the helplessness of the conventional order of politicians before the revolutionary challenges of the twentieth century; it also reflected the rejection, whether through pessimism or aesthetic revulsion, of the 'plebeian' solution of communism. ' Dynamism has become a necessity,' Mosley wrote in *The Alternative*. ' Only higher men can match, and dwell with, the forces which the mind of present man has created. '[17] All this was already explicit in Shaw; it was also the lesson Mosley drew from the failure of existing men and institutions to cope with the great depression and avert the supreme tragedy of another war.

Also at the level of thought Mosley is clearly searching for a philosophy capable of reconciling England and Germany, democracy and fascism in a new European creed. The democratic camel and the fascist lion of Nietzsche's *Three Metamorphoses* must give way to something higher – the child: ' a forgetfulness, a new beginning '. This was Mosley's Europe.

At the personal level, Mosley's new doctrine of higher forms, as he came to call it, provided him with both a critique of his actions in the 1930s and a justification for what he had been trying to do all his life. It deepened his awareness of certain things, without deflecting him from his purpose. Fascism's fault, and by implication his own, as he came to see it, was too much paganism and not enough Christianity. He saw that in its hunger for action it had been too willing to sacrifice liberty and trample on the rights of others. It had tended to ' exult in violence for its own sake. I was probably guilty in not doing enough to stop it. ' To his son Nicholas he wrote in 1958: ' The faults, so far, have been the faults of adolescence, coupled with a driving sense of urgency in desperate situations. A desperate child is capable of any horror. Movements can begin as children and then can become adult. . . . We are faced here with the problem of producing a leadership and a movement which is adult; the old Platonic problem of making men fit for power. It should not be insuperable with the aid of modern knowledge – including the new self knowledge . . . people evolve from experience. ' This is the closest Mosley has ever come to admitting that he was not fit for the kind of power he sought in the 1930s, and that some of the thrusts of the psychology he had been reading in prison had gone home. One can be cynical about all this. Eric Bentley writes: ' The immoralist, in search of the abnormal and the illicit, makes of vice his first subject of study, but when in time vice becomes normal, virtue in its turn acquires a morbid fascination, and normality seems Bohemian. '[18] One can take this view of Mosley: morality which most educated people find normal seems to have come to him rather late in the day. But I think an alternative view fits his case better: it is easy for the low-spirited to be good, but very difficult for the high-spirited, for energy and imagination are amoral. This in the last resort is the problem of his life. Yet the very problem pinpoints the practical difficulty of his philosophy, namely that ' there is a sheer lack of any class of higher men '[19] – men fit for the power that Mosley would like them – and himself – to exercise.

And even assuming that the higher men exist, there remains the problem which baffled and defeated Shaw: how to get them into the higher jobs. ' Is it necessary to make men mad before you can get them to do anything? ' Mosley went on in the same letter. ' Is serious achievement impossible without the dynamism of frenzy – is Apollo helpless before Dionysus?' – or Faust without Mephisto-pheles? Was it necessary to ' stir the nether world to uproar ', to bring tumult to the State, to get things done? And if it was, how were the movement and the men ever to become adult? To this Mosley did, and could, give no answer. Christian love could become the method only ' when the higher men are not underneath but on top', he wrote to Nicholas in a war-time letter. Till then it would be necessary to say with *Zarathustra* that ' Love hath an end.'

Chapter 26

The Vision Splendid

AFTER FIVE years of forced war-time inactivity, Mosley was determined to get back into active politics as soon as possible. But he eased himself back gradually, determined to give the Government no excuse to pass fresh legislation to curtail his activities. Indeed, for the first three years after the war, those activities were largely confined to farming an eleven-hundred-acre estate at Crowood, near Ramsbury, Wiltshire.

His first political action was to form a publishing company which in 1946 produced *My Answer*, a reprint of *Tomorrow We Live*, with a long introduction defending his opposition to the War. Churchill's speech at Fulton, Missouri, had, he said, justified up to the hilt his pre-war contention ' that to fight Germany, where no British interest was involved, would be to create a Communist danger to threaten every British interest '.[1] *My Answer* set the tone of much of Mosley's post-war polemics: as well as a future to be gained, there was a past to be justified, defended or explained away, a past which Mosley recognised now constituted a new and major barrier between him and the British people. With his old supporters, Mosley kept in touch by means of a monthly News Letter commenting on current affairs (1946–7). He also addressed private meetings of his supporters organised into Book and Thought clubs. Even these limited activities were not carried out without difficulty. Printing unions made trouble about the printing of the News Letter; attempts to revive a newspaper were foiled by the simple expedient of refusing a paper quota.[2] Irate proprietors of halls cancelled meetings of ' the Modern Thought ' groups when they learned the identity of their guest speaker.[3]

In October 1947 came *The Alternative*, the statement of the post-war faith which, like *The Greater Britain*, was clearly intended to re-launch the political movement. To a conference of Mosleyite book clubs on 15 November 1947 at the Memorial Hall, Farringdon Street – site of the New Party's first public meeting sixteen years before – Mosley explained the new idea: ' If they linked the Union of Europe with the development of Africa in a new system of two continents, they would build a civilization which surpassed, and a force which equalled, any power in the world. . . . From that union would be born a civilization of continuing creation and ever unfolding beauty that would withstand the tests of time.' On 8 February 1948, the decisive step was taken: Mosley returned to active politics as leader

of the Union Movement, campaigning for ' Europe a Nation '.   In
this concept he found a final faith which reconciled the two powerful
urges of his life: to build his ' land fit for heroes ' and to heal the
wounds of the First World War.

To understand its place in Mosley's thought one must go back
to the conflict, presented in Chapter 2, between socialism and
imperialism.   Both had developed in the late nineteenth century
in response to the incipient breakdown of *laissez-faire* capitalism.
Underconsumptionist and marxist socialists wanted to create the
market which modern industry required by redistributing wealth;
imperialists wanted to create it by excluding foreign imports from
a protected area.   Liberals of all kinds basically believed that the
free market would automatically equate supply and demand, whatever deviations from it they were prepared to accept in practice.

Mosley had joined this debate from the left-wing side in politics
in the 1920s.   In his *Revolution by Reason* (1925) he had demanded
the nationalisation of the banking system to expand credit and
direct ' new money ' to the ' necessitous areas of poverty ' – a mixture
of Keynes and Hobson.   In 1930 he had urged direct government
investment to stimulate demand. Both proposals involved a high
degree of national planning.   Both were directed to the problem
of inadequate demand arising from within the domestic economy.
But already by 1925 Mosley was aware of deflationary pressures
originating from outside the domestic economy.   The proposal of
a floating exchange-rate and the suggestion that Britain should buy
less from abroad were both designed to shield the ' reflated '
national economy from deflationary pressure exerted through the
balance of payments.   A visit to America convinced Mosley that a
controlled private-enterprise system could provide high and increasing wages provided that the economy was largely self-contained.
The depression which hit Britain from outside in 1930 reinforced
this line of thought.   By 1930 Mosley was talking of ' insulating '
Britain from the ' chaos of world markets '.   Since Britain could not
be self-sufficient like America, insulation had to be broadened, and
Mosley went on to speak of ' a conscious control and direction of the
united economic resources of our Commonwealth for the benefit of
the Commonwealth as a whole '.   Here he established contact with
the tradition of Joseph Chamberlain and the economic imperialists
on the right of politics, and broke decisively with marxism.   He
chose empire as the unit of economic community because it was
' there ' (which the marxist world-state plainly was not), and because social imperialism seemed an ideology capable of mobilising
the radical right and the working class behind a ' united ' recovery
effort.

We have now reached the political economy of fascism.   The
reconciling institutions of the corporate state (themselves fore-

shadowed in Mosley's proposals for a national economic council in 1925 and the New Party's commodity boards) were to be entrusted with the task of ' deliberately raising demand as science increased the power to produce '.   There was to be a planned and complementary exchange of goods between Britain and the self-governing dominions.   The colonial empire (India and Africa) was to be kept as an exclusive preserve for endangered British exports like Lancashire cotton, on the eighteenth century mercantilist model.   Evolution, Mosley argued, was creating not the marxist or even the liberal world-state but a world of great units, collectively organised to maximise their power and welfare.

This ' social imperial ' solution to the problems of the modern world broke down internationally in the Second World War; and in Britain had failed by 1939 to emerge as a conscious alternative to the old régime.*   The attempts by Germany, Italy and Japan to acquire their own empires by methods at once direct and brutal united, it is true, the chauvinist right and the moral left as Mosley had hoped, but in opposition to, not in support of, fascist economics. Mosley's argument that self-contained empires would abolish the causes of war ignored the problem of how to move peacefully from one state of international power-distribution to another.   The instinctive opposition of conservative forces to any changes in the world *status quo* could have been overcome only had the alternative systems which the fascist powers tried to create been unshakeably rooted in a ' universalist ' conception and been inaugurated by methods which did not affront the conscience of the non-fascist world and thus unite chauvinism and morality behind a defence of the existing order.   In other words, Hitler's attempt to adapt Europe to the new reality of its ' dwarfing ' by the rising superpowers of America and Russia[4] could have succeeded only had it been attempted by political methods and informed by a genuine European idealism rather than by the conception of German imperialism.   The heroic and barbaric values embodied in the Nazi enterprise totally overshadowed the rational and humane ends to which, according to Mosley, fascism was basically directed.   The triumph of the moral conceptions of the Allies, which dealt a death-blow not only to the putative fascist empires but also (though this was not so clearly recognised at the time) to the existing European colonial empires, eliminated ' social imperialism ' from history.   It cleared the way for the Anglo-American attempt to restore the essentials of a single-world trading community.   It also cleared the way for Mosley to bring together this ' rational ' economics with his passionate longing

*This is not to deny the reality of the Ottawa system established in 1932.   But for most British leaders, as well as the bulk of the intellectual establishment, ' bloc ' economics remained a ' second-best ' solution, to be scrapped as soon as it was possible to re-create a single-world economic community.

for European reconciliation, born in the trenches of 1914–18, into
a new system which would transcend the barbarities of fascist
imperialism.

European union thus represents for Mosley on the one side the
fusion of socialism and mercantilism in a new voluntarist setting; on
the other side, the political expression of that realisation of a common
heritage, a common fate, first obscurely awakened in the ' comradeship of the trenches ' in 1914–18, when even the common soldier
felt himself part, if only momentarily, of a new European aristocracy born under fire. It became for Mosley a final faith because
it eliminated in his view two radical defects of his earlier plans.
The first was the element of imperialism. The new Europe was to
be created by consent. On 16 October 1948 Mosley proposed
as a first step towards creating ' Europe a Nation ' the election of a
European assembly by universal suffrage in which ' every European
shall be able to vote for any other European '.* In the developed
plan, a European government would be subject to dismissal by a
European parliament: there would be liberty of opposition and the
preservation of basic human rights. A European nation thus
created by consent would have established an undeniable moral
and legal basis for its existence and would thus have overcome a
central marxist (and, for that matter, liberal) objection to empires:
that established by the sword, and ruled by the sword, they would
inevitably perish by the sword as subject peoples revolted against
foreign domination and as one forcible division of the world gave
way to another.† In the concept of executive action to equate
demand and supply in a non-imperial self-contained area Mosley
believed he had finally discovered a secure answer both to the
marxist law of immiseration and to the leninist law of perpetual
imperial struggle for the ' division and redivision ' of the world.

The second defect of Mosley's fascist plan was that it had left out
of account his longing for European reconciliation. It provided
for no institutions to maintain European peace. Indeed, by its
assumption of a number of European empires, each with their own

---

*Mosley fared no better than earlier advocates of European unity in defining
exactly what he meant by Europe. Although he toyed with the idea of a union
stretching from the Atlantic to the Urals, in practice his Europe meant the non-
communist countries, plus the ' lost lands ' following a Soviet withdrawal. ' We
will secure the liberation of the enslaved lands of Eastern Europe, the union of
the German people and the restoration of their territory, freedom . . . for the
Baltic, Balkan and Polish peoples ' (*Union*, 22 Oct 1949).

†There was, of course, always a strong voluntarist element in the imperial schemes
of both Joseph Chamberlain and Mosley since they presupposed in part voluntary
bargains between Britain and the dominions; but the ' imperial ' element was
clearly to be paramount in the economic arrangements which Britain would
make with its colonial empire.

colonial spheres, it perpetuated the division of Europe.   After the
war, Mosley conceded that fascism had been ' too nationalistic '.
European unity had become a condition of European independence.
Unless a new European patriotism could be born, European history
would come to an end.   ' Europe a Nation ' thus represented for
Mosley a synthesis of the economic and spiritual, hitherto sundered
in his thought.   Common culture would make possible voluntary
political and economic union which was required not only to secure
higher standards of life but to preserve European independence in
a world of superpowers.

This is the fully evolved post-war idea.   Admittedly to describe
it in these terms suggests a much cleaner break from the imperialist
and fascist past than in fact occurred.   Mosley's Europe was to
include Africa.   In one of the rare reports of a Mosley speech in the
post-war years Mervyn Jones commented in 1949 that Mosley's
purpose ' is to make each eager youngster envisage himself, suitably
clad in khaki shorts and topee and carrying a whip or revolver,
striding magisterially across a vast plantation where countless black
backs bend in rhythm '.[5]   This is typically unfair.   Nevertheless,
it is perfectly true that in Mosley's immediate post-war blueprint
Africa was to be the ' empire of Europe ', an empire that was to fulfil
a variety of functions.   First, by providing Europe with its raw
materials, it would complete the self-sufficient system and thus enable Europe to live ' independently of foreign doles '.[6]   Secondly,
Africa's great value in Mosley's eyes was as the forcing-ground for
European unity.   Its development would be carried out by a
joint-stock company of European nations and thus union would be
' promoted in high degree by a common task and mutual interest '.
Through the development of Africa, Germany and Italy could be
reintegrated into the European family.[7]   Thirdly, Mosley had a
Faustian vision of Africa: the vision of the heroic technician ' opening up ' the still-dark continent, reclaiming marshes and deserts
for the uses of man, cutting tunnels, canals, railways and highways
through natural obstacles.[8]   Finally, Africa was to provide the soil
for European colonisation in a Spenglerian ' renewal '.   ' Just
think what could be done, and in how short a time ', Mosley
enthused in a Kensington Town Hall speech of 17 October 1949,

> if the energies of Englishmen, Frenchmen, Germans and
> Italians, and all the other European peoples, great and small,
> were pooled and directed by common consent and purpose to
> win wealth from the richest Continent on Earth.   What
> material happiness could be achieved and what spiritual
> satisfaction!   The plough would replace the sword; sweat
> would pour but not blood; construction would rise above
> destruction; brotherhood above vendetta; and Union above

division. A new civilisation will be born in that achievement. Within it will continue and develop the endless diversity and invention of the European genius in measureless contribution to the future welfare of mankind.

Africa might be the elixir of life for the exhausted spirit of Faustian man in his gilded megalopolis; but what about the Africans themselves? Where did they fit into the vision splendid?

It is a sign of Mosley's increasing awareness of the moral dimension that he soon repudiated the idea of the ' old colonialism ', still barely questioned by the Conservatives. In April 1948 he endorsed a plan by Oswald Pirow, a former South African cabinet minister and founder in 1940 of a pro-Nazi New Order, for dividing Africa into black and white areas. At a joint press conference in London, Mosley and Pirow rejected the policy of ' keeping the Negro within white territory ' as ' sweated labour ' for finance capitalism under the guise of multi-racialism and advocated allocating two-thirds of sub-Saharan Africa to black states and one-third to white states. ' In effect ', Pirow said, ' it means a segregation, not of the Native, but of the White Man.' Pirow's scheme rested on three propositions which he considered ' axiomatic ' : (1) that colour was not the test of civilization; (2) that equal rights cannot be withheld from a civilised person solely on account of the colour of his skin; and (3) that equal rights between black majorities and white minorities in the same state ' must inevitably lead to . . . the disappearance of Western civilization '. Mosley made a strong distinction between his proposals and South Africa's apartheid policy, which he nevertheless thought might develop into something better. ' A genuine apartheid, a real separation of the two peoples into two nations which enjoy equal opportunity and status . . . is a strong contradiction to the bogus apartheid which seeks to keep the negro within white territory but segregated into black ghettoes which are reserves of sweated labour living in wretched conditions. . . . Hysterical propaganda has made the term apartheid cover both concepts, although they are entirely opposed .'[9]

In 1953 Mosley was attracted by another scheme–a united Europe should give its black subjects equal rights in a Eur-African political system, the greater numbers in Europe ensuring a permanent white majority. The whites, he insisted, would not stand for equality of citizenship ' within an area so limited that it would finally produce a black majority '. Either they would leave altogether, in which case Africa would be lost for Europe, ' or they will fight it to the death. . . . Are Europe and America either prepared to lose from Western Civilization the wealth of Africa . . . or to send troops to shoot down white settlers? '[10] Under the new plan, Africa would be divided into black and white states with a two-tier franchise (as in

Europe): one for their own countries, another for Europe-Africa as a whole.[11]

It is fascinating to watch Mosley grappling with the problem of satisfying black African aspirations while retaining Africa within the framework of a European political economy. At least it can be said that he started to tackle the real problems of colonial Africa's future sooner than either the orthodox right who looked forward to years more of the ' old colonialism ' or the orthodox left for whom ' one man, one vote ' and constitutions on the Westminster model were the complete panacea. The first ignored the future, and the second ignored the past. As always Mosley tried to combine the two. In fact, something not unlike Mosley's division of Africa between black and white is being worked out today, though with much less clarity and much less white area than he would have liked; and, above all, without guarantee against what he would regard as the exploitation of black Africa by Western finance in order eventually to undercut the high-wage economies of Europe.

There is another sense in which Mosley's post-war Europe was tied to his own past. It was projected against the background of a mortal communist threat, both external and internal. In his philosophic writings Mosley looked forward to the day when life could evolve into ' higher forms ' without the stimulus of pain and disaster. But this could only happen when the ' higher types ' were in charge. Mosley's Europe would be born in economic collapse and revolutionary upheaval: the familiar fascist scenario transposed from a national to a European setting. For all the modification which his ideas had undergone, Mosley remained true to his conception of himself as a man of crisis; and his Europe, like his England, would be reborn in crisis.

The *deus ex machina* in this case was world communism spearheaded by Russia. In his suggestive essay, ' European Unity in Thought and Action ', Geoffrey Barraclough observed that it has always been much easier to unite Europe *against* something than *for* something. Russia and communism occupied the same place in Mosley's thought as the Saracens had at the time of the Crusades: Europe was to unite against the threat of Asia – an idea born, as we have seen, in the First World War. This threat was both material and spiritual: Russian military power was the secular arm of world communism. Against this double – and connected – threat (for Mosley envisaged a combination of external Soviet pressure and internal political guerilla action fomented by communist parties) Europe must be armoured both by a military shield, which implied a pooling of military resources,[12] and by an ' idea ' capable of winning the masses from communism. The Soviet military threat led Mosley, in common with a number of others (for instance, Bertrand Russell[13]), to advocate at the time of the Berlin crisis

(1948) an ultimatum to Russia to renounce the manufacture of nuclear weapons and to give up its gains in eastern Europe on threat of atomic bombardment.[14]   As the Soviets developed a nuclear capacity to match America's in a new balance of terror, and with the growth of NATO's conventional forces, Mosley started concentrating on the ideological aspects of the confrontation.

The Russians, he argued, in his essay ' The European Situation ' (1950), would launch ' not a war of States but a war of politics reinforced by violence '.   The age of nuclear stalemate would usher in the era of the urban guerilla, fomenting industrial sabotage, striking against the ' nerve centres of opposing governments . . . which . . . have been softened by internal propaganda and thoroughly permeated by highly-placed agents in the key positions of administration and defence.'[15]   This scenario was influenced by Mosley's early experience of the Irish troubles (now reinterpreted to suit his new ideological stance), his brushes with the communists in the 1930s, and the revelation after the war of communist spies and sympathisers in high places – this was the time of Klaus Fuchs, Alger Hiss, and Burgess and Maclean.   Its background was a decaying capitalist system unable either to offer its populations a spiritual idea or, in the end, to stave off economic disaster.   ' The coming struggle ', Mosley wrote in 1954, ' will be a battle of ideas. It is clearly possible only for those who have an idea to take an effective part in such a contest.'

It was here that fascism, transposed into a wider context, and purged of its ' adolescent ' barbarities, still had a vital part to play. It is Mosley's continuing emphasis not only on the need for a new economic system, but also for a ' new idea', a new set of values, a new type of man, that pinpoints the origins of his Europe, and sets it apart from the anti- or non-fascist European movement started after the war.[16]   Mosley's Europe had its origins in the kind of fascist solidarity which led William Joyce to Berlin and which had thrown up ' collaborators ' all over Europe.   Although Mosley, for reasons we have suggested, was not prepared to accept European unification on German terms, his post-war idea was already foreshadowed in Marcet Déat's proclamation in 1943 of a ' solidary community of European nations ', a ' European socialism ' and a ' European duty against the evils of bolshevism and capitalism '[17] and in the manifesto of Mussolini's ill-fated Republic of Salo the same year, which called for the ' realisation of a European Community, with a federation of all nations ' and the development, for the benefit of European peoples and of the natives, of Africa's natural resources.[18]   It was not till much later that Mosley could tear himself away sufficiently from his fascist perspective on contemporary history to see virtue in the efforts being made by the ' other side ' to realise his own aims; and to see himself consciously

as an *avant-garde* philosopher of the actual Europe being constructed rather than the exponent of that ' alternative ' Europe which
continued to exist in the fantasies of the defeated fascists.

The basis of his post-war political orientation was his continuing
belief in the inevitability of economic collapse – a belief which has
survived to this day.   Mosley had no more faith than in the 1930s
in the survival chances of the liberal economic system, even on the
improved Keynesian and Bretton Woods model.   His basic idea
was still that the system of finance capitalism set up a chronic
tendency for demand to fall short of productive capacity, and thus
for the system to collapse into depression.   He started predicting
this collapse as soon as the war ended. ' [Gaitskell and Wilson] must
know ', he wrote in 1953, ' that the policy of exporting capital goods,
which they so strongly advocate, must lead in the end to the equipment of their competitors and the self-sufficiency of markets to which
Britain now sends goods and from which we obtain raw materials.'
Labour's policy was simply to reinstate nineteenth century capitalism with America replacing Britain as the world's chief money-
lender.   ' The only contact of that policy with any form of socialism
is that the programme is entirely according to Marx . . . the only
surprise is that the causative chain should again be set in motion by
the two economic experts of the Labour Party.'[19]   By 1958 he
recognised that collapse had been staved off by American capital
outflows ' on an unprecedented scale '.[20]   This had obscured the
basic dilemma that ' every country cannot at the same time sell
more than it buys on world markets' by keeping the European
countries in artificial surplus.   But spiralling domestic and world
inflation would only make the collapse more severe when it came.
It was in such conditions of crisis that the opportunity would arise
to construct the new system of ' European socialism ' and divide up
the rest of the world rationally into continental systems – the Soviet
Bloc, China, North America, East Asia, etc.

From today's perspective these gloomy prognostications seem far
less fanciful than they did ten years ago (not to mention Mosley's
1930s proposal for making Britain self-sufficient in energy by extracting oil from coal).   The Bretton Woods system which depended,
as Mosley saw, on American capital exports, collapsed in 1971, thus
transforming the whole structure of economic, political and military
interdependence based on American monetary hegemony into an
increasingly explicit competitive relationship between the major
capitalist blocs – America, Europe and Japan.[21]   Protectionist sentiment has flared everywhere against the operations of that most
sophisticated modern instrument of finance capitalism, the multi-
national corporation.   The class-struggle, hopefully banished by
the affluence of the 1950s and 1960s, once more rears its ugly head,
calling for the construction of a rational industrial order.   It is too

early to say that the world is approaching 1929, but the trend is
certainly in that direction.   Once again, the criticism of Mosley is
not in his analysis, which has been astonishingly prescient, but in
the political conclusion he drew from it, namely, that he should hold
himself in reserve for the crisis.   As a result his warnings and
alternatives have gone unheeded; and if and when the situation
develops into one from which he might conceivably derive benefit
the politician of the single situation will be dead or incapa-
citated.

Mosley's decision to pin his hopes on the ' crisis ' meant, as it
had in the 1930s, the rejection of the politics of ' normality '.
Instead he set out to sell Europe-Africa to the British people surrounded by familiar faces from his immediate past: Raven Thomson
(secretary till his death in 1955), ' Mick ' Clarke, Jeffrey Hamm
(who succeeded Thomson as secretary), Robert Row, Alfred
Flockhart, Tommy Moran, Hector McKechnie, Victor Burgess
and others.   Neil Francis-Hawkins did not resume an active role
and died soon afterwards.   Clarke and Moran also dropped out.
With the exception of the flamboyant Dan Harmston, who organised the Smithfield porters against coloured immigration in 1968
and 1972,[22] Union Movement threw up no new popular leader in
the post-war years.

Indeed, the prevalence of the ' old guard ' soon gave it a depres-
singly familiar look.   Like the Bourbons, the fascists seemed to have
learnt nothing and forgotten nothing.   Jeffrey Hamm, a Welshman
by birth and schoolmaster by profession, had been arrested in the
war and imprisoned under Regulation 18B.   In 1946 he organised
a British League of Ex-Servicemen and Women in the East End
of London which became the main active force in the new Union
Movement.   Naturally, the revival of the fascists reactivated a
violent opposition from communists and Jews (Jewish bodies such as
the 43 Group and the Association of Jewish Ex-Servicemen taking
the lead) and this in turn revived the ' quarrel with the Jews ',
though on a much narrower front.   Officially, the Jewish Question
no longer existed.   Pre-war policy proposals were dropped.   Jews
were even welcome to join Union Movement.   But the consistent
fights with Jews at meetings and processions in Hackney and elsewhere (at one meeting Hamm's head was split open by a brick[23])
brought back much of the old anti-semitic truculence.   There were
references to ' freshly imported Spivs ' and ' Communist aliens '.[24]
Of the Board of Deputies, *Union* wrote on 2 April 1949, ' These
gentlemen are certainly enjoying their little hour which the efforts
of Britain won for them.   Some memory of the nemesis of history
might suggest to them that they are enjoying it too well.'   The
alleged link between the 43 Group and Jewish terrorist organisations
fighting British forces in Palestine was used to suggest that Union

Movement was fighting the same battle as 'our lads' in the Middle East.[25]

Nevertheless, it would be wrong to imply that Union Movement was simply the post-war version of the old British Union. By adopting the European cause, Mosley renounced the old nationalist support which had sustained the pre-war Movement: much of this now went to the late A. K. Chesterton's League of Empire Loyalists (1954). The fact that Mosley encouraged his movement's anti-semitism to die away by refusing to recognise a Jewish question meant that anti-semites sought other pastures. Here the running was made by Colin Jordan, Arnold Leese's spiritual heir, who founded the White Defence League which merged with John Bean's National Labour Party into the British National Party in 1960.* (Later the Empire Loyalists and the B.N.P. came together in the National Front pledged to combat coloured immigration and entry into the Common Market.) In other words, Mosley deliberately renounced much of his old chauvinist, racialist following and tried to win new converts, and a new type of convert, to new ideas. In particular he was much more chary than of old in getting involved with cranks and extremists who would discredit him: his cold-shouldering of the American Francis Parker Yockey who tried to interest him in the ' liberation of Britain and Europe from the regime of the inner-Traitor and the outer-Enemy ' is a case in point.† Although at the time the period 1947–50 looked like a simple revival of fascism, one can now see it as a process of extrication from the dead hand of pre-war fascism and a rededication to a new, and more moderate, crusade.

In other ways, too, Union Movement was different from British Union. Although both idea and movement were projected against an anticipated background of capitalist disintegration and struggle against communism, the atmosphere was much less military than before the war. It was never an ex-serviceman's movement as the pre-war one had been: the Second World War was not Mosley's war. There was much less centralisation. Above all, Mosley was

---

*Colin Jordan complained that Mosley's Union Movement ' is not and never has been a genuine racialist organization ' (*Combat*, Dec 1960). Mosley's comment on Colin Jordan: ' There is always something tragically comic in the spectacle of live dwarves posturing in the clothes of dead giants ' (*National European*, Aug 1965).

†Yockey apparently sent Mosley a copy of his monumental Spenglerian tome *Imperium* in the late 1940s. It was another variation on the theme of the coming destruction of the West at the hands of Asia as a result of an ' inner Culture-Disease ' planted by the Jews. Yockey saw Hitler's Third Reich as a ' premature ' Imperium and devoted his efforts to campaigning for a new one which would restore the supremacy of Western civilization. He died in prison in 1960.

only intermittently active.   Union Movement was never the centre of his life as the B.U. had been.   From 1946–50 he farmed in Wiltshire; after 1950 he was in England only for relatively short periods. From his first ' retirement ' in 1950 one can see the beginning of a painful struggle by a proud and opinionated man to disengage himself not only from the policies of the past but from the political methods of the past, which was not finally accomplished till 1966. Under these circumstances, and with the legacy of the past and the affluence of the present as additional handicaps, Union Movement never achieved the strength or impetus of the pre-war organisation. In 1964 one observer estimated 1500 active Mosley supporters and 10,000–15,000 sympathisers.[26] This would seem about right for the early 1960s when the Movement probably reached its peak. After Mosley's own retirement from the leadership it declined into what looks like a small society for the propagation of Mosley's memory.

An increasing part of Mosley's time was spent in propagating his European ideas abroad.   On his first European trip in 1949 – the Government had refused to return his passport before then – he had bought a house at Orsay, just outside Paris, appropriately named (though not by him) 'Temple de la Gloire'.   A palladian structure of great beauty, it was designed by the Madeleine's architect, Vignon, in commemoration of General Moreau's victory at Hohenlinden. Here Mosley lived increasingly from the 1950s onwards (there was an interlude in Ireland) learning to ' think and feel as a European '. A prophet without honour in his own country, his book *The Alternative* had given him a considerable audience among what the fascist intellectual Maurice Bardèche called ' these bands of lost soldiers who recognized each other in the murk of injustice and hatred '. Mosley's post-war efforts took him on the familiar neo-fascist trail to Franco's Spain, Perón's Argentina and Verwoerd's South Africa, as well as to Italy where a neo-fascist movement was established soon after the war.   He met Perón himself, Serrano Suñer, Franco's former foreign minister, Filipo Anfuso, Mussolini's last foreign minister; and he got to know Italian M.S.I. leaders like Giorgio Almirante,   Alwise Loridan and Ponce de León.   He came into contact with the more attractive survivors of the fascist generation: military heroes like Mussolini's rescuer Otto Skorzeny, the German air ace Ulrich Rudel (whose memoirs, with an introduction by Douglas Bader, were published by Mosley's publishing house), the Italian naval hero Prince Junio Valerio Borghese, and the Wehrmacht's *partizankrieg* expert Arthur Erhardt, later publisher of *Nation Europa*. He met S.S. survivors who were ' passionately European and entirely supported my advanced European ideas '[27] as well as First World War intellectuals like Ernst Jünger.   The quest for an alternative Europe took Mosley to a number of conferences in search of a common creed capable of uniting the various neo-fascist movements into a European-wide political force. In 1962, Mosley presented his ' alternative ' European programme to a meeting of neo-fascist leaders at Venice: a ' common government for purposes of foreign policy, defence, economic policy, finance and scientific development ', to be elected by a ' free vote of the whole people of Europe '; the economic leadership of such a government through a ' wage–price ' policy; negotiations for American and Russian military disengagement ' until mutual disarmament can be secured by the initiative of a European leadership ': division of Africa into black and white states. This 'Declaration of Venice' was initialled on 1 March by Mosley on behalf of Union Movement, Giovanni Lanfre and others on behalf of the Italian M.S.I., von Thadden on behalf of the German Reichspartei, and Jean Thiriart on behalf of Jeune-Europe (Belgium).[28] Once more one is sadly struck by the practical remoteness of all this from what was actually happening.

To clothe the European idea in flesh and blood, to create a body of European thought, was the ambitious aim of the *European*, a monthly ' journal of opposition ' which Mosley founded in March 1953, and which his wife Diana edited for the six years of its life. Mosley's aim of starting a forum of debate in which his position could be defended and attacked so that ' truth ' would emerge was only partially realised. Opponents steered well clear of the *European*, if indeed they even heard of it, so that such debate as took place was within fascist and neo-fascist circles of thought, revolving round the relative importance of nationalism and Europeanism, the practicability of syndicalism (the old left–right split in fascism), the importance of race, etc. There was no debate on economic policy. At no time since Mosley's Memorandum was subjected to Treasury examination in 1930 have his economic plans received searching scrutiny from professional economists or politicians – the penalty of his self-imposed isolation. One could argue that both sides have been losers from this deafening non-communication.

Despite these limitations, the *European* was an impressive achievement. Mosley himself wrote a number of fascinating essays under his own name and in addition contributed a regular commentary on world affairs under the pen name ' European '. Taken as a whole, these are his best polemical writings, clear and pungent, with shafts of wit, even humour, beginning to break through the underlying bitterness: Mosley is starting to mellow and look on human failings with a certain indulgence. The *European* also attracted some excellent and serious writers: Desmond Stewart, who had become a sympathiser as an Oxford undergraduate in 1947,[29] Ezra Pound, Roy Campbell, Henry Williamson, Hugo Charteris. There was a group of young writers interested in Pound: Alan Neame, Noel

Stock, Peter Whigham and Denis Goacher. They later gravitated to *Agenda*, a Poundian poetry-cum-criticism magazine. A. James Gregor, who has since made a name for himself in political science, wrote essays on syndicalism and race, notable for their extraordinary proliferation of footnotes. Foreign contributors included the French writers Jacques Brousse, Henri Gilbert and Michel Mohrt, as well as that echo from the past, Dr Otto Strasser. Robin Adair upheld the cause of *haute cuisine* in a regular feature, ' The European at Table '. As in all Mosley's enterprises, there was a strong family connection: Diana wrote book reviews, Nicholas contributed an attack on the heroic ideal which had so attracted him earlier, Alexander did some translations.

The grand theme of the *European* was Europe – its rationale, its structure, its tasks. But Mosley also provided a penetrating analysis of the problems facing Britain. Nor did he deviate from his conviction, first awakened in the First World War, that a new type of man, a new set of values in life and statesmanship, was required to secure the future out of the travails of the present. A few leading themes may be briefly discussed.

It was in the 1950s that Mosley spelt out more fully what he meant by ' European Socialism '. Assuming the viable area had been created, how was it to be organised? In the 1920s and 1930s he had advocated, in essence, an economy planned all the way down. In the 1950s he rejected this as too ' bureaucratic '. The final simplification of all his previous schemes was what he called a ' wage–price mechanism ' or, as it would now be called, a compulsory prices and incomes policy. As far as I know, Mosley was the first politician to make this the central instrument of economic management,* and certainly the first to think of applying it on a European scale. (The economist, Dr Thomas Balogh, was the intellectual pioneer of this approach round about this time: was Mosley influenced by him?)

Mosley first began talking of the need for a wage–price policy in 1955 as an alternative to Britain's Stop–Go policy. By 1957 he was seeing it as the ideal instrument for equating supply and demand in his ' viable ' European economy: indeed, the full potential of such an instrument could be realised only in a system independent of world markets.† He defined it as ' a definite, conscious and deliberate economic leadership by government ' in order to ' foresee, forestall, command and direct events rather than always play the role of their surprised and helpless victim '.[30] Naturally

---

*John Wheatley had advocated a planned incomes policy in 1926.
†In 1957 Mosley distinguished between the ' positive ' uses of the wage–price policy to secure even growth in a self-contained system and its ' negative ' form of a wage-price freeze to hold down costs in order to compete on world markets (*European*, Sept 1957).

it presupposed a European government. To put common market before common government, Mosley argued, was to negate all the real possibilities opened up by European union – a refrain later to be taken up by Servan-Schreiber.

What Mosley proposed, briefly, was that a European government should determine the main lines of reward in all the main European industries with the aim of (1) equalizing wages in competing industries to eliminate undercutting; (2) raising wages as science increased the power to produce; and (3) shaping 'the whole economy in the fashion desired'. The price side of the mechanism would be applied 'only where monopoly conditions prevailed'.[31]

This was to be one pillar of his 'European socialism'. The other was a 'synthesis of private enterprise and syndicalism' – an outgrowth of his earlier guild socialist and corporatist ideas. In his essay 'European Socialism' (1951) Mosley laid down three stages for the development of industrial ownership. A new industry ' is best launched, and brought to the point of established success, by a single creative individual ' who should be ' relieved of the main burdens of taxation ' and given every freedom and encouragement to use his drive and energy. At the second ' intermediate ' stage, when the industry had become ' too large for personal management but not yet ripe enough to be syndicalized ', it should be owned jointly by workers and shareholders (co-partnership). Finally, when industries become so big ' that they have passed beyond any kind of private management and are now controlled by officials of monopoly capitalism or by the officials of the state ' they would revert ' to the workers who would take the place of the shareholders'. The industry would become ' their industry and they can do what they will '. In this way Mosley hoped to reconcile private initiative with satisfaction of the quest for status which ' to an almost fantastic degree . . . rises above the question of mere reward '. In political terms, he was not unaware of the advantages of an attack which can ' roll up the left flank of labour by its syndicalism [and] the right flank of conservatism by its support for the creative individual . . . '. As always he liked to think of himself in the ' hard centre ' ready to take over the ' soft centre ' of a disintegrating liberalism.

What would Mosley's economy be like in practice? He argues that it retains the principles of a free economy, defined as a system in which ' men should be persuaded to do what has to be done by the inducement of reward ' rather than by coercion. But the point about a free economy is that ' what has to be done ' is determined by the market. In Mosley's system it would be determined by the Government, since he himself admits that under the ' wage–price mechanism ' it would be ' possible quite clearly to decide which industries continued and which ceased to exist.... The flow of labour could be controlled as directly as the flow of water by differential levels. ... It is the most potent instrument for shaping the future development of industry which could be devised.'[32] The nearest parallel to Mosley's scheme is, not surprisingly, a war economy in which the Government takes all the main decisions, but leaves industry in private hands. This must be modified, however, by the proposal for workers' ownership which certainly reflects Mosley's dislike of ' mandarin socialism ' and possibly his attempt to check the concentration of economic power in the hands of the State. This proposal, as well as a further one for the abolition of inherited wealth,[33] suggests a considerable redistribution of income to the working class. Indeed, this is also the aim of the ' wage–price ' mechanism, which seeks to raise consumption relative to saving. This in turn implies a fall in the share of the national income going to profits and therefore a fall in the rate of growth. The picture which emerges is that of a rather sluggish, high-consumption society, with a small, fast-growing sector of advanced technology created and run by an élite of creative entrepreneurs: a modern parallel, and at a much higher level of affluence, to a seventeenth century mercantilist economy. It is an intriguing idea.

Mosley's antagonism to international capitalism was not just economic, but political. He believed it produced conflict, not harmony, creating vested interests in far-away countries which inevitably dragged governments into ' foreign quarrels ' which were none of their business. Thus the essential condition of peace was an agreed division of economic and political interests between potential rivals. The key to Mosley's plan for a settlement with Russia was contained in this 1950 phrase ' hold Europe; leave Asia '. He had long believed communism was an Asiatic creed: its future plainly lay in Asia, not in Europe. Thus he wanted Europe and America to renounce any political, military or economic interest in Asia. ' It is reasonable to assume ', he wrote in 1958, ' that the American citizen and taxpayer will not wish American armies to go plunging for ever about the mainland of Asia in order to prevent by force the spread of the communist doctrine among Eastern peoples.'[34] As always, he was premature. Even more striking was his insistence that Western leaders should engage Russian leaders in continual dialogue and debate with the dual object of winning a durable peace and winning the battle for the soul of the West. He was constantly urging them to exploit creatively the opportunities opened by Russia's disarmament proposals. In particular he was irked by the West's refusal to respond to Khruschev's many-times-repeated offer to withdraw Russian troops from the satellite countries if the United States withdrew theirs from Western Europe: in his view a golden opportunity for independence which found the Europeans

unready for emancipation from the American–Russian tutelage.*
In 1957 he complained that:

> no proposals of the Russians are now ever taken seriously.
> This journal, on the other hand, has urged throughout that
> every Russian proposal should be taken with deadly serious-
> ness and subjected to the test of a definite method. A
> Russian *démarche* should immediately be debated in public
> in the full glare of world publicity, and tested with a relentless
> cross-examination until its clear meaning is revealed. It
> would then be exposed as a piece of propaganda nonsense
> which could do the Soviet cause no good, or would be estab-
> lished as a definite offer from which the Soviets would find it
> very difficult to retreat without loss of prestige and damage to
> the local Communist Parties of the world. The West would
> then either score a propaganda success or register a solid
> advance towards peace, disarmament and the real security
> we seek.

' Continual athleticism of mind and spirit ' was needed in the
' long wrestle with the Soviets to win the peace and a commanding
influence in the minds of men '.[35]

Similarly, Mosley urged a British withdrawal from the Middle
East. His policy of holding Europe, leaving Asia, ' automatically
eliminates exhausting commitments like the Suez Canal ', he wrote
early in 1954. It is not clear where the Arab world fitted into
Mosley's ' blocs '. It was never intended as part of his Europe-
Africa system. On the other hand, the Arabs were ' a sister people
. . . natural allies of the West in the struggle for independence
against Communism '. Thus he was particularly disenchanted by
the West's alienation of the Arabs by its support of Israel, both at
Suez and after. When the Americans went into the Lebanon in
1958, and the British followed into Jordan, he was particularly out-
spoken. ' Why – what for?' he asked. ' Is there any answer,
except that these countries are very close to Israel – and it might be
awkward for Israel if they fell into the wrong hands? The excuse

---

*Khruschev in May 1955 proposed the liquidation of all foreign bases in Europe.
He was quoted by *The Times* of 19 November 1956 as saying: ' If you withdraw
your troops from Germany, France and Britain – I am speaking of American
troops – we will not stay one day in Poland, Hungary and Rumania.' Coral
Bell and Adam Ulam are sceptical of any real possibility of reaching agreement
with the Soviets after 1954, though neither goes as far as Walter Laqueur in dismissing Russian proposals as ' mere propaganda moves '. The decisive obstacle
to American–Soviet disengagement was the fear of Germany – on both sides of
the Iron Curtain. It is hard to judge how much progress could have been made
with the Russian proposals because the Americans never took them up, and
there was no ' Europe ' to take them up.

given is that we are pledged to defend them from aggression. But what shred of evidence exists that we are defending these foreign governments against anything except a rising of their own peoples?' Far from his attitude being ' anti-semitic ' Mosley said that ' we would not permit the Arabs to walk into Palestine and cut two million Jewish throats '. But short of that the British Government ' should look after Britain and let the Jews look after themselves '.[36] Mosley rejected root and branch the idea of a new Holy Alliance of conservative powers rushing in to suppress revolution wherever it reared its ugly head – an attitude that sustained his adamant opposition to the Vietnam war.

Many of Mosley's ideas have come to pass not because President Nixon and Dr Henry Kissinger read his writings but because he heard the ' hoof beat of history '. His dream of a united Europe yet remains to be realised. He frequently and eloquently expressed his belief in Europe's right to independence and greatness. Comparing Europe to America and Russia he asked: ' Can it really be denied that we are larger in numbers, at least the equal in science and technique, at least the equal in energy, and possibly firmer in character because we have lived longer and done more? And if so, can anyone explain with clear reason why we should cling to America and shiver in fear of Russia without ever a serious thought of exerting the giant strength of Europe, first to restore the balance of the world and then to lead it to a new level of security and happiness? '[37] He traced the trouble to the ' fear of living with the Germans. . . . That fear inhibits the making of Europe and compels us to live as divided dependants of America '.[38] Yet ' a Germany integrated with Europe is not a menace but a source of strength by any standards, except those of a man with a pathological disposition towards the constitutionally feeble '.[39] Mosley's desire to fling away the American crutch never betrayed him into the shrill anti-Americanism of certain sections of the Left or of Gaullism. America had restored Europe in an act of ' unparalleled generosity '. Such an act alone ruled out mean feelings.[40] Nevertheless, he keenly felt the humiliation of dependence. ' Are we fallen so low that the Europe of Caesar, of Frederick, of Bonaparte and Nelson cannot even lift a finger . . . unless the word of command is given in an American accent?'[41] It was ' the division of Europe alone which stops all good things '.

Mosley felt even more keenly the humiliation of Britain's accelerating decline. The most scornful language in the *European* is reserved for the failings of British statesmanship; particularly for its refusal to ' enter fully and completely into European life '. ' The excuse was that such participation . . . would jeopardise the Commonwealth. The result is a scattered and divided Commonwealth protected from Soviet pressure by special arrangements with

America from which Britain is excluded' (August 1954). He was no more tolerant of the other failures of declining empire. The only reason for the British decision to hold Cyprus was that they had always been in the Mediterranean. ' The chicken with its head cut off makes the familiar movements long after the body has ceased to live. We need new thoughts as a preliminary to new life' (November 1955).

Nor were domestic prospects any brighter. Under the régime of the ' runaway Butler ' Britain had ' inflated itself into a crisis before the world depression had even begun ' like ' the man who was billed for a championship fight but got so drunk that he looks like falling on his face before the fight begins' (September 1955). The Government had neither the ' mind nor the will ' to devise a ' wage and salary policy' (December 1955). Instead they ' inflated because they had no courage; they now deflate because they have no ideas' (April 1956). The British taxation system was hopeless: ' a premium is placed on inability and a penalty on ability ' (March 1956). Labour's policy only made things worse. Of Bevan, Mosley wrote, ' He wants to intensify the policy of the welfare state until nature itself is denied. His ambition is always to make two false teeth appear when only one tooth grew before' (May 1953). Yet, while refusing to put its own affairs in order, Britain continued to act like a great power on borrowed money: ' The old lady cannot forever cadge enough with one hand to cover the largesse she scatters with the other in order to create the present illusion of past grandeur. . . . The basic figures are so simple that even a Tory can add them up; they mean smash -- it is only a matter of time' (July 1957). Mosley's most comprehensive assessment of Britain's postwar decline was given in the last issue of *European* (February 1959) in a telling comparison with Germany:

> Germany has concentrated on doing possible things which are within its strength, and Britain has tried to do impossible things which are quite beyond its individual strength. Germany has used the immense energy of a highly gifted and very hard working people in a maximum productive effort at highly competitive prices which have piled up a very large surplus in its balance of payments. Britain has dissipated the effort of the British people in trying to support at the same time a welfare state which is a heavier proportionate burden than that of America; backward black colonies which perhaps used to be exploited by us . . . but now very thoroughly exploit us by demanding large sums in respect of sterling balances or by way of fresh loans to finance a development more rapid than they can assimilate; a military burden which is supposed to make an overtaxed

island an effective competitor with America and Russia; and finally a currency which is not only responsible for all this but for financing more than half the world's trade. A year's reading of all the profoundest obfuscations of the economists will not make the causes of our present situation any clearer than a short consideration of those salient and obvious facts.

' A great country does not fall so far and so fast without defeat in war ', Mosley concluded, ' unless a deep moral rot has first occurred; the immense mistakes of recent policy could not have happened in a society which was free from an organic disease of the mind and spirit. '[42]

The fault, as always, Mosley located in the British ruling class. ' When Destiny calls for a cohort of Caesars, who have been trained beyond personal ambition in a Platonic Academy, "Democracy" inevitably produces a gaggle of Grocks, ' he had declared loftily in *The Alternative*. The age required a new order of ' men of creative realism '. How were they to be produced? Youth was definitely not the answer, Mosley decided, as he approached his sixtieth year. Resisting the clamour for the resignation of the eighty-year-old Winston Churchill he wrote in a light vein, ' It is rumoured that he sometimes dozes a little in Cabinet; but who would not go to sleep while some of them were talking? Stalin, during the early days of windy discussions in revolutionary committees, used to lie down and sleep on the kitchen table till the comrades had blown off steam . . . his slumbers were not the sign of exhaustion but of revolutionary realism. His colleagues may have reason to congratulate themselves that Sir Winston is not like Lord Melbourne, who grew so wakeful in his old age, that he could not even sleep in Cabinet. It may be that some men of that age can work less than formerly; but as the late J. L. Garvin said . . . "six hours of [Lloyd George] are worth more than sixteen hours a day of any of the others".'[43] More seriously, Mosley wrote in his autobiography: ' The human tragedy is that we all die just as we are acquiring a little sense ', an idea of Shaw whose *Back to Methuselah* was a plea for men to live longer and a faith that ultimately they would do so by a simple act of will.

If longevity was, for the vital, the only secure guarantee of wisdom, a certain maturity might nevertheless be achieved by the right way of life which would in turn create the right attitude to life. Mosley never set down his thoughts on the right preparation or training for a statesman in any systematic way, vitally important though he believed that to be. If he had any general philosophy of development it was the belief that in the individual, as in society, growth is brought about by a clash of opposites. The condition

for individual development was the full expression of *all* the individual's contradictory powers: through the clash between them
a balanced character would ultimately be achieved. This is
why he was so attracted to the Greek notion that *every* power in
nature had its tutelary deity. Mosley based his philosophy of
life to a large extent on his own nature, which characteristically
alternated between pleasure and duty, reflection and action. He
sought to transcend the dichotomy between the puritan and the
libertine, the thinker and the doer, by the concept of the athlete;
someone who has drunk deeply of life, but who imposes upon himself
a voluntary discipline for a definite purpose, and thus creates his
own character to fulfil his destiny. The statesman, according to
Mosley, should be like the athlete who has trained himself to ' peak '
at the right moment. What Mosley is arguing is that the statesman should have served his apprenticeship in many varied life
situations, not just locked up in politics, Whitehall, business or the
universities: doubtless a truism, but one which the specialisation
of modern life makes increasingly elusive.

The highest statesmen had thus come to possess a passionate
' will to achievement ' in which high purpose was combined with
complete realism in action and execution. British statesmanship
on the contrary had recently exhibited the reverse quality of a
moral hysteria in which action could take place at all only under
the impact of temporary passion, which was bound to deflect it
from the true purposes of action. The classic examples in Mosley's
life were Neville Chamberlain's avalanche of guarantees to eastern
Europe in March–April 1939, and Eden's ' hysterical stampede '
into Suez in 1956. Mosley's comment on the latter might apply
just as well to the former: ' Nothing was thought out in advance.
Every move was the result not of plan but of impulse. '[44]

But the trouble went even deeper. Pondering the disparity
between recent British conduct in war and peace, Mosley wrote:
' It becomes more and more remarkable that our present governing class can take nothing seriously except a war; they can blow
up anything, but build nothing.' Could it be that democracy
could tolerate greatness only to rescue it from the disasters of
mediocrity, never to lead it to high achievement? In *The Alternative* Mosley referred to Britain as the ' nation with the Oedipus
Complex ' by which he meant the instinctive urge to strike down
anyone who seemed capable of leading it, except in war. This
problem was posed in acute form by the career of Churchill.

To Mosley, Churchill is the supreme British example of the
great man who can under modern conditions be let loose only to
destroy, never to create. The war he saw as Churchill's Faustian
pact with Mephistopheles. ' Thus alone did he disarm the life-
long prejudice of Conservative leaders against him; those who

covered him with vile and lying abuse in his striving for constructive achievement became his fawning sycophants when he resigned himself to be the instrument of catastrophe. . . .' For Churchill's bargain with Mephistopheles was not, in Mosley's view, ennobled by a worthy purpose. He was a hero in the classic Greek sense: ' If you decide to be heroic, in terms of your own character, it does not matter what it is about; by being brave you become a hero. . . .' But ' it matters terribly to other people, for you may, in the heroic mood, either take life or save it, be an instrument of the highest good or the deepest evil. . . . Churchill could express the heroic mood in a drive to fatality, but he could not guide and direct it to high achievement. '[45]

Consideration of the Churchill phenomenon brought Mosley to the question posed by Nietzsche: what were the social conditions for the nurture and creative expression of genius? His answer was the same as Nietzsche's: breaking the hold of egalitarianism, the belief that all men were created equal and should be treated alike. Mosley is an unabashed élitist. His whole thesis of politics was simply that the existing élites were decadent and would have to be replaced by new ones.

The chief problem as he saw it was to combine the claims of the mass with the encouragement of genius in the individual: only in this way could the highest aim of his European system – ' a civilisation of continuing creation and ever unfolding beauty ' – be secured. All his plans have had the dual character of seeking to improve the conditions of the majority while encouraging the truly outstanding person to express what is in him. No society, Mosley believed, which accepted the principle of equality could do justice to the need for ' continuing creation '; not because outstanding people necessarily required privileged treatment as an incentive to create, but because any society which on principle denies their claim to privileged treatment has come to deny the need for the outstanding; as Mosley would see it, has come to lose its evolutionary drive to ' higher forms '.

Mosley's answer to equality, therefore, was function. In *The Alternative* he elaborated on the classic Greek notion of justice as the ' completion ' with which every section of the community ' expresses its particular virtue in it and fulfils its specific function ' and quoted Aristotle to the effect that nothing is more unjust than to ' treat unequals equally '.[46] These functions were not to be confused with hereditary classes. There must be equal opportunities for all in the State of the future. But, once this opportunity had been given, the outstanding must in turn be given their head.

The relationship between this concept of acknowledging outstanding achievement and creating a civilization of higher forms is clear. Outstanding men and women are themselves ' higher forms ': it was this aspect of Mosley's doctrine which made him attractive to Colin Wilson, author of *The Outsider*, and philosopher of evolutionary existentialism. ' He is far and away the most intelligent politician I have ever met,' Wilson wrote of Mosley in 1959,[47] a comment which no doubt contributed to Wilson's rapid loss of esteem with the literary establishment. Outstanding persons also served as examples to mankind on its upward ascent: they revealed men as they might become. Desmond Stewart wrote: ' It is not arrogance, fascism, boy-scoutism, snobbery . . . to assert that there are men and women more beautiful, more valorous and more strong than the rest of us, and that to admire such people is beneficial for ourselves and for society. . . . The admiration of the noble draws us upwards. '[48] Finally, higher types were the instruments bringing higher life into existence. Mosley never believed that the old order of politicians were or could be such instruments. In 1956 he wrote ' the rhythm of this age is profoundly different ' from that of the pre-1914 world ' or else our whole thesis of present existence is wrong. If this is a period which can be fitted by these men and these measures we shall be greatly mistaken. '[49] He concluded in 1972: ' To meet the social dangers of our age it will be necessary again to evoke the heroic mood; not for the universal destruction which war now threatens, but at last for the high purpose of creative peace. '[50]

Chapter 27

A New Beginning?

IN A revealing interview in 1959, Mosley described himself as 'what Goethe called the educated soldier – that is, a man capable equally of reflection and action. In my case I tend to submerge myself completely in either quality. In action, all my reflective qualities disappear. In reflection, I withdraw entirely and the thought of then having to return to action is highly disagreeable. I have to make myself do it each time.'[1] Mosley's life, in fact, reveals two kinds of oscillations – between grass-roots and élite politics, and between reflection and action. The first half of the 1950s had been a period of reflection: basically, the elaboration of the European Idea, and its relationship to the problems of the economy, peace and social justice. The constructive task of the *European* was essentially fulfilled by 1956 though it survived till the beginning of 1959. Already he was writing to Nicholas in 1955, ' I have a feeling that before long, the rush may begin again, though I am usually premature. But, when it does, all charm of life flies, as well as all sense! – for a long season. ' On 20 March 1956 he addressed his first major public meeting in five years at Kensington Town Hall: 600 people turned up. It was almost back to old times with 1500 at the Manchester Free Trade Hall in November 1956. A *Daily Telegraph* reporter wrote after a Finsbury Town Hall meeting: ' But after all these years I thought some of the fizz might have gone out of him. Not a bit of it. Alone, he held a packed proletarian audience – only a few velvet collars – for 75 minutes, pulverising each party in turn.' A series of meetings in London, Birmingham and Coventry completed the autumn speaking-tour, with the Suez crisis giving it an immediate focus. There was a university meeting at Cambridge and a debate at the Oxford Union under the presidency of Brian Walden (now Labour M.P. for All Saints, Birmingham) the following year. There were the usual protests: in Birmingham a fierce scuffle developed when a Union Movement lorry with the slogan ' Mosley stands for Workers Ownership ' was attacked by strikers.[2] In the same period Union Movement gained respectable votes in municipal elections in Shoreditch and the old Mosley stamping-ground in East London.

Why Mosley should have felt that the hour of action was fast approaching in the Britain of the 1950s basking in the first sunshine of the affluent society is a little difficult to understand. Al-

ways sensitive to impending collapse, he may have noted the first
faint rumblings of trouble in the Eden administration of the mid-
1950s.[3]   Perhaps he felt that ten years without major crisis was
about as long as capitalism could manage.   Perhaps he was just
itching to get back into the fray.

He returned at an opportune moment.   Suez and Hungary
offered temporary excitements; but it is clear in retrospect that
what set Union Movement up in business again in a small way
was coloured immigration, which became an important issue in
fringe politics in the mid-1950s.   It was in this period that the first
substantial immigration of Jamaicans to Britain started; and for
a number of years Union Movement, with the idiosyncratic
exception of Cyril Osborne, the M.P. for Louth, had the field
virtually to itself in drawing attention to this phenomenon, and
the social tensions inherent in it, which did not really hit the public
and the political system till the celebrated Notting Hill race riots
of September 1958.

Until 1960 coloured immigration into England was almost
entirely from the West Indies.   It was caused by the acute labour
shortage of a full-employment economy which led employers
actively to recruit immigrant labour.   This was a familiar pattern
all over Europe.   However, there was an important difference
in England's case.   Foreign immigration for purposes of work
and/or settlement was severely restricted by the Aliens Act, passed
in 1905; this restriction did not, however, apply to Commonwealth citizens who entered as British subjects, just as any other
British subjects returning to their country.   High unemployment
in the West Indies, consequent, so Mosley always claimed, on the
Labour Government's Black Pact with Cuba in 1951 under which
Britain undertook to switch sizeable purchases of sugar from the
British West Indies to Cuba, led many Jamaicans to exercise their
rights to live and work in Britain and bring in their families as well.[4]
Once it started to be challenged, this Open Door policy in reverse
acquired powerful supporters.   The pro-immigration lobby united
economic liberals inside and outside the Government who regarded
national frontiers as archaic obstacles to economic integration with
internationalists who regarded them as obstacles to the brotherhood of man.[5]   There was the powerful Labour Party commitment to the Commonwealth, partly the expression of its belief
in multiracialism, partly the result of what Paul Foot calls an
' inverted chauvinism ' which saw Commonwealth citizens as
Britain's ' children ',[6] partly the result of deep guilt-feelings
about empire.   The strength of this establishment sentiment was
sufficient to hold up legislation to control the inflow of immigrants
till 1962, and to weaken the Act then passed by omitting any
control on the entry of dependants.   It was sufficient throughout

the 1950s and most of the 1960s to brand as wicked racialists any who, like Mosley or Enoch Powell, attempted to make immigration a political issue, despite the opinion-poll evidence of continuing majority opposition to coloured immigration from the late 1950s onwards. (The leaderships of all three parties were determined to keep immigration ' out of politics '.)   In 1968 a further measure was passed by the Labour Government to check the threatened arrival of Kenyan Asians who had previously been granted the option of British nationality; it was not till 1971 that the entry of Commonwealth citizens was put on a similar footing to that of ' aliens ' in a final symbolic winding-up of empire.   By this time, Britain had absorbed at least one million coloured immigrants in twenty years.   The White Man's Burden, which had never been more than a phrase in Britain's period of greatness, became a reality in its period of decline.   But, whether one regards the result as progress or nemesis, most people today would agree that it was both a mistake and an injustice to allow the principle of *laissez-faire* to govern mass migrations of people in the middle of the twentieth century: an injustice both to the immigrants and to the ' natives ' in this strange reversal of history.

Mosley's attack on coloured immigration was more principled than his attack on Jews in the 1930s.   For one thing, it was, in the main, an attack on immigration, not on immigrants.   The Union Movement pamphlet, *The Coloured Invasion*, distributed at the time of the Notting Hill riots of 1958, declared: ' Most coloured immigrants are decent folk.   They are victims of a vicious system which they cannot understand.'   The ' vicious system ' was the exploitation of cheap labour in the interests of capitalism – the economic underpinning of the idealistic vision of multiracialism. From 1929 when as a minister he carried through Parliament provisions against the exploitation of native labour, through the 1930s when he protested against capitalist exploitation of natives in South Africa, to the Mosley–Pirow proposals of the 1940s with their rejection of ' keeping the Negro within white territory as sweated labour ', Mosley has consistently repudiated the capitalist view of blacks, coloureds (not to mention indigenous whites) as cheap labour to lower production costs and maximise efficiency. It was one strand in his rejection of the whole capitalist philosophy of economic integration, which he invariably regarded as a euphemism for keeping up profits by lowering the price of labour. Thus, in economic terms, Mosley's objection to importing labour was exactly the same as his objection to exporting capital: both were designed to undercut high wage-systems, and both cut across his aim of making Britain part of a high-wage European system. He saw Labour's support for coloured immigration and multiracialism as yet another instance of the way in which international socialism was invariably to be found on the side of the most predatory forces of international capitalism.

However, there is no doubt that Mosley rejected the ideal of multiracialism as well as the economic lever by which it was being realised, the attempt to replace the ' bright-hued differences of nature's vital plan ' with the ' dull grey amalgam of contemporary decadence ' as he put it in 1965.   It would be wrong to describe his position as racialist, though he did make use of genetic arguments from time to time, particularly those of the Oxford biologist, C. D. Darlington, against ' wide outcrosses '.[7] His preferred notion was that indiscriminate intermingling was contrary to ' nature ' – a formulation which conveniently obscured, by straddling both positions, the old argument between genetic and social conditioning.   Although Mosley recognised that science was forcing communities into ever-larger aggregations, he firmly believed that the way forward was through a gradual extension of kinship to ethnically and culturally related groups, not through arbitrary ' outcrosses ' with quite different peoples: the legal fiction that Europeans were ' aliens ' while Asians and Africans were British struck him in particular as a dangerous piece of nonsense with disastrous implications for Britain's future.   Equally he now disagrees with the tendency to make foreigners of the British-descended peoples in the former Dominions.

Mosley declared himself against coloured immigration before any real question of exploiting the issue arose – before there was a problem.   In a statement issued on 27 February 1952 Mosley defined his attitude to the thin initial trickle of West Indian immigration.   ' I have already stated ', he wrote, ' that I am strongly against any offensive abuse of Negroes. '   Britain must live with them ' as friendly neighbours '.   But this did not mean an ' admixture of races '.   It meant ' apartheid ', defined as the separation of black and white peoples.   Such was his policy in Africa. The same principles must apply to Britain.   ' Therefore we must prevent the residence of Negroes in Britain. '   All European countries applied rules of this sort to stop foreigners from residing and working in their countries without special permission.   These rules must be applied to Britain.   Negroes would be allowed in for the purpose of study and as visitors or tourists.   The ' small numbers ' already resident would not be affected.   ' We do not want bad blood made, but we will not have precisely the conditions created in Britain which we are out to prevent in Africa. It is no solution of the problem to exchange trouble in Africa for trouble in England. '   The policy at this point involved no deportation.   It meant simply enacting in 1952 the laws which were brought in ten years later in response to public pressure, after the

colour problem had been created. Six years later the policy was:
(1) restriction of immigration to students; (2) guaranteed markets
for all the sugar, fruit and tobacco the West Indies could supply,
plus massive injections of capital into West Indian housing and
local industry; and (3) wider powers to deport immigrants convicted of offences.[8] West Indians, Mosley declared at Trafalgar
Square in 1958, would ' rather be back in the sunshine than in the
November fogs of London '. A West Indian in the audience
expressed his enthusiastic agreement. ' That's right, boss. You
buy our sugar and I'll take the sunshine. '[9]

By 1959, in preparation for his fight at North Kensington,
Mosley developed for the first time the policy of repatriating the
West Indians ' with fares paid . . . to good jobs with good wages '.[10]
' Jamaica for the Jamaicans and Britain for the British. I say let
the Jamaicans have their country back – and let us have ours. '[11]
It was much less clear how Mosley was going to get the Asians
back to Asia.* In the late 1960s Union Movement became
interested in the possibility of resettling large numbers of
immigrants, both West Indian and Asian, in the South American
state of Guyana, which already had a population of Asians
and West Indians, and whose black government seemed at any
rate receptive to the idea of large-scale West Indian resettle-
ment.[12]

Although Mosley has never renounced his plan for the compulsory repatriation of most coloured immigrants, his attitude
gradually mellowed. In 1965 he appeared at a press conference
with a Nigerian bomber pilot and an Indian Oxford graduate
to launch an Associate Movement of coloured people ' who had
expressed their agreement and desire to co-operate with Union
Movement's constructive policy for the return of post-war immigrants to their homelands '.[13] Little more was heard of this
curious venture. ' Cases of hardship or of special service to
Britain would naturally be treated in humane, friendly and appreciative fashion ', Mosley wrote at the same time, adding ' we
would even hope to persuade some to stay who perform such
service '. At the height of the civil rights campaign in America,
Mosley was quick to spot that the goals of white liberals and many
black Americans were not identical. In 1963 he addressed him-

*Repatriation of Asians was apparently linked to his policy of using European
agricultural surpluses to end famine in Asia (*National European*, May 1965). It
is important to note, though, that when Mosley developed his repatriation
proposals in the late 1950s the immigrant population was largely West Indian.
According to Home Office estimates quoted by Paul Foot, *Immigration and
Race in British Politics* (1965) p. 126, net Commonwealth immigration between
1953 and 1959 broke down as follows: 134,000 from the West Indies, 27,300
from India and 14,560 from Pakistan.

self to Black America in the following terms:

> In conditions where we cannot have separate countries, let
> us have separate communities.   In America you want ' civil
> rights ': if that means equal voting rights, equal education
> with separate teaching, equal right to work and pay ac-
> cording to qualification and skill – the answer is, yes cer-
> tainly.   But if you mean the right to force your way into
> white schools, homes and clubs which do not want you,
> to impose your presence on white communities that do not
> want you, the answer is no.   Conversely we whites will not
> force our way into your communities of which your new
> negro intellectuals will teach you to be equally proud and
> even jealous.   In public life, in factory and street, often in
> sport and play we will work and live in friendship side by
> side.   In private life with children and in the home, no
> man has right to impose his presence on another.   We must
> each develop our community and be proud of it.

It is not yet clear that he, much less his followers, would accept this
as a possible model for community relations in Britain.

It was not so much the enunciation of this policy as the use
Mosley made of the colour issue in sensitive areas of north London
and elsewhere in the 1950s that raised the cry that he was stirring
up racial hatred.   In August 1958, race rioting broke out in
Nottingham.   On 24 August of that year came the famous Notting
Hill incident in London as a result of which nine ' Teddy
boys ' were given exemplary sentences of four years each by Mr
Justice Salmon for ' nigger bashing '.   In a tense situation, Jeffrey
Hamm, the Union Movement's secretary, made a speech on
immigration outside Latimer Road underground station on 2
September.   Mosley was abroad at the time, but the T.U.C.
accused him of ' fanning the flames of racial violence '.   In fact,
according to *The Times* report of 3 September, Hamm said ' nothing that could be construed as an appeal to violence, and limited
himself to repeating that all immigration should be stopped '.
In an analysis of the situation in Notting Hill, *The Times* of 8
September concluded that ' although the riots appear to be to
the advantage of the [Union] movement there is no evidence
that the party are the cause of them. . . . Their propaganda . . . is
directed towards diverting racial hatred to anti-Government
feeling rather than inciting violence. '   Hamm himself claimed
that he had tried to produce a calming effect.   At the same time,
he refused to condemn the Teddy boys who, he said, ' were the
target of those who had grown old too early and have forgotten
or prefer to forget the wild indiscretions of their own youth '.
With his blazing eyes and uncompromising statements, Hamm

evidently did not strike the reporters who interviewed him as a calming influence.[14]

Youths in 'Teddy boy' clothes and hairstyles (including Mosley's own two teenage sons, Alexander and Max) had for some time been prominent on Union Movement occasions. Mosley characteristically sprang to the defence of the Teds as 'fine types'. The Teddy movement, he wrote, 'is vital and, in comparison with many of its critics, also virile, which is what youth should be'. Teddy boy leaders often had 'high intelligence'. Their reactions 'are mostly the normal, healthy reactions of vigorous young men' to the 'corrupt and finally destructive values of a rotten society'. Their best place was 'in a serious political movement . . . determined to secure . . . revolutionary changes . . . by . . . legal and constitutional means'.[15] This was by no means the general opinion at the time, though in retrospect it can be seen that sensationalist media unthinkingly dubbed all Teddy boys as 'thugs' in much the same way as the label was indiscriminately applied to all fascists in the 1930s.[16] It was far from being welcome to Mosley's own intellectual admirers. The events of Notting Hill revealed a split in Union Movement which has always haunted Mosley's political career, between those who, in *The Times*'s words, 'seem to have a genuine desire to see his policies instituted . . .' and those who 'like fighting Communists and painting slogans on railway bridges'.[17]

To the intellectuals attracted by his European idealism and his doctrine of the Hero, Mosley suddenly became a Hero, if not with feet of clay, at least with feet planted in some pretty unappetising soil. The subject matter of the *European*, all the way down to Robin Adair's fastidious cuisine, appeared to have little enough in common with Teddy boys bashing black men. A Sartre might solve the problem of commitment by aligning himself with the evolutionary force of the proletariat: but not all Mosley's eloquence on the theme of Nature's renewal could persuade intellectuals that the life-force was embodied in the long drapes of the lumpenproletarian Teds. 'But *why* allow his followers to use these methods?' asked Colin Wilson in 1959. 'It seems to me not only a bad thing to do, but from the political standpoint, silly and incompetent. In many ways, Mosley shows a disturbing lack of insight into his own time. . . .'[18] From Mosley's son Nicholas came a cry of anguish:

> I have such an admiration for what you write and say, that I cannot bear to see the whole structure of thought and prophecy seeming to be led towards the ditch by exactly the same blind force that ruined and destroyed it before the war. I sometimes complain that history repeats itself, yet I am

bewildered that it can do so in this immediate and despairing way.[19]

The events of 1958 marked Nicholas' final disillusionment with his father's politics, indeed with all revolutionary political action. ' I see clearly ', he wrote many years after, ' that while the right hand dealt with grandiose ideas and glory, the left hand let the rat out of the sewer. '[20]   This is perhaps unfair.   But Mosley had got himself into his usual impossible position.   The only way he could get the publicity needed to give him a fresh political start was by using an issue like immigration; but it was publicity of a kind likely to discredit him even further in the minds of all ' reason-able ' men.   Thus Mosley was held fast in his self-inflicted embrace with the Establishment's outcasts; while the larger European policies which might have attracted the reputable people went un-read and unheard.   This was his basic political dilemma to which he only started to face up in the mid-1960s.

More immediately Mosley tried to re-enter Parliament for the first time since 1931, as Union Movement candidate for North Kensington in the 1959 general election, no doubt to prove, as in the East End in 1936, that he had a political following and therefore a right to exist in an area where he was accused simply of stirring up trouble.   At his adoption meeting in Argyll Hall on 6 April 1959, he expounded his plans before an enthusiastic audience of about 600.   ' His point by point analysis of how Britain could solve its economic difficulties by pulling out of world markets and uniting a Europe of 300 million people and using Africa as the source of raw materials and as a market for manufactured goods was enthused over by a section of teenage cheerleaders who looked the most un-likely to understand what it was all about, ' sourly noted one local correspondent.[21]   ' If you elect Mosley the whole world will sit up and take notice, ' the Union Movement challenged North Kensington's electors, without much exaggeration.[22]

Mosley campaigned on his full programme, but with special emphasis on the housing problem, which was acute, on coloured immigration into the area, and the connection between the two. Union Movement publicity made great play with the ' savage sentences ' passed on the nine Teddy boys the previous autumn, pointing out with pride how it had organised petitions for their reduction.   It claimed that when Mosley visited derelict houses and complained the Council rapidly arranged repairs or moved tenants to better quarters.   The floating Irish population was wooed as usual with appeals to Mosley's record in 1920, and with his policy for uniting Ireland, and attacks on ' gerrymandering ' and imprisonment without trial in Northern Ireland.[23]   This espousal of the main planks in the subsequent Ulster Civil Rights

Movement was not just tactical: there were many Irish and Catholics in Union Movement, as in the pre-war B.U.F. Jeffrey Hamm was an ardent advocate of Irish unification; and the Irish run like a bright thread through Mosley's chequered career. Mosley himself campaigned vigorously, chiefly from a truck with a powerful amplification system and two tall trumpets, stepping up his rate of out-of-door meetings to four a day in the actual campaign. ' A neat, impressive figure, despite a slight stoop, and a frozen, vulpine smile, Sir Oswald still radiated some of the aura of a major political personality,' wrote Keith Kyle. 'He possessed a mellifluous flow of language and, when interrupted, an instantaneous command of invective.'[24]

The same writer notes that Mosley's speeches incorporated a ' high road ' and a ' low road '. The high road included advocating ' compulsory free passage back to the West Indies for the immigrants, combined with heavy British investment to build up local West Indian employment and the purchase of all British sugar from Jamaica '. The low road led, by contrast, ' through sordid tales of sexual offences by coloured men, spiced with such nasty remarks as that West Indians provided cheap labour because they could at a pinch live off a tin of Kit-E-Kat a day '. Mosley's more ardent listeners, according to Kyle, consisted of ' wizened old men, wan spinsters, and duck-tailed teddy boys . . . intrigued to hear a man of education and breeding clothe in fancy words their fouler thoughts '. Though there is evidently some truth in this picture, it is distorting in a subtle and characteristic way, partly by putting too much weight on a platform joke (Kit-E-Kat), but much more seriously by ignoring any possible effect of Mosley's ' high line' which, apart from its European idealism, must have been an education in itself in economics and world affairs.*

*Sir Oswald Mosley has commented as follows:
In North Kensington when the coloured immigration problem was still easily remediable, I stood for a constructive and humane policy, was invariably polite to their questioners, and entered their houses when invited for reasonable discussion with their intelligent leaders. However, during the passages in speeches to which exception is taken, I certainly gave illustration of events which had already occurred when adolescents were uprooted and thrown into a foreign land with a foreign moral climate. The threefold increase in violent crimes during the last decade to which they have certainly contributed their quota of particular offences would appear to justify such warnings to the mass of the British people in the early stages of that development. I always emphasise, as I did again recently and briefly on British television, that when coloured immigrants are here they should be treated with the utmost courtesy and kindness. What is utterly wrong is to have no constructive solution but to rely on a mixture of bullying and bribery to drive them out. Much more could be said about what you call my high road and my low road in politics. It is perfectly true that I have always maintained in real politics a man must be equally at home at lunch

However, not all the eloquence at Mosley's command could persuade the electors of North Kensington to return him to Parliament.   On the basis of a pre-election canvass he persuaded himself that he would get a third of the votes and thus scrape home against the three other contenders.   In fact, he got 2821 or eight per cent of the votes cast and lost his deposit for the first time in his life.*   It was a tremendous shock and humiliation.   He could not believe that the British people had rejected him and asked the High Court to order an inspection of the ballot papers.   His supporters talked of a ' frame-up ' to stop him getting back into Parliament.   The case collapsed through lack of evidence.   Gradually the shock wore off and he consoled himself with the thought that the ' new movement ' had always done badly in moments of tranquillity.   It was the absence of that elusive ' crisis ' that had brought his efforts to nought.

Although the crisis refused to come, Mosley continued to campaign.   Kensington Town Hall was still available most of the time; and between 1959 and 1962 he held seven open-air meetings in Trafalgar Square, drawing large crowds of the curious and the loyal.   There was still occasional ' sport ' for his followers, as when in white military-looking raincoat he led his supporters from Charing Cross to Trafalgar Square where Hugh Gaitskell, Jeremy Thorpe, Lord Altrincham and Father Trevor Huddleston were speaking in support of a new Boycott Campaign against South Africa.[25]   Union Movement fought the odd by-election.   One, at Moss Side, Manchester, in 1961, in which its candidate was a former long-distance runner called Hesketh, provoked the following rather sad reflections:

A striking feature of yesterday's meeting was the almost repetitive pattern set by the speakers.   They start with a reference to Sir Oswald and his valiant war record, continue with a condemnation of the Coalition Government for ' ratting on the ex-servicemen ', and then describe at inordinate length the failure of the ' old gang ' to cope with the Depression and

---

with Keynes or in the evening of an East End pub, at an Oxford high table or at a rowdy street-corner meeting.   The art of practical politics is to give high ideas form and garments which the mass of the people can understand by illustrations from their daily lives and personal awareness.   When some fine old worker pays you the greatest possible compliment after a speech with the words – ' You have been saying what I have been thinking all my life ' – it is a particular satisfaction to know that you have touched some deep chord in his being with a translated and developed sequence of European thought which may have begun with Heraklitus.   What Goethe called *Ganzheit* is essential in politics.

*The results were: G. Rogers (Lab.), 14,925; R. Bulbrook (Con.), 14,048; M. Hydleman (L.), 3118; O. Mosley (U.M.), 2821.

unemployment. This section of the harangue becomes almost indistinguishable from speeches made by far-left Marxists who haven't recovered from the 1930s. There then follows a long passage about the B.U.F., the futility of World War II and the iniquity of imprisoning Mosley under 18B, with much reference in this respect to the different treatment accorded to Lloyd George, Fox and Pitt when they opposed war. Finally the speech gets into the coming crisis and depression – far-left undertones again – and the need for Europe a Nation, and also Africa for the Blacks (well 2/3rds of Africa for the Blacks). Finally a wind-up about the brightly coloured threads of civilisation. . . . [26]

What kept Mosley going? In a revealing piece in 1963 he described seeing the French film *1914–1918*:

. . . the fatuous German royalties – so ridiculously pleased with themselves . . . evoked memories of the pompous idiocy, the pleasure-yielding futility of the politicians on the other side. . . . They soon made way for the long-excluded phenomenon of will and energy who was Clemenceau, and for the dynamic genius of Lenin whose speaking revealed both a vast contempt for the system and the men he was overthrowing and a passionate belief in his cause and his companions. Running through all like a leitmotif was a brilliantly selected still of French poilus: in their midst a simple soldier whose expression combined manly resolution and a dedicated resignation to death with that sense of the ultimate pathos, the infinite waste of it all which was the epitaph of the doomed generation.

I left the cinema strangely feeling both very old and very young, and found myself saying as of yore, we shall get them yet. . . .[27]

But ' they ', in fact, had once more got him. On 1 March 1962, as we have seen, Mosley and other European ' neo-fascists ' had signed their European Declaration at Venice. This event, it seems, temporarily reactivated the old Jewish–Communist alliance. Violence was switched on again. On 12 May 1962 Robert Row, editor of *Action*, and another Union Movement official, Keith Gibson, were beaten up at their headquarters by members of the Yellow Star organisation. Mosley's Trafalgar Square meeting of 22 July was broken up even before he had got there. On 31 July, the sixty-five-year-old Mosley was knocked down and kicked on the ground as he was about to address a meeting in Ridley Road, Dalston; the peculiar arrangement of the police vehicles making it impossible for his supporters to prevent the assault. He was saved from serious injury only by holding one of his assailants on top of

him till he was rescued by his son Max.   With his usual courage he
got up and tried to address the meeting which was then closed by
the police: two old opponents, Lord Longford and Victor Gollancz,
courageously wrote to *The Times* condemning the assault on Mosley.
On 5 August 1962 the *Sunday Telegraph* reported that 'Jews are
planning a nation-wide campaign . . . against Sir Oswald Mosley's
Union Movement'.   Deputations were sent to the Home Office;
threats were made to sweep fascism off the streets; the 43 Group was
revived as the 62 Group; Jewish shopkeepers and businessmen in
the East End supplied funds.   'With Communists taking advantage
of the situation, a new wave of violence could result.'[28]

In the House of Commons it was assumed by Jo Grimond, George
Brown and others that Mosley had suddenly returned to the platform
after years of absence and that his reappearance had unleashed the
violence.   As the *Sunday Telegraph* editorial of 5 August 1962 put
it, 'Mosley himself is a provocation, and he does not need to
open his mouth to provoke violence.'   But this view does not
explain how it was, as the home secretary, Mr Henry Brooke, told
the House, that 'for the last two years the Union Movement and
some of these other . . . bodies have been holding meetings
and there has been no disorder'.[29]   Mosley, as we have seen, had
been coming regularly to Trafalgar Square and also speaking
frequently in the Ridley Road.   How had he suddenly become more
provocative in 1962 than in 1961?   The Venice meeting and the
scare of a European 'fascist revival' was the precipitating cause,
but the violence was helped along by the presence of television
cameras, and by the intervention of organisations like Colin
Jordan's British National Party (Colin Jordan was in fact arrested
at Trafalgar Square under the Public Order Act earlier in July
for attempting to justify Hitler's policy toward the Jews).   In the
upshot, Trafalgar Square and most major halls were again closed
to Mosley, and the violence, deprived of opportunity, died down
again.

Although Mosley still spoke occasionally, and stood once more
for Parliament, at Shoreditch and Finsbury in 1966, polling 1600
or 4.6 per cent of the votes cast, the era of the mass Mosley meetings
was finally drawing to a close.   Following the fiasco at Shoreditch,
Mosley gave up the leadership of the Union Movement.   It was
partly a concession to age; partly a confession that thirty-six years
of 'grass-roots' campaigning had ended in failure.   He sensed
belatedly that mass movements and mass meetings were things of
the past.   As a means of communicating policies they had become
hopelessly inefficient – especially as the Press never reported what
he said in any case.   To his followers he explained that if he was to
'get them yet' a new approach was needed.   The key to publicity,
and hence to power and influence, was the Press and television.

But he could get into neither if he went on speaking in shabby halls and at street corners. So he announced his 'withdrawal' from 'party warfare'.

There was no thought of retirement. At seventy, Mosley felt his powers waxing, not waning. Men mature with age, like good wines, he engagingly explained to a visiting journalist. Another wrote that at seventy-one 'he looks a very rugged 55'. He still lived like an 'athlete in light training'. The problem was to sell the new 'mature' Mosley and his European ideas to the British public.

In 1966 he launched his latest – and probably final – campaign. He began to call for 'a government of union drawn from everything vital in the country.' This was a development of an early theme – the Centre or Coalition Party idea of the 1920s. The next step was to get him and his ideas discussed again. Mosley's last appearance on B.B.C. had been at the time of Olympia in 1934. In 1935 the Government had told the B.B.C. that scheduled talks by him and Harry Pollitt, the communist leader, were 'not in the national interest', and the B.B.C. had weakly backed down: a curious commentary on the robust independence of this public institution.[30] More recently, Sir Hugh Carleton-Greene, director-general of the B.B.C., had been heard to remark that Mosley would appear only over his dead body. This was the kind of challenge that Mosley loved to accept. He started an action for libel against the B.B.C. over a comment made about him, explaining frankly that his object was simply to secure the right to defend himself on any programme in which his past was being discussed. This right was finally conceded in 1968 after Lord Chief Justice Parker had remarked on the curious system whereby 'someone who has the ear of the whole nation can say things and the unfortunate subject has no means of answering back in the same medium'.[31] A tempestuous appearance on the David Frost show, with old East End opponents like 'Solly' Kaye prominent in the audience, marked the end of the I.T.V. ban as well. But for Mosley these were only the first steps in his campaign to discuss the contemporary issues that consumed him.

The second stage in his self-attempted rehabilitation was the publication of his autobiography, *My Life*, in October 1968. It was a sign of the thaw that had already set in that he was able to secure a reputable publisher (Nelson), and that non-contentious extracts were serialised in *The Times*. A rather more contentious review in the same journal by the Conservative M.P., Norman St. John Stevas (21 October 1968), accepting Mosley's defence on the charge of anti-semitism, evoked a correspondence between Mosley and Bernard Levin, notable for the enormous length of the letters on both sides. *My Life* was widely and favourably reviewed. 'A superb political thinker, the best of our age,' enthused A. J. P.

Taylor. Michael Foot spoke of 'the deep-laid middle-class love of mediocrity and safety-first which consigned political genius to the wilderness and the nation to the valley of the shadow of death'. 'The best-written volume of memoirs emanating from my generation' was the verdict of Sir Colin Coote.[32] Mosley struck an adroit balance between the past and the future: the last chapter is significantly entitled 'Policies for Present and Future'.

In the unwritten language of British political forms, the autobiography was accepted for what it was: the opening of negotiations for peace with the British Establishment. Mosley had few cards to play beyond an ability which could not be denied: the response to the returning sinner was not ungenerous. A long 'Panorama' programme with the late James Mossman was the first concession: it attracted $8\frac{1}{2}$ million viewers, a record for that time, and impressive evidence of the continuing interest in Mosley's personality and career. Early in 1969 came an I.T.V. 'Face the Press' programme in the North which got 69 per cent of the audience in competition with the B.B.C.'s 'Twenty-Four Hours' and news summary; when the programme was shown in London a week later it got 47 per cent, compared with a typical 30 per cent.[33] He was allowed an occasional non-controversial article in the *Daily Telegraph Magazine;* more recently he seems to have found something of a forum in *Books and Bookmen.*

Progress was excruciatingly slow for an elderly man: the next major television appearance was not till 1971 in an A.T.V. documentary, 'A Kind of Exile' (27 July). The following night Mosley appeared in BBC2's 'Late Night Line-up' to discuss the Common Market with Richard Crossman. In a clash between two skilful swordsmen, Mosley had the distinct edge in the first half of the programme when Crossman attempted to identify his European ideas with those of Hitler; but in the second part Crossman made a distinct comeback when he failed to elicit any clear reply to the question why there should be any role or future for Mosley, in view of the Heath government's espousal of the European idea. The atmosphere of the past hung heavy over the discussion of the future: Crossman's clever questioning revealed the gulf which forty years in the political wilderness had opened up between Mosley's thought and language and the issues and style of contemporary politics. At the age of seventy-four Mosley had to relearn the art of clothing his old–new ideas in the contemporary idiom. The publication of the American edition of *My Life* in February 1972 (by Arlington House) produced more reviews (warmer the further West the journal) and numerous television and radio appearances in the United States, including one on William Buckley's 'Firing Line'. Finally, a brief appearance in the B.B.C. documentary 'If Britain Had Fallen' in September 1972 led to an article in *The Listener* of 21

September which is the best short defence of his anti-war policy of the late 1930s.

The reviews, articles and television appearances gave Mosley new contacts in the world of the media and an opportunity to mend broken political fences. Forty years on the Mosley ' conversations ' are in full swing at private lunches and dinners in London and Orsay. The range of his political, academic and journalistic acquaintances is surprisingly large, and to each member of this select circle comes his *Broadsheet*, elaborating his thoughts on contemporary problems; thoughts transmitted in an almost illegible hand, or on tapes, to his secretariat in London, for printing and distribution all over the world.

The worsening economic situation gave him plenty of opportunities for restating old themes in new settings. ' The breakdown of Bretton Woods gives Britain a supreme opportunity to take the initiative in rapid construction of an European system,' he wrote after the crisis of August 1971.[34] He chaffed Nicholas Kaldor for advocating floating exchange-rates: ' Such valuable erudition should not in the end be reduced to the simple proposition – down with Europe, and up with the banana republic. ' [35] Inflation, he warned sternly, would have to be cured by creating mass unemployment but then using the unemployed to rebuild the slums and create new public amenities: ' it may in the end even prove an advantage for some proportion of manpower to be employed in stopping pollution instead of promoting surplus growth '.[36] The skilful way in which he united the environment issue with the fight against inflation shows that the master of combinations has lost none of his old touch. Naturally Mosley had his solution for the Irish problem as well: a redrawing of the Ulster borders so as to transfer most of the Catholic population from North to South.[37]

These were some of the great policies waiting to be carried out: but they required ' a change of mind and character in government which dares to give a clear lead and tell the nation in plain language what needs to be done '; a ' union of men and women drawn from every vital source in the nation and adequate to win the confidence of the country '. In such a union Mosley, too, was prepared to ' serve our country '.

Does Mosley really believe that the British people will recall him to lead them, people ask in amazement, adding that if he does he really must be mad. Even if the crisis does come, there is a much more obvious Man of Destiny waiting in the wings – Enoch Powell. Taxed with his intentions, Mosley replies that he seeks only the role of a ' peddler of ideas ' on television and in the Press; adding ' obviously, like other Englishmen, I am ready with my compatriots wherever they may be, if wanted, to serve our country '.[38] The role of advocate and propagandist for ' European Government ' –

the central plank of his post-war policy – undoubtedly attracts him; whether it has shut out the tremendous call of power, the power not just to advocate but to construct, is doubtful. For Mosley ideas have always been *prologemena* to action.

That he feels he has a contribution to make is undeniable. Frustration channels a still-abundant physical and mental vitality, to which the years have added tolerance and wisdom, into strenuous activity. The old flame ignited by the First World War still burns brightly; it will be extinguished only with his death or incapacity. As ever he looks to events to vindicate his profound conviction that ' a different order of character and resolution ' is required to master the problems of the world into which he was born. This attitude to life will always make him the eternal contemporary of some, the eternal enemy of others, long after the particular problems to which he devoted his own life have passed away. The future will assess his place and contribution in relation to its own needs, purposes and possibilities. Today's biographer can do no better than end with one of his own favourite passages from *Faust*:

> Whoever strives
> Can be redeemed.

Notes

Abbreviations

BU   British Union
BUF   British Union of Fascists
HC Deb.   *Parliamentary Debates, House of Commons*
ML   Sir Oswald Mosley, *My Life* (1968)
MP   Mosley Papers
OM   Sir Oswald Mosley
PRO   Public Record Office
UM   Union Movement

Chapter 1. Feudal Livery

1. *Mosley Family: memoranda*, ed. Ernest Axon (1902).
2. Sir Oswald Mosley, *Family Memoir*, where there is no mention of the privateering expedition.
3. Quoted in W. E. A. Axon, *Lancashire Gleanings*, pp. 12 ff.
4. These details are taken from *The History of the Castle, Priory and Town of Tutbury, in the County of Stafford*, written by OM's great-great-grandfather Sir Oswald Mosley in 1832.
5. For an account of this episode which includes some touching letters from Anne Mosley on her son's behalf, see John Booker's *History of the Ancient Chapels of Didsbury and Chorlton*, pp. 147 ff.
6. *ML*, p. 2.
7. H. R. G. Greaves, 'Personal Origins and Interrelations of the Houses of Parliament', in *Economica*, ix (1929) p. 81; quoted in F. M. L. Thompson, *British Landed Society in the Nineteenth Century*, p. 63.
8. Ibid. p. 27.
9. See E. Tangye Lean, *The Napoleonists: a study in political disaffection 1760–1960*, p. 234.
10. Thompson, *British Landed Society*, pp. 22–4.
11. This account is largely based on Arthur Redford's *A History of Local Government in Manchester*, vol. i, pp. 66 ff., 131–49, 182 ff. For a more general perspective, see Karl Polanyi, *The Great Transformation*, p. 66.
12. For an account of this case, in addition to Sir Oswald Mosley's *Family Memoir*, see *Annals of Manchester*, ed. W. E. A. Axon.
13. Richard Cobden, *Incorporate Your Borough* (1837); quoted in Redford, *Local Government in Manchester*, vol. ii, pp. 13–14.
14. Ibid. i 149; ii 9–24, 94.
15. See also *ML*, pp. 7, 21.
16. Ibid. p. 13.
17. Ibid. p. 22
18. See Colin Wilson, *New Pathways in Psychology* (1972); also David Hackett Fischer, *Historians' Fallacies* (1971) pp. 213–15.
19. *ML*, p. 11.

20. Reminiscences of Mrs Jessie Shercliff, 1943; for the battle of the pews, see also F. A. Slaney, *The History of St Mary's Church, Rolleston* (1960).
21. Quoted in Robert A. Nisbet, *The Sociological Tradition* (1967) p. 191.
22. *ML*, p. 191.
23. For a brilliant sketch of the transition to Victorian England, see Mario Praz, ' The Victorian Mood: a reappraisal ', in *The Nineteenth Century World*, ed. Guy Métraux and François Crouzet.
24. A. K. Chesterton, *Portrait of a Leader*, p. 13.
25. *ML*, p. 27.
26. Ibid. p. 35.
27. This account of Winchester is based on J. D'E. E. Firth, *Winchester*.
28. *ML*, p. 25.
29. Ibid. p. 30.
30. Ibid. p. 31.
31. Of 339 recruits in 1891, about half were the sons of army and naval officers, 102 of professional and businessmen, 29 of churchmen and 54 of peers, baronets and ' private gentlemen '. Brig. Sir John Smythe, *Sandhurst*, pp. 261–2. See also Hugh Thomas, *The Story of Sandhurst*, for a general survey of Sandhurst.
32. *ML*, pp. 41–2.
33. Letter to the author.
34. Viscount Montgomery, *Memoirs* (1958), pp. 24–5.

Chapter 2. The Challenge to Liberalism

1. H. Stuart Hughes, *Consciousness and Society: the reorientation of European social thought 1890–1930*, p. 14.
2. Hans Rosenberg, ' Political and Economic Consequences of the Great Depression ', in *Economic History Review*, vol. I, no. 13 (1943).
3. H. Feis, *Europe the World's Banker 1870–1914* (1930) p. 14.
4. E. J. Hobsbawm, *Industry and Empire*, p. 127.
5. R. S. Sayers, *A History of Economic Change in England 1880–1939*, p. 5.
6. S. B. Saul, *The Myth of the Great Depression 1873–1896*, p. 33.
7. Quoted in Keith Hutchinson, *The Decline and Fall of British Capitalism*, p. 91.
8. Sayers, *History of Economic Change*, p. 14.
9. A. L. Levine discusses these explanations and adds more of his own in his *Industrial Retardation in Britain 1880–1914*. An example of the contemporary genre is Paul Einzig's *Decline and Fall? Britain's Crisis in the Sixties* (1969).
10. Corelli Barnet, *The Collapse of British Power*, p. 26. For Barnet, as for Gibbon, the villain is Christianity.
11. Quoted in Charles E. McLelland, *The German Historians and England: a study in nineteenth century views*, p. 184.
12. The eighteenth-century writer Joseph Harris, quoted in Edmund Whittaker, *History of Economic Ideas*, p. 296.
13. W. J. Ashley, *The Tariff Problem* (1903).
14. Feis, *Europe the World's Banker*, p. 4.
15. Quoted in W. H. B. Court, *British Economic History*, p. 462.
16. Peter Mathias, *The First Industrial Nation*, pp. 329–30. Mathias notes how the British-financed American railway-lines ran from mid-west to the east coast – exactly the lines tapping the wheat belt and the middle western hog- and cattle-rearing areas in the Chicago hinterland.

17. Ibid. p. 319.
18. V. I. Lenin, *Imperialism, the Highest Stage of Capitalism* (International Publishers ed.) p. 101.
19. Margaret Cole, *The Story of Fabian Socialism*, p. 10.
20. Quoted in A. M. M. McBriar, *Fabian Socialism and English Politics 1884–1914*, p. 13.
21. Bernard Semmel, *Imperialism and Social Reform*, p. 21.
22. McBriar, *Fabian Socialism*, p. 49.
23. See Robert Skidelsky, *Politicians and the Slump; the Labour Government of 1929–31*, pp. 48–9.
24. See Melvin Richter, *The Politics of Conscience: T. H. Green and his age*, especially ch. VII. The title shows what it was all about.
25. Julian Amery, *Life of Joseph Chamberlain*, vol. v, p. 317. Amery admirably sums up the issues involved in his ch. CI of the same volume entitled 'The Fiscal Revolution in Perspective'.
26. Joseph Chamberlain, quoted in André Maurois, *The Edwardian Era*, pp. 164–5.
27. Cole, *Fabian Socialism*, p. 102.
28. Quoted in McBriar, *Fabian Socialism*, p. 132.
29. Semmel, *Imperialism*, p. 82.
30. McBriar, *Fabian Socialism*, p. 132.
31. Semmel, *Imperialism*, pp. 72–5.
32. For the best introduction to Shaw's ideas, see Eric Bentley's *Bernard Shaw*.

Chapter 3. A Special Kind of Experience

1. *ML*, p. 49.
2. R. Bellamy, 'We Marched with Mosley' (MS.).
3. *ML*, p. 57.
4. Ibid. p. 47.
5. Ibid. p. 59.
6. Ibid. p. 60.
7. Sayers, *History of Economic Change*, p. 49.
8. A. J. P. Taylor, *English History 1914–1945*, pp. 113–14.
9. *ML*, p. 70.
10. Quoted in Reginald Pound, *The Lost Generation*, p. 93.
11. *ML*, pp. 229–30.
12. *European*, Aug 1954.
13. *ML*, p. 74.
14. Ibid. p. 90.
15. See 'My Notebook', in *Harrow Observer*, 26 July 1918; also *ML*, p. 88.
16. Ibid. 9 Aug 1918.
17. Taylor, *English History*, p. 127.
18. *Harrow Observer*, 13 Dec 1918.
19. Ibid. 11 Oct 1918.
20. Ibid. 25 Oct 1918.
21. Ibid. 8 Nov 1918.
22. Ibid. 11 Oct 1918.
23. Ibid. 13 Dec 1918.
24. Ibid. 8 Nov 1918.
25. Ibid. 8 Nov 1918.

26. Ibid. 13 Dec 1918.
27. Ibid. 13 Dec 1918.
28. Ibid. 3 Jan 1919.
29. Ibid. 8 Nov 1918.

Chapter 4.   The Young Crusader

1. Montague Smith, ' The Story of Sir Oswald Mosley ', in *Daily Mail*, 30 May 1930.
2. *HC Deb.*, vol. 112, cols 671-4.
3. Ibid. vol. 123, col. 111.
4. Ibid. vol. 130, cols 2323–5.
5. *Daily Mail*, 24 July 1919.
6. *Manchester Dispatch*, 7 July 1919.
7. *ML*, p. 101.
8. *Financial News*, 26 Apr 1919.
9. *ML*, p. 91.
10. See C. Coote, *Editorial*, pp. 101, 103.
11. *ML*, p. 24.
12. Leonard Mosley, *Curzon: the end of an epoch*, p. 199.
13. Curzon Papers (unclassified).
14. MP (unclassified).

Chapter 5.   ' Still the Swine Won't Talk '

1. Address to Harrow electors, 1922.
2. McBriar, *Fabian Socialism*, p. 145.
3. *Harrow Observer*, 11 June 1920.
4. *HC Deb.*, vol. 143, col. 534; address to Harrow electors, 1922.
5. *ML*, p. 148.
6. *HC Deb.*, vol. 130, cols 1313, 1590; vol. 132, cols 138, 142.
7. Address to Harrow electors, 1922.
8. Interview in *Ways and Means*, Dec 1920.
9. See *Harrow Gazette*, 15 Oct 1920, for the text of the memorandum he circulated to M.P.s.
10. Quoted in *ML*, p. 157.
11. *HC Deb.*, vol. 133, col. 1048.
12. Ibid. vol. 133, cols 1008–13.
13. Ibid. vol. 134, col. 542.
14. Ibid. vol. 135, cols 518–24.
15. MP: Peace with Ireland Council, Statement of Aims, Including Peace Policy.
16. Ibid.
17. *HC Deb.*, vol. 139, col. 165.
18. MP: Peace with Ireland Council.
19. *HC Deb.*, vol.138, cols 1991–2; interjections by courtesy of the *Morning Post*, 4 Mar 1921.
20. *ML*, p. 156.
21. *HC Deb.*, vol. 139, col. 168.
22. MP: Peace with Ireland Council.   In his memoirs OM writes: ' My own opinion . . . is that the decisive factor [in securing the defeat of the Government's Irish policy] was our organisation of the Bryce Commission ' (*ML*,

p. 155). In fact, there was no Bryce Commission. Lord Bryce was merely chairman of a committee to try to get a commission together. After a large number of refusals to serve, the attempt was abandoned. It remains true, however, that the Peace with Ireland Council did collect a good deal of information which would have been damaging had it been published.

23. Lord Beaverbrook, *The Decline and Fall of Lloyd George*, p. 84.

Chapter 6.   The Very Independent Member

1. Beatrice Webb, *Diaries*, ed. Margaret Cole, vol. I, *1912–24*, pp. 242–3.
2. *HC Deb.*, vol. 143, cols 530–6.
3. Ibid. vol. 153, col. 2096.
4. Cecil Papers, B.M. 51163, ff. 4–5.
5. Cecil to Cowdray, 9 July 1921.
6. Scott to Cecil, 2 Sept 1921.
7. For an account of this curious episode, see Maurice Cowling, *The Impact of Labour*, pp. 102–4.
8. *ML*, p. 146.
9. He received an ' emphatic ' vote of confidence on 11 Oct 1921 and again on 4 May 1922.
10. *Harrow Observer*, 18 May 1923.
11. Unsigned article, ' Press Ethics ', in *Harrow Gazette*, 12 Nov 1920.
12. *Harrow Observer*, 13 Oct 1922.
13. Ibid. 15 Sept 1922.
14. Ibid. 21 July 1922.
15. Ibid. 25 Aug 1922.
16. Ibid. 1 Sept 1922.
17. Address to Harrow electors, Oct 1922.
18. *ML*, p. 165.
19. *Harrow Observer*, 10 Nov 1922; transposed into direct speech.
20. Ibid. 3 Nov 1922; transposed into direct speech.
21. *ML*, p. 165.
22. *Westminster Gazette*, 30 May 1923.
23. H. H. Asquith, *Letters to a Friend, second series, 1922–7*, pp. 61–2.
24. *East London Advertiser*, 9 June 1923.
25. *HC Deb.*, vol. 160, cols 1604–6.
26. Ibid. vol. 161, cols 2433–4.
27. Ibid. vol. 160, cols 405–6.
28. Ibid. vol. 161, col. 1365.
29. 15 July 1923; 19 June 1923; 26 June 1923.
30. *HC Deb.*, vol. 161, col. 1363.
31. *Middlesex and Buckinghamshire Advertiser*, 23 Nov 1923.
32. *Middlesex County Times*, 8 Dec 1923.
33. *HC Deb.*, vol. 169, col. 370.
34. *Ealing Gazette*, 14 April 1923.

Chapter 7.   Revolution by Reason

1. *Portrait of the Labour Party*, pp. viii–x.
2. *Birmingham Town Crier*, 25 July 1924.
3. *ML*, p. 175.

4. Ibid. p. 177.
5. 7 Nov 1924.
6. *ML*, p. 125.
7. *Birmingham Town Crier*, 12 Sept 1924.
8. Letter to the *Morning Post*, 17 July 1928.
9. E. Bentley, *A Century of Hero-worship*, p. 149.
10. Society for the Study of Labour History, *Bulletin No. 18*, Spring 1969.
11. Hugh Thomas, *John Strachey*, p. 46.
12. John Strachey, *Revolution by Reason* (1925) p. vii. This interpretation of Strachey was suggested to me by Miss Deirdre Whiteside, a student of mine at Barnard College, Columbia. It is largely confirmed by Mr Thomas's biography.
13. Thomas, *Strachey*, p. 110.
14. *ML*, p. 185.
15. Thomas, *Strachey*, p. 49.
16. See R. S. Sayers, ' The Return to Gold, 1925 ', reprinted in *The Gold Standard and Unemployment Policies between the Wars*, ed. Sidney Pollard, pp. 90, 94–5.
17. J. M. Keynes, *Tract for Monetary Reform* (1923) pp. 36–7.
18. See the *Nation*, 24 May 1924.
19. Keynes, *Tract*, p. 143.
20. I.L.P. *Annual Report*, 1925, pp. 155–7.
21. *The Times*, 22 April 1925.
22. Ibid. 20 April 1925.
23. *Staffordshire Sentinel*, 1 Aug 1925.
24. *Birmingham Town Crier*, 8 May 1925.
25. Ibid. 10 July 1925.
26. Robert Boothby, *I Fight to Live*, p. 24.
27. OM, *Revolution by Reason*, pp. 16–17.
28. Ibid. pp. 16–17.
29. Ibid. p. 15.
30. Ibid. pp. 20–2.
31. Ibid. p. 12.
32. Ibid. pp. 22–3.
33. Ibid. pp. 23, 27.
34. Ibid. p. 27.
35. I.L.P. *Annual Report*, 1926, p. 86.
36. *New Leader*, 7 Oct 1927.
37. Hugh Dalton, *Call Back Yesterday*, p. 174.
38. Labour Party Conference *Annual Report*, 1927, pp. 246–8.
39. Webb, *Diaries*, vol. II, *1924–32*, p. 68.
40. Ibid. p. 89.
41. Philip Snowden, *Autobiography*, vol. II, p. 876.
42. *New Leader*, April 1927.
43. OM, ' The Labour Party's Financial Policy ', in *Socialist Review*, Sept 1927, p. 33.
44. Henry Pelling, *Popular Politics and Society in Late Victorian England*, p. 5.
45. Thomas Jones, *Whitehall Diary*, vol. I, p. 274.
46. Third Congress of the Labour and Socialist International, *Report and Proceedings*, vol. III, sect. VI, pp. 42–3.
47. L. T. Hobhouse, *Liberalism*, p. 114.

Chapter 8. The Dandy of the Revolution

1. *Daily News*, 10 Aug 1925.
2. *Birmingham Town Crier*, 4 June 1926.
3. *ML*, p. 192.
4. Quoted from the *Miner* in *Birmingham Town Crier*, 27 Oct 1926.
5. For OM's present views, see his review of Christopher Farman's *The General Strike*, in *Books and Bookmen*, April 1973.
6. *Westminster Gazette*, 17 Dec 1926.
7. *New Leader*, 28 Dec 1926.
8. Georg Brandes, *Ferdinand Lassalle*, p. 37.
9. *Daily Express*, 7, 8 Dec 1926.
10. See *Birmingham Daily Mail*, 16 Dec 1926; *Daily Express*, 7 Dec 1926; *Morning Post*, 7 Dec 1926.
11. *Daily Express*, 13 Dec 1926.
12. *Birmingham Daily Mail*, 4 Dec 1926.
13. *Birmingham Town Crier*, 10 Dec 1926.
14. See *Daily Telegraph*, 9 Dec 1926.
15. *Birmingham Gazette and Express*, 17 Dec 1926.
16. Edmund Burke, *Reflections on the French Revolution* (New York, 1937) p. 185.
17. See W. G. Runciman, *Relative Deprivation and Social Justice*, and David Marquand, ' The Politics of Deprivation ', in *Encounter*, April 1969.
18. The Tawney remark is given by Royden Harrison in ' Labour Government: then and now ', in *Political Quarterly*, June 1970, pp. 67–81.
19. *Morning Post*, 17 Dec 1926.
20. *Birmingham Post*, 10 Dec 1926.
21. Ibid. 16 Dec 1926.
22. Ibid. 14 Dec 1926.
23. Ibid. 15 Dec 1926.
24. *Star*, 15 Dec 1926.
25. *Morning Post*, 23 Dec 1926.
26. *Birmingham Post*, 23 Dec 1926.
27. Ellen Wilkinson, *Peeps at Politicians* (1930) pp. 38–40.
28. *Daily Express*, 5 May 1927.
29. Report of the National Administrative Council Meeting, in *New Leader*, 6 July 1928.
30. For the Cook–Maxton manifesto, see R. E. Dowse, *Left in the Centre*, pp. 142–3; R. K. Middlemas, *The Clydesiders*, pp. 218–21.
31. Snowden, *Autobiography*, vol. ii, p. 876.
32. ' Smethwick Notes ', in *Birmingham Town Crier*, 3 Aug 1928.
33. *Scotsman*, 9 Nov 1925.
34. Society for the Study of Labour History, *Bulletin No. 18*, Spring 1969.
35. *Birmingham Town Crier*, 4 June 1929.
36. Ibid. 23 Dec 1927.
37. National Executive Council Minutes, 26 April 1929; *Birmingham Town Crier*, 14 June 1929.
38. See Baroness Ravensdale, *In Many Rhythms*, p. 138; also *Birmingham Town Crier*, 17 May 1929.
39. ' Smethwick Notes ', in ibid. 31 May 1929.
40. *Labour Magazine*, 1 April 1931.
41. C. L. Mowat, *Britain between the Wars*, pp. 351–2.

42. Kingsley Martin, *Harold Laski*, p. 76.
43. *Labour Magazine*, 1 May 1929.

Chapter 9. The Day of Judgment

1. See Skidelsky, *Politicians and the Slump*, p. 77.
2. Jones, *Whitehall Diary*, vol. II, *1926–1930*, p. 187.
3. Gregory Blaxland, *J. H. Thomas: a life for unity*, p. 225.
4. Ibid. p. 221.
5. PRO: CAB. 27/389. DU(29).
6. Those with a taste for such matters can follow the great Whitehall saga of wood versus steel telephone-cases and telegraph-poles in CAB 27/389/90.
7. *ML*, p. 234.
8. For the parliamentary proceedings, see *HC Deb.*, vol. 230, cols 515–26, 681–778, 861–76.
9. For these various quotations, see ibid. 230, cols 293, 393, 520, 769.
10. Snowden, *Autobiography*, vol. II, p. 760.
11. For the work of the Retirement Pensions Committee, see PRO: CAB 27/391, 402; CAB 24/207; see also the Lansbury Papers (London School of Economics), Boxes 19–20. The only previously published account is to be found in Skidelsky, *Politicians and the Slump*, pp. 95–9.
12. See ibid. p. 43.
13. Ibid. p. 154.
14. Lansbury Papers, Box 20.
15. For Maybury's obstructive attitude, see PRO: CAB 24/212.
16. See Skidelsky, *Politicians and the Slump*, pp. 56–7.
17. PRO: CAB 24/206.
18. See Skidelsky, *Politicians and the Slump*, pp. 151–3.
19. For his cabinet report on his Canadian trip on 25 Sept 1929, see PRO: CAB 24/205.
20. J. H. Thomas, *My Story*, p. 170.
21. Keynes Papers, Correspondence 1930.
22. For details of these affecting exchanges, see Thomas, *My Story*, pp. 170-2.
23. MP: OM to MacDonald, 22 Feb 1930.
24. Ibid.: MacDonald to OM, 25 Feb 1930.
25. OM, *The Greater Britain* (1934 ed.) pp. 59–60.
26. *HC Deb.*, vol. 234, cols 94–102.
27. *Birmingham Gazette*, 26 Feb 1930.
28. *HC Deb.*, vol. 234, col. 1642.
29. Harold Nicolson's Diaries, MS., 15 Jan 1930.
30. Ibid. 12 Mar 1930.

Chapter 10. The New Deal that Wasn't

1. PRO: CAB 24/209, 211.
2. The fact was that there was almost no activity then in progress; see Skidelsky, *Politicians and the Slump*, p. 153.
3. E. Halévy, *Era of Tyrannies*, p. 196.
4. Jones, *Whitehall Diary*, vol. II, p. 260.
5. *HC Deb.*, vol. 239, col. 1434.
6. Boothby, *I Fight to Live*, p. 91.
7. These extracts from the Cabinet Committee discussions are taken from Jones, *Whitehall Diary*, vol. II, pp. 256–60.

8. W. F. Mandle, ' Sir Oswald Mosley's Resignation from the Labour Government ', in *Historical Studies*, 10 (1963.)
9. *Life in Britain between the Wars*, ed. Peter Quennell, pp. 194–5.
10. For a fuller account of this meeting, see Skidelsky, *Politicians and the Slump*, pp. 185–8.
11. See *HC Deb.*, vol. 239, cols 1348–72.
12. Webb, *Diaries*, vol. II, 29 May 1930.
13. For this belated examination of Mosley's proposals, see PRO: Treasury Papers 175/42.

Chapter 11. Workers of the Empire, Unite!

1. Letter of resignation, 20 May 1930.
2. Webb, Diaries, MS., 29 May 1930.
3. Letter to the author, 13 May 1971.
4. M. Foot, *Aneurin Bevan*, vol. I, p. 121.
5. *Daily Herald*, 23 June 1930.
6. *Forward*, 31 May 1930.
7. Samuel Beer, *Modern British Politics*, p. 149.
8. The *functional* importance of socialism in the Labour Party has been grasped in an important essay by V. Bogdanor, in *The Age of Affluence*, ed. V. Bogdanor and R. Skidelsky.
9. *New Statesman*, 5 Sept 1931.
10. John Strachey, *The Menace of Fascism*, p. 156.
11. W. J. Brown, *So Far*, p. 158.
12. Nicolson Diaries, MS., 15 Feb 1930.
13. Ibid. 2 July 1930.
14. *Liverpool Echo*, 29 May 1930.
15. *Sunday Chronicle*, 25 May 1930.
16. 31 May 1930.
17. ' What I Am Fighting For ', in *Sunday Express*, 25 May 1930.
18. *HC Deb.*, vol. 239, cols 1351–2.
19. Ibid. vol. 241, col. 1348.
20. Beaverbrook to OM, 17 July 1930.
21. See *Manchester Guardian*, 21 July 1930; *Birmingham Post*, 22 Oct 1930.
22. *Sunday Pictorial*, 9 Nov 1930.
23. Oliver Baldwin, *The Questing Beast: an autobiography*, p. 241.
24. Hugh Massingham, in *Sunday Telegraph*, 21 Aug 1966.
25. F. Brockway, *Inside the Left*, p. 210; for another comment on MacDonald's speech see MacNeill Weir, *The Tragedy of Ramsay MacDonald*, p. 244.
26. Sir John Foster Fraser, in *Sunday Graphic*, 12 Oct 1930.
27. Brockway, *Inside the Left*, p. 212.
28. For the Llandudno Conference debates, see Annual Report of the Labour Party, 1930, pp. 179–204.
29. Interview with Allan Young, 1 Aug 1970.
30. For the speech as a whole, see *HC Deb.*, vol. 244, cols 67–81.
31. Ibid. cols 86–7, 94, 117.
32. Ibid. cols 172–4.
33. Ibid. cols 236–7, 583–4.
34. Ibid. cols 756–7, 761.
35. *Star*, 21 Nov 1930.

36. *HC Deb.*, vol. 244, cols 101, 104.

37. Ibid. cols 779–81.

38. *New Leader*, 18 July 1930.

39. *HC Deb.*, vol. 244, col. 508.

40. Ibid, col. 810.

41. *Sunday Express*, 11 Jan 1931.

42. National Executive Council Minutes, 25, 26 Nov 1930.

43. Passfield Miscellaneous Letters, Cole to Beatrice Webb, 9 Dec 1930.

44. *Daily Herald*, 8 Dec 1930.

45. *Evening Standard*, 4 Dec 1930.

46. Letter to the author, 21 Dec 1962.

47. *Manchester Guardian*, 8 Dec 1930.

48. *New Leader*, 12 Dec 1930.

49. *The Times*, 11, 13, 17 Dec 1930; *Weekend Review*, 27 Dec 1930.

50. *Observer*, 7 Dec 1930.

51. *Church Times, Christian Science Monitor, Methodist Recorder* and *Church of Ireland Gazette* all gave the Manifesto unstinted praise: 11, 12 Dec 1930.

52. *Manchester Guardian*, 10 Dec 1930.

53. *New Leader*, 19 Dec 1930.

54. *The Times*, 10 Dec 1930.

55. *Nation and Athenaeum*, 13 Dec 1930.

56. *Yorkshire Post*, 14 Feb 1931.

57. *Daily Mail*, 17 Dec 1930.

58. *ML*, p. 345.

59. Nicolson Diaries, MS., 4 Feb 1931.

60. *Birmingham Town Crier*, 6 Mar 1931.

61. *Birmingham Gazette*, 27 Feb 1931; report by the national agent, Mr Shepherd, 28 Feb 1931, in the MacDonald Papers; *Birmingham Town Crier*, 6 Mar 1931.

62. Foot, *Bevan*, vol. I, p. 133.

63. *ML*, pp. 262–3.

Chapter 12.   Exit John Strachey

1. *Manchester Guardian*, 16 Mar 1931.

2. BUF, *Oswald Mosley and British Fascism*, p. 157.

3. *A National Policy*, p. 29.

4. Harold Nicolson, *Diaries*, p. 76: 30 May 1931.

5. Nicolson Diaries, MS., 22 July 1931.

6. Nicolson, *Diaries*, pp. 72, 74; 29 Apr, 6 May 1931.

7. Minutes of the Birmingham branch of I.L.P., 9 Apr 1931.

8. Nicolson, *Diaries*, p. 53: 11 June 1930.

9. *Evening Standard*, 22 Apr 1931.

10. *Manchester Evening News*, 25 Apr 1931.

11. Nicolson, *Diaries*, p. 71: 27 Apr 1931.

12. John Strachey, *The Menace of Fascism* (1933).

13. E. Nolte, *Three Faces of Fascism*, p. 203; see especially pp. 202–8.

14. Nicolson, *Diaries*, p. 75: 28 May 1931.

15. *ML*, pp. 284–5.

16. See John Strachey, in *Weekend Review*, 20 June 1931; E. F. Melville, in *Fortnightly Review*, May 1931.

17. Nicolson Diaries, MS., 20 July 1931.

18. See John Strachey, in *Weekend Review*, 20 June 1931; also Nicolson Diaries, MS., 17 July 1931.
19. *Manchester Guardian*, 16 May 1931.
20. This account is taken from Nicolson Diaries, MS., 5–7 July 1931; Jack Jones, *Unfinished Journey*, pp. 263–4; *Manchester Guardian*, 9 June 1931.
21. *Political Quarterly*, vol. II (1931).
22. Ibid. See also R. Butt, *The Power of Parliament*, p. 136.
23. See *Birmingham Post*, 29 Aug 1931.
24. *HC Deb.*, vol. 254, col. 2147.
25. Nicolson Diaries, MS., 23 July 1931; also Nicolson, *Diaries*, pp. 82–3: 23 July 1931.

Chapter 13.   Hold High the Marigold!
 1. Nicolson Diaries, MS., 22 July 1931.
 2. *Daily Herald*, 27 Aug 1931.
 3. *The Times*, 28 Aug 1931.
 4. Nicolson Diaries, MS., 31 Aug 1931; see also Nicolson, *Diaries*, p. 88: 26 Aug 1931.
 5. Nicolson Diaries, MS., 25 Sep 1931.
 6. *HC Deb.*, vol. 256, cols 72–82.
 7. Ibid. cols 156–7.
 8. Nicolson Diaries, MS., 12 Sept 1931.
 9. *The Times*, 11 Sept 1931.
10. For an account of the Glasgow meeting, see Nicolson, *Diaries*, p. 91; *The Times*, 21 Sept 1931.
11. *HC Deb.*, vol. 256, cols 1319–23.
12. See Nicolson, *Diaries*, p. 93: 1 Oct 1931; also Nicolson Diaries, MS., 28 Sept, 2 Oct 1931; *News Chronicle*, 24 Sept 1931.
13. *Action*, 8 Oct 1931.
14. *Manchester Guardian*, 26 Oct 1931.
15. *Glasgow Daily Record*, 21 Oct 1931.
16. *Action*, 22 Oct 1931.
17. James Lees-Milne, *Another Self*, p. 97.
18. *Manchester Guardian*, 29 Oct 1931.
19. Nicolson Diaries, MS., 28 Sept 1931.
20. Nicolson, *Diaries*, p. 96: 2 Nov 1931.

Chapter 14.   Part-time Saviour
 1. Nicolson, *Diaries*, p. 88: 26 Aug 1931.
 2. Ibid. pp. 97–8: 11 Dec 1931; also Nicolson Diaries, MS., for same date and 1 Feb 1932.
 3. Nicolson, *Diaries*, p. 98: 11 Dec 1931.
 4. Nicolson Diaries, MS., 4 Dec 1931.
 5. Nicolson, *Diaries*, p. 106: 6 Jan 1932.
 6. Ibid. p. 107: 18 Jan 1932.
 7. Nicolson Diaries, MS., 6 Jan 1932.
 8. *Daily Mail*, 1 Feb 1932.
 9. Nicolson, *Diaries*, p. 31: 31 Aug 1931.
10. Ibid. p. 114: 5 Apr 1932.
11. Ibid. p. 114: 15 Apr 1932.
12. Ibid. p. 111: 2 Mar 1932.

13. Colin Cross, *The Fascists in Britain*, p. 57.
14. Ibid. p. 67.
15. 24 Jan 1933.
16. Ravensdale, *In Many Rhythms*, pp. 141–2.
17. MP: Lloyd George to OM, 22 Sept 1934.
18. Nicolson Diaries, MS., 11 Oct 1933.

Chapter 15.   The Return of the Demons

 1. George Orwell, *The Road to Wigan Pier* (New York, 1961) pp. 162–4.
 2. *ML*, p. 287.
 3. Nolte, *Three Faces of Fascism*, p. 456.
 4. Semmel, *Imperialism*, pp. 246–57.
 5. *Fascist Quarterly*, vol. II, no. 1.
 6. OM, *The Alternative*, pp. 24, 27–8.
 7. *British Union Quarterly*, vol. I, no. 3.
 8. *Fascist Quarterly*, vol. II, no. 2.
 9. Ibid. vol. II, no. 3.
10. This point is well brought out in regard to Germany by T. W. Mason, in ' The Primacy of Politics ', in *The Nature of Fascism*, ed. S. J. Woolf, pp. 165–95.
11. OM, in *Weekend Review*, 24 Jan 1931.
12. Strachey, *Revolution by Reason*, p. 127.
13. Quoted in E. H. Carr, *The October Revolution*, pp. 6–7 and n.
14. OM, *Greater Britain*, pp. 105–6.   All quotations are from the 1932 edition unless otherwise stated.
15. Ibid. p. 106.
16. Ibid. p. 93.
17. Ibid. p. 93.
18. Ibid. p. 88.
19. OM, *Greater Britain* (1934) p. 131.
20. OM, *Tomorrow We Live*, pp. 28–30.
21. J. F. C. Fuller, *Towards Armageddon*, pp. 54–76.
22. OM, in *Daily Herald*, 25 Mar 1925.
23. OM, *Greater Britain*, pp. 93–5.
24. Quoted in Nigel Harris, *Competition and the Corporate Society*, p. 55.
25. *Spectator*, 16 Feb 1934, p. 225.
26. OM, *Tomorrow We Live*, p. 11.
27. Ibid. pp. 37–8.
28. Ibid. pp. 33–7.
29. Ibid. p. 45.
30. Ibid. p. 7.
31. *Action*, 11 Sept 1937.
32. OM, *Tomorrow We Live*, p. 37.
33. OM, *The Age of Plenty*, vol. I, no. 1(1934) p. 8.
34. OM, *Tomorrow We Live*, p. 15.
35. *Action*, 27 June 1937.
36. O. Spengler, *The Decline of the West* (1932 ed.) vol. I. p. 44.
37. Reprinted as ' The Philosophy of Fascism ', in *Fascist Quarterly*, vol. I, no. 1. (1935).
38. OM, *Tomorrow We Live*, p. 77.
39. *Fascist Quarterly*, vol. I, no. 3, p. 258.
40. ' James Drennan ', *BUF, Oswald Mosley and British Fascism*, p. 43.

41. *Action*, 30 Dec 1937.
42. Ibid. 12 Feb 1938.
43. *Blackshirt*, 26 Oct 1934.
44. Georg Brandes, *Frederick Nietzsche: an essay in aristocratic radicalism* (1914) p. 37.
45. OM, *Tomorrow We Live*, p. 16.
46. OM, *Fascism: 100 questions asked and answered*, Q. 20.
47. Ibid. Q. 21.
48. Ibid. Q. 24.
49. OM, *Tomorrow We Live*, p. 23.
50. Raven Thomson, in *Fascist Quarterly*, vol. i, no. 1, p. 27.
51. OM, *Fascism*, Q. 14.
52. OM, ' The Philosophy of Fascism ', p. 56.

Chapter 16.   The Anatomy of a Movement

1. Unpublished MS: 'The British Union of Fascists in Yorkshire 1934–1940 ', Trevelyan Scholarship Project (1960).
2. *Cavalcade*, 13 Nov 1937.
3. W. F. Mandle, 'The Leadership of the British Union of Fascists,' in *Australian Journal of Politics and History*, Dec 1966, pp. 362–3.
4. See Fuller, *Towards Armageddon*.
5. See Thompson, *English Landed Society*, ch. 12, on 'radicalisation' of the aristocracy.
6. *Action*, 15 Oct 1938.
7. *Blackshirt*, 26 April 1935.
8. *Daily Herald*, 21 July 1933; *Daily Telegraph*, 30 Sept 1933.
9. MP: transcript of speech.
10. Quoted in *Evening News*, 7 Nov 1934.
11. See R. Benewick, *Political Violence and Public Order*, pp. 267–8.
12. *Daily Mail*, 2 May 1934.
13. *Blackshirt*, 28 Dec 1934.
14. Colin Cross, *Fascists in Britain*, p. 137.
15. BU: Constitution and Rules, sect. v, p. 67.
16. *Blackshirt*, 18 Jan 1935.
17. Ibid. 22 Mar 1935.
18. Cross, *Fascists in Britain*, p. 137.
19. *Blackshirt*, 24 May 1935.
20. Cross, *Fascists in Britain*, p. 138.
21. *Blackshirt*, 11 Oct 1935.
22. This account is taken from ' The British Union of Fascists in Yorkshire 1934–1940 '.
23. *Action*, 21 May 1936.
24. Ibid. 6 May 1936.
25. Ibid. 9 Oct 1937.
26. Ibid. 6 Mar 1936.
27. Ibid. 2 July 1938.
28. *National Newsagent, Bookseller and Stationer*, 18 Feb 1939.
29. See *Daily Herald* ,14, 23 Dec 1938.
30. *Scotsman*, 4 Apr 1938; *Action*, 9 Apr 1938.
31. *Blackshirt*, 3 Jan 1936.
32. *Action*, 19 Dec 1936.
33. ' Who Backs Mosley, Fascist Promises and Fascist Performances ', Labour Research Department, summer 1934.

34. Benewick, *Political Violence*, p. 199, gives the sum as £100,000; see *ML*, p. 347.
35. MP: 1940 unclassified.
36. See Cross, *Fascists in Britain*, pp. 131–2; Benewick, *Political Violence*, pp. 109–10.
37. PRO: CAB 66/35.
38. *HC Deb.*, vol. 363, cols. 966–7.
39. Benewick, *Political Violence*, p. 303.

Chapter 17.   Leaders and Fellow-travellers

1. *Leeds Mercury*, 25 April 1934.
2. *News Chronicle*, 23 April 1934.
3. *Yorkshire Post*, 27 April 1934.
4. *Grimsby Evening Telegraph*, 18 Feb 1936.
5. *Southend Times*, 14 April 1937.
6. *Blackshirt*, 2 Nov 1934; 29 Mar 1935.
7. This quotation is taken from *Mosley: the facts*, p. 91.
8. This quotation is taken from ibid. p. 93.
9. J. A. Cole, *Lord Haw-Haw–and William Joyce*, p. 45.
10. *Action*, 23 Jan 1937.
11. Ibid. 18 June 1936.
12. *Jewish Chronicle*, 7 Dec 1934.
13. *ML*, p. 332.
14. *Fascist Week*, 17 Nov 1933.
15. *The Listener*, 21 Oct 1965; see also George Orwell, 'Inside the Whale', in *Collected Essays* (Mercury Books, 1961) pp. 145–9.
16. Douglas Jerrold, *Georgian Adventure*, p. 299.
17. Ibid. pp. 323–4.
18. See *The Best of Hugh Kingsmill*, ed. Michael Holroyd, p. 19; also T. S. Eliot, *Selected Prose*, ed. John Hayward, pp. 43–4.
19. *Action*, 2 April 1936.
20. John Harrison, *The Reactionaries*, p. 94.
21. Noel Stock, *The Life of Ezra Pound*, p. 350.
22. ' In Praise of Guy Fawkes ', reprinted in *Bernard Shaw: platform and pulpit*, ed. Dan H. Laurence, pp. 242–3.
23. Alastair Hamilton, *The Appeal of Fascism*, p. 270.
24. See particularly ' In Praise of Guy Fawkes ', pp. 244, 251, 254–5.
25. Hugh Ross Williamson, *Who Is for Liberty?*, p. 218.
26. Ibid. pp. 238–9.
27. See *European*, Oct 1953.
28. Quoted in *Radio Times*, 17 Aug 1972.
29. *European*, June 1954, pp. 56–7.
30. Beverley Nichols, *Men Do Not Weep*, pp. 21–2.

Chapter 18. The Politics of Confrontation

1. *Daily Telegraph*, 23 Dec 1932.
2. *Manchester Guardian*, 24 Oct 1932.
3. *News Chronicle, Glasgow Evening Citizen*, 7 Dec 1932.
4. For accounts of this meeting, including OM's own version, see *Manchester Guardian*, 13, 14, 15 Mar 1933.
5. *Sussex Daily News*, 14 Nov 1934.
6. See Cross, *Fascists in Britain*, p. 84; Benewick, *Political Violence*, p. 214.   This was less true after 1937.

7. *Daily Worker*, 29 Jan 1930.

8. R. Palme Dutt, *Fascism and Social Revolution*, p. 82.

9. For these accounts, see *Daily Herald*, 4 June 1932; *Manchester Guardian*, 6 June 1932; *Forward*, 11 June 1932.

10. For a vivid description of these tactics, see Douglas Hyde, *I Believed*, pp. 39 ff.

11. Henry Pelling, *The British Communist Party*, p. 39.

12. PRO: MEPOL 2/3077.

13. For details, see Bob Darke, *Cockney Communist*, especially ch. 4.

14. MP: memorandum on the *Star* libel action, 1934.

15. *New Statesman*, 16 June 1934.

16. *Oldham Evening Chronicle*, 25 Jan 1935.

17. *Manchester Guardian*, 7 Jan 1935.

18. *Action*, 3 July 1937.

19. *Blackshirt*, 13 June 1936.

20. See Special Branch reports for April 1937, Oct 1938: PRO: MEPOL 2/3043.

21. The same is true of other countries. In Spain the left unleashed violence against José Primo de Rivera's Falange to force it to ' choose ' the right. (See Stanley G, Payne, *Falange: a history of Spanish fascism*, pp. 52 ff.) As in England, one of the earliest left-wing tactics was to attack falangist newsvendors.

22. See ' Mandrake ', in *Sunday Telegraph*, 28 July 1963.

23. *Daily Mail*, 23 April 1934.

Chapter 19.   The Beast Unchained?

1. *Daily Worker*, 9 June 1934.

2. Ibid. 28 May 1934.

3. Ibid. 26 May 1934.

4. These Special Branch reports can be seen in PRO: MEPOL 2/4319.

5. Benewick, *Political Violence*, pp. 181–2.

6. Statement of Sgt Thompson.

7. Quoted in Frederic Mullaly, *Fascism inside England*, p. 36.

8. *The Listener*, 13 June 1934.

9. *Spectator*, 15 June 1934.

10. Mullaly, *Fascism inside England*, p. 38.

11. *Fascists at Olympia*, compiled by ' Vindicator ' (Gollancz, 1934), *Eye-witnesses at Olympia* (Union of Democratic Control, 1934). Both are reproduced in Mullaly, *Fascism inside England*, pp. 34–7 and 91–100.

12. Quoted in BUF, *Red Violence and Blue Lies*, p. 36.

13. *Daily Telegraph*, 11 June 1934.

14. Quoted in *Red Violence and Blue Lies*, p. 17.

15. *Sunday Pictorial*, 24 June 1934.

16. MP: unclassified.

17. All this testimony is to be found in PRO: MEPOL 2/4319.

18. *New Statesman*, 16 June 1934.

19. Letter to *Manchester Guardian*, 15 June 1934.

20. P. Toynbee, *Friends Apart*, p. 21.

21. *ML*, p. 299.

22. *Sheffield Daily Telegraph*, 29 June 1934.

23. Weber, *Action Française*, p. 146.

Chapter 20. Who Was then the Englishman?

1. For details of these groups, see Mrs Hilary Blume, ' A Study of Anti-Semitic Groups in Britain 1918–1940 ', M.Phil. thesis, Sussex University, 1971.

2. For a general discussion, see J. W. Parkes, *The Jewish Problem in the Modern World* (1939).

3. Rather the reverse; e.g., a meeting at the Marcus Samuel Hall, Stamford Hill, London, in 1923 when OM appeared with Miss Nettie Adler, Rev. S. Levy, Rabbi Harris Cohen, the Rev. J. Shapiro and several other well-known Jews to discuss the League of Nations from the Jewish point of view (*Daily Herald*, 18 Mar 1935).

4. Nicolson Diaries, MS.; Nicolson's letter to Cynthia Mosley, dated 9 Sept 1932, is in MP.

5. *Jewish Chronicle*, 6 Jan 1933.

6. A. K. Chesterton and Joseph Leftwich, *The Tragedy of Antisemitism*, p. 65.

7. Ibid. p. 65.

8. These details are taken from PRO: MEPOL 2/3069.

9. *Jewish Chronicle*, 4 Aug 1933.   See also 15 June 1934 (after Olympia), 7 Sept 1934 and 14 Nov 1934, when Lord Melchett urged Jews to stay away from fascist meetings. One motive of Jewish leaders was to prevent Jews from being popularly identified with communists. (Neville Laski, *Jewish Rights and Jewish Wrongs* (1939) p. 135.)

10. *Blackshirt*, 30 Sept, 18 Nov 1933.

11. Information about the boycott can be found in *Keesing's Contemporary Archives Weekly Diary of World Events, 1931–4*, pp. 729–30; *Jewish Chronicle*, 28 July, 4 Aug 1933; ' A Blow at Oppression: the Jewish anti-Nazi boycott 1933–9 ', in *Weiner Library Bulletin*, no. 1 (1960), which claims great success for the boycott in damaging the German economy.   For a contrary – and probably more accurate – view, see Stephen S. Wise, *Challenging Years: the autobiography of Stephen Wise*, p. 260.   S. Salomon, *The Jews of Britain*, pp. 86–95, gives British details.   For BUF views on the boycott, see *Blackshirt*, 1 Nov 1935, 29 Aug 1936, 23 Jan 1937.

12. See *Jewish Chronicle*, 10 Nov, 24 Nov 1933, for both quotations.

13. The Beckett libel case raises the interesting question of how much of the scurrilous anti-semitic material that went into the two BUF newspapers, *Action* and *Blackshirt*, OM saw and approved. Today he claims that constant travelling made him incapable of exercising effective supervision of the papers (*ML*, p. 342).   In the Camrose libel case he claimed that he had not seen the article in question because he was ill with influenza at the time. Beckett, who had by this time left the movement, stated on the contrary that ' The proofs were read, the article instructed and approved by a certain individual.' (Harold Hobson and others, *The Pearl of Days: an intimate memoir of the Sunday Times, 1822–1972*, p.197).   OM's claim is also denied by another *Action* editor, A. K. Chesterton, who likewise says OM scrutinised all the material going in (*Jewish Chronicle*, 13 Dec 1968).

14. *ML*, pp. 346–7.   See also a comment by Kingsley Martin on Rothermere and advertisers in *Political Quarterly*, Mar 1934.   Randolph Churchill wrote: ' I have seen the *Daily Mail* abandon the support of Sir Oswald Mosley in the thirties under the pressure of Jewish advertisers' (*Spectator*, 27 Dec 1963). Since Randolph Churchill worked for Lord Rothermere at the time this statement is not without weight.

15. OM at the Albert Hall, quoted in *Blackshirt*, 2 Nov 1934. His speech is transcribed verbatim in this issue.

16. Chesterton and Leftwich, *Tragedy of Antisemitism*, p. 65.

17. *Action*, 7 Nov 1936.

18. The most comprehensive collection of these phrases is to be found in OM's speech at the Sheffield Town Hall, reported in *Blackshirt*, 2 Aug 1935.

19. Ibid. 17 May 1935.

20. *Western Daily Press*, 17 May 1935.

21. OM, *Fascism*, QQ. 95–9.

22. OM, *Tomorrow We Live*, p. 65.

Chapter 21. The Campaign in East London

1. For the clothing industry, see *Evening Standard*, 3 Nov 1936; for a *Daily Herald* analysis of the furniture trade, see the issues of 14 and 23 Dec 1938.

2. For an interesting account of the origins of Marks & Spencers, see an interview with Lord Sieff in the *Observer* colour supplement, 30 June 1968.

3. *Blackshirt*, 30 May 1936.

4. Bernard Gainer, *The Alien Invasion*, p. 44.

5. Clement Bruning, in *Blackshirt*, 4 Oct 1935.

6. *New Statesman*, 7 Nov 1936.

7. For the best account, see Gainer, *Alien Invasion*.

8. *Action*, 6 Mar 1937.

9. *HC Deb.*, vol. 309, cols 1596–8.

10. Benewick, *Political Violence*, p. 217.

11. These figures are compiled from the monthly police reports on the East End, 1936–9. PRO: MEPOL 2/3043.

12. *Evening Standard*, 2, 5, Nov 1936.

13. PRO: MEPOL 2/3125.

14. For several such cases, see PRO: MEPOL 2/3085–7.

15. PRO: MEPOL 2/3087.

16. Hyde, *I Believed*, p. 141.

17. PRO: MEPOL 2/3109.

18. PRO: MEPOL 2/3043. Sir Philip Game's report to the Home Office submitted at the beginning of Oct 1936, together with the Special Branch report for the same month, gives the following account of the dissension within BU at this time:

> The British Union of Fascists (Sir Oswald Mosley) has given a definite warning to its speakers to refrain from attacking the Jews at public meetings, it being emphasised that arrests of its members for Jew baiting is likely to do the Fascist movement in this country more harm than good.
>
>   . . . an influential section of the British Union of Fascists' leading officials strongly deprecates any suggestion that the party should modify its policy . . . and is urging the necessity for showing the country that fascists are not afraid of facing imprisonment for speaking what they believe to be the truth about the Jews. On September 15th, William JOYCE (Director of Propaganda) called together the principal Party speakers and delivered to them what amounted to a tirade against Jews and the attitude taken up by the Government on anti-semitism. While he advised them to refrain from indulging in personal abuse of Jews (expressions such as 'filthy swine', etc.) he

exhorted them not to retreat in the face of Police persecution and declared that, if necessary, all Fascist speakers should be prepared to face imprisonment rather than comply with the dictum of the authorities that they were not to attack Jewry. Large scale arrests would, in his opinion, inevitably tend to intensify antagonism towards Jews.

In the absence of Sir Oswald Mosley this section have evolved a plan for deliberately courting prosecution by the delivery of a carefully prepared anti-Semitic speech by one of the party leaders at a large rally, possibly that to be held on October 4th.

19. PRO: MEPOL 2/3115.
20. *Liverpool Post*, 28 Sept 1936.
21. PRO: MEPOL 2/3043: Sept 1936.
22. PRO: MEPOL 2/3125.
23. PRO: MEPOL 2/3043: Oct, Nov 1936.
24. Ibid.: Nov 1936.
25. Ibid.
26. Ibid.: June 1937. Neville Laski, President of the Board of Deputies, warned against ' Jewish mushroom organisations which had sprung up . . . ostensibly to fight anti-semitism, but which were in reality nothing but " rackets " ' (Oct 1936 report).
27. PRO: MEPOL 2/3043: July 1937.
28. Ibid.: Oct 1936.
29. *Blackshirt*, 10 Oct 1936.
30. See ' Jack Spot ', in *Sunday Times Magazine*, 8 Aug 1965; Brian McConnell and others, *The Evil Firm – the Rise and Fall of the Brothers Kray*, pp. 57–8; also *Sunday Chronicle*, 16 Jan 1955, for Jack Spot's personal reminiscences of this occasion.
31. PRO: MEPOL 2/3043: Nov 1936.
32. Ibid.: Nov 1937.
33. *Blackshirt*, 25 April 1936.
34. PRO: MEPOL 2/3043: Mar 1937.
35. Ibid.
36. BU did not improve on its March results in the borough elections of October 1937. See Benewick, *Political Violence*, pp. 283–4.

Chapter 22. The Government Steps In

1. Memorandum by the Home Secretary to the Cabinet, 25 May 1934. PRO: CAB 24/249.
2. Critchley had promised Mosley the hall. The Assistant Commissioner replied that he should keep his word, but impose a bond so large that it would be impossible for Mosley to pay. This he did. The Assistant Commissioner comments: ' Critchley impressed me as being anxious to meet us and would willingly get out of his promise, but he wanted to shield himself behind us ' (PRO: MEPOL 2/3073).
3. The police were not usually as direct as at the White City. A more usual tactic was for a municipal authority to insert into a letting agreement a clause specifying the presence of police as a condition for booking. The police would then say they could not come, or alternatively that they would expect a large fee for their services. PRO: MEPOL 2/3083.
4. PRO: MEPOL 2/3077.

5. See PRO: MEPOL 2/3104.
6. See *Action*, 25 June 1936, for a verbatim report of the trial in the Oxford Police Court.
7. *Oxford Mail*, 26 May 1936.
8. *Manchester Daily Dispatch*, 29 June 1936.
9. *Manchester Guardian*, 20 July 1936.
10. *Manchester Daily Dispatch*, 28 Sept 1936.
11. *Oldham Evening Chronicle and Standard*, 29 Sept 1936.
12. The Public Order Act can be found in *Public Acts and Measures* (1936) pp. 60–7.
13. *HC Deb.*, vol. 317, col. 1388.
14. Ibid. col. 1351.
15. Memorandum by the Home Secretary (Sir John Simon) to the Cabinet, 12 Oct 1936. PRO: CAB 24/264.
16. *Action*, 17 Oct 1936.
17. *ML*, p. 303.
18. For the judgments in the two cases, see Costin and Watson, *The Law and the Working of the Constitution*, vol. II, pp. 297–8, 315–17.
19. R. A. Cline, in *Spectator*, 24 Aug 1962.
20. See Benewick, *Political Violence*, p. 180.
21. *Political Quarterly*, Jan 1937.
22. Memorandum by the home secretary (Sir John Gilmour) to the Cabinet, 11 July 1934. PRO: CAB 24/250.

Chapter 23. The Peace of Europe

1. Winston S. Churchill, *The Second World War*, vol. I, p. 163.
2. OM, *Greater Britain*, pp. 140, 143–6.
3. *New Statesman*, 15 July 1933.
4. ' The World Alternative ', in *Fascist Quarterly*, July 1936, pp. 383–4.
5. Ibid. p. 392.
6. *Action*, 18 Jan 1940.
7. See *The Origins of the Second World War*, ed. Esmonde M. Robertson, for the views of H. W. Koch and Alan Bullock (pp. 163–4, 220).
8. Ibid. p. 162.
9. Alan Bullock, *Hitler: a study in tyranny*, p. 540.
10. Bullock, *Hitler*, p. 308.
11. K. Middlemas, *Diplomacy of Illusion*, ch. 5, especially pp. 160 ff., 175–6.
12. OM, *Tomorrow We Live*, p. 67.
13. OM, *Alternative*, pp. 114–24.
14. OM, *The British Peace – How to Get It* (1939).
15. OM, *Fascism*, Q. 90.
16. Taylor, *Beaverbrook*, p. 344.
17. Churchill, *Second World War*, vol. I, pp. 162–5.
18. For the most detailed discussion of these conflicts, see K. Middlemas and John Barnes, *Baldwin*, pp. 829–41; for the liveliest, Barnet, *Collapse*, pp. 350 ff.
19. *Daily Mail*, 29 Aug 1935.
20. Middlemas and Barnes, *Baldwin*, p. 838.
21. Churchill, *Second World War*, vol. I, p. 137.
22. *Action*, 14 May 1936.
23. The Peace Ballot was hopeless as a scientific test of opinion (see Barnet, *Collapse*, pp. 359–60).

24. *Notts Guardian*, 9 Mar 1936.
25. *Action*, 14 May 1936.
26. OM, *Tomorrow We Live*, p. 69.
27. *Action*, 25 June 1936.
28. Ibid. 18 Nov 1937.
29. Ibid. 24 July 1937, 6 Jan 1938.
30. Raven Thomson, in *Action*, 26 Dec 1936.
31. Churchill, *Second World War*, vol. i, p. 176.
32. See ibid. vol. i, pp. 162 ff. See also Baldwin's remarks to the French Ambassador on the eve of the Abyssinian crisis: ' The British people have always countenanced dictatorships as long as the dictatorships concern themselves with domestic affairs of their own countries. When dictatorships have shown an urge to sally forth from home, to poke their noses beyond their own frontiers, and to disturb the peace, Great Britain had been compelled, sooner or later, to intervene in order to free the world from the danger of the dictatorships. That is what England did with Napoleon. That is what England did with Wilhelm II. That is what England will do with Mussolini. . . . ' Quoted in Middlemas and Barnes, *Baldwin*, p. 857.
33. F. Gannon, *The British Press and Germany, 1936–39*, p. 294.
34. *Action*, 26 Feb 1938.
35. Ibid. 5 Mar 1938.
36. Ibid. 19 March 1938.
37. Ibid. 17 Sept 1938.
38. A. J. P. Taylor, *The Origins of the Second World War* (Penguin ed.) p. 195.
39. *Action*, 3 Sept 1938.
40. Ibid. 24 Sept 1938.
41. Taylor, *Second World War*, p. 223.
42. *Action*, 26 Nov 1938.
43. Ibid. 17 Dec 1938.
44. Ibid. 8 Apr 1939.
45. Ibid. 29 July 1939.
46. Ibid. 22 Apr 1939.
47. Ibid. 13 May 1939.
48. Quoted in ibid. 20 May 1939.
49. *Forward*, 3 June 1939.
50. Letter dated 17 July in author's possession.
51. OM at Ridley Road, Hackney, 8 Oct 1939.
52. OM, in *Action*, 9 May 1940.
53. Ibid. 25 Jan 1940.
54. Ibid. 5 Oct, 9 Nov, 16 Nov, 23 Nov 1939; 25 Jan, 18 Apr, 9 May, 16 May 1940.

Chapter 24. Churchill's Guest

1. Cross, *Fascists in Britain*, p. 193.
2. PRO: CAB 65/7.
3. Note by Tom Harrisson from the Mass Observation Archive: ' Attitudes to Oswald Mosley in the Thirties and early Forties '.
4. PRO: CAB 66/35.
5. Quoted by Paul Addison in *Lloyd George: twelve essays*, ed. A. J. P. Taylor, p. 371.

6. C. F. Clayton, *The Wall Is Strong*.
7. See *The Times*, 10 Aug, 8 Nov 1940.
8. *HC Deb.*, vol. 367, cols 837 ff.
9. Ibid. col. 867.
10. Churchill, *Second World War*, vol. II, p. 627.
11. MP: OM to Stokes, 15 Jan 1941.
12. Churchill, *Second World War*, vol. III, pp. 749–50.
13. PRO: CAB 66/20 WP (41) 279.
14. PRO: CAB 65/34: April 1943.
15. Quoted by Herbert Morrison: *HC Deb.*, vol. 395, col. 467.
16. Taylor, *Beaverbrook*, p. 551.
17. HC Deb., vol. 395, col. 406.
18. PRO: CAB 65/40.
19. *HC Deb.*, vol. 395, col. 1660.
20. For the whole debate, see ibid. cols 395–478.
21. Cross, *Fascists in Britain*, p. 91.

Chapter 25. The Faustian Riddle

1. E. H. Carr, *The October Revolution*, p. 58.
2. Humphrey Trevelyan, *Goethe and the Greeks*, p. 43.
3. C. M. Bowra, *The Greek Experience*, p. 46.
4. G. Lowes Dickinson, *The Greek View of Life* (1929) p. 27.
5. Bowra, *Greek Experience*, p. 50.
6. Quoted in ibid. p. 127.
7. E. Heller, *The Disinherited Mind*, p. 73.
8. Bowra, *Greek Experience*, p. 36.
9. Trevelyan, *Goethe*, p. 72.
10. Quoted in ibid. p. 169.
11. Quoted in Heller, *Disinherited Mind*, p. 75.
12. Trevelyan, *Goethe*, p. 247.
13. F. M. Stawell and G. Lowes Dickinson, *Goethe and Faust*, p. 243.
14. Introduction to Goethe's *Faust* (Euphorion Books, 1949) p. 6.
15. OM, *Alternative*, pp. 307–10.
16. Ibid. p. 313.
17. Ibid. p. 151.
18. Eric Bentley, *A Century of Hero-worship*, p. 248.
19. Ibid. p. 188.

Chapter 26. The Vision Splendid

1. *My Answer*, p. 29.
2. See *Union*, 13 Mar 1948.
3. See *Daily Mail*, 23 Sept 1946.
4. Geoffrey Barraclough, *An Introduction to Contemporary History*, p. 32.
5. ' Still Trying ', in *New Statesman and Nation*, 22 Oct 1949.
6. For OM's early post-war views on Africa, see *The Alternative*, pp. 164 ff.; *Union*, 13 Mar 1948; Jeffrey Hamm, in *Union*, 2 April 1949; and ' D.S. ' (Desmond Stewart?), in *Union*, 20 Mar 1949.
7. *The Alternative*, p. 179.
8. *European*, Sept 1955.
9. These quotations are from *ML*, p. 485; Pirow, ' Why I came to Britain ',

in *Union*, 17 April 1948; ' Pirow Proposals ', in *European*, Aug 1953; OM, in *European*, April 1954.

10. *European*, April 1954.

11. See *Mosley: policy and debate*, pp. 38, 40.

12. OM speech (transcript), 15 Nov 1947.

13. ' Either we must have a war against Russia before she has the atom bomb or we will have to lie down and let them govern us. . . . Anything is better than submission ' (Bertrand Russell, in *Observer*, 21 Nov 1948).

14. *Union*, 3 July 1948.

15. *European*, Oct 1954.

16. For the post-war European movement, see Lord Gladwyn, *The European Idea*; Arnold Zurcher, *The Struggle to Unite Europe 1940–1958*; Andrew and Francis Boyd, *Western Union;* and Henri Brugmans, *L'Idée Européenne*.

17. Quoted in Weber, *Varieties of Fascism*, p. 185.

18. Quoted in A. James Gregor, *The Ideology of Fascism*, pp. 388–9.

19. *European*, May 1953.

20. OM, *Europe: faith and plan*, p. 27.

21. For the best account of this breakdown, see D. Calleo and B. Rowland, *America and the World Political Economy*, pp. 3–4.

22. *Daily Mail*, 25 April 1968; *Daily Express*, 25 Aug 1972.

23. *Union*, 4 Sept 1948; Victor Burgess had been beaten up a couple of months previously (ibid. 3 July 1948).

24. e.g., ibid. 3 Dec 1949.

25. ' Sgt. Major Flynn spoke first of his experiences with terrorists in Palestine, receiving a most sympathetic and attentive hearing. . . . Victor Burgess . . . voiced the protest of Union Movement against alien gangsterism which denied to the people of Brixton the opportunity of hearing the Union Movement case ' (ibid. 3 July 1948).

26. Michael Hamlyn, in *Sunday Times*, 17 June 1964.

27. *ML*, p. 439.

28. Ibid. pp. 434–8. Angelo Del Boca and Mario Giovana, *Fascism Today*, p. 84, say that OM attended a conference at Malmö, Sweden, in 1951. This appears to be a complete invention. Like all books on contemporary fascism, this one is full of the most grotesque errors.

29. On 23 Oct 1947 Desmond Stewart moved the resolution ' that this House would deplore legislation to curb fascist activities in this country ' at the Oxford Union. Rather surprisingly, it was carried by 350 votes to 178.

30. OM, *Europe*, p. 43.

31. The fullest exposition of the ' wage–price ' mechanism is to be found in ibid. pp. 43 ff.

32. Letter to the author.

33. OM's actual suggestion was that a man should be allowed to pass on wealth he has created to his children, but his children should not be allowed to pass on *that* wealth to their children.

34. OM, *Europe*, p. 92.

35. *European*, May 1957.

36. Ibid. June 1953.

37. OM, *Europe*, p. 86.

38. Ibid. p. 86.

39. *European*, Feb 1958.

40. OM, *Europe*, p. 86.
41. *European*, Jan 1959.
42. Ibid. July 1954.
43. Ibid. Nov 1954.
44. *European*, Oct 1956.
45. Ibid. May 1955.
46. OM, *The Alternative*, p. 53.
47. Colin Wilson, in *Twentieth Century*, Dec 1959.
48. Desmond Stewart, in *European*, June 1953.
49. Ibid. Jan 1956.
50. Preface to the American edition of *ML*.

Chapter 27. A New Beginning?

1. ' Return of the Man in Black ', in *John Bull*, 5 Sept 1959.
2. *Birmingham Post*, 26 July 1956.
3. See *European*, Sept 1955.
4. For West Indian views at the time, see *Manchester Guardian*, 13 June 1952; *New Statesman* (letter from Mr Frank Hill) 1 Oct 1955.
5. For economic views, see the *Economist* line, quoted in Andrew Roth, *Enoch Powell: Tory Tribune* (1970) p. 209; examples of Labour internationalist sentiment are given in Paul Foot, *Immigration and Race in British Politics* (1965) pp. 113, 117; e.g., James Callaghan, who in 1946 talked of the ' artificial segregation of nation from nation '.
6. Ibid. pp. 190 ff.
7. *Mosley: right or wrong*, p. 120.
8. *The Coloured Invasion* (UM, 1958).
9. *Action*, 11 July 1958.
10. *Mosley: right or wrong*, p. 115.
11. Quoted in *North Kensington Leader*, May 1959.
12. *Daily Mirror*, 23 Sept 1967; *Action*, 15 Sept 1969.
13. *National European*, May 1965.
14. For the ' race riots ' of Aug/Sept 1958, see *Daily Sketch*, 3 Sept 1958, and *The Times*, 26 Aug and 12, 16 Sept 1958.
15. *European*, Oct 1958.
16. For a good account of the Teddy Boy movement, see Paul Rock and Stanley Cohen, ' The Teddy Boy ', in *The Age of Affluence*, ed. V. Bogdanor and R. Skidelsky.
17. *The Times*, 8 Sept 1958.
18. *Twentieth Century*, Dec 1959.
19. Nicholas Mosley to OM, 3 Oct 1958.
20. Interview in *Guardian*, 29 June 1971.
21. *Shepherd's Bush Gazette*, 8 April 1959.
22. *North Kensington Leader*, May 1959.
23. Ibid. Feb/Mar 1959.
24. D. E. Butler and Richard Rose, *The British General Election of 1959*, p. 179.
25. *Manchester Guardian*, 29 Feb 1960.
26. Private information.
27. *Action*, 10 May 1963.
28. *Sunday Telegraph*, 5 Aug 1962; *The Times*, 3 Aug 1962. For the 62 Group, see *Sunday Times*, 19 Feb 1967.

29. *The Times*, 3 Aug 1962.
30. See the account in *Sunday Times*, 13 July 1972, based on the Cabinet Papers.
31. High Court of Justice, Queen's Bench Division, 16 Feb 1966. Constantine FitzGibbon relates (*The Times*, 15 June 1968) that when compiling a feature for the B.B.C. in 1965 on British fascism he was told on ' no account to record the voice of Sir Oswald Mosley ' and that OM was ' permanently banned from the B.B.C.'
32. See *Observer*, 20 Oct 1968; *Evening Standard*, 22 Oct 1968; *Sunday Telegraph*, 20 Oct 1968.
33. Private information.
34. *Broadsheet*, no. 9 (16 Sept 1971).
35. Ibid. no. 7 (26 April 1971).
36. Ibid. unnumbered (27 Nov 1970).
37. Ibid. nos. 10, 16 (8 Oct 1971, 12 Sept 1972).
38. Ibid. no. 15 (30 June 1972).

Bibliography

Primary Sources

Access to Mosley's private papers has been limited. How much exists, or where they are located, is difficult to say. Mosley himself never kept a diary, though his mother did. He also wrote frequently to his mother from school and from the front line in the First World War. When she died in 1949, her personal papers appear to have come into the possession of Mosley's younger brother John, who did not seem to know much either about their whereabouts or their contents. In any case, both he and the youngest brother Edward took the view that private family history should not go beyond the family, especially when the persons concerned are still alive. So it will be up to some future biographer to wrest the secrets of Mosley's childhood and youth from these sources, if by that time they still exist.

Mosley's own attitude is different. He is as uninterested in his personal past as he is in other people's. Also, in the course of a long, tempestuous life, he has moved house so many times – privately as well as politically – that his papers have become hopelessly scattered – in England, France and Ireland. Much has undoubtedly been lost or destroyed. Some fascist records were seized by the police in 1940 and never returned. Others were hidden and hit by bombs. Individual members of the British Union of Fascists or post-war Union Movement appropriated papers which they are either still guarding or which in turn they have lost or destroyed. Mosley's Irish house burnt down in 1954. One can only hope that someone will, before it is too late, set about organising a proper archive of material relating to Mosley's own life and his political activities. They have become part of English history, and therefore historical records of them ought not to be lost through carelessness or through that exaggerated concern for not revealing information to ' the enemy ' which still characterises veterans of the fascist struggle.

Still, I have not drawn a complete blank. Mosley himself has generously made available letters written to him or his first wife, Cynthia, in the 1920s and early 1930s. (I have not, however, been able to see any of his correspondence with people still alive, or with Bertrand Russell in the 1950s.) His eldest son Nicholas has also kindly allowed me to use the letters that passed between him and his father between 1941 and 1958. The difficulty here has been to decipher Mosley's handwriting. Harold Nicolson's unpublished papers, including not only his diary but some correspondence with Mosley, are the most important sources for the New Party and the beginnings of fascism. I have also been able to see an important collection of political papers relating chiefly to the internal affairs of both the British Union of Fascists and Union Movement, but containing interesting material on Mosley's war-time imprisonment, and a file on Mosley's early work for the Peace with Ireland Council in 1921. The Curzon Papers give an illuminating picture of the young Mosley at the time of his marriage to Cynthia Curzon. There is a letter from Mosley to Lord Robert Cecil in the Cecil Papers, which also contain some interesting material on the Centre Party project of 1920 – in which Mosley was involved. The historian Hugh Thomas, biographer of John Strachey, has allowed me to use two letters from Mosley to Strachey in 1926. From the

Franklin D. Roosevelt Library (Hyde Park, New York) I was able to get a number of letters passing between the Mosleys and Franklin Roosevelt the same year. No doubt many letters from or to Mosley will come to light once he or his correspondents die.

The availability of official government papers for the inter-war years has also been of great help. I have used them extensively for Mosley's career as a minister in 1929-30, for the Government's attitude to fascism in the 1930s and for Mosley's imprisonment 1940-3. In particular, the files of the Metropolitan Police relating to public disturbances and to East London in the 1930s have been especially helpful – this is the first time I am aware of their being used. How much still remains closed under the Hundred-year Rule is impossible to say. But I cannot believe that it will yield much of significance. I have also seen the minutes of the League of Nations Union for the period 1919-24, the Labour Party's National Executive Committee for the years 1924-31 as well as the minutes of the Birmingham Borough Labour Party and of the Birmingham I.L.P. for the same period. There is little of value in them: minutes are rarely written with the historian in mind.

The relative lack of personal papers has imposed special difficulties. Some biographies almost write themselves, the biographer doing little more than providing a running commentary on the ample material. Here the biographer has had to do most of the work himself. I do not regret this, for the challenge posed by writing about Mosley is a challenge not of description, but of interpretation, not just of Mosley's life but of what has happened to England in the last seventy years and of his relationship to those events.

The primary published sources on Mosley's life are the newspapers, weekly and monthly journals (both in Britain and abroad) and the volumes of *Hansard* (from 1919 to 1931). I am indebted to Mosley's office for furnishing me with thirty volumes of press cuttings covering the years 1919-40, and for making available numerous cuttings for the post-war period. In addition the *Harrow Observer* and the *Birmingham Town Crier* are the best sources for those two respective episodes in Mosley's career; and the *New Leader* is well worth studying not only for his own articles but for the I.L.P. in the 1920s. Many journals with material on Mosley – *Westminster Gazette, Nation and Athenaeum, Fortnightly Review, Weekend Review, Saturday Review, Everyman,* etc. – are now defunct, the *New Statesman* and *Spectator* being the sole significant survivors of that multitude of political weeklies which once catered to the needs of an imperial ruling class. The journals of the pre-war New Party and British Union of Fascists, and Mosley's post-war Union Movement –*Action, Blackshirt, Fascist Week, Union* and *National European* for the newspapers; *Fascist Quarterly, British Union Quarterly, Age of Plenty* and the *European* for the periodicals – are the chief primary sources for Mosley's post-1931 political career. Mosley contributed to them all; they reveal a great deal about the ideas he espoused and the movement he led.

Mosley has probably spoken and written more than any British politician this century except Churchill. The following are his books and most important essays: *Revolution by Reason* (1925) described by Sidney Pollard as an ' isolated *tour de force* '; ' The Labour Party's Financial Policy ', in *Socialist Review*, September 1927; ' Mr Lloyd George and Unemployment ', in *Labour Magazine*, April 1929; ' From Tory to Labour ', in *Labour Magazine*, May 1929; ' Old Parties or New ', in *Political Quarterly*, January-March 1932; *The Greater Britain* (1932), which Harold Nicolson thought an ' amazing achievement '; *Taxation and the People* (1933); ' The Philosophy of Fascism ', in *Fascist Quarterly*, January 1935; ' The World Alternative ', in *Fascist Quarterly*, July 1936; *Fascism: 100 questions asked and answered* (1936); *Tomorrow We Live* (1938), the most lucid introduction to Mosley's ideas in the 1930s; *The British Peace: how to get it* (1940); *My Answer* (1946); *The Alternative* (1947), the most philosophical of Mosley's books, reflecting his war-time prison-reading; *The European Situation: the third force* (1950); *European Socialism* (1951); introduction to Goethe's *Faust*, trans. Bayard Taylor (Euphorion Books, 1952); review of Erich Heller's *The Disinherited Mind*, in *European*, April 1953; *Policy and Debate* (1954); ' The Problem of Power: government of tomorrow ', in *European*, July 1955; ' Automation: problem and solution ', in *European*, October 1955; ' Wagner and Shaw: a synthesis', in *European*, March 1956; review of Colin Wilson's *The Outsider*, in *European*, February 1957; *Europe: faith and plan* (1958), also published in French, German and Italian; *Mosley: right or wrong?* (1961), the most accessible statement of his post-war policies; *My Life* (1968); and ' Democracy ', in *Eboracum* (York University), 1 December 1970. *Mosley: the facts* (1958) is a useful compilation by friends of speeches and writings. The most interesting of Mosley's post-war writings are to be found in his commentaries and articles in the *European*, a monthly journal which ran from 1953 to 1959. In addition, there have been the Mosley News Letters (1946–7), his ' Analysis ' column in *Action* and *National European*, and since 1970 his privately circulated Broadsheets. With the exception of *My Life* all his books and articles after 1931 have been published by his own publishing companies – Greater Britain Publications, Action Press, Sanctuary Press, Mosley Publications, Euphorion Books. Since 1935 or there-abouts none of these publications have been generally available in bookshops. It would be interesting to know how well they sold.

Secondary Sources

My Life is Mosley's autobiography. There has been only one previous biography, or rather hagiography – A. K. Chesterton's *Oswald Mosley: portrait of a leader* (1938) – although there is a considerable amount of biographical material in 'James Drennan'(pseud.), *BUF, Oswald Mosley and British Fascism*(1934), and Colin Cross, *The Fascists in Britain* (1961). R. Reynell Bellamy's ' We Marched with Mosley ' is an unpublished inside account of British fascism by an admirer of Mosley with much useful biographical information, especially on Mosley's child-hood and First World War experiences. E. Tangye Lean's *The Napoleonists: a study in political disaffection 1760–1960* (1970) has some interesting biographical detail and makes some fascinating connections between Mosley and other ' Napo-leonists '. The best general books covering the central period of Mosley's life are C. L. Mowat, *Britain between the Wars 1918–1940* (1955), and A. J. P. Taylor, *English History 1914–1945* (1965). Samuel Beer, *Modern British Politics* (1965), is the best on its subject. Peter Quennell has edited a useful collection of essays, *Life in Britain between the Wars* (1970). For a brilliant economic background see Karl Polanyi, *The Great Transformation* (1944).

Mosley's career spanned so many political parties and touched on so many political and philosophical issues that it is best to discuss the secondary sources I have found most helpful under definite headings.

Mosley's Ancestry, Childhood and Youth

Important sources for Mosley's ancestry are: Sir Oswald Mosley, *Family Memoir* (1849), an idealised, pious retrospect; W. E. A. Axon's *Lancashire Gleanings* (1883); *Mosley Family: memoranda*, ed. Ernest Axon (1902); and *Annals of Manchester* ed.

W. E. A. Axon (1886). All these works, together with John Booker's *History of the Ancient Chapels of Didsbury and Chorlton* (1857) may be found in the Manchester City Central Public Library. F. A. Slangley has an account of Mosley's grandfather's quarrel with the local Rector in his *History of St Mary's Parish Church, Rolleston* (1960). For the origins of the Mosley family fortunes I have consulted W. J. Ashley, *An Introduction to English Economic History and Theory* (1893); Lawrence Stone, ' The Anatomy of the Elizabethan Aristocracy ', in *Economic History Review*, vol. 18 (1948); Hugh Trevor Roper, ' The Elizabethan Aristocracy: an anatomy anatomised ', in *Economic History Review*, 2nd ser. vol. 3 (1951); *Social Change and Revolution in England 1540–1640*, ed. Lawrence Stone (1965). Lord Morley's *Life of Richard Cobden* (1881) has details of Cobden's quarrel with the Mosleys' ' feudal livery ' in Manchester; see also Arthur Redford, *The History of Local Government in Manchester*, 3 vols (1939–40). For the English country gentleman, the two most important books are G. E. Mingay, *English Landed Society in the Eighteenth Century* (1968), and F. M. L. Thompson, *English Landed Society in the Nineteenth Century* (1963). For the transformation from the aristocratic to the bourgeois life-style, there is a good essay by Mario Praz, ' The Victorian Mood: a reappraisal ', in *The Nineteenth Century World*, ed. Guy Métraux and François Crouzet (1963). For a history of Winchester see J. D'E. Firth, *Winchester* (1936); for Sandhurst, Brigadier Sir John Smythe, *Sandhurst* (1961), and Hugh Thomas, *The Story of Sandhurst* (1961). Sir Robert Bruce Lockhart has some reminiscences of Mosley at Sandhurst in his *Your England* (1955).

Background and War

For late nineteenth-century politics and ideas, the indispensable background to much of what later crystallised into fascism, the following are particularly helpful: H. Stuart Hughes, *Consciousness and Society: the reorientation of European social thought 1890–1930* (1958) and Geoffrey Barraclough's *Introduction to Contemporary History* (1967), full of provoking ideas. The Great Depression of 1873–96 has been summarised in S. B. Saul's *The Myth of the Great Depression of 1873–1896* (1969); its political consequences in Hans Rosenberg, ' Political and Economic Consequences of the Great Depression of 1873–1896 in Central Europe ', in *Economic History Review*,1,13 (1943). Edmund Whittaker has a good section on mercantilism in his *History of Economic Ideas* (1935). Late nineteenth-century views of the economists on the trade-cycle are discussed by T. W. Hutchison, in his *A Review of Economic Doctrines 1870–1929* (1953). There is a particularly useful essay on marxist economics by Martin Bronfenbrenner in *Marx and Modern Economics*, ed. D. Horowitz (1968). Two indispensable sources are J. A. Hobson, *Imperialism* (1902), and V. I. Lenin, *Imperialism, the highest stage of capitalism* (1916). For proto-fascist movements and thought, see Eugen Weber, *Varieties of Fascism* (1964), and also his *Action Française* (1962). A. James Gregor, *The Ideology of Fascism* (1969), has an interesting discussion on late nineteenth-century precursors. The most useful books on Britain's *fin-de-siècle* dilemmas are: E. J. Hobsbawm, *Industry and Empire* (1969); R. S. Sayers, *A History of Economic Change in England 1880–1939* (1967); A. L. Levine, *Industrial Retardation in Britain, 1880–1914* (1967); Keith Hutchinson, *The Decline and Fall of British Capitalism* (1966); Peter Mathias, *The First Industrial Nation* (1969); Corelli Barnett, *The Collapse of British Power* (1972); and W. H. B. Court, *British Economic History 1870–1911, Commentary and Documents* (1965). For British political reactions see: A. M. McBriar, *Fabian Socialism and English Politics 1884–1914* (1962); Margaret Cole, *The Story of Fabian Socialism* (1961); L.T. Hobhouse, *Liberalism* (1911). Bernard Semmel, *Imperialism aud Social Reform* (1960), provides an excellent guide through the political maze of social imperialism, as well as having a chapter on Mosley as the heir to Joseph Chamberlain. See also Julian Amery's lucid chapter 'The Fiscal Revolution in Perspective' in J. L. Garvin and J. Amery, *Life of Joseph Chamberlain*, vol. v (1969). Eric Bentley's *Bernard Shaw* (1957) is important for Shaw's political ideas. S. T. Glass, *The Responsible Society: the ideas of Guild Socialism* (1966), is useful.

R. Reynell Bellamy, 'We Marched with Mosley' (unpublished MS.), has a good section on Mosley's war experiences. For the mentality or myth of the war generation the best sources are: Reginald Pound, *The Lost Generation of 1914* (1965); Robert Graves and Alan Hodge, *The Long Weekend, a social history of Great Britain 1918–1939* (1963 ed.); and *The Collected Poems of Wilfred Owen*, edited with an introduction and notes by C. Day Lewis (1964). The most persistent novelist of the war generation is Mosley's friend Henry Williamson. Mosley appears as Sir Hereward Birkin in *The Phoenix Generation* (1961). Arthur Marwick has written a good article, 'The Impact of the First World War on British Society', in *Journal of Contemporary History*, January 1968.

Mosley in Parliament 1918–24

Colin Coote's *Editorial* (1965) and Leonard Mosley's *Curzon: the last phase* (1960) give glimpses of Mosley at the start of his parliamentary career; the latter has useful information on Curzon's unbelievably complicated financial tangles and his first wife's Leiter background; Baroness Ravensdale, *In Many Rhythms* (1953), is useful on the Curzon family background; there are many puzzled comments on Mosley himself showing that Cynthia Mosley's elder sister found her brother-in-law as baffling as did most of his contemporaries. Lord Robert Cecil has written a dull autobiography, *All the Way* (1949); Beaverbrook's considerably more entertaining *The Decline and Fall of Lloyd George* is useful for the Irish troubles. On the Lloyd George coalition the chief source is Maurice Cowling, *The Impact of Labour* (1971); Kenneth Morgan has an elegant essay in *Lloyd George: twelve essays*, ed. A. J. P. Taylor (1971). Peter K. Cline, 'Reopening the Case of the Lloyd George Coalition and Postwar Economic Transition', in *Journal of British Studies*, November 1970, is helpful, despite its extraordinary title. Philip Abrams, 'The Failure of Social Reform 1918–1920', in *Past and Present*, April 1963, explains just that. There are a couple of brief but illuminating references to Mosley just before he joined the Labour Party in H. H. Asquith, *Letters to a Friend* (1934).

Mosley in the Labour Party 1924–31

Catherine Ann Cline, *Recruits to Labour: the British Labour Party 1914–1931* (1963), is suggestive on the differences between aristocratic and bourgeois recruits to the Labour Party. For an incisive portrait of Ferdinand Lassalle, Mosley's socialist hero, see Georg Brandes, *Ferdinand Lassalle* (1911). Egon Wertheimer, the London correspondent of *Vorwaerts*, is extremely sharp on Mosley in his *Portrait of the Labour Party* (1929); it is also the best portrait of the Labour Party in that period, though it cannot match John Scanlon's witty and ironic handling of a tragic theme in his *Decline and Fall of the Labour Party* (1932). Ralph Milliband, *Parliamentary Socialism: a study in the politics of labour* (1961), gives a left-wing critique of 'Parliamentarism' in the 1920s. There are sketches of Mosley and other incidentally useful insights in Fenner Brockway, *Inside the Left* (1942); John Paton, *Left Turn* (1937); W. J. Brown, *So Far* (1943); and Oliver Baldwin, *The Questing Beast* (1932). James Lees-Milne's extremely funny autobiography *Another Self*

(1970) has a brief glimpse of Mosley in 1931. A fictionalised, though only intermittently perceptive, portrait of Mosley is to be found in a novel by John Strachey's
sister, Amabel Williams-Ellis, *The Wall of Glass* (1927). (It is noteworthy that this
and Wyndham Lewis's much more distinguished *The Apes of God* (1930) both contain unpleasant, stereotyped portraits of Jews, which helps mark the distance
between the interwar years and present attitudes to the subject.) A. P. Nicholson
has captured Mosley much more successfully in *Who Goes Home?* (1931). Beatrice
Webb's *Diaries*, ed. Margaret Cole, 2 vols (1956), are an important source for
Mosley and the Labour Party in the 1920s and early 1930s. On the whole he
comes out better than do most other Labour politicians, e.g. Ramsay MacDonald
– ' a magnificent substitute for a leader '. Ellen Wilkinson provides lightweight
but intelligent glimpses of Mosley and many other public figures in her *Peeps at
Politicians* (1930); James Johnston's *A Hundred Commoners* (1931) is a political journalist's view of the Westminster scene: there is a good impression of Mosley in the
late 1920s. Hugh Dalton's *Call Back Yesterday* (1953) gives the Labour Establishment view of Mosley. There is a personal impression of Mosley at this time in Sir
George Catlin's *For God's Sake, Go!* (1972). Hugh Thomas, *John Strachey* (1973),
is good on the personal relationship between Mosley and Strachey.

For Mosley's economic proposals the chief source apart from his own writings
is John Strachey's *Revolution by Reason* (1925); Robert Boothby, *I Fight to Live* (1947),
has an interlude in Venice with Strachey and the Mosleys when *Revolution by Reason*
was under discussion. R. K. Middlemas, *The Clydesiders* (1965) is particularly
good on that neglected figure, John Wheatley. There is a useful Ph.D. dissertation by Cairns King Smith, ' A Comparison of the Philosophy and Tactics of the
Independent Labour Party with those of the Labour Party of England, 1924–1931 '
(Chicago University, 1936). Robert E. Dowse, *Left in the Centre* (1965), is a sympathetic account of the I.L.P. with some incidental information on Mosley. It is
characteristic of the tendency to obliterate Mosley from the annals of the Labour
Party that one hardly gathers from this book that Mosley was one of the leaders of
the I.L.P. and played an important role in shaping its policy. Kingsley Martin,
Harold Laski (1953), is the source for the story that MacDonald wanted to make
Mosley foreign secretary in 1929. Mosley was greatly influenced by Keynes
and Shaw. He certainly read Keynes' *Tract for Monetary Reform* (1923) and his
Economic Consequences of Mr Churchill (1925). He later referred frequently to Shaw's
Caesar and Cleopatra (1899) and *Back to Methuselah* (1921). He read Shaw's *The
Perfect Wagnerite* (1898) on his way to India in 1924; and attended a reading party
at the Astors in 1928 when Shaw read his new play *The Applecart*. In the late 1920s
he was fascinated by the character of Julius Caesar and annotated the passages
dealing with Caesar in Theodore Mommsen's *The History of the Roman Republic*,
trans. W. P. Dickson, 5 vols (1901).

  The Gold Standard and Employment Policies Between the Wars, ed. Sidney Pollard
(1970) (especially the editor's introductory essay), and Donald Winch, *Economics
and Policy* (1969), have some interesting discussions on economic attitudes in the
inter-war years, including the period of the Labour Government of 1929–31. For
these two years the main source is Robert Skidelsky, *Politicians and the Slump* (1967).
Goronwy Rees, *The Great Slump: capitalism in crisis* (1970), is a bright account,
which errs like practically everything written on this period by Oxford and Cambridge dons who lived through it in attributing the misfortunes of governments at
the time to intellectual errors which could be corrected only when Keynes had
published his *General Theory* (1936): a view of the matter which, incidentally,

Keynes himself, Roosevelt and Hitler never shared. For one moderately, and another extremely, hostile view of Mosley in government, see Thomas Jones, *Whitehall Diaries*, ed. K. Middlemas, vol. II (1969), and Viscount Snowden, *Autobiography*, 2 vols (1934). Gregory Blaxland, *J. H. Thomas, a life for unity* (1964), is naïve but useful on its hero as employment minister 1929–30. Raymond Postgate's *Life of George Lansbury* (1951) is well written, but facts are not his strong point. John Rhodes, a postgraduate of Sussex University, has written a first-rate M.A. thesis: 'The Mosley Memorandum: a study in economic policy and decision-making'. J. A. Cross and R. K. Alderman, *Tactics of Resignation* (1967), and W. F. Mandle, 'Sir Oswald Mosley's Resignation from the Labour Government,' in *Historical Studies*, 10 (1963), both contain analyses of varying quality on Mosley's resignation. Aneurin Bevan's brief association with Mosley is traced in Michael Foot's excellently written *Aneurin Bevan*, vol. I, revised ed. (1966); for Mosley and the Other Club, see Colin R. Coote's book, *The Other Club* (1971). For the New Party the main sources are: Harold Nicolson's *Diaries*, vol. I, ed. Nigel Nicolson (1961); John Strachey, *The Menace of Fascism* (1933); Robert Skidelsky's essay 'Great Britain', in *European Fascism*, ed. S. J. Woolf (1968), and W. F. Mandle, 'The New Party', in *Historical Studies, Australia and New Zealand*, vol. 12 (1966); Ronald Butt, *The Power of Parliament* (1964), gives an account of attitudes to Parliament in the early 1930s, with some details of Mosley's New Party proposals for parliamentary reform.

Mosley and Fascism 1932–45

The books on fascism outside Britain are legion. For fascism in general I have found the following particularly helpful: Eugen Weber, *Varieties of Fascism* (1964); Ernst Nolte, *The Three Faces of Fascism* (1965); A. J. Gregor, *The Ideology of Fascism* (New York, 1969); P. F. Drucker, *The End of Economic Man* (1939); *European Fascism* (1968) and *The Nature of Fascism* (1968), both edited by S. J. Woolf; Alastair Hamilton, *The Appeal of Fascism* (1971); and Walter Laqueur and George L. Mosse (eds), 'International Fascism 1920–1945', in *Journal of Contemporary History*, vol. II, no. 1 (1966). A hostile but interesting contemporary assessment is Ellen Wilkinson and Edward Conze, *Why Fascism?* (1934). Important English marxist analyses are found in John Strachey's *The Coming Struggle for Power* (1932), the same author's *The Nature of Capitalist Crisis* (1935) and Rajani Palme Dutt's *Fascism and Social Revolution* (1934). (Strachey revised his views of fascist economics – 'can capitalism plan?' – to some extent in part IV of *The Strangled Cry* (1962).) Marxist views are summarised in John M. Cammett, 'Communist Theories of Fascism, 1920–1935', in *Science and Society*, XXI (1967). W. E. D. Allen wrote a fascinating analysis in terms of English history, *BUF, Oswald Mosley and British Fascism* (1934), under the pseudonym of 'James Drennan'. Nigel Harris' book, *Competition and the Corporate Society* (1972), has an intriguing section on the spread of corporatist ideas in the Conservative Party in the 1930s. No one can understand the immediate intellectual background to fascism without reference to Oswald Spengler's *The Decline of the West*, first published in 1918, whose gloomy prognostications Mosley explicitly set out to controvert.

The literature on British fascism is generally unsatisfactory. With the exception of Colin Cross, *The Fascists in Britain* (1961), excellent within its limits, none of the recent writers have that indispensable quality of sympathy. They write to condemn, and the result is that they fail to understand. Despite its scholarly apparatus, Robert Benewick's *Political Violence and Public Order* (1969) has little to commend it as an intellectual enterprise: not only is the analysis itself full of *non sequiturs*, but quite often it has little relation to the facts which the author himself presents. W. F. Mandle's *Antisemitism and the British Union of Fascists* (1968) is vitiated by some extraordinary omissions which one must charitably attribute to the fact that, working from Australian libraries, he did not have access to all the available sources. David Schermer's *Blackshirts: fascism in Britain* (1971) is an uninspired amalgamation of everyone else's mistakes, with none of their redeeming virtues. For a book of illustrated history, the photographic reproductions are appalling. Frederic Mullaly's *Fascism inside England* (1946) appears to be written from a pro-Communist Party point of view; as does W. A. Rudlin's *The Growth of Fascism in Great Britain* (1935): this is worth looking at, however, for the characteristic far-left view in the 1930s that Mosley's followers were the storm troops of the National Government. *Who Backs Mosley?* (Labour Research Department, 1934) has much useful information and tendentious argument; the same is true of *Mosley Fascism: the man, his policy and methods* (1935), produced by the same organisation. Mosley was mentioned or described in many pre-war books and articles, one of the most balanced being Rom Landau's *Love for a Country* (1939).

On the intellectuals and fascism, Alastair Hamilton's book, already mentioned, has a (weak) chapter on fascist-inclined intellectuals: Belloc, Chesterton, Shaw, Wyndham Lewis, Ezra Pound, etc. A much more brilliant insight into the intellectual appeal of fascism is afforded by the discussion of Carlyle, Nietzsche, Wagner, Spengler and others in Eric Bentley's, *Cult of the Superman* (1947) – American title, *A Century of Hero-Worship* (1957). John Harrison, *The Reactionaries* (1966), has chapters on Yeats, D. H. Lawrence, Eliot, Wyndham Lewis, Pound: the chief deficiency of this book is its title. Neal Wood's *Communism and British Intellectuals* (1959) is excellent. For individuals sympathetic to Mosley and/or fascism in the 1930s, the following works among many may be mentioned: J. A. Cole, *Lord Haw-Haw – and William Joyce* (1964); T. S. Eliot, *Selected Prose*, ed. John Hayward (1953); J. F. C. Fuller, *Empire Unity and Defence* (1934) and *Towards Armageddon* (1937); A. K. Chesterton, *Why I left Mosley* (1938); Douglas Jerrold, *Georgian Adventure* (1938); Wyndham Lewis, *Left Wings over Europe* (1936); Jessica Mitford, *Hons and Rebels* (1960); Beverley Nichols, *News of England* (1938) and *Men Do Not Weep* (1941); John Scanlon, *Very Foreign Affairs* (1938), *But Who Has Won?* (1939); G. B. Shaw, ' In Praise of Guy Fawkes ', in *Where Stands Socialism Today?* (1933); Alexander Raven Thomson, *Civilisation as Divine Superman* (1932) and *The Coming Corporate State* (1937); Noel Stock, *The Life of Ezra Pound* (1970); Hugh Ross Williamson, *Who Is for Liberty?* (1939) (his *A.D. 33 – a tract for the times* (1941) was read and admired by Mosley in prison); Jorian Jenks, *Spring Comes Again* (1939). Henry Williamson's novel *The Phoenix Generation* (1965) has already been mentioned.

The politics of confrontation in the 1930s gave rise to much comment, mostly in the various journals. See particularly the *New Statesman*, 16 June 1934, 24 and 31 October 1936, 9 October 1937; *Spectator*, 27 April and 15 June 1934, 9 October 1936, 8 October 1937; *Saturday Review*, 16 June 1934; *Round Table*, June 1934, January 1937. For the Communist Party, Douglas Hyde, *I Believed: the autobiography of a former British communist* (1951), and Henry Pelling, *The British Communist Party: a historical profile* (1958), should be consulted. Kenneth Newton, *The Sociology of British Communism* (1969), has some tactful explanations of Jewish support for the Communist Party. On the Olympia meeting of 7 June 1934, *Red*

Violence and Blue Lies (1934) is the fascist reply to the charges made in ' Vindicator ', *Fascists at Olympia* (1934) and *Eye-Witnesses at Olympia* (1934). Philip Toynbee, *Friends Apart* (1954), has some personal reminiscences of Olympia. For the communist version of Cable Street, see Phil Piratin, *Our Flag Stays Red* (1948).

Anti-semitism, too, has a vast literature. The books I have found particularly helpful on the general aspects include Bernard Lazare, *Anti-semitism* (1967); Warner Sombart, *The Jews and Modern Capitalism* (New York, 1969; first English edition 1913); Hannah Arendt, *The Origins of Totalitarianism* (1951); James Parkes, *The Emergence of the Jewish Problem 1878–1939* (1946) and *The Jewish Problem in the Modern World* (1938). For Jewish immigration to Britain, Bernard Gainer's *The Alien Invasion* (1972) is excellent. See also *A Minority in Britain: social studies of the Anglo-Jewish community*, ed. Maurice Freedman (1955). Neville Laski's *Jewish Rights and Jewish Wrongs* (1939) is the official Jewish defence to anti-semitic charges in the 1930s. Anti-Jewish literature of the inter-war years includes Lt- Col. A. H. Lane, *The Alien Menace*, 3rd ed. (1932), and ' M. G. Murchin ' (pseud.), *Britain's Jewish Problem* (1939). Hilaire Belloc, *The Jews* (1922), gives a Catholic view of the Jewish impact on European life, and particularly the Jewish influence on the Russian Revolution. For the ' conspiracy ' theme see, for instance, Nesta Webster, *World Revolution* (1921; revised ed. 1971). Norman Cohn, *Warrant for Genocide* (1967), examines this notion in relation to the Protocols of the Elders of Zion. Andrew Sharf, *The British Press and Jews under Nazi Rule* (1964), is somewhat one-sided. Stephen S. Wise, *Challenging Years* (New York, 1949), has some material on the anti-Nazi economic boycott. There is a B.Litt. thesis by Mrs Hilary Blume on ' Anti-Semitic Groups in Britain 1918–1940 ' (Sussex University, 1971). An unusual debate through correspondence between A. K. Chesterton and Joseph Leftwich, *The Tragedy of Anti-Semitism* (1948), makes a brief reference to the Mosley movement.

An impressive statement of the non-interventionist tradition in British foreign politics is William Harbutt Dawson's *Richard Cobden and Foreign Policy* (1926). Also good is A. J. P. Taylor, *The Troublemakers* (1957). His recent *Beaverbrook* (1972) discusses, and supports, Beaverbrook's ' imperial isolationist ' stand in the 1930s. The opposite view can be found in Winston Churchill's *The Second World War*, vol. I, *The Gathering Storm* (1948), a sustained argument in favour of the balance of power. E. H. Carr's *The Twenty Years Crisis* (1939) is a brilliant attack on the utopianism of Woodrow Wilson, Lord Robert Cecil, etc. It is particularly strong on the relations between politics and economics in the inter-war period. J. F. Naylor, *Labour's International Policy* (1969), is naïve.

Unlike the First World War, the causes of the Second World War have not produced a distinguished interpretative literature. In general, the wickedness of the Nazis has been held to remove the need for any more detailed justification for Britain's decision to fight Hitler, and criticism has been chiefly directed at its refusal to do so earlier. For a long time ' revisionists ' could not get any sort of hearing. The writings of Harry Elmer Barnes, Charles Callan Tansill and D. L. Hoggan were regarded at best as wildly eccentric, at worst as evil: it is a fact that Hoggan's *Der erzwungene Krieg* (1963) has been unable to find an English-language publisher. The first important academic breakthrough was A. J. P. Taylor's *Origins of the Second World War* (the 1963 ed. has his ' Second Thoughts '). By 1965 D. C. Watt could talk about the ' rise of a revisionist school ' (*Political Quarterly*, April–June 1965). The release of the British Cabinet Papers has greatly altered the context of the debate, with much more emphasis now placed on the military factor and Britain's appalling strategic dilemmas: examples are Michael Howard, *The Continental Commitment* (1970); R. K. Middlemas, *Diplomacy of Illusion* (1972); and Corelli Barnett, *The Collapse of British Power* (1972). No published writer has yet attempted to integrate the economic with the political and strategic aspects of international relations in the 1930s. A long-overdue start on this has been made by Kendall Myers, ' A Rationale for Appeasement ' (Ph. D. dissertation, School of Advanced International Studies, Washington, 1972). Simon K. Newman's ' Chamberlain's Diplomatic Revolution? The origins of the British guarantee to Poland ' (Ph. D. dissertation, School of Advanced International Studies, Washington, 1973) is the best account yet of that unbelievable episode. The state of present published research is summarised in two volumes: *The Origins of the Second World War*, ed. Esmonde M. Robertson (1971) and *The Origins of the Second World War: A .J. P. Taylor and his critics*, ed. W. R. Louis (1970). For the time being the best introduction to Hitler's foreign policy remains Alan Bullock, *Hitler: a study in tyranny* (1952). Of all the revisionist books, the one that most closely approaches the argument against the war and its probable consequences set out in chapter 20 of Mosley's *My Life* (restated in the *Listener*, 21 September 1972) is William Henry Chamberlin, *America's Second Crusade* (1950). At present what one can say is that, though the evaluation of the war, its origins and its consequences remains and will continue to remain the subject of intense debate, most of Mosley's detailed criticisms of British policy in the 1930s, particularly on the failure to rearm, the Abyssinian crisis and the Polish guarantee, are receiving increasing scholarly support.

Churchill's view of Mosley's imprisonment can be traced in the various appendixes to his *Second World War*. David Littlejohn, *The Patriotic Traitors* (1971), disposes of the view that European fascist parties were fifth columnists. C. F. Clayton, *The Wall Is Strong* (1958), contains impressions of Mosley and British fascists by a former governor of Brixton Prison. Norman Longate's book *If Britain Had Fallen* (1972) examines the claim that British Union was prepared to resist a German invasion.

Mosley Since the Second World War

Mosley's prison reading should be included here, for this laid the foundation of his post-war philosophy. In prison Mosley discovered the Greeks. He read the Greek tragedians and philosophers; he also read Werner Jaeger's *Paedeia*, 3 vols (1934–47); G. Lowes Dickinson's *The Greek View of Life* (1910); Humphry Trevelyan's *Goethe and the Greeks* (1941). For a further account of the Greek view of life, see C. M. Bowra, *The Greek Experience* (1957). For the early Greek philosophers who so fascinated Mosley, particularly Heraclitus, the founder of dialectical thinking, see John Burnet's *Early Greek Philosophy* (1892) and Rex Warner's *The Greek Philosophers* (1958). Mosley has praised R. H. S. Crossman's *Plato Today* (1937), possibly because he is mentioned in it. Wolfgang Leppmann's *Winckelmann* (1971) is a biography of the founder of German neo-classicism. F. Stawell and G. Lowes Dickinson's *Goethe and Faust* (1928) is the best introduction I have read to that tremendous subject; also to be recommended is George Lukacs, *Goethe and His Age*, trans. Robert Andrew (1968). For a short introduction to Nietzsche, Georg Brandes, *Friedrich Nietzsche: a study in aristocratic radicalism* (first English ed. 1914), is unsurpassed; Walter Kaufman's *Nietzsche: philosopher, psychologist, antichrist*, revised ed. (1968), is the standard modern scholarly account. A book dealing with these thinkers, together with Spengler, Kafka and others, which greatly impressed Mosley in the 1950s is Erich Heller's *The Disinherited Mind* (1952). Mosley also gained something from Arnold Toynbee's *Study of History* because it suggested a ' response ' to the ' challenge ' of decline.

It is impossible to furnish anything like a comprehensive bibliography for all the issues of peace and war touched upon by Mosley since 1945. The best introduction to Mosley's post-war thinking (Mosley and his circle) is to be found in the volumes of the *European*, the monthly political-cum-literary journal edited by his wife Diana from 1953 to 1959. In evaluating the quality of Mosley's post-war thinking on economics I have profited from David Calleo and Benjamin Rowland's notable contribution, *America and the World Political Economy* (1973). Mention should be made of Calleo's earlier books: *Britain's Future* (1968) and *The Atlantic Fantasy* (1970). For international relations, particularly relations with the Soviets, the most helpful books have been Coral Bell's *Negotiation from Strength: a study in the politics of power* (1962) and *The Debatable Alliance: an essay in Anglo-American relations* (1964); and Adam Ulam, *The Rivals: America and Russia since World War II* (New York, 1971) and *Expansion and Coexistence: the history of Soviet foreign policy 1917–1967* (New York, 1968). Interestingly, from about 1950 onwards Mosley has been consistently more ' left-wing ' on dealing with the Soviets and China than the Anglo-Saxon establishments, till President Nixon caught up in 1971–2. On Mosley's prophecy of the age of the ' urban guerilla ' one might cite a vast supporting ' counter-insurgency ' literature: e.g. Ian Greig, *The Assault on the West* (1968), and Robert Moss, *Urban Guerillas* (1972).

The literature on European integration and Britain's relationship to it has also been enormous. The best account is still Miriam Camps, *Britain and the European Community 1955–63* (1964). Mosley read and found himself in general agreement with Franz Josef Strauss' *Challenge and Response: a programme for Europe* (1969). Saul B. Cohen's *Geography and Politics in a Divided World* (1964) is interesting on the possibility of regional blocs and racial partition in southern Africa.

Immigration into Britain has occasioned an enormous literature, but no reliable general statistics. Nicholas Deakin, *Colour Citizenship and British Society* (1970), reports on race relations. A survey by Paul Foot, *Immigration and Race in British Politics* (1965), mentions Mosley's movement, while his *The Rise of Enoch Powell* (1969) debunks the ' opportunism ' of Mosley's rival on this issue. The North Kensington intervention is unsympathetically described by Ruth Glass in *Newcomers: the West Indians in London* (1960), and Keith Kyle has a section or the attempt to return to Parliament in *The British General Election of 1959*, ed. D. E. Butler and R. Rose (1960). In ' Colour and the 1966 General Election ', in *Race*, July 1966, Nicholas Deakin claims that immigration had no significant political impact when Union Movement candidates, including Mosley, stood again for election. Mosleyite policy was originally outlined by Robert Row in *The Colour Question in Britain* (1959). Mosley has never delved deeply into ethnological science, but in defending his ' functional ' view of racial differences has relied on biologists such as C. D. Darlington, author of *Genetics and Man*, revised ed. (1966), and contributor to *Race and Modern Science*, ed. Robert E. Kuttner (New York, 1967).

Very few books deal with Mosley's post-war activities. George Thayer, *The British Political Fringe* (1965), and Dennis Eisenberg, *The Re-emergence of Fascism* (1967), are as hostile to him as they are factually unreliable. Angelo Del Boca and Mario Giovana are no better in their *Fascism Today: a world survey* (1970), which even describes how Mosley tried to become a local councillor in 1953!

Index